汉语语法难点释疑

郑懿德　马盛静恒
刘月华　杨甲荣

华语教学出版社
北　京

First Edition 1992
Second Printing 1996

ISBN 7-80052-202-4

Published by Sinolingua
24 Baiwanzhuang Road, Beijing 100037, China
Printed by Beijing Foreign Languages Printing House
Distributed by China International
Book Trading Corporation
35 Chegongzhuang Xilu, P.O. Box 399
Beijing 100044, China

Printed in the People's Republic of China

序

1983年7月，中国和美国汉语教师代表团在北京举行了学术讨论会，双方代表除了交流研究成果和教学经验以外，经过认真讨论，确定了十三项合作研究的项目，"'了''着''过''是……的''在''呢'研究"就是其中的一项。此项研究任务最后落实由郑懿德（北京语言学院）、马盛静恒（美国麻省维廉大学）、刘月华（北京语言学院）、杨甲荣（中央民族学院）四位老师承担，并确定郑懿德、马盛静恒分别为中、美双方的负责人。这个研究项目历经五年，现在业已完成，其研究成果，包括有关的研究文献和为美国学生编写的语法难点教材及练习。现将后者汇集成册，定名为《汉语语法难点释疑》，即将交付出版。

当前，世界汉语教学正处于一个大发展的时期，我国的对外汉语教学事业以前所未有的速度向前发展。当前对外汉语教学面临的任务很多，其中最紧迫、最突出的是教材建设。在对外汉语的教材建设中，在眼下适用于国外的教材很少的情况下，尤其要考虑国外的需要，有步骤有重点地编写出版适应各主要国家和地区需要的各个层次、各种类型的教材。《汉语语法难点释疑》以美国学生和以英语为母语或媒介语的汉语学习者为对象，选择重要的语法难点作深入的研究和较详细的讲解，这样的教材尚属罕见。

如何编写对外汉语的教材，编写什么样的语法教材才能切合外国学生的需要呢？对外汉语教学的实践经验告诉我们，很重要的一条是教材要有针对性和实用性，要能针对一定教学对象的特点和需要。一部好的对外汉语教材，除了对语法体系、概貌作简明系统的介绍外，应把相当的力量花在解决外国人学汉语的主要难点上，对出现频率高、用法复杂、容易误用的语法点应着力描写，并尽可能作些对比。比如本书的“了”“着”“过”“是……的”“在”“呢”这些语法难点，还有象量词的用法，各类补语的用法，特殊动词谓语句（如“把”字句、“被”字句等）的用法，以及词语尤其是虚词的用法（在句子里的作用），格式的用法（适用的场合）和变化（加减其中的成分、变换其中的次序）等等，都应重点阐释。

本书的四位编著者都是多年从事对外汉语语法教学的老师，他们看到，外国学生渴望的是教他们运用已经掌握的一定数量的词语，造出符合汉语语法的句子，以达到交际的目的。确实，对外汉语教学的语法教材应适应教学对象的需要，有别于供汉族人使用的语法教材。为本族人编写的语法教材是为那些在开始学习研究语法之前已经掌握了自己的语言的人服务的，而为非本族人编写的语法教材则是为了更好地帮助学习者掌握运用一种目的语。这就要求教材、教法都能适应第二语言的教学需要，采用适合于非本族学生学习语言的方式，使语法理论和知识的学习侧重于掌握汉语语法规则，提高汉语实际水平。本书编著者在详细讲解语法难点的用法之后，还设计了丰富多样的练习，每引入一个语法点，就配有相应的练习，学生可以及时通过练习检查自己是否已经学会使用这些知识，教员也可以从中了解学生是否已经掌握这些知识。本书从讲解内容到练习，难易兼备，照顾到了各种程度学生的需要。

这是一个中美合作的科研项目。在教材和练习编写之前，双方编著者从资料搜集入手，做了许多与课题有关的基础研究工作。例如：1. 查阅中美主要汉语语法书、工具书，汉语教科书，公开发表的论文、美国博士论文，编写有关研究资料索引；2. 挑选较有价值的研究资料汇编成参考书；3. 分别从在美学生和来华留学生中搜集以英语为母语的学习者运用这些汉语语法点的病句。在吸收前人的研究成果、了解学生的困难和需要的基础上，开展了综合性的科学研究，最后才结合自己的教学经验动手编写教材。因此，对所选择的六个语法条目，都作了比较详细的描写，尤其是对使用条件(如什么时候可用，什么时候不可用，什么时候可用可不用)的探讨，有些是过去的语法著作未用过重墨的。因此，此书不仅对学习汉语的外国人有帮助。也可供汉语教师和汉语语法研究者参考。

作为一个尝试，本教材的编写目的能否圆满地实现，还有待于在教学实践中加以检验。鉴于迄今为止，专为外国人编写的汉语语法教材尚不多见，我希望能有更多的适合非汉族人学习的汉语语法著作问世，以适应不断发展的对外汉语教学事业的需要。

这个项目从提出到实施的整个过程，我都比较了解。因此在本项目完成、《汉语语法难点释疑》即将付梓之际，四位编著者要我作序。我很高兴见到又一项中美合作研究项目结出成果，对外汉语教材又添新作，就欣然写这些作为赞助。是为序。

吕必松

1988年9月

编写说明

以汤瑞哲先生为团长、李又安女士为副团长的美国汉语教师代表团和以吕必松先生为团长、林焘先生为副团长的中国汉语教师代表团于1983年7月20日至23日、27日至28日在北京举行了学术讨论会。会上确定了十三个合作研究项目。《汉语语法难点释疑》为合作项目的第二项。

我们从教学实践中感到，教外国人学习汉语语法主要是教给学生语法规则，而不是语法理论知识。因此，编写教材的基本出发点不是让学生学会多少语法术语、语法理论，而在于注重提高运用语言的实际能力。

教外国人学习汉语语法与教汉族人学习汉语语法的难点重点都不尽相同。汉语是缺少严格意义的形态变化的语言，但象本项目研究的"了""着""过""是……的""在""呢"这六个语法点，是汉语用以表示时态的语法点，这几个语法点出现频率高，用法比较复杂，外国人误用率很高，因此，当在美国执教多年的马盛静恒教授提出合作编写这几个语法难点释疑的项目时，立即得到中国同行的赞同。几年来，我们在大量搜集、阅读、吸收现有的有关研究成果的基础上，编写了这本为以英语为母语的学生服务的《汉语语法难点释疑》，力求采用外国学生容易掌握的方法，详解它们的用法规律，尽可能说明它的使用条件，即什么时候可用，什么时候不用，什么时候可用可不用。全书本着精讲多练、讲练结合的实用性原则，编有大量的练习，每引进一步，随即配上一个练习，旨在指导外国人真正有效地掌握这六个语法难点的正确用法。六个条目之间也进行了适当的横向和纵向的对比。为了便于外国人学习，例句及练习均标有汉语拼音，书后附有练习答案。练习有易有难，由易及难，可供大学一年级至三年级的学生学习及老师教学之用。

本书执笔分工如下：1.“了”的用法——马盛静恒；2.“着”的用法——刘月华；3.“过”的用法——刘月华；4.“是……的”的用法——杨甲荣；5.“在”的用法——郑懿德；6.“呢”的用法——郑懿德。卫德泉同志曾参加过本书第一阶段的有关研究资料的搜集工作。

编写者诚挚地希望使用本书的教师和学生们提出意见和建议，以便再版时修订使其完善。

编　者

1988 年 8 月

目　录

壹、"了"的用法

贰、“着”的用法

叁、“过”的用法

肆、“是……的”的用法

伍、“在”的用法

陆、“呢”的用法

壹、“了”的用法

“了”字是对外汉语教学中的一个重点，也是外国学生学习汉语的难点，因为：

1. “了”字的出现频率很高，用途也很多。
2. “了”字本身没有固定的意义，其意义依句型、副词、时间词以及动词的性质而定。
3. “了”字的用途常为语言环境、说话人的主观看法、方言以及体裁所左右。
4. “了”字的某些功用与学生母语有相近或相似的地方，学生常因母语的干扰而误用。
5. 对“了”字的知识了解不够透澈。
6. 缺乏有系统的教材及练习。

本教材提供“了”字的基本知识及用法。共分十二单元。

一、“了”表示情况的改变

在这一个单元里，“了”字都出现在句尾，表示前后情况的改变。请看下面的例子：

(1) 天气很热。

Tiānqì hěn rè.

(2) 天气热了。

Tiānqì rè le.

例 1 说明天气很热，例 2 不但说明天气热，而且表示过去天气不热，现在热了，与以前不同了。

练习一

（一）　形容词＋"了"

请把下面句子的意思写出来：

例：A. 东西贵了。

Dōngxi guì le.

A'. 东西从前不贵，现在贵。

Dōngxi cóngqián bú guì, xiànzài guì.

B. 东西不贵了。

Dōngxi bú guì le.

B'. 东西从前贵，现在不贵。

Dōngxi cóngqián guì, xiànzài bú guì.

1. 肉便宜了。

Ròu piányi le.

______________________________________。

2. 我母亲老了。

Wǒ mǔqin lǎo le.

______________________________________。

3. 功课不多了。

Gōngkè bù duō le.

______________________________________。

4. 孩子高了。

Háizi gāo le.

______________________________________。

5. 学生不用功了。

Xuésheng bú yònggōng le.

________________________________。

（二） 关系动词＋宾语＋“了”

请把下面句子的意思写出来：

例：A. 这个地方叫百花山了。

Zhège dìfang jiào Bǎihuā Shān le.

A'. 这个地方现在叫百花山，从前不叫百花山。

Zhège dìfang xiànzài jiào Bǎihuā Shān, cóngqián bú jiào Bǎihuā Shān.

B. 这个地方不叫百花山了。

Zhège dìfang bú jiào Bǎihuā Shān le.

B'. 这个地方现在不叫百花山，从前叫百花山。

Zhège dìfang xiànzài bú jiào Bǎihuā Shān, cóngqián jiào Bǎihuā Shān.

1. 小王不是教员了。

Xiǎo Wáng bú shi jiàoyuán le.

________________________________。

2. 高小姐是老何的爱人了。

Gāo xiǎojiě shì lǎo Hé de àiren le.

________________________________。

3. 他不是我的男朋友了。

Tā bú shì wǒ de nán péngyou le.

________________________________。

4. 孩子不象爸爸了。

Háizi bǔ xiàng bàba le.

________________________________。

5. 他是美国人了。

Tā shì Měiguórén le.

____。

（三） 心理状态的动词＋宾语＋“了”

请把下面句子的意思写出来：

例：A. 张小姐喜欢他了。

Zhāng xiǎojiě xǐhuan tā le.

A'. 张小姐现在喜欢他，可是从前不喜欢他。

Zhāng xiǎojiě xiànzài xǐhuan tā, kěshì cóngqián bù xǐhuan tā.

B. 张小姐不喜欢他了。

Zhāng xiǎojiě bù xǐhuan tā le.

B'. 张小姐现在不喜欢他，可是从前喜欢他。

Zhāng xiǎojiě xiànzài bù xǐhuan tā, kěshì cóngqián xǐhuan tā.

1. 他爱中国了。

Tā ài Zhōngguó le.

____。

2. 我想（念）我父母了。

Wǒ xiǎng(niàn) wǒ fùmǔ le.

____。

3. 我不想吃饭了。

Wǒ bù xiǎng chīfàn le.

____。

4. 小李讨厌他的女朋友了。

Xiǎo Lǐ tǎoyàn tā de nǚ péngyou le.

____。

5. 他不恨他的父亲了。

Tā bú hèn tā de fùqin le.

______________________________。

（四） 表状态的动词＋“了”

请把下面句子的意思写出来：

例：A. 我饿了。

Wǒ è le.

A'. 刚才我不饿，现在饿了。

Gāngcái wǒ bú è, xiànzài è le.

B. 我不饿了。

Wǒ bú è le.

B'. 刚才我饿，现在我不饿了。

Gāngcái wǒ è, xiànzài wǒ bú è le.

1. 妈妈累了。

Māma lèi le.

______________________________。

2. 他病了。

Tā bìng le.

______________________________。

3. 那个老人耳朵不聋了。

Nàge lǎorén ěrduo bù lóng le.

______________________________。

4. 孩子都不困了。

Háizi dōu bú kùn le.

______________________________。

5. 他醉了。

Tā zuì le.

______________________________。

（五） 能愿动词＋动词＋宾语＋“了”

请把下面句子的意思写出来：

例：A. 我愿意做事了。

Wǒ yuànyi zuò shì le.

A'. 我从前不愿意，现在愿意了。

Wǒ cóngqián bú yuànyi，xiànzài yuànyi le.

B. 我不愿意做事了。

Wǒ bú yuànyi zuò shì le.

B'. 我从前愿意做事，现在不愿意做。

Wǒ cóngqián yuànyi zuò shì，xiànzài bú yuànyi zuò.

1. 我们不能够买汽车了。

Wǒmen bù nénggòu mǎi qìchē le.

________________________________。

2. 我可以做这个练习了。

Wǒ kěyǐ zuò zhège liànxí le.

________________________________。

3. 他不敢说英语了。

Tā bù gǎn shuō Yīngyǔ le.

________________________________。

4. 你应该预备功课了。

Nǐ yīnggāi yùbèi gōngkè le.

________________________________。

5. 我们都会看中国报了。

Wǒmen dōu huì kàn Zhōngguó bào le.

________________________________。

（六） 可能补语＋“了”

请把下面句子的意思写出来：

例：A. 我看得懂中文报了。

Wǒ kàn de dǒng Zhōngwén bào le.

A'. 我从前看不懂中文报，现在看得懂。

Wǒ cóngqián kàn bù dǒng Zhōngwén bào, xiànzài kàn de dǒng.

B. 我看不懂中文报了。

Wǒ kàn bù dǒng Zhōngwén bào le.

B'. 我从前看得懂中文报，现在看不懂。

Wǒ cóngqián kàn de dǒng Zhōngwén bào, xiànzài kàn bù dǒng.

1. 现在我们都吃得饱了。

Xiànzài wǒmen dōu chī de bǎo le.

________________________________。

2. 我看不见黑板上的字了。

Wǒ kàn bú jiàn hēibǎn shàng de zì le.

________________________________。

3. 学生听得懂老师说的话了。

Xuésheng tīng de dǒng lǎoshī shuō de huà le.

________________________________。

4. 我们买得起那个车了。

Wǒmen mǎi de qǐ nàge chē le.

________________________________。

5. 你说的话，我听不清楚了。

Nǐ shuō de huà, wǒ tīng bù qīngchu le.

________________________________。

（七） 时间词/年龄/重量＋“了”

请把下面句子的意思写出来：

例：五点钟了。

Wǔ diǎn zhōng le.

刚才不是五点钟，现在是五点钟。

Gāngcái bú shì wǔ diǎn zhōng, xiànzài shì wǔ diǎn zhōng.

1. 七点半了。

Qī diǎn bàn le.

______________________________________。

2. 已经星期三了。

Yǐjing Xīngqīsān le.

______________________________________。

3. 我十六岁了。

Wǒ shíliù suì le.

______________________________________。

4. 我母亲八十岁了。

Wǒ mǔqin bāshí suì le.

______________________________________。

5. 孩子十磅了。

Háizi shí bàng le.

______________________________________。

二、"太/最……了"强调主观见解

"了"不但可以表示前后情况的不同，也可以跟副词"太"或"最"同时出现，肯定了已经出现的状况，强调说话人的主观见解。

请比较下面两个句子：

(1) 中文太难。

Zhōngwén tài nán.

(2) 中文太难了。

Zhōngwén tài nán le.

第一个句子跟第二个句子意思一样，所不同的是第二句的语气较重。

练习二

一、请把"了"加在下面各句句尾，以加强主观的见解。

例：这么说最好。

Zhème shuō zuì hǎo.

这么说最好了。

Zhème shuō zuì hǎo le.

1. 小李最聪明。

Xiǎo Lǐ zuì cōngming.

2. 这个问题太难解决。

Zhège wèntí tài nán jiějué.

3. 房子太小。

Fángzi tài xiǎo.

4. 东西太贵。

Dōngxi tài guì.

5. 小王认为他的女朋友最漂亮。

Xiǎo Wáng rènwéi tā de nǚ péngyou zuì piàoliang.

6. 中国人口太多。

Zhōngguó rénkǒu tài duō.

7. 今天最冷。

Jīntiān zuì lěng.

二、请把下面的句子翻译成英文,注意这些句子句尾都有“了”。

1. 他的讲演有意思极了。

Tā de jiǎngyǎn yǒu yìsi jí le.

2. 那个人坏透了。

Nàge rén huàitòu le.

3. 这个办法好极了。

Zhège bànfǎ hǎojí le.

4. 小李这个人太好了。

Xiǎo Lǐ zhège rén tài hǎo le.

5. 今天冷死了。

Jīntiān lěngsǐ le.

三、“快/就要……了”表示情况就要改变

当“了”与“快/就要”同时在句子里出现表示某种情况就要改变,比如说“饭快好了”的意思是“饭马上就好了”。

练 习 三

一、请按照下面的句子回答问题：

例：火车快要到了。

Huǒchē kuàiyào dào le.

问题：火车现在在没在这儿？

回答：没有。

1. 就要下雨了。

Jiù yào xià yǔ le.

问题：现在下没下雨？

回答：

2. 饭就好了。

Fàn jiù hǎo le.

问题：饭现在好了没有？

回答：

3. 还有一刻钟就可以出去了。

Hái yǒu yí kè zhōng jiù kěyǐ chūqu le.

问题：(1)现在可以不可以出去？

回答：

问题：(2)还有多久就可以出去？

回答：

4. 病人快死了。

Bìngrén kuài sǐ le.

问题：(1)病人现在死了没有？

回答：

问题：(2)病人还能活很久吗？

回答：

二、请在下面的句子里表示时间的词或副词下面画一条线：

例：我们就要下课了。

Wǒmen jiù yào xiàkè le.

1. 我们明天就要考试了。

Wǒmen míngtiān jiù yào kǎoshì le.

2. 再有三天就放假了。

Zài yǒu sān tiān jiù fàngjià le.

3. 孩子快要睡着了。

Háizi kuàiyào shuì zháo le.

4. 客人十点钟就要走了。

Kèren shí diǎn zhōng jiù yào zǒu le.

5. 马上就要上课了。

Mǎshàng jiù yào shàngkè le.

6. 我一会儿就做完了。

Wǒ yíhuìr jiù zuòwán le.

7. 他夏天就要毕业了。

Tā xiàtiān jiù yào bìyè le.

8. 明天他就来了。

Míngtiān tā jiù lái le.

9. 明天就是星期六了。

Míngtiān jiùshi Xīngqīliù le.

10. 那件事快做完了。

Nà jiàn shì kuài zuòwán le.

三、把下面的句子译成英文：

1. 谁快要来了？

Shuí kuàiyào lái le?

2. 他们就要结婚了吗？

Tāmen jiù yào jiéhūn le ma?

3. 这个字我快学会了。
Zhège zì wǒ kuài xuéhuì le.

4. 他们一会儿就来了。
Tāmen yíhuìr jiù lái le.

5. 那个病人快死了。
Nàge bìngrén kuài sǐ le.

四、把下面的句子译成中文：

1. We're about to eat.

2. It will soon be 10 o'clock.

3. He is about to leave.

4. My friend will come from China soon.

5. I am going to China soon.

四、"动词＋了＋时量词语＋（名词）＋了"表示某种活动到目前为止已进行了若干时间

如果句子里有两个"了"，一个在动词的后面，一个在句子的最

后面，而且一定有时间量词，这种句子的意思是到说话的时间为止某个活动已经进行了多少时间了。比如说“他看了两个钟头的书了”意思是说到目前为止他已经看了两个钟头的书，也许他还要继续看下去，也许他觉得两个钟头已经太多了不要再看下去了。

请注意下面句子的问题回答：

小王学了三年中文了。

Xiǎo Wáng xuéle sān nián Zhōngwén le.

问题：(1)上面的句子里有几个“了”字？

回答：有两个。

问题：(2)第一个“了”字在什么词的后面？

回答：在动词后面。

问题：(3)第二个“了”字呢？

回答：在句子的最后面。

问题：(4)这个句子里的时间词是什么？

回答：三年。

问题：(5)时间词是在动词的前面还是后面？

回答：后面。

问题：(6)从上面的句子我们知道小李是几年前开始学中文的？

回答：三年前。

问题：(7)我们知道不知道他以后还要不要学中文？

回答：不知道。

问题：(8)为什么？

回答：因为他可以说：我不要再学了。他也可以接着说：我还想再学。

练 习 四

一、请在下面句子中的“了”字下面点一个点(.)，表时量词语下面画一条线：

例：你等了我多久了？

Nǐ děngle wǒ duō jiǔ le?

1. 我等了你半天了。

Wǒ děngle nǐ bàntiān le.

2. 你来了多少时候了？

Nǐ láile duōshao shíhou le?

3. 我来了一年半了。

Wǒ láile yì nián bàn le.

4. 你在美国住了多久了？

Nǐ zài Měiguó zhùle duō jiǔ le?

5. 你已经看了几个钟头的书了？

Nǐ yǐjing kànle jǐ gè zhōngtóu de shū le?

二、按照下面的句子回答问题：

李教授教了十年书了。

Lǐ jiàoshòu jiāole shí nián shū le.

问题：(1)上面的句子里有几个“了”字？

回答：

问题：(2)句子里的时间词是什么？

回答：

问题：(3)那个时间词在什么词的前面？

回答：

问题：(4)李教授是什么时候开始教书的？

回答：

问题：(5)他现在还在教书吗？

回答：

问题：(6)我们知道不知道他以后还要不要教书？

回答：

三、请把下面的句子译成英文：

1. 我们坐了几个钟头的飞机了？

Wǒmen zuòlè jǐ ge zhōngtóu de fēiji le?

2. 我们已经走了五个钟头了还没到。

Wǒmen yǐjing zǒule wǔ gè zhōngtóu le hái méi dào.

3. 你在这儿等了多久了？

Nǐ zài zhèr děngle duō jiǔ le?

4. 差不多两个半钟头了。

Chà bu duō liǎng gè bàn zhōngtóu le.

5. 你们在中国住了多久了？

Nǐmen zài Zhōngguó zhùle duō jiǔ le?

四、请把下面的句子翻译成中文：

1. He has been studying for four hours, he doesn't want to study any more.

2. I've already taught for more than 20 years.

3. We have been living here for more than six years.

4. They have already driven for four days.

5. We've lived in the hotel for four months.

五、"动词＋了＋数量词＋（名词）＋了"表示某种活动到目前为止已经完成了若干数量

这个句型跟第四单元不同的是句子里的时间词改为数量词了。例如说"我买了三本书了"这个句子的意思是到说话的时间为止"我"已经买了三本书了。也许"我"打算买五本，现在已经买了三本了，还得再买两本。也许认为"我"买三本书已经太多了，不想再买了。

请注意下面句子的问题及回答：

小王吃了三碗饭了。

Xiǎo Wáng chīle sān wǎn fàn le.

问题：(1)上面的句子里有几个"了"字？

回答：有两个。

问题：(2)第一个"了"字在什么词的后面？

回答：在动词的后面。

问题：(3)第二个"了"字在哪儿？

回答：在句子的最后面。

问题：(4)句中的数量词是什么？

回答："三碗"。

问题：(5)小王已经吃了几碗饭了？

回答：三碗。

问题：(6)从上面的句子知道不知道小王还要不要再吃饭？

回答：不知道。

问题：(7)这样的句型，不能用表示过去的时间词，如"去

年”、“昨天”等，为什么？

回答：因为这样的句型表示“活动一直进行到现在”，所以不能用表示过去的时间词。

问题：(8)这样的句型可以用什么时间词呢？

回答：可以用“今天”、“今年”、“现在”等。

问题：(9)如果在句子里没有时间词呢？

回答：如果没有时间词就表示“到说话的时候”或“到目前为止”。

问题：(10)什么副词常常出现在这种句型里？

回答：“已经”。

练习五

一、请在下面的句子中的“了”字下面点一个点(．)，数量词下面画一条线(——)。

例：你看了几次电影了？

Nǐ kànle jǐ cì diànyǐng le?

1. 我看了两次电影了。

Wǒ kànle liǎng cì diànyǐng le.

2. 今天我已经上了两节课了。

Jīntiān wǒ yǐjing shàngle liǎng jié kè le.

3. 我已经吃了两块糖了，不能再吃了。

Wǒ yǐjing chīle liǎng kuài táng le, bù néng zài chī le.

4. 妈妈已经给了我五百块钱了，不能再跟她要了。

Māma yǐjing gěile wǒ wǔbǎi kuài qián le, bù néng zài gēn tā yào le.

5. 我们喝了两瓶酒了，还要再喝吗？

Wǒmen hēle liǎng píng jiǔ le, hái yào zài hē ma?

二、请把下面的句子译成英文：

1. 我已经花了两百块钱了，不能再花了。

Wǒ yǐjing huāle liǎng bǎi kuài qián le, bù néng zài huā le.

2. 他已经结了三次婚了。

Tā yǐjing jiéle sān cì hūn le.

3. 老师讲了好几遍了，他还是不懂。

Lǎoshī jiǎngle hǎo jǐ biàn le, tā háishi bù dǒng.

4. 你已经买了几所房子了？

Nǐ yǐjing mǎile jǐ suǒ fángzi le?

5. 你教了几年中文了？

Nǐ jiāole jǐ nián zhōngwén le?

三、请把下面的英文译成中文：

1. That child has already sung three songs. He still want to sing one more.

2. Mr Tian has already bought one car. He still wants to buy another.

3. I have read three books today, I don't want to read any more.

4. We've walked 10 miles. How far do we still have to go?

5. You've already invited 10 friends. How many more are you go-

ing to invite?

六、"动词＋了＋时量词语＋(名词)"表示某种活动在过去曾经进行了若干时间

当"了"出现在动词的后面，而且句子里有时量词语，则表示某种活动曾在过去进行过若干时间；如果，句子中没有明确的时间词，就不知道这个活动是在过去什么时候发生的。比如说"他学了两个月的法文"，从这个句子我们只知道"他"在过去学过两个月的法文，而且现在不学了，但是"他"在过去什么时候学的却不知道了。

请注意下面句子的问题与回答：

小李学了三年中文。

Xiǎo Lǐ xuéle sān nián zhōngwén.

问题：(1)上面句子里有几个"了"字？

回答：就有一个。

问题：(2)这个"了"字在什么词的后面？

回答：在动词的后面。

问题：(3)动词跟"了"的后面有什么词？

回答：有时量词跟名词。

问题：(4)小李学了几年中文？

回答：三年。

问题：(5)从上面的句子里可以不可以知道小李是什么时候学的中文？

回答：不知道。

问题：(6)如果要想说明小李在什么时候学了三年中文怎么办？

回答：可以加上确定的时间，如“他在中国的时候”“从1956年到1959年”等。

问题：(7)小李现在还在学中文吗？

回答：他已经不学了。

练习六

一、按照下面的句子回答问题：

小钱的父母在纽约住了三年。

Xiǎo Qián de fùmǔ zài Niǔyuē (New York) zhùle sān nián.

问题：(1)上面的句子里有几个“了”字？

回答：

问题：(2)“了”字在什么词的后面？

回答：

问题：(3)“了”字后面是什么词？

回答：

问题：(4)小钱的父母现在还住在纽约吗？

回答：

问题：(5)由这个句子能不能知道小钱的父母什么时候在纽约住过三年？

回答：

二、把下面的句子译成英文：

1. 你上礼拜做了几个钟头的事？

Nǐ shàng lǐbài zuòle jǐ gè zhōngtóu de shì?

2. 你去年在纽约住了多久？

Nǐ qùnián zài Niǔyuē (New York) zhùle duō jiǔ?

3. 你学了几年中文？
Nǐ xuéle jǐ nián Zhōngwén？

4. 你在中国的时候教了几年书？
Nǐ zài Zhōngguó de shíhou jiāole jǐ nián shū？

5. 你一共学了几年中国画儿？
Nǐ yígòng xuéle jǐ nián Zhōngguóhuàr？

三、把下面的句子译成中文：

1. I worked 20 hours last week.

2. Last year, I stayed in New York for nine months.

3. I studied Chinese for six years.

4. I taught two years while I was in China.

5. I studied Chinese painting for more than two years.

七、"动词＋了＋数量词＋(名词)"表示某种活动在过去完成的数量

这个句型跟第六单元所不同的是说到某种活动的次数或质量而不是时间。例如：

(1) 他看了三次电影。

Tā kànle sān cì diànyǐng.

(2) 他买了五本书。

Tā mǎile wǔ běn shū.

第一个句子是说那个人在过去某段时间里曾看过三次电影。第二句是说“他”在过去曾买过五本书，但是“他”是在过去什么时候看的电影，什么时候买的书却不知道。

请注意下面句子的问题与回答：

小王买了三本书。

Xiǎo Wáng mǎile sān běn shū.

问题：(1)上面句子里有几个“了”字？

回答：就有一个。

问题：(2)这个“了”字在什么词的后面？

回答：在动词的后面。

问题：(3)动词跟“了”字的后面有什么词？

回答：有数量词跟名词。

问题：(4)小王买了几本书？

回答：三本。

问题：(5)他那三本书是什么时候买的？我们知道吗？

回答：不知道。

问题：(6)如果要想说明小王在什么时候买了三本书怎么办？

回答：可以在句子里加上确定的过去时间词，如“昨天”、“去年”、“我在中国的时候”等。

练 习 七

一、请在下面句子中的"了"字下面点一个点(.),数量词下面画一条线(——)。

1. 上星期我们参观了一个工厂。

Shàng xīngqī wǒmen cānguānle yí gè gōngchǎng.

2. 前年我们买了一辆旧汽车。

Qiánnián wǒmen mǎile yí liàng jiù qìchē.

3. 那天来了几位客人?

Nà tiān láile jǐ wèi kèren?

4. 昨天晚上我看了一个电影。

Zuótiān wǎnshang wǒ kànle yí gè diànyǐng.

5. 她买了几件新衣服。

Tā mǎile jǐ jiàn xīn yīfu.

二、请把下面的句子译成英文:

1. 李教授写了两本历史书。

Lǐ jiàoshòu xiěle liǎng běn lìshǐ shū.

2. 每人买了一本字典。

Měi rén mǎile yì běn zìdiǎn.

3. 他杀了一个女人。

Tā shāle yí gè nǚrén.

4. 去年他到欧洲去了一个多月。

Qùnián tā dào Ōuzhōu qùle yí gè duō yuè.

5. 他刚才休息了一会儿。

Tā gāngcái xiūxile yíhuìr.

三、请把下面的句子译成中文：

1. I drank two bowls of soup last night.

2. It rained a little yesterday morning.

3. His parents bought a house in Boston last year.

4. I wrote two hundred characters yesterday.

5. I saw two movies last month.

八、“时间词＋没(有)＋动词＋了”表示某种活动有若干时间没有发生

当“了”出现在时间词、“没(有)”、动词的后面，这个句子表示某种活动到目前为止已经有多久没发生了。比如说“我三天没吃中国菜了”，意思是从三天前开始到现在“我”已经有三天没吃中国菜了。

(一) 请注意下面句子的问题及回答：

小李三天没(有)喝酒了。

Xiǎo Lǐ sān tiān méi (yǒu) hē jiǔ le.

问题：(1)上面句子里的“了”字在哪儿？

回答：在句子的最后面。

问题：(2)时间词在动词的前边还是后边？

回答：前边。

问题：(3)小李最后一次喝酒是在几天以前？

回答：三天以前。

问题：(4)小李几天没有喝酒了？

回答：三天。

(二) 请比较下面两个句子：

(1) 小王两天没(有)吃饭了。

Xiǎo Wáng liǎng tiān méi (yǒu) chīfàn le.

(2) 小王两天没(有)吃饭。

Xiǎo Wáng liǎng tiān méi(yǒu) chīfàn.

问题：(1)第一个句子跟第二个句子有什么不同？

回答：第二个句子没有"了"。

问题：(2)从第二个句子我们可以知道小王在什么时候两天没吃饭吗？

回答：不知道。我们只知道他在过去曾有两天没吃饭，但是不知道在什么时候。

问题：(3)副词"已经"只可以在第一个，还是第二个句型中出现？

回答：第一个。

问题：(4)时间词，如"过去"、"去年"、"昨天"等表示过去的时间只能在哪个句型中出现？

回答：第二个。

练习八

一、请在下面句子的时间词下面画一条线(——)，动词下面画一个点(．)，“了”字下面画一个圈(。)。

例：我们八年没有见面了。

Wǒmen bā nián méiyou jiànmiàn le.

1. 孩子两天没回家了。

Háizi liǎng tiān méi huí jiā le.

2. 那个学生已经三天没来上课了。

Nàge xuésheng yǐjing sān tiān méi lái shàngkè le.

3. 小田已经有两次没来考试了。

Xiǎo Tián yǐjing yǒu liǎng cì méi lái kǎoshì le.

4. 到明年四月，我就三年没做事了。

Dào míngnián sìyuè, wǒ jiù sān nián méi zuò shì le.

5. 已经一个月没下雨了。

Yǐjing yí gè yuè méi xià yǔ le.

二、改错：

1. 他没吃两天饭了。

Tā méi chī liǎng tiān fàn le.

2. 我们明天一天没看书了。

Wǒmen míngtiān yì tiān méi kàn shū le.

3. 我去年一天没喝酒了。

Wǒ qùnián yì tiān méi hē jiǔ le.

4. 他每星期(有)一天不做事了。

Tā měi xīngqī (yǒu) yì tiān bú zuò shì le.

5. 我没看三个钟头的电视了。

Wǒ méi kàn sān ge zhōngtóu de diànshì le.

三、把下面的句子译成英文：

1. 我们差不多五年没见面了。

Wǒmen chà bu duō wǔ nián méi jiànmiàn le.

2. 我好几天没吃中国饭了。

Wǒ hǎo jǐ tiān méi chī Zhōngguófàn le.

3. 那个孩子已经有三天没洗澡了。

Nà gè háizi yǐjing yǒu sān tiān méi xǐzǎo le.

4. 他跟他太太两天没说话了。

Tā gēn tā tàitai liǎng tiān méi shuō huà le.

5. 一个多月没下雨了。

Yí gè duō yuè méi xià yǔ le.

四、请把下面的句子译成中文：

1. Last month he didn't come to class for a week.

2. He hasn't been to class for a week.

3. He hasn't gone home for more than 10 years.

4. He didn't write to his parents while he was in China.

5. It has been five years since I last saw him.

九、"动词＋了＋宾语＋了"表示某种活动已经完成了，也表示事态有了变化

当句子里有两个"了"，一个在动词后面，一个在宾语后面，没有时间词或数量词是表示某种活动已经完成了，也表示事态有了变化。如"他买了车了"意思是从前没车，现在有了，"他"买车的活动已经完成了。

请注意下面句子的问题及回答：

孩子们都吃了饭了。

Háizimen dōu chīle fàn le.

问题：(1)上面的句子里有几个"了"字？

回答：有两个。

问题：(2)第一个"了"字在什么词的后面？

回答：在动词的后面。

问题：(3)第二个"了"呢？

回答：在句尾宾语的后面。

问题：(4)我们知道孩子们什么时候吃饭吗？

回答：不知道。

问题：(5)从上面的句子我们知道不知道孩子吃了多少饭？

回答：不知道。

问题：(6)从上面的句子只能知道什么？

回答：只知道孩子吃了饭了。

十、“动词＋宾语＋了表示某种活动”已经完成或表示情况的改变

当句子里只有一个“了”而这个“了”是在动词及宾语的后面，这种句子可能会有两个意思，比方说“他喝酒了”，这个句子可以解释为他从前不喝酒，现在喝酒了——表示情况的改变；也可以解释为“他喝酒的活动已经完成了”——动作的完成。如果说话时的情况清楚，那么句子的意思就明确了；否则在动词后面再加一个“了”字才可以只表示动作的完成。如说“他喝了酒了”。

请注意下面句子的问题及回答：

我们听录音了。

Wǒmen tīng lùyīn le.

问题：(1) 上面的句子里有几个“了”字？

回答：只有一个。

问题：(2) 那个“了”字在句子的什么地方？

回答：在句子的最后、宾语的后面。

上面这个句子在不同的情况下可能有两个不同的意思：一个是听录音的活动已经完成了；一个是“我们”从前不听录音，现在听了。例如：如果老师问：

你们听录音了没有？

学生可以回答：

我们听录音了。(动作完成了)

如果老师知道学生一直不听录音，就给学生讲了听录音的重要性，几天后老师问：

你们现在还不听录音吗？

学生可以回答：

我们听录音了。(情况改变了)

比较下面的句子,看“动词+‘了’+宾语+‘了’”与“动词+宾语+‘了’”的异同:

(1) 孩子吃了饭了。

Háizi chīle fàn le.

(2) 孩子吃饭了。

Háizi chīfàn le.

问题:(1)第一个句子跟第二个句子有什么不同?

回答:第一个句子有两个“了”字,第二个句子只有一个“了”字。

问题:(2)第二个句子比第一个句子少了哪个“了”字?

回答:少了动词后面的“了”字。

问题:(3)第一个句子跟第二个句子意思有什么不同?

回答:这两个句子都可以说明孩子吃饭的活动已经完成,但是第二个句子也可能说明情况的改变。比方说,从前孩子“不愿吃饭”,或“不会吃饭”,或“没有开始吃饭”,可是现在“吃饭”了。

问题:(4)既然第二个句型也可以表示动作已经完成,为什么还要用第一个句型呢?

回答:为了避免句子的意思不清楚。

问题:(5)如果情况很清楚,动词后面的“了”字是不是可以省略呢?

回答:是的。所以“动词+‘了’+宾语+‘了’”的句型也可以写作:动词+(“了”)+宾语+“了”。

练习九

一、请把下列句子译成英文：

1. 我已经买(了) 报纸了，你不必买了。

Wǒ yǐjing mǎi(le) bàozhǐ le, nǐ bú bì mǎi le.

2. 我昨天在路上遇见(了)老张了。

Wǒ zuótiān zài lù shang yùjiàn(le) Lǎo Zhāng le.

3. 你吃饭了吗?我吃了。

Nǐ chīfàn le ma? Wǒ chī le.

4. 你喜欢吃中国饭了吗？我喜欢吃了。

Nǐ xǐhuan chī Zhōngguófàn le ma? Wǒ xǐhuan chī le.

5. 这个问题你们讨论了没有？我们讨论了。

Zhège wèntí nǐmen tǎolùnle méiyǒu? Wǒmen tǎolùn le.

6. 学生都预备功课了。

Xuésheng dōu yùbèi gōngkè le.

a.

b.

7. 他吃牛肉了。

Tā chī niúròu le.

a.

b.

8. 我写信了。

Wǒ xiě xìn le.

a.

b.

9. 我写了信了。

Wǒ xiěle xìn le.

10. 学生都下(了)车了。

Xuésheng dōu xià(le) chē le.

二、请把下面的句子译成中文：

1. Have you eaten?

2. Mr Zhang went to the store.

3. I took a bus today.

4. He bought a pen yesterday.

5. Mrs Li sold her old car.

6. All of those students did their homework.

7. I have paid him (the money).

8. Have you sung (the song)?

9. Have you bought the watch he liked?

10. I've already bought that watch.

十一、“了”在结果补语、“被”字句、“把”字句中表示活动的完成

当“了”出现在结果补语、“被”字句、“把”字句句尾都表示某项活动的完成。请看下面的例句。

（一） 动词＋结果补语＋“了”

“了”字在结果补语后面表示活动的完成。

例：这本书我看完了。

Zhè běn shū wǒ kànwǎn le.

“了”字在结果补语象“完”、“好”、“见”等后面都表示活动的结果及完成。

练 习 十

一、请在下面句子中的结果补语下面画一条线（——），并把句子译成英文：

1. 这些生字我都记住了。

Zhèxiē shēngzì wǒ dōu jìzhu le.

2. 那个作业我已经写完了。

Nàge zuòyè wǒ yǐjing xiěwán le.

3. 东西他都卖光了。

Dōngxi tā dōu màiguāng le.

4. 屋子收拾干净了。

Wūzi shōushi gānjìng le.

5. 汽车已经修理好了。

Qìchē yǐjing xiūlǐ hǎo le.

二、请把下面的句子译成中文：

1. He opened the door.

2. Two days ago, the tickets were all sold out.

3. You've pronounced this character incorrectly.

4. I saw him yesterday.

5. I have finished the job.

（二）“被”＋主语＋动词＋结果补语＋“了”

“了”字在“被”字句中出现时表示活动的完成。

例：钱都被人拿走了。

Qián dōu bèi rén názǒu le.

当“了”出现在被动句句尾时，表示某种活动已经完成。

练习十一

一、请把下面的句子译成英文：

1. 他被大家说服了。

Tā bèi dàjiā shuōfú le.

2. 她女儿被人带走了。

Tā nǚ'ér bèi rén dàizǒu le.

3. 一条小狗被车轧死了。

Yì tiáo xiǎo gǒu bèi chē yàsǐ le.

4. 车被人偷走了。

Chē bèi rén tōuzǒu le.

5. 这件事情被他发现了。

Zhè jiàn shìqing bèi tā fāxiàn le.

二、请把下面的句子译成中文：

1. Our conversation was overheard by them.

2. He was often beaten by his parents.

3. My watch has been stolen.

4. I was scolded by my mother.

5. The dog was killed by the farmer.

(三) "把"＋宾语＋动词＋"了"

"了"字在把字句中表示行动的完成。

例：李小姐把她的房子卖了。

Lǐ xiǎojiě bǎ tā de fángzi mài le.

练习十二

一、请把下面的句子译成英文：

1. 孩子们把糖都吃了。

Háizimen bǎ táng dōu chī le.

2. 父母把汽车送给我了。

Fùmǔ bǎ qìchē sònggěi wǒ le.

3. 我把钱全给他了。

Wǒ bǎ qián quán gěi tā le.

4. 学生把书放在桌子上了。

Xuésheng bǎ shū fàngzài zhuōzi shàng le.

5. 我把功课做好了。

Wǒ bǎ gōngkè zuòhǎo le.

二、请把下面的句子译成中文：

1. She tidied up the living room.

2. I forgot his name.

3. I wrote that character wrong.

4. He broke the teacup.

5. I ate all of the apples.

三、改正下面的错句：

1. 那本书被人偷走。

Nà běn shū bèi rén tōuzǒu.

2. 孩子被妈妈打。

Háizi bèi māma dǎ.

3. 他把糖吃。

Tā bǎ táng chī.

4. 我把那张地图借。

Wǒ bǎ nà zhāng dìtú jiè.

5. 衣服洗。

Yīfu xǐ.

6. 他的父亲被人杀。

Tā de fùqīn bèi rén shā.

7. 这几个字我忘记。

Zhè jǐ ge zì wǒ wàngjì.

8. 信已经写。

Xìn yǐjing xiě.

9. 他把椅子搬进。

Tā bǎ yǐzi bānjìn.

10. 菜都被孩子吃。
Cài dōu bèi háizi chī.

十二、复习题

一、把下面的句子译成英文：

1. 我懂中文。
Wǒ dǒng Zhōngwén.

2. 我懂中文了。
Wǒ dǒng Zhōngwén le.

3. 他们没有钱。
Tāmen méiyǒu qián.

4. 他们没有钱了。
Tāmen méiyǒu qián le.

5. 爸爸不想做买卖。
Bàba bù xiǎng zuò mǎimai.

6. 爸爸不想做买卖了。
Bàba bù xiǎng zuò mǎimai le.

7. 他是美国人。
Tā shì Měiguórén.

8. 他是美国人了。

Tā shì Měiguórén le.

9. 学生都听得懂英语。

Xuésheng dōu tīng de dǒng Yīngyǔ.

10. 学生都听得懂英语了。

Xuésheng dōu tīng de dǒng Yīngyǔ le.

二、把下面的句子译成中文：

1. I can (know how to) speak Chinese now.

2. He doesn't like his wife any more.

3. The children are all grown up now.

4. I can not study any more.

5. Now I know his name.

6. I am hungry (now).

7. What time is it now?

8. This watch is broken (now).

9. It's not early any more (i.e. It's getting late.).

10. He is now much taller than I am.

三、请按照每句后面英文的意思决定需要不需要加"了"字，如需要请写"了"字，如不需要请画一个"×"。

1. 他喜欢吃中国饭______。
   Tā xǐhuan chī Zhōngguófàn ______.
   (He likes to eat Chinese food.)
2. 我的车坏______。
   Wǒ de chē huài ______.
   (My car is broken.)
3. 她不喜欢她的男朋友______。
   Tā bù xǐhuan tā de nán péngyou ______.
   (She doesn't like her boy friend anymore.)
4. 我妹妹不聪明______。
   Wǒ mèimei bù cōngming ______.
   (My (younger) sister is not smart.)
5. 你母亲好______吗？
   Nǐ mǔqin hǎo ______ ma?
   (Has your mother recovered?)
6. 张先生不在书店里______。
   Zhāng xiānsheng bú zài shūdiàn lǐ ______.
   (Mr Zhang is no longer at book store.)
7. 我不记得你的名字______。
   Wǒ bú jì de nǐ de míngzi ______.
   (I can't remember your name now.)
8. 你们有车______吗？
   Nǐmen yǒu chē ______ ma?
   (Do you have a car now?)

9. 汽车现在都小______。

Qìchē xiànzài dōu xiǎo ______.

(Cars have gotten smaller now.)

10. 那个橘子坏______。

Nàge júzi huài ______。

(That orange is spoiled.)

四、请把下面的句子翻译成英文：

1. 别忘了把书带来。

Bié wàngle bǎ shū dàilai.

2. 孩子们都大了，父母都老了。

Háizimen dōu dà le，fùmǔ dōu lǎo le.

3. 我的车坏了，怎么修也修不好。

Wǒ de chē huài le，zěnme xiū yě xiū bù hǎo.

4. 我们一学会说话就学写字了。

Wǒmen yì xuéhuì shuōhuà jiù xué xiězì le.

5. 学生真聪明，一学就会了。

Xuésheng zhēn cōngming，yì xué jiù huì le.

6. 天气太冷了，别出去了！

Tiānqì tài lěng le，bié chūqu le！

7. 我们已经学了三个月的中文了。

Wǒmen yǐjing xuéle sān gè yuè de Zhōngwén le.

8. 他昨天喝了三瓶啤酒。

Tā zuótiān hēle sān píng píjiǔ.

9. 钱都被人偷走了。

Qián dōu bèi rén tōuzǒu le.

10. 弟弟把糖都吃完了。

Dìdi bǎ táng dōu chīwán le.

11. 我一吃就知道这个菜坏了。

Wǒ yì chī jiù zhīdao zhège cài huài le.

12. 张小姐太漂亮了。

Zhāng xiǎojiě tài piàoliang le.

13. 我的钱都用完了。

Wǒ de qián dōu yòngwán le.

14. 火车快要开了。

Huǒchē kuàiyào kāi le.

15. 他这几天忙极了，别去看他了。

Tā zhè jǐ tiān mángjí le, bié qù kàn tā le.

16. 他喝了两瓶酒了，不能再喝了。

Tā hēle liǎng píng jiǔ le, bù néng zài hē le.

17. 我给他打了五个电话了，都没打通。

Wǒ gěi tā dǎle wǔ ge diànhuà le, dōu méi dǎtōng.

18. 要是明天下雨,我就不去了。

Yàoshi míngtiān xià yǔ, wǒ jiù bú qù le.

19. 要是我有钱,我就到欧洲去旅行了。

Yàoshi wǒ yǒu qián, wǒ jiù dào Ōuzhōu qù lǚxíng le.

20. 他一来了我就走了。

Tā yì láile wǒ jiù zǒu le.

五、请把下面的句子译成中文:

1. I am not going any more.

2. He went to China last week.

3. My sister is much taller than before.

4. What time is it now? It's 4:15 now.

5. This book is too expensive. Don't buy it.

6. My brother is going to graduate from college very soon.

7. I went home right after class.

8. He has seen three movies this week.

9. Where did he go?

10. He went to school.

11. Have you told your father?

12. I'll go home right after I buy the book.

13. I went home right after I saw the movie.

14. Did you study last week? No, I didn't.

15. I don't want to drink wine anymore.

16. I learned a little Chinese when I was in China.

17. I know how to drive now.

18. He understands English now.

19. He is better now.

20. I teach three hours every day.

贰、"着"的用法

动态助词"着"可用在动词和形容词后表示状态和动作的持续。

一、"动词＋'着'"表示事物存在的状态

(一)"动作动词＋'着'"表示状态

有些动词通常表示一种动作,如"放、摆、挂、扛、穿、戴"等。

(1) 小明往墙上挂一幅画儿。

Xiǎo Míng wǎng qiáng shàng guà yì fú huàr.

(2) 妈妈给毛毛穿新衣服。

Māma gěi Máomao chuān xīn yīfu.

此类动作完成后,受动作影响的事物会保持动作的状态,这种状态要用"着"来表示:

(1) 画在墙上挂着。

Huà zài qiáng shàng guàzhe.

(2) 新衣服毛毛穿着呢。

Xīn yīfu Máomao chuānzhe ne.

在上述句子里,"挂着"表示"画儿"存在的状态,"穿着"表示"新衣服"存在的状态。

如说话人谈论的不是受动作影响的事物,而是要描写一个处所,说明那个处所有什么事物,并说明它以什么状态存在,就可以把处所词放在句首,用下列句式表示:

(1) 墙上挂着一幅画儿。

Qiáng shàng guàzhe yì fú huàr.

（2）毛毛身上穿着新衣服。

Máomao shēn shàng chuānzhe xīn yīfu.

这种句子叫存现句。存现句是描写性的。我们可以用存现句描写一间屋子的陈设：

（3）屋子中间放着一张床，靠墙摆着一套沙发，沙发前放着一张茶几，茶几上摆着一个花瓶。

Wūzi zhōngjiān fàngzhe yì zhāng chuáng, kào qiáng bǎizhe yí tào shāfā, shāfā qián fàngzhe yì zhāng chájī, chájī shàng bǎizhe yí gè huāpíng.

也可以描写景物：

（4）村外种着一片桃树，树上结着很多桃子。树下站着一些摘桃的农民。

Cūnwài zhòngzhe yí piàn táoshù, shù shàng jiēzhe hěn duō táozi. Shùxià zhànzhe yìxiē zhāi táo de nóngmín.

还可以描写人的穿着打扮：

（5）这个姑娘头上戴着花围巾，身上穿着红羽绒服，手上戴着皮手套。

Zhège gūniang tóu shàng dàizhe huā wéijīn, shēn shàng chuānzhe hóng yǔróngfú, shǒu shàng dàizhe pí shǒutào.

（二）"着"与"在"的比较

"动词＋'着'"表示一种状态，是描写性的；"'在'＋动词"是叙述性的，表示动作的进行。比较：

（1）A. 他穿着一件红毛衣。

Tā chuānzhe yí jiàn hóng máoyī.

B. 他在穿那件红毛衣。

Tā zài chuān nà jiàn hóng máoyī.

（2）A. 墙上挂着一幅山水画儿。

Qiáng shàng guàzhe yì fú shānshuǐ huàr.

B. 他在往墙上挂一幅山水画儿。

Tā zài wǎng qiáng shàng guà yì fú shānshuǐ huàr.

(3) A. 门开着。

Mén kāizhe.

B. 他在开门。

Tā zài kāi mén.

(4) A. 院子里种着很多花。

Yuànzi li zhòngzhe hěn duō huā.

B. 他正在院子里种花。

Tā zhèngzài yuànzi li zhòng huā.

如果句子里有表示动作发生的处所的介词"'在'+名词"词组，表示动作进行的"在"就与介词"在"合一，见例4. B。

(三)此类句子的结构特点：

1. 动词前不能加"在"。例如：

(1) * 他身上在穿着一件红毛衣。

Tā shēn shàng zài chuānzhe yí jiàn hóng máoyī.

(2) * 墙上在挂着一幅山水画儿。

Qiáng shàng zài guàzhe yì fú shānshuǐ huàr.

(3) * 门外在开着很多牡丹花。

Mén wài zài kāizhe hěn duō mǔdān huār.

(4) * 院子里在种着很多树。

Yuànzi li zài zhòngzhe hěn duō shù.

2. "着"的前后不能加其它成分，如补语，其它的动态助词("了"、"过")等。下面的句子是不对的：

(1) * 湖边上长满着果树。

Húbiān shàng zhǎng mǎn zhe guǒshù.

(2) * 他身上穿着了一件新毛衣。

Tā shēnshàng chuānzhe le yí jiàn xīn máoyī.

(3) * 桌上放着过一瓶花。

Zhuō shàng fàngzhe guo yì píng huā.

(4) * 山上开遍着鲜花。

Shān shàng kāibiàn zhe xiānhuā.

3. 可以出现在这种句子里的动词多表示手的动作。如：挂、放、摆、盖、蒙、系、摞、堆、搭、架、带、戴、留、藏、含、刻、写、涂、雕刻、补、打、钉、晒、洒、晾、插等。

练习一

一、按图描写一段话，要求尽可能用"着"：

1. 人物

2. 风景

3. 房间

二、把下列句子翻译成汉语：

1. There is a book (placed) on the desk.
   He put the book on the desk.

2. Xiao Ming is wearing a new cap.
   Xiao Ming put his cap on his head.

3. The elder sister is holding a bunch of flowers.
   The elder sister put a bunch of flowers in the vase.

4. The students are writing characters in their exercise books.
   Many characters are written in the exercise book.

5. There grow many trees at the entrance.
   People are planting trees at the entrance.

6. An oil painting was hung on the wall.
   He hung the oil painting on the wall.

7. The teacher is standing in the front of the classroom.
   There are many students sitting in the classroom.

8. The father is wearing a black overcoat.
   The father is putting on his overcoat.

三、判断正误：

1. A. 花瓶里在插很多鲜花。
   Huāpíng li zài chā hěn duō xiānhuā.

B. 花瓶里插着很多鲜花。

Huāpíng li chāzhe hěn duō xiānhuā.

2. A. 小明头上戴帽子。

Xiǎo Míng tóu shàng dài màozi.

B. 小明头上戴着帽子。

Xiǎo Míng tóu shàng dàizhe màozi.

3. 甲：你在干什么呢？

Nǐ zài gàn shénme ne?

乙：A. 我在穿衣服。

Wǒ zài chuān yīfu.

B. 我穿着衣服。

Wǒ chuānzhe yīfu.

4. 甲：你在晒被子吗？

Nǐ zài shài bèizi ma?

乙：A. 对，我晒着被子。

Duì, wǒ shàizhe bèizi.

B. 对，我在晒被子。

Duì, wǒ zài shài bèizi.

5. A. 桌子上堆满着书。

Zhuōzi shàng duī mǎn zhe shū.

B. 桌子上堆着书。

Zhuōzi shàng duīzhe shū.

C. 桌子上堆满了书。

Zhuōzi shàng duī mǎn le shū.

6. A. 柜子里挂着了几件衣服。

Guìzi li guàzhe le jǐ jiàn yīfu.

B. 柜子里挂了几件衣服。

Guìzi li guàle jǐ jiàn yīfu.

C. 柜子里挂着几件衣服。

Guìzi li guàzhe jǐjiàn yīfu.

7. 甲：我的帽子呢？

Wǒ de màozi ne?

乙：A. 你在戴帽子。

Nǐ zài dài màozi.

B. 你戴着呢。

Nǐ dàizhe ne.

C. 你头上戴着帽子。

Nǐ tóu shàng dàizhe màozi.

8. 甲：我刚买的那张画呢？

Wǒ gāng mǎi de nà zhāng huàr ne?

乙：A. 墙上挂着一幅画儿。

Qiáng shàng guàzhe yì fú huàr.

B. 在墙上挂着呢。

Zài qiáng shàng guàzhe ne.

C. 挂在墙上了。

Guà zài qiáng shàng le.

二、表示人的姿态

有些动词表示人的动作，这些动作可以持续，结果成为一种状态——人的姿态，这时要加上“着”。如：

(1) 他低着头，想了很长时间。

Tā dīzhe tóu, xiǎngle hěn cháng shíjiān.

(2) 我弯着腰，看了半天。

Wǒ wānzhe yāo, kànle bàntiān.

（3）他们俩手拉着手。

Tāmen liǎ shǒu lāzhe shǒu.

上述动词前可以加上“在”，如：

（1）他在低着头。

Tā zài dīzhe tóu.

（2）他在弯着腰。

Tā zài wānzhe yāo.

（3）他们俩在手拉着手。

Tāmen liǎ zài shǒu lāzhe shǒu.

有一些动词也可以构成存现句，把处所词放在句首。例如：

（1）A. 他背着一个受伤的男孩。

Tā bēizhe yí gè shòushāng de nánháir.

B. 他背上背着一个受伤的男孩。

Tā bèi shàng bēizhe yí gè shòushāng de nánháir.

（2）A. 一个陌生人在椅子上坐着。

Yí gè mòshēng rén zài yǐzi shàng zuòzhe.

B. 椅子上坐着一个陌生人。

Yǐzi shàng zuòzhe yí gè mòshēng rén.

（3）A. 纪念碑在广场中间矗立着。

Jìniànbēi zài guǎngchǎng zhōngjiān chùlìzhe.

B. 广场中间矗立着人民英雄纪念碑。

Guǎngchǎng zhōngjiān chùlìzhe Rénmín Yīngxióng Jìniànbēi.

（4）A. 病人在床上躺着。

Bìngrén zài chuáng shàng tǎngzhe.

B. 床上躺着个病人。

Chuáng shàng tǎngzhe ge bìngrén.

构成存现句后就不能再加“在”了。

构成此类句子动词主要是人体动作动词，如“站、立、坐、蹲、躺、跪、扛、抱、举”等。

练习二

一、判断正误：

1. A. 我进门的时候，她怀中正抱了一个孩子。

   Wǒ jìn mén de shíhou, tā huái zhōng zhèng bàole yí gè háizi.

   B. 我进门的时候，她怀中正抱着一个孩子。

   Wǒ jìn mén de shíhou, tā huái zhōng zhèng bàozhe yí gè háizi.

2. A. 一本书放着在桌子上。

   Yì běn shū fàngzhe zài zhuōzi shàng.

   B. 桌子上放着一本书。

   Zhuōzi shàng fàngzhe yì běn shū.

3. A. 他围着一条新围巾。

   Tā wéizhe yì tiáo xīn wéijīn.

   B. 他在围着一条新围巾。

   Tā zài wéizhe yì tiáo xīn wéijīn.

4. A. 椅子上坐着一个小姑娘。

   Yǐzi shàng zuòzhe yí gè xiǎo gūniang.

   B. 椅子上在坐着一个小姑娘。

   Yǐzi shàng zài zuòzhe yí gè xiǎo gūniang.

5. A. 那个人在墙角蹲着。

   Nàge rén zài qiángjiǎo dūnzhe.

   B. 那个人蹲着在墙角。

   Nàge rén dūnzhe zài qiángjiǎo.

6. A. 他在床上躺着看书。

Tā zài chuáng shàng tǎngzhe kàn shū.

B. 他躺着在床上看书。

Tā tǎngzhe zài chuáng shàng kàn shū.

7. A. 他在低着头想事情。

Tā zài dīzhe tóu xiǎng shìqing.

B. 他在想事情低着头。

Tā zài xiǎng shìqing dīzhe tóu.

8. A. 我进来的时候，他正在躺着。

Wǒ jìnlai de shíhou, tā zhèng zài tǎngzhe.

B. 床上在躺着一个病人。

Chuáng shàng zài tǎngzhe yí gè bìngrén.

二、把下面的句子变成存现句：

例1：画儿在墙上挂着。

Huàr zài qiáng shàng guàzhe.

墙上挂着一幅画儿。

Qiáng shàng guàzhe yì fú huàr.

例2：把画儿挂在墙上。

Bǎ huàr guà zài qiáng shàng.

墙上挂着一幅画儿。

Qiáng shàng guàzhe yì fú huàr.

1. 把书放在桌子上。

Bǎ shū fàng zài zhuōzi shàng.

2. 收音机在桌子上摆着。

Shōuyīnjī zài zhuōzi shàng bǎizhe.

3. 把帽子戴在头上。

Bǎ màozi dài zài tóu shàng.

4. 衣服在柜子里挂着。

Yīfu zài guìzi li guàzhe.

5. 把字写在本子上。

Bǎ zì xiě zài běnzi shàng.

6. 钟在墙上挂着。

Zhōng zài qiáng shàng guàzhe.

7. 把画印在书的封面上。

Bǎ huàr yìn zài shū de fēngmiàn shàng.

8. 花在花瓶里插着。

Huār zài huāpíng li chāzhe.

三、"动词+'着'"表示动作的持续

(一)"着"用在表示动作的动词后,表示一个动作在持续进行。例如:

(1) 汽车在公路上飞快地开着,我们离目的地越来越近了。

Qìchē zài gōnglù shàng fēikuài de kāizhe, wǒmen lí mùdìdì yuè lái yuè jìn le.

(2) 雨不停地下着,下了一整天了。

Yǔ bù tíng de xiàzhe, xiàle yì zhěng tiān le.

(3) 孩子们笑着,唱着,高兴极了。

Háizimen xiàozhe, chàngzhe, gāoxìng jí le.

(4) 女儿在讲事情的经过,他静静地听着。

Nǚ'ér zài jiǎng shìqing de jīngguò, tā jìngjìng de tīngzhe.

从表达方面来说,这种句子不是叙述性的,即不是叙述一个动作在进行,而是描写性的,即通过对人物持续进行的动作行为的描述,来描写人物的姿态、心理、状态。正因为如此,此类句子动词前常常有描写性的状语。如例1."飞快地"描写汽车跑的状态,例2."不停地"描写天气下雨的状态,例4."静静地"描写"他听"的状态。

表示动作持续的“着”多出现于文学作品，口语中较少使用。

（二）句子的结构特点

1. 因为“着”表示动作的持续，所以上文一般要交代这个动作已在进行或将要进行的必然性和可能性。这种“着”很少出现于一篇文章或一段话的开头。例如：

（1）现在是立冬前后，快晌午了，太阳溶化着大道两旁树枝上的霜花，水不断地滴落在她的头上。

Xiànzài shì lìdōng qiánhòu, kuài shǎngwǔ le, tàiyáng rónghuàzhe dàdào liǎngpáng shùzhī shàng de shuānghuā, shuǐ búduàn de dīluò zài tā de tóu shàng.

“立冬前后”、“快晌午了”是“霜花”“溶化着”的条件。

（2）东郭先生赶着驴，在路上慢慢地走着。

Dōngguō xiānsheng gǎnzhe lǘ, zài lù shàng mànmàn de zǒuzhe.

这句话的上文交代了东郭先生已赶驴上路。

（3）她心里怦怦地跳动，整个身子听着院子里的响声。

Tā xīn li pēngpēng de tiàodòng, zhěng gè shēnzi tīngzhe yuànzi li de xiǎngshēng.

这句话的上文交代了院子里有响声，所以引起她注意。

2. 因为“着”表示动作的持续，所以必然与一个确定的时间相联系。即“着”表示在某一确定的时间里行为动作在持续进行。见以上各例。如果叙述过去的事件，就表示在过去某个时间，动作已在进行。例如：

（1）去年春节前，我回到了故乡。当时家家都忙碌着，准备着。在农村，过春节可是一件大事。

Qùnián Chūnjié qián, wǒ huídào le gùxiāng. Dāngshí jiājiā dōu mánglùzhe, zhǔnbèizhe. Zài nóngcūn, guò Chūnjié kě shì yí jiàn dà shì.

这个句子里的“着”表示过去——去年春节前，“忙碌”、“准备”的动作在持续。

(2) 昨天下午我去幼儿园的时候，看见孩子们正在院子里唱着，笑着，很高兴。

Zuótiān xiàwǔ wǒ qù yòu'éryuán de shíhou, kànjiàn háizimen zhèng zài yuànzi li chàngzhe, xiàozhe, hěn gāoxìng.

在这种句子里，不仅要交代动作发生的时间——过去的某一时刻，而且还要把叙述时间由现在改为过去，这就是例(1)中出现“当时”、例(2)中出现“我去幼儿园的时候看见”的原因。否则叙述时间——现在——与动作持续的时间——过去——将发生冲突，句子就站不住了：

*昨天下午孩子们唱着，笑着，高兴极了。

Zuótian xiàwǔ háizimen chàngzhe, xiàozhe, gāoxìng jí le.

3. 只有表示可持续进行的动作动词才能用“着”，如“走、跑、画、唱、吃、喝、哭、笑、看、听”等。

(三)“着”与“在”、“……呢”比较

“在”或“……呢”表示动作的进行，即表示人物正在进行什么动作，是叙述性的。如果要问一个人正在做什么，问话和答话都只能用“在”、“……呢”。例如：

(1) 甲：刘明在干什么？

Liú Míng zài gàn shénme?

乙：刘明在听英语广播。

Liú Míng zài tīng Yīngyǔ guǎngbō.

(2) 甲：老王哪儿去了？

Lǎo Wáng nǎr qù le?

乙：老王打球呢。

Lǎo Wáng dǎ qiú ne.

而“着”是描写性的，上述句子不能用“着”替换“在”：

(1') 甲：* 小刘干着什么？

Xiǎo Liú gàn zhe shénme?

乙：* 小刘听着英语广播。

Xiǎo Liú tīngzhe Yīngyǔ guǎngbō.

(2') 甲：老王哪儿去了？

Lǎo Wáng nǎr qù le?

乙：* 老王打着球。

Lǎo Wáng dǎzhe qiú.

练习三

、用所给的词组成句子：

例：雪　下　不停地　着

雪不停地下着。

1. 小明　着　笑　不停地
2. 他　看　呆呆地　着　书上的字
3. 外面　雨　正在　着　下
4. 人们　议论　着　纷纷
5. 孩子们　跳　高兴地　着
6. 他们俩　握　手　着　用力地

二、判断正误：

1. A. 昨天下午他们讨论着旅行的问题。

Zuótiān xiàwǔ tāmen tǎolùnzhe lǚxíng de wèntí.

B. 昨天下午我去找他们的时候，他们正在讨论旅行的问题。

Zuótiān xiàwǔ wǒ qù zhǎo tāmen de shíhou, tāmen zhèng zài tǎolùn lǚxíng de wèntí.

2. A. 甲：他在干什么？

Tā zài gàn shénme？

乙：他在写字。

Tā zài xiě zì.

B. 甲：他干着什么？

Tā gànzhe shénme？

乙：他写着字。

Tā xiězhe zì.

3. A. 甲：小李呢？

Xiǎo Lǐ ne？

乙：他吃着饭。

Tā chīzhe fàn.

B. 甲：小李呢？

Xiǎo Lǐ ne？

乙：他吃饭呢。

Tā chī fàn ne.

4. A. 他们现在上着课。

Tāmen xiànzài shàngzhe kè.

B. 他们现在在上课呢。

Tāmen xiànzài zài shàngkè ne.

四、"动词＋'着'"表示伴随动作

（一）"着"可以用在连动句的第一个动词前，表示伴随的动作，这是一种很常见的用法。比如甲跟乙握手，握手时甲面带笑容，可以说：

（1）甲笑着跟乙握手。

Jiǎ xiàozhe gēn Yǐ wòshǒu.

一个人喜欢吃饭时看报,可以说:

(2) 他喜欢吃着饭看报。

Tā xǐhuān chīzhe fàn kàn bào.

类似的句子如:

(3) 连长拍着桌子说:"你们为什么不服从我的命令。"

Liánzhǎng pāizhe zhuōzi shuō: "Nǐmen wèishénme bù fúcóng wǒ de mìnglìng."

(4) 他们吃着饭商量事情。

Tāmen chīzhe fàn shāngliang shìqing.

(5) 小芳照着镜子梳头。

Xiǎo Fāng zhàozhe jìngzi shūtóu.

(6) 李刚总是哼着歌走路。

Li Gāng zǒng shì hēngzhe gē zǒu lù.

这类句子不能用"在"替换"着":

(1') * 甲在笑跟乙握手。

Jiǎ zài xiào gēn Yǐ wòshǒu.

(2') * 他在喜欢吃饭看报。

Tā zài xǐhuan chīfàn kàn bào.

(3') * 连长在拍桌子说……

Liánzhǎng zài pāi zhuōzi shuō...

(4') * 他们在吃饭商量事。

Tāmen zài chīfàn shāngliang shì.

(5') * 小芳在照镜子梳头。

Xiǎo Fāng zài zhào jìngzi shūtóu.

(6') * 李刚总是在哼歌走路。

Lǐ Gāng zǒng shì zài hēng gē zǒu lù.

这是因为两个动词的关系不是并列的,去掉第一个动词后的"着",

其伴随性就无法体现。

有的句子第一动词与第二动词的位置可以颠倒，不过颠倒后的主次关系就改变了。如：

(1) 他看着报吃饭。

Tā kànzhe bào chīfàn.

他吃着饭看报。

Tā chīzhe fàn kàn bào.

(2) 他唱着歌走路。

Tā chàngzhe gē zǒulù.

他走着路唱歌。

Tā zǒuzhe lù chàng gē.

这样的句子去掉“着”，在第一动词后加上一个停顿，可变成两个分句：

(1′)他看报，吃饭。

Tā kàn bào, chī fàn.

(2′)他唱歌，走路。

Tā chàng gē, zǒulù.

如果两个动词中有一个通常总表示另一个的伴随动作，就不能做上述变换。比如一个动词表示表情、姿势，另一动词表示说话、走路、握手等动作性较强的动作：

(3) 老王笑着跟老李握手。

Lǎo Wáng xiàozhe gēn Lǎo Lǐ wòshǒu.

*老王握着手跟老李笑。

Lǎo Wáng wòzhe shǒu gēn Lǎo Lǐ xiào.

(4) 连长拍着桌子大声喊。

Liánzhǎng pāizhe zhuōzi dàshēng hǎn.

*连长大声喊拍着桌子。

Liánzhǎng dàshēng hǎn pāizhe zhuōzi.

(5) 小姑娘总是哼着歌走路。

Xiǎo gūniang zǒngshì hēngzhe gē zǒulù.

＊小姑娘总是走着路哼歌。

Xiǎo gūniang zǒngshì zǒuzhe lù hēng gē.

(6) 他笑着对我点头。

Tā xiàozhe duì wǒ diǎn tóu.

＊他点着头对我笑。

Tā diǎnzhe tóu duì wǒ xiào.

上述句子一般也不能加“在”：

(3') ＊老王在笑着跟老李握手。

Lǎo Wáng zài xiàozhe gēn Lǎo Lǐ wòshǒu.

(4') ＊连长在拍着桌子大声喊。

Liánzhǎng zài pāizhe zhuōzi dàshēng hǎn.

(5') ＊小姑娘在哼着歌走路。

Xiǎo gūniang zài hēngzhe gē zǒulù.

(6') ＊他在笑着对我点头。

Tā zài xiàozhe duì wǒ diǎn tóu.

(二)有些连动句，第一动词后加“着”表示方式或状态，第二动词表示原因或目的。例如：

(1) 孩子们闹着去北海。

Háizimen nàozhe qù Běihǎi!

(2) 老王急着去开会，饭也没吃完。

Lǎo Wáng jízhe qù kāihuì, fàn yě méi chī wán.

(3) 大家忙着准备考试。

Dàjiā mángzhe zhǔnbèi kǎoshì.

(4) 刚进腊月，孩子们就吵着要买新年礼物了。

Gāng jìn Làyuè, háizimen jiù chǎozhe yào mǎi Xīnnián lǐwù le.

例1意思是：孩子们为去北海而闹；例2的意思是：老王因为去开会而着急；例3意思是：大家因为准备考试而忙；例4意思是：孩子们为了买新年的礼物而吵。

（三）如果一个人在说话的同时或稍晚一点开始了另一个动作，可以用“说”后加上“着”来表示。例如：

（1）“妈妈太累了，我自己走。”小江说着从妈妈怀里挣脱出来。

"Māma tài lèi le, wǒ zìjǐ zǒu." Xiǎo Jiāng shuōzhe cóng māma huái li zhèngtuō chūlai.

（2）“大家准备好了吗？”老师说着走进教室。

"Dàjiā zhǔnbèi hǎo le ma?" Lǎoshī shuōzhe zǒujìn jiàoshì.

（3）“你以后还敢撒谎吗？”爸爸说着，打了儿子一个耳光。

"Nǐ yǐhòu hái gǎn sāhuǎng ma?" Bàba shuōzhe, dǎle érzi yí gè ěrguāng.

练习四

一、用所给的词组成句子：

1. 张三　哭　说　着　“我再也不敢了。”
2. 他　红　脸　着　不说话
3. 小明　背　书包　着　上学
4. 李四　开　灯　着　睡觉
5. 妹妹　闹　要去看电影　着
6. 小刚　正　写信　忙着　给母亲
7. “到了。”　陈明　下了自行车　说　着
8. 弟弟　喊　拍手　着　“真好！”

二、判断正误：

1. A. 我跟老师握着手很紧。

Wǒ gēn lǎoshī wòzhe shǒu hěn jǐn.

B. 我跟老师紧紧地握着手。

Wǒ gēn lǎoshī jǐnjǐn de wòzhe shǒu.

2. A. 爸爸静静地听着我说，不时点点头。

Bàba jìngjìng de tīngzhe wǒ shuō, bùshí diǎndiǎn tóu.

B. 爸爸在静静地听我说，不时点点头。

Bàba zài jìngjìng de tīng wǒ shuō, bùshí diǎndiǎn tóu.

3. A. 连长看着战士脸色苍白，心里很难过。

Liánzhǎng kànzhe zhànshì liǎnsè cāngbái, xīnli hěn nánguò.

B. 连长看着战士苍白的脸，心里很难过。

Liánzhǎng kànzhe zhànshi cāngbái de liǎn, xīn li hěn nánguò.

4. A. 船上的人，有的照着相，有的唱着歌，有的划着船，十分热闹。

Chuán shàng de rén, yǒude zhàozhe xiàng, yǒude chàngzhe gē, yǒude huázhe chuán, shífēn rènào.

B. 船上的人，有的在照相，有的在唱歌，有的在划船，十分热闹。

Chuán shàng de rén, yǒude zài zhàoxiàng, yǒude zài chàng gē, yǒude zài huá chuán, shífēn rènào.

5. A. 他失败了，低着头走回座位。

Tā shībài le, dīzhe tóu zǒu huí zuòwèi.

B. 他失败了，低头走回座位。

Tā shībài le, dī tóu zǒu huí zuòwèi.

6. A. 听了老师的话，我看他，感动得流下了眼泪。

Tīngle lǎoshī de huà, wǒ kàn tā, gǎndòng de liúxià le yǎnlèi.

B. 听了老师的话，我看着他，感动得流下了眼泪。

Tīngle lǎoshī de huà, wǒ kànzhe tā, gǎndòng de liúxià le yǎnlèi.

五、"着"的成句作用

（一）有些动词，所表示的动作动作性不强，不能单独作谓语，更不能单独构成句子，组句时要加上"着"，表示动作在持续。例如：

（1）他在床上躺着。

Tā zài chuáng shàng tǎngzhe.

*他在床上躺。

Tā zài chuáng shàng tǎng.

（2）这封信我一直珍藏着。

Zhè fēng xìn wǒ yìzhí zhēncángzhe.

*这封信我一直珍藏。

Zhè fēng xìn wǒ yìzhí zhēncáng.

（3）老师在教室前边站着。

Lǎoshī zài jiàoshì qiánbian zhànzhe.

*老师在教室前边站。

Lǎoshī zài jiàoshì qiánbian zhàn.

此类动词多表示人体的动作、姿势。

（二）有些动词构成祈使句时，也要求用"着"或其它成份。例如：

（1）你等着/一下，我马上就回来。

Nǐ děngzhe/yíxià, wǒ mǎshàng jiù huílai.

*你等，我马上就回来。

Nǐ děng, wǒ mǎshàng jiù huílai.

（2）你看着点儿/一下，别叫猫偷吃了。

Nǐ kànzhe diǎnr/yíxià, bié jiào māo tōu chī le.

* 你看,别叫猫偷吃了。

Nǐ kàn, bié jiào māo tōu chī le.

(3) 你们听着,没有我的命令,谁也不许走。

Nǐmen tīng zhe, méiyǒu wǒ de mìnglìng, shuí yě bù xǔ zǒu.

* 你们听,没有我的命令,谁也不许走。

Nǐmen tīng, méiyǒu wǒ de mìnglìng, shuí yě bù xǔ zǒu.

(4) 下次再来,想着来看看我们。

Xià cì zài lái, xiǎngzhe lái kànkan wǒmen.

* 下次再来,想来看看我们。

Xià cì zài lái, xiǎng lái kànkan wǒmen.

此类动词有:仰、搁、托、捧、扶、挨、搂、伸、缩、披、呆、记、拿、举等。

形容词有一部分构成祈使句时,也要求或可以加"着":

(1) 慢着,我还有话要说呢。

Mànzhe, wǒ hái yǒu huà yào shuō ne.

* 慢,我还有话要说呢。

Màn, wǒ hái yǒu huà yào shuō ne.

(2) 稳着点儿,别慌!

Wěn zhe diǎnr, bié huāng!

* 稳点儿,别慌!

Wěn diǎnr, bié huāng!

(3) 机灵(着)点儿!

Jīling (zhe) diǎnr!

(4) 细致(着)点儿!

Xìzhì (zhe) diǎnr!

例3、4可去掉"着"。

练 习 五

一、将下列句子译成英文：

1. 你们在这儿等着，哪儿也别去。

   Nǐmen zài zhèr děngzhe, nǎr yě bié qù.

2. 躺着，别起来！

   Tǎngzhe, bié qǐlai.

3. 带着大衣，天快冷了。

   Dàizhe dàyī, tiān kuài lěng le.

4. 快着点儿，要晚了。

   Kuàizhe diǎnr, yào wǎn le.

5. 小心着点儿，别碰着头。

   Xiǎoxīnzhe diǎnr, bié pèngzhe tóu.

6. 小芳闹着叫爸爸带她去公园。

   Xiǎo Fāng nàozhe jiào bàba dài tā qù gōngyuán.

7. 我急着赶飞机，觉都没睡好。

   Wǒ jízhe gǎn fēijī, jiào dōu méi shuìhǎo.

8. 孩子们正忙着准备考试。

   Háizimen zhèng mángzhe zhǔnbèi kǎoshì.

二、判断正误：

1. A. 孩子们在教室里静静地坐。

   Háizimen zài jiàoshì li jìngjìng de zuò.

   B. 孩子们在教室里静静地坐着。

   Háizimen zài jiàoshì li jìngjìng de zuòzhe.

2. A. 这几本书我一直保存。

   Zhè jǐ běn shū wǒ yìzhí bǎocún.

   B. 这几本书我一直保存着。

Zhè jǐ běn shū wǒ yìzhí bǎocúnzhe.

3. A. 你们等着，我一会儿就来。

Nǐmen děngzhe, wǒ yíhuìr jiù lái.

B. 你们等，我一会儿就来。

Nǐmen děng, wǒ yíhuìr jiù lái.

4. A. 扶他！

Fú tā!

B. 扶着他！

Fúzhe tā!

5. A. 别在地上蹲，快起来！

Bié zài dì shàng dūn, kuài qǐlai.

B. 别在地上蹲着，快起来！

Bié zài dì shàng dūnzhe, kuài qǐlai.

6. A. 记，这件事对谁也不能说！

Jì, zhè jiàn shì duì shuí yě bù néng shuō.

B. 记着，这件事对谁也不能说！

Jìzhe, zhè jiàn shì duì shuí yě bù néng shuō.

7. A. 拿着，给你妈带去！

Názhe, gěi nǐ mā dàiqu.

B. 拿，给你妈带去！

Ná, gěi nǐ mā dàiqu.

8. A. 你们听，今天晚上谁也不许离开！

Nǐmen tīng, jīntiān wǎnshàng shuí yě bù xǔ líkai.

B. 你们听着，今天晚上谁也不许离开！

Nǐmen tīngzhe, jīntiān wǎnshàng shuí yě bù xǔ lí kai.

六、"着"的其他用法

(一)动词后加“着”，连用两次，后面再接其他动词，表示前一个动作正在进行当中，后一个动作就发生了，这时第一个动作自然就停止了，有“不知不觉”的意味。例如：

(1) 他想着想着笑了起来。

Tā xiǎngzhe xiǎngzhe xiàole qǐlai.

(2) 孩子哭着哭着睡着了。

Háizi kūzhe kūzhe shuìzháo le.

(3) 老人说着说着唱了起来。

Lǎorén shuōzhe shuōzhe chàngle qǐlai.

(4) 小马跑着跑着停了下来。

Xiǎo mǎ pǎozhe pǎozhe tíngle xiàlai.

这种句子的第二部分也可以是动词的否定形式或形容词：

(5) 汽车开着开着慢了下来。

Qìchē kāizhe kāizhe mànle xiàlai.

(6) 他喝着喝着脸红了起来。

Tā hēzhe hēzhe liǎn hóngle qǐlai.

(7) 小李吃着吃着不吃了。

Xiǎo Lǐ chīzhe chīzhe bù chī le.

(8) 他讲着讲着不讲了。

Tā jiǎngzhe jiǎngzhe bù jiǎng le.

第二部分为形容词的句子，出现形容词所表现的状态后，第一动词所表示的动作不一定停止进行。

(二)有的动词加“着”不加“着”意思相同，加“着”只有缓和语气的作用：

(1) 这次会议有一百多人参加，代表着二十多个国家的汉语教师。

Zhè cì huìyì yǒu yìbǎi duō rén cānjiā, dàibiǎozhe èrshí duō gè guójiā de Hànyǔ jiàoshī.

（2）他的演说充满着热情和信心。

Tā de yǎnshuō chōngmǎnzhe rèqíng hé xìnxīn.

（3）这个事件有着巨大的国际影响。

Zhège shìjiàn yǒuzhe jùdà de guójì yǐngxiǎng.

（4）这个地方也存在着不少问题。

Zhège dìfāng yě cúnzàizhe bù shǎo wèntí.

这种用法存在于书面语。

（三）作词缀，主要是介词的词缀，无意义。如“趋着、沿着、顺着、随着、朝着、向着、为着”；“怎么着”；“接着”等。

（四）“着呢”用在形容词后，表示程度高，是一种口语现象。例如：

（1）今天冷着呢。

Jīntiān lěngzhe ne.

（2）这个电影好看着呢，你一定要看！

Zhège diànyǐng hǎokànzhe ne，nǐ yídìng yào kàn！

（3）那个地方远着呢，你别去了。

Nàge dìfang yuǎnzhe ne，nǐ bié qù le.

（4）他们的日子过得舒服着呢。

Tāmen de rìzi guò de shūfuzhe ne.

叁、"过"的用法

一、"过"的意义

"过"表示曾经有某种经验，曾进行某一动作或存在某一状态，用"过"时，该动作已不进行或该状态已不存在。例如：

(1) 我去过北京。

Wǒ qùguo Běijīng.

（现在"我"在东京）

(2) 他爸爸当过工人。

Tā bàba dāngguo gōngrén.

（现在"他爸爸"不是工人）

(3) 小明看过《红楼梦》。

Xiǎo Míng kànguo《Hónglóumèng》.

（"小明"现在没在看《红楼梦》）

(4) 王云的妈妈我看见过。

Wáng Yún de māma wǒ kànjiànguo.

（现在"我"不是正在看"王云的妈妈"）

(5) 小刚以前胖过。

Xiǎo Gāng yǐqián pàngguo.

（"小刚"现在不胖）

(6) 我的眼睛近视过，后来治好了。

Wǒ de yǎnjīng jìnshiguo, hòulái zhìhǎo le.

"了"也可以表示曾经进行某一动作或存在某一状态，但用"了"时，该动作或状态可能不再进行或不存在，也可能仍在进行或仍存在：

（1）我昨天去书店买了两本书。

Wǒ zuótiān qù shūdiàn mǎile liǎng běn shū.

（“我”现在没买书）

（2）过去小刚胖了一阵子，后来又瘦了。

Guòqù Xiǎo Gāng pàngle yízhènzi, hòulái yòu shòu le.

（3）这本书我看了一天了，今天晚上就能看完。

Zhè běn shū wǒ kànle yì tiān le, jīntiān wǎnshang jiù néng kànwán.

（“我”现在正在看）

（4）这朵花红了好几天了，现在颜色还是这么好看。

Zhè duǒ huār hóngle hǎo jǐ tiān le, xiànzài yánsè hái shì zhème hǎokàn.

（“花”仍很红）

例1、2中的“了”可以用“过”替换：

（1'）我昨天去书店买过两本书。

Wǒ zuótiān qù shūdiàn mǎiguo liǎng běn shū.

（2'）过去小刚胖过一阵子，后来又瘦了。

Guòqù Xiǎo Gāng pàngguo yízhènzi, hòulái yòu shòu le.

例3、4中的“了”不能用“过”替换：

（3）＊这本书我看过一天了，今天晚上就能看完。

Zhè běn shū wǒ kànguo yì tiān le, jīntiān wǎnshang jiù néng kànwán.

（4）＊这朵花红过好几天了，现在颜色还是这么好看。

Zhè duǒ huār hóngguo hǎo jǐ tiān le, xiànzài yánsè hái shì zhème hǎokàn.

练 习 一

一、用"过"及所给的词语组句。

例如：

去　那个地方

我去过那个地方。

Wǒ qùguo nàge dìfang.

那个地方我去过。

Nàge dìfang wǒ qùguo.

1. 看　这个电影

2. 吃　芒果

3. 喝　茅台

4. 爱　这个姑娘

5. 热　这个地方

6. 想念　妈妈

二、用"过"或"了"填空：

1. 这朵花在瓶子里养____三天了，现在还开得很好。

Zhè duǒ huār zài píngzi li yǎng ____ sān tiān le, xiànzài hái kāi de hěn hǎo.

2. 那个地方我去____，我对那儿很熟悉。

Nàge dìfang wǒ qù ____, wǒ duì nàr hěn shúxi.

3. 这个电影我看____，不想看了。

Zhège diànyǐng wǒ kàn ____, bù xiǎng kàn le.

4. 什么地方我只要去____一次就记住了。

Shénme dìfang wǒ zhǐyào qù ____ yí cì jiù jìzhù le.

二、什么时候用"过"？(I)

一个人什么时候需要告诉别人他自己或别的什么人有某种经验——曾进行某动作或存在某状态呢？也就是说，在什么场合用"过"呢？比如，什么时候一个人问另外一个人"你去过上海吗？"这句话要解决这个问题，必须把用"过"的句子放在一个具体的语言环境中去考察。请看下边一段对话：

(1) 王：老张，你去过上海吗？

Wáng：Lǎo Zhāng, nǐ qùguo Shànghǎi ma?

张：去过，去年还去过一次。

Zhāng：Qùguo, qùnián hái qùguo yí cì.

王：我后天去上海，不知道那儿现在气候怎么样？我带什么衣服去合适？

Wáng：Wǒ hòutiān qù Shànghǎi, bù zhīdào nàr xiànzài qìhòu zěnmeyàng? Wǒ dài shénme yīfu qu héshì?

张：现在五月中，那儿已经热了，带单衣就可以了。

Zhāng：Xiànzài Wǔyuè zhōng, nàr yǐjing rè le, dài dānyī jiù kěyǐ le.

从这段对话中可以看出，老王要问老张的主要不是“去过上海没有”，而是要问“现在去上海穿什么衣服合适”，但他不知道老张是否具备回答这个问题的条件——是否去过上海、了解上海的气候，所以才问“去过上海吗”。

从另一个方面来说如果在老张回答“去过”之后，老王不说话了，老张一定会感到奇怪，会问：“你问我去过上海没有干嘛？”因为他觉得老王的问话没有完。

从上面的分析可以看出，用“过”的短语、分句或句子在语意上是不能自足的，即它不负载说话人要传达的最终信息。与包含“过”的句子的同时，总是存在一个语意上与之有直接联系的、负载最终信息的句子（短语、分句），后者有时不出现，但听话人可以意会。例如：

（2）病人：大夫，我肚子疼。

Bìngrén：Dàifu，wǒ dùzi téng.

大夫：大便正常吗？

Dàifu：Dàbiàn zhèngcháng ma？

病人：有点腹泻。

Bìngrén：Yǒu diǎnr fùxiè.

大夫：你吃过什么不干净的东西吗？

Dàifu：Nǐ chīguo shénme bù gānjìng de dōngxi ma？

病人：今天早晨我喝了一杯剩牛奶。

Bìngrén：Jīntiān zǎochén wǒ hēle yì bēi shèng niúnǎi.

大夫：牛奶没放在冰箱里，是不是？

Dàifu：Niúnǎi méi fàng zài bīngxiāng li，shì bú shì？

病人：对。

Bìngrén：Duì.

大夫：牛奶变质了。你知道肚子为什么疼了吧？不要紧，吃点药就好了。

Dàifu：Niúnǎi biànzhì le. Nǐ zhīdao dùzi wèishénme téng le ba？Búyàojǐn，chī diǎnr yào jiù hǎo le.

在上边这段话里，大夫所以问“你吃过什么不干净的东西吗？”是为了了解病人肚子疼的原因。

(3)（在书店里）

甲：这本书好吗？

Jiǎ：Zhè běn shū hǎo ma？

乙：我没看过，不知道，买一本看看吧。

Yǐ：Wǒ méi kànguo，bù zhīdào，mǎi yì běn kànkan ba.

乙所以说“我没看过”，是为了向甲说明不能给甲一个满意回答的原因。

(4) 小明：小丽，告诉你，坐飞机特别有意思。

Xiǎo Míng：Xiǎo Lì，gàosù nǐ，zuò fēijī tèbié yǒuyìsi.

小丽：是吗？怎么有意思？

Xiǎo Lì：Shì ma？Zěnme yǒuyìsi？

小明：嗯……在飞机上往下看，地球象个小皮球。

Xiǎo Míng：Ng... zài fēijī shang wǎngxià kàn，dìqiú xiàng ge xiǎo píqiú.

妈妈：小明，别瞎吹了，你坐过飞机吗？小丽别信他的。

Māma：Xiǎo Míng，bié xiā chuī le，nǐ zuòguo fēijī ma？Xiǎo Lì bié xìn tā de.

妈妈这句话的意思是：“你没坐过飞机，所以你不知道坐飞机的情况，你刚才说的都是瞎话，吹牛。”这个意思，小明小丽是可以意会的。

练习二

、填空：

1. 甲：杭州好玩吗？

Jiǎ：Hángzhōu hǎowánr ma？

乙：我没去____杭州，不知道。

Yǐ：Wǒ méi qù ____ Hángzhōu，bù zhīdào.

2. 甲：这家饭馆菜做得好吗？

Jiǎ：Zhè jiā fànguǎnr cài zuò de hǎo ma？

乙：不知道，我没在这儿吃____饭。

Yǐ：Bù zhīdào，wǒ méi zài zhèr chī ____ fàn.

3. 甲：你会说汉语吗？

Jiǎ：Nǐ huì shuō Hànyǔ ma？

乙：我学____几个月汉语，会说一点儿。

Yǐ：Wǒ xué ____ jǐ ge yuè Hànyǔ，huì shuō yìdiǎnr.

4. 甲：这个字你认识吗？

Jiǎ：Zhège zì nǐ rènshi ma？

乙：这个字我好象学____，不过忘了。

Yǐ：Zhège zì wǒ hǎoxiàng xué ____，búguò wàng le.

5. 甲：你喜欢巴金的作品吗？

Jiǎ：Nǐ xǐhuan Bā Jīn de zuòpǐn ma？

乙：我看____巴金的《家》，很喜欢。

Yǐ：Wǒ kàn ____ Bā Jīn de《Jiā》，hěn xǐhuan.

6. 甲：你看____京戏吗？

Jiǎ：Nǐ kàn ____ Jīngxì ma？

乙：看____。

Yǐ：Kàn ____.

甲：你给我介绍一下京戏的乐器好吗？

Jiǎ：Nǐ gěi wǒ jièshào yí xià Jīngxì de yuèqì hǎo ma？

乙：对不起，我只在台下看____戏，没去____后台，连京戏用什么乐器都没见____,怎么给你介绍呢?

Yǐ:Duìbùqǐ, wǒ zhǐ zài tái xià kàn ____ xì, méi qù ____ hòutái, lián Jīngxì yòng shénme yuèqì dou méi jiàn ____, zěnme gěi nǐ jièshào ne?

三、什么时候用“过”?(II)

(一) “过”出现在说明事情的原因、前提的句子里。例如:

(1) 他吃过不识字的苦,所以特别爱学习。

Tā chīguo bù shí zì de kǔ, suǒyǐ tèbié ài xuéxí.

(2) 你是知识分子,喝过墨水,起出来的名字一定好听。

Nǐ shì zhīshì fènzǐ, hēguo mòshuǐr, qǐ chūlai de míngzi yídìng hǎotīng.

(3) 由于他演过戏,动作象猴子,加上他又姓侯,所以人家都叫他“猴子”。

Yóuyú tā yǎnguo xì, dòngzuò xiàng hóuzi, jiāshang tā yòu xìng Hóu, suǒyǐ rénjiā dōu jiào tā "hóuzi".

(4) 你既然看过这个电影,那么我就不给你买票了。

Nǐ jìrán kànguo zhège diànyǐng, nàme wǒ jiù bù gěi nǐ mǎi piào le.

例1是说:因为他不识字,吃了很多苦头,所以(现在)特别爱学习;例2是说:“你念过书”,给孩子起的名字一定比没念过书的人起的名字好听;例3中包含“过”的分句说明“人家叫他猴子的原因”;例4包含“过”的句子说明“我不给你买票的原因”。

(二) “过”出现在说明人、事物或其间的关系的句子里。例如:

(1) 他当过兵,打过仗,受过磨炼,十分勇敢坚强。

Tā dāngguo bīng, dǎguo zhàng, shòuguo móliàn, shífēn

yǒnggǎn jiānqiáng.

(2) 小张和小李从来没吵过架。

Xiǎo Zhāng hé Xiǎo Lǐ cónglái méi chǎoguo jià.

(3) 多少年没这么热过了,今年的气候特别反常。

Duōshao nián méi zhème règuo le, jīnnián de qìhòu tèbié fǎncháng.

(4) 这所大学出过好几任总统。

Zhè suǒ dàxué chūguo hǎo jǐ rèn zǒngtǒng.

此类句子中包含“过”的部分(短语、分句等)表述的是人或事物的具体经历,跟它相关的部分(有时不出现)表示抽象的性质、关系。如例1通过“当兵”、“打仗”、“受磨炼”这些具体经历,说明“他”的性格——十分勇敢坚强;例2通过“小张和小李从来没吵过架”这种具体事实,说明他们二人的关系好;例3通过“多少年没这么热”,说明“今年气候异常”;例4通过“这所大学出过几任总统”这个具体事实,说明该大学不同寻常。

练习三

请用“过”完成句子:

1. 甲:这是一封中文信,你能给我翻译一下吗?

Jiǎ: Zhè shì yì fēng Zhōngwén xìn, nǐ néng gěi wǒ fānyì yíxia ma?

乙:对不起,我__________,翻译不出来。

Yǐ: Duìbùqǐ, wǒ __________, fānyì bù chū lái.

2. 甲:你知道鲁迅吗?

Nǐ zhīdào Lǔ Xùn ma?

乙:鲁迅是中国伟大的文学家,我__________。

Lǔ Xùn shì Zhōngguó wěidà de wénxuéjiā，wǒ

______.

3. 小李______，不知道长城什么样。

Xiǎo Lǐ ______, bù zhīdào Chángchéng shénmeyàng.

4. 王刚：这种衣服穿着凉快吗？

Wáng Gāng：Zhè zhǒng yīfu chuānzhe liángkuai ma？

李华：不知道，我______。

Lǐ Huá：Bù zhīdào，wǒ ______.

5. 甲：王老师乒乓球打得非常好。

Wáng lǎoshī pīngpāngqiú dǎ de fēicháng hǎo

乙：你怎么知道？

Nǐ zěnme zhīdào？

甲：今天下午我还跟他______。

Jīntiān xiàwǔ wǒ hái gēn tā ______.

乙：这不能说明问题，你的乒乓球打得太不怎么样了。

Zhè bù néng shuōmíng wèntí，nǐ de pīngpāngqiú dǎ de tài bù zěnmeyàng le.

6. 甲：你的女朋友很漂亮。

Nǐ de nǚ péngyou hěn piàoliang.

乙：你怎么知道？

Nǐ zěnme zhīdào？

甲：我______她的照片。

Wǒ ______ tā de zhàopiàn.

乙：在哪儿？

Zài nǎr？

甲：在你的桌子上。

Zài nǐ de zhuōzi shang.

乙：那是我妹妹！

Nà shì wǒ mèimei.

四、“过”与“了”用法比较

“了”表示动作、状态的实现，与“过”在用法上有所不同，“了”可以出现在说明原因、前提的句子中，如：

(1) 甲：咱们的新老师姓什么？

Zánmen de xīn lǎoshī xìng shénme?

乙：刚才我问了校长，他姓赵。

Gāngcái wǒ wènle xiàozhǎng, tā xìng Zhào.

(2) 甲：你饿了吧？吃点东西吗？

Nǐ è le ba? Chī diǎnr dōngxi ma?

乙：我刚才吃了两片面包，还不饿。

Wǒ gāngcái chīle liǎng piànr miànbāo, hái bú è.

以上两个答句中的“了”可以用“过”替换，如：

(1) 乙：刚才我问过校长，他姓赵。

Gāngcái wǒ wènguo xiàozhǎng, tā xìng Zhào.

(2) 乙：我刚才吃过两片面包，还不饿。

Wǒ gāngcái chīguo liǎng piànr miànbāo, hái bú è.

但“了”还可以出现在客观地叙述动作、状态发生的句子中，在这种句子中，传达的最终信息，也不要求有另外的语意相关的句子。例如：

(3) 这一天天气很好，刚八点，孩子们就涌进了公园。

Zhè yì tiān tiānqì hěn hǎo, gāng bā diǎn, háizimen jiù yǒngjìn le gōngyuán.

(4) “同志，我买《新华字典》。”

售货员立刻把字典递给了他。

"Tóngzhì, wǒ mǎi《Xīnhuá Zìdiǎn》."

Shòuhuòyuán lìkè bǎ zìdiǎn dìgěi le tā.

(5) 昨天我去百货大楼，先在二楼买了一件衣服、一双鞋，后来去三楼买了一条床单、一对枕头，最后在一楼买了些化妆品。

Zuótiān wǒ qù Bǎihuò Dàlóu, xiān zài èr lóu mǎile yí jiàn yīfu, yì shuāng xié, hòulái qù sān lóu mǎile yì tiáo chuángdān, yí duì zhěntou, zuìhòu zài yīlóu mǎile xiē huàzhuāngpǐn.

(6) 那个地方很美：山上长满了树，树上开满了花。山下修了一个停车场，停车场上停满了汽车。

Nàge dìfang hěn měi: shān shang zhǎngmǎn le shù, shùshang kāimǎn le huā. Shān xià xiūle yí ge tíngchēchǎng, tíngchēchǎng shang tíngmǎn le qìchē.

这些句子里的"了"不能换成"过"。

"过"总是通过过去发生的动作、状态来说明解释当前的事理、人物；"了"则可以纯粹叙述某一特定时间发生的事件、动作，而不涉及另外一个时间的人物、事件。因此，如果你要客观地叙述一个人在某一时间进行了某一（或某些）动作，或描写某人某处出现了什么状态，就应该用"了"。

练习四

一、用"过"或"了"填空：

1. 医生：你打_____青霉素吗？对青霉素过敏吗？

Nǐ dǎ _____ qīngméisù ma? Duì qīngméisù guòmǐn ma?

病人：打_____，不过敏。

Dǎ _____, bú guòmǐn.

2. 甲：你昨天都干什么了？

Nǐ zuótiān dōu gàn shénme le?

乙：上午看____两个钟头书，下午看____一场电影。

Shàngwǔ kàn ____ liǎng gè zhōngtóu shū, xiàwǔ kàn ____ yì chǎng diànyǐng.

3. 甲：西安的秦始皇陵大不大？

Xī'ān de Qín Shǐhuáng Líng dà bú dà?

乙：我没去____西安，不知道。

Wǒ méi qù ____ Xī'ān, bù zhīdào.

4. 小刘看____《红楼梦》、《三国演义》、《水浒传》，中文水平相当高。

Xiǎo Liú kàn ____《Hónglóumèng》,《Sān Guó Yǎnyì》,《Shuǐhǔ Zhuàn》, zhōngwén shuǐpíng xiāngdāng gāo.

5. 我已经吃____饭了，不吃了。

Wǒ yǐjing chī ____ fàn le, bù chī le.

6. 柯恩去____广州、上海、重庆、昆明、青岛、哈尔滨等很多地方，他很喜欢中国。

Kē'ēn qù ____ Guǎngzhōu, Shànghǎi, Chóngqìng, Kūnmíng, Qīngdǎo, Hā'ěrbīn děng hěn duō dìfang, tā hěn xǐhuan Zhōngguó.

二、根据所给的句子，选择正确答案。

例：小李学过汉语。

Xiǎo Lǐ xuéguo Hànyǔ.

A. 小李现在在学汉语。( )

Xiǎo Lǐ xiànzài zài xué Hànyǔ.

B. 小李现在没在学汉语。(√)

Xiǎo Lǐ xiànzài méi zài xué Hànyǔ.

1. 玛丽结过婚。

Mǎlì (Mary) jiéguo hūn.

A. 玛丽现在和丈夫一起生活。(　)

Mǎlì (Mary) xiànzài hé zhàngfu yìqǐ shēnghuó.

B. 玛丽现在是单身。(　)

Mǎlì (Mary) xiànzài shì dānshēn.

2. 小张学了三年英语了,再有一年就毕业了。

Xiǎo Zhāng xuéle sān nián Yīngyǔ le, zài yǒu yì nián jiù bìyè le.

A. 小张正在学英语。(　)

Xiǎo Zhāng zhèngzài xué Yīngyǔ.

B. 小张现在没在学英语。(　)

Xiǎo Zhāng xiànzài méi zài xué Yīngyǔ.

3. 你当过老师吗?

Nǐ dāngguo lǎoshī ma?

A. "你"现在是老师。(　)

"Nǐ" xiànzài shì lǎoshī.

B. "你"现在不是老师。(　)

"Nǐ" xiànzài bú shì lǎoshī.

4. 约翰去过中国。

Yuēhàn (John) qùguo Zhōngguó.

A. 约翰现在在中国。(　)

Yuēhàn (John) xiànzài zài Zhōngguó.

B. 约翰现在不在中国。(　)

Yuēhàn (John) xiànzài bú zài Zhōngguó.

5. 飞机刚刚降落在机场。

Fēijī gānggāng jiàngluò zài jīchǎng.

A. 飞机现在不在机场。(　)

Fēijī xiànzài bú zài jīchǎng.

B. 飞机现在在机场。(　)

Fēijī xiànzài zài jīchǎng.

6. 我刚到中国的时候想过家，而且想得厉害。

Wǒ gāng dào Zhōngguó de shíhou xiǎngguo jiā, érqiě xiǎng de hěn lìhai.

A. “我”现在很想家。( )

"Wǒ" xiànzài hěn xiǎng jiā.

B. “我”现在不太想家。( )

"Wǒ" xiànzài bú tài xiǎng jiā.

7. 雨下了一个小时了。

Yǔ xiàle yí ge xiǎoshí le.

A. 现在可能还在下雨。( )

Xiànzài kěnéng hái zài xià yǔ.

B. 现在一定不下雨了。( )

Xiànzài yídìng bú xià yǔ le.

8. 他们有过孩子，那个孩子很可爱。

Tāmen yǒuguo háizi, nàge háizi hěn kě'ài.

A. 他们的孩子死了。( )

Tāmen de háizi sǐ le.

B. 他们的孩子在上学。( )

Tāmen de háizì zài shàngxué.

C. 他们现在没有孩子。( )

Tāmen xiànzài méiyǒu háizi.

五、“过”与时间状语

用“过”时，前边的状语多数不指明确定的时间，如“以前、从前、过去”等等，而且常常不出现时间状语，表示的是说话以前的某一时间。例如：

（1）从前他吃过这种鱼。

Cóngqián tā chīguo zhè zhǒng yú.

（2）甲：你离开家以后，再也没回去吗？

Nǐ líkāi jiā yǐhòu, zài yě méi huíqu ma?

乙：不，以前回去过，这几年因为忙，没回去。

Bù, yǐqián huíquguo, zhè jǐ nián yīnwèi máng, méi huíqu.

（3）甲：这本书刘红看过吗？她要是没看过就借给她看吧。

Zhè běn shū Liú Hóng kànguo ma? Tā yàoshi méi kànguo jiù jiè gěi tā kàn ba.

乙：她可能没看过，我给她送去。

Tā kěnéng méi kànguo, wǒ gěi tā sòngqu.

（4）甲：你学过什么外语？

Nǐ xuéguo shénme wàiyǔ.

乙：英语、法语。

Yīngyǔ, Fǎyǔ.

有时，“过”前的状语表示一个确定的时间：

（5）甲：你昨天找过我吗？

Nǐ zuótiān zhǎoguo wǒ ma?

乙：昨天下午找过你，你不在。

Zuótiān xiàwǔ zhǎoguo nǐ, nǐ bú zài.

甲：有事吗？

Yǒu shì ma?

乙：通知你明天开会。

Tōngzhī nǐ míngtiān kāihuì.

当“过”前的状语表示确定的时间时，常常用于证实或反驳。例如：

(6) 甲：我叫你经常去看看他，你为什么不去？

Wǒ jiào nǐ jīngcháng qù kànkan tā, nǐ wèishénme bú qù.

乙：我常去，今天早晨还去过。

Wǒ cháng qù, jīntiān zǎochén hái qùguo.

(7) 甲：中国菜很好吃，你吃过吗？

Zhōngguócài hěn hǎochī, nǐ chīguo ma?

乙：吃过，上个月我还在中国吃过。

Chīguo, shàng ge yuè wǒ hái zài Zhōngguó chīguo.

(8) 甲：小张是不是病了，怎么好几天没见他了？

Xiǎo Zhāng shì bú shì bìng le, zěnme hǎo jǐ tiān méi jiàn tā le?

乙：没病，刚才我还见过他来取信。

Méi bìng, gāngcái wǒ hái jiànguo tā lái qǔ xìn.

在用"了"的句子里，最常出现的状语是表示确定时点的：

(1) 今天早晨我们班来了一位新同学。

Jīntiān zǎochén wǒmen bān láile yí wèi xīn tóngxué.

(2) 昨天下午两点，小张送来了一份报告。

Zuótiān xiàwǔ liǎng diǎn, Xiǎo Zhāng sòngláile yí fèn bàogào.

(3) 去年老王生了两次病。

Qùnián Lǎo Wáng shēngle liǎng cì bìng.

(4) 十月二十八号晚七点三十分，那个地区发生了一次大地震。

Shíyuè èrshíbā hào wǎn qī diǎn sānshí fēn, nàge dìqū fāshēngle yí cì dà dìzhèn.

包含"了"的句子的状语也可以是表示不确定的时点的，常见的有以下三种句式：

A. 表示先后发生的几个动作：

（1）他每天吃了睡，睡了吃，什么正经事都不干。

Tā měi tiān chīle shuì, shuìle chī, shénme zhèngjing shì dōu bú gàn.

（2）你什么时候写完了作业，什么时候叫你出去玩。

Nǐ shénme shíhou xiěwánle zuòyè, shénme shíhou jiào nǐ chūqu wánr.

B. 动词后有数量词：

（3）那个地方我一共去了两次。

Nàge dìfang wǒ yígòng qùle liǎng cì.

（4）甲：你们已经学了多少汉字了？

Nǐmen yǐjing xuéle duōshao Hànzì le?

乙：一千五。

Yì qiān wǔ.

C. 句末有"了"或有后续句：

（5）甲：你告诉老师什么时候回国了吗？

Nǐ gàosù lǎoshī shénme shíhou huí guó le ma?

乙：已经给他写了信了。

Yǐjing gěi tā xiěle xìn le.

（6）这件事我已经通知了小李，你去通知小赵吧。

Zhè jiàn shì wǒ yǐjing tōngzhīle Xiǎo Lǐ, nǐ qù tōngzhī Xiǎo Zhào ba.

（7）你们吃了饭再走吧。

Nǐmen chīle fàn zài zǒu ba.

练 习 五

一、填适当的时间状语：

1. ____________，我看过很多中国电影。

____________, wǒ kànguo hěn duō Zhōngguó diànyǐng.

2. 我____________写了三封信。

Wǒ ____________ xiěle sān fēng xìn.

3. 他____________给我来了一个电话。

Tā ____________ gěi wǒ láile yí ge diànhuà.

4. 他____________喜欢过一个日本女孩子。

Tā ____________ xǐhuanguo yí ge Rìběn nǚ háizi.

5. 张老师____________教过许多美国学生。

Zhāng lǎoshī ____________ jiāoguo xǔduō Měiguó xuésheng.

6. ____________我要去上海开会。

____________ wǒ yào qù Shànghǎi kāihuì.

7. 老马____________来找过你，说有重要的事。

Lǎo Mǎ ____________ lái zhǎoguo nǐ, shuō yǒu zhòngyào de shì.

8. ____________他得过一场大病。

____________ tā déguo yì chǎng dà bìng.

六、"过"可以结合的词语

"过"可以结合的词语面很广，可以结合动词、形容词、动词短语。例如：

1. 这个孩子姓过王，后来改姓刘了。

Zhège háizi xìngguo Wáng, hòulái gǎi xìng Liú le

2. 这个地方从来没干净过。

Zhège dìfang cónglái méi gānjìngguo.

3. 我到南京去找过他，他离开那儿了。

Wǒ dào Nánjīng qù zhǎoguo tā, tā líkāi nàr le.

4. 他欺骗、侮辱过这个孩子。

Tā qīpiàn, wūrǔguo zhège háizi.

什么样的词语不能与“过”结合呢?

如果一个词,它表示的动作或状态对当事者来说是不可改变的,该词就不能与“过”结合,可以分两类:

A. 有的动作或状态,对当事者来说是必然的,而且在当事者存在期间只有一次,表示这种动作的词就不能与“过”结合。比如一个人只出生一次,所以不能说“这个孩子出生过”。“开幕”、“闭幕”对于一次会议,“毕业”对于一个人的一个阶段的学习,都属此类。“死”对一个人来说只有一次,但为什么可以说“他死过三次”呢?这是因为这里说的“死”是假死,不是真正的医学上的死。还可以说“他死过三个孩子”。在这个句子里“死”的是孩子,而不是“他”,因孩子可以有几个,“死”就可以有几次,即当事者不止一人。

B. 认知意义动词,如“认识”、“知道”、“懂”、“明白”等。

在否定句里 A、B 两类动词可以与“过”结合。

练习六

一、判断正误(不限一正):

1. A. 我从来没吃过中国饭。

Wǒ cónglái méi chīguo Zhōngguó fàn.

B. 我从来没吃了中国饭。

Wǒ cónglái méi chīle Zhōngguó fàn.

2. A. 来中国以后,我生过两次病。

Lái Zhōngguó yǐhòu, wǒ shēngguo liǎng cì bìng.

B. 来中国以后,我生了两次病。

Lái Zhōngguó yǐhòu, wǒ shēngle liǎng cì bìng.

3. A. 他病了以后，我去医院看过他。

Tā bìngle yǐhòu, wǒ qù yīyuàn kànguo tā.

B. 他病了以后，我去医院看他。

Tā bìngle yǐhòu, wǒ qù yīyuàn kàn tā.

4. A. 张文去上海过，李红没去上海过。

Zhāng Wén qù Shànghǎi guo, Lǐ Hóng méi qù Shànghǎi guo.

B. 张文去过上海，李红没去过上海。

Zhāng Wén qùguo Shànghǎi, Lǐ Hóng méi qùguo Shànghǎi.

5. A. 我从来没看见他这样不讲理。

Wǒ cónglái méi kànjiàn tā zhèyàng bù jiǎnglǐ.

B. 我从来没看见过他这样不讲理。

Wǒ cónglái méi kànjiànguo tā zhèyàng bù jiǎnglǐ.

C. 我从来没看见他这样不讲理过。

Wǒ cónglái méi kànjiàn tā zhèyàng bù jiǎnglǐ guo.

6. A. 以前他买了一件大衣，很难看，就扔掉了。

Yǐqián tā mǎile yí jiàn dàyī, hěn nánkàn, jiù rēngdiào le.

B. 以前他买过一件大衣，很难看，就扔掉了。

Yǐqián tā mǎiguo yí jiàn dàyī, hěn nánkàn, jiù rēngdiào le.

二、改病句：

1. 他上午买过火车票，下午就走了。

Tā shàngwǔ mǎiguo huǒchē piào, xiàwǔ jiù zǒu le.

2. 这个人没有找你过，你不必多心。

Zhège rén méiyou zhǎo nǐ guo, nǐ búbì duōxīn.

3. 他从北京大学毕过业，又去语言学院工作。

Tā cóng Běijīng Dàxué bìguo yè, yòu qù Yǔyán Xuéyuàn

gōngzuò.

4. 长城我一次也没去了。

Chángchéng wǒ yí cì yě méi qù le.

肆、"是……的"的用法

现代汉语中有一种谓语部分由"是……的"格式构成的句子。我们管带有这种格式的句子叫"是……的"句。

在"是……的"句中，可以把"是……的"看作一个整体结构。它象一个活动的框子套在谓语上。需要的时候套上去，不需要可以省去，并不影响句子的基本意思。它在句子里只说明意义的重点，或表示某种语气。因此从本质上看，"是……的"句也还是一般的动词谓语句、形容词谓语句，或主谓谓语句。

从"是……的"结构在句子中的作用来看，"是……的"句有两类：一、说明句子意义重点的"是……的"句；二、表示语气的"是……的"句。

一、说明意义重点的"是……的"句

（一）"是……的"句说明的意义重点

（1）客人是什么时候走的？

Kèren shì shénme shíhou zǒu de ?

客人是七点钟走的。

Kèren shì qī diǎnzhōng zǒu de.

（2）客人什么时候走？

Kèren shénme shíhou zǒu?

客人七点钟走。

Kèren qī diǎnzhōng zǒu.

比较这两组句子可以看出：有"是……的"结构的句子表示事

情发生在过去，动作已经完成，客人已经走了。它要着重说明的不是动作本身，而是动作发生的时间。客人是在七点钟走的。

当说话的双方都已知道某一动作已经在过去完成了，想要着重指出与这个动作有关的某一方面的内容，比如动作完成的时间、地点、方式、动作的施事者或受事者等等，就可以用“是……的”句。这类“是…… 的”句的谓语主要是动词、动词短语和以动词作谓语的主谓短语。

练习一

一、朗读下面的对话，体会“是……的”句表示的意义重点。

1. 王华什么时候来北京？

Wáng Huá shénme shíhou lái Běijīng?

他下星期来。

Tā xià xīngqī lái.

他已经来了，他是昨天来的。

Tā yǐjing lái le, tā shì zuótiān lái de.

2. 晚上你几点睡？

Wǎnshang nǐ jǐ diǎn shuì?

我十点睡，不过昨天是十二点才睡的。

Wǒ shí diǎn shuì, búguò zuótiān shì shí'èr diǎn cái shuì de.

3. 联欢会在哪儿开？

Liánhuān huì zài nǎr kāi?

以前是在教室里开的，这次也在教室开吧。

Yǐqián shì zài jiàoshì li kāi de, zhè cì yě zài jiàoshì kāi ba.

4. 你的作业都做完了吗？

Nǐ de zuòyè dōu zuòwán le ma？

都做完了，我的作业是昨天晚上做的。

Dōu zuòwán le，wǒ de zuòyè shì zuótiān wǎnshang zuò de.

5. 你跟谁一起学习？

Nǐ gēn shuí yìqǐ xuéxí？

昨天我是跟王丽一起学习的，今天我要和张明一起学习。

Zuótiān wǒ shì gēn Wáng Lì yìqǐ xuéxí de，jīntiān wǒ yào hé Zhāng Míng yìqǐ xuéxí.

二、朗读下面的句子，看看每组的两个句子表示的意义重点有什么不同。

1. a 我们八点钟上课。

Wǒmen bā diǎnzhōng shàng kè.

b 我们是八点钟上的课，已经学习了一个小时了。

Wǒmen shì bā diǎnzhōng shàng de kè，yǐjing xuéxíle yí gè xiǎoshí le.

2. a 日本学生昨天回国了。

Rìběn xuésheng zuótiān huí guó le.

b 日本学生是昨天回国的。

Rìběn xuésheng shì zuótiān huí guó de.

3. a 王华坐飞机去美国。

Wáng Huá zuò fēijī qù Měiguó.

b 王华是坐飞机去的美国。

Wáng Huá shì zuò fēijī qù de Měiguó.

4. a 玛丽跟同学们一起去颐和园。

Mǎlì gēn tóngxuémen yìqǐ qù Yíhéyuán.

b 玛丽是和同学们一起去颐和园的。

Mǎlì shì hé tóngxuémen yìqǐ qù Yíhéyuán de.

5. a 他们在哪儿吃午饭？

Tāmen zài nǎr chī wǔfàn?

b 他们是在哪儿吃的午饭？

Tāmen shì zài nǎr chī de wǔfàn?

（二）表示意义重点的“是……的”句的几种句式

1. 着重指出动作发生的时间、地点、目的等内容的“是……的”句。这种句子，在“是……的”结构中的动词前一定有表示这方面内容的状语。全句意义的重点是由状语表达的。因此，句子的重音也落在状语上。

主语∥是＋状语＋动词＋的

（1）我是前天来的。

Wǒ shì qiántiān lái de.

（指出动作在过去发生的时间）

（2）王华是从上海来的。

Wáng Huá shì cóng Shànghǎi lái de.

（指出动作在过去发生的地点）

（3）他们是坐汽车来的。

Tāmen shì zuò qìchē lái de.

（指出方式）

(4) 他是对我说的，你别生气。

Tā shì duì wǒ shuō de, nǐ bié shēngqì.

(指出对象)

(5) 新房子是为工人盖的。

Xīn fángzi shì wèi gōngrén gài de?

(指出目的)

这种句子如用特殊疑问句提问，疑问代词应该问句子中所强调的状语部分。

(1) 你是什么时候来的？

Nǐ shì shénme shíhou lái de?

(2) 王华是从哪儿来的？

Wáng Huá shì cóng nǎr lái de?

(3) 他们是怎么来的？

Tāmen shì zěnme lái de?

(4) 他是对谁说的？

Tā shì duì shuí shuō de?

"是……的"结构里的动词如果带名词宾语，宾语的位置一般在"的"后，有时也可在"的"前。如果宾语是代词则宾语一般都在"的"前。

主语//是＋动词＋的＋宾语(名词)

你是什么时候上的大学？

Nǐ shì shénme shíhou shàng de dàxué?

我是一九六四年上的大学。

Wǒ shì 1964 nián shàng de dàxué.

主语//是＋动词＋宾语(代词)＋的

你是什么时候看见他的？

Nǐ shì shénme shíhou kànjiàn tā de?

我是昨天看见他的。

Wǒ shì zuótiān kànjiàn tā de.

动词后面有趋向补语“来”或“去”时，如宾语在趋向补语“来”“去”前面，“的”紧跟“来”“去”放在句尾。如宾语在“来”“去”后面，“的”也随“来”“去”挪到宾语前。如：

(1) 我是五点半回学校来的。

Wǒ shì wǔ diǎn bàn huí xuéxiào lái de.

(2) 张丽是昨天打电话来的。

Zhāng Lì shì zuótiān dǎ diànhuà lái de.

(3) 张丽是昨天打来的电话。

Zhāng Lì shì zuótiān dǎlái de diànhuà.

练习二

一、朗读下面的“是……的”句，注意句子的重音，并说明各句意思的重点：

1. 火车是八点钟开的。

Huǒchē shì bā diǎnzhōng kāi de.

2. 毕业典礼是在礼堂举行的。

Bìyè diǎnlǐ shì zài lǐtáng jǔxíng de.

3. 礼物是为孩子们买的。

Lǐwù shì wèi háizimen mǎi de.

4. 玛丽是在哪儿学的中文？

Mǎlì shì zài nǎr xué de Zhōngwén.

5. 他是在北京学的中文。

Tā shì zài Běijīng xué de Zhōngwén.

6. 老师是打铃以后进教室去的。

Lǎoshī shì dǎ líng yǐhòu jìn jiàoshì qù de.

7. 中华人民共和国是一九四九年建立的。

Zhōnghuá Rénmín Gònghéguó shì yī jiǔ sì jiǔ nián jiànlì de.

8. 委员会是由十五个人组成的。

Wěiyuánhuì shì yóu shíwǔ gè rén zǔchéng de.

9. 老师们是昨天走的，学生是今天才去的。

Lǎoshīmen shì zuótiān zǒu de, xuésheng shì jīntiān cái qù de.

10. 这消息我是今天才知道的。

Zhè xiāoxi wǒ shì jīntiān cái zhīdao de.

11. 这件事你是什么时候告诉他的？

Zhè jiàn shì nǐ shì shénme shíhou gàosu tā de?

12. 我是昨天才听说的。

Wǒ shì zuótiān cái tīngshuō de.

13. 我是在王府井买的洗衣机。

Wǒ shì zài Wángfǔjǐng mǎi de xǐyījī.

14. 去年张老师是和外国学生一起去参观的。

Qùnián Zhāng lǎoshī shì hé wàiguó xuésheng yìqǐ qù cānguān de.

15. 我是上个月写去的信，最近没去信。

Wǒ shì shàng gè yuè xiěqù de xìn, zuìjìn méi qù xìn.

二、朗读下面的会话，体会“是……的”句的用法，并记住它们：

A：您是从哪个国家来的？

Nín shì cóng nǎge guójiā lái de?

B：我是从美国来的。

Wǒ shì cóng Měiguó lái de.

A：您是什么时候来的？

Nín shì shénme shíhou lái de?

B：我是昨天刚到的。

Wǒ shì zuótiān gāng dào de.

A：是坐飞机来的吗？

Shì zuò fēijī lái de ma?

B：是。

shì.

A：你汉语说得挺不错，是在美国什么大学学的？

Nǐ Hànyǔ shuō de tǐng bú cuò，shì zài Měiguó shénme dàxué xué de?

B：我不是在大学学的汉语。

Wǒ bú shì zài dàxué xué de Hànyǔ.

A：那你是怎么学的？

Nà nǐ shì zěnme xué de?

B：我是跟一个中国朋友学的。

Wǒ shì gēn yí gè Zhōngguó péngyou xué de.

A：学了多长时间？

Xuéle duō cháng shíjiān?

B：我是从1987年开始学的，到现在已经快三年了。

Wǒ shì cóng yī jiǔ bā qī nián kāishǐ xué de，dào xiànzài yǐjing kuài sān nián le.

* * *

一个小女孩问她妈妈："妈妈，爸爸是在什么地方生的？"

Yí gè xiǎo nǚháir wèn tā māma："Māma，bàba shì zài shénme dìfang shēng de?"

"爸爸是在上海生的。"

"Bàba shì zài Shànghǎi shēng de."

"您也是在上海生的吗？"

"Nín yě shì zài Shànghǎi shēng de ma?"

"不，我是在北京生的。"

"Bù，wǒ shì zài Běijīng shēng de?"

"妈妈，我是在哪儿生的？"

"Māma, wǒ shì zài nǎr shēng de?"

"你是在广州生的。"

"Nǐ shì zài Guǎngzhōu shēng de."

"那么,咱们三个人是怎么认识的呢?"

"Nàme, zánmen sān gè rén shì zěnme rènshi de ne?

* * *

A:你是刚理的发吧?

Nǐ shì gāng lǐ de fà ba?

B:对,我是昨天刚理的发,你看怎么样?

Duì, wǒ shì zuótiān gāng lǐ de fà, nǐ kàn zěnmeyàng?

A:挺漂亮,你是在哪儿理的?

Tǐng piàoliang, nǐ shì zài nǎr lǐ de?

B:是在王府井四联理发馆理的。

Shì zài Wángfǔjǐng Sìlián lǐfàguǎn lǐ de.

A:这个理发馆一定很不错,刚才我看见王华了,他也是在那儿理的发。

Zhège lǐfàguǎn yídìng hěn búcuò, gāngcái wǒ kàn jiàn Wáng Huá le, tā yě shì zài nàr lǐ de fà.

B:我正找王华呢,你是在哪儿看见他的?

Wǒ zhèng zhǎo Wáng Huá ne, nǐ shì zài nǎr kànjiàn tā de?

A:我是在图书馆看见他的。

Wǒ shì zài túshūguǎn kànjiàn tā de.

三、用下面的词语作强调动词状语的"是……的"句:

1. 1776年7月4日

1776 nián 7yuè 4 rì

2. 跟中国朋友一起

gēn Zhōngguó péngyou yìqǐ

3. 哪儿

nǎr

4. 坐船　坐火车

zuò chuán zuò huǒchē

5. 在商店里

zài shāngdiàn li

6. 从北京

cóng Běijīng

7. 怎么

zěnme

8. 为孩子们

wèi háizimen

9. 对大家

duì dàjiā

10. 慢慢地

mànmānde

四、把下面的句子改成特指疑问句：

1. 我是上星期刚认识的玛丽。

Wǒ shì shàng xīngqī gāng rènshi de Mǎlì.

2. 这些书是从图书馆借的。

Zhèxiē shū shì cóng túshūguǎn jiè de.

3. 我们是在家里玩的。

Wǒmen shì zài jiā li wán de.

4. 我们是在一起开会认识的。

Wǒmen shì zài yìqǐ kāihuì rènshi de .

5. 这个代表团是由校长和教授组成的。

Zhège dàibiǎotuán shì yóu xiàozhǎng hé jiàoshòu zǔchéng de.

6. “们”字是由“亻”和“门”两个部分组成的。

″们″zì shì yóu ″亻″ hé ″门″ liǎng gè bùfen zǔchéng de.

7. 雨是半夜下的。

Yǔ shì bànyè xià de.

8. 代表团是坐飞机来中国的。

Dàibiǎotuán shì zuò fēijī lái Zhōngguó de.

9. 这些东西是从家乡带来的。

Zhèxiē dōngxi shì cóng jiāxiāng dàilái de.

10. 小华是上星期寄来的信。

Xiǎohuá shì shàng xīngqī jìlái de xìn.

2. 着重指出过去已完成了的动作的施事者(即完成动作的人)的"是……的"句。这样的句子,在"是……的"结构中的常是一个主谓短语。这个主谓短语的谓语是动词,主谓短语的主语就是句子要强调的重点,说话时重音也落在它上面。而全句的主语在意义上则是主谓短语中动词的受事。

主语//是+主谓短语+的

这主意是谁出的?

Zhè zhǔyi shì shuí chū de?

这主意是王华出的。

Zhè zhǔyi shì Wáng Huá chū de.

信是谁寄来的?

Xìn shì shuí jìlai de?

信是我女儿寄来的。

Xìn shì wǒ nǚ'ér jìlai de.

3. 上面句式2可以换成另一种格式,而强调的重点不变。把全句的主语挪到句尾,作主谓短语中动词的宾语,意思不会变化,因为主语本来在意义上就是动词的受事。主谓短语中的主语本来就是动作的施事者。这样,句子以"是"开头,要着重说明的仍是"是"后面的成分,即动作的施事者。重音也还落在它上面。

是+主语//动词+的+宾语

是谁出的主意?

Shì shuí chū de zhǔyi ?

是王华出的主意。

Shì Wáng Huá chū de zhǔyi.

是谁寄来的信?

Shì shuí jìlai de xìn?

是我女儿寄来的信。

Shì wǒ nǚ·ér jìlai de xìn.

句式2、3两种格式能强调同一成分。作动词受事的词语，前面如有较长的定语，常常放在句首。如定语简单或没定语，则可放在句尾作宾语。

是谁出的主意？

Shì shuí chū de zhǔyi?

这种不得人心的坏主意是谁出的？

Zhè zhǒng bù dé rénxīn de huài zhǔyi shì shuí chū de？

4. 着重指出已完成了的动作的受事者的"是……的"句。这种句子，"是……的"中间是动词，动词的宾语在"的"后，全句要强调的意义重点就是这个宾语。句子的重音也落在宾语上。

主语//是＋动词＋的＋宾语

我是骑的自行车，他是坐的汽车，结果我们一起到家。

Wǒ shì qí de zìxíngchē, tā shì zuò de qìchē, jiéguǒ wǒmen yìqǐ dào jiā.

我是去的大连，他是去的上海，我没看见他。

Wǒ shì qù de Dàlián, tā shì qù de Shànghǎi, wǒ méi kànjian tā.

5. 指出一个动作是产生某一结果的原因的"是……的"句。这种句子，"是……的"结构中间是一个动词。全句的主语在意义上是动作所产生的结果。全句要强调说明的是产生这一结果的原因。因此，说话时句子的重音落在"是……的"中的动词上。

主语//是＋动词＋的

他头疼是哭的。

Tā tóu téng shì kū de.

老人生病是气的。

Lǎorén shēngbìng shì qì de.

动词后面如有宾语，则动词还要在宾语后面重复一次。全句的重音应落在重复的动词上。

主语//是＋动词＋宾语＋动词(重复)＋的

他头疼是喝酒喝的。

Tā tóu téng shì hē jiǔ hē de.

腿疼是爬山爬的。

Tuǐ téng shì pá shān pá de.

以上几种说明意义重点的"是……的"句，在使用中，常常可以把"是"省去，意思不会发生变化。比如：①你是哪天来的？你哪天来的？②我是六号来的。我六号来的。各组中的两句话意思一样，特别是第3句式放在句首的"是"更是常常略去。比如：是谁出的主意？王华出的主意。不过句式5中的"是"却是不能省略的。"他头疼是哭的"不能说成"他头疼哭的"。

这种说明意义重点的"是……的"句的否定形式是"不是……的"。它所否定的不是动作本身，而是句子所着重说明的与动词有关的部分。

新同学不是昨天来的，是今天来的。

Xīn tóngxué bú shì zuótiān lái de, shì jīntiān lái de.

我不是去的大连，是去的上海。

Wǒ bú shì qù de Dàlián, shì qù de Shànghǎi.

第一句否定的是动作发生的时间。已经来了，不过不是昨天来的。第二句否定的是动词的宾语。已经去了，不过不是去的大连。

练 习 三

一、朗读下面的句子，说出各句的意思重点，读对句子的重音：

1. 安娜不是在语言学院学的汉语，他是在北大学的。

Ānnà bú shì zài Yǔyán Xuéyuàn xué de Hànyǔ, tā shì zài Běi-Dà xué de.

2. 昨晚我们是看的话剧，不是看的电影。

Zuówǎn wǒmen shì kàn de huàjù, bú shì kàn de diànyǐng.

3. 他胳臂疼是划船划的。

Tā gēbei téng shì huá chuán huá de.

4. 是你关的窗户吗？玻璃怎么破了？

Shì nǐ guān de chuānghu ma? Bōli zěnme pò le?

5. 这件事是经理同意的，别人不知道。

Zhè jiàn shì shì jīnglǐ tóngyì de, biéren bù zhīdao.

6. 我是要的橘子水，你却送来了啤酒。

Wǒ shì yào de júzi shuǐ, nǐ què sòngláile píjiǔ.

7. 今天早上你们是吃的什么？

Jīntiān zǎoshang nǐmen shì chī de shénme?

8. 大家都是吃的面条，只有她是吃的面包。

Tàjiā dōu shì chī de miàntiáo, zhǐyǒu tā shì chī de miànbāo.

9. 这件衣服褪色了，不是洗的，是晒的。

Zhè jiàn yīfu tuì sè le, bú shì xǐ de, shì shài de.

10. 你们几位是不是一起来的？

Nǐmen jǐ wèi shì bú shì yìqǐ lái de?

11. 不，我是一个人来的。

Bù, wǒ shì yí gè rén lái de.

12. 他耳朵聋是打针打的。

Tā ěrduo lóng shì dǎ zhēn dǎ de.

13. 是谁炒的菜？太咸了！

Shì shuí chǎo de cài? Tài xián le!

14. 张丽炒的。

Zhāng Lì chǎo de.

15. 你是怎么去的颐和园？

Nǐ shì zěnme qù de Yíhéyuán?

16. 我是骑自行车去的，他们是走着去的。

Wǒ shì qí zìxíngchē qù de, tāmen shì zǒuzhe qù de.

二、读熟下面的会话，体会"是……的"句的用法：

A：张丽，你的裙子真漂亮。

Zhāng Lì, nǐ de qúnzi zhēn piàoliang.

B：谢谢。

Xièxie

A：是你男朋友送的吧？

Shì nǐ nán péngyou sòng de ba?

B：不，是我妈妈送的。

Bù, shì wǒ māma sòng de.

A：她是在哪儿买的裙子？

Tā shì zài nǎr mǎi de qúnzi?

B：不是在北京买的，是在上海买的。

Bú shì zài Běijīng mǎi de, shì zài Shànghǎi mǎi de.

A：哦！她是什么时候去上海的？

Ò! Tā shì shénme shíhou qù Shànghǎi de?

B：是上个月去的。

Shì shàng gè yuè qù de.

A：可惜我不知道，要不我也请她带一条。

Kěxī wǒ bù zhīdao, yàobu wǒ yě qǐng tā dài yì tiáo.

* * *

A：张丽，你好，你去哪儿？

Zhāng Lì, nǐ hǎo, nǐ qù nǎr?

B：你好，我带我妹妹去动物园了。她刚来北京。

Nǐ hǎo, wǒ dài wǒ mèimei qù Dòngwùyuán le, tā gāng lái Běijīng.

A：是吗！她是从哪儿来的？

Shì ma! Tā shì cóng nǎr lái de?

B：她从四川来的。

Tā cóng Sìchuān lái de.

A：那你得带她好好玩玩儿啦。

Nà nǐ děi dài tā hǎohāo wánrwanr la.

B：那当然啦。前天是去的长城，昨天是去的天坛，今天去的动物园。明天该去颐和园了。

Nà dāngrán la. Qiántiān shì qù de Chángchéng, zuótiān shì qù de Tiāntán, jīntiān qù de Dòngwùyuán, míngtiān gāi qù Yíhéyuán le.

A：真去了不少地方，你累了吧。

Zhēn qùle bù shǎo dìfang, nǐ lèi le ba.

B：不，前两天不是我陪她玩的，天坛是我爱人陪她去的，我大女儿陪她去的长城。

Bù, qián liǎng tiān bú shì wǒ péi tā wánr de, Tiāntán shì wǒ àiren péi tā qù de, wǒ dà nǚ'ér péi tā qù de Chángchéng.

A：真有意思，祝你们玩得高兴。

Zhēn yǒu yìsi, zhù nǐmen wánr de gāoxìng.

* * *

A：马克，想不到在北京看见你。

Mǎkè, xiǎng bu dào zài Běijīng kànjiàn nǐ.

B：你好，我是跟我们国家的贸易代表团来的。我当翻译。

Nǐ hǎo, wǒ shì gēn wǒmen guójiā de màoyì dàibiǎotuán lái de. Wǒ dāng fānyì.

A：你到了北京，怎么不来我家呢？

Nǐ dàole Běijīng, zěnme bù lái wǒ jiā ne?

B：天天想去看你，可是一点儿时间也没有，身体也不太好。

Tiāntiān xiǎng qù kàn nǐ, kěshì yìdiǎnr shíjiān yě méi yǒu,

shēntǐ yě bú tài hǎo.

A：真的，嗓子都哑了。

Zhēnde，sǎngzi dōu yǎ le.

B：嗓子哑是说话说的。

Sǎngzi yǎ shì shuōhuà shuō de.

A：你当翻译真辛苦。好象眼睛也红了。

Nǐ dāng fānyì zhēn xīnkǔ，hǎoxiàng yǎnjīng yě hóng le.

B：眼睛红是熬夜熬的。

Yǎnjīng hóng shì áoyè áo de.

A：今晚来我家吃饭吧。

Jīnwǎn lái wǒ jiā chī fàn ba.

B：对不起，今晚还有事。

Duìbuqǐ，jīnwǎn hái yǒu shì.

A：明晚怎么样？

Míngwǎn zěnmeyàng？

B：好，明晚一定来。

Hǎo，míngwǎn yídìng lái.

三、用“是……的”句回答下面的问题：

1. 是谁买的电影票？

Shì shuí mǎi de diànyǐngpiào.

2. 张丽是怎么去大连的？

Zhāng Lì shì zěnme qù Dàlián de？

3. 你们中午是吃的中餐还是吃的西餐？

Nǐmen zhōngwǔ shì chī de zhōngcān háishi chī de xīcān？

（用肯定、否定两种形式回答）

4. 王华和张丽都是学的文学吗？

Wáng Huá hé Zhāng Lì dōu shì xué de wénxué ma?

（用肯定、否定两种形式回答）

5. 王华和张丽是唱的什么歌？

Wáng Huá hé Zhāng Lì shì chàng de shénme gē?

6. 这张画是谁画的？

Zhè zhāng huàr shì shuí huà de?

7. 这件事你是怎么知道的？

Zhè jiàn shì nǐ shì zěnme zhīdao de?

8. 他怎么头痛啦？

Tā zěnme tóu tòng la?

9. 这篇文章是你写的吗？

Zhè piān wénzhāng shì nǐ xiě de ma?

（用肯定、否定两种形式回答）

10. 你是在上海遇见他的吗？

Nǐ shì zài Shànghǎi yùjian tā de ma?

（用肯定、否定两种形式回答）

四、根据下面句子的意思重点，把它们改为"是……的"式特指疑问句：

1. 今天没买肉，他们是吃的素菜。

Jīntiān méi mǎi ròu, tāmen shì chī de sùcài.

2. 小王的对象是他姐姐介绍的。

Xiǎo Wáng de duìxiàng shì tā jiějie jièshào de.

3. 是小明打破的玻璃。

Shì Xiǎo Míng dǎpò de bōli.

4. 雨是半夜下的。

Yǔ shì bànyè xià de.

5. 我是在书店买的地图。

Wǒ shì zài shūdiàn mǎi de dìtú.

6. 讲师团是由三位教授率领的。

Jiǎngshītuán shì yóu sān wèi jiàoshòu shuàilǐng de.

7. 颐和园是一七五〇年开始修建的。

Yíhéyuán shì 1750 nián kāishǐ xiūjiàn de.

8. 我女儿是学的音乐。

Wǒ nǚ'er shì xué de yīnyuè.

9. 牙疼是吃糖吃的。

Yá téng shì chī táng chī de.

10. 工作主要是小王做的。

Gōngzuò zhǔyào shì Xiǎo Wáng zuò de.

五、按照提示的重点，把下面的句子改成“是……的”句：

1. 我以前学习汉语。（没学历史）

Wǒ yǐqián xuéxí Hànyǔ.

2. 我走着来。（没坐车）

Wǒ zǒuzhe lái.

3. 我们都不在家，谁做饭了？

Wǒmen dōu bú zài jiā, shuí zuò fàn le?

4. 我一个人来。（没跟别人一起来）

Wǒ yí gè rén lái.

5. 我写信告诉他。（不是打电话）

Wǒ xiě xìn gàosu tā.

6. 我在书桌上找到了这枝笔。（不是在椅子上）

Wǒ zài shūzhuo shàng zhǎodàole zhè zhī bǐ.

7. 小明买这张票。（不是别人）

Xiǎo Míng mǎi zhè zhāng piào.

8. 你在哪儿上车？

Nǐ zài nǎr shàng chē?

9. 为皇帝母亲的生日修建了颐和园。（不是为别的事）

Wèi huángdì mǔqin de shēngrì xiūjiàn le Yíhéyuán.

10. 我在北京看见了张丽。(不是在上海)

Wǒ zài Běijīng kànjiànle Zhāng Lì.

(三)区分"是……的"和"了"

"是……的"句有时会和带有动态助词"了"的句子相混,把"玛丽是在美国生的。"说成"玛丽在美国生了。"因为它们都在动词谓语句中使用,并且它们所表示的动作都是过去已经完成或发生了的。因此,有必要区分"是……的"和"了"在句中的不同作用。

A:王华去日本了,你知道吗?

Wáng Huá qù Rìběn le, nǐ zhīdao ma?

B:我不知道,他是什么时候走的?

Wǒ bù zhīdao, tā shì shénme shíhou zǒu de?

A:他是上个月走的。

Tā shì shàng ge yuè zǒu de.

B:他是不是坐船去的?

Tā shì bu shì zuò chuán qù de?

A:他不是坐船去的,是坐飞机去的。

Tā bú shì zuò chuán qù de, shì zuò fēijī qù de.

B:他妈妈去没去?

Tā māma qù méi qù?

A:他妈妈没去。

Tā māma méi qù.

可以看出1. 动词后面用"了"的句子是说明过去已发生了的动作或行为。而用"是.....的"的句子则是着重指出动作、行为发生的时间、地点、方式等有关的内容。2."是……的"的否定形式是"不是……的","了"则用"没"否定。3. 它们的正反疑问句的形式也不同。

我们把这两种形式放在一起来比较，是为了区分它们，免得用错。这两种形式并不总是可以互相替换的。有不少句子只有其中的一种形式，换成另一形式，意思就会发生变化或根本不能成立了。

我是吃了饭来的。

Wǒ shì chīle fàn lái de.

* 我吃了饭来了。

Wǒ chīle fàn lái le.

第二句不能成立。

你是怎么去颐和园的？

Nǐ shì zěnme qù Yíhéyuán de?

你怎么去颐和园了？

Nǐ zěnme qù Yíhéyuán le?

第一句问的是去颐和园的方式，坐车还是走着。第二句则是问去颐和园的原因。两句话之间并无联系。

练习四

一、下面各组中的两句话意义有什么不同？请为问句作出答案，为陈述句配上问题：

1. a 他昨天来了。

Tā zuótiān lái le.

b 他是昨天来的。

Tā shì zuótiān lái de.

2. a 昨天半夜下雨了。

Zuótiān bànyè xià yǔ le.

b 昨天是半夜下的雨。

Zuótiān shì bànyè xià de yǔ.

3. a 小王是七点起床的吗？

Xiǎo Wáng shì qī diǎn qǐchuáng de ma?

b 小王七点起床了吗？

Xiǎo Wáng qī diǎn qǐchuáng le ma?

（用否定形式）

4. a 这些窗户不是去年修理的。

Zhèxiē chuānghu bú shì qùnián xiūlǐ de.

b 这些窗户去年没修理。

Zhèxiē chuānghu qùnián méi xiūlǐ.

5. a 我们不是上星期六看的电影。

Wǒmen bú shì shàng Xīngqīliù kàn de diànyǐng.

b 我们上星期六没看电影。

Wǒmen shàng Xīngqīliù méi kàn diànyǐng.

二、朗读下面的几段话，体会用"了"的句子和用"是……的"的句子意思上的差别：

日本姑娘美子第一次来中国旅行。她是和几个朋友一起来的。他们在北京住了一个星期。游览了长城、故宫、北海等名胜古迹，还看了一次京戏。不过，时间不够没能去香山。美子还买了不少中国特产，是和朋友们一起在王府井买的。他们还吃了有名的烤鸭，是在全聚德吃的。大家都说：这次旅行太有意思了；明年暑假一定再来。今天早上他们已经回国了。来的时候，他们是坐的飞机，回去是坐的船。

Rìběn gūniang Měizǐ dì-yī cì lái Zhōngguó lǚxíng. Tā shì hé jǐ ge péngyou yìqǐ lái de. Tāmen zài Běijīng zhùle yí gè xīngqī, yóulǎnle Chángchéng, Gùgōng, Běihǎi děng míngshèng gǔjì, hái kànle yí cì Jīngxì. Búguò, shíjiān búgòu méi néng qù Xiāngshān. Měizǐ hái mǎile bù shǎo Zhōngguó tèchǎn, shì hé péngyoumen yìqǐ zài Wángfǔjǐng mǎi de. Tāmen hái chīle yǒumíng de kǎoyā, shì zài Quánjùdé chī de. Dàjiā dōu shuō: Zhècì lǚxíng tài yǒu yìsi le; míngnián shǔjià yídìng zài lái. Jīntiān zǎoshang tāmen yǐjing huí guó le. Lái de shíhou, tāmen shì zuò de fēijī, huíqu shì zuò de chuán.

* * *

A：你昨天来了吗？

Nǐ zuótiān lái le ma?

B：我来了，你不在。

Wǒ lái le, nǐ bú zài.

A：你是什么时候来的？是早上来的吗？

Nǐ shì shénmen shíhou lái de? Shì zǎoshang lái de ma?

B：不是早上来的，我十二点来的。

Bú shì zǎoshang lái de, wǒ shí'èr diǎn lái de.

A：哦！十二点我去食堂了。真对不起，我还以为你没来呢。

O! shí'èr diǎn wǒ qù shítáng le. Zhēn duìbuqǐ, wǒ hái yǐwéi nǐ méi lái ne.

* * *

A：听说你最近去了日本，是吗？

Tīngshuō nǐ zuìjìn qùle Rìběn, shì ma?

B：是，你怎么知道的？

Shì, nǐ zěnme zhīdao de?

A：是老王告诉我的。

Shì Lǎo Wáng gàosu wǒ de.

B：对，我是和老王一起去的。我们在东京住了十天，参观了不少地方。

Duì, wǒ shì hé Lǎo Wáng yìqǐ qù de. Wǒmen zài Dōngjīng zhùle shí tiān, cānguānle bù shǎo dìfang.

A：去了别的城市没有？

Qùle biéde chéngshì méiyou?

B：没去。

Méi qù.

A：是日中友好协会邀请你们的吗？

Shì Rì-Zhōng Yǒuhǎo Xiéhuì yāoqǐng nǐmen de ma?

B：不是日中友协请的，是东京外国语大学请的。

Bú shì Rì-Zhōng yǒu-xié qǐng de, shì Dōngjīng Wàiguóyǔ Dàxué qǐng de.

三、把下面用“了”的句子改为“是……的”句，并说明意思有什么变化：

1. 1949年10月1日中华人民共和国成立了。

1949 nián 10 yuè 1 rì Zhōnghuá Rénmín Gònghéguó chénglì le.

2. 上星期天下午，我们去了北海公园。

Shàng Xīngqītiān xiàwǔ, wǒmen qùle Běihǎi Gōngyuán.

3. 他骑车走了。

Tā qí chē zǒu le.

4. 王华跟他母亲一起去南方了。

Wáng Huá gēn tā mǔqin yìqǐ qù nánfāng le.

5. 我在王府井看见了安娜。

Wǒ zài Wángfǔjǐng kànjianle Ānnà.

6. 屋里太冷了。谁把窗户打开了？

Wūli tài lěng le. Shuí bǎ chuānghu dǎkāi le?

7. 他喝茶喝得睡不着觉了。

Tā hē chá hē de shuì bù zháo jiào le.

8. 张丽没坐公共汽车去。

Zhāng Lì méi zuò gōnggòng qìchē qù.

9. 他们在礼堂里举行了婚礼。

Tāmen zài lǐtáng li jǔxíngle hūnlǐ.

10. 我们十年前就认识他了。

Wǒmen shí nián qián jiù rènshi tā le.

四、把下面几段话中的错句子挑出来并改正：

1. 我们班来了一个新同学。他昨天来。他的名字叫郑琳达。他的中国话说得不太好。我问他："你是什么时候来中国的？"他说："我是上个月刚来了。""你的父亲、母亲是美国人吗？""我的父亲、母亲都是中国人。他们是1948年去美国的，已经在美国住了三十多年了。"我说："欢迎你来学习汉语，你有什么困难，我一定帮助你。"他高兴地说："谢谢，我要在中国是学习一年的。"

Wǒmen bān láile yí gè xīn tóngxué. Tā zuótiān lái. Tā de míngzi jiào Zhèng Líndá. Tā de Zhōngguóhuà shuō de bú tài hǎo. Wǒ wèn tā: "Nǐ shì shénme shíhou lái Zhōngguó de?" Tā shuō: "Wǒ shì shàng gè yuè gāng lái le." "Nǐ de fùqin, mǔqin shì Měiguórén ma?" "Wǒ de fùqin, mǔqin dōu shì Zhōngguórén. Tāmen shì 1948 nián qù Měiguó de, yǐjing zài Měiguó zhùle 30 duō nián le." Wǒ shuō: "Huānyíng nǐ lái xuéxí Hànyǔ, nǐ yǒu shénme kùnnan, wǒ yídìng bāngzhù nǐ." Tā gāoxìng de shuō: "Xièxie, wǒ yào zài Zhōngguó shì xuéxí yì nián de."

* * *

2. A:请问这本书是在哪儿买的?

Qǐngwèn zhè běn shū shì zài nǎr mǎi de?

B:我是从图书馆借了。

Wǒ shì cóng túshūguǎn jiè le.

A:我也去图书馆了,可是没借到。

Wǒ yě qù túshūguǎn le, kěshì méi jièdào.

B:我是上星期借了。听说王府井新华书店也有这本书,你可以去看看。

Wǒ shì shàngxīngqī jiè le. Tīngshuō Wángfǔjǐng Xīnhuá Shūdiàn yě yǒu zhè běn shū, nǐ kěyǐ qù kànkan.

A:我已经去过三次了也没看见。

Wǒ yǐjing qùguo sān cì le yě méi kànjian.

B:我看完了一定借给你。

Wǒ kànwánle yídìng jiègěi nǐ.

A:太好了!我是什么时候可以去你家拿的呢?

Tài hǎo le! Wǒ shì shénme shíhou kěyǐ qù nǐ jiā ná de ne?

B:后天下了课来好吗?

Hòutiān xiàle kè lái hǎo ma?

A:好,谢谢你。

Hǎo xièxie nǐ.

二、表示语气的“是……的”句

（一）“是……的”句表示的语气

例：玛丽会来吗？

Mǎlì huì lái ma?

（1）玛丽会来。

Mǎlì huì lái.

（2）玛丽是会来的。

Mǎlì shì huì lái de.

这些节目怎么样？

Zhèxiē jiémù zěnmeyàng?

（1）这些节目很精彩。

Zhèxiē jiémù hěn jīngcǎi.

（2）这些节目是很精彩的。

Zhèxiē jiémù shì hěn jīngcǎi de.

第一组问答中，第(1)句回答只一般地说明玛丽可能来。第(2)句的谓语上套上了“是……的”，就加上了肯定语气。说话人表示确实知道玛丽是会来的。第二组问答中，第(1)句回答是一般地说节目好。第(2)句加强了肯定语气，说话者表示自己确实认为节目很精彩。

说话的人在叙述自己对某一件事的看法、见解，或对某一事加以解释、说明的同时，表示自己的情绪、口气，就可以用表示语气的“是……的”句。它主要表示加强肯定、确认的语气，有时也可表示缓和、委婉的语气。

这类句子的“是……的”结构中间，除了动词、动词短语、主谓短语外，还有形容词、助动词和某些副词。不论谓语是什么，加上

"是……的"结构后,"的 "总是在句尾。

(二)表示语气的"是……的"句的几种句式

1.单独的形容词、动词、助动词作谓语时,"是……的"结构套在单词谓语上。说话时句子的重音也落在这个单词谓语上。

主语//是+单词谓语+的

钱是有的,不到紧急的时候不能用。

Qián shì yǒu de, bú dào jǐnjí de shíhou bù néng yòng.

其实,他是明白的,不愿说就是了。

Qíshí, tā shì míngbai de, bú yuàn shuō jiùshì le.

你不来是可以的,可孩子得来。

Nǐ bù lái shì kěyǐ de, kě háizi děi lái.

2."是……的"结构中间的谓语是动词结构时,有三种形式是常见的:动词前有助动词,说话时重音落在助动词上。

主语//是+助动词+动词+的

我是愿意帮助他们的。

Wǒ shì yuànyì bāngzhù tāmen de.

不愉快的事是可能发生的。

Bù yúkuài de shì shì kěnéng fāshēng de.

动词后有可能补语。套上"是……的"结构后,句子重音落在整个动补结构上,如:

主语//是+动+可能补语+的

这么多事一天是干不完的。

Zhème duō shì yì tiān shì gàn bu wán de.

只要大家安静,老师的话是听得见的。

Zhǐyào dàjiā ānjìng, lǎoshī de huà shì tīng de jiàn de.

有时动词的前后既有助动词又有可能补语。如:

主语//是+助动词+动词+可能补语+的

他的打算是可以看得出来的。

Tā de dǎsuàn shì kěyǐ kàn de chūlái de.

这点儿东西他是应该搬得动的。

Zhè diǎn dōngxi tā shì yīnggāi bān de dòng de.

3. 句子的谓语如是主谓结构，套上“是……的”时，不能把主谓结构整个放在“是……的”中间，而应把“是”插在主谓结构的主语与谓语之间，“的”字仍在句尾：

主语//主语＋是＋谓语＋的

这儿的规章制度大家是知道的。

Zhèr de guīzhāng zhìdù dàjiā shì zhīdao de.

这些道理人们是懂得的。

Zhèxiē dàolǐ rénmen shì dǒngdé de.

这种句子的主语，在意义上是谓语中动词的受事。因此也可把主语挪到后面作宾语，“的”仍在句尾。

主语//是＋动词＋宾语＋的

大家是知道这儿的规章制度的。

Dàjiā shì zhīdao zhèr de guīzhāng zhìdù de.

人们是懂得这些道理的。

Rénmen shì dǒng dé zhèxiē dàolǐ de.

挪动之后句子所表示的语气并没有变。重音都落在动词上。

表示语气的“是……的”句的否定形式是把“是……的”结构中的成分改成否定形式。

在这样的教室里上课，老师的话是听不见的。

Zài zhèyàng de jiàoshì li shàngkè, lǎoshī de huà shì tīng bu jiàn de.

如果在“是……的”前再用“不”来否定一次，就成为双重否定形式，用来委婉地或强调地肯定某一件事。如：

大家安静一点，老师的话不是不能听见的。

Dàjiā ānjìng yì diǎnr, lǎoshī de huà bú shì bù néng tīngjiàn de.

（三）区分两种“是……的”句

“是……的”结构在不同的句子形式中起的作用不同，构成了两种“是……的”句，怎样区分这两类“是……的”句呢？

1. 指出意义重点的“是……的”句的谓语，即在“是……的”结构里的成分是动词、动词短语或以动词为谓语的主谓短语。表示语气的“是……的”句的谓语除动词和动词短语外，也有形容词、形容词短语、能愿动词、副词等。

2. 即使谓语都是动词，情况也不同。指出意义重点的句子，动词前面常有表示时间、地点、方式的状语，也就是句子要强调的重点。表示语气的句子，动词前常有能愿动词，动词后常有可能补语。

3. 宾语的位置也是区分两种句子的标志之一。指出意义重点的“是……的”句宾语可以在“的”前也可在“的”后。强调语气的句子，宾语只能在“的”前，“的”字总是在句尾。

4. 这两类句子的否定形式也不同。指出意义重点的否定形式是“不是…… 的”，它所否定的不是动作本身，而是句子所要强调指出的与动词有关的内容。表示语气的“是……的”句的否定形式是把“是……的”结构中的成分变为否定。

从句子的结构上科学地分辨这两类“是……的”句，对于正确理解和掌握它们是十分必要的，但更重要的是多练习多实践，在实际语言环境中体察分辨不同句式的特点，养成语感，才能真正运用自如。

练 习 五

一、朗读下面表示语气的“是……的”句，读对句子的重音，体会它所表示的语气：

1. 他们是很想学英语的，就是没人教。

Tāmen shì hěn xiǎng xué Yīngyǔ de, jiùshi méi rén jiāo.

2. 工人们是会同意我的意见的，不必担心。

Gōngrénmen shì huì tóngyì wǒ de yìjian de, búbì dānxīn.

3. 别着急，问题不是不能解决的。

Bié zháojí, wèntí bú shì bù néng jiějué de.

4. 这么点儿路我是走得动的，不用坐车了。

Zhème diǎnr lù wǒ shì zǒu de dòng de, bú yòng zuò chē le.

5. 人们是不愿意听空话的，他们要求解决实际问题。

Rénmen shì bú yuànyì tīng kōnghuà de, tāmen yāoqiú jiějué shíjì wèntí.

6. 对学习，大家都是很认真的。

Duì xuéxí, dàjiā dōu shì hěn rènzhēn de.

7. 让大家都知道我们的困难，是很必要的。

Ràng dàjiā dōu zhīdao wǒmen de kùnnan, shì hěn bìyào de.

8. 对我们的要求是很严格的。

Duì wǒmen de yāoqiú shì hěn yángé de.

9. 这么简单的问题，你是应该懂的。

Zhème jiǎndān de wèntí, nǐ shì yīnggāi dǒng de.

10. 我是从来不抽烟的。

Wǒ shì cónglái bù chōu yān de.

11. 人是老实的，不过太老实了也办不了大事。

Rén shì lǎoshi de, búguò tài lǎoshi le yě bàn bù liǎo dà shì.

12. 我的心情你是不能理解的。

Wǒ de xīnqíng nǐ shì bù néng lǐjiě de.

13. 这些问题不是不能解决的，他们就是不愿意管。

Zhèxiē wèntí bú shì bù néng jiějué de, tāmen jiùshi bú yuànyì guǎn.

14. 一个人是吃不完这么多菜的。

Yí gè rén shì chī bù wán zhème duō cài de.

15. 只要多练习，汉语是能学得好的。

Zhǐyào duō liànxí, Hànyǔ shì néng xué de hǎo de.

二、把下面的句子改成表示语气的“是……的”句：

1. 下雨王华就不会来了。

Xià yǔ Wáng Huá jiù bú huì lái le.

2. 时间太少，这么多题目作不完。

Shíjiān tài shǎo, zhème duō tímù zuò bù wán.

3. 鸦片战争以后，中国人民生活很痛苦。

Yāpiàn zhànzhēng yǐhòu, Zhōngguó rénmín shēnghuó hěn tòngkǔ.

4. 这本书的内容很重要，请大家认真阅读。

Zhè běn shū de nèiróng hěn zhòngyào, qǐng dàjiā rènzhēn yuèdú.

5. 玛丽很不愿意离开中国。

Mǎlì hěn bú yuànyì líkāi Zhōngguó.

6. 北京的冬天很冷，大家注意别感冒了。

Běijīng de dōngtiān hěn lěng, dàjiā zhùyì bié gǎnmào le.

7. 这演讲应该听，不过跟我们关系不大，所以我们没去听。(双重否定)

Zhè yǎnjiǎng yīnggāi tīng, búguò gēn wǒmen guānxì bú dà,

suǒyǐ wǒmen méi qù tīng.

8. 他很想来看你，可惜没时间了。

Tā hěn xiǎng lái kàn nǐ, kěxī méi shíjiān le.

9. 从学校回家，不坐车我走得了。

Cóng xuéxiào huí jiā, bú zuò chē wǒ zǒu de liǎo.

（否定形式）

10. 杰克能学好汉语，你别着急。

Jiékè néng xuéhǎo Hànyǔ, nǐ bié zháojí.

三、分辨下面的“是……的”句哪些是指出意义重点的，哪些是表示语气的：

1. 我是寄的挂号信，不会丢。

Wǒ shì jì de guàhàoxìn, bú huì diū.

2. 这本书是五十年代出版的，现在买不到了。

Zhè běn shū shì wǔshí niándài chūbǎn de, xiànzài mǎi bu dào le.

3. 楼下的声音这儿是听不见的

Lóu xià de shēngyīn zhèr shì tīng bu jiàn de.

4. 这件衣服是不是去年做的？

Zhè jiàn yīfu shì bu shì qùnián zuò de?

5. 这些年中国的农业发展是很快的。

Zhèxiē nián Zhōngguó de nóngyè fāzhǎn shì hěn kuài de.

6. 他肩膀疼是挑水挑的。

Tā jiānbǎng téng shì tiāo shuǐ tiāo de.

7. 琳达的汉语是学得不错的，只是发音稍差一点儿。

Líndá de Hànyǔ shì xué de búcuò de, zhǐshì fāyīn shāo chà yìdiǎnr.

8. 学生们是怎么去颐和园的？

Xuéshengmen shì zěnme qù Yíhéyuán de?

9. 解放前，我家的生活是很困难的。

Jiěfàng qián, wǒ jiā de shēnghuó shì hěn kùnnan de.

10. 外国人是很喜欢这些工艺品的。

Wàiguó rén shì hěn xǐhuan zhèxiē gōngyìpǐn de.

11. 这些事不是不能商量的，你别着急。

Zhèxiē shì bú shì bù néng shāng liang de, nǐ bié zháojí.

12. 这些问题不是大家一起商量的，我不知道。

Zhèxiē wèntí bú shì dàjiā yìqǐ shāngliang de, wǒ bù zhīdào.

13. 这几件事都是办不到的，你不必再说了。

Zhè jǐ jiàn shì dōu shì bàn bu dào de, nǐ búbì shuō le.

14. 小王是哪天离开北京的？

Xiǎo Wáng shì nǎ tiān líkāi Běijīng de?

15. 他们想去是可以的，不过要听老师的话。

Tāmen xiǎng qù shì kěyǐ de, búguò yào tīng lǎoshī de huà.

四、按照要求改写下面的“是……的”句：

1. 琳达是在美国上的大学。（特指疑问句）

Líndá shì zài Měiguó shàng de dàxué.

2. 只要认真复习，你是能考好的。

Zhǐyào rènzhēn fùxí, nǐ shì néng kǎohǎo de.

3. 王华是会回去的。（否定句）

Wáng Huá shì huì huíqu de.

4. 他发烧是洗冷水澡洗的。

Tā fāshāo shì xǐ lěngshuǐ zǎo xǐ de.

5. 这些活儿今天是干得完的。（否定句）

Zhèxiē huór jīntiān shì gàn de wán de.

6. 他的两个孩子都上大学了，儿子是学的物理，女儿是学的外语。

Tā de liǎng gè háizi dōu shàng dàxué le, érzi shì xué de wùlǐ, nǚ'ér shì xué de wài yǔ.

（特指疑问句）

7. 菜是小王的母亲做的。（否定句）

Cài shì Xiǎo Wáng de mǔqin zuò de.

8. 他的目的人们是看不清楚的。(肯定句)
Tā de mùdì rénmen shì kàn bù qīngchu de.

9. 其实生产定额并不高，只要好好干，不是不可能达到的。(肯定句)
Qíshí shēngchǎn dìng'é bìng bù gāo，zhǐyào hǎohāo gàn，bú shì bù kěnéng dádào de.

10. 冰箱太重了，是我们六个人一起抬上来的。(疑问句)
Bīngxiāng tài zhòng le，shì wǒmen liù gè rén yìqǐ tái shànglai de.

五、按照情景和提示的要求写出正确的"是……的"句：

1. A：你好，我叫安娜，是美国留学生。
Nǐhǎo，wǒ jiào Ānnà，shì Měiguó liúxuéshēng.

B：噢！你学中文吗？
O！Nǐ xué Zhōngwén ma？

A：(安娜学中医)
(Ānnà xué Zhōngyī)

B：你是哪天到北京的？
Nǐ shì nǎ tiān dào Běijīng de？

A：(前天)
(Qiántiān)

B：生活习惯吗？
Shēnghuó xíguàn ma？

A：还不太习惯。

Hái bú tài xíguàn.

B：（刚到新环境，生活不习惯很自然。）

（Gāng dào xīn huánjìng, shēnghuó bù xíguàn hěn zìrán.）

A：这所学校的外国学生好象不太多。

Zhèsuǒ xuéxiào de wàiguó xuésheng hǎoxiàng bú tài duō.

B：（很多，不过现在都出去旅行了。）

（Hěn duō, bú guò xiànzài dōu chūqu lǚxíng le.）

2. A：你的毛衣真漂亮，是王府井买的吗？

Nǐ de máoyī zhēn piàoliang, shì Wángfǔjǐng mǎi de ma？

B：（妈妈做的）

（Māma zuò de）

A：你妈妈真会做衣服。

Nǐ māma zhēn huì zuò yīfu.

B：（很会做，每一件都漂亮。）

（Hěn huìzuò, měi yí jiàn dōu piàoliang.）

3. A：张丽，来打兰球吧。

Zhāng Lì, lái dǎ lánqiú ba.

B：我腿疼，打不了。

Wǒ tuǐ téng, dǎ bu liǎo.

A：为什么腿疼？

Wèi shénme tuǐ téng？

B：（爬山）

（Pá shān）

4. A：昨晚你们是不是看京戏去了？

Zuówǎn nǐmen shì bu shì kàn Jīngxì qùle？

B：是。

Shì.

A：（在哪儿？）

（Zài nǎr？）

B：（人民剧场）

（Rénmín Jùchǎng）

A：你觉得京戏怎么样？

Nǐ juéde Jīngxì zěnmeyàng？

B：（唱腔好听，服装美）

（Chàngqiāng hǎotīng，fúzhuāng měi）

A：听说你对京戏很内行，下次一起去好吗？

Tīngshuō nǐ duì Jīngxì hěn nèiháng，xià cì yìqǐ qù hǎo ma？

5. A：已经六点半了，玛丽怎么还不来？

Yǐjing liù diǎn bàn le，Mǎlì zěnme hái bù lái？

B：她昨天答应来了吗？

Tā zuótiān dāying lái le ma？

A：答应了。

Dāying le.

B：（一定会来）

（Yídìng huì lái）

六、根据下面的提示写出带有各种"是……的"句的对话：

1. 琳达告诉王华，她刚从成都回来，在成都住了两个星期。去的时候坐火车，回来时坐船。坐船在长江航行非常有意思，三峡风光非常美。四川菜很辣，不过她也喜欢吃。四川小吃也很不错。

Líndá gàosu Wáng Huá ，tā gāng cóng Chéngdū huílai，zài Chéngdū zhùle liǎng gè xīngqī. Qù de shíhou zuò huǒchē，huílai shí zuò chuán. Zuò chuán zài Cháng Jiāng hángxíng fēicháng yǒu yìsi，Sānxiá fēngguāng fēicháng měi. Sìchuān cài hěn là，bú guò tā yě xǐhuan chī. Sìchuān xiǎochī yě hěn búcuò.

2. 琳达和王华聊天，琳达告诉王华前几天她的父亲母亲来了，他们来北京旅行。琳达陪他们游览了很多地方。昨天去了长城，前天去了故宫，上星期去了香山和颐和园。他们还在东来顺吃了涮羊肉。她的父亲母亲觉得这次旅行真有意思。

Líndá hé Wáng Huá liáotiānr，Líndá gàosu Wáng Huá qián jǐ tiān tā de fùqin mǔqin láile，tāmen lái Běijīng lǚxíng. Líndá péi tāmen yóu lǎn le hěn duō dìfang. Zuótiān qùle Chángchéng，qiántiān qùle Gùgōng，shàng xīngqī qùle Xiāngshān hé Yíhéyuán. Tāmen hái zài Dōngláishùn chīle shuàn yángròu. Tā de fùqin mǔqin juéde zhè cì lǚxíng zhēn yǒu yìsi.

3. 琳达和王华聊天，她告诉王华，她买了好几本小说，有鲁迅的、茅盾的和丁玲的。琳达想：自己的汉语水平不高，看这些小说一定有很多困难。

Líndá hé Wáng Huá liáotiānr，tā gàosu Wáng Huá，tā mǎile hǎo jǐ běn xiǎoshuōr，yǒu Lǔ Xùn de，Máo Dùn de hé Dīng Líng de.

Líndá xiǎng: Zìjǐ de Hànyǔ shuǐpíng bù gāo, kàn zhè xiē xiǎoshuōr yídìng yǒu hěn duō kùnnan.

4. 同学们都希望明天别考试了。他们这几天游泳游得太累了。可是张老师一定不会同意。王华却说：也不一定。只要把理由说清楚，张老师也可能会同意。

Tóngxuémen dōu xīwàng míngtiān bié kǎoshì le. Tāmen zhè jǐ tiān yóuyǒng yóu de tài lèi le, Kěshì zhāng lǎoshī yídìng bú huì tóngyì. Wáng Huá què shuō: Yě bù yídìng. Zhǐyào bǎ lǐyóu shuō qīngchu, Zhāng lǎoshī yě kěnéng huì tóngyì.

5. 星期天，琳达、玛丽、木村在宿舍里做饭。他们谈到买了些什么菜，在哪儿买的菜，什么菜好吃，什么不好吃，哪个国家的菜好吃，谁做的菜好吃等等。

Xīngqītiān, Líndá, Mǎlì, Mùcūn zài sùshè li zuò fàn. Tāmen tándào mǎile xiē shénme cài, zài nǎr mǎi de cài, shénme cài hǎochī, shénme bù hǎo chī, nǎge guójiā de cài hǎochī, shuí zuò de cài hǎochī děngděng.

伍、"在"的用法

现代汉语里，"在"可以是动词，如：

他在家。

Tā zài jiā.

可以是介词，如：

在他的帮助下，小李进步很快。

Zài tā de bāngzhù xià, Xiǎo Lǐ jìnbù hěn kuài.

也可以是副词，如：

他在研究语法。

Tā zài yánjiū yǔfǎ.

本节要谈的是副词的"在"，它修饰动词。

一、"在"的意义：

"在"的本义是居、存，即存在的意思。存在本身是一个历程的进行、绵延。汉语里动词本身不表示"时""态"或"体"，但时间副词"在"可以放在动词的前边，表示动作、行为在进行中或状态在持续中，如：

他在看书。

Tā zài kàn shū.

十几张嘴同时在问，在叫。

Shíjǐ zhāng zuǐ tóngshí zài wèn, zài jiào.

风在吼，马在叫，黄河在咆哮。

Fēng zài hǒu, mǎ zài jiào, Huáng Hé zài páoxiāo.

“在”着重呈现动作的持续进行还没有完结的状况，在语法意义上，比较接近英语的“-ing”，不论这个动作或行为什么时间开始，什么时间结束，它甚至可用于修饰无始无终的动作或行为。如：

他们在表演汉语节目。

Tāmen zài biǎoyǎn Hànyǔ jiémù.

他在练毛笔字。

Tā zài liàn máobǐ zì.

地球在绕着太阳转。

Dìqiú zài ràozhe tàiyáng zhuàn.

各种物质的分子总是在不停地运动着。

Gè zhǒng wùzhì de fēnzǐ zǒng shì zài bùtíng de yùndòngzhe.

“在”可以表示动作的反复进行或长期持续，它可受表示情况的重复或再现、表频率、表时间、表持续以及表周遍意义的副词修饰。这类副词有：“又、还、也、常常、经常、时常、已经、总、时时、都、全、一直”等等。如：

你又在作诗了么？

Nǐ yòu zài zuò shī le me?

他一直在研究美术史。

Tā yìzhí zài yánjiū měishùshǐ.

你还在琢磨这个问题呀？

Nǐ hái zài zuómo zhège wèntí ya?

我们都在夸你呢。

Wǒmen dōu zài kuā nǐ ne.

练　习　一

一、找出下列句中副词性的“在”，在（　）内画个“√”：

1. 他生在纽约，长在华盛顿。（　）

Tā shēng zài Niǔyuē (New York), zhǎng zài Huáshèngdùn (Washington).

2. 苹果放在冰箱里了。(　)

Píngguǒ fàng zài bīngxiāng li le

3. 孩子在找他妈妈。(　)

Háizi zài zhǎo tā māma.

4. 他在写信。(　)

Tā zài xiě xìn.

5. 张先生在图书馆。(　)

Zhāng xiānsheng zài túshūguǎn.

6. 同学们在黑板上练汉字。(　)

Tóngxuémen zài hēibǎn shàng liàn Hànzì.

7. 他们累了，在休息呢。(　)

Tāmen lèi le, zài xiūxi ne.

8. 脚下有我们富饶的油海在激荡。(　)

Jiǎo xià yǒu wǒmen fùráo de yóuhǎi zài jīdàng.

9. 他在床上躺着。(　)

Tā zài chuáng shang tǎngzhe.

10. 约翰教授住在北京饭店。(　)

Yuēhàn (John) jiàoshòu zhù zài Běijīng Fàndiàn.

二、用所给的词语造句：

1. 研究　汉语语法　在　一直　他们
2. 一直　她　当　在　翻译
3. 在　还　孩子们　考试
4. 王先生　买卖　做　在　也
5. 中国饭　做　在　张小姐

三、你能找出下列这段话中的时间副词“在”吗？

我难得慢慢地骑着车子，在华灯齐放的长安街上驶过。心里有一种说不出来的滋味在折腾着。难道我是在恋爱了么？不，这不叫恋爱！小说上有过这样的故事，这叫单恋！在恋爱的是她，还有那个漂亮的小伙子。

Wǒ nándé mànman de qízhe chēzi，zài huádēng qí fàng de Cháng'ān Jiē shang shǐguo. Xīn li yǒu yì zhǒng shuō bù chulai de zīwèi zài zhētengzhe. Nándào wǒ shì zài liàn'ài le me？Bù，zhè bú jiào liàn'ài！Xiǎoshuō shang yǒuguo zhèyàng de gùshi，zhè jiào dān liàn！Zài liàn'ài de shì tā，hái yǒu nàge piàoliang de xiǎohuǒzi.

四、请给下列句子补上时间副词"在"：

1. 这是一个身材高大，头发长，眼球白多黑少的人，看人总像渺视。

   Zhè shì yí gè shēncái gāodà，tóufa cháng，yǎnqiú bái duō hēi shǎo de rén，kàn rén zǒng xiàng miǎoshì.

2. 听！又是一阵炮声，死神狂吼。

   Tīng！Yòu shì yí zhèn pào shēng，sǐshén kuáng hǒu.

3. 山谷里一团火光闪动。

   Shāngǔ li yì tuán huǒ guāng shǎndòng.

4. 好象有人小声哭泣。

   Hǎoxiàng yǒu rén xiǎo shēng kūqì.

5. 谁吹笛子？这么动听！

   Shuí chuī dízi？Zhème dòngtīng！

二、"在"的使用条件

"在"的使用条件，即动词什么时候可以加"在"，什么时候不能加"在"，可以从动词本身的性质、意义和动词短语的组成情况加以考察。

（一）从动词本身的性质和意义看

1. 表示行为动作的动词（这类动词占动词的多数），如“跑、吃、洗、说、看、学习、研究、表演”等，不论单独使用或有限制地组成动词短语，都可以受“在”的修饰，表示动作或行为在进行中，例如：

他在看。

Tā zài kàn.

珍妮在学习。

Zhēnní(Jane) zài xuéxí.

大家都在说：“他可是个好人！”

Dàjiā dōu zài shuō："Tā kě shì ge hǎorén!"

2. 表示状态的动词，一般不受“在”的修饰。

（1）“饿、病、瞎、皱、瘸、僵、醉、麻、聋、哑、疯、乏、塞、通、醒”等状态动词不表示动作，单独使用时不受“在”的修饰，如不能说“在醉”“在麻”“在瘸”。

（2）“躺、坐、站、跪、蹲、靠、趴、倚”等表示身体姿势的动词，表示相对静止的状态，单独使用时，不受“在”的修饰，如不说“在躺”“在坐”“在站”。只有在加了“着”表示状态持续态时，才能加“在”，如可说“在躺着”“在坐着”“在跪着”“在蹲着”。

（3）部分表心理状态的动词，如“爱、恨、喜欢、佩服、相信”等不表示什么动作，单独使用时不受“在”的修饰，但有的带了宾语后，可受“在”的修饰，如“我知道他在恨我”“三年过去了，他还在爱她”。

3. 有些表示行为动作的动词，如“关、开、插、雇、写、贴、种、埋、拖”等，附上“着”表示行为动作后果（或成效）的状态，这时不受“在”的修饰，请比较：

表示动作意义	表示状态意义
他关门。	门关着。

Tā guān mén.	Mén guānzhe.
他在关门。	* 门在关着。
Tā zài guān mén.	Mén zài guānzhe.
他写字。	黑板上写着字。
Tā xiě zì.	Hēibǎn shang xiězhe zì.
他在写字。	* 黑板上在写着字。
Tā zài xiě zì.	Hēibǎn shang zài xiězhe zì.
他贴邮票。	信封上贴着邮票。
Tā tiē yóupiào.	Xìnfēng shang tiēzhe yóupiào.
他在贴邮票。	* 信封上在贴着邮票。
Tā zài tiē yóupiào.	Xìnfēng shang zài tiēzhe yóupiào.
他插花。	花瓶里插着花。
Tā chā huā.	Huāpíng li chāzhe huā.
他在插花。	* 花瓶里在插着花。
Tā zài chā huā.	Huāpíng li zài chāzhe huā.

4. 特殊动词"是""有""象""在",以及动词"姓、成为、具有、属于、隶属、等于、善于、包含、包括、该、欠、显、差、多、含有、具备、牵涉、适合、符合、缺乏、类似、充满、区别、重视、轻视、值得、蕴藏"等不表示什么动作,不受"在"的修饰,例如不能说:

*他在是这个公司的董事长。

Tā zài shì zhège gōngsī de dǒngshìzhǎng.

*中国也在有自己的电子工业。

Zhōngguó yě zài yǒu zìjǐ de diànzǐ gōngyè.

*这些财产在属于他。

Zhèxiē cáichǎn zài shǔyú tā.

*地下在蕴藏着丰富的宝藏。

Dìxia zài yùncáng zhe fēngfù de bǎozàng.

5. 一些非自主动词（或称感知动词），如“觉得、知道、发现、认识、感觉、听见、闻见、看见、遇到、遇见”等，不受“在”的修饰。

6. 无进行过程或持续过程的动词，如“死、停、到、懂、去、来、完、剩、结束、开始、撤销、放弃、遗漏、到达、停止、破裂、拉倒、出发、否决、通过、决定、取缔、丢失、遗失、准许、禁止”等，不受“在”的修饰。

7. 助动词如“能、会、敢、得(děi)、肯、应、要、应该、应当、必须”等，以及一些表示意愿的动词，如“愿意、需要、希望、赞成、拥护”等，不受“在”的修饰。

8. 动词带后缀“了”“过”，不受“在”的修饰。因为“了”表示动作处于完成的状态，“过”表示动作完毕或曾经发生、曾经经历过某事，因此不能与表示动作正在进行的“在”并用，如：

他看了/过那篇文章。

Tā kànle/guo nà piān wénzhāng.

*他在看了/过那篇文章。

Tā zài kànle/guo nà piān wénzhāng.

他查了/过资料。

Tā chále/guo zīliào.

*他在查了/过资料。

Tā zài chále/guo zīliào.

练 习 二

一、下列动词前哪些可以加“在”，哪些不能加“在”，请分别用“√”

"×"表示：

跑（　　）看（　　）吃（　　）有（　　）
pǎo kàn chī yǒu

洗（　　）问（　　）藏（　　）跳（　　）
xǐ wèn cáng tiào

死（　　）到（　　）能（　　）像（　　）
sǐ dào néng xiàng

知道（　　）喜欢（　　）停止（　　）具备（　　）
zhīdao xǐhuān tíngzhǐ jùbèi

包括（　　）应该（　　）决定（　　）觉得（　　）
bāokuò yīnggāi juédìng juédé

二、判断正误：

1. A. 门锁着。
Mén suǒzhe.
B. 门在锁着。
Mén zài suǒzhe.

2. A. 玛丽小姐买苹果。
MǎLì xiǎojiě mǎi píngguǒ.
B. 玛丽小姐在买苹果。
MǎLì xiǎojiě zài mǎi píngguǒ.

3. A. 我在需要你的帮助。
Wǒ zài xūyào nǐ de bāngzhù.
B. 我需要你的帮助。
Wǒ xūyào nǐ de bāngzhù.

4. A. 他睡觉。
Tā shuìjiào.
B. 他在睡觉。
Tā zài shuìjiào.

5. A. 我发现她特别爱说笑话。

Wǒ fāxiàn tā tèbié ài shuō xiàohuà.

B. 我在发现她特别爱说笑话。

Wǒ zài fāxiàn tā tèbié ài shuō xiàohuà.

6. A. 我在决定到中国去学习汉语。

Wǒ zài juédìng dào Zhōngguó qù xuéxí Hànyǔ.

B. 我决定到中国去学习汉语。

Wǒ juédìng dào Zhōngguó qù xuéxí Hànyǔ.

7. A. 黑板上写着字。

Hēibǎn shàng xiězhe zì.

B. 黑板上在写着字。

Hēibǎn shàng zài xiězhe zì.

8. A. 他开始研究《红楼梦》。

Tā kāishǐ yánjiū《Hónglóumèng》.

B. 他在开始研究《红楼梦》。

Tā zài kāishǐ yánjiū《Hónglóumèng》.

9. A. 你找什么呢?

Nǐ zhǎo shénme ne?

B. 你在找什么呢?

Nǐ zài zhǎo shénme ne?

10. A. 他成为美国有名的汉学家。

Tā chéngwéi Měiguó yǒumíng de hànxuéjiā.

B. 他在成为美国有名的汉学家。

Tā zài chéngwéi Měiguó yǒumíng de hànxuéjiā.

三、朗读下面的句子,看看哪个句子的"在"用得合适,哪个用得不合适,在句末括号内用"√""×"表示:

1. 我在希望能有机会到中国看看长城。( )

Wǒ zài xīwàng néng yǒu jīhuì dào Zhōngguó kànkan

chángchéng.

2. 张小姐在打电话，请稍等会儿。(　)

Zhāng xiǎojiě zài dǎ diànhuà，qǐng shāo děng huìr.

3. 世界上许多国家在探索国际政治经济新秩序问题。(　)

Shìjiè shàng xǔduō guójiā zài tànsuǒ guójì zhèngzhì jīngjì xīn zhìxù wèntí.

4. 时间很奇妙，分分秒秒都不停止，人生永远在失去的就是时间，婴儿也在失去他们的时间。(　)

Shíjiān hěn qímiào，fēnfēn-miǎomiǎo dōu bù tíngzhǐ，rénshēng yǒngyuǎn zài shīqù de jiùshì shíjiān，yīng'ér yě zài shīqù tāmen de shíjiān.

5. 我在她的门上敲了半天，她的门在锁着。(　)

Wǒ zài tā de mén shàng qiāole bàntiān，tā de mén zài suǒzhe.

6. 他以为对方在开玩笑，没有理睬。(　)

Tā yǐwéi duìfāng zài kāi wánxiào，méiyǒu lǐcǎi.

7. 他在感冒，不能去上课了。(　)

Tā zài gǎnmào，bù néng qù shàngkè le.

8. 他在同意我的旅行计划。(　)

Tā zài tóngyì wǒ de lǚxíng jìhuà.

9. 我连手表也不带，反正不管看不看，时间都一样在消逝。(　)

Wǒ lián shǒubiǎo yě bú dài，fǎnzheng bùguǎn kàn bu kàn，shíjiān dōu yíyàng zài xiāoshì.

10. 她一看见他的眼睛，顿时便觉得浑身的怒火在燃烧。(　)

Tā yí kànjian tā de yǎnjīng，dùnshí biàn juédé húnshēn de nùhuǒ zài ránshāo.

四、在下列各句中的适当的位置上加上时间副词"在"：

1. 我起初以为对方开玩笑，或是喝醉酒，可是他既没喝酒，也开不出玩笑来，因为他正担心那头16岁的印度象兰尼的健康。

Wǒ qǐchū yǐwéi duìfāng kāi wánxiào, huò shì hēzuì jiǔ, kěshì tā jì méi hē jiǔ, yě kāi bu chū wánxiào lai, yīnwèi tā zhèng dānxīn nà tóu shíliù suì de Yìndùxiàng Lánní de jiànkāng.

2. 桥牌活动室里十多位年轻人正聚精会神地打桥牌。

Qiáopái huódòngshì li shí duō wèi niánqīng rén zhèng jùjīng-huìshén de dǎ qiáopái.

3. 这些日子，这个愣小子学打算盘。

Zhèxiē rìzi, zhège lèng xiǎozi xué dǎ suànpan.

4. 一场热烈的讨论还进行着。

Yì cháng rèliè de tǎolùn hái jìnxíngzhe.

5. 她好象是洗澡，可是不管我怎么叫门，她都没有反应，而且门是反锁着。

Tā hǎoxiàng shì xǐzǎo, kěshì bùguǎn wǒ zěnme jiào mén, tā dōu méiyǒu fǎnyìng, érqiě mén shì fǎn suǒzhe.

（二）从动词短语的组成情况看

这部分所讨论的各式动词短语，其中动词的使用条件，仍受第一部分所谈的条件的限制。

1.“在”与并列式的动词或动词短语

“在”可以修饰并列式的动词或动词短语，如：

这时候，人力车，马车，汽车，都在奔走响动。

Zhè shíhòu, rénlìchē, mǎchē, qìchē, dōu zài bēnzǒu xiǎngdòng.

他看见一些中小学生背着书包在玩牌、打架。

Tā kànjiàn yìxiē zhōng xiǎo xuésheng bēizhe shūbāo zài wánr

pái, dǎjià.

2. “在”与偏正式的动词短语

A. “在”可以修饰偏正式的动词短语，如：

风在猛烈地刮着。

Fēng zài měngliè de guāzhe.

大家都在刻苦地钻研。

Dàjiā dōu zài kèkǔ de zuānyán.

B. 介名短语可以修饰动词短语，组成偏正式的动词短语。有一部分由介名短语充当修饰语的偏正式动词短语，可以受“在”的修饰，如：

他在向我招手致意。

Tā zài xiàng wǒ zhāoshǒu zhìyì.

队伍在向后方撤退。

Duìwǔ zài xiàng hòufāng chètuì.

他在朝天开枪。

Tā zài cháo tiān kāi qiāng.

一对恋人在沿着湖边散步。

Yí duì liànrén zài yánzhe hú biān sànbù.

他在对我翻白眼。

Tā zài duì wǒ fān báiyǎn.

他在冲我发火。

Tā zài chòng wǒ fāhuǒ.

阿里在跟我开玩笑。

Ālǐ zài gēn wǒ kāi wánxiào.

他在为大伙儿办事。

Tā zài wèi dàhuǒr bàn shì.

观众在为他的高超演技喝彩。

Guānzhòng zài wèi tā de gāochāo yǎnjì hècǎi.

他在给我们介绍情况。

Tā zài gěi wǒmen jièshào qíngkuàng.

强盗们在趁火打劫。

Qiángdàomen zài chènhuǒdǎjié.

上述例句中，是由介词"向、朝、沿着、对、冲、跟、为、给、趁"组成的介名短语修饰动词或动词短语，组成偏正式动词短语，受"在"的修饰。

C. 由介词"在、自、当、对于、比、由于、连"等组成的介名短语充当修饰语的偏正式动词短语不受"在"的修饰。如：

* 他在在宿舍写信。

Tā zài zài sùshè xiě xìn.

* 他在对于这个问题作了分析。

Tā zài duìyú zhège wèntí zuòle fēnxī.

D. "在"也不能修饰由"从"组成的介名短语充当修饰语的偏正式动词短语，如：

* 他在从我家门口经过。

Tā zài cóng wǒ jiā ménkǒu jīngguò.

* 兔子在从洞里爬出。

Tùzi zài cóng dòng li pá chū.

这时的"从"跟表处所词语组合，指处所、来源。

但是"在"可以修饰由"从…向…"构成的介名短语充当修饰语的偏正式动词短语，如：

卫星在从东向西移动。

Wèixīng zài cóng dōng xiàng xī yídòng.

我们在从胜利走向胜利。

Wǒmen zài cóng shènglì zǒuxiàng shènglì.

这时的"从"指发展、变化。

一般说来，单纯表示原因，表示处所、时间的起点，表示过去时间的起点，表示事件发生的时间、处所，表示涉及的事物，表示人、事物、行为之间的对待关系等一类的介词组成的介名短语，不受“在”的修饰。保留有动作意味的介词，如引进施动者，表示遵从某种标准，表示利用条件或机会，引进动作的对象或范围等一类的介词组成的介名短语，可受“在”的修饰。而且什么样的介名短语可以受“在”的修饰，这跟介名短语所修饰的动词的情况也有关系：不受“在”修饰的动词短语，它受介名短语修饰后同样不受“在”的修饰，试比较：

他在开玩笑。	* 他在没关系。
Tā zài kāi wánxiào.	Tā zài méi guānxi.
他跟我开玩笑。	他跟这事没关系。
Tā gēn wǒ kāi wánxào.	Tā gēn zhè shì méi guānxi.
他在跟我开玩笑。	* 他在跟这事没关系。
Tā zài gēn wǒ kāi wánxiào.	Tā zài gēn zhè shì méi guānxi.

上述例句中，动词短语“没关系”不受“在”的修饰，它受介名短语“跟这事”修饰后，组成偏正式的动词短语“跟这事没关系”，因为不说“在没关系”，所以也不说“在跟这事没关系”。

练 习 三

一、找出下列句子中正确的句子：

1. A. 我们在从香港走。
   Wǒmen zài cóng Xiānggǎng zǒu.
   B. 我们从香港走。
   Wǒmen cóng Xiānggǎng zǒu.
2. A. 他在给孩子们讲故事。
   Tā zài gěi háizimen jiǎng gùshi.
   B. 他给孩子们讲故事。

Tā gěi háizimen jiǎng gùshi.

3. A. 从我开始，一人说一句。

Cóng wǒ kāishǐ, yì rén shuō yí jù.

B. 在从我开始，一人说一句。

Zài cóng wǒ kāishǐ, yì rén shuō yí jù.

4. A. 这事刚好被你遇到了。

Zhè shì gānghǎo bèi nǐ yùdào le.

B. 这事刚好在被你遇到了。

Zhè shì gānghǎo zài bèi nǐ yùdào le.

5. A. 这个意见被大家否决了。

Zhège yìjiàn bèi dàjiā fǒujué le.

B. 这个意见在被大家否决了。

Zhège yìjiàn zài bèi dàjiā fǒujué le.

二、在适当的地方填上时间副词“在”：

1. 她常常梦见孩子胖乎乎的小脸向自己微笑。

Tā chángcháng mèngjiàn háizi pànghūhū de xiǎo liǎn xiàng zìjǐ wēixiào.

2. 我知道，我妈妈一直为我担心。

Wǒ zhīdao, wǒ māma yìzhí wèi wǒ dānxīn.

3. 他给小狗洗澡呢。

Tā gěi xiǎo gǒu xǐzǎo ne.

4. 大家都朝前看。

Dàjiā dōu cháo qián kàn.

5. 一个女大学生替她看家。

Yí gè nǚ dàxuéshēng tì tā kān jiā.

6. 他跟他的太太打电话。

Tā gēn tā de tàitai dǎ diànhuà.

7. 在五十年代，全世界的画家包括苏联画家在内，都奔跑、探索、创新。

Zài wǔshí niándài, quán shìjiè de huàjiā bāokuò Sūlián huàjiā zài nèi, dōu bēnpǎo, tànsuǒ, chuàngxīn.

8. 世界上许多国家都引进、试种我国的杂交水稻。

Shìjiè shàng xǔduō guójiā dōu yǐnjìn, shì zhòng wǒ guó de zájiāo shuǐdào.

9. 黄河呵,您的儿女向您倾诉心中的爱。

Huáng Hé a, nín de érnǚ xiàng nín qīngsù xīnzhōng de ài.

10. 大家都为这件事烦恼。

Dàjiā dōu wèi zhè jiàn shì fánnǎo.

3.“在”可以修饰述宾式动词短语,但有些限制:

A. 宾语只受实指的数量词(除“一”外)修饰时,不受“在”的修饰。请比较:

他在洗衣服。

Tā zài xǐ yīfu.

*他在洗三件衣服。

Tā zài xǐ sān jiàn yīfu.

他在画图。

Tā zài huà tú.

*他在画五幅图。

Tā zài huà wǔ fú tú.

B. 如果宾语另受描写性或限制性的定语修饰时,可以受“在”的修饰:

他在洗那三件(借来的)衣服。

Tā zài xǐ nà sān jiàn (jièlái de)yīfu.

他在画五幅方言地图。

Tā zài huà wǔ fú fāngyán dìtú.

他在为展览馆画两幅大型壁画。

Tā zài wèi zhǎnlǎnguǎn huà liǎng fú dàxíng bìhuà.

C. 如果是先总述后分述的句子，总述部分也可以不受限制地用“在”修饰：

他在编两本词典，一本是英汉的，一本是汉英的。

Tā zài biān liǎng běn cídiǎn, yì běn shì Yīng-Hàn de, yì běn shì Hàn-Yīng de.

D. 宾语受非实指的数量词修饰时，动词前可加“在”，“在”着重表示动作在进行中，而不表示动作所涉及的宾语的数量：

我在洗一件衣服。

Wǒ zài xǐ yí jiàn yīfu.

我在洗两件衣服。

Wǒ zài xǐ liǎng jiàn yīfu.

我在洗几件衣服。

Wǒ zài xǐ jǐ jiàn yīfu.

我在洗一些衣服。

Wǒ zài xǐ yìxiē yīfu.

“一”“两”可以是实指，如“今天的作业只有一/两道题”；也可以是虚指，如“你等我会儿，我跟他说一/两句话”。以上例句中的“一”“两”表示不定量而并非实指，数量词“一件、两件、几件”及“一些”等，一般轻读。“一”“两”的意义跟“几”“一些”“若干”相当，上述例句都可以用来回答“你在干什么？”的问题。

E. 带准宾语的述宾式短语，不受“在”的修饰：

＊在看一次

zài kàn yí cì

＊在踢一脚

zài tī yì jiǎo

* 在放一枪

zài fàng yì qiāng

* 在等一会儿

zài děng yíhuìr

* 在休息半个钟头

zài xiūxi bàn ge zhōngtóu

* 在住两年

zài zhù liǎng nián.

F. 带存现宾语的述宾式短语，不受“在”的修饰。因为存现宾语表示存在、出现或消失的事物，带存现宾语的动词加“着”表示动作所产生的状态，因此不受表示动作或行为在进行中的时间副词“在”的修饰，如：

* 台上在坐着很多人。

Tái shàng zài zuòzhe hěn duō rén

* 幕后在走出一个人。

Mù hòu zài zǒuchū yí ge rén

* 树上在飞走一只鸟。

Shù shàng zài fēizǒu yì zhī niǎo

练 习 四

一、判断正误：

1. A. 本子上写着名字。

Běnzi shàng xiězhe míngzi.

B. 本子上在写着名字。

Běnzi shàng zài xiězhe míngzi.

2. A. 他在做五道数学题。

Tā zài zuò wǔ dào shùxuétí.

B. 他在做今天刚布置的那五道数学题。

Tā zài zuò jīntiān gāng bùzhì de nà wǔ dào shùxuétí.

3. A. 她在看一本小说。

Tā zài kàn yì běn xiǎoshuō.

B. 她在看四本小人书。

Tā zài kàn sì běn xiǎorénshū.

4. A. 我休息三天。

Wǒ xiūxi sān tiān.

B. 我在休息三天。

Wǒ zài xiūxi sān tiān.

5. A. 我在买苹果。

Wǒ zài mǎi píngguǒ.

B. 我在买三斤苹果。

Wǒ zài mǎi sān jīn píngguǒ.

6. A. 他在打一小时球。

Tā zài dǎ yì xiǎoshí qiú.

B. 他在打球。

Tā zài dǎ qiú.

7. A. 墙上在挂着几幅名画。

Qiáng shàng zài guàzhe jǐ fú míng huà.

B. 墙上挂着几幅名画。

Qiáng shàng guàzhe jǐ fú míng huà.

8. A. 黑影里站着四五个人。

Hēi yǐng li zhànzhe sì-wǔ gè rén.

B. 黑影里在站着四五个人。

Hēi yǐng li zài zhànzhe sì-wǔ gè rén.

9. A. 他在买三束鲜花。

Tā zài mǎi sān shù xiānhuā.

B. 他在买一些鲜花。

Tā zài mǎi yìxiē xiānhuā.

10. A. 他砍一刀，我砍一刀。

Tā kǎn yì dāo, wǒ kǎn yì dāo.

B. 他在砍一刀，我在砍一刀。

Tā zài kǎn yì dāo, wǒ zài kǎn yì dāo.

二、看图说说他们现在都在干什么？

三、下列各句的述宾结构中，哪些能受"在"的修饰？

1. 哦，我觉得我象做梦。

Ò, wǒ juédé wǒ xiàng zuòmèng.

2. 你有水果刀吗？

Nǐ yǒu shuǐguǒdāo ma?

3. 你的儿子鼓动罢工，是吗？

Nǐ de érzi gǔdòng bàgōng, shì ma?

4. 你是笑话我么？

Nǐ shì xiàohua wǒ me?

5. 他等你呢，快去吧！

Tā děng nǐ ne, kuài qù ba!

6. 老二，你去一趟吧！

Lǎo Èr, nǐ qù yí tàng ba!

7. 她听见孩子哭。

Tā tīngjian háizi kū.

8. 谁敲门呀？

Shuí qiāo mén ya?

9. 我们休息五分钟吧。

Wǒmen xiūxi wǔ fēnzhōng ba.

10. 他夸奖他太太能干。

Tā kuājiǎng tā tàitai nénggàn.

四、找出下面句子里的时间副词"在"：

1. 点点灯光似浮动的航标，

Diǎndiǎn dēngguāng sì fúdòng de hángbiāo,

在湖里，在湖岸，难以辨出——

Zài hú li, zài hú àn, nányǐ biàn chū—

是牧场老妈妈在捻羊毛？

Shìmùchǎng lǎomāma zài niǎn yángmáo?

是林区小伙子在磨板斧？

Shì línqū xiǎohuǒzi zài mó bǎnfǔ?

2. 沙漠里在炼焦、炼铁，

Shāmò li zài liàn jiāo, liàn tiě,

黄河上在修桥、筑坝；

Huáng Hé shàng zài xiū qiáo, zhù bà;

一阵春雨进车窗，

Yí zhèn chūnyǔ jìn chē chuāng,

陇中又在修渠迎绿化。

Lǒngzhōng yòu zài xiū qú yíng lǜhuà.

3. 小黄鹂和小山雀在枝叶茂盛的果树林里飞来飞去，跟着妈妈捕捉害虫。秋天，果树上结满了果子。一阵风吹过，红通通的海棠，黄澄澄的梨，都轻轻地点着头，在感谢黄鹂和山雀呢。

Xiǎo huánglí hé xiǎo shānquè zài zhīyè màoshèng de guǒshù lín li fēi lái fēi qù, gēnzhe māma pǔzhuō hàichóng. Qiūtiān, guǒshù shàng jiēmǎn le guǒzi. Yí zhèn fēng chuīguo, hóngtōngtōng de hǎitáng, huángdēngdēng de lí, dōu qīngqīng de diǎnzhe tóu, zài gǎnxiè huánglí hé shānquè ne.

五、请把下面的句子翻译成英语：

1. 一进房间，他就发现王老师在等他。

Yí jìn fángjiān, tā jiù fāxiàn Wáng lǎoshī zài děng tā.

2. 你在讲什么？

Nǐ zài jiǎng shénme?

3. 画的右边，有一个老太太在读报。

Huà de yòubian, yǒu yí gè lǎo tàitai zài dú bào.

4. 昨晚七点到九点我们在打扫大礼堂。

Zuó wǎn qī diǎn dào jiǔ diǎn wǒmen zài dǎsǎo dà lǐtáng.

5. 她在唱中国民歌。

Tā zài chàng Zhōngguó mín'gē.

6. 你在等谁呢?我在等我妹妹。

Nǐ zài děng shuí ne? Wǒ zài děng wǒ mèimei.

7. 她在研究《汉语语法手册》。

Tā zài yánjiū《Hànyǔ Yǔfǎ Shǒucè》.

8. 昨晚我没出去,我在给我母亲写信。

Zuó wǎn wǒ méi chūqu, wǒ zài gěi wǒ mǔqin xiě xìn.

9. 她在穿衣服,请稍候。

Tā zài chuān yīfu, qǐng shāo hòu.

10. 你在干什么?——我在洗衣服。

Nǐ zài gàn shénme? —Wǒ zài xǐ yīfu.

4. "在"不能修饰述补式短语。因为"在"表示动作、行为的进行或持续,而补语的作用在于说明动作的结果或状态。

* 我在看见他。

Wǒ zài kànjian tā.

* 阿里在听懂我的话。

Ālǐ zài tīngdǒng wǒ de huà.

* 他在喝醉。

Tā zài hēzuì.

* 他在递过来一杯咖啡。

Tā zài dì guolai yì bēi kāfēi.

5. 由介词“在”组成的介名短语作状语或补语时，动词不受“在”的修饰，请比较：

列车在绿色的原野上奔驰。

Lièchē zài lǜsè de yuányě shàng bēnchí.

* 列车在绿色的原野上在奔驰。

Lièchē zài lǜsè de yuányě shàng zài bēnchí.

列车奔驰在绿色的原野上。

Lièchē bēnchí zài lǜsè de yuányě shàng.

* 列车在奔驰在绿色的原野上。

Lièchē zài bēnchí zài lǜsè de yuányě shàng.

练　习　五

一、判断正误：

1. A. 老师，我听懂了您的话。

Lǎoshī, wǒ tīng dǒngle nín de huà.

B. 老师，我在听懂您的话。

Lǎoshī, wǒ zài tīngdǒng nín de huà.

2. A. 他在拿出钥匙。

Tā zài náchu yàoshi.

B. 他拿出钥匙。

Tā náchu yàoshi.

3. A. 他在花园里在浇花。

Tā zài huāyuán li zài jiāo huā.

B. 他在花园里浇花。

Tā zài huāyuán li jiāohuā.

4. A. 小二黑伸出头来一看。

Xiǎo Èrhēi shēnchū tóu lai yí kàn.

B. 小二黑在伸出头来一看。

Xiǎo Èrhēi zài shēnchū tóu lai yí kàn.

5. A. 我们留学生在学会汉字了。

Wǒmen liúxuéshēng zài xué huì hànzì le.

B. 我们留学生学会汉字了。

Wǒmen liúxuéshēng xué huì hànzì le.

6. A. 水倒在杯子里。

Shuǐ dào zài bēizi li.

B. 水在倒在杯子里。

Shuǐ zài dào zài bēizi li.

7. A. 他在宿舍在打扑克。

Tā zài sùshè zài dǎ pūkè.

B. 他在宿舍打扑克。

Tā zài sùshè dǎ pūkè.

8. A. 他在记住一个生词。

Tā zài jìzhu yí gè shēngcí.

B. 他在记一个生词。

Tā zài jì yí gè shēngcí.

9. A. 来中国以后，我学到很多东西。

Lái Zhōngguó yǐhòu, wǒ xuédào hěn duō dōngxi.

B. 来中国以后，我在学到很多东西。

Lái Zhōngguó yǐhòu, wǒ zài xuédào hěn duō dōngxi.

10. A. 名字写在本子上。

Míngzi xiě zài běnzi shàng.

B. 名字在写在本子上。

Míngzi zài xiě zài běnzi shàng.

二、改正病句：

1. 我在吃得惯中国菜，而且越来越爱吃。

Wǒ zài chī de guàn Zhōngguócài, érqiě yuè lái yuè ài chī.

2. 小李在拿出来的书是跟我昨天买的一样。

Xiǎo Lǐ zài ná chulai de shū shì gēn wǒ zuótiān mǎi de yíyàng.

3. 他边看通知边点头，我知道他已经在看懂这个通知。

Tā biān kàn tōngzhī biān diǎntóu, wǒ zhīdao tā yǐjing zài kàndǒng zhège tōngzhī.

4. 唇膏在抹在嘴唇上。

Chúngāo zài mǒ zài zuǐchún shàng.

5. 这朵花正好在圣诞节在开。

Zhè duǒ huā zhènghǎo zài Shèngdànjié zài kāi.

6. 他在打通电话。

Tā zài dǎtōng diànhuà.

7. 我找他的时候他在床上在看报。

Wǒ zhǎo tā de shíhou tā zài chuáng shàng zài kàn bào.

8. 他在听到家乡地震的消息，急得不得了。

Tā zài tīngdào jiāxiāng dìzhèn de xiāoxi, jí de bù dé liǎo.

9. 他在黑板上在写字。

Tā zài hēibǎn shàng zài xiě zì.

10. 垃圾在倒在马路上是不文明的。

Lājī zài dào zài mǎlù shàng shì bù wénmíng de.

6. “在”与连动式短语

“在”能否修饰连动式的短语，情况比较复杂，在这里只作简单的介绍。

连动式短语是一种构造复杂的短语，施动者联系两个或两个以上的动词或动词短语，如果用“在”修饰，“在”一般用在连动式短语中的第一个动词或动词短语前。动词短语的限制条件见前，动词的限制条件，同于“动词本身的性质和意义”部分。连动式短语是多种多样的，有的能受“在”的修饰，有的则不能：

A. 几个动作先后发生的连动式短语，不受“在”的修饰，如：

他下地开门出去。

Tā xià dì kāi mén chūqu.

* 他在下地开门出去。

Tā zài xià dì kāi mén chūqu.

他推门进去。

Tā tuī mén jìnqu.

* 他在推门进去。

Tā zài tuī mén jìnqu.

B. 第二个动词、动词短语表示第一个动词、动词短语的目的或第一个动词、动词短语表示第二个动词、动词短语的方式、工具的连动式短语，可受“在”的修饰，如：

医生在想办法救活她。

Yīshēng zài xiǎng bànfǎ jiùhuó tā.

他在打电话请医生。(以上 $V(p)_2$是 Vp_1的目的)

Tā zài dǎ diànhuà qǐng yīshēng.

他在扯着嗓子喊。

Tā zài chězhe sǎngzi hǎn.

他在捂着嘴笑。

Tā zài wǔzhe zuǐ xiào.

他在掐着指头算。

Tā zài qiāzhe zhǐtou suàn.

你们简直在闭眼瞎来。(以上 Vp_1是 $V(p)_2$的方式)

Nǐmen jiǎnzhí zài bì yǎn xiā lái.

他在用毛笔一笔一笔地描。

Tā zài yòng máobǐ yì bǐ yì bǐ de miáo.

护士在用棉签洗擦伤口。(以上 Vp_1是 $V(p)_2$的工具)

Hùshi zài yòng miánqiān xǐ cā shāngkǒu.

C. 第一个动词或动词短语表示第二个动词或动词短语活动的状态的连动式短语,不受“在”的修饰,如:

他笑着说。

Tā xiàozhe shuō.

* 他在笑着说。

Tā zài xiàozhe shuō.

他红着脸说。

Tā hóngzhe liǎn shuō.

* 他在红着脸说。

Tā zài hóngzhe liǎn shuō.

D. 几个动作同时进行的连动式短语，不受“在”的修饰，如：

在这儿吃吧，咱们吃着谈。

Zài zhèr chī ba, zánmen chīzhe tán.

* 在这儿吃吧，咱们在吃着谈。

Zài zhèr chī ba, zánmen zài chīzhe tán.

他喝着酒看电视。

Tā hēzhe jiǔ kàn diànshì.

* 他在喝着酒看电视。

Tā zài hēzhe jiǔ kàn diànshì.

* 他在喝酒看电视。（这种句式成立，但已由连动句式变成联合式动词短语作谓语句）

Tā zài hē jiǔ kàn diànshì.

E. 动词加“了”“过”“起来”等的连动式短语，不受“在”的修饰，如：

我喝了两口烧酒壮壮胆子。

Wǒ hēle liǎng kǒu shāojiǔ zhuàngzhuang dǎnzi.

* 我在喝了两口烧酒壮壮胆子。

Wǒ zài hēle liǎng kǒu shāojiǔ zhuàngzhuang dǎnzi.

他立刻雇了三轮车去看简素华。

Tā lìkè gùle sānlúnchē qù kàn Jiǎn Sùhuá.

* 他立刻在雇了三轮车去看简素华。

Tā lìkè zài gùle sānlúnchē qù kàn Jiǎn Sùhuá.

他吃过午饭上学去了。

Tā chīguo wǔfàn shàngxué qù le.

* 他在吃过午饭上学去了。

Tā zài chīguo wǔfàn shàngxué qù le.

这孩子哭起来没完。

Zhè háizi kū qilai méi wán.

* 这孩子在哭起来没完。

Zhè háizì zài kū qilai méi wán.

F. 连动式短语中有一种类型是，动$_1$和动$_2$从肯定、否定两个方面说明一件事。动$_2$带否定副词“不”或“没(有)”，表示对前一个动作的持续或对前一个动作进行描写。这样的连动式短语，不受“在”的修饰，如：

阿毛拉着奶奶的衣角不放。

Āmáo lāzhe nǎinai de yī jiǎo bú fàng.

* 阿毛在拉着奶奶的衣角不放。

Āmáo zài lāzhe nǎinai de yī jiǎo bú fàng.

张素素却板起脸儿不笑。

Zhāng Sùsù què bǎnqi liǎnr bú xiào.

张素素却在板起脸儿不笑。

Zhāng Sùsù què zài bǎnqi liǎnr bú xiào.

G. 动$_1$和动$_2$是同一个动词的连动式短语，不受“在”的修饰，如：

他喝酒喝醉了。

Tā hē jiǔ hēzuì le.

* 他在喝酒喝醉了。

Tā zài hē jiǔ hēzuì le.

他抓工作抓得很紧。

Tā zhuā gōngzuò zhuā de hěn jǐn.

* 他在抓工作抓得很紧。

Tā zài zhuā gōngzuò zhuā de hěn jǐn.

这类短语通常动$_1$带宾语，动$_2$是动结式复合动词或带“得”加补语，从意义上看，动$_2$对动$_1$有补充说明作用，这和第4个问题有关，所以不受“在”的修饰。

7.“在”与兼语式短语。

凡是动词或动词短语符合上面谈过的使用条件的兼语式短语，都可以受“在”的修饰，如：

你是惹我生气么？

Nǐ shì rě wǒ shēngqì me?

你是在惹我生气么？

Nǐ shì zài rě wǒ shēngqì me?

他教我学汉语。

Tā jiāo wǒ xué Hànyǔ.

他在教我学汉语。

Tā zài jiāo wǒ xué Hànyǔ.

连省里的报纸都表扬你们创造了新记录。

Lián shěng li de bàozhǐ dōu biǎoyáng nǐmen chuàngzào le xīn jìlù.

连省里的报纸都在表扬你们创造了新记录。

Lián shěng li de bàozhǐ dōu zài biǎoyáng nǐmen chuàngzào lc xīn jìlù.

练 习 六

一、判断正误：

1. A. 他推车出门买东西。

Tā tuī chē chū mén mǎi dōngxi.

B. 他在推车出门买东西。

Tā zài tuī chē chū mén mǎi dōngxi.

2. A. 他在到飞机场接人。

Tā zài dào fēijīchǎng jiē rén.

B. 他到飞机场接人。

Tā dào fēijīchǎng jiē rén.

3. A. 她扔下孩子走了。

Tā rēngxia háizi zǒu le.

B. 她在扔下孩子走了。

Tā zài rēngxia háizi zǒu le.

4. A. 他坐飞机去纽约。

Tā zuò fēijī qù Niǔyuē (New York).

B. 他在坐飞机去纽约。

Tā zài zuò fēijī qù Niǔyuē(New York).

5. A. 他家养了一只猫捉老鼠。

Tā jiā yǎngle yì zhī māo zhuō lǎoshǔ.

B. 他家在养了一只猫捉老鼠。

Tā jiā zài yǎngle yì zhī māo zhuō lǎoshǔ.

6. A. 他放出鸡去寻食吃。

Tā fàngchu jī qu xún shí chī.

B. 他在放出鸡去寻食吃。

Tā zài fàngchu jī qu xún shí chī.

7. A. 他卖了家具回娘家了。

Tā màile jiājù huí niángjia le.

B. 她在卖了家具回娘家了。

Tā zài màile jiājù huí niángjia le.

8. A. 楼前盖了两排车棚存放自行车。

Lóu qián gàile liǎng pái chēpéng cúnfàng zìxíngchē.

B. 楼前在盖了两排车棚存放自行车。

Lóu qián zài gàile liǎng pái chēpéng cúnfàng zìxíngchē.

9. A. 她在笑起来那样的动人。

Tā zài xiào qilai nàyàng de dòngrén.

B. 她笑起来那样的动人。

Tā xiào qilai nàyàng de dòngrén.

10. A. 他叫我们规矩点儿。

Tā jiào wǒmen guīju diǎnr.

B. 他在叫我们规矩点儿。

Tā zài jiào wǒmen guīju diǎnr.

二、把下列的词语组成句子：

1. 在　他　脱险　他们　营救

zài　tā　tuōxiǎn　tāmen　yíngjiù

2. 他　组织　在　大家　表演　节目

tā　zǔzhī　zài　dàjiā　biǎoyǎn　jiémù

3. 在　迎接　院子　打扫　他　客人

zài　yíngjiē　yuànzi　dǎsǎo　tā　kèren

4. 在　他　母亲　劝　他　药　喝

zài　tā　mǔqin　quàn　tā　yào　hē

5. 他　出租汽车　在　电话　打　叫

tā　chūzūqìchē　zài　diànhuà　dǎ　jiào

三、改病句：

1. 她在哭着出去了。

   Tā zài kūzhe chūqu le.

2. 他在上课上累了。

   Tā zài shàngkè shànglèi le.

3. 参观访问在使我们有很大收获。

   Cānguān fǎngwèn zài shǐ wǒmen yǒu hěn dà shōuhuò.

4. 她在笑着告诉我们她男朋友来了。

   Tā zài xiàozhe gàosu wǒmen tā nán péngyou lái le.

5. 她在进城买飞机票。

   Tā zài jìn chéng mǎi fēijī piào.

四、根据所给的情节，用"在"修饰动词回答问题：

1. 珍妮：喂，喂，请转452分机。喂，您是王大夫吗？我的同屋苏珊心脏病发作了，请您来一下好吗？

   Zhēnní (Jane)：Wèi，wèi，qǐng zhuǎn 452 fēnjī. Wèi，nín shì Wáng dàifu ma？Wǒ de tóngwū Sū Shān xīnzàngbìng fāzuò le，qǐng nín lái yí xià hǎo ma？

   问：珍妮在干什么呢？

   Zhēnní zài gàn shénme ne？

   答：

2. 约翰：你复习功课呀？

Yuēhàn (John)：Nǐ fùxí gōngkè ya？

珍妮：是的，明天要期中考试了。

Zhēnní (Jane)：Shìde，míngtiān yào qīzhōng kǎoshì le.

问：珍妮在干什么？

Zhēnní zài gàn shénme？

答：

五、把下面的句子翻译成中文，注意使用时间副词"在"：

1. We have been looking for a good cook，and we have not found one yet.

2. I am learning to speak English.

3. He is calling for a taxi.

4. They are compiling a Chinese-English dictionary.

5. She was watching TV at 8 o'clock yesterday evening.

6. She was reading an English magazine when I came in.

7. My brother was repairing a radio yesterday evening.

8. Don't disturb him. He is learning his lessons.

9. Stop that. You are being ridiculous.

10. He is talking with Lao Wang.

11. Opening the drawer he took out a dictionary.

12. The news made her happy.

13. The doctor advised him to take a good rest.

14. He will not let her go to the dance.

六、下列的连动句中，哪些可以加“在”？哪些不能加“在”？请在句末括号内用“√”“×”表示：

1. 我（　）去问。（　）

   Wǒ qù wèn.

2. 他（　）拉着我的手说：“你唱得真好哇！”（　）

   Tā lāzhe wǒ de shǒu shuō: "Nǐ chàng de zhēn hǎo wa!"

3. 她（　）用梳子一遍一遍地梳着头。（　）

   Tā yòng shūzi yí biàn yí biàn de shūzhe tóu.

4. 他们（　）坐飞机去上海。（　）

   Tāmen zuò fēijī qù Shànghǎi.

5. 我（　）有理由不同意。（　）

   Wǒ yǒu lǐyóu bù tóngyì.

6. 他（　）回宿舍取作业。（　）

   Tā huí sùshè qǔ zuòyè.

7. 他（　）想办法说服她。（　）

   Tā xiǎng bànfǎ shuōfú tā.

8. 小王（　）拿起一支笔在本子上写起来。（　）

   Xiǎo Wáng náqi yì zhī bǐ zài běnzi shàng xiě qilai.

9. 她（　）等着见您。（　）

Tā děngzhe jiàn nín.

10. 他（　）轻轻地推门出去。（　）

Tā qīngqīng de tuī mén chūqù.

三、"在""正""正在"用法比较

时间副词"在"与"正""正在"用在动词前均可表示动作进行或状态持续，如：

同学们在写汉字。

Tóngxuémen zài xiě Hànzì.

同学们正写汉字呢。

Tóngxuémen zhèng xiě Hànzì ne.

同学们正在写汉字。

Tóngxuémen zhèngzài xiě Hànzì.

它们常能相互替换，但不是在任何情况下都能任意替换，它们之间用法还是有区别的：

1. "正"着重指动作的时间，强调动作在发生和进行时刻；"在"着重指动作在持续或进行中所处的状态，"正在"既指时间又指状态。如：

她正过马路，一辆摩托车飞驶过来。

Tā zhèng guò mǎlù, yí liàng mótuōchē fēi shǐ guòlai.

她坐在床上，愁眉苦脸地好象在想什么办法。

Tā zuò zài chuáng shàng, chóu méi kǔ liǎn de hǎoxiàng zài xiǎng shénme bànfǎ.

同学们正在准备考试。

Tóngxuémen zhèngzài zhǔnbèi kǎoshì.

2. 当“正”在动词前表示该动作的发生和进行的时刻与另一动作的发生和进行的时刻处于同一时点上，受副词“正”修饰的动作是极短暂的，动作几无进行过程或持续过程，这种情况“正”不能用“在”替换，如：

阿里正投篮，客队一队员打手犯规。

Ālǐ zhèng tóulán, kè duì yí duìyuán dǎ shǒu fànguī.

我正眨眼，突然灯灭了。

Wǒ zhèng zhǎyǎn, tūrán dēng miè le.

主人正出门，客人来了。

Zhǔrén zhèn chū mén, kèren lái le.

我正打哈欠，一只蚊子飞进口中。

Wǒ zhèng dǎ hāqian, yì zhī wénzi fēi jìn kǒu zhōng.

3. “正”也可修饰有一定持续过程的或一定延续时间的动作，这时的“正”虽可用“在”替换，但用“正”时，具体动作本身是一个时段，说话的人把它抽象成一个时点，用“在”表示某一动作持续状态。请比较：

他们在开会，我们稍等会儿。

Tāmen zài kāihuì, wǒmen shāo děng huìr.

他们正开会，我们稍等会儿。

Tāmen zhèng kāihuì, wǒmen shāo děng huìr.

他们在开会，我们没事儿。

Tāmen zài kāihuì, wǒmen méi shìr.

* 他们正开会，我们没事儿。

Tāmen zhèng kāihuì, wǒmen méi shìr.

以上四句中，第一、三两句表示动作在进行，状态在持续。第二句说话的人把时段抽象成时点。第四句不对，因为“正”不用来表时段。

4. “正”后不能用单一动词，“在”“正在”不限：

我们在讨论。

Wǒmen zài tǎolùn.

我们正在讨论。

Wǒmen zhèngzài tǎolùn.

* 我们正讨论。

Wǒmen zhèng tǎolùn.

我们正讨论，他走进来了。

Wǒmen zhèng tǎolùn, tā zǒu jìnlai le.

5. “在”后不能用介词“从”，“正”“正在”不限：

太阳正从东方升起。

Tàiyang zhèng cóng dōngfāng shēngqǐ.

太阳正在从东方升起。

Tàiyang zhèngzài cóng dōngfāng shēngqǐ.

* 太阳在从东方升起。

Tàiyang zài cóng dōngfang shēngqǐ.

6. “在”可受表反复进行或长期持续的副词、形容词如“常常、一直、还、经常”等修饰，“正”和“正在”不行：

我一直在等她。

Wǒ yìzhí zài děng tā.

* 我一直正等她。

Wǒ yìzhí zhèng děng tā.

* 我一直正在等她。

Wǒ yìzhí zhèngzài děng tā.

7. 由介词“在”组成介名短语作状语或补语时，动词只受“正”的修饰，不受“在”“正在”的修饰：

那时我在纽约住。

Nà shí wǒ zài Niǔyuē (New York) zhù.

那时我正在纽约住。

Nà shí wǒ zhèngzài Niǔyuē (New York) zhù.

*那时我正在在纽约住。

Nà shí wǒ zhèngzài zài Niǔyuē (New York) zhù.

*那时我在在纽约住/*在纽约在住

Nà shí wǒ zài zài Niǔyuē (New York) zhù/zài Niǔyuē zài zhù.

那时我住在纽约。

Nà shí wǒ zhù zài Niǔyuē (New York).

那时我正住在纽约。

Nà shí wǒ zhèng zhù zài Niǔyuē (New York).

*那时我正在住在纽约。

Nà shí wǒ zhèngzài zhù zài Niǔyuē (New York).

*那时我在住在纽约。

Nà shí wǒ zài zhù zài Niǔyuē (New York).

练习七

一、用"在""正""正在"填空：

1. 我(　　)想吃中国菜，他就给我端来了。

   Wǒ(　　)xiǎng chī Zhōngguó cài, tā jiù gěi wǒ duānlai le.

2. 物质的分子总(　　)不停地运动。

   Wùzhì de fēnzǐ zǒng (　　) bù tíng de yùndòng.

3. 我(　　)走到展览会门口，碰到了阿芳。

   Wǒ (　　) zǒu dào zhǎnlǎnhuì ménkǒu, pèngdào le Ā Fāng.

4. (　　)说着，新媳妇就端出一盘炒鸡蛋。

   (　　) shuōzhe, xīn xífu jiù duānchu yì pán chǎo jīdàn.

5. 都说好了，她怎么还不来呢？这简直是(　　)开玩笑。

   Dōu shuōhǎo le, tā zěnme hái bù lái ne? Zhè jiǎnzhí shì (　　)

kāi wánxiào.

6. 几天来，这家省级新闻单位，(　　)进行一项紧张而颇具诱感力的工作——评定职称.

Jǐ tiān lái, zhè jiā shěngjí xīnwén dānwèi, (　　)jìnxíng yí xiàng jǐnzhāng ér pō jù yòuhuòlì de gōngzuò — píngdìng zhíchēng.

7. 十五年来，我一直(　　)练笔，(　　)写作。

Shíwǔ nián lái, wǒ yì zhí(　　) liànbǐ, (　　)xiězuò.

8. 他(　　)设计一种新的服装式样。

Tā (　　) shèjì yì zhǒng xīn de fúzhuāng shìyang.

9. 病魔每时每刻都(　　)折磨着她，威胁着她的生命。

Bìngmó měi shí měi kè dōu (　　) zhémozhe tā, wēixiézhe tā de shēngmìng.

10. 我经常(　　)想，怎么才能更好地帮助留学生提高汉语水平呢？

Wǒ jīngcháng (　　) xiǎng, zěnme cái néng gèng hǎo de bāngzhù liúxuéshēng tígāo Hànyǔ shuǐpíng ne?

二、判断正误：

1. A. 汉语水平在提高。(　　)

Hànyǔ shuǐpíng zài tígāo.

B. 汉语水平正提高。(　　)

Hànyǔ shuǐpíng zhèng tígāo.

C. 汉语水平正在提高。(　　)

Hànyǔ shuǐpíng zhèngzài tígào.

2. A. 约翰又在练口语了。(　　)

Yuēhàn (John) yòu zài liàn kǒuyǔ le.

B. 约翰又正练口语了。(　　)

Yuēhàn (John) yòu zhèng liàn kǒuyǔ le.

C. 约翰又正在练口语了。( )

Yuēhàn (John) yòu zhèngzài liàn kǒuyǔ le.

3. A. 我去的时候,他正从楼上下来。( )

Wǒ qù de shíhou, tā zhèng cóng lóu shang xiàlai.

B. 我去的时候,他正在从楼上下来。( )

Wǒ qù de shíhou, tā zhèngzài cóng lóu shang xiàlai.

C. 我去的时候,他在从楼上下来。( )

Wǒ qù de shíhou, tā zài cóng lóu shang xiàlai.

4. A. 你又在忙什么呢?( )

Nǐ yòu zài máng shénme ne?

B. 你又正忙什么呢?( )

Nǐ yòu zhèng máng shénme ne?

C. 你又正在忙什么呢?( )

Nǐ yòu zhèngzài máng shénme ne?

5. A. 他一直正研究语法。( )

Tā yìzhí zhèng yánjiū yǔfǎ.

B. 他一直在研究语法。( )

Tā yìzhí zài yánjiū yǔfǎ.

C. 他一直正在研究语法。( )

Tā yìzhí zhèngzài yánjiū yǔfǎ.

6. A. 他们俩正在屋里说话呢。( )

Tāmen liǎ zhèngzài wū li shuōhuà ne.

B. 他们俩在屋里说话呢。( )

Tāmen liǎ zài wū li shuōhuà ne.

7. A. 他还在找你。( )

Tā hái zài zhǎo nǐ.

B. 他还正在找你。( )

Tā hái zhèngzài zhǎo nǐ.

8. A. 警察在注意他们。(　)
Jǐngchá zài zhùyì tāmen.
B. 警察正注意他们。(　)
Jǐngchá zhèng zhùyì tāmen.
C. 警察正在注意他们。(　)
Jǐngchá zhèngzài zhùyì tāmen.

9. A. 我经常正考虑这个问题。(　)
Wǒ jīngcháng zhèng kǎolǜ zhège wèntí.
B. 我经常在考虑这个问题。(　)
Wǒ jīngcháng zài kǎolǜ zhège wèntí.
C. 我经常正在考虑这个问题。(　)
Wǒ jīngcháng zhèngzài kǎolǜ zhège wèntí.

10. A. 他总在写信。(　)
Tā zǒng zài xiě xìng.
B. 他总正写信。(　)
Tā zǒng zhèng xiě xìn.
C. 他总正在写信。(　)
Tā zǒng zhèngzài xiě xìn.

三、改正病句中带点的词：

1. 三年来，我家的收入逐年正增加。
Sān nián lái, wǒ jiā de shōurù zhú nián zhèng zēngjiā.

2. 星期六晚上，他又正在跳舞了。
Xīngqīliù wǎnshang, tā yòu zhèngzài tiào wǔ le.

3. 你说九点来，我一直正在等你。
Nǐ shuō jiǔ diǎn lái, wǒ yìzhí zhèngzài děng nǐ.

4. 我们走进会场时，在轮到他演讲。

Wǒmen zǒu jìn huìchǎng shí, zài lún dào tā yǎnjiǎng.

5. 我在走着，突然有人喊我的名字。

Wǒ zài zǒuzhe, tūrán yǒu rén hǎn wǒ de míngzi.

6. 到中国以来，我的体重正增加。

Dào Zhōngguó yǐlái, wǒ de tǐzhòng zhèng zēngjiā.

7. 我去找他时他在出门。

Wǒ qù zhǎo tā shí tā zài chū mén.

8. 我经常正盼望着你来。

Wǒ jīngcháng zhèng pànwàngzhe nǐ lái.

9. 我们正在去长城，你也跟我们一块儿去吧。

Wǒmen zhèngzài qù Chángchéng, nǐ yě gēn wǒmen yíkuàir qù ba.

10. 去年这时候，我正在在北京语言学院学习。

Qùnián zhè shíhou, wǒ zhèngzài zài Běijīng Yǔyán Xuéyuàn xuéxí.

11. 他正在坐在办公室里看报。

Tā zhèngzài zuò zài bàngōngshì li kàn bào.

12. 他时常正在写信。

Tā shícháng zhèngzài xiě xìn.

四、请把下列句子译成中文：

1. While we were talking with our teacher, Dick came up.

2. We were picking cotton when it began to rain.

3. He is always writing letters.

4. When he came, I was reading an English newspaper.

5. Look, the children are swimming happily.

6. Shc was doing some shopping when I met her.

7. I was doing my lessons when John came.

8. He is showing the foreign guests round the city.

9. He was writing an article yesterday evening.

10. The students were cleaning the classroom when Professor Wang came in.

11. I was entering the workshop when I heard somebody call after me.

12. He is writing a letter.

四、“在”与“着”用法比较

(一)“在”与“着”表示的意义不同:“在”表示进行意义,表示动作在进行中和状态在持续中;“着”不用来表示进行意义,而是表示动作的进行态和状态的持续态。请比较:

他在穿大衣。(“在”表示穿大衣的动作正在进行。)

Tā zài chuān dàyī.

他穿着大衣。(“着”表示“穿”这个动作结果状态的继续,大衣在他身上。)

Tā chuānzhe dàyī.

(二)“在”与“着”用法不同:

“在”用在动词的前面,“着”用在动词的后面。“在”与“着”用法的不同,可以从以下一些方面具体加以分别。

1. 只表示动作进行的用“在”不用“着”:

看!火车在过山洞。

Kàn! Huǒchē zài guò shāndòng.

*看!火车过着山洞。

Kàn! Huǒchē guòzhe shāndòng.

2. 只表示动作的进行态和状态的持续态的用“着”不用“在”。如:

武松敲着桌子叫道。

Wǔ Sōng qiāozhe zhuōzi jiào dào.

*武松在敲桌子叫道。

Wǔ Sōng zài qiāo zhuōzi jiào dào.

3. 询问正在进行的情况,不论提问还是回答,只用“在”,不用“着”:

谁在闹?

Shuí zài nào?

兰兰在闹。

Lánlán zài nào.

*谁闹着?

Shuí nàozhe?

*兰兰闹着。

Lánlán nàozhe.

他在干什么?

Tā zài gàn shénme?

他在洗衣服。

Tā zài xǐ yīfu.

*他干着什么?

Tā gànzhe shénme?

*他洗着衣服。

Tā xǐzhe yīfu.

4. 状态动词不能加“在”可加“着”;存现句的动词都是表状态意义的,因此,存现句的动词不能加“在”,可以加“着”,请比较:

黑板上写着字。

Hēibǎn shang xiězhe zì.

*黑板上在写字。

Hēibǎn shang zài xiězì.

台上坐着主席团。

Tái shang zuòzhe zhǔxítuán.

*台上在坐主席团。

Tái shàng zài zuò zhǔxítuán.

桌子上摆着很多书。

Zhuōzi shàng bǎizhe hěn duō shū.

*桌子上在摆很多书。

Zhuōzi shang zài bǎi hěn duō shū.

5. 表示姿势的动词，表现某种相对静止的状态，可加“着”不可加“在”，加“着”后才可加“在”：

他躺着。

Tā tǎngzhe.

* 他在躺。

Tā zài tǎng.

他在躺着。

Tā zài tǎngzhe.

他坐着。

Tā zuòzhe.

* 他在坐。

Tā zài zuò.

他在坐着。

Tā zài zuòzhe.

6. 连动句中，动$_1$是描述动$_2$的状态的，动$_1$只能用“着”，不能用“在”：

张三张着嘴睡觉。

Zhāng Sān zhāngzhe zuǐ shuìjiào.

* 张三在张嘴睡觉。

Zhāng Sān zài zhāng zuǐ shuìjiào.

他微笑着说。

Tā wēixiàozhe shuō.

* 他在微笑说。

Tā zài wēixiào shuō.

7. 两种活动同时进行的连动式短语可用“着”不可用“在”：

他喝着啤酒看电视。

Tā hēzhe píjiǔ kàn diànshì.

＊他在喝啤酒看电视。

Tā zài hē píjiǔ kàn diànshì.

上面例句中的第二句话也可以说，但短语就改变为联合式短语了。

8. 动$_1$表示动$_2$的工具或动$_2$表示动$_1$的目的的连动句，用“在”不用“着”：

他在用纱布包扎伤口。

Tā zài yòng shābù bāozā shāngkǒu.

＊他用着纱布包扎伤口。

Tā yòngzhe shābù bāozā shāngkǒu.

医生在想办法救活她。

Yīshēng zài xiǎng bànfǎ jiù huó tā.

＊医生想着办法救活她。

Yīsheng xiǎngzhe bànfǎ jiùhuó tā.

9. “着”可用在命令句中，要求对方继续保持某种原有的情况，“在”则不行：

穿着雨衣！

Chānzhe yǔyī！

＊在穿雨衣！

Zài chuān yǔyī！

带着钱！

Dàizhe qián！

＊在带钱！

Zài dài qián！

10. “在”可表示反复进行或长期持续的活动，“着”不行：

罗杰瑞先生在研究汉语方言。

Luó Jiéruì xiānsheng zài yánjiū Hànyǔ fāngyán.

＊罗杰瑞先生研究着汉语方言。

Luó Jiéruì xiānsheng yánjiūzhe Hànyǔ fāngyán.

珍妮在写小说。

Zhēnní zài xiě xiǎoshuō.

*珍妮写着小说。

Zhēnní xiě zhe xiǎoshuō.

练　习　八

一、下列句子中哪些“在”“着”用得对？

1. A. 地上扔着许多果皮。

Dì shàng rēngzhe xǔduō guǒpí.

B. 地上在扔许多果皮。

Dì shàng zài rēng xǔduō guǒpí.

2. A. 床上在躺一个小孩儿。

Chuáng shàng zài tǎng yí gè xiǎoháir.

B. 床上躺着一个小孩儿。

Chuáng shàng tǎngzhe yí gè xiǎoháir.

3. A. 小张在干什么？小张在扫地。

Xiǎo Zhāng zài gàn shénme? Xiǎo Zhāng zài sǎo dì.

B. 小张干着什么？小张扫着地。

Xiǎo Zhāng gànzhe shénme? Xiǎo Zhāng sǎozhe dì.

4. A. 老师在握我的手说：“欢迎你再来中国！”

Lǎoshī zài wò wǒ de shǒu shuō:"Huānyíng nǐ zài lái Zhōngguó!"

B. 老师握着我的手说：“欢迎你再来中国！”

Lǎoshī wòzhe wǒ de shǒu shuō: "Huānyíng nǐ zài lái Zhōngguó!"

5. A. 你瞧，小兰兰在洗手绢。

Nǐ qiáo, Xiǎo Lánlan zài xǐ shǒujuàn.

B. 你瞧，小兰兰洗着手绢。

Nǐ qiáo, Xiǎo Lánlan xǐzhe shǒujuàn.

6. A. 他在拍小刘的肩膀说……

Tā zài pāi Xiǎo Liú de jiānbǎng shuō...

B. 他拍着小刘的肩膀说……

Tā pāizhe Xiǎo Liú de jiānbǎng shuō…

7. A. 拿着！别丢了。

Názhe! Bié diū le.

B. 在拿！别丢了。

Zài ná! Bié diū le.

8. A. 他在修理自行车。

Tā zài xiūlǐ zìxíngchē.

B. 他修理着自行车。

Tā xiūlǐzhe zìxíngchē.

9. A. 你看着，别让他跑了。

Nǐ kānzhe, bié ràng tā pǎo le.

B. 你在看，别让他跑了。

Nǐ zài kān, bié ràng tā pǎo le.

10. A. 她坐着讲课。

Tā zuòzhe jiǎngkè.

B. 她在坐讲课。

Tā zài zuò jiǎngkè.

二、把下列句子译成英文：

1. 下雪了吗？

Xià xuě le ma?

2. 张林到家时，他妹妹正在做作业。

Zhāng Lín dào jiā shí, tā mèimei zhèngzài zuò zuòyè.

3. 我进来时她在看一本中文杂志。

Wǒ jìnlai shí tā zài kàn yì běn zhōngwén zázhì.

4. 一个警察扶着老太太过了马路。

Yí gè jǐngchá fúzhe lǎotàitai guòle mǎlù.

5. 司机在擦车。

Sījī zài cā chē.

6. 桌子上面挂着一盏灯。

Zhuōzi shàngmian guàzhe yì zhǎn dēng.

7. 不要靠门站着。

Bú yào kào mén zhànzhe.

8. 商店还开着门吗？

Shāngdiàn hái kāizhe mén ma?

9. 我在读一本很有趣的书。

Wǒ zài dú yì běn hěn yǒuqù de shū.

10. 旗子上写着："我们要面包！"

Qízi shàng xiězhe: "Wǒmen yào miànbāo!"

11. 带着你的雨伞，以防下雨。

Dàizhe nǐ de yǔsǎn, yǐ fáng xià yǔ.

12. 他正在门里面站着。

Tā zhèngzài mén lǐmiàn zhànzhe.

三、请把下列句子译成中文：

1. Look! A train is passing over the bridge!

2. She was not conscoiously telling a lie.

3. She is doing her grammar exercises.

4. The nurse was giving him an injection.

5. Is she having her supper?

6. We are having a Chinese class.

7. She is reading today's newspaper.

8. The invalid is gathering strength.

9. Whom are you talking to?

10. Gas molecules are always moving.

陆、“呢”的用法

“呢”可以表示陈述语气，也可以表示疑问语气。“呢”用在陈述句尾，可以表示动作的进行或持续的状态，也可以表示说话人的确认、强调、褒贬等的态度；用在疑问句中，可使询问的语气变得委婉、缓和；“呢”也用来连续上下文，还可以表示停顿。

下面我们将结合“呢”的常用句式，分别论述“呢”的这些“表态”功能。

一、“呢”的用法

（一）“呢”用于陈述句句尾，表示动作的进行或持续状态。“呢”的这种用法，其语法意义比较接近英语的“-ing”。例如：

他上课呢。

Tā shàngkè ne.

He is having class.

玲玲睡觉呢。

Língling shuìjiào ne.

Lingling is sleeping.

看！火车过隧道呢。

Kàn! Huǒchē guò suìdào ne.

Look! The train is passing through a tunnel.

外头下雪呢。

Wàitou xià xuě ne.

It is snowing outside.

他们开会呢。

Tāmen kāihuì ne.

They are having a meeting.

1."呢"常跟"着"相配,动词之前常有"正""在""正在"等,如:

请等会儿,他吃着饭呢。

Qǐng děng huìr, tā chīzhe fàn ne.

他正看书呢,灯忽然灭了。

Tā zhèng kàn shū ne, dēng hūrán miè le.

他在哭呢,你劝劝他吧。

Tā zài kū ne, nǐ quànquan tā ba.

医生正在给他做手术呢。

Yīshēng zhèngzài gěi tā zuò shǒushù ne.

他老婆气得嚷起来了,他还在喝酒呢。

Tā lǎopo qì de rǎng qǐlai le, tā hái zài hē jiǔ ne.

2. 动+着+呢

A."动+着+呢",动词多是表动态的,去掉"着"字,句子的基本意思不变。请比较:

他吃着饭呢。

Tā chīzhe fàn ne.

他吃饭呢。

Tā chī fàn ne.

他正开着门呢。

Tā zhèng kāizhe mén ne.

他正开门呢。

Tā zhèng kāi mén ne.

别吵他,他正背着电话号码呢。

Bié chǎo tā, tā zhèng bèizhe diànhuà hàomǎ ne.

别吵他,他正背电话号码呢。

Bié chǎo tā, tā zhèng bèi diànhuà hàomǎ ne.

正说着呢，你就来了。

Zhèng shuōzhe ne, nǐ jiù lái le.

正说呢，你就来了。

Zhèng shuō ne, nǐ jiù lái le.

我们正商量着呢。

Wǒmen zhèng shāngliangzhe ne.

我们正商量呢。

Wǒmen zhèng shāngliang ne.

B. “动＋着＋呢”也可表示静止状态，这时的“着”字必不可少。例如：

雨伞在手上拿着呢。

Yǔsǎn zài shǒu shang názhe ne.

*雨伞在手上拿呢。

Yǔsǎn zài shǒu shang ná ne.

门开着呢。

Mén kāizhe ne.

*门开呢。

Mén kāi ne.

黑板上写着字呢。

Hēibǎn shang xiězhe zì ne.

*黑板上写字呢。

Hēibǎn shang xiě zì ne.

他在墙根儿蹲着呢。

Tā zài qiánggēnr dūnzhe ne.

*他在墙根儿蹲呢。

Tā zài qiánggēnr dūn ne.

他一看，门锁着呢。

Tā yí kàn, mén suǒzhe ne.

* 他一看,门锁呢。

Tā yí kàn, mén suǒ ne.

3. “还没……呢”“没……呢”,“呢”表示某处状况的继续,着重指出动作虽然还没有发生,但是可以预料将来是要发生的。例如:

天还没亮呢。

Tiān hái méi liàng ne.

他还没起床呢。

Tā hái méi qǐchuáng ne.

事情还没完呢。

Shìqing hái méi wán ne.

没走呢,还在那儿呢。

Méi zǒu ne, hái zài nàr ne.

所谓“将来”,往往只是一种意图,就是要做出某种动作,但是在说话的时候,还没来得及实现:

我还没洒水呢,他就扫起地来了。

Wǒ hái méi sǎ shuǐ ne, tā jiù sǎo qǐ dì lái le.

田大哥还没开口呢,田大嫂先说开了。

Tián dàgē hái méi kāikǒu ne, Tián dàsǎo xiān shuō kāi le.

才说要去找你呢,正好你来了。

Cái shuō yào qù zhǎo nǐ ne, zhènghǎo nǐ lái le.

练 习 一

一、指出下列句中的“呢”,哪些是表示动作的进行或状态的持续的:

1. 你怎么不去呢。

Nǐ zěnme bú qù ne.

2. 同学们都在上课呢。

Tóngxuémen dōu zài shàngkè ne.

3. 三个孩子都扒着门缝往外看呢。

Sān gè háizi dōu bāzhe mén fèngr wǎng wài kàn ne.

4. 你知道不知道他的家在哪儿呢？

Nǐ zhīdao bù zhīdao tā de jiā zài nǎr ne?

5. 他们开着会呢。

Tāmen kāizhe huì ne.

6. 你为什么不告诉他呢？

Nǐ wèi shénme bú gàosù tā ne?

7. 上午呢，我要上课；下午呢，我也没时间。

Shàngwǔ ne, wǒ yào shàngkè; xiàwǔ ne, wǒ yě méi shí jiān.

8. 他们正找你呢，快去吧！

Tāmen zhèng zhǎo nǐ ne, kuài qù ba!

9. 他要是不说呢？

Tā yàoshì bù shuō ne?

10. 其实呢，他自己也不想去。

Qíshí ne, tā zìjǐ yě bù xiǎng qù.

11. “等一会儿吧！”巡警也很客气。“里边拿人呢！”

"Děng yíhuìr ba!" Xúnjǐng yě hěn kèqì. "Lǐbian ná rén ne!"

12. 他听录音呢，找他有事吗？

Tā tīng lùyīn ne, zhǎo tā yǒu shì ma?

13. 谈那些干什么呢？

Tán nàxiē gàn shénme ne?

14. 李先生在门内坐着往外看呢。

Lǐ xiānsheng zài mén nèi zuòzhe wǎng wài kàn ne.

15. 这消息真不真呢?

Zhè xiāoxi zhēn bù zhēn ne?

二、下列各组句子中,哪个是对的?

1. A. 他在黑板上写字呢。

Tā zài hēibǎn shang xiě zì ne.

B. 黑板上写着字呢。

Hēibǎn shang xiězhe zì ne.

C. 黑板上写字呢。

Hēibǎn shang xiě zì ne.

2. A. 他蹲在外边儿呢。

Tā dūn zài wàibianr ne.

B. 他在外边儿蹲呢。

Tā zài wàibianr dūn ne.

C. 他在外边儿蹲着呢。

Tā zài wàibianr dūnzhe ne.

3. A. 门上贴着对联儿呢。

Mén shang tiēzhe duìliánr ne.

B. 对联儿在门上贴呢。

Duìliánr zài mén shang tiē ne.

C. 对联儿在门上贴着呢。

Duìliánr zài mén shang tiēzhe ne.

4. A. 请打开箱子。

Qǐng dǎkāi xiāngzi.

B. 箱子开着呢。

Xiāngzi kāizhe ne.

C. 箱子开呢。

Xiāngzi kāi ne.

5. A. 插着门儿呢。

Chāzhe ménr ne.

B. 插门儿呢。

Chā ménr ne.

C. 门儿插呢。

Ménr chā ne.

(二)"呢"表示说话人的态度和感情。

1. 表示确认,有强调、指示或夸张的语气,使对方信服或对进一步的信息感兴趣。常见的句式有:

A. "在……呢""有……呢",如:

她在后边呢,就回来。

Tā zài hòubian ne, jiù huílai.

他在家呢,请进吧!

Tā zàijiā ne, qǐng jìn ba!

有我呢,他不敢委曲你。

Yǒu wǒ ne, tā bù gǎn wěiqū nǐ.

他家有游泳池呢!

Tā jiā yǒu yóuyǒngchí ne!

他呀,银行里有上万元的存款呢!

Tā ya, yínháng li yǒu shàng wàn yuán de cúnkuǎn ne!

B. "还……呢"

这个问题我还不懂呢。

Zhège wèntí wǒ hái bù dǒng ne.

让着她点儿,她还是个小孩儿呢。

Ràngzhe tā diǎnr, tā háishì gè xiǎoháir ne.

现在我还不去呢。

Xiànzài wǒ hái bú qù ne.

快睡吧，明天还要起早呢。

Kuài shuì ba, míngtiān hái yào qǐ zǎo ne.

还早呢，怕什么！

Hái zǎo ne, pà shénme!

C. "才……呢"

晚场电影八点才开始呢。

Wǎnchǎng diànyǐng bā diǎn cái kāishǐ ne.

你才糊涂呢，明天上什么课都不知道。

Nǐ cái hútu ne, míngtiān shàng shénme kè dōu bù zhīdao.

你给我看了我才信呢！

Nǐ gěi wǒ kànle wǒ cái xìn ne!

上海才热闹呢！

Shànghǎi cái rènao ne!

西伯利亚才冷呢！

Xībólìyà cái lěng ne!

D. "可……呢"

北京的名胜古迹可多呢！

Běijīng de míngshèng gǔjì kě duō ne!

中国菜可香呢！

Zhōngguó cài kě xiāng ne!

哈尔滨的冰景可美呢！

Hā'ěrbīn de bīng jǐng kě měi ne!

侨乡的元宵节可热闹呢！

Qiáo xiāng de Yuánxiāo Jié kě rènao ne!

这种布可结实呢！

Zhè zhǒng bù kě jiēshi ne!

"呢"肯定事实之外，还可以表示赞扬、夸奖或是责备、讥笑的感情，如：

别看他不言不语的，会开飞机呢。

Bié kàn tā bù yán bù yǔ de, huì kāi fēijī ne.

约翰会烧中国菜呢。

Yuēhàn huì shāo Zhōngguó cài ne.

还说要帮我干活呢，连个人影儿都不见。

Hái shuō yào bāng wǒ gàn huó ne, lián gè rényǐngr dōu bú jiàn.

连这个都不懂，还是个大学生呢。

Lián zhège dōu bù dǒng, háishì gè dàxuéshēng ne.

“呢”作为表夸张语气词，它是往大的方面夸张，与它相对的“罢了”，是往小里夸张，试比较：

两元钱呢，这么一双筷子。

Liǎng yuán qián ne, zhème yì shuāng kuàizì.

（一双筷子就两元钱，太贵了。）

两元钱罢了，丢了就丢了。

Liǎng yuán qián bàle, diūle jiù diū le.

（只丢了两元钱，不算多。）

你别小看他，人家还会做诗呢。

Nǐ bié xiǎokàn tā, rénjia hái huì zuò shī ne.

（会做诗，不能小看）

他就会做两首诗罢了，别的会什么？

Tā jiù huì zuò liǎng shǒu shī bàle, bié de huì shénme?

（会写点诗不算什么）

三个人呢，煮这点儿饭怎么够吃呵？

Sān gè rén ne, zhǔ zhèdiǎnr fàn zěnme gòu chī a?

（人多饭太少）

三个人罢了，煮这么多饭怎么吃得了？

Sān gè rén bàle, zhǔ zhème duō fàn zěnme chīde liǎo?

（人少饭太多）

2. “呢”用在有疑问词或疑问式的句中，使询问的语气较为委婉、缓和：

A. 用于特指问句，句中含有“谁”“怎么”“什么”“为什么”“哪”等疑问词：

你说谁？

Nǐ shuō shuí?

你说谁呢？

Nǐ shuō shuí ne?

你为什么不去？

Nǐ wèi shénme bú qù?

你为什么不去呢？

Nǐ wèi shénme bú qù ne?

他怎么说？

Tā zěnme shuō?

他怎么说呢？

Tā zěnme shuō ne?

你干什么？

Nǐ gàn shénme?

你干什么呢？

Nǐ gàn shénme ne?

B. 用于选择问句的并列的各项目的后边，末一项可以不用：

你今天去还是明天去？

Nǐ jīntiān qù háishì míngtiān qù?

你今天去呢还是明天去(呢)？

Nǐ jīntiān qù ne háishì míngtiān qù(ne)?

你现在学英语还是学法语？

Nǐ xiànzài xué Yīngyǔ háishì xué Fǎyǔ?

你现在学英语呢还是学法语(呢)?

Nǐ xiànzài xué Yīngyǔ ne háishì xué Fǎyǔ(ne)?

你对这件事是赞成是反对还是漠不关心?

Nǐ duì zhè jiàn shì shì zànchéng shì fǎnduì háishì mò bù guānxīn?

你对这件事是赞成呢反对呢还是漠不关心(呢)?

Nǐ duì zhè jiànshì shì zànchéng ne fǎnduì ne háishì mò bù guānxīn (ne)?

C. 用于正反问句:

你去不去?

Nǐ qù bú qù?

你去不去呢?

Nǐ qù bú qù ne?

他肯不肯来?

Tā kěn bù kěn lái?

他肯不肯来呢?

Tā kěn bù kěn lái ne?

D. 用于反问句,句中常有"哪里""怎么""何必"与之呼应:

我怎么敢说?

Wǒ zěnme gǎn shuō?

我怎么敢说呢?

Wǒ zěnme gǎn shuō ne?

你何必生气?

Nǐ hébì shēngqì?

你何必生气呢?

Nǐ hébì shēngqì ne?

E. 是非问句不能用"呢",只能用"吗":

他身体好吗?

Tā shēntǐ hǎo ma?

* 他身体好呢?

Tā shēntǐ hǎo ne?

你懂了吗?

Nǐ dǒngle ma?

* 你懂了呢?

Nǐ dǒngle ne?

(三)“呢”用来连续上下文:

1. 询问与上文相关连的问题,常用在对话中,如:

他是美国人,你呢?(你是哪国人?)

Tā shì Měiguó rén, nǐ ne? (Nǐ shì nǎ guó rén?)

他会拉提琴,你呢?(你会不会呢?)

Tā huì lā tíqín, nǐ ne? (Nǐ huì bú huì ne?)

大家都来了,小王呢?(小王在哪儿?)

Dàjiā dōu lái le, Xiǎo Wáng ne? (Xiǎo Wáng zài nǎr?)

老张呢,他也来吗?(他怎么样呢?)

Lǎo Zhāng ne, tā yě lái ma? (Tā zěnmeyàng ne?)

2. 引起下文,常用在对话中:

你做什么呢?我做飞机模型呢。

Nǐ zuò shénme ne? Wǒ zuò fēijī móxíng ne.

他不肯呢?(即:要是他不肯,该怎么办呢?)

Tā bù kěn ne? (Jí: Yàoshi tā bù kěn, gāi zěnme bàn ne?)

后来呢?(即:后来怎么样呢?)

Hòulái ne? (Jí: Hòulái zěnmeyàng ne?)

3. 连续上下文:

你爸爸看书呢,别打搅他。

Nǐ bàba kàn shū ne, bié dǎjiǎo tā.

小点儿声,素素在这儿睡觉呢。

Xiǎo diǎnr shēng, Sùsù zài zhèr shuìjiào ne.

(四)"呢"表示停顿

1. 放在要突出的成分之后，引起对方注意，含有"要说""论到""至于"的意思，"呢"后可以是逗号，也可以无逗号，如：

大学会直接向教育部请示，我们呢只能听教育局的。

Dàxué huì zhíjiē xiàng jiàoyùbù qǐngshì, wǒmen ne zhǐ néng tīng jiàoyùjú de.

他自己呢也很会吹嘘，一提起身世，他便告诉人家他爸爸是驻外大使。

Tā zìjǐ ne yě hěn huì chuīxū, yì tí qǐ shēnshì, tā biàn gàosu rénjia tā bàba shì zhù wài dàshǐ.

我呢，没时间去，他呢，又死活不肯去，真不好办。

Wǒ ne, méi shíjiān qù, tā ne, yòu sǐhuó bù kěn qù ,zhēn bù hǎo bàn.

其实呢，他自己也很明白。

Qíshí ne, tā zìjǐ yě hěn míngbai.

2. 用在假设小句之后：

你要是不想去呢，就别去算了。

Nǐ yàoshi bù xiǎng qù ne, jiù bié qù suàn le.

你要是非说不可呢，就说两句。

Nǐ yàoshi fēi shuō bùkě ne, jiù shuō liǎng jù.

练 习 二

一、说说下列各句中的"呢"表示什么样的感情、态度：

1. 他会六种语言呢！

Tā huì liù zhǒng yǔyán ne!

2. 还是个大人呢，连小妞妞都不如。

Hái shì gè dàren ne, lián Xiǎo Niūniu dōu bùrú.

3. 看样子有七八十里地呢。

Kàn yàngzi yǒu qī-bāshí lǐ dì ne.

4. 他是个语言学博士呢！

Tā shì gè yǔyánxué bóshì ne!

5. 你吃不吃呢？

Nǐ chī bù chī ne?

6. 他会用汉语唱中国歌呢！

Tā huì yòng Hànyǔ chàng Zhōngguó gē ne!

7. 你为什么不去呢？

Nǐ wèi shénme bú qù ne?

8. 奥运会上他得过两枚金牌呢！

Àoyùnhuì shàng tā déguò liǎng méi jīnpái ne!

9. 王府井大街可热闹呢！

Wángfǔjǐng dàjiē kě rènao ne!

10. 你为什么不说呢？

Nǐ wèi shénme bù shuō ne?

二、给下列各句填上“呢”或“吗”：

1. 这样说对不对（　）？

Zhèyàng shuō duì bú duì (　)?

2. 明天走（　）？

Míngtiān zǒu（　）？

3. 这象话（　）？

Zhè xiànghuà (　)?

4. 就他知道，是（　）？

Jiù tā zhīdao, shì (　)?

5. 你问我是哪国人（　）？

Nǐ wèn wǒ shì nǎ guó rén (　)?

6. 我是去（　），还是不去（　）？

Wǒ shì qù (　), háishi bú qù (　)?

7. 你不知道她叫什么名字（　）？

Nǐ bù zhīdao tā jiào shénme míngzi (　)?

8. 他起床了（　）？

Tā qǐchuáng le（　）？

9. 他要是不说（　）？

Tā yàoshi bù shuō (　)?

10. 你到过中国（　）？

Nǐ dàoguo Zhōngguó (　)?

11. 她还到长江游过泳（　）！

Tā hái dào Cháng Jiāng yóu guò yǒng (　)!

12. 你见过美国总统（　）？

Nǐ jiànguo Měiguó zǒngtǒng (　)?

13. 签证什么时候才能下来（　）？

Qiānzhèng shénme shíhou cái néng xiàlái（　）？

14. 你认识她（　）？

Nǐ rènshi tā (　)?

15. 你有没有时间(　)?

Nǐ yǒu méi yǒu shíjiān (　)?

二、“呢”与“了”的对比

“呢”与“了”都可表示某种状态,但二者有区别:“呢”表示动作的持续状态;“了”表示变化,表示新情况的出现,即强调由一种状态转入另一种状态,强调某一新的动作或状态的出现。试比较:

下雨呢!(原来就下雨,现在还在下。)

Xià yǔ ne!

下雨了!(原来不下雨,现在下雨了。)

Xià yǔ le!

灯亮着呢。(灯一直亮着。)

Dēng liàngzhe ne.

灯亮了。(灯原来不亮,现在亮了。)

Dēng liàng le.

有“呢”的句子常与表示状态持续的助词“着”共存,而表示变化的“了”,由于不能和持续性的概念相容,因而也不能与“着”共存:

门开着呢。

Mén kāizhe ne.

*门开着了。

Mén kāizhe le.

正想着呢。

Zhèng xiǎngzhe ne.

*正想着了。

Zhèng xiǎngzhe le.

三、“呢”与“的”的对比

“呢”与“的”都可以表示确认、肯定的语气，但它们是有区别的：“的”是说事实确凿、毫无疑问，“呢”是说事实显然，一望而知；“的”偏于申说己见，表示一定如此，“呢”偏于叫别人信服自己的估计。如：

我也要去的，待会儿见。（我要去是毫无疑问的。）
Wǒ yě yào qù de, dāi huìr jiàn.

我也要去呢，你等我一会儿。（我马上就要去。）
Wǒ yě yào qù ne, nǐ děng wǒ yíhuìr.

这套家具一千元买不来的。（我买过，我知道。）
Zhè tào jiāju yìqiān yuán mǎi bù lái de.

这套家具一千元买不来呢！（不信你试试看。）
Zhè tào jiāju yìqiān yuán mǎi bù lái ne!

练 习 三

一、指出下列各组句子中带点的字的语义差别：

1. A. 我学汉语了。
Wǒ xué Hànyǔ le.

B. 我学汉语呢。
Wǒ xué Hànyǔ ne.

2. A. 池子里养鱼呢。
Chízi li yǎng yú ne.

B. 池子里养鱼了。
Chízi li yǎng yú le.

3. A. 他吃饭了。

Tā chīfàn le.

B. 他吃饭呢。

Tā chīfàn ne.

4. A. 这些粮食够吃一年的。

Zhèxiē liángshi gòu chī yì nián de.

B. 这些粮食够吃一年呢。

Zhèxiē liángshi gòu chī yì nián ne.

C. 这些粮食够吃一年了。

Zhèxiē liángshi gòu chī yì nián le.

D:这些粮食够吃一年罢了。

Zhèxiē liángshi gòu chī yìnián bàle.

5. A. 这个地方不缺海鲜的。

Zhège dìfang bù quē hǎixiān de.

B. 这个地方不缺海鲜呢。

Zhège dìfang bù quē hǎixiān ne.

C. 这个地方不缺海鲜了。

Zhège dìfang bù quē hǎixiān le.

6. A. 下雪呢。
Xià xuě ne.

B. 下雪了。
Xià xuě le.

7. A. 二三里地呢。
Èr-sān lǐ dì ne.

B. 二三里地罢了。
Èr-sān lǐ dì bàle.

8. A. 车开了。
Chē kāi le.

B. 车开着呢。
Chē kāizhe ne.

9. A. 这么好的房子，此地很难找到呢。
Zhème hǎo de fángzi, cǐ dì hěn nán zhǎodào ne.

B. 这么好的房子，此地很难找到的。
Zhème hǎo de fángzi, cǐ dì hěn nán zhǎodào de.

10. A. 他会走钢丝的。
Tā huì zǒu gāngsī de.

B. 他会走钢丝呢！

Tā huì zǒu gāngsī ne!

二、请把下列句子翻译成英文：

1. 他吃过早饭了。

2. 他吃早饭呢。

3. 要下雪了。

4. 外边下着雪呢！

5. 他想听听广播。

6. 他听广播呢。

7. 他听过广播了。

8. 他吃辣椒的。

9. 他吃辣椒了。

10. 他吃辣椒呢。

练习参考答案

“了”的练习答案

练　习　一

(一)1. 肉从前不便宜,现在便宜了。
2. 我母亲从前不老,现在老了。
3. 从前功课多,现在不多。
4. 孩子从前不高,现在高了。
5. 学生从前用功,现在不用功。

(二)1. 小王现在不是教员,从前是。
2. 高小姐现在是老何的爱人,从前不是。
3. 他现在不是我的男朋友,从前是。
4. 孩子现在不象爸爸,从前象。
5. 他现在是美国人,从前不是。

(三)1. 他现在爱中国,可是从前不爱。
2. 现在我想(念)我父母,可是从前不想。
3. 我本来想吃饭,现在不想吃了。
4. 小李现在讨厌他的女朋友了,可是从前喜欢她。
5. 从前他恨他的父亲,现在不恨了。

(四)1. 刚才妈妈不累,现在累了。
2. 本来他没病,现在病了。
3. 从前那个老人耳朵聋,现在不聋了。
4. 刚才孩子们困,现在不困了。

5. 刚才他没醉，现在醉了。

(五)1. 我们从前能够买汽车，现在不能了。

2. 我本来不会做这个练习，现在可以做了。

3. 他从前敢说英文，现在不敢说。

4. 你本来不必预备功课，现在应该预备了。

5. 从前我们不会看中国报，现在会看了。

(六)1. 从前我们都吃不饱，现在吃得饱了。

2. 从前我看得见黑板上的字，现在看不见了。

3. 学生从前听不懂老师说的话，现在听得懂了。

4. 我们从前买不起那个车，现在买得起了。

5. 你说的话，我以前听得清楚，现在听不清楚了。

(七)1. 刚才不是七点半，现在是七点半。

2. 昨天不是星期三，今天是星期三。

3. 我去年不是十六岁，今年十六岁。

4. 我母亲去年不是八十岁，今年八十岁。

5. 孩子从前不到十磅，现在到十磅了。

练 习 二

一、1. 小李最聪明了。

2. 这个问题太难解决了。

3. 房子太小了。

4. 东西太贵了。

5. 小王认为他的女朋友最漂亮了。

6. 中国人口太多了。

7. 今天最冷了。

二、1. His speech is very interesting.

2. That man is very bad.

3. This method is excellent.

4. This man, Xiao Li, is a very good person.

5. It's extremely cold today.

练 习 三

一、1. 没有。

2. 没有。

3. (1)不可以。

(2)还有一刻钟。

4. (1)没有。

(2)不能。

二、1. 就要

2. 再、三天、就

3. 快要

4. 十点钟、就要

5. 马上、就要

6. 一会儿、就

7. 夏天、就要

8. 明天、就

9. 明天、就、星期六

10. 快

三、1. Who will be here soon?

2. Are they going to get married soon?

3. I've nearly learned this character.

4. They'll be here soon.

5. The patient is dying.

四、1. 我们快要吃饭了。

2. 快要十点了。

3. 他就要走了。

4. 我的朋友很快就要从中国来了。

5. 我就要去中国了。

练 习 四

一、1. 等了　　半天

2. 来了　　多少时候

3. 来了　　一年半

4. 住了　　多久

5. 看了　　几个钟头

二、1. 有两个"了"字。

2. "十年"。

3. 在名词"书"的前面。

4. 李教授是十年前开始教书的。

5. 还在教书。

6. 不知道。

三、1. How many hours have we been on the plane?

2. We've been walking for five hours and yet we haven't arrived.

3. How long have you been waiting here?

4. Nearly two and a half hours.

5. How long have you been living in China?

四、1. 他已经学了四个钟头了，他不想再学了。

2. 我已经教了二十多年书了。

3. 我们已经在这儿住了六年多了。

4. 他们已经开了四天车了。

5. 我们已经在这个旅馆住了四个月了。

练 习 五

一、1. 看了　　两次

2. 上了　　两节

3. 吃了　　两块

4. 给了　　五百块

5. 喝了　　两瓶

二、1. I've already spent 200 yuan. I'm not going to spend any more.

2. He was married three times.

3. Though the teacher has explained several times, still he doesn't understand.

4. How many houses have you bought?

5. How many years have you been teaching Chinese?

三、1. 那个孩子已经唱了三首歌了,他还想再唱一首。

2. 田先生已经买了一辆小车了,他还想再买一辆。

3. 今天我已经看了三本书了,不想再看了。

4. 我们已经走了十英里路了,还要走多远?

5. 你已经请了十个朋友了,还要再请几个?

练 习 六

一、1. 只有一个。

2. 在动词的后面。

3. 时量词。

4. 现在不住在纽约。

5. 不能。

二、1. How many hours did you work last week?

2. How long did you stay in New York last year?

3. How many years did you study Chinese?

4. How many years did you teach when you were in China?

5. How many years did you learn Chinese painting all together?

三、1. 上星期我工作了二十小时。

2. 去年我在纽约住了九个月。

3. 我学了六年中文。

4. 我在中国的时候教了两年书。

5. 我学了两年多中国画。

练　习　七

一、1. 参观了　一个

2. 买了　一辆

3. 来了　几位

4. 看了　一个

5. 买了　几件

二、1. Professor Li wrote two history books.

2. Everyone bought a dictionary.

3. He killed a woman.

4. He stayed in Europe for a month last year.

5. He had a short rest just now.

三、1. 昨天晚上我喝了两碗汤。

2. 昨天早晨下了一点儿雨。

3. 去年，他父母在波士顿买了一座房子。

4. 昨天我写了二百个字。

5. 上个月，我看了两部电影。

练　习　八

一、1. 两天　回　了
　　2. 三天　来　上　了
　　3. 两次　来　考试　了
　　4. 三年　做　了
　　5. 一个月　下　了

二、1. 他两天没吃饭了。
　　2. 我们昨天一天没看书了。
　　我们明天一天不看书。
　　3. 我去年一年没喝酒了。
　　4. 他每星期(有)一天不做事。
　　5. 我三个钟头没看电视了。

三、1. We haven't seen each other for nearly five years.
　　2. I haven't had Chinese food for quite a few days.
　　3. The child hasn't taken a bath for three days.
　　4. He and his wife haven't spoken to each other for two days.
　　5. It hasn't rained for more than a month.

四、1. 上个月他有一个星期没来上课。
　　2. 他有一个星期没去上课了。
　　3. 他有十多年没回家了。
　　4. 在中国的时候,他没有给父母写过信。
　　5. 从我最后一次见到他,到现在已经五年了。

练　习　九

一、1. I've already bought the newspaper, you don't have to buy it.
　　2. I met Lao Zhang in the street yesterday.

3. Have you had your breakfast (lunch, supper)? Yes, I have.

4. Have you come to be fond of Chinese food?

Yes, I have.

5. Have you discussed this question?

Yes, we have.

6. a. The students have prepared for the lesson.

b. All the students prepared for the lesson.

7. a. Now he started to have beef.

b. He ate beef.

8. a. I wrote a letter.

b. I have written the letter.

9. I have written the letter.

10. The students have got off (the bus).

二、1. 你吃饭了吗？

2. 张先生去百货商店了。

3. 今天我坐公共汽车了。

4. 昨天他买了一支钢笔。

5. 李太太卖掉了她的旧汽车。

6. 所有的学生都做了作业(了)。

7. 我给他钱了。

8. 你唱(那支歌)了吧？

9. 你买了他喜欢的那只手表了吗？

10. 我已经买了那只手表了。

练 习 十

一、(1)住

I have learnt these new words by heart.

(2)<u>完</u>

I've finished that homework.

(3)<u>光</u>

He has sold all these things.

(4)<u>干净</u>

The room has been tidied up.

(5)<u>好</u>

The bus has been repaired.

二、(1)他打开了门。

(2)两天前票就售完了。

(3)这个字你读错了。

(4)昨天我看见他了。

(5)我干完了这项工作。

练习十一

一、(1) He was persuaded by others.

(2) His daughter was taken away by someone.

(3) A dog was killed by a car.

(4) The car was stolen.

(5) This (matter) was discovered by him.

二、(1)我们的谈话被他们听见了。

(2)他经常挨父母打。

(3)我的手表被偷了。

(4)我被妈妈训了一顿。

(5)哪只狗被农夫杀死了。

练习十二

一、1. The children ate all the sweets.
2. My parents gave the car to me.
3. I gave him all the money.
4. The student put the book on the table.
5. I've finished my homework.

二、1. 她把起居室收拾干净了。
2. 我把他的名字忘了。
3. 我把那个字写错了。
4. 他把茶杯打破了。
5. 我把苹果都吃了。

三、1. 那本书被人偷走了。
2. 孩子被妈妈打了。
3. 他把糖吃了。
4. 我把那张地图借来了。
5. 衣服洗了。
6. 他的父亲被人杀了。
7. 这几个字我忘记了。
8. 信已经写了。
9. 他把椅子搬进来了。
10. 菜都被孩子吃光了。

十二 复 习 题

一、1. I know Chinese.
2. Now I have learnt Chinese.
3. They don't have money.
4. They haven't got any more money now.

5. My father doesn't want to do business.

6. My father doesn't want to do business any more.

7. He is American.

8. He has become an American now.

9. All the students understand English.

10. The students understand English now.

二、1. 我会说汉语了。

2. 他不再喜欢他的妻子了。

3. 孩子们都长大了。

4. 我不能再学习了。

5. 现在我知道他的名字了。

6. 我饿了。

7. 几点了？

8. 这表坏了。

9. 已经不早了。

10. 他现在比我高多了。

三、1. ×　　2. 了

3. 了　　4. ×

5. 了　　6. 了

7. 了　　8. 了

9. 了　　10. 了

四、1. Don't forget to bring the book!

2. The children have all grown up. Their parents are getting old.

3. There's something wrong with my car, and it can't be repaired anymore.

4. As soon as we learnt to speak, we started learning to write characters.

5. The students are very clever. They are quick at learning (it).

6. It's rather cold outside. Don't go out.
7. We have been learning Chinese for three months.
8. He drank three bottles of beer yesterday.
9. All the money was stolen.
10. My brother ate all of the sweets.
11. As soon as I ate the food, I know it has gone bad.
12. How pretty Miss Zhang is!
13. I've spent all my money.
14. The train is about to pull out.
15. He has been very busy these days. Please don't go to see him.
16. He has drunk two bottles of wine. He can't drink any more.
17. I phoned him five times, but didn't get through.
18. If it rains tomorrow, I am not going.
19. If I had enough money, I would have gone to Europe for a trip.
20. As soon as he came, I left.

五、1. 我不想再去了。
2. 上星期他去中国了。
3. 我妹妹比以前高多了。
4. 几点了?四点一刻了。
5. 这本书太贵了,别买了。
6. 我哥哥(弟弟)很快就要大学毕业了。
7. 一下课,我就回家了。
8. 这星期,他看了三部电影了。
9. 他去哪儿了?
10. 他上学了。
11. 你告诉你父亲了吗?
12. 我买了这本书就回家。

13. 我看完电影就回家了。
14. 上星期你学习了吗?没有。
15. 我不想再喝(葡萄)酒了。
16. 我在中国的时候,学了一点儿中文。
17. 我会开车了。
18. 他会英文了。
19. 他好点儿了。
20. 我每天教三个小时的课。

"着"的练习答案

练 习 一

一、1. 人物

这位姑娘很年轻。头上戴着一顶时髦的白帽子,耳朵上戴着闪闪发光的耳环,还戴着一副太阳镜。她身上穿着一件花衬衫,下边穿着一条黑裙子。肩上挎着一个黑色的小皮包,手里拿着一架照像机。

2. 风景

林子左边有一座小山,山坡上种着果树。山下有一条小河,河上架着一座小石桥。桥头竖着一块石碑,上面刻着三个字:赵州桥。河边盖着一排新楼,楼四周种着许多花草。河上隐约地可看见几艘小船。

3. 房间

我的房间不太大,里边东西很多。窗前放着一张桌子,桌子上摆着我的小录音机。桌子前边摆着一把椅子。左边靠墙放着一张床,床上铺着花床单。右边靠墙摆着一个大衣柜,大衣柜上有一面大镜子。大衣柜旁边是一个小书架,上边摆满了书。书架顶上放着一个花瓶，里边插着一束花。窗户大开着，门关着。

二、1. 桌子上放着一本书。
他把书放在桌子上。
2. 小明戴着一顶新帽子。
小明把帽子戴在头上。
3. 姐姐手里拿着一束鲜花。
姐姐把一束鲜花插在花瓶里。
4. 学生们在练习本上写字。
练习本上写着很多字。
5. 门口种着很多树。
人们正在门口种树。
6. 墙上挂着一幅油画。
他把油画挂在墙上。
7. 老师站在教室的前边。
教室里坐着许多学生。
8. 爸爸穿着黑色的大衣。
爸爸在穿大衣。

三、1. B
2. B
3. 乙 A
4. 乙 B
5. B、C
6. C、B
7. 乙 B
8. 乙 B、C

练　习　二

一、1. B

2. B

3. A

4. A

5. A

6. A

7. A

8. A

二、1. 桌子上放着一本书。

2. 桌子上摆着一个收音机。

3. 头上戴着一顶帽子。

4. 柜子里挂着一些衣服。

5. 本子上写着一些字。

6. 墙上挂着一个钟。

7. 书的封面印着画儿。

8. 花瓶里插着一束花。

练 习 三

一、1. 小明不停地笑着。

2. 他呆呆地看着书上的字。

3. 外面正在下着雨。

4. 人们纷纷议论着。

5. 孩子们高兴地跳着。

6. 他们俩用力地握着手。

二、判断正误：

1. B

2. A

3. B

4. B

练　习　四

一、1. 张三哭着说:“我再也不敢了。”

2. 他红着脸,不说话。

3. 小明背着书包上学。

4. 李四开着灯睡觉。

5. 妹妹闹着要去看电影。

6. 小刚正忙着给母亲写信。

7. “到了。”陈明说着下了自行车。

8. 弟弟拍着手喊着:“真好!”

二、1. B　　2. A

3. B　　4. B

5. A　　6. B

练　习　五

一、1. You all wait here, (and) don't go anywhere.

2. Lie (stay) in bed, (and) don't get up.

3. Take your overcoat with you, (for) it's getting cold.

4. Be quick, (or) we'll be late.

5. Be careful, (and) mind not to hurt your head.

6. Xiao Fang was keeping on at her father to take her to a park.

7. As I was in a hurry to catch the plane, I didn't even sleep well.

8. The children are busy preparing for the examination.

二、1. B

2. B

3. A

4. B

5. B

6. B

7. A

8. B

“过”的练习答案

练 习 一

一、1. 我看过那个电影。
　　或 那个电影我看过。
　2. 我吃过芒果。
　　或 芒果我吃过。
　3. 我喝过茅台。
　　或 茅台我喝过。
　4. 我爱过这个姑娘。
　　或 这个姑娘我爱过。
　5. 这个地方热过。
　6. 我想念过妈妈。

二、1. 了　　2. 过
　3. 过　　4. 过

练 习 二

一、1. 了　　2. 过

3. 过　　　4. 过
5. 过　　　6. 过、过
7. 过、过、过

练　习　三

1. 没学过中文
2. 看过他的作品
3. 没去过长城
4. 没穿过这种衣服
5. 打过球
6. 见过

练　习　四

一、1. 过　过　　　2. 了　了
3. 过　　　4. 过
5. 了　　　6. 过
二、1. B　　　2. A
3. B　　　4. B
5. B　　　6. B
7. A　　　8. A、C

练　习　五

一、1. 以前　　从前
2. 昨天
3. 刚才、昨天(确定时间)

4. 从前、过去

5. 过去、从前

6. 明天、下个月(确定时间)

7. 上午、刚才(确定时间)

8. 以前、去年

练　习　六

一、1. A　　2. A、B

3. A　　4. B

5. B、C　　6. B

二、1. 他上午买了火车票,下午就走了。

2. 这个人没找过你,你不必多心。

3. 他从北京大学毕业以后,就去语言学院工作了。

4. 长城我一次也没去过。

"是……的"的练习答案

练　习　一

一、1. 指出动作在过去发生的时间

2. 指出动作在过去发生的时间

3. 指出动作在过去发生的处所

4. 指出动作在过去发生的时间

5. 指出动作在过去发生的方式

二、1. a. 陈述某一事实

b. 指出动作在过去发生的时间

2. a. 动作已完成

b. 指出动作在过去发生的时间

3. a. 陈述某一事实

b. 指出动作在过去发生的方式

4. a. 陈述某一事实

b. 指出动作在过去发生的方式

5. a. 询问某事

b. 询问动作在过去发生的处所

练 习 二

一、1. 重音在“八点钟” 指出动作在过去发生的时间

2. 重音在“礼堂” 指出动作在过去发生的处所

3. 重音在“孩子们” 指出过去动作的目的

4. 重音在“哪儿” 询问动作在过去发生的处所

5. 重音在“北京” 指出动作在过去发生的处所

6. 重音在“打铃以后” 指出动作在过去发生的时间

7. 重音在“一九四九年” 指出动作在过去发生的时间

8. 重音在“十五个人” 指出过去动作的施动者

9. 重音在“昨天”“今天” 指出动作在过去发生的时间

10. 重音在“今天” 指出动作在过去发生的时间

11. 重音在“什么时候” 询问动作在过去发生的时间

12. 重音在“昨天” 指出动作在过去发生的时间

13. 重音在“王府井” 指出动作在过去发生的处所

14. 重音在“外国学生” 指出动作在过去发生的方式

15. 重音在“上个月” 指出动作在过去发生的时间

四、1. 你是什么时候认识玛丽的？

2. 这些书是从哪儿借的？

3. 你们是在哪儿玩儿的？

4. 你们是怎么认识的？
5. 这个代表团是由什么人组成的？
6. “们”字是由哪两部分组成的？
7. 雨是什么时候下的？
8. 代表团是怎么来中国的？
9. 这些东西是从哪儿带来的？
10. 小华是什么时候寄来的信？

练 习 三

一、1. 重音在“语言学院”“北大”　指出动作在过去发生的处所
2. 重音在“话剧”“电影”　指出过去动作的受事者
3. 重音在“划”　指出动作结果的原因
4. 重音在“你”　指出过去动作的施事者
5. 重音在“经理”　指出过去动作的施事者
6. 重音在“桔子水”　指出过去动作的受事者
7. 重音在“什么”　询问过去动作的受事者
8. 重音在“面条”“面包”　指出过去动作的受事者
9. 重音在“洗”“晒”　指出动作结果的原因
10. 重音在“一起”　询问过去动作的方式
11. 重音在“一个人”　指出动作在过去发生的方式
12. 重音在“打”　指出动作结果的原因
13. 重音在“谁”　询问过去动作的施事者
14. 重音在“张丽”　指出过去动作的施事者
15. 重音在“怎么”　询问过去动作的方式
16. 重音在“骑自行车”“走着”指出动作在过去发生的方式

三、1. 是琳达买的电影票。
2. 张丽是坐船去大连的。

3. 我们不是吃的西餐，是吃的中餐。
4. 他们不是学的文学，是学的历史。
5. 他唱的是日文歌。
6. 这张画是王华画的。
7. 这件事我是从小王那儿知道的。
8. 他头疼是干活儿累的。
9. 这篇文章是王华写的，不是我写的。
10. 我不是在上海遇见他的，是在北京遇见他的。

四、1. 今天没买肉，他们吃的什么？
2. 小王的对象是谁介绍的？
3. 是谁打破的玻璃？
4. 雨是什么时候下的？
5. 你是买的什么？
6. 讲师团是由谁率领的？
7. 颐和园是什么时候开始修建的？
8. 你女儿是学的什么？
9. 你是怎么牙疼的？
10. 工作主要是谁做的？

五、1. 我以前是学习的汉语。
2. 我是走着来的。
3. 我们都不在家，是谁做的饭？
我们都不在家，饭是谁做的？
4. 我是一个人来的。
5. 我是写信告诉他的。
6. 我是在书桌上找到这枝笔的。
7. 是小明买的票。
这张票是小明买的。
8. 你是在哪儿上的车？

9. 颐和园是为皇帝母亲的生日修建的。

10. 我是在北京看见的张丽。

练　习　四

一、1. a. 他昨天来了没有？

b. 他是不是昨天来的？

2. a. 昨天半夜下雨没下雨？

b. 昨天是不是半夜下的雨？

3. a. 小王不是七点起床的。

b. 小王七点还没起床。

4. a. 这些窗户是不是去年修理的？

b. 这些窗户去年修理了没有？

5. a. 你们是不是上星期六看的电影？

b. 你们上星期六看没看电影？

三、1. 中华人民共和国是1949年成立的。

2. 我们是上星期天下午去的北海。

3. 他是骑车走的。

4. 王华是跟他母亲去南方的。

5. 我是在王府井看见的安娜。

6. 屋里太冷了，是谁把窗户打开的？

7. 他睡不着觉是喝茶喝的。

8. 张丽不是坐公共汽车去的。

9. 他们是在礼堂举行的婚礼。

10. 我们是七年前认识他的。

四、1. a. 他昨天来。×

他是昨天来的。

b. 我是上个月刚来了。×

我是上个月刚来的。

c. 谢谢，我要在中国是学习一年的。×

谢谢，我要在中国学习一年。

2. a. 我是从图书馆借了。×

我是从图书馆借的。

b. 我是上星期借了。×

我是上星期借的。

c. 我是什么时候可以去你家拿的呢。×

我什么时候可以去你家拿呢？

练　习　五

二、1. 下雨王华是不会回来的。

2. 时间太少，这么多题目是做不完的。

3. 鸦片战争后，中国人民的生活是很痛苦的。

4. 这本书的内容是很重要的，请大家认真阅读。

5. 玛丽是很不愿意离开中国的。

6. 北京的冬天是很冷的，大家注意不要感冒了。

7. 这演讲不是不应该听的，不过跟我们关系不大，所以我们没去。

8. 他是很想来看你的，可惜没时间了。

9. 从学校回家，不坐车，我是走不了的。

10. 杰克是能学好汉语的，你别着急。

三、1. 指出意义重点

2. 指出意义重点

3. 语气

4. 指出意义重点

5. 语气

6. 指出意义重点
7. 语气
8. 指出意义重点
9. 语气
10. 语气
11. 语气
12. 指出意义重点
13. 语气
14. 指出意义重点
15. 语气

四、1. 琳达是在哪儿上的大学？
2. 只要认真复习，你不是不能考好的。
3. 王华是不会回去的。
4. 他发烧是不是洗冷水澡洗的？
5. 这些活儿今天是干不完的。
6. 他的两个孩子都上大学了，他们是学的什么专业？
7. 菜不是小王的母亲做的。
8. 他的目的人们是看得清楚的。
9. 其实生产定额并不高，只要好好干，是可能达到的。
10. 冰箱是几个人抬上来的？

五、1. 不，我是学中医的。
前天到的。
刚到新环境，生活不太习惯是很自然的。
外国学生很多的。
2. 不，是妈妈做的。
是的，她做的衣服每一件都很漂亮的。
3. 爬山爬的。
4. 在哪儿看的？

在人民剧场看的。

京戏的唱腔很好听的，服装也很美。

听说你对京戏是很内行的，下次一起去好吗？

5. 她一定会来的。

“在”的练习答案

练 习 一

一、1.（×） 2.（×）

3.（√） 4.（√）

5.（×） 6.（×）

7.（√） 8.（√）

9.（×） 10.（×）

二、1. 他们一直在研究汉语语法。

2. 她一直在当翻译。

3. 孩子们还在考试。

4. 王先生也在做买卖。

5. 张小姐在做中国饭。

三、在折腾着

难道我是在恋爱了么？

在恋爱的是他

四、1. 看人总象在渺视

2. 死神在狂吼

3. 火光在闪动

4. 有人在小声哭泣

5. 谁在吹笛子

练 习 二

一、跑(√)　看(√)　吃(√)　有(×)
洗(√)　问(√)　藏(×)　跳(√)
死(×)　到(×)　能(×)　像(×)
知道(×)　喜欢(√)　停止(×)　具备(×)
包括(×)　应该(×)　决定(×)　觉得(×)

二、1. A　2. A、B
3. B　4. A、B
5. A　6. B
7. A　8. A
9. A、B　10. A

三、1.(×)　2.(√)
3.(√)　4.(√)
5.(×)　6.(√)
7.(×)　8.(×)
9.(√)　10.(√)

四、1. 我起初以为对方在开玩笑……
2.……正聚精会神地在打桥牌。
3. 这个愣小子在学打算盘。
4. 一场热烈的讨论还在进行着。
5. 她好象是在洗澡……

练 习 三

一、1. B　2. A、B
3. A　4. A
5. A

二、1. 她常常梦见孩子胖乎乎的小脸在向自己微笑。

2. ……我妈妈一直在为我担心。

3. 他在给狗洗澡呢。

4. 大家都在朝前看。

5. 一个女大学生在替她看家。

6. 他在跟他的太太打电话。

7. ……全世界的画家……都在奔跑、探索、创新。

8. 世界上许多国家都在引进、试种我国的杂交水稻。

9. ……您的儿女在向您倾诉心中的爱。

10. 大家都在为这件事烦恼。

练　习　四

一、这是星期日上午，法国留学生安娜和哈雷在打网球，日本留学生铃木常昭和伊藤加代子在打太极拳，美国留学生约翰在跑步，刚果留学生和中国学生在聊天儿。

二、1. A　　2. B

3. A　　4. A

5. A　　6. B

7. B　　8. A

9. B　　10. A

三、1. 哦，我觉得我象在做梦。

3. 你的儿子在鼓动罢工，是吗？

4. 你是在笑话我么？

5. 他在等你呢，快去吧！

8. 谁在敲门呀？

10. 他在夸奖他太太能干。

四、1. 在捻羊毛。

在磨板斧？

2. 在炼焦、炼铁，

在修桥、筑坝；

在修渠迎绿化。

3. 在感谢黄鹂和山雀呢。

五、1. On entering the room, he found Professor Wang waiting for him.

2. What are you talking about?

3. On the right side of the picture, an old woman is reading a newspaper.

4. We were cleaning the auditorium from 7 to 9 last night.

5. She is singing a Chinese folk song.

6. Who are you waiting for? I'm waiting for my sister.

7. He is studying *A Handbook of Chinese Grammar*.

8. I didn't go out last night. I was writing to my mother.

9. She is dressing. Wait a moment please.

10. What are you doing? --I'm doing some washing.

练 习 五

一、1. A　　2. B

3. B　　4. A

5. B　　6. A

7. B　　8. B

9. A　　10. A

二、1. 我吃得惯中国菜……

2. 小李拿出来的书……

3. ……我知道他已经看懂这个通知。

4. 唇膏抹在嘴唇上。

5. 这朵花正好在圣诞节开。

6. 他在打电话/他打通了电话/他打通电话了

7. ……他在床上看报

8. 他听到……

9. 他在黑板上写字。

10. 垃圾倒在马路上……

练 习 六

一、1. A　　2. B

3. A　　4. A

5. A　　6. A

7. A　　8. A

9. B　　10. A、B

二、1. 他们在营救他脱险。

2. 他在组织大家表演节目。

3. 他在打扫院子迎接客人。

4. 他在劝他母亲喝药。

5. 他在打电话叫出租汽车。

三、1. 她哭着出去了。

2. 他上课上累了。

3. 参观访问使我们有很大收获。

4. 她笑着告诉我们她男朋友来了。

5. 她进城买飞机票。

四、1. 珍妮在打电话请医生给苏珊看病。

2. 珍妮在复习功课准备明天的期中考试。

五、1. 我们一直要找个好炊事员,现在还没有找着。

2. 我在学说英语。

3. 他在打电话叫车。

4. 他们在编一本汉英辞典。

5. 昨晚八点钟她在看电视。

6. 我进来时她在看一本英文杂志。

7. 我哥哥昨天晚上在修理收音机。

8. 不要打搅他,他在做功课呢。

9. 算了吧,你又在招人家笑话了。

10. 他在和老王谈话。

11. 他打开抽屉拿出一本词典来。

12. 这消息使她高兴。

13. 医生劝他好好休息。

14. 他不会让她去跳舞。

六、1. (×)　2. (×)

3. (√)　4. (×)

5. (×)　6. (×)

7. (√)　8. (×)

9. (√)　10. (×)

练　习　七

一、1. 正　2. 在

3. 正　4. 正

5. 在　6. 正在

7. 在、在　8. 正在

9. 在　10. 在

二、1. A、C　2. A

3. A、B　4. A

5. B　　　　6. A、B

7. A　　　　8. A、B、C

9. B　　　　10. A

三、1. 在　　　　2. 在

3. 在　　　　4. 正

5. 正　　　　6. 在

7. 正　　　　8. 在

9. ∅　　　　10. 正/∅

11. 正　　　　12. 在

四、1. 我们正/正在和老师谈话时，迪克走了过来。

2. 我们正在摘棉花，忽然天下雨了。

3. 他总是在写信。

4. 他来的时候，我正在看一张英文报纸。

5. 看，孩子们正在高高兴兴地游泳。

6. 她正在买东西时，我遇见了她。

7. 约翰来的时候我正/正在做功课。

8. 他正在陪外宾游览市区。

9. 他昨天晚上在写文章。

10. 王老师走进教室时，学生们正在打扫教室。

11. 我正走进车间，忽然听见背后有人叫我。

12. 他在写信。

练　习　八

一、1. A　　　　2. B

3. A　　　　4. B

5. A　　　　6. B

7. A　　　　8. A

9. A　　　　10. A

二、1. Is it snowing?

2. When Zhang Lin got home, his younger sister was doing her homework.

3. She was reading a Chinese magazine when I came in.

4. A policeman helped the old woman across the street.

5. The driver is cleaning the car.

6. There is a lamp hanging over the table.

7. Don't stand against the door.

8. Is the shop still open?

9. I'm reading a very interesting book.

10. On the banners were the words: "We want bread!"

11. Take your umbrella with you lest it should rain.

12. He was standing just inside the door.

三、1. 看！有辆火车在过桥呢！

2. 她不是在有意说谎。

3. 她正在做语法练习。

4. 护士正在给他打针呢。

5. 她在吃晚饭吗？

6. 我们正在上汉语课。

7. 她正在看今天的报纸。

8. 病人的体力正在恢复。

9. 你在跟谁说话？

10. 气体分子总是在不断地运动着。

"呢"的练习答案

练 习 一

一、1.（×）	2.（√）	3.（√）
4.（×）	5.（√）	6.（×）
7.（×）	8.（√）	9.（×）
10.（×）	11.（√）	12.（√）
13.（×）	14.（√）	15.（×）

二、1. A（√）	B（√）	C（×）
2. A（√）	B（×）	C（√）
3. A（√）	B（×）	C（√）
4. A（√）	B（√）	C（×）
5. A（√）	B（√）	C（×）

练习二

一、1. 赞扬、夸奖	2. 责备、讥笑
3. 强调	4. 确认、夸赞
5. 疑问	6. 确认、夸赞
7. 疑问	8. 确认、夸赞
9. 确认、夸张	10. 疑问

二、1. 呢	2. 吗
3. 吗	4. 吗
5. 吗	6. 呢、呢
7. 吗	8. 吗
9. 呢	10. 吗
11. 呢	12. 吗
13. 呢	14. 吗
15. 呢	

练　习　三

一、1. A. 表示变化。以前没学，现在学了。

B. 动作进行或持续。正在学汉语。

2. A. 鱼正养在池子里。

B. 表示变化。池子里原来不养鱼，现在养鱼了。

3. A. 表示变化。本来不吃饭，现在吃了。

B. 表示动作进行或持续。

4. A. 表示肯定。用“的”加强了肯定的语气。

B. 确认、夸张。表示粮食之多足够吃上一年。

C. 表示数量变化的幅度达到了某种标准。

D. 夸张。表示粮食之少只够吃上一年。

5. A. 肯定事实。

B. 确认、夸张。

C. 表示变化。

6. A. 状态的持续。雪原来就在下。

B. 表示新情况的出现。原来没下雪。

7. A. 夸张。路太远。

B. 夸张。只不过二三里地，很近。

8. A. 表示新情况的出现。车原来没开。

B. 状态的持续。车一直在开着。

9. A. 偏重于说服别人，叫人相信所说的事实。

B. 偏重申说己见，表示一定是这样。

10. A. 偏重申说己见，我见过，我知道确实如此。

B. 夸赞、说服别人相信。

二、1. He has had his breakfast.

2. He is having his breakfast.

3. It is going to snow.

4. It is snowing outside.
5. He wants to listen to the radio.
6. He is listening to the radio.
7. He has listened to the radio.
8. He is used to having some hot peppers.
9. He has had some hot peppers. (Now he starts to have some hot peppers.)
10. He is eating some hot peppers.

责任编辑　贾寅淮
封面设计　朱　丹

汉语语法难点释疑

郑懿德　马盛静恒
刘月华　杨甲荣

*

华语教学出版社出版
（中国北京百万庄路24号）
邮政编码 100037
春雷印刷厂印刷
中国国际图书贸易总公司发行
（中国北京车公庄西路35号）
北京邮政信箱第399号　邮政编码 100044
1992年（大32开）第一版
1996年第二次印刷
（汉英）
ISBN 7-80052-202-4/H · 198（外）
01910
9-CE-2616P

NINTH EDITION

MACROECONOMICS

Theories and Policies

Richard T. Froyen

University of North Carolina Chapel Hill

PEARSON
Prentice Hall

Pearson Education International

Editor-in-Chief: Eric Svendsen
Acquisitions Editor: Chris Rogers
Product Development Manager: Ashley Santora
Project Manager, Editorial: Mary Kate Murray
Editorial Assistant: Vanessa Bain
Marketing Manager: Andrew Watts
Marketing Assistant: Ian Gold
Senior Managing Editor: Judy Leale
Project Manager, Production: Ana Jankowski
Permissions Project Manager: Charles Morris
Senior Operations Supervisor: Arnold Vila
Operations Specialist: Michelle Klein
Cover Design: Margaret Kenselaar
Creative Director: Jayne Conte
Cover Illustration/Photo: Getty Images, Inc.
Composition/Full-Service Project Management: Aptara, Inc. / Puneet Lamba
Printer/Binder: Courier/Westford/Phoenix Color Corp./Hagerstown
Typeface: 10/12 Times

Credits and acknowledgments borrowed from other sources and reproduced, with permission, in this textbook appear on appropriate page within text.

Pearson Education Ltd., London
Pearson Education Singapore, Pte. Ltd
Pearson Education Canada, Inc.
Pearson Education–Japan
Pearson Education Australia PTY, Limited
Pearson Education North Asia Ltd., Hong Kong
Pearson Educación de Mexico, S.A. de C.V.
Pearson Education Malaysia, Pte. Ltd.
Pearson Education Upper Saddle River, New Jersey

PEARSON
Prentice Hall

10 9 8 7
ISBN-13: 978-0-13-712971-3
ISBN-10: 0-13-712971-8

To Linda, Katherine, Sara, and Andrea

Brief Contents

Contents

Preface

The term macroeconomics was first used by the Norwegian economist Ragnar Frisch in 1933. Macroeconomics is clearly the younger sibling of the economics family. It is no coincidence that macroeconomics emerged as a major branch of economics amid the chaotic conditions of the Great Depression of the 1930s. The severe economic problems of the time lent importance to the subject matter of macroeconomics—the behavior of the economy as a whole. A book by John Maynard Keynes, *The General Theory of Employment, Interest, and Money,* developed a framework in which to systematically consider the behavior of aggregate economic variables such as employment and output. During the two decades following World War II, Keynes's followers elaborated and extended his theories. From the first there were skeptics, perhaps most notably Milton Friedman, but Keynesian economics became the orthodox mode of thinking about macroeconomic questions.

The years since the late 1960s, however, have witnessed major challenges to Keynesian economics. In the 1970s there was increased interest in *monetarism,* the body of theory Milton Friedman and others had developed beginning in the 1940s. A new school of macroeconomic theory, the *new classical* economics, also came on the scene during the 1970s. In the 1980s, Keynesian policy prescriptions came under attack from a group called the *supply-side* economists. The 1980s also witnessed the development of two new lines of macroeconomic research: the *real business cycle* theory and the *new Keynesian* economics.

Many of the post-1970 developments in macroeconomics have been the result of dissatisfaction with the Keynesian theory and the policy prescriptions that follow from it. In addition to controversy, however, the past three decades have seen what all would agree is progress in our theories of the macroeconomy. There have been significant improvements in the handling of expectations, in our understanding of labor market institutions, in accounting for the macroeconomic implications of various market structures, in the modeling of open economies, and in accounting for the ultimate sources of economic growth.

In this book I have tried to explain macroeconomics, inclusive of recent developments, in a coherent way but without glossing over the fundamental disagreements among macroeconomists on issues of both theory and policy. The major modern macroeconomic theories are presented and compared. Important areas of agreement as well as differences are discussed. An attempt is made to demonstrate that the controversies among macroeconomists center on well-defined issues that are based on theoretical differences in the underlying models.

FEATURES

Distinguishing features of the approach taken here include the following:

- An up-to-date summary of the Keynesian position, including research that has come to be called the *new Keynesian economics*.
- A detailed analysis of the challenges to the Keynesian position by the monetarists, new classical economists, and real business cycle theorists.
- An extensive treatment of monetary policy that considers both optimal tactics (the instrument problem) and possible optimal strategies (e.g., inflation targets). For both monetary and fiscal policy questions, policy issues are closely related to the theories we consider.
- An analysis of the post-1970 slowdown in U.S. output growth, capital formation, and growth in labor productivity. Within this context of intermediate-run growth, the views of the supply-side economists and their critics are examined. Also within this context of the determinants of rates of intermediate-run economic growth, we consider whether there are signs that the productivity slowdown of the 1970s has been reversed. Is there a "new economy" developing in the new century?
- A consideration of the determinants of long-run economic growth. Both the neoclassical growth model and recent models of endogenous growth are discussed.
- Consideration of foreign exchange rate determination and the International Monetary System. Monetary and fiscal policy effects in the open economy are analyzed within the framework of the Mundell–Fleming model.

ORGANIZATION

Part I (Chapters 1 and 2) discusses the subject matter of macroeconomics, recent behavior of the U.S. economy, and questions of measurement. Part II (Chapters 3–8) begins our comparison of macroeconomic models. We start with the classical system and then go on to the Keynesian model. Part III considers challenges to the Keynesian system and rebuttals to these challenges. Chapter 9 examines monetarism and the issues in the monetarist Keynesian controversy. Chapter 10 examines alternative views of the unemployment–inflation trade-off and the *natural rate* theory. Chapter 11 presents the new classical theory with its central concepts of *rational expectations* and market clearing. In Chapter 12 two newer directions in macroeconomic research are examined. One, very strongly rooted in the classical tradition, is the real business cycle theory. The second, the new Keynesian economics, is, as its name suggests, firmly in the Keynesian tradition. Chapter 13 summarizes and compares the different models considered in Parts II and III.

Part IV considers open-economy macroeconomics. Chapter 14 focuses on exchange rate determination and the international monetary system. Chapter 15 utilizes the Mundell–Fleming model to examine the effects of monetary and fiscal policy in the open economy.

Part V deals with macroeconomic policy. Chapters 16 and 17 focus on monetary policy. Chapter 18 considers fiscal policy.

Part VI lengthens the time horizon of the analysis beyond the short run. Chapter 19 is concerned with growth over intermediate–run periods of a decade or two. Chapter 20 considers long-run equilibrium growth.

NEW IN THE NINTH EDITION

- The chapters with the most significant revisions are those on monetary policy and economic growth. Revisions of the two chapters on monetary policy place greater emphasis on interest rates and inflation targeting strategies and less on money. The chapter on long-run economic growth has expanded coverage of endogenous growth models.
- The chapter on long-run growth has also been moved out of Part II. It is now placed together with the chapter on intermediate-run growth to form Part VI.
- New Perspectives have been added, including ones covering the possible trade-offs between equity and efficiency, the advantages and disadvantages of the Federal Reserve's adoption of inflation targeting, and the normative aspects of economic growth. Other Perspectives have been updated and revised.
- As in the previous edition, an attempt has been made to shorten and streamline the text. The chapters on consumption and investment and on money demand have been dropped. (They will still be available on the website for the book.) In the chapters in Parts II and III on economic models, material that is less relevant than when first written has been shortened or deleted. I believe that 90 percent of the new edition can be covered within a one-semester course.

ANCILLARIES

- *Instructor's Manual with Test Bank:* This resource manual provides the instructor with detailed chapter summaries, answers to end-of-chapter questions, and a complete test bank. For each chapter, there are 50 to 70 multiple-choice questions as well as 10 to 15 problems and essay questions. The Instructor's Manual is avail able for download at http://www.prenhall.com/froyen. Further resources for both students and instructors may also be found on the companion website.

ACKNOWLEDGMENTS

I am especially grateful to Sharon Erenburg, Eastern Michigan University, for extensive comments and contributions that helped in revisions for this edition as well as the previous one. Reviewers recruited by Prentice Hall also provided many useful suggestions. These reviewers are Peter Hess, Davidson College; Brice Sutton, St. Louis University; Darryl Getter, U.S. Naval Academy; Charles R. Britton, University of Arkansas; Lara Bryant, University of North Carolina, Chapel Hill; Anthony J. Laramie, Boston College; Masha Rahnama, Texas Tech University; and Kristin A. Van Gaasbeck, University of California, Davis.

Many people have been helpful in preparing the various editions of this book. I have benefited from comments by Roger Waud, Art Benavie, Alfred Field, and Pat Conway, all from the University of North Carolina, as well as by Lawrence Davidson and Williard Witte, Indiana University; Dennis Appleyard, Davidson College; Alfred Guender, University of Canterbury; Homer Erekson, Miami University; Allin Cottrell,

Wake Forest University; David Van Hoose, Baylor University; Michael Bradley, George Washington University; Art Goldsmith, Washington and Lee University; Sang Sub Lee, Freddie Mac; David Bowles, Clemson University; Michael Loy and Lawrence Ellis, Appalachian State University; and Rody Borg, Jacksonville University.

I want to thank Michael Aguilar and John Kavekos for their careful research assistance on this revision.

I am also grateful to Chris Rogers and Mary Kate Murray at Prentice Hall for their editorial cooperation on this revision.

PART ONE

Introduction and Measurement

CHAPTER 1

Introduction

CHAPTER 2

Measurement of Macroeconomic Variables

Part I discusses the subject matter of macroeconomics, the behavior of the U.S. economy, and the measurement of macroeconomic variables. Chapter 1 defines macroeconomics and traces the macroeconomic trends in the United States since World War II. The chapter then poses some central questions in macroeconomics. Chapter 2 deals with measurement and defines the main macroeconomic aggregates. Central to this task is an examination of the U.S. national income accounts.

CHAPTER 1

Introduction

1.1 WHAT IS MACROECONOMICS?

This book examines the branch of economics called *macroeconomics*. The British economist Alfred Marshall defined economics as the "study of mankind in the ordinary business of life; it examines that part of individual and social action which is most closely connected with the attainment and with the use of the material requisites of well-being."[1] In macroeconomics, we study this "ordinary business of life" in the aggregate. We look at the behavior of the economy as a whole. The key variables we study include total output in the economy, the aggregate price level, employment and unemployment, interest rates, wage rates, and foreign exchange rates. The subject matter of macroeconomics includes factors that determine both the levels of these variables and how the variables change over time: the rate of growth of output, the inflation rate, changing unemployment in periods of expansion and recession, and appreciation or depreciation in foreign exchange rates.

Macroeconomics is policy oriented. It asks, to what degree can government policies affect output and employment? To what degree is inflation the result of unfortunate government policies? What government policies are *optimal* in the sense of achieving the most desirable behavior of aggregate variables, such as the level of unemployment or the inflation rate? Should government policy attempt to achieve a *target level* for foreign exchange rates?

For example, we might ask to what degree government policies were to blame for the massive unemployment during the Great Depression of the 1930s or for the simultaneously high unemployment and inflation of the 1970s. What role did "Reaganomics" play in the sharp decline in inflation and rise in unemployment in the early 1980s? To what degree have government policies been responsible for the sharp decline in the average inflation rate in the United States and other industrialized countries that occurred over the past two decades?

Economists disagree on policy questions. In part, the controversy over policy questions stems from differing views of the factors that determine the key variables mentioned previously. Questions of theory and policy are interrelated. Our analysis examines different macroeconomic theories and the policy conclusions that follow from those theories. It would be more satisfying to present *the* macroeconomic theory and policy prescription. Satisfying, but such a presentation would be misleading because there are fundamental differences among schools of macroeconomics. In comparing different theories, however, we see that there are substantial areas of agreement as well as disagreement. Controversy does not mean chaos. Our approach is to isolate key issues that divide macroeconomists and to explain the theoretical basis for each position.

[1] Alfred Marshall, *Principles of Economics*, 8th ed. (New York: Macmillan, 1920), p. 1.

We analyze macroeconomic orthodoxy as it existed when the 1970s began, what is termed *Keynesian economics.* The roots of Keynesian theory as an attack on an earlier orthodoxy, *classical economics,* are explained. We then examine the challenges to the Keynesian position, theories that have come to be called *monetarism* and the *new classical economics.* Finally, we consider two recent theories. One, strongly rooted in the classical tradition, is the *real business cycle theory.* The other, the *new Keynesian theory,* is, as its name suggests, in the Keynesian tradition. How each theory explains the events from the 1970s to the present, as well as the policies each group of economists propose to provide for better future economic performance, is a central concern of our analysis.

1.2 POST–WORLD WAR II U.S. ECONOMIC PERFORMANCE

Our tasks here are to sketch the broad outline of U.S. macroeconomic performance over the post–World War II period and to suggest some central questions addressed in our later analysis.

Output

Figure 1-1 shows the growth rate of output for the United States for the years 1953–2006. The output measure in the figure is *real* **gross domestic product (GDP)**. Gross domestic product measures current production of goods and services; *real* means that the measures in Figure 1-1 have been corrected for price change. The data measure growth in the quantity of goods and services produced.

gross domestic product (GDP)
a measure of all currently produced final goods and services

The data in the figure show considerable variation in GDP growth over the past five decades. During the 1960s, there was steady, relatively high growth in GDP. In all other decades, there were years of negative growth; GDP declined in at least 1 year.

FIGURE 1-1 Annual Percentage Change in Real GDP, 1953–2006

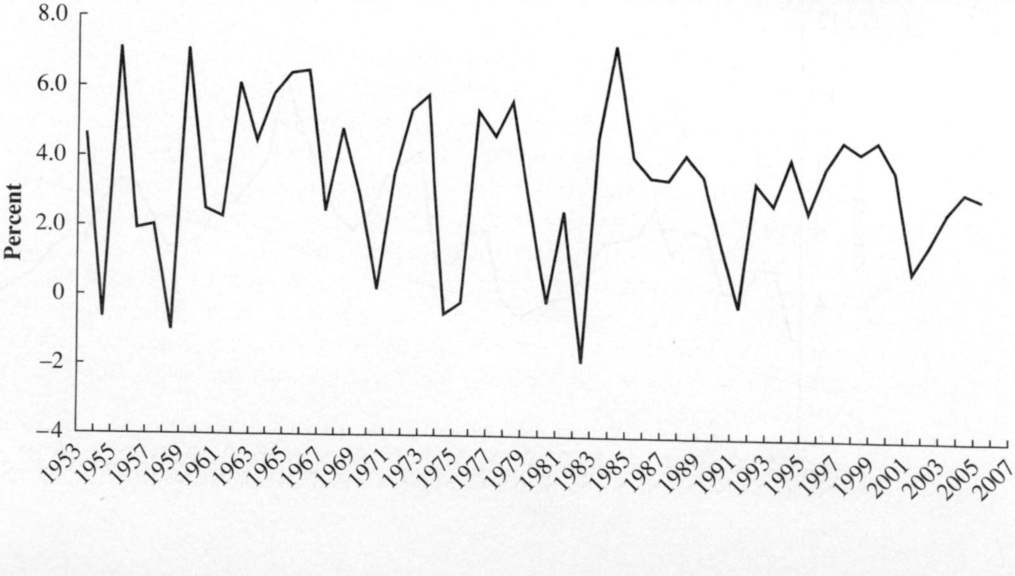

TABLE 1-1 Real GDP Growth in the United States, Average Percentage Change for Selected Periods

Years	*Percent*
1953–69	3.8
1970–81	2.7
1982–95	3.0
1996–2006	3.2

Table 1-1 summarizes growth trends over the past half century. The table indicates a decline of about 1 percentage point in the GDP growth rate in the post-1970 period. There are some signs of a reversal of this growth slowdown starting in the mid-1990s. Beginning in the late 1980s output growth appears to have become less volatile than in the previous three decades. This can be seen in Figure 1-1.

Unemployment

unemployment rate the number of unemployed persons expressed as a percentage of the labor force

Figure 1-2 shows the U.S. **unemployment rate** for each year since 1953. The unemployment rate is the percentage of the labor force that is not employed.

The slower output growth in the post-1970 period is reflected in rising unemployment during these years, as can also be seen in Table 1-2, which shows average unemployment rates for selected periods. In the late 1990s there seemed to be a reversal of this trend as the unemployment rate fell to a 30-year low of just under 4 percent. Then as output growth slowed after 2000, the unemployment rate rose to nearly 6 percent. Although this rate is not

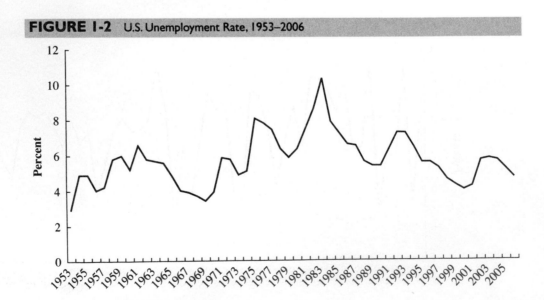

FIGURE 1-2 U.S. Unemployment Rate, 1953–2006

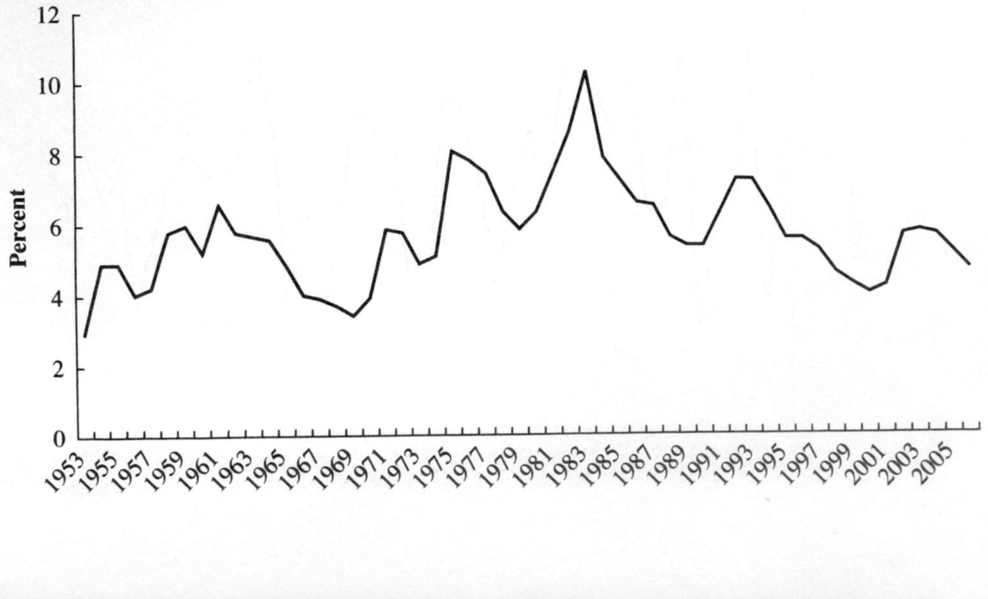

TABLE 1-2 U.S. Unemployment Rate, Averages for Selected Periods

Years	*Percent*
1953–69	4.8
1970–81	6.4
1982–95	6.9
1996–2006	5.0

inflation
a rise in the general level of prices

price index
a measure of the aggregate price level relative to a chosen base year

consumer price index (CPI)
a measure of the retail prices of a fixed "market basket" of several thousand goods and services purchased by households

especially high by the standard of previous recessions, unemployment did remain high even as output growth picked up after 2002, causing talk of a "jobless recovery."

Inflation

Figure 1-3 shows the rate of **inflation** for 1953–2006. To calculate the rate of inflation, we use a **price index** that measures the aggregate (or general) price level relative to a base year. The inflation rate is then computed as the percentage rate of change in the price index over a given period. In Figure 1-3 the inflation rate is measured by the **consumer price index (CPI)**; other price indices are considered in the next chapter. The CPI measures the retail prices of a fixed "market basket" of several thousand goods and services purchased by households.

It can be seen from the figure and from Table 1-3 that the inflation rate was low and relatively stable in the 1950s and early 1960s. In the late 1960s, an upward trend in inflation is apparent. This upward trend continued and intensified in the 1970s. The early 1980s were a

FIGURE 1-3 U.S. Inflation Rate, 1953–2006

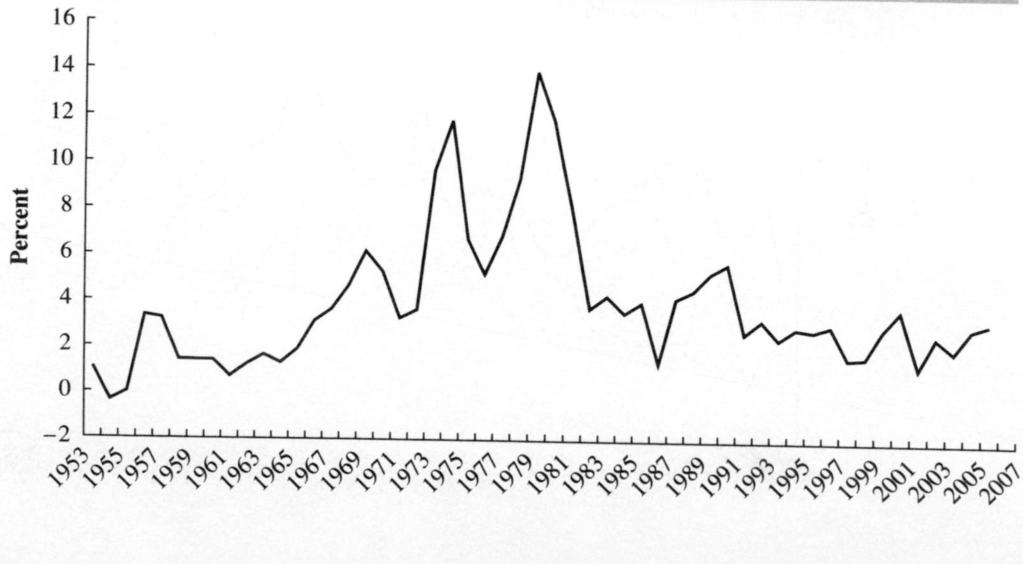

TABLE 1-3 U.S. Inflation Rate, Averages for Selected Periods

Years	*Percent*
1953–60	1.4
1961–69	2.6
1970–81	8.0
1982–95	3.8
1996–06	2.6

period of *disinflation*, meaning a decline in the inflation rate. The inflation rate remained fairly low throughout the 1980s. There was an upward blip in the inflation rate in 1990, partly due to a sharp rise in energy prices after Iraq's invasion of oil-rich Kuwait. This was reversed as energy prices fell with the allied victory in the Persian Gulf War in early 1991. Inflation then remained low, though another rise in energy prices moved it up somewhat in 2003–6.

Inflation and Unemployment

Figure 1-4 plots the annual unemployment rate for 1953–2006 together with the annual inflation rate during that same time period. Note that in the early portion of this period, through the late 1960s, there is a negative relationship between the inflation rate and the unemployment rate; years of relatively high inflation are years of relatively low unemployment. In the period since 1970, no such simple relationship is evident. During parts of the 1970s—for example, 1973–75—the unemployment and

FIGURE 1-4 U.S. Unemployment and Inflation Rates, 1953–2006

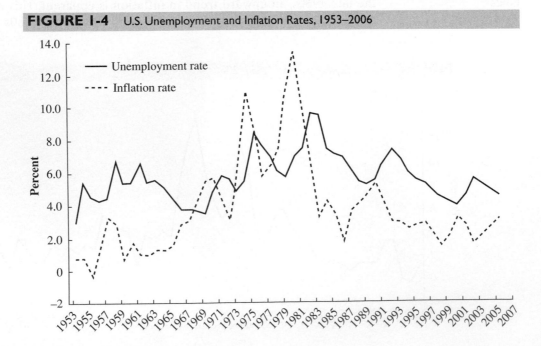

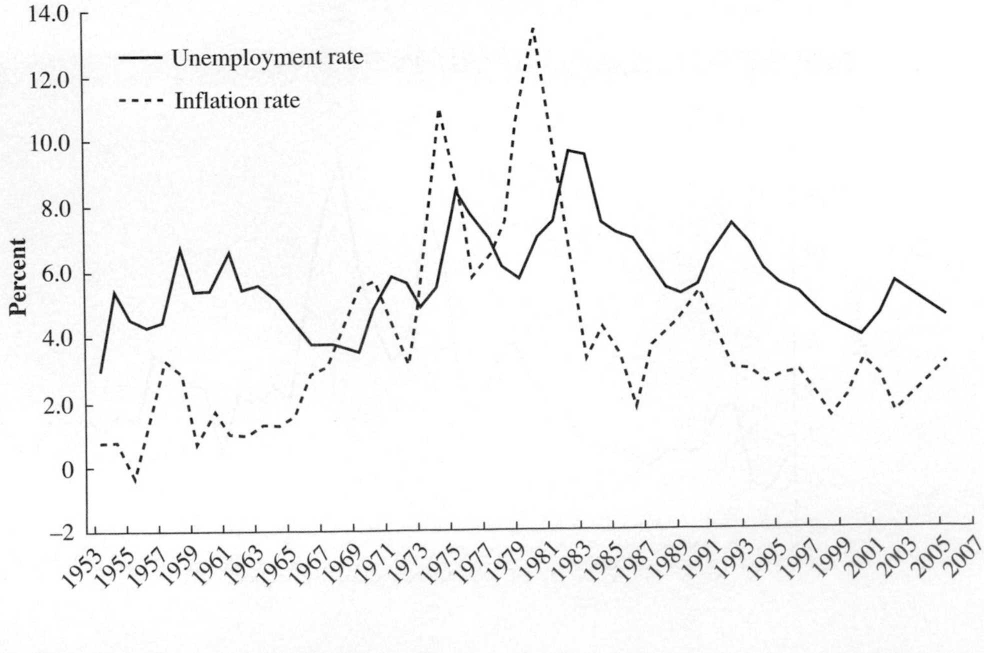

inflation rates both rose sharply. In the early 1980s, the negative relationship seemed to return, with unemployment rising sharply as inflation declined. Later in the 1980s, the inflation rate remained low while the unemployment rate steadily declined. Between 1990 and 1991, the unemployment rate rose and the inflation rate fell, but the behavior of the inflation rate appears to have been due to factors connected with the Persian Gulf War rather than any underlying unemployment-inflation relationship. From 1992 to 1999, both the inflation and unemployment rates fell. Beginning in 2001, unemployment rose as the inflation rate fell. Both series reversed course in 2003, again moving in opposite directions.

These changes in the relationship between the inflation rate and the unemployment rate can be seen in Figure 1-5. In parts *a* and *b* of the graph, the inflation rate is measured on the vertical axis and the unemployment rate on the horizontal axis. Part *a* is for the years 1953–69, and the negative relationship between the two variables is evident. Part *b* is for 1970–2006, and for these years there is no apparent relationship between inflation and unemployment.

FIGURE 1-5*a* Relationship Between Inflation and Unemployment, 1953–69

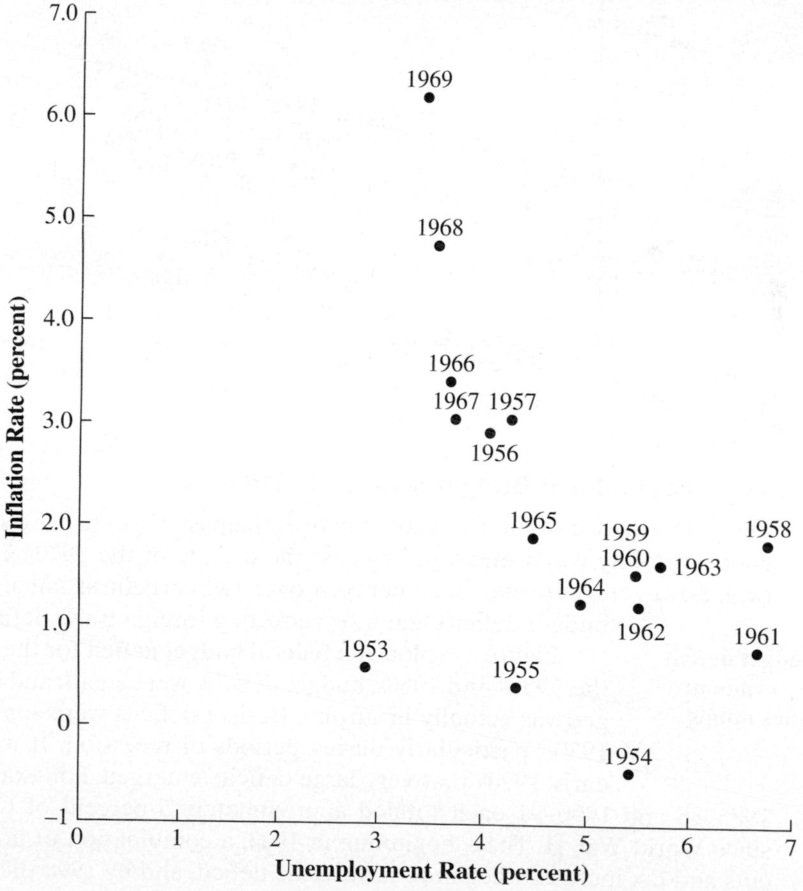

FIGURE 1-5*b* Relationship Between Inflation and Unemployment, 1970–2006

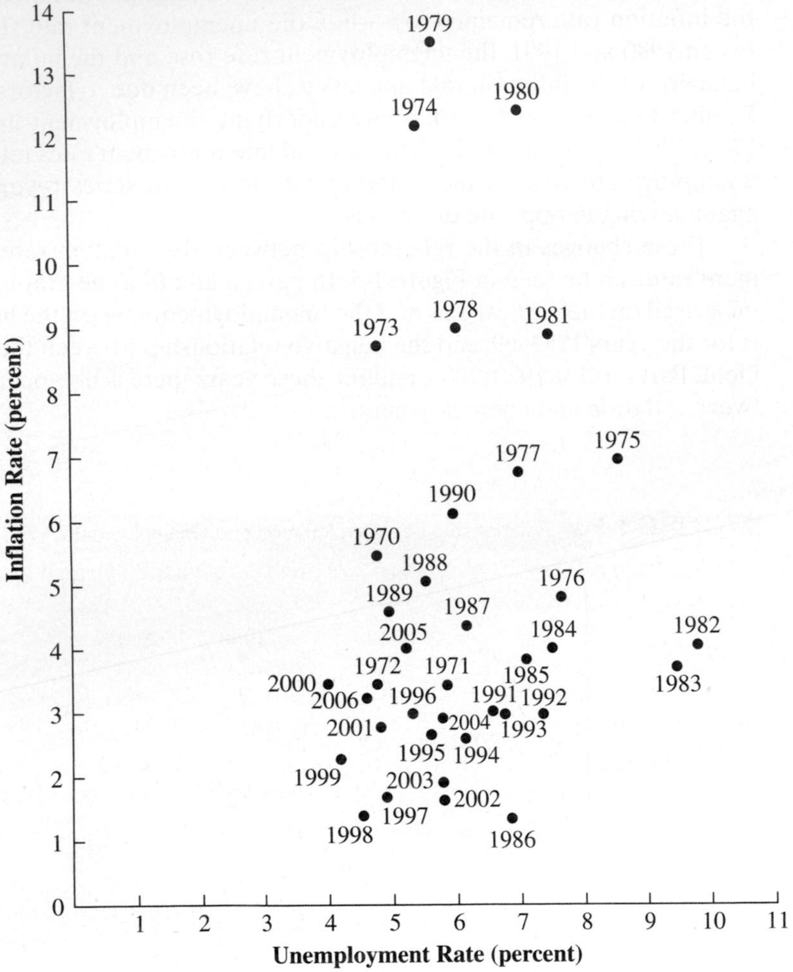

The U.S. Federal Budget and Trade Deficits

The performance of the U.S. economy over the past 25 years has on average been quite good, certainly when measured against the decade of the 1970s. For much of the period, however, there has been concern over two structural imbalances: large federal budget deficits and a skyrocketing foreign trade deficit.

federal budget deficit federal government tax revenues minus outlays

Figure 1-6 plots the **federal budget deficit** for the years 1953–2005. In the 1950s and 1960s, budget deficits were small, and sometimes the budget was actually in surplus. Budget deficits were somewhat larger in the 1970s, particularly during periods of recession. It was in the 1980s and early 1990s that very large deficits emerged. For example, the deficits of 1985–86 and 1990–91 each totaled approximately 5 percent of GDP, a level unseen since World War II. Then, beginning in 1993, a combination of government spending cuts and tax increases began to reduce the deficit, and by 1998 the budget moved into

FIGURE 1-6 U.S. Federal Budget Deficit, 1953–2005

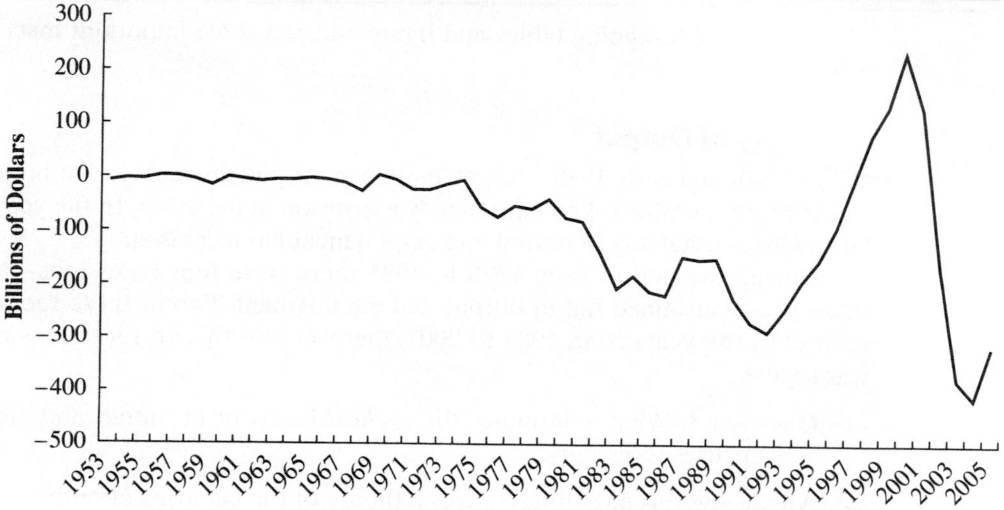

surplus. Early in the new century, however, the budget moved dramatically back into deficit, with deficits similar in magnitude to those of the 1980s and 1990s.

trade deficit the excess of imports over exports

Figure 1-7 shows the U.S. merchandise **trade deficit** for the years since 1953. The trade deficit is the excess of U.S. imports over exports. The United States began to run trade deficits in the 1970s, but as with federal budget deficits, it was in the 1980s that the trade deficit ballooned, rising to over $150 billion in 1988. The trade deficit then declined for a few years, but it began to rise in the mid-1990s, exceeding $260 billion by 1999, rising to over $500 billion by 2003 and then to over $700 billion in 2005.

FIGURE 1-7 U.S. Balance on Goods and Services, 1953–2005

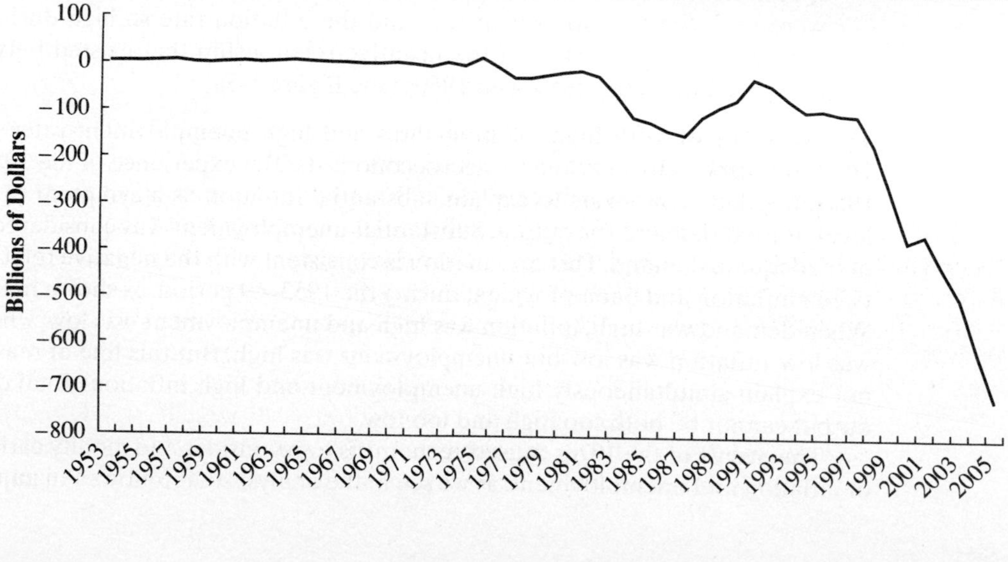

1.3 CENTRAL QUESTIONS IN MACROECONOMICS

The data in the foregoing tables and figures suggest some important macroeconomic questions.

Instability of Output

In the 1970s and early 1980s, output, employment, and unemployment became significantly more unstable following a steady expansion in the 1960s. In the years since the late 1980s, the stability of output and employment has increased.

During the period from 1970 to 1984 there were four recessions—times when there was a sustained fall in output and employment. Two of these recessions were severe. In the years from 1985 to 2007, there were only two recessions and neither was severe.

Question 1: What determines the *cyclical* behavior of output and employment? What causes recessions?

Answering this question requires a theory of the behavior of output and employment over periods of 1 to 4 years, a theory of the cyclical behavior of output and employment.

Movements in the Inflation Rate

In our overview of the U.S. economy, we have seen that there have been significant variations in inflation over time. The 1970s was the period of the "great peacetime inflation." Both before and after that period, the rate of inflation was much lower.

Question 2: What are the determinants of the rate of inflation? What role do macroeconomic policies play in determining inflation?

The Output–Inflation Relationship

Question 3: What relationship exists between inflation and unemployment? Why were both the unemployment rate and the inflation rate so high during much of the 1970s? What became of the negative relationship that existed between these two variables in the 1950s and 1960s (see Figure 1-5a)?

The presence of both high inflation rates and high unemployment rates during the 1970s was especially puzzling to macroeconomists. The experience of the 1950s and the 1960s had led economists to explain substantial inflation as a symptom of too high a level of total demand for output. Substantial unemployment was considered the result of inadequate demand. This explanation is consistent with the negative relationship between inflation and unemployment during the 1953–69 period, as shown in Figure 1-5a. When demand was high, inflation was high and unemployment was low; when demand was low, inflation was low but unemployment was high. But this line of reasoning cannot explain simultaneously high unemployment and high inflation. Total demand for output cannot be both too high and too low.

The events of the 1970s caused economists to reconsider and modify earlier theories of inflation and unemployment, as we see in the analysis that follows. An important part

aggregate demand the sum of the demands for current output by each buying sector of the economy: households, businesses, the government, and foreign purchasers of exports

of this reconsideration of existing theory concerns the role of total demand for output, what is termed **aggregate demand**, in determining output, employment, and inflation.

Additional questions about the relationship between inflation and unemployment were raised by the behavior of the two variables in the mid- to late 1990s. As unemployment fell to low levels, many economists expected rising inflation. Instead, inflation remained low. Why?

All in all, the relationship between unemployment and inflation has been much more complex in the post-1970 period than in earlier years. The macro economic theories we consider try to explain why.

Growth Slowdown and Turnaround?

What explains the decline in the growth rate of output, as measured by GDP, over the years after 1970? As we saw in Table 1-1, output grew at an average annual rate of 3.8 percent for the 1953–69 period compared with 2.7 percent for 1970–81 and 3.0 percent for 1982–95. Accompanying the decline in output growth were declines in growth of labor productivity and real wages. By the mid-1990s, many Americans, especially young people, were complaining about the shortage of good jobs.

Over much of the period, there was also the question of the shortage of jobs per se. Together with the slower growth after 1970, the unemployment rate was higher than in the 1950s or 1960s. It should be noted, however, that the rise in the average U.S. unemployment rate after 1970 was much less marked than in most of Europe. In fact, by 2000, the U.S. unemployment rate had returned to below 5 percent, whereas unemployment rates in countries such as Germany, France, and Italy were still near post–World War II record highs.

Moreover, in the United States during the 1990s, there were signs that the growth slowdown was being reversed. A mild recession in 2001 was a bump in what seemed to be a road to higher growth in output and labor productivity.

Question 4: What determines the rate of growth in output over periods of one or two decades? Over longer periods such as a century?

One can ask this question for one country across time periods or across countries. Why have some countries grown very rapidly and some more slowly?

Implications of Deficits and Surpluses

As the U.S. federal budget deficit rose rapidly in the 1980s, observers speculated about their effects. The *Financial Times* asked whether the economy was headed for a "rendezvous with disaster." Others believed that the deficit posed problems of a subtler, long-term kind more akin to "termites in the basement" than "the wolf at the door." As the budget moved into surplus in the late 1990s, the problem receded. There was actually concern about the huge projected surpluses, which implied that the national debt would be retired completely by 2012. The concern was unwarranted.

Today we are once again concerned with large current and projected future deficits. Given the debt the country will pile up, how will the government commitment to the retiring baby boom generation, in terms of Social Security benefits and Medicare, be financed? Will government borrowing to finance the deficits raise interest rates and retard investment and growth?

The rapidly growing U.S. trade deficit has also been a cause of concern. The United States effectively borrows from abroad to finance this deficit. Thus, continuing deficits have been mirrored by a growing U.S. foreign debt. Many worry about the effects of the deficits and debt on the future stability of the dollar and of U.S. asset markets.

1.4 CONCLUSION

There is no shortage of questions. The chapters that follow present theories that try to explain the data discussed here and provide answers to the questions we have raised. Prior to examining these theories, in Chapter 2 we consider the measurement of the major macroeconomic variables of interest.

KEY TERMS

- gross domestic product (GDP) 3
- unemployment rate 4
- inflation 5
- price index 5
- consumer price index (CPI) 5
- federal budget deficit 8
- trade deficit 9
- aggregate demand 11

REVIEW QUESTIONS AND PROBLEMS

1. What are some of the important variables that constitute the subject matter of macroeconomics? How does macroeconomics differ from microeconomics, the other major branch of economic theory?
2. Summarize the behavior of the inflation and unemployment rates since 1990. Did the movements of these rates over this period more closely resemble those of the 1970s or those of the 1950s and 1960s?
3. There were several shifts in the output-inflation relationship over the 1953–2002 period. Explain the nature of these shifts.
4. Using the *Economic Report of the President* or other sources for the most recent years, update the data in Tables 1-1 to 1-3.
5. Summarize the behavior of U.S. federal government budget deficits and U.S. merchandise trade deficits since 1953. Does this behavior suggest a relationship between the two deficits? Perhaps at some times and not at others?

CHAPTER 2

Measurement of Macroeconomic Variables

Now what I want is, Facts. Teach these boys and girls nothing but Facts. Facts alone are wanted in life. Plant nothing else, and root out everything else. You can only form the minds of reasoning animals upon Facts; nothing else will ever be of any service to them. . . . Stick to the Facts, sir![1]

In subsequent chapters, we examine macroeconomic models. These models are simplified representations of the economy that attempt to capture important factors determining aggregate variables such as output, employment, and the price level. Elements of the models are theoretical relationships among aggregative economic variables, including policy variables. As a prelude to understanding such relationships, this chapter begins by defining the real-world counterparts of the variables in our models. It also considers accounting relationships that exist among these variables because we use these relationships to construct our models. We begin by describing the key variables measured in the national income accounts.

2.1 THE NATIONAL INCOME ACCOUNTS

Economists read with dismay of Presidents Hoover and then Roosevelt designing policies to combat the Great Depression of the 1930s on the basis of sketchy data such as stock price indices, freight car loadings, and incomplete indices of industrial production. Comprehensive measures of national income and output did not exist at that time. The Depression emphasized the need for such measures and led to the development of a comprehensive set of national income accounts.[2]

Like the accounts of a business, national income accounts have two sides: a product side and an income side. The product side measures production and sales. The income side measures the distribution of the proceeds from sales.

[1]Charles Dickens, *Hard Times* (New York: Norton, 1966), p. 1

[2]Nobel Prize–winning economists Simon Kuznets and Richard Stone played pioneering roles in the development of national income accounting. See Simon Kuznets, *National Income and Its Composition, 1919–38* (New York: National Bureau of Economic Research, 1941). During World War II, the Commerce Department took over the maintenance of the national income accounts. National income accounts data are published in the *Survey of Current Business.* A description of recent revisions in the national income accounts is "Preview of the Comprehensive NIPA Revision: Changes in Definitions and Classifications," *Survey of Current Business* (June 2003), pp. 17–34.

On the product side there are two widely reported measures of overall production: gross domestic product (GDP), which we looked at in Chapter 1, and gross national product (GNP). They differ in their treatment of international transactions. GNP includes earnings of U.S. corporations overseas and U.S. residents working overseas; GDP does not. Conversely, GDP includes earnings in the United States of foreign residents or foreign-owned firms; GNP excludes those items. For example, profits earned in the United States by a foreign-owned firm would be included in GDP but not in GNP.

For the United States, there is little difference between these two measures because relatively few U.S. residents work abroad, and the overseas earnings of U.S. firms are about the same as the U.S. earnings of foreign firms. The difference between GNP and GDP is large for a country such as Pakistan, with a large number of residents working overseas, or Canada, where there is much more foreign investment than there is Canadian investment abroad. In 1991, the U.S. national income accountants shifted emphasis from GNP to GDP. Our explanation of the product side of the national accounts therefore concentrates on GDP. The GNP concept enters into the discussion at a later point.

On the income side of the national accounts, the central measure is national income, although we also discuss some related income concepts.

2.2 GROSS DOMESTIC PRODUCT

gross domestic product (GDP)
measure of all currently produced final goods and services

Gross domestic product (GDP) is a measure of all currently produced final goods and services evaluated at market prices. Some aspects of this definition require clarification.

Currently Produced

GDP includes only currently produced goods and services. It is a flow measure of output per time period—for example, per quarter or per year—and includes only goods and services produced during this interval. Market transactions such as exchanges of previously produced houses, cars, or factories do not enter into GDP. Exchanges of assets, such as stocks and bonds, are examples of other market transactions that do not directly involve current production of goods and services and are therefore not in GDP.

Final Goods and Services

Only the production of final goods and services enters GDP. Goods used to produce other goods rather than being sold to final purchasers—what are termed *intermediate goods*—are not counted separately in GDP. Such goods show up in GDP because they contribute to the value of the final goods they are used to produce. Counting them separately is double counting. For example, we would not want to count the value of flour used in making bread separately and then again when the bread is sold.

capital goods
capital resources such as factories and machinery used to produce other goods

However, two types of goods used in the production process are counted in GDP. The first is currently produced **capital goods**—business plant and equipment purchases. Such capital goods are ultimately used up in the production process, but within the current period only a portion of the value of the capital good is used up in production. This portion,

depreciation portion of the capital stock that wears out each year

termed **depreciation**, can be thought of as embodied in the value of the final goods that are sold. Not including capital goods separately in GDP would be equivalent to assuming that they depreciated fully in the current time period. In GDP, the whole value of the capital good is included as a separate item. In a sense this is double counting because, as just noted, the value of depreciation is embodied in the value of final goods. At a later point, we will subtract depreciation to construct a *net* output measure.

The other type of intermediate goods that is part of GDP is *inventory investment*—the net change in inventories of final goods awaiting sale or of materials used in the production process. Additions to inventory stocks of final goods belong in GDP because they are currently produced output. These additions should be counted in the current period as they are added to stocks so that the timing of national product is defined correctly; they should not be counted later, when they are sold to final purchasers. Inventory investment in materials similarly belongs in GDP because it also represents currently produced output whose value is not embodied in *current* sales of final output. Notice that inventory investment can be negative or positive. If final sales exceed production—for example, because of a rundown of inventories (negative inventory investment)—GDP will fall short of final sales.

Evaluated at Market Prices

GDP is the value of goods and services determined by the common measuring rod of market prices. This is the trick to being able to measure apples plus oranges plus railroad cars plus. . . . But this does exclude from GDP goods that are not sold in markets, such as the services of homemakers or the output of home gardens, as well as nonreported output from illegal activities, such as the sale of narcotics, gambling, and prostitution.[3] Also, because it is a measure of the value of output in terms of market prices, GDP, which is essentially a quantity measure, is sensitive to changes in the average price level. The same physical output will correspond to a different GDP level as the average level of market prices varies. To correct for this, in addition to computing GDP in terms of current market prices, a concept termed *nominal GDP*, the national income accountants also calculate *real GDP*, which is the value of domestic product in terms of constant prices. The way the latter calculation is made is discussed later in this chapter.

GDP can be broken down into the components shown in Table 2-1. The values of each component for selected years are also given in the table. The data in the table suggest a number of trends and patterns.

consumption household sector's demand for output for current use

The **consumption** component of GDP consists of the household sector's purchases of currently produced goods and services. Consumption can be broken down into consumer durable goods (e.g., automobiles, televisions), nondurable consumption goods (e.g., foods, beverages, clothing), and consumer services (e.g., medical services, haircuts). Consumption is the largest component of GDP, comprising between 65 and 70 percent of GDP in recent years.

[3]For some services that are not sold on the market, the Commerce Department does try to *impute* the market value of the service and include it in GDP. An example is the services of owner-occupied houses, which the Commerce Department estimates on the basis of rental value.

TABLE 2-1 Nominal GDP and Its Components, Selected Years (billions of dollars)

	GDP	*Consumption*	*Investment*	*Government Purchases of Goods and Services*	*Net Exports*
1929	103.7	77.5	16.5	9.4	0.4
1933	56.4	45.9	1.7	8.7	0.1
1939	92.0	67.2	9.3	14.7	0.8
1945	223.0	119.8	10.8	93.2	−0.9
1950	294.3	192.7	54.1	46.9	0.7
1960	527.4	332.3	78.9	113.8	2.4
1970	1,039.6	648.9	152.4	237.1	1.2
1980	2,795.6	1,762.9	477.9	569.7	−14.9
1990	5,803.2	3,831.5	861.7	1,181.4	−71.4
2000	9,824.6	6,683.7	1,755.4	1,751.0	−365.5
2006	13,246.6	9,268.9	2,212.5	2,527.7	−762.5

Note: Components may not sum to the total due to rounding error.
SOURCE: Bureau of Economic Analysis, Department of Commerce.

investment part of GDP purchased by the business sector plus residential construction

The **investment** component of GDP in Table 2.1 consists of three subcomponents. The largest of these is business fixed investment. Business fixed investment consists of purchases of newly produced plant and equipment—the capital goods discussed previously. The second subcomponent of investment is residential construction investment, the building of single- and multifamily housing units. The final subcomponent of investment is inventory investment, which is the change in business inventories. As noted, inventory investment may be positive or negative. In 2006, inventory investment was $49.6 billion, meaning that there was an increase in that amount of inventories during that year.

Over the years covered by Table 2-1, investment was a volatile component of GDP, ranging from 3.0 percent of GDP in 1933 to 18.4 percent of GDP in 1950. This volatility of investment behavior has implications for the macroeconomic models considered later.

The figures in Table 2-1 are *gross* rather than net, meaning that no adjustment for depreciation has been made. The investment total in the table is gross investment, not net investment (net investment equals gross investment minus depreciation). In 2006, for example, depreciation, which is also called the *capital consumption allowance*, was $1,576.9 billion, two-thirds of gross investment.[4]

government purchases goods and services that are the part of current output that goes to the government sector—the federal government as well as state and local governments

The next component of GDP in the table is **government purchases** of goods and services. This is the share of the current output bought by the government sector, which includes the federal government as well as state and local governments. It is important to note that not all government expenditures are part of GDP because not all government expenditures represent a demand for currently produced goods and services.

[4]In 1933, depreciation was $7.6 billion. Because gross investment was only $1.7 billion, *net* investment was negative. This means that the capital stock declined in that year because gross investment was insufficient to replace the portion of the capital stock that wore out.

Government transfer payments to individuals (e.g., Social Security payments) and government interest payments are examples of expenditures that are not included in GDP. The table shows that government's share of GDP has increased in the post–World War II period relative to the prewar period. In 1929, government purchases of goods and services were 9.1 percent of total output. Not surprisingly, in 1945, the government component of output, swollen by the military budget during World War II, rose to 42 percent. In the postwar period, the government sector did not return to its prewar size. Government purchases of goods and services were approximately 20 percent of GDP in 1960 and 1990. Between 1990 and 2006, there was a slight decline to 19 percent of GDP. Trends in the size of the government budget—both purchases of goods and services and other components not included in the national income accounts—are analyzed in a later chapter when we consider *fiscal* or government budget policy.

net exports
total (gross) exports minus imports

The final component of GDP given in Table 2-1 is **net exports**. Net exports equal total (gross) exports minus imports. These items represent the direct contribution of the foreign sector to GDP. Gross exports are currently produced goods and services sold to foreign buyers. They are a part of GDP. Imports are purchases by domestic buyers of goods and services produced abroad and should not be counted in GDP. Imported goods and services are, however, included in the consumption, investment, and government spending totals in GDP. Therefore, we need to subtract the value of imports to arrive at the total value of domestically produced goods and services. Net exports remain as the (net) direct effect of foreign-sector transactions on GDP. As the table shows, net exports were strongly negative in 2006, reflecting the large U.S. trade deficit.

Read Perspectives 2-1.

2.3 NATIONAL INCOME

We turn now to the income side of the national accounts. In computing national income, our starting point is the GNP total, not GDP. The reason is that, as explained earlier, GNP includes income earned abroad by U.S. residents and firms but excludes earnings of foreign residents and firms from production in the United States. This is the proper starting point because we want a measure of the income of U.S. residents and firms.

To go from GDP to GNP, we add foreign earnings of U.S. residents and firms. We then subtract earnings in the United States by foreign residents and firms. This calculation results in a GNP of $13,296.5 billion compared with a GDP of $13,246.6 billion. As noted previously, there is little difference between these two production measures for the United States.

national income
sum of the earnings of all factors of production that come from current production

National income is the sum of factor earnings from current production of goods and services. Factor earnings are incomes of factors of production: land, labor, and capital. Each dollar of GNP is one dollar of final sales, and if there were no charges against GNP other than factor incomes, GNP and national income would be equal. There are, in fact, some other charges against GNP that cause national income and GNP to diverge, but the two concepts are still closely related. The adjustments required to go from GNP to national income, with figures for the year 2006, are shown in Table 2-2.

PERSPECTIVES 2-1

WHAT GDP IS NOT

GDP is the most comprehensive measure of a nation's economic activity. Policymakers use GDP figures to monitor short-run fluctuations in economic activity as well as long-run growth trends. It is worthwhile, however, to recognize important limitations of the GDP concept.

NONMARKET PRODUCTIVE ACTIVITIES ARE LEFT OUT

Because goods and services are evaluated at market prices in GDP, nonmarket production is left out (e.g., noted earlier, for instance, homemaker services). Intercountry comparisons of GDP overstate the gap in production between highly industrialized countries and less-developed nations, where largely agrarian nonmarket production is of greater importance.

THE UNDERGROUND ECONOMY IS LEFT OUT

Also left out of GDP are illegal economic activities and legal activities that are not reported to avoid paying taxes—the *underground economy.* Gambling and the drug trade are examples of the former. Activities not reported to avoid paying taxes take many forms; for example, repairmen who are paid in cash for services may under-report or fail to report the income. It is hard to estimate the size of the underground economy for obvious reasons. Rough estimates for the United States range from 5 to 15 percent of GDP.

GDP IS NOT A WELFARE MEASURE

GDP measures production of goods and services; it is not a measure of welfare or even of material well-being. For one thing, GDP gives no weight to leisure. If we all began to work 60-hour weeks, GDP would increase, yet would we be better off?

GDP also fails to subtract for some welfare costs of production. For example, if production of electricity causes acid rain, and consequently water pollution and dying forests, we count the production of electricity in GDP but do not subtract the economic loss from the pollution. In fact, if the government spends money to try to clean up the pollution, we count that too!

GDP is a useful measure of the overall level of economic activity, not of welfare.

GDP AND HAPPINESS

If it is not a welfare measure, one would not expect GDP to measure happiness. In recent years, however, there has been a great deal of interest in the relationship, or lack of relationship, between GDP and happiness. Surveys show that GDP and happiness, measured by "life satisfaction," have little relationship. People in Ghana are more satisfied with their lives than people in the Unites States; those in Nigeria are as satisfied as those in France. While surveys may be unreliable, other evidence also indicates little relationship between GDP and various measures of happiness. Perhaps relative income in a society is more important than absolute income. Alternatively, income relative to past income may matter. In surveys early in this century, people in the former Soviet republics were least satisfied with their lives. Their incomes had on average declined.

In the Himalayan kingdom of Bhutan, the government has focused on gross national happiness (GNH), not GDP. The United Nations provides indices of social welfare as alternatives to standard measures of GDP. It would take us too far afield to consider these alternatives, but note that happiness is another thing that GDP is not.

TABLE 2-2 Relationship of GNP and National Income, 2006 (billions of dollars)

GNP	13,276.5
Minus: Depreciation	1,576.9
Net national product	11,699.6
Minus: Indirect taxes and other	992.7
National income	10,706.9

SOURCE: Bureau of Economic Analysis, Department of Commerce.

The first charge against GNP that is not included in national income is depreciation. The portion of the capital stock used up must be subtracted from final sales before national income is computed; depreciation represents a cost of production, not factor income. Making this subtraction gives us **net national product (NNP)**, the net production measures referred to earlier. From this total, both indirect taxes—sales and excise taxes—and the net amount of some additional items labeled "other" in the table are subtracted to yield national income. An indirect tax such as a sales tax represents a discrepancy between the market price of a product, which includes the tax (the amount entered in GNP), and the proceeds of the seller, from which factor incomes are paid. The "other" category in Table 2-2 includes minor adjustments for additional discrepancies between factor earnings and the market prices of items included in GNP.

net national product GNP minus depreciation

Figure 2-1 shows the components of national income (factor payments) as shares of the total for 1959 and for 2006. In 2006 labor's share, which includes wages and salaries as well as supplements (benefits), was 64 percent of national income. This is not

FIGURE 2-1 Shares of National Income

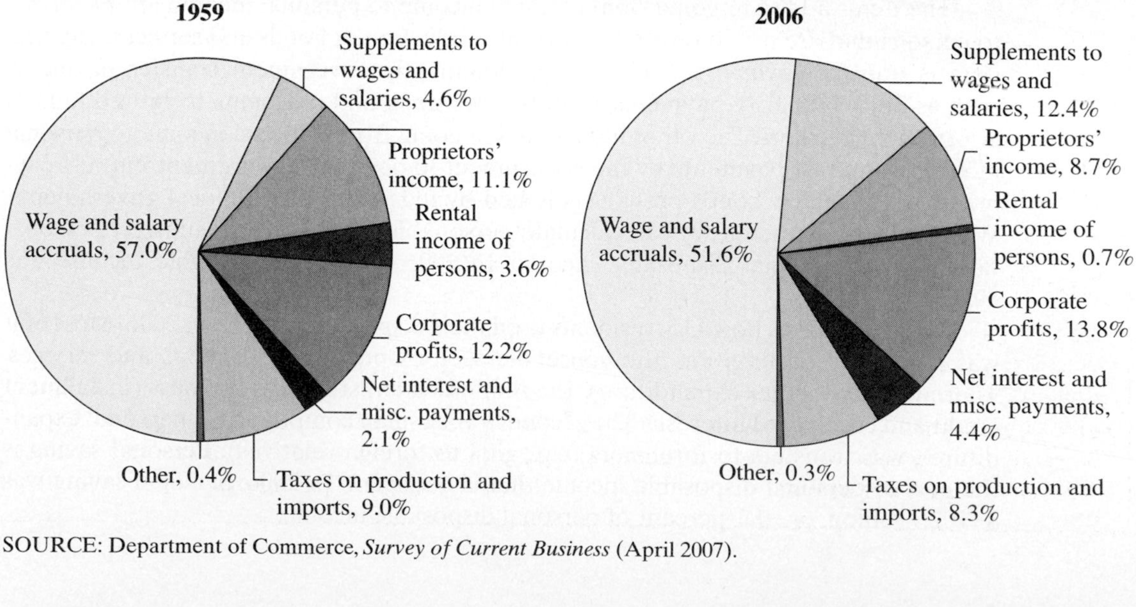

SOURCE: Department of Commerce, *Survey of Current Business* (April 2007).

much different from the percentage in 1959. Today a greater part of labor compensation is, however, in benefits and less in wages and salaries.

Corporate profits were between 12 and 14 percent of national income in both years. The other main components of national income are proprietors' income, which is the income of unincorporated businesses, rental income, and interest income. (Figure 2-1 also shows the tax component that was netted out in Table 2-2.)

2.4 PERSONAL AND DISPOSABLE PERSONAL INCOME

National income measures income earned from current production of goods and services. For some purposes, however, it is useful to have a measure of income received by *persons* regardless of source. For example, consumption expenditures by households are influenced by income. The relevant income concept is all income received by persons. Also, we want a measure of income after deducting personal tax payments. **Personal income** is the national income accounts measure of the income received by persons from all sources. When we subtract personal tax payments from personal income, we get disposable (after-tax) personal income.

personal income
measure of income received by persons from all sources

To go from national income to personal income, we subtract elements of national income that are not received by persons and add income of persons from sources other than current production of goods and services. The details of the necessary adjustments are not central to our focus. In brief, they are the following. The first of the main items subtracted from national income in going to personal income are the parts of corporate profits in the national income accounts that are not paid out as dividends to persons. These portions include corporate profits tax payments and undistributed profits (retained earnings). Also subtracted from national income in computing personal income are contributions to Social Security by the employer and employee. These payroll taxes are included in the employee compensation term in national income but go to the government, not directly to persons.

The items added in going from national income to personal income are payments to persons that are not in return for current production of goods and services. The first item is *transfer payments.* These are predominantly government transfer payments such as Social Security payments, veterans' pensions, and payments to retired federal government workers. The other item added in going from national income to personal income is interest payments by the government to persons. Government interest payments are made on bonds previously issued by federal, state, and local governments. With these adjustments, we can calculate personal income. We then subtract personal taxes to get personal disposable income. In 2006, personal disposable income was \$9,522.8 billion.

Table 2-3 shows how U.S. residents used their disposable income in 2006. Most of it was spent for consumption, the household sector's purchases of goods and services. There were two other expenditures. The first was interest paid to business (installment credit and credit card interest). The second, a very small component of personal expenditures, was transfers to foreigners (e.g., gifts to foreign relatives). Personal saving is the part of personal disposable income that is not spent. In 2006, personal saving was \$−102.7 billion, or −1.1 percent of personal disposable income.

TABLE 2-3 Disposition of Personal Disposable Income, 2006 (billions of dollars)

Personal disposable income	9,522.8
Less	
Personal consumption expenditures	9,268.9
Interest paid to business	230.3
Personal transfer payments to foreigners (net)	126.3
Personal saving	−102.7

SOURCE: Bureau of Economic Analysis, Department of Commerce.

A negative personal saving rate means that personal outlays exceeded disposable income. The year 2006 was only the second time that this occurred in the post–World War period. The other year was 2005. A negative personal saving rate does not mean that national saving was zero. There is also saving by the business sector. Nor does a negative personal saving rate imply that household wealth was declining in 2006. The price of existing assets held by households was rising during that year. Capital gains on existing assets are not included in national (or personal) income. The low, and in 2005–6 negative, saving rate has, however, been a cause of concern in the United States. We take up this question later in the book.

Read Perspectives 2-2.

2.5 SOME NATIONAL INCOME ACCOUNTING IDENTITIES

The interrelationships among GDP, national income, and personal income form the basis for some accounting definitions or *identities* that are used to construct the macroeconomic models considered in later chapters. In deriving these identities, we simplify the accounting structure by ignoring a number of items discussed previously.

The simplifications we impose are as follows:

1. The foreign sector will be omitted. This means that we drop the net exports term from GDP (see Table 2-1) and the net foreign transfers item from personal outlays in breaking down the disposition of personal income (see Table 2-3). The foreign sector is reintroduced into our models later, when we consider questions of international macroeconomics. In excluding the foreign sector, we also exclude foreign earnings of U.S. residents and firms, as well as U.S. earnings of foreign residents and foreign-owned firms. GNP and GDP are thus equal. The terms *GNP* and *GDP* are used interchangeably except where we reintroduce the foreign sector.
2. Indirect taxes and the other discrepancies between GNP and national income are ignored (see Table 2-2). We assume that national income and national product or output are the same. The terms *national income* and *output* are used interchangeably throughout this book.
3. Depreciation is ignored (except where explicitly noted). Therefore, gross and net national product are identical.
4. Several simplifications are made in the relationship between national income and personal disposable income. We assume that all corporate profits are paid out as dividends; there are no retained earnings or corporate tax payments. We assume

PERSPECTIVES 2-2

NATIONAL INCOME ACCOUNTS FOR ENGLAND AND WALES IN 1688

National income accounts provide a profile of the economic life of a country. Although it is only in the post–World War II years that governments systematically kept these accounts, there are estimates from previous eras. These are of interest in charting the changes that economies have undergone.

Tables 2-4 and 2-5 show the national GNP and income accounts for England and Wales (combined) for 1688, the year of the Glorious Revolution. They were compiled by Gregory King, and more than a century passed before administrative records allowed such calculations to be repeated. In terms of completeness and consistency, King's calculations remained unique until the twentieth century.[a]

Table 2-4 shows that for England and Wales in 1688 relative to the 2006 U.S. economy, consumption was a much larger fraction of total national product (90 percent versus 70 percent). Investment and government spending were much smaller fractions of output. Imports and exports were each about 10 percent of GNP, somewhat smaller than in most modern economies. Still, this was an "open" economy with significant foreign trade.

The figures in Table 2-5 for the components of national income show that in England and Wales in 1688, wages and salaries comprised a much smaller fraction and rents, profits, and interest a much larger one relative to the U.S. economy today. Wages and salaries were 37 percent of national income versus a current 64 percent. Rents, profit, and interest were nearly three times higher as a share of national income in England and Wales in 1688 than in the United States today.

Overall, the picture of England and Wales in 1688 is one of an agrarian economy. It is estimated that 70 to 80 percent of the population was engaged in agriculture. But it was an open economy, and there was significant investment. The picture is not one of a subsistence economy. Estimates from other sources suggest that per capita income at the time was perhaps one-eighth of that for England and Wales today.

TABLE 2-4 GNP of England and Wales, 1688 (millions of pounds)

Consumption	46.0
Investment	1.7
Government purchases	2.4
Exports	5.1
Less imports	−4.4
GNP	50.8

TABLE 2-5 Components of National Income for England and Wales, 1688 (millions of pounds)

Wages and salaries	17.7
Rents	13.0
Profits and interest	14.7
Cottagers and paupers	2.6
National income	48.0

[a]The estimates in the tables are taken from Phyllis Deane and W. A. Cole, *British Economic Growth: 1688–1959* (London: Cambridge University Press, 1967, p. 2). The estimates are based on King's original manuscripts and worksheets as well as other contemporaneous sources.

that all taxes, including Social Security contributions, are assessed directly on households. Consequently, we can specify personal disposable income as national income (or output) minus tax payments (Tx) plus government transfers (Tr), which include government interest payments. Letting *net* taxes (T) equal tax payments minus transfers,

$$T \equiv \text{Tx} - \text{Tr} \tag{2.1}$$

we have (personal) disposable income Y_D equal to national income (Y) minus net taxes:

$$Y_D \equiv Y - \text{Tx} + \text{Tr} \equiv Y - T$$

With these simplifications, we have the following accounting identities. GDP (Y) is defined as

$$Y \equiv C + I_r + G \tag{2.2}$$

that is, as consumption (C) plus *realized investment* (I_r) plus government purchases of goods and services (G).[5] The subscript (r) on the investment term is included because we want to distinguish between this realized investment total that appears in the national income accounts and the *desired* level of investment spending.

From the income side of the national income accounts, again using simplifications 1 to 4 *and ignoring interest paid to business* (in Table 2-3), we have the identity

$$Y_D \equiv Y - T \equiv C + S \tag{2.3}$$

which states that, with the simplifying assumptions we have made, all disposable income, which equals national income (Y) minus *net* tax payments ($T \equiv$ tax payments minus transfers), goes for consumption expenditures or personal saving (S). We can write (2.3) as

$$Y \equiv C + S + T$$

and, because Y is both national income and output, we can combine (2.2) and (2.3) to write

$$C + I_r + G \equiv Y \equiv C + S + T$$

This identity states that expenditures on GDP ($C + I_r + G$) by definition equal dispositions of national income ($C + S + T$).

2.6 MEASURING PRICE CHANGES: REAL VERSUS NOMINAL GDP

nominal GDP
GDP measured in current dollars

So far, the figures we have been discussing are for **nominal GDP**, which measures currently produced goods and services evaluated at current market prices. GDP is the value of currently produced goods and services measured in market prices, so it will change when the overall price

[5]It is important to distinguish identities such as (2.1) and (2.2), which are indicated by the three-bar symbol ($\equiv$), and equations, which are indicated with the usual equal sign (=). Identities are relationships that follow from accounting or other definitions and therefore hold for any and all values of the variables.

level changes as well as when the actual volume of production changes. For many purposes, we want a measure of output that varies only with the quantity of goods produced. Such a measure would, for example, be most closely related to employment.

The GDP measure that changes only when quantities, not prices, change is termed *real GDP*. The traditional way of constructing real GDP is to measure output in terms of constant prices from a base year. Using 2000, for example, we can compute the value of GDP in 1960, 1980, or 2006 in terms of the price level or value of the dollar in 2000. Changes in GDP in 2000-valued dollars then provide a measure of quantity changes between these years. Measuring real GDP in terms of prices from a base year, however, has several shortcomings, which we will discuss. Consequently, in 1995 the U.S. Bureau of Labor Statistics began to construct an alternative real GDP measure called *chain-weighted real GDP*. We consider the two procedures in turn.

Real GDP in Prices from a Base Year

Column 1 of Table 2-6 shows nominal GDP for selected years. Column 2 shows the value of real GDP as measured in 2000 prices for each of these years. In 2000, real and nominal income are the same because base-year prices are current prices. In prior years, when current prices were lower than 2000 prices, real GDP was higher than nominal GDP. Conversely, in the years after 2000, when prices were higher, nominal GDP exceeded real GDP.

Table 2-6 shows that real GDP often behaves quite differently from nominal GDP. Nominal GDP changes whenever the quantity of goods produced changes *or* when the market price of those goods changes; real GDP changes only when production changes. Therefore, when prices are changing dramatically, the movements of the two measures diverge sharply. The table shows, for example, that while nominal GDP rose by approximately $250 billion from 1973 to 1975, real GDP declined. Again, between 1979 and 1980, there was a rapid increase in nominal GDP but a fall in real GDP. In

TABLE 2-6 Nominal GDP, Real GDP, and Implicit GDP Deflator, Selected Years

	Nominal GDP (Billions of Current Dollars)	*Real GDP (Billions of 2000 Dollars)*	*Implicit GDP Deflator ((Column 1/Column 2)*100)*
1960	526.4	2,501.8	21.0
1970	1,038.5	3,771.9	27.5
1973	1,382.7	4,341.5	31.8
1974	1,500.0	4,319.6	34.7
1975	1,638.3	4,311.2	38.0
1979	2,563.3	5,173.4	49.5
1980	2,789.5	5,161.7	54.0
1990	5,803.1	7,112.5	81.6
1996	7,816.9	8,328.9	93.9
1998	8,747.0	9,066.9	96.5
2000	9,817.0	9,817.0	100.0
2002	10,469.6	10,048.8	104.2
2005	12,455.8	11,048.6	112.7
2006	13,246.6	11,415.3	116.0

SOURCE: Bureau of Economic Analysis, Department of Commerce.

both periods, real GDP declined because production of goods and services declined. Prices, however, rose rapidly enough in these inflationary years to make nominal GDP rise.

Now consider the numbers in column 3 of Table 2-6, which gives the ratio of nominal GDP to real GDP (nominal GDP ÷ real GDP), where the ratio is multiplied by 100 (following the procedure in the national income accounts). The ratio of nominal GDP to real GDP is a measure of the value of current production in current prices (e.g., in 2006) relative to the value of the *same* goods and services in prices for the base year (2000). Because the same goods and services appear at the top and bottom, the ratio of nominal GDP to real GDP is just the ratio of the current price level of goods and services relative to the price level in the base year. It is a measure of the aggregate (or overall) price level, which in the previous chapter we called a **price index**. This index of the prices of goods and services in GDP is called the **implicit GDP deflator**.

price index measures the aggregate price level relative to a chosen base year

implicit GDP deflator index of the prices of goods and services included in GDP

We measure changes in the aggregate price level by comparing values of the implicit GDP deflator in different years. First, compare the implicit price deflator between the base year, 2000, and 2006. In the base year, real and nominal GDP are the same, and the implicit price deflator has a value of 100. From Table 2-6, we see that in 2006 the value of the implicit GDP deflator was 116. This means that GDP at current prices in 2006 (nominal GDP) was 16 percent higher than the same goods and services valued at 2000 prices. The aggregate price level, as measured by the GDP deflator, rose 16 percent between 2000 and 2006.

We can also use the implicit GDP deflator to measure price changes between two years, neither of which is the base year. Between 2005 and 2006, the implicit GDP deflator rose from 112.7 to 116. As measured by this index, the percentage rise in the aggregate price level (or rate of inflation) between 2005 and 2006 was

$$[(116.0 - 112.7) \div 112.7] \times 100 = 2.9\%$$

Before going on, consider how the GDP deflator got its name. The ratio of nominal to real GDP is termed a *deflator* because we can divide nominal GDP by this ratio to correct for the effect of inflation on GDP—to deflate GDP. This follows because

$$\text{GDP deflator} = \frac{\text{nominal GDP}}{\text{real GDP}}$$

$$\text{real GDP} = \frac{\text{nominal GDP}}{\text{GDP deflator}}$$

The GDP deflator is an *implicit* price index in that we first construct a quantity measure, real GDP, and then compare the movement in GDP in current and constant dollars to gauge the changes in prices. We do not *explicitly* measure the average movement in prices. Two examples of explicit price indices are considered in the next section.

Chain-Weighted Real GDP

Two problems arise when real GDP is measured using prices in a base year. One problem is that every time the base year changes, the weights given to different sectors are changed and history is rewritten. When, for example, the base year was changed from 1996 to 2000, the recessions of the 1970s took on a slightly different pattern.

A second, more serious problem involves changes in relative prices and consequent substitutions among the product categories contained in GDP. For example, in the years since 2000, the relative price of personal computers has been falling, and consumers have shifted expenditures toward computer purchases. If in calculating real GDP we use the higher 2000 prices to weight the computer component, computers will be overestimated as a GDP component.

To address these problems, the Bureau of Economic Analysis (BEA), the government agency that maintains the national income accounts, in 1995 introduced a new chain-weighted measure of real GDP. Instead of using prices in a base year as weights, the chain-weighted measure uses the average of prices in a given year and prices in the previous year. Thus, real GDP in 2006 is calculated using 2005 and 2006 prices as weights. In effect, the base moves forward each year to eliminate the problem caused by relative price–induced substitutions such as those in the computer example. Moreover, history will not be rewritten by arbitrary changes in the base year. Once the chain-weighted measure has been calculated, it remains fixed.

2.7 THE CONSUMER PRICE INDEX AND THE PRODUCER PRICE INDEX

Because the GDP deflator measures changes in the prices of all currently produced goods and services, it is the most comprehensive measure of the rate of price change. Two other price indices are widely reported, however, and have their uses and advantages.

consumer price index (CPI) measures the retail prices of a fixed "market basket" of several thousand goods and services purchased by households

The **consumer price index (CPI)** measures the retail prices of a fixed "market basket" of several thousand goods and services purchased by households. The CPI is an explicit price index in the sense that it directly measures movements in the weighted average of the prices of the goods and services in the market basket through time. The CPI is the price index most relevant to consumers because it measures the prices of goods and services directly purchased by them. Many government pensions, including Social Security benefits, and some wage rates are indexed to the CPI, meaning that they have provisions for automatic increases geared to increases in the CPI.

producer price index (PPI) measures the wholesale prices of approximately 3,000 items

Another widely reported price index is the **producer price index (PPI)**, which measures the wholesale prices of approximately 3,000 items. Because items sold at the wholesale level include many raw materials and semifinished goods, movements in the PPI signal future movements in retail prices, such as those measured in the CPI. Both the CPI and the PPI have the advantage of being available monthly, whereas the implicit GDP deflator is available only quarterly.

Figure 2-2 shows the annual inflation rates for the years 1967–2004 as measured by the three price indices we have discussed. In terms of broad movement in the inflation rate, the three indices show similar patterns. The acceleration of inflation in the 1973–75 and 1979–80 periods is evident in each series, as is the disinflation in the post-1980 years. There are, however, some differences in the three series that reflect their different composition. The PPI, for example, gives a larger weight to raw materials than

FIGURE 2-2 Three Measures of Inflation, 1967–2004

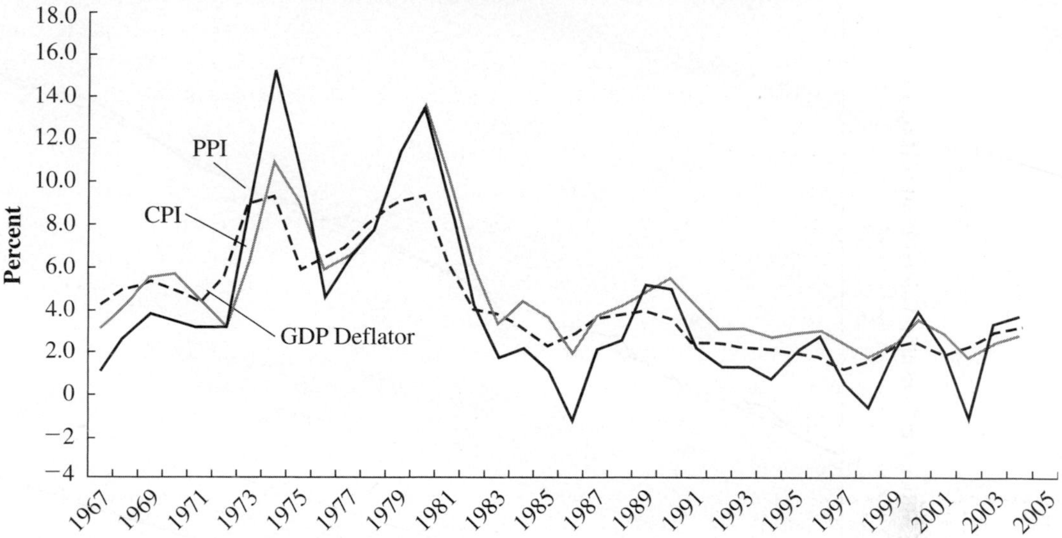

either of the others and therefore rose substantially more than the CPI or GDP deflator in 1973 and 1974, when agricultural and crude oil prices skyrocketed. Conversely, when these raw material prices declined during the 1982–86 period and again in 1996–97, the decline in the inflation rate registered by the PPI was the largest among the three inflation measures.

2.8 MEASURES OF CYCLICAL VARIATION IN OUTPUT

Most of this book focuses on short-run, or cyclical, movements in output and employment—fluctuations over periods of perhaps one to four years. Over these periods, fluctuations in output and employment come primarily from variations in actual output around **potential output**, which is defined as the level of output that the economy could produce at high rates of resource utilization. Such short-run movements in output consist of changes in the utilization rates of labor and capital. It is in the longer run that growth of potential output, which implies growth in the available quantity of factors of production (capital and labor), becomes an important determinant of output growth. We have already discussed the measurement of actual real output (GDP); what remains is to explain the measurement of potential real output and thus the deviations of *actual* GDP from *potential* GDP.

potential output level that would be reached if productive resources (labor and capital) were being used at benchmark high levels

A problem arises in measuring potential output. What are sustainable high levels of resource allocation? In the 1960s, the President's Council of Economic Advisors, which at the time compiled the official estimates of potential output, simply estimated the level of output that corresponded to a 4 percent unemployment rate. In later years,

FIGURE 2-3 Potential (Trend) and Actual GDP

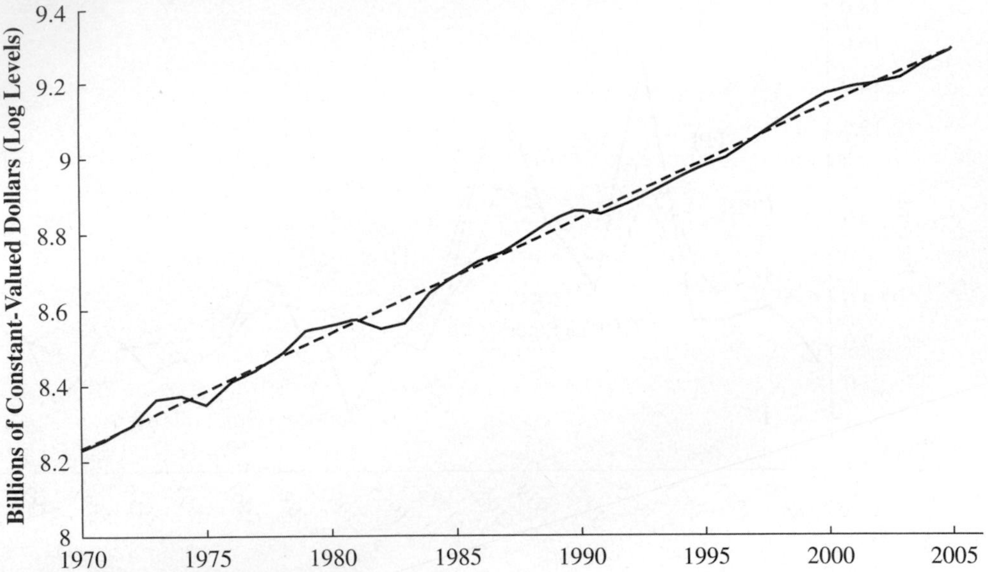

economists and policymakers concluded, based in part on the experience of the 1960s, that 4 percent was too low an unemployment rate to be sustained without a buildup of inflationary pressure. In the 1980s, an unemployment rate in the range of 5.5 to 6 percent was often used as a benchmark high-employment level. But in recent years, there has been less certainty that any one unemployment rate is an appropriate benchmark; by 2000, for example, the unemployment rate had dipped below 4 percent without any apparent development of inflationary pressure.

Fortunately for our current purpose of broadly describing the cyclical movements in output over recent decades, the precise measure of a benchmark high-employment level, and thus of potential output, is not important. For policy questions concerning how low we might expect the unemployment rate to be reduced, the proper benchmark unemployment rate is important.

Figure 2-3 shows plots of actual and potential GDP, where potential GDP is measured simply by the trend (or average) rate of growth in GDP. Because, as discussed in Chapter 1, there was a slowdown in trend growth in the post-1970 period, we restrict our discussion to the 1970–2006 period.

The brief recession of 1970 was followed by a robust recovery that pushed output above the trend line by 1973. Then came the severe recession of 1973–75, when output fell nearly 5 percent below potential output. There was another sharp drop when trend output fell below potential output during the recession of 1981–82. This was followed by a long period of expansion and then a less severe recession in 1990–91. The period 1991–2000 was one of sustained expansion. GDP then declined in a recession in 2001. The recovery that followed has lasted through 2007.

Fluctuations in actual output around potential output, as illustrated in Figure 2-2, together with the associated variations in other macroeconomic aggregates, form the subject matter for much of the analysis to come.

Read Perspectives 2-3.

PERSPECTIVES 2-3

DATING BUSINESS CYCLES

We have talked about recessions as periods when actual output falls well below potential output and unemployment rises above the high-employment benchmark, but precisely how do we measure when recessions begin and end? For example, if output begins to decline in January, rises a bit in February, and then begins a sustained decline in March, did the recession begin in January or in March? Also, the date when unemployment begins to increase may not coincide with the start of the output decline.

There is no precise way to date recessions or expansions. Judgments must be made. In the United States, the closest we come to an official dating of business cycles is that done by the Business Cycle Dating Group of the National Bureau of Economic Research (NBER), a private research organization. Table 2-7 shows the NBER dating of post–World War II U.S. business cycles. The *peak* measures the end of an expansion, and the *trough* gives the end of each recession. On average, expansions lasted just under 50 months and recessions just over 10 months. None of the postwar recessions came near the 43-month contraction period that began the Great Depression of the 1930s. The economic expansion that began in March 1991 and ended in March 2001 was the longest of the post–World War II period (120 months).

TABLE 2-7 Postwar U.S. Business Cycles

Peak	*Trough*	*Length (Months) of Expansion*	*Recession*
November 1948	October 1949	37	11
July 1953	May 1954	45	10
August 1957	April 1958	39	8
April 1960	February 1961	24	10
December 1969	November 1970	106	11
November 1973	March 1975	36	16
January 1980	July 1980	58	6
July 1981	November 1982	12	16
July 1990	March 1991	92	8
March 2001	November 2001	120	8

2.9 Conclusion

monetary policy central bank's use of control of the money supply and interest rates to influence the level of economic activity

We have now discussed the real-world counterparts to the central variables that appear in the models of the next section—with one exception. The exception is money. The quantity of money is a key variable in all the models we consider later. Control of the quantity of money through **monetary policy** is one important type of stabilization policy. The definition of money turns out to be somewhat more complicated than it seems at first glance and is best put off until later, when questions of money supply and demand are examined in detail. For now, it is adequate to use

money whatever is commonly accepted as payment in exchange for goods and services (and payment of debts and taxes)

the term **money** in our models to mean the stock of currency plus "checkable" deposits (deposits on which checks may be written).

We return to questions of measurement at several later points. In addition to further discussion of the empirical definition of money, we need to consider foreign exchange rates and measures of our international transactions (Chapter 14) and go into more detail concerning the federal government budget (Chapter 18). Some other variables (e.g., the wage rate and the interest rate) are defined as they are encountered in our analysis.

This chapter began with one of Charles Dickens's characters admonishing a teacher to "Stick to the Facts." But Conrad's Lord Jim complains "They wanted facts. Facts! They demanded facts from him, as if facts could explain anything." At this point we turn to explaining, rather than just measuring, the behavior of macroeconomic variables.

KEY TERMS

- gross domestic product (GDP) 14
- capital goods 14
- depreciation 15
- consumption 15
- investment 16
- government purchases 16
- net exports 17
- national income (NI) 17
- net national product 19
- personal income 20
- nominal GDP 23
- pricc index 25
- implicit GDP deflator 25
- consumer price index (CPI) 26
- producer price index (PPI) 26
- potential output 27
- monetary policy 29
- money 30

REVIEW QUESTIONS AND PROBLEMS

1. Define the term *gross domestic product.* Explain which transactions in the economy are included in GDP.
2. What is the difference between GNP and GDP?
3. Define the term *national income.* Why is national income not equal to GNP?
4. Define the terms *personal income* and *personal disposable income.* Conceptually, how do these income measures differ from national income? Of what use are these measures?
5. Three price indices were considered in this chapter: the GDP deflator, the CPI, and the PPI. Explain the differences among these different measures of the price level.
6. Using the data in Table 2-6, compute the percentage change in the price level between 1960 and 1970, between 1973 and 1996, and between 1960 and 2006.
7. Explain the concept of chain-weighted real GDP. What problems with the previous measure of real GDP led to the introduction of this new measure?
8. Explain the concept of *potential output.* Why is potential output difficult to measure?
9. Suppose a worker's income was $15,000 in 1960 and $45,000 in 2006. Using the GDP deflator as a price index, calculate whether the worker's real income had increased or decreased over this period.

PART TWO

Classical Economics and the Keynesian Revolution

The chapters in this part begin our analysis of macroeconomic models. We start with the classical model and then turn to the Keynesian model that developed as an attack on the classical system—the so-called Keynesian revolution.

CHAPTER 3

Classical Macroeconomics (I): Output and Employment

3.1 THE STARTING POINT

The term *macroeconomics* originated in the 1930s. That decade witnessed substantial progress in the study of aggregative economic questions. The forces that determine income, employment, and prices had been receiving greater attention since the turn of the twentieth century, after a long period in which microeconomic questions dominated the field of economics. The world Depression that began in 1929 added urgency to the study of macroeconomic questions. The products of this research were theories of the "business cycle" and policy prescriptions for stabilizing economic activity. One theory and set of policy conclusions swept the field and became a new orthodoxy in macroeconomic thought. The book containing this theory was *The General Theory of Employment, Interest and Money*, by John Maynard Keynes, and the process of change in economic thinking that resulted from this work has been called the *Keynesian revolution*. But revolution against what? What was the old orthodoxy? Keynes termed it "classical economics," and it is this body of macroeconomic thought that we study in this chapter and the next.

The ideas that formed the Keynesian revolution, as well as the evolution of these ideas in the post-Keynesian period, are central to our analysis. A prerequisite for this analysis is a knowledge of the classical system that Keynes attacked. Classical theory also plays a positive role in the later development of macroeconomics. Although many early Keynesian writers viewed the classical theory as ready for the scrap heap of outmoded ideas, overreaction subsided with time, and modern Keynesian economics contains many ideas that originated with the classical economists. The classical model also provides the starting point for challenges that have been mounted against the Keynesian theory by *monetarists, new classical economists*, and *real business cycle theorists*.

Keynes used the term *classical* to refer to virtually all economists who had written on macroeconomic questions before 1936. More conventional terminology distinguishes between two periods in the development of economic theory before 1930. The first, termed *classical*, is the period dominated by the work of Adam Smith (*Wealth of Nations*, 1776), David Ricardo (*Principles of Political Economy*, 1st ed., 1817), and John Stuart Mill (*Principles of Political Economy*, 1st ed., 1848). The second, termed the *neoclassical period*, had as its most prominent English representatives Alfred Marshall (*Principles of Economics*, 8th ed., 1920) and A. C. Pigou (*The Theory of Unemployment*, 1933). Keynes believed that the macroeconomic theory of the two periods was homogeneous enough to be dealt with as a whole.

To classical economists, the equilibrium level of output at any time was a point of *full employment* or, in terms of the variables described in Chapter 2, a point when actual output was equal to potential output. Equilibrium for a variable refers to a state in which all the forces acting on that variable are in balance and, consequently, there is no tendency for the variable to move from that point. It was an important tenet of classical economists that only full-employment points could be positions of even short-run equilibrium. Absent full employment, classical economists assumed that forces not in balance were acting to bring output to the full-employment level. Classical equilibrium economics examined the factors that determined the level of full-employment output along with the associated levels of other important aggregates, such as employment, prices, wages, and interest rates.

3.2 THE CLASSICAL REVOLUTION

Classical economics emerged as a revolution against a body of economic doctrines known as *mercantilism*. Mercantilist thought was associated with the rise of the nation-state in Europe during the sixteenth and seventeenth centuries. Two tenets of mercantilism were (1) bullionism, a belief that the wealth and power of a nation were determined by its stock of precious metals, and (2) the belief in the need for state action to direct the development of the capitalist system.

Adherence to bullionism led countries to attempt to secure an excess of exports over imports in order to earn gold and silver through foreign trade. Methods used to secure this favorable balance of trade included export subsidies, import duties, and development of colonies to provide export markets. State action was believed to be necessary to cause the developing capitalist system to further the interests of the state. Foreign trade was carefully regulated, and the export of bullion was prohibited to serve the ends of bullionism. The use of state action was also advocated on a broader front to develop home industry, to reduce consumption of imported goods, and to develop both human and natural resources.

In contrast to the mercantilists, classical economists emphasized the importance of *real* factors in determining the "wealth of nations" and stressed the optimizing tendencies of the free market in the absence of state control. Classical analysis was primarily *real* analysis; the growth of an economy was the result of increased stocks of the factors of production and advances in techniques of production. Money played a role only in facilitating transactions as a *means of exchange*. Most questions in economics could be answered without analyzing the role of money. Classical economists mistrusted government and stressed the harmony of individual and national interests when the market was left unfettered by government regulations, except those necessary to ensure that the market remained competitive. Both of these aspects of classical economics—the stress on real factors and the belief in the efficacy of the free-market mechanism—developed in the course of controversies over long-run questions concerning the determinants of economic development. These classical positions on long-run issues were, however, important in shaping classical economists' views on short-run questions.

The attack on bullionism led classical economists to stress that money had no intrinsic value. Money was important only for the sake of the goods it could purchase. Classical economists focused on the role of money as a means of exchange. Another role money had played in the mercantilist view was as a spur to economic activity. In the short run, mercantilists argued, an increase in the quantity of money would lead to an increase in demand for commodities and would stimulate production and employment. For classical economists to ascribe this role to money in determining real variables, even in the short run, was dangerous in light of their deemphasis of the importance of money.

The classical attack on the mercantilist view of the need for state action to regulate the capitalist system also had implications for short-run macroeconomic analysis. One role for state action in the mercantilist view was to ensure that markets existed for all goods produced. Consumption, both domestic and foreign, must be encouraged to the extent that production advanced. The classical response is stated by John Stuart Mill:

> In opposition to these palpable absurdities it was triumphantly established by political economists that consumption never needs encouragement.[1]

As in other areas, classical economists felt that the free-market mechanism would work to provide markets for any goods that were produced: "The legislator, therefore, need not give himself any concern about consumption."[2] The classical doctrine was that, in the aggregate, production of a given quantity of output will generate sufficient demand for that output; there could never be a "want of buyers for all commodities."[3] Consequently, classical economists gave little explicit attention to factors that determine the overall demand for commodities, which in Chapter 1 we termed **aggregate demand**.

aggregate demand sum of the demands for current output by each of the buying sectors of the economy: households, businesses, the government, and foreign purchasers

Thus, two features of the classical analysis arose as part of the attack on mercantilism:

1. Classical economics stressed the role of real as opposed to monetary factors in determining output and employment. Money had a role in the economy only as a means of exchange.
2. Classical economics stressed the self-adjusting tendencies of the economy. Government policies to ensure an adequate demand for output were considered by classical economists to be unnecessary and generally harmful.

We turn now to the model constructed by classical economists to support these positions.

3.3 PRODUCTION

production function summarizes the relationship between total inputs and total outputs assuming a given technology

A central relationship in the classical model is the aggregate **production function**. The production function, which is based on the technology of individual firms, is a relationship between the level of output and the level of factor inputs. For each level of inputs, the production function shows the resulting level of output and is written as

$$Y = F(\overline{K}, N) \tag{3.1}$$

[1] J. S. Mill, "On the Influence of Consumption on Production," in *Essays on Economics and Society*, vol. 4 of *Collected Works* (Toronto: University of Toronto Press, 1967), p. 263.

[2] Ibid., p. 263.

[3] Ibid., p. 276.

TABLE 3-1 The Relationship Between Output, Fixed Capital Stock, and Labor

	N = Labor	*Y = Output*	$\Delta Y/\Delta N$ = *MPN*	
A	0	0		
B	1	10	10	Constant returns
C	2	20	10	
D	3	28	8	Diminishing returns
E	4	33	5	
F	5	34	1	
G	6	32	−2	Negative returns

On line A, 0 units of labor (N) are hired, and total output (Y) is 0.

On line B, 1 unit of labor (N) is hired, and total output (Y) is 10 units. $\Delta Y/\Delta N$, the change in output given a change in labor, is 10/1 = 10. This is the MPN. The MPN of worker 1 is 10, since output increased by 10 units when labor increased by 1 unit.

On line C, 2 workers are hired, and total output (Y) is 20 units. $\Delta Y/\Delta N$, the change in output given a change in labor, is (20 − 10)/1 = 10. The MPN of worker 2 is the same as the MPN of worker 1, since output increased by 10 units when labor increased by one unit. This is the area of constant returns to scale.

On line D, 3 workers are hired, and total output (Y) is 28 units. $\Delta Y/\Delta N$, the change in output given a change in labor, is (28 − 20)/1 = 8. The MPN of worker 3 is 8 units. The increase in output when worker 3 was hired is less than the MPN of worker 2.

This is the area of diminishing returns to scale. In this area on the production function, total output increases as an additional unit of labor is hired, but marginal output diminishes.

Output increases at a diminishing rate due to the law of diminishing returns.

This law states that as variable inputs (in this case, homogeneous labor) are added to a fixed input (the capital stock, which is being held constant), beyond some point, the amount by which output increases will diminish.

On line E, 4 workers are hired, and output (Y) is 33 units. The MPN of worker 4 is 5 units.

On line F, 5 workers are hired, and output (Y) is 34 units. The MPN of worker 5 is 1 unit.

On line G, 6 workers are hired, and output (Y) is 32 units. This is the area of negative returns. The MPN of worker 6 is negative (−2). At this point, both total output and marginal output decreased. Firms would not hire in the area of negative returns to scale.

where Y is output, $\overline{K}$ is the stock of capital (plant and equipment), and N is the quantity of the homogeneous labor input.[4] For the short run, the stock of capital is assumed to be fixed, as indicated by the bar over the symbol for capital. The state of technology and the population are also assumed to be constant over the period considered. For this short-run period, output varies solely with variations in the labor input (N) drawn from the fixed population.

The numbers in Table 3-1 illustrate the fundamental relationship between a change in labor input and the resulting change in output, holding the capital stock $\overline{K}$ constant. The values from Table 3-1 are plotted in Figures 3-1*a* and 3-1*b*.

[4]Functional notation such as that used in (3.1) will be used at numerous points in our analysis. In each case, such equations mean that the function involved (in this case F) is a relationship that determines a unique value of the left-hand variable (in this case Y) for each combination of the levels of the *arguments* of the function (in this case K and N).

FIGURE 3-1 Production Function and MPN Curves

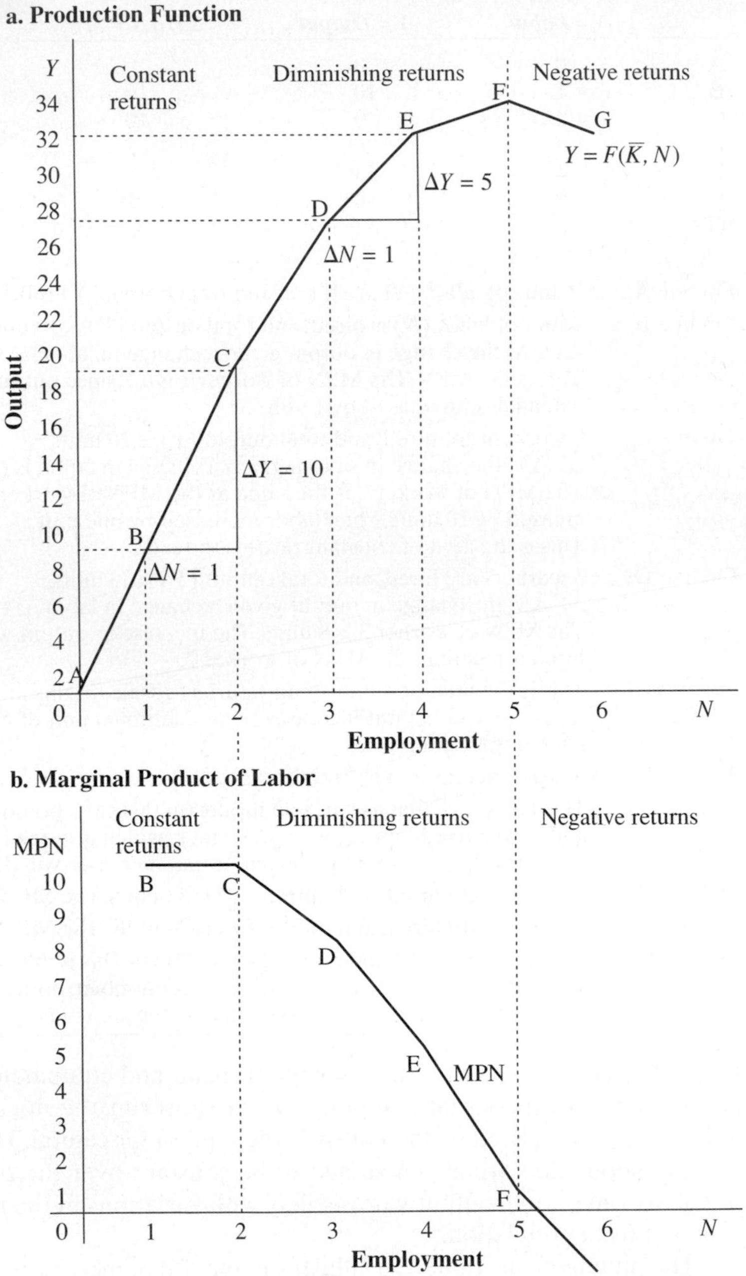

In Figure 3-1*a*, the production function, $Y = F(\overline{K}, N)$, indicates the output that would be produced by the efficient utilization of each level of labor input. As drawn, the production function has several characteristics. At low levels of labor input, the function is a straight line. The slope of the line gives the increase in output for a given increment in labor input, so this straight-line (constant-slope) portion of the production function exhibits constant returns to scale. For very low levels of labor utilization, it might be presumed that additional workers could be applied to a given amount of plant and equipment without a fall in the productivity of the last worker hired. For the most part, however, we consider situations where adding additional labor will result in increased total output, but where the size of the increases to output declines as more labor is employed. This portion of the production function exhibits diminishing returns to scale. Negative returns to scale occur when additional labor input results in decreased total output. Firms would not operate on this portion of the production function, since hiring additional labor results in a decrease in total output.

In Figure 3-1*b*, we plot the change in output given a change in labor input. This is the **marginal product of labor (MPN)**. The MPN is the slope of the production function ($\Delta Y/\Delta N$) in Figure 3-1*a*.[5]

marginal product of labor (MPN) the addition to total output due to the addition of a unit of labor (the quantity of other inputs being held constant)

In the range of constant returns to scale, as N increases, the slope of the line is flat. As more workers are hired, however, the slope becomes negative, indicating that while the marginal product of each worker hired is positive, it is less than the marginal product of the previous worker. This area represents diminishing returns to scale. The marginal product of the additional worker is below the horizontal axis in the area of negative returns to scale.

The short-run production function plotted in Figure 3-1*a* is a technological relationship that determines the level of output given the level of labor input (employment). The capital stock, along with the existing level of technology and skill level of the workforce, is being held constant. Classical economists assumed that the quantity of labor employed would be determined by the forces of demand and supply in the labor market.

3.4 EMPLOYMENT

The hallmark of classical labor market analysis is the assumption that the market works well. Firms and individual workers optimize. They have perfect information about relevant prices. There are no barriers to the adjustment of money wages; the market *clears*.

Labor Demand

The purchasers of labor services are firms. To see how the aggregate demand for labor is determined, we begin by considering the demand for labor on the part of an individual firm, denoted the *i*th firm. In the classical model, firms are perfect competitors that choose their output so as to maximize profits. In the short run, output is varied solely by changing the labor input so that choice of the level of output and quantity of the labor input are one decision. The perfectly competitive firm will increase output until the marginal cost of producing a unit of output is equal to the marginal revenue received from its sale. For the perfectly competitive firm, marginal revenue is equal to

[5] The differencing symbol Δ (delta) indicates the change in the variable it precedes (e.g., ΔY is the change in Y).

product price (P).[6] Because labor is the only variable factor of production, the marginal cost of each additional unit of output is the marginal labor cost. Marginal labor cost equals the money wage divided by the number of units of output produced by the additional unit of labor. We defined the units of output produced by the incremental unit of labor employed as the MPN. Thus, marginal cost for the ith firm (MC_i) is equal to the money wage (W) divided by the marginal product of labor for that firm (MPN_i).[7]

$$MC_i = \frac{W}{MPN_i} \tag{3.2}$$

The condition for short-run profit maximization in the purely competitive market is

$$P = MC_i \tag{3.2a}$$

Substituting the expression for marginal cost (MC) from equation (3.2) into equation (3.2*a*) shows the short-run profit-maximizing position for the firm buying labor in the market for inputs:

$$P = W/MPN_i \tag{3.3}$$

Multiplying both sides of equation (3.3) by MPN and dividing both sides by P gives the expression

$$MPN_i = \frac{W}{P} \tag{3.4}$$

The profit maximization condition in equation (3.4) can be explained as follows: The firm will hire up to the point where the additional output obtained by hiring one more worker (MPN) is just equal to the real wage (W/P) paid to hire that worker.

The condition for profit maximization in equation (3.4) is illustrated in Figure 3-2. The demand for labor schedule for the firm, plotted against the real wage, is the MPN schedule from Figure 3-1. The labor demand curve is downward-sloping due to the law of diminishing returns. At a real wage such as 8.0 (e.g., a money wage of \$8 and a product price of \$1), the firm will hire 3 workers. At a quantity of labor below 3, say 2, the MPN (10) exceeds the real wage (8.0). The payment to the worker in real terms is less than the real product produced. Profits will be increased by hiring additional units of labor. Alternatively, at quantities of labor input above 3, if the real wage is 8, the real wage is above the MPN. The payment to labor exceeds the real product of the marginal worker, and marginal cost exceeds product price. The firm will reduce labor to increase profit.

---

[6]A perfectly competitive firm faces a horizontal product demand curve. By assumption, the firm is so small a portion of the market that its increase in output can be sold without depressing the product price. The analysis could be reformulated for the firm facing a downward-sloping demand curve without substantially changing the conclusions that we reach in this chapter. The question of whether firms are in fact perfect competitors does, however, have important implications at future points in our analysis.

[7]The i subscript does not appear on the price or wage variables because these are uniform across firms. MPN_i for each firm is derived from the production function for each firm, assumed to be identical over all firms; that is,

$$Y_i = F(\overline{K}_i, N_i)$$

for each firm.

FIGURE 3-2 Labor Demand for a Firm

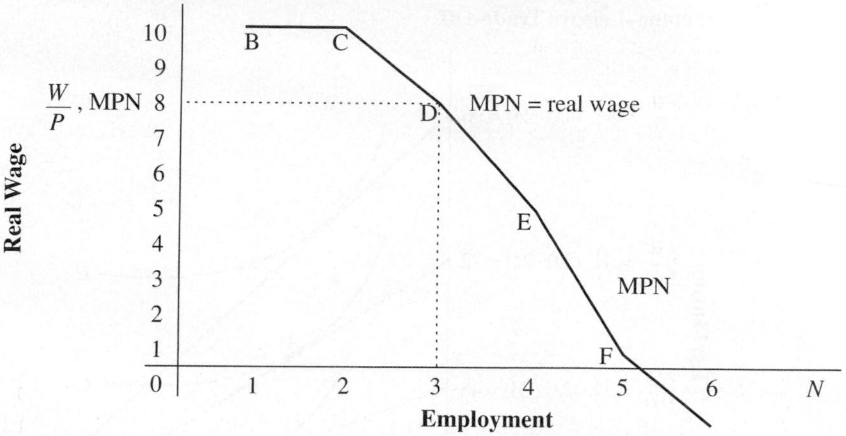

The condition for profit maximization is met at the point where the real wage (W/P) is equated with the MPN, as shown in equation (3.4). If the real wage is 8, then the firm will maximize profits by hiring 3 workers, since the MPN is 8.0. This is shown at point D on the graph of the demand for labor, MPN. In order to get the firm to hire more labor, the real wage must fall since the additional output produced by each additional worker is declining.

Thus, the profit-maximizing quantity of labor demanded by a firm at each real wage is given by the labor input that equates the real wage and the MPN. The marginal product curve is the firm's demand curve for labor. The implication is that labor demand depends inversely on the level of the real wage. The labor demand curve is downward-sloping due to the law of diminishing returns. The higher the real wage, for example, the lower the level of labor input that will equate the real wage to the MPN. In Figure 3-2, if the wage were 5, instead of 8, labor demand would be 4 instead of 3. The demand curve for labor is an economy-wide aggregation of the individual firms' demand curves. For each real wage, this curve will give the sum of the quantities of labor input demanded by the firms in the economy. We write this aggregate labor demand function (N^d) as

$$N^d = f\left(\frac{W}{P}\right) \qquad (3.5)$$
$$(-)$$

where in the aggregate, as with individual firms, an increase in the real wage lowers the demand for labor.

Labor Supply

The last relationship necessary for determining employment and output in the classical system is the labor supply curve. Labor services are supplied by individual workers. Classical economists assumed that the individual attempts to maximize utility (or satisfaction). The level of utility depends positively on both real income, which gives the individual command over goods and services, and leisure. There is, however, a trade-off between the two goals because income is increased by work, which reduces available leisure time.

Consider, for example, how individual j allocates one 24-hour period between leisure hours and hours worked: (N_j^s) is the individual's supply of labor. Figure 3-3

FIGURE 3-3 Individual Labor Supply Decision

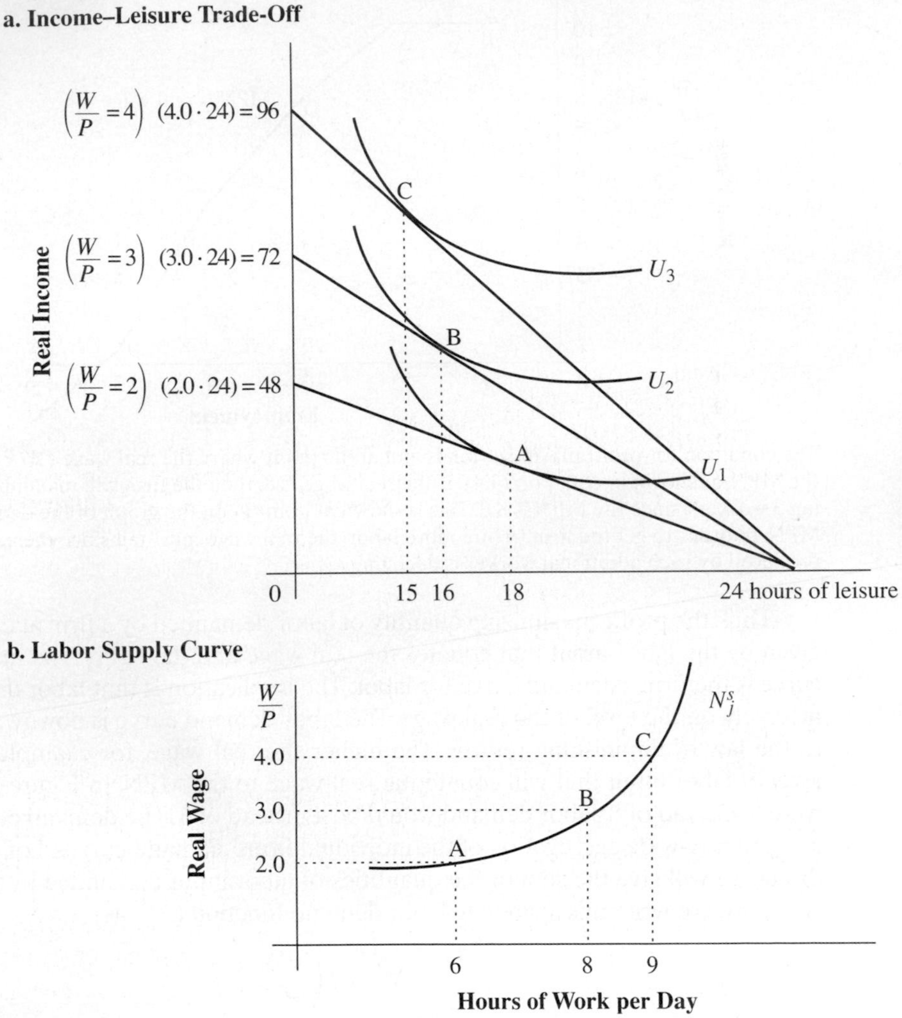

Part *a* depicts the individual's labor–leisure choice. The individual will supply labor (N_j^s) up to the point where the rate at which labor may be traded for leisure in the marketplace, which is given by the real wage (W/P), is equated with the rate at which the individual is willing to trade labor (give up leisure) in return for income, which is measured by the slope of the individual's indifference curves (U_1, U_2, U_3). At a real wage of 2.0, the individual will choose 18 hours of leisure, point A on the income–leisure trade-off graph. Hours of work chosen will then be 6 (24 hours in the day − 18 hours of leisure). This is shown at point A on the labor supply curve. At a real wage of 3.0, the individual will choose 16 hours of leisure, point B on the income–leisure trade-off graph. Hours of work chosen will then be 8 (24 hours in the day − 16 hours of leisure). This is shown at point B on the labor supply curve. At a real wage of 4.0, the individual will choose 15 hours of leisure, point C on the income–leisure trade-off graph. Hours of work chosen will then be 9 (24 hours in the day − 15 hours of leisure). This is shown at point C on the labor supply curve.

illustrates the choice facing the individual. On the horizontal axis, we measure hours of leisure per day. The maximum, of course, is 24 hours. The horizontal intercept, where the individual chooses no labor and all leisure, is 24. The number of hours worked are, therefore, 24 minus the number of hours of leisure selected. Real income is measured on the vertical axis and is equal to the real wage, W/P, multiplied by the number of hours the individual works. Each vertical intercept is the real wage multiplied by 24 hours in the day, which would occur if the individual chose all labor and zero leisure—i.e., ($W/P \cdot 24$). The curved lines in the graph (labeled U_1, U_2, U_3) are indifference curves. Points along one of these curves are combinations of income and leisure that give equal satisfaction to the individual; hence, the person is indifferent as to which point along a given curve is selected. The slope of the indifference curve gives the rate at which the individual is willing to trade off leisure for income—that is, the increase in income the person would have to receive to be just as well off after giving up a unit of leisure. In fact, the cost of choosing each hour of leisure is the real wage, W/P, since the individual is choosing not to work for each hour of leisure. In addition, all points along U_2, for example, yield greater satisfaction to the individual than any point on U_1, since any point on an indifference curve that sits farther to the right indicates a larger income, given leisure (or the same number of hours worked). Therefore, the individual attempts to achieve the "northernmost" possible indifference curve. The higher the real wage, the higher the satisfaction the individual can select (represented by an indifference curve that sits farther to the right).

The straight-line rays originating at the point of 24 hours on the horizontal axis give the budget lines facing the individual. Starting from 24 hours (no work, all leisure), the individual can trade off leisure for income at a rate equal to the hourly real wage, W/P. The slope of the budget line is the real wage. The higher the real wage, the steeper the budget line, reflecting the fact that at a higher real wage, an individual who increases hours of work by 1 unit (moves one unit to the left along the horizontal axis) will receive a larger increment of income (move farther up the vertical axis along the budget line) than he or she would have received at the lower real wage. Three budget lines, corresponding to real wage rates of 2.0, 3.0, and 4.0, are shown in Figure 3.3*a*. Notice that at a higher real wage, the individual can choose an indifference curve that yields greater satisfaction.

In Figure 3-3*b*, we construct the labor supply curve for the *j*th individual. This supply curve consists of points such as A, B, and C from Figure 3-3*a*, giving the amount of labor the individual will supply at each real wage. This aggregate labor supply curve can be written as

$$N^s = \underset{(+)}{g}\left(\frac{W}{P}\right) \tag{3.6}$$

Two features of the classical labor supply theory require further comment. First, note that the wage variable is the real wage. Labor supply is determined by the real wage, not the money wage. The worker receives utility ultimately from consumption, and in making the labor–leisure decision, the individual is concerned with the command over goods and services received for a unit of labor. For example, starting at point C on the income–leisure trade-off graph, if the money wage is $4 and the price is 1.0, the real wage is 4.0 ($\frac{4}{1}$) and the individual will choose 15 hours of leisure and work 9 hours (point C on the labor supply curve). If the money wage is still $4, but the price is now 2.0, the individual's real wage is 2.0 ($\frac{4}{2}$). The individual will now select point A on the income–leisure trade-off graph, choosing 18 hours of leisure. Hours of work decrease to 6 (24 − 18), which is point A on the labor supply curve. Clearly, as the *real wage increases* (decreases), leisure decreases (increases) and *hours of work increase* (decrease). This is the significance of equation (3.6). Since the real wage (W/P) is measured along the vertical axis on the labor supply curve, if either the money wage or price (or both) change, the number of hours worked are determined by moving along the labor supply curve.

Second, by the construction of Figure 3-3, the labor supply curve is positively sloped; more labor is assumed to be supplied at higher real wage rates. This relation reflects the fact that a higher real wage rate means a higher price for leisure in terms of foregone income. At this higher price, we assume that the worker will choose less leisure. This effect is analogous to the *substitution effect* in the theory of consumer demand. There is another effect: the equivalent of *the income effect* in consumer demand theory. As the real wage increases, the worker is able to achieve a higher level of real income. At higher levels of real income, leisure may become more desirable relative to further increments in income. With successive increases in the real wage, a point may be reached at which the worker chooses to supply less labor as the real wage increases and consumes more leisure. At this point, the income effect outweighs the substitution effect; the labor supply curve assumes a negative slope and bends back toward the vertical axis. Almost certainly, at extremely high wage rates, we would reach a backward-bending portion of the labor supply curve, and perhaps wage rates need not be so "extremely" high. Although the empirical evidence on this question is inconclusive, we will assume that for wage rates observed in industrialized nations, the aggregate labor supply curve does have a positive slope; the substitution effect outweighs the income effect.

3.5 EQUILIBRIUM OUTPUT AND EMPLOYMENT

So far, the following relationships have been derived:

$$Y = F(\bar{K}, N) \text{ (aggregate production function)} \tag{3.1}$$

$$N^d = f\left(\frac{W}{P}\right) \text{ (labor demand schedule)} \tag{3.5}$$

$$N^s = g\left(\frac{W}{P}\right) \text{ (labor supply schedule)} \tag{3.6}$$

These relationships, together with the equilibrium condition for the labor market,

$$N^s = N^d \tag{3.7}$$

determine output, employment, and the real wage. In common terminology, output, employment, and the real wage are designated as the *endogenous variables* in the model to this point, where an endogenous variable is one that is determined within the model.

Equilibrium within the classical model is illustrated in Figure 3-4. Graph *a* shows the determination of the equilibrium levels of employment (N_0) and the real wage $(W/P)_0$ at the point of intersection between the aggregate labor demand and labor supply curves. This equilibrium level of labor input (N_0) results in an equilibrium level of output (Y_0) given by the production function, as shown in Figure 3-4*b*.

FIGURE 3-4 Classical Output and Employment Theory

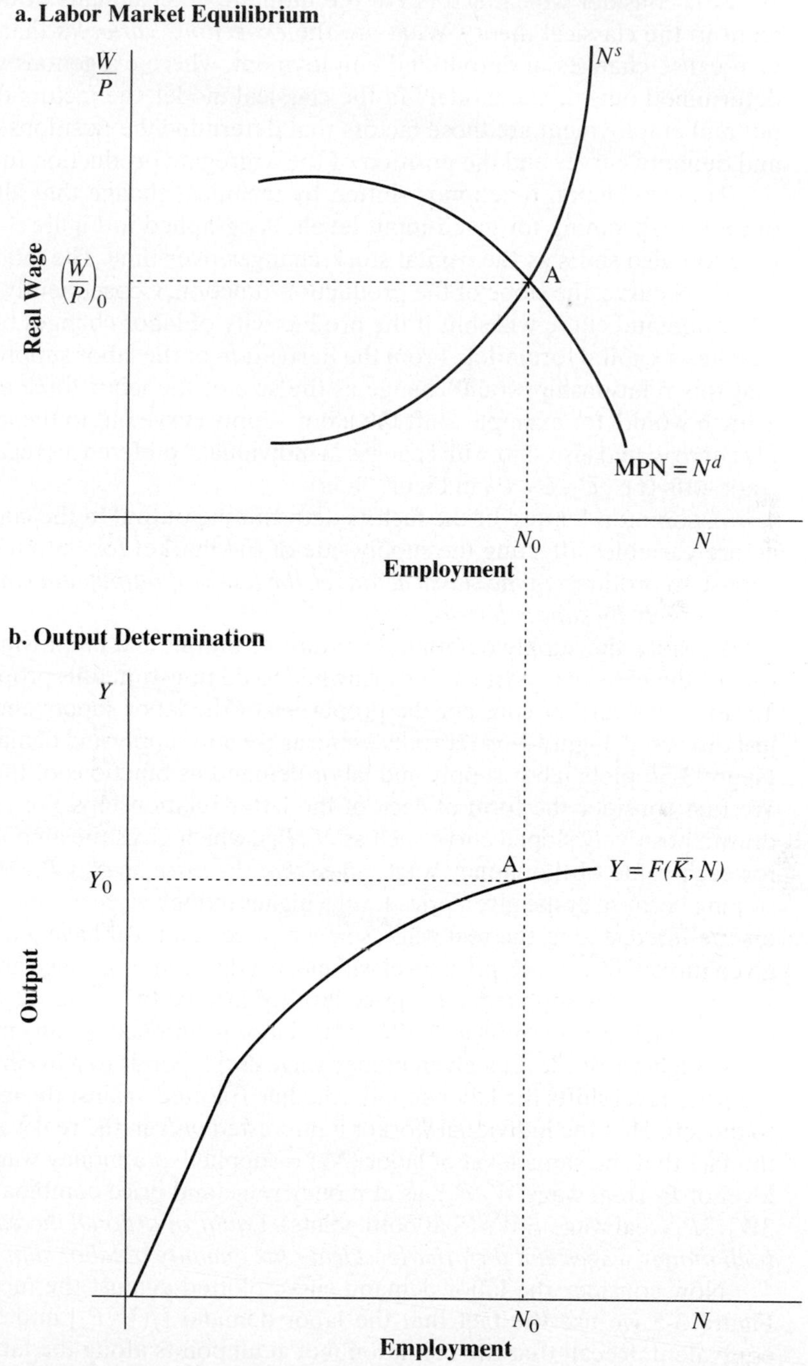

Part *a* depicts labor market equilibrium at the real wage $(W/P)_0$ at equilibrium point A. In the aggregate, labor supply equals labor demand, $N^d = N^s$. Equilibrium employment is N_0. Substitution of equilibrium employment into the production function in part *b* determines equilibrium aggregate output, Y_0 at point A.

The Determinants of Output and Employment

We now consider which factors are the ultimate determinants of output and employment in the classical theory. What are the *exogenous variables* that, when changed, in turn cause changes in output and employment, where exogenous variables are those determined outside the model? In the classical model, the factors that determine output and employment are those factors that determine the positions of the labor supply and demand curves and the position of the aggregate production function.

The production function is shifted by technical change that alters the amount of output forthcoming for given input levels. As graphed in Figure 3-4*b*, the production function also shifts as the capital stock changes over time. The labor demand curve is the MPN curve, the slope of the production function. Consequently, the position of the labor demand curve will shift if the productivity of labor changes because of technical change or capital formation. From the derivation of the labor supply curve, one can see that this relationship would change as the size of the labor force changes. Population growth would, for example, shift the labor supply curve out to the right. The labor supply curve would also shift with changes in individuals' preferences regarding labor–leisure trade-offs (i.e., U_1, U_2, U_3 in Figure 3-3*a*).

A common feature of the factors determining output in the classical model is that all are variables affecting the supply side of the market for output—the amount firms choose to produce. *In the classical model, the levels of output and employment are determined solely by supply factors.*

Because the supply-determined nature of output and employment is a crucial feature of the classical system, it is worthwhile to demonstrate this property more formally. To do so, we further consider the properties of the labor supply and demand functions just discussed. Figure 3-5*a* reproduces the aggregate supply and demand curves for labor. Figure 3-5*b* plots labor supply and labor demand as functions of the money wage (W). We first consider the form of each of the latter relationships. For labor supply, we can draw a positively sloped curve such as $N^s(P_1)$, which gives the amount of labor supplied for each value of the money wage, *given that the price level is* P_1. The curve is upward-sloping because at the given price level a higher money wage is a higher real wage. Workers are interested in the real wage, so each price level will have a different curve. For a given money wage each price level will mean a different real wage and, hence, a different amount of labor supplied. At a price level of $2P_1$, or twice that of P_1, the labor supply curve in Figure 3-5*b* shifts to $N^s(2P_1)$; less labor is supplied for any money wage because at the higher price level a given money wage corresponds to a lower real wage. A rise in the price level shifts the labor supply schedule (plotted against the money wage) upward to the left. That the individual worker is interested *only* in the real wage can be seen from the fact that the same level of labor (N_1) is supplied at a money wage of W_1 and a price level of P_1 (real wage W_1/P_1), as at money wage and price combinations of $2W_1, 2P_1$ or $3W_1, 3P_1$ (real wage = W_1/P_1 at both points). *Equiproportional increases (or decreases) in both money wages and the price level leave the quantity of labor supplied unchanged.*

Now consider the labor demand curve plotted against the money wage, where in Figure 3-5 we use the fact that the labor demand [$f(W/P)$] and MPN schedules are equivalent. Recall that the condition met at all points along the labor demand curve is

$$\frac{W}{P} = \text{MPN} \tag{3.8}$$

FIGURE 3-5 Labor Market Equilibrium and the Money Wage

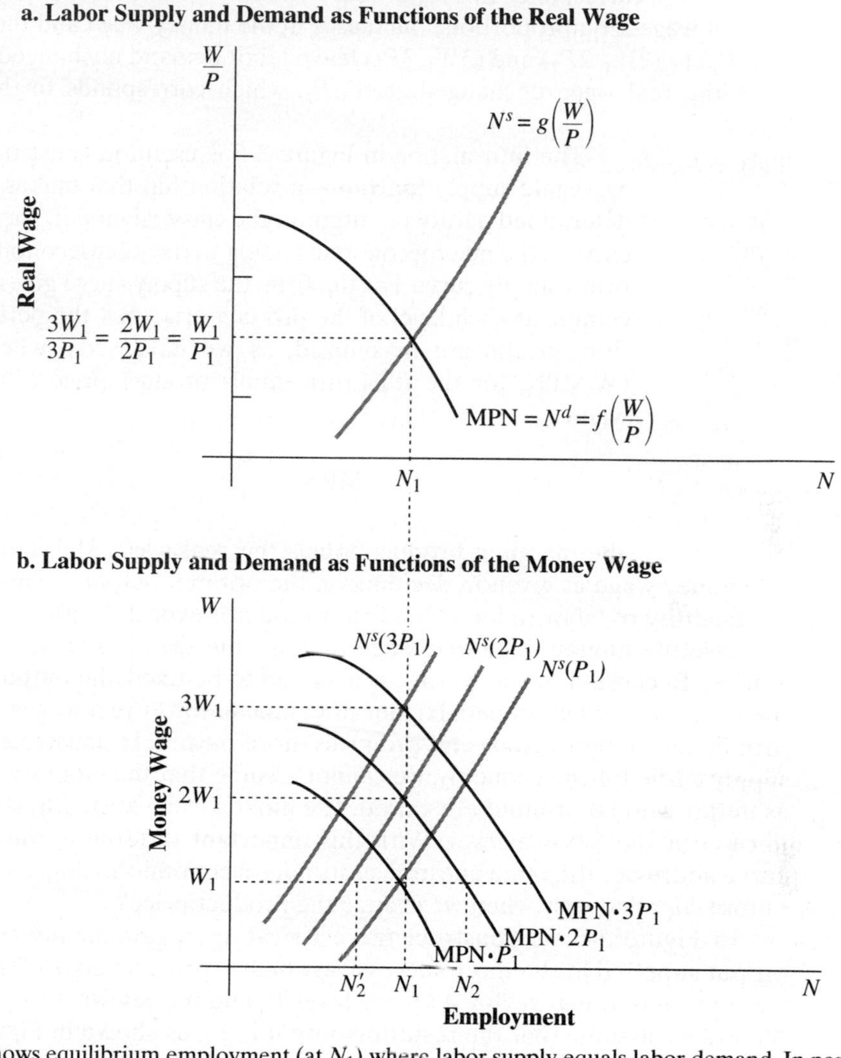

Part *a* shows equilibrium employment (at N_1) where labor supply equals labor demand. In part *b* labor supply and demand are plotted as functions of the money wage. Increases in the price level (from P_1 to $2P_1$, then to $3P_1$) shift the labor supply and demand schedules upward proportionately. The money wage rises proportionately with the price level (from W_1 to $2W_1$, then to $3W_1$). The real wage and level of employment are unchanged.

If we want to know the quantity of labor that will be demanded at any money wage, as was the case for the quantity supplied, the answer depends on the price level. Given the money wage, the firm will choose the level of employment at which

$$W = \text{MPN} \cdot P \tag{3.9}$$

At successively higher price levels ($P_1, 2P_1, 3P_1$) the labor demand curve plotted against the money wage shifts to the right (from $\text{MPN} \cdot P_1$ to $\text{MPN} \cdot 2P_1$ to $\text{MPN} \cdot 3P_1$).

For a given money wage, more labor is demanded at higher price levels because that money wage corresponds to a lower real wage rate.[8] The demand for labor depends on the real wage. Equiproportional increases in the money wage and the price level from (W_1, P_1) to $(2W_1, 2P_1)$ and $(3W_1, 3P_1)$ leave labor demand unchanged at level N_1. They leave the real wage unchanged at W_1/P_1, which corresponds to the demand N_1 in Figure 3-5a.

aggregate supply function macroeconomic analog to the individual market supply curve, which shows the output forthcoming at each level of product price. The aggregate supply curve shows the total output firms will supply at each value of the aggregate price level

The information in Figure 3-5 is useful in constructing the classical **aggregate supply function**—a relationship that makes clear the supply-determined nature of output in the classical model. The aggregate supply curve is the macroeconomic analog to the microeconomic concept of the firm's supply curve. For the firm, the supply curve gives the output forthcoming at each level of the product price. For the perfectly competitive firm, profits are maximized, as we have seen, where marginal cost (W/MPN_i for the ith firm) equals product price (P), or equivalently, where

$$\text{MPN}_i = \frac{W}{P} \tag{3.10}$$

the marginal product equals the real wage. The individual firm takes the money wage as given in deciding on the optimal output to supply and therefore the quantity of labor to hire. One firm would not expect its effort to hire more labor to cause the money wage to change because the firm is a small part of the overall market. Because the money wage is assumed to be fixed, the output supply curve for the firm is positively sloped. Higher prices mean lower real wages; consequently, the firm demands more labor and produces more output. In constructing the aggregate supply curve for the economy, we cannot assume that the money wage remains fixed as output and labor input are varied. The money wage must adjust to maintain equilibrium in the labor market. With this important difference, the aggregate supply curve addresses the same question as its microeconomic analog: How will the level of output supplied vary when we change the product price?

In Figure 3-6 we construct the classical aggregate supply function. Consider output supplied at the three successively higher price levels, P_1, $2P_1$, and $3P_1$, which were plotted in Figure 3-5. At price level P_1 and money wage W_1, employment was N_1 and we assume that the resulting output is Y_1, as shown in Figure 3-6.[9] How will output supplied vary as we go to a price level of $2P_1$? At a price level of $2P_1$, if the money wage remained at W_1, we can see from Figure 3-5*b* that labor demand would increase to N_2. The higher price would mean a lower real wage, and firms would try to expand both employment and output. The money wage will not, however, remain at W_1. At a price level of $2P_1$ the labor supply curve in Figure 3-5*b* will have shifted to $N^s(2P_1)$, and at a money wage of W_1, labor supply will be only N_2'

[8] Equation (3.9) has a simple interpretation. For profit maximization, the money wage paid to the incremental worker (W) must just equal the worker's contribution to the firm's revenue. The worker's contribution to money revenues equals his or her marginal product multiplied by the product price ($\text{MPN} \cdot P$), which is termed the *marginal revenue product*.

[9] This output level is read from the production function given in Figure 3-4.

FIGURE 3-6 Classical Aggregate Supply Curve

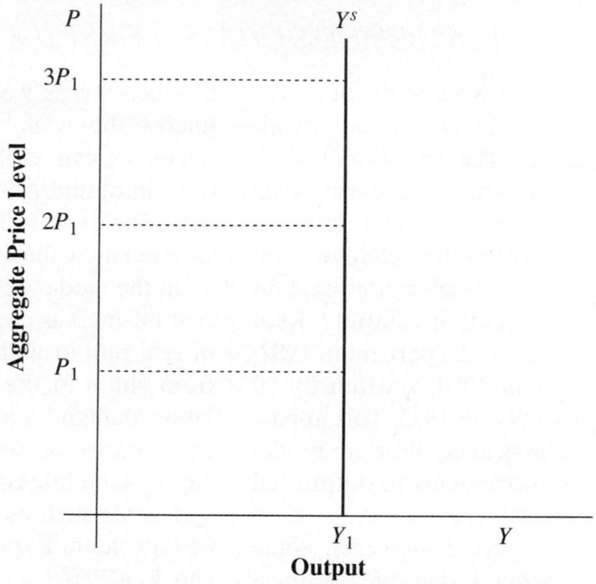

The vertical classical aggregate supply curve reflects the fact that higher values of the price level require proportionately higher levels of the money wage for labor market equilibrium. The real wage, employment, and therefore level of output are the same at $P_1, 2P_1$, and $3P_1$.

units. There will be an excess demand for labor equal to $(N_2 - N'_2)$ units and the money wage will rise.

The process at work here is one of some firms responding to higher prices by attempting to expand employment and production. To expand employment, they raise money wages in an effort to bid workers away from other firms. Firms that lag in the process of raising money wages suffer higher quit rates and lose workers. This process of rising money wages will stop only when the money wage has increased sufficiently to reequilibrate supply and demand in the labor market. As can be seen in Figure 3-5*b*, reequilibration occurs at a money wage of $2W_1$, where the money wage has increased proportionately with the price level. At this point, the initial real wage is restored and employment is back at its original level. Consequently, output supplied at price level $2P_1$ is equal to Y_1, the output level for price level P_1. At a still higher price level of $3P_1$, the money wage rises to $3W_1$, but again, output is unchanged at Y_1. The aggregate supply curve is vertical. Higher prices provide a spur to output only if they are not matched by proportionately higher money wages—only if they lower the real wage. Given the assumptions we have made, however, equilibrium in the labor market requires that money wages rise proportionately with prices to maintain the equilibrium real wage in that market.

The vertical aggregate supply curve illustrates the supply-determined nature of output in the classical model. For output to be in equilibrium, we must be on the supply curve; output must be at Y_1.

PERSPECTIVES 3-1

REAL BUSINESS CYCLES: A FIRST LOOK

It was argued in Section 3.5 that the determinants of output in the classical model are all supply-side variables. The traditional view had been that these supply-side variables change only slowly over time. But if output is determined by variables that change only slowly, how can the classical model explain sharp cyclical movements in output? Real GDP, for example, fell by 2.5 percent in 1982, rose by 6.8 percent in 1984, and fell by 30 percent between 1929 and 1933. This apparent failure of the classical equilibrium model to explain cyclical movements in output led to the Keynesian revolution.

In the post-1980 period, however, some economists have argued that the business cycle *is* caused by changes in *real* supply-side variables, much along classical lines. These economists do not accept the view that supply-side factors change only slowly over time. They believe that changes in technology and shocks that affect capital formation and labor productivity, as well as disturbances that influence the availability and prices of natural resources, can explain the short-run fluctuations in output as well as its long-run growth path. The models these economists have constructed are called *real business cycle* models.

In the model described in this chapter, the real business cycle theorists see fluctuations in real output and employment as resulting from shifts in the production function and labor demand schedules in Figure 3-4. If preferences of workers change, the labor supply schedule could also shift.

Events such as the OPEC (Organization of Petroleum Exporting Countries) oil-price shock in 1974 led all economists to recognize that at times supply-side shocks can affect the cyclical behavior of output. Still, the view that real supply-side factors can fully explain the business cycle is controversial. We will consider real business cycle models in detail in Chapter 12.

Factors That Do Not Affect Output

Now consider the factors that will *not* affect output and employment in the classical model. Because output and employment are supply-determined, the level of aggregate demand will have *no* effect on output. As John Stuart Mill advised the legislator, "He need not give himself concern over the demand for output." Factors such as the quantity of money, level of government spending, and level of demand for investment goods by the business sector are all demand-side factors that have no role in determining output and employment. The case of government tax policy is more complex. Changes in taxes, to the degree that they affect the demand side, will not affect output or employment. But changes in tax rates also have incentive or supply-side effects that do matter for output and employment, as we will see in Chapter 4.

Read Perspectives 3-1.

3.6 CONCLUSION

The striking feature of the classical model is the supply-determined nature of output and employment. This property follows from the vertical aggregate supply curve. The classical aggregate supply curve is vertical because of the assumptions we have made about the labor market. It is worthwhile to recognize explicitly the nature of these assumptions. In general, the foregoing portrayal of the labor and product markets can be characterized by the term *auction market*. Labor and output are assumed to be traded in markets that are continually in equilibrium and in which all participants make decisions based on announced real wage rates and product prices. Two assumptions implicit in this classical representation of the labor market are as follows:

1. Perfectly flexible prices and wages
2. Perfect information on the part of all market participants about market prices

For whatever time period we assume that the equilibrium model determines employment and output, equilibrium must be achieved. If such a model is to explain employment and output in the short run, prices and wages must be perfectly flexible in that time period.

The auction market characterization of the labor market also requires that market participants have perfect information about market prices. Both suppliers and purchasers of labor must know the relevant trading prices. This condition requires that when selling and buying labor at a given money wage (W), both workers and employers know the command over commodities that will result from such a wage (W/P).

These two assumptions, essential for the nature of the classical equilibrium theory of employment and output, are the elements of the classical theory that Keynes attacked. Before considering that attack, we discuss other major elements of the classical theory.

Key Terms

- aggregate demand 34
- production function 34
- marginal product of labor (MPN) 37
- aggregate supply function 46

Review Questions and Problems

1. In what respects was the classical attack on mercantilism important in shaping classical economists' views on macroeconomic questions?
2. Explain the concept of an aggregate production function. How would you expect the production function in Figure 3-1 to be affected by an increase in the average and marginal productivity of labor for a given output level, owing, for example, to increased education of the labor force? How would such a shift in the production function affect the levels of output and employment in the classical model?
3. Explain the classical theories of labor supply and demand. Why is the labor demand schedule downward-sloping when plotted against the real wage, whereas the labor supply schedule is upward-sloping on the same graph?
4. Suppose that the public's taste changes in such a way that leisure comes to be more desirable than commodities. How would you expect such a change to affect output, employment, and the real wage in the classical model?
5. We termed the classical view of the labor market an *auction market*. What assumptions underlie this characterization?

6. In microeconomics, we expect the supply curve for the firm to slope upward to the right when drawn against price. The classical aggregate supply curve is based on this microeconomic theory of the firm but is vertical. Why?
7. What are the major determinants of output and employment in the classical system? What role does aggregate demand have in determining output and employment?
8. Suppose that, due for example to reconstruction after a war, the capital stock of a nation increases. Use the graphical framework of Figure 3-4 to illustrate the effect that the increase in the capital stock would have on output, employment, and the real wage in the classical model.

CHAPTER 4

Classical Macroeconomics (II): Money, Prices, and Interest

In this chapter we complete the discussion of the classical model. We analyze the classical theory of aggregate price level determination, which brings in the demand side of the model. Determination of the interest rate is also discussed. Next, we consider the policy conclusions that emerge from the classical model—classical views on monetary and fiscal policy.

4.1 THE QUANTITY THEORY OF MONEY

To understand the determination of the price level in the classical system, we analyze the role of money. In the classical theory, the quantity of money determines aggregate demand, which in turn determines the price level.

The Equation of Exchange

quantity theory of money
classical theory stating that the price level is proportional to the quantity of money

velocity of money
rate at which money *turns over* in GDP transactions during a given period: that is, the average number of times each dollar is used in GDP transactions

The starting point for the classical **quantity theory of money** is the equation of exchange, an identity relating the volume of transactions at current prices to the supply of money times the turnover rate of each dollar. This *turnover rate* for money, which measures the average number of times each dollar is used in transactions during the period, is called the **velocity of money**. In the form used by the American quantity theorist Irving Fisher, this identity is expressed as

$$MV_T \equiv P_T T \qquad \textbf{(4.1)}$$

where M is the quantity of money, V_T is the transactions velocity of money, P_T is the price index for the items traded, and T is the volume of transactions. This relationship is an identity because of the *ex post* definition of velocity. If, for example, over a given period the value of transactions in current dollars ($P_T T$) were \$3,600 billion and the money supply (M) were \$300 billion, we define the transactions velocity (or turnover rate) of money as the number of times the average dollar was used in transactions:

$$V_T \equiv \frac{P_T T}{M} = \frac{3{,}600}{300} = 12 \qquad \textbf{(4.2)}$$

The transaction variable (T) includes not only sales and purchases of newly produced goods but also exchanges of previously produced goods and financial assets. Another expression of the equation of exchange focuses only on income transactions:

$$MV \equiv PY \qquad \textbf{(4.3)}$$

M is again the quantity of money, and V is now the income velocity of money, the number of times the average dollar is used in a transaction involving current output. The price index for currently produced output is given by P and the level of current output by Y. Again, this relationship would be an identity as long as income velocity was defined residually, as the level necessary to make the equality hold:

$$V \equiv \frac{PY}{M} \tag{4.4}$$

In equation (4.3), the variables are easier to measure and are central to our concerns, so we focus on this form of the equation.

The equation of exchange is a truism and does not explain the variables it contains. Fisher and other quantity theorists, however, postulated that the *equilibrium* values of the elements in the equation of exchange, with the exception of the price level, are determined by other forces. Thus, the equation of exchange determines the price level. As Fisher put it:

> We find that, under the conditions assumed, the price level varies (1) directly as the quantity of money in circulation (M), (2) directly as the velocity of its circulation (V), (3) inversely as the volume of trade done by it (T). The first of these three relations is worth emphasis. It constitutes the "quantity theory of money."[1]

Output is a measure of real economic activity. As we saw in Chapter 3, classical economists regarded this variable as supply-determined. Most simply, money was assumed to be a metallic money such as gold, but considering paper money and bank deposits does not seriously complicate the analysis. The important assumption was that the quantity of money was exogenously controlled by the monetary policy authority.

Fisher argued that, in equilibrium, the velocity of money was determined by the payment habits and payment technology of society. For example, factors such as the average length of the pay period, the practice of using charge accounts or bank charge cards, and the prevalence of trade credit among businesses all affect the velocity of circulation. Shorter pay periods lead to smaller average money holdings over the pay period for any given income level, and hence an increase in velocity. Frequent use of charge accounts by consumers or trade credit by businesses also increases velocity, the number of transactions per unit of money. According to Fisher and other quantity theorists, *the equilibrium level of velocity was determined by such institutional factors and could be regarded as fixed for the short run.*

If velocity is predetermined and not simply defined residually to equate MV and PY, the equation of exchange is not merely a definition. With output fixed from the supply side, the equation of exchange now expresses a relationship of proportionality between the exogenously given money supply and the price level:

$$M\bar{V} = P\bar{Y} \tag{4.5}$$

or

$$P = \frac{\bar{V}}{\bar{Y}}M \tag{4.6}$$

[1] Irving Fisher, *The Purchasing Power of Money* (New York: Macmillan, 1922), p. 29.

The bar over the V and Y indicates that these terms can be taken as given. Equation (4.6) indicates the dependence of the price level on the supply of money. A doubling of M doubles P, or a 10 percent increase in M leads to a 10 percent increase in P. This is the basic result of the quantity theory of money: *The quantity of money determines the price level.*

The Cambridge Approach to the Quantity Theory

The mathematics of the quantity theory may be clear from equations (4.5) and (4.6), but what about the economics? How do changes in the money supply affect the price level? This question can be answered more easily after considering another variant of the quantity theory: the Cambridge approach.

Cambridge approach a version of the quantity theory of money that focuses on the demand for money ($M^d = kPY$)

The **Cambridge approach**, named after Cambridge University, the academic home of its originators, Alfred Marshall and A. C. Pigou, also demonstrated a proportional relationship between the quantity of money and the aggregate price level. The foundation of this relationship was, however, less mechanistic than the transactions, or Fisherian (after Irving Fisher), version of the quantity theory. Marshall began by focusing on the individual's decision on the optimal amount of money to hold. Some money will be held because of the convenience that money provides in transactions compared with other stores of value. Money also provides security by lessening the possibility of inconvenience or bankruptcy from failing to meet unexpected obligations. But as Pigou noted, "Currency held in the hand yields no income," so money will be held only insofar as its yield in terms of convenience and security outweighs the income lost from not investing in productive activity or the satisfaction lost by not simply using the money to purchase goods to consume. On these criteria, how much money will it be optimal to hold?

Marshall and the other Cambridge economists assumed that the demand for money would be a proportion of income. The Cambridge equation is written as

$$M^d = kPY \tag{4.7}$$

Money demand (M^d) is assumed to be a proportion (k) of nominal income, the price level (P) times the level of real income (Y). The desirable property of money is its usefulness for transactions, so it follows that the demand for money depends on the level of transactions, which may be supposed to vary closely with income. The proportion of income that would be optimal to hold in the form of money (k) is assumed to be stable in the short run, depending, as in the Fisherian formulation, on the payment habits of the society.

In equilibrium, the exogenous supply of money must equal the quantity of money demanded:

$$M = M^d = kP\overline{Y} \tag{4.8}$$

With k fixed in the short run and real output ($\overline{Y}$) determined, as before, by supply conditions, the Cambridge equation also reduces to a proportional relationship between the price level and the money supply. As in the Fisherian approach, the quantity of money determines the price level.

The formal equivalence of the Cambridge equation and Fisher's version of the equation of exchange can be seen by rewriting equation (4.8) as

$$M\frac{1}{k} = P\overline{Y} \tag{4.9}$$

By comparing this with Fisher's equation (4.5), we can see that the two formulations are equivalent, with V equal to $1/k$. For example, if individuals wish to hold an amount equal to one-fourth of the nominal income in the form of money, the number of times the average dollar is used in income transactions will be four.

Although the two formulations of the quantity theory are formally equivalent, the Cambridge version represents a step toward more modern monetary theories. The Cambridge focus was on the quantity theory as a theory of the demand for money. The proportional relationship between the quantity of money and the price level resulted from the fact that the proportion of nominal income people wished to hold in the form of money (k) was constant and the level of real output was fixed by supply conditions. Following up on Pigou's analysis of the alternatives to holding wealth in the form of money, Keynes attacked the quantity theory by providing a new theory of money demand.

In addition, the Cambridge focus on money demand leads to an answer to the question about the way money affects the price level. Let us suppose that we begin at equilibrium and then consider the effects of doubling the quantity of money. Initially, there is an excess of money supply over the amount demanded. Individuals try to reduce their money holdings to the optimal proportion of their income by putting this excess into alternative uses of consumption and investment. They increase their demand for commodities. This increased demand for commodities puts upward pressure on prices. In the language of classical economists, there is too much money chasing too few goods. If output is unchanged, as it would be in the classical model, and k is constant, a new equilibrium will be reached only after the price level is doubled. At that point, nominal income, and hence money demand, will have doubled. This was the link in the classical system between money and prices; an excess supply of money led to increased demand for commodities and upward pressure on the price level.

The Classical Aggregate Demand Curve

The quantity theory is the *implicit* theory of the aggregate demand for output within the classical system. We can use the quantity theory to construct the classical aggregate demand curve in Figure 4-1. For concreteness, we assign numerical values to the variables with which we are concerned. Let the value of k be one-fourth so that velocity is 4. Initially, let the supply of money be 300 units. In order for either equation (4.8) or (4.5) to hold, $P \times Y$ (nominal income) must be equal to 1,200 (4×300). In Figure 4-1, with price on the vertical axis and real output on the horizontal axis, the line labeled Y^d ($M = 300$) connects all the points where $P \times Y$ equals 1,200 units.[2] Points lying on the schedule, for example, are real income levels of 300 and 600 with accompanying price levels of 4.0 and 2.0, respectively.

Now consider a higher value of the money supply of, for example, 400 units. To satisfy either equation (4.8) or (4.5), with k still equal to one-fourth ($V = 4$), $P \times Y$ must now equal 1,600. The schedule Y^d ($M = 400$) corresponding to a value of M equal to 400 lies above and to the right of the Y^d ($M = 300$) schedule and shows all $P \times Y$ combinations of 1,600. *An increase in the money supply shifts the aggregate demand curve to the right.*

For a given supply of money, we trace out a downward-sloping aggregate demand curve that can be put together with the vertical aggregate supply curve in Figure 3-6 to

[2]The schedule Y^d ($M = 300$) and other aggregate demand curves are constructed so that the product of the value of the variable on the vertical axis times the value of the variable on the horizontal axis ($P \times Y$) is equal at all points along the schedule. Such a curve is a rectangular hyperbola.

FIGURE 4-1 Classical Aggregate Demand Curve

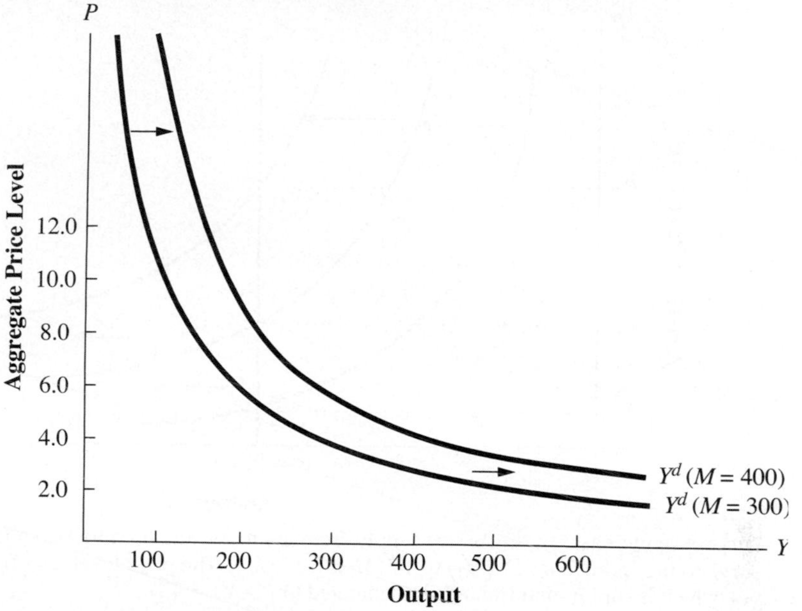

The classical aggregate demand curve plots combinations of the price level (P) and output (Y) consistent with the quantity theory equation $PY = M\bar{V}$, for a given money supply (M) and fixed velocity ($\bar{V}$). With $M = 300$ and velocity assumed to be 4, points such as $P = 12.0$ and $Y = 100$ or $P = 6.0$ and $Y = 200$ ($PY = 1{,}200 = MV$ in each case) lie along the aggregate demand curve. An increase in the money supply to $M = 400$ shifts the aggregate demand curve to the right.

illustrate the determination of price and output in the classical model. This is done in Figure 4-2.

Figure 4-2 reproduces the vertical aggregate supply curve (Y_1^s) from Figure 3-6 and shows several aggregate demand curves [$Y^d(M_1)$, $Y^d(M_2)$, $Y^d(M_3)$] drawn for successively higher values of the money supply (M_1, M_2, M_3). As just explained, increasing the money supply shifts the aggregate demand curve upward to the right. Because the supply curve is vertical, increases in demand do not affect output. Only the price level increases. Also note that for a given value of k (or V), *a change in the quantity of money is the only factor that shifts the aggregate demand curve*. Because the equilibrium value of k (or V) was considered to be stable in the short run, aggregate demand varied only with the supply of money.

The classical theory of aggregate demand has been termed an *implicit* theory. The theory is not explicit in the sense that it focuses on the components of aggregate demand and explains the factors that determine their level. Instead, in the classical theory, a given value of MV [or $M(1/k)$] implies the level of $P \times Y$ that is required for equilibrium in the money market—for money demand to equal the existing money supply. If money demand exceeds (falls short of) money supply, there will be a spillover to the commodity market as individuals try to reduce (increase) their expenditures on commodities. Points along the Y^d schedule are points at which firms and households are in equilibrium with regard to their money holdings and, therefore, are also at equilibrium rates of expenditures on commodities.

Read Perspectives 4-1.

FIGURE 4-2 Aggregate Supply and Demand in the Classical System

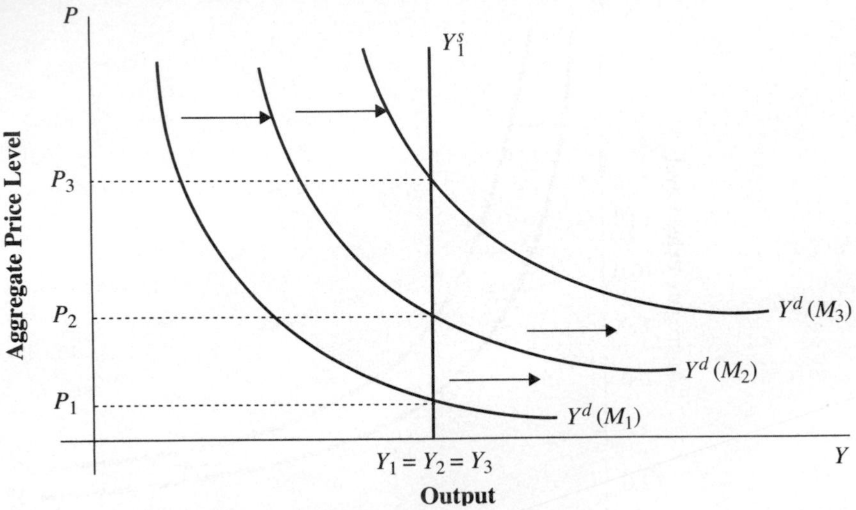

Successive increases in the money supply, from M_1 to M_2 and then to M_3, shift the aggregate demand curve to the right, from $Y^d (M_1)$ to $Y^d (M_2)$ to $Y^d (M_3)$. The price level rises from P_1 to P_2 to P_3. Output, which is supply-determined, is unchanged ($Y_1 = Y_2 = Y_3$).

4.2 THE CLASSICAL THEORY OF THE INTEREST RATE

In the classical system, the components of aggregate demand—consumption, investment, and government spending—play their explicit role in determining the interest rate. It is, in fact, the interest rate that guarantees that exogenous changes in the particular components of demand do not affect aggregate demand.

The equilibrium interest rate in the classical theory was the rate at which the amount of funds individuals desired to lend was just equal to the amount others desired to borrow. For simplicity, we assume that borrowing consists of selling a standard bond, a promise to pay certain amounts in the future. Lending consists of buying such bonds. Later, we consider the properties of bonds in more detail, but for now, the simplest assumption is that the standard bond is a *perpetuity*, a bond that pays a perpetual stream of interest payments with no return of principal. The rate of interest measures the return to holding bonds and, equivalently, the cost of borrowing. The interest rate depends on the factors that determine the levels of bond supply (borrowing) and bond demand (lending).

In the classical system, the suppliers of bonds were the firms, which financed all investment expenditures by the sale of bonds, and the government, which might sell bonds to finance spending in excess of tax revenues.[3]

The level of the government deficit (excess of spending over revenues), as well as the portion of the deficit the government might choose to finance by selling bonds to

[3]The word *might* is used concerning the government's sale of bonds to finance a deficit because, as will be explained in Section 4.3, the alternative of financing the deficit by printing money is available to the government. Also note that *investment* refers to expenditure by firms on plant, durable equipment, and inventories—investment in the national income accounts sense. The term *investment* does *not* refer to the purchase of financial assets such as bonds.

PERSPECTIVES 4-1

MONEY IN HYPERINFLATIONS

The relationship between money and the price level postulated by the quantity theory can be seen clearly during hyperinflations. A hyperinflation is a period when the price level explodes. When this happens, the money supply *always* explodes as well. This can be seen in Table 4-1, which shows the monthly inflation rates and growth rates in the money supply from four hyperinflations. In each case, the extremely high inflation rate (19,800 percent per month for Hungary) is matched by an extremely high rate of growth in the money supply (12,200 percent for Hungary).

Table 4-2 shows inflation and money growth rates for several countries that have experienced high and sustained inflation rates during a more recent period. Here again there is a strong positive relationship between inflation and money growth.

As we will see in later chapters, many economists do not accept the quantity theory of money as applied to economies in normal circumstances. The data in Tables 4-1 and 4-2 do, however, illustrate an implication of the quantity theory on which there is general agreement: Sustained very high inflation rates require accommodating high money growth rates.

TABLE 4-1 Inflation and Money Growth in Four Hyperinflations

	Time Period	*Inflation Rate (Monthly, Percent)*	*Money Growth Rate (Monthly, Percent)*
Germany	August 1922 to November 1923	322	314
Greece	November 1943 to November 1944	365	220
Hungary	August 1945 to July 1946	19,800	12,200
Poland	January 1923 to January 1924	81	72

SOURCE: Philip Cagan: "The Monetary Dynamics of Hyperinflation," in Milton Friedman, ed., *Studies in the Quantity Theory of Money* (Chicago: University of Chicago Press, 1956), p. 26. Reprinted by permission of the University of Chicago Press.

TABLE 4-2 Inflation and Money Growth in Several High Inflation Economies, 1985–95

	Inflation Rate (Annual, Percent)	*Money Growth Rate (Annual, Percent)*
Nicaragua	962	836
Brazil	875	996
Peru	399	389
Argentina	256	258

SOURCE: World Bank.

the public, are exogenous policy variables. In the classical model, the level of business investment was a function of the expected profitability of investment projects and the rate of interest. The expected profitability of investment projects was assumed to vary with expectations of product demand over the life of these projects, and the state of these expectations was subject to exogenous shifts.

For a given expected profitability, investment expenditures varied inversely with the interest rate. Classical economists explained this relationship as follows. A firm would have a number of possible investment projects offering various expected returns. It could rank these projects in order of the level of expected profits. The rate of interest represents the cost of borrowing funds to finance these investment projects. At a high interest rate, fewer projects will be profitable, net of interest costs. At successively lower rates of interest (lower borrowing costs), more and more projects will become profitable, net of interest costs, and investment will increase. We look at investment in more detail later but obtain the same general result. Investment depends inversely on the rate of interest. Thus, on the supply (borrowing) side of the bond market, the government bond supply is exogenous, and the business supply of bonds equals the level of investment expenditure. Investment varies inversely with the interest rate and is also influenced by exogenous shifts in the expected profitability of investment projects.

On the demand (lending) side of the bond market are the individual savers who purchase the bonds. In the classical model, saving was taken to be a positive function of the rate of interest. The act of saving is the act of forgoing current consumption to have a command over goods in a future period, a trade-off of current consumption for future consumption. As the interest rate increases, the terms of the trade-off become more favorable. A dollar saved today will earn a higher interest return for the saver, a greater command over consumption goods in future periods. Classical economists assumed that individuals would take advantage of this more favorable trade-off; they would save more at higher rates of interest.

But saving need not go into bonds; money is also a potential store of wealth. Because money paid no interest, classical economists assumed that bonds would be preferred as a store of wealth. As discussed previously, some money would be held for the convenience and security it offered. However, wealth accumulated through new saving would be held in bonds. Classical economists believed that people might shift their wealth into the form of money in times of severe general economic distress. At such times, with bank panics and bankruptcies prevalent, people might worry about bond default and hoard money, but in normal times the classical assumption was that saving was a demand for bonds.

Determination of the interest rate is illustrated in Figure 4-3. Saving (S) is plotted as an upward-sloping function of the rate of interest. Saving provides the demand for bonds, or as the classical economists called it, the *supply of loanable funds*. Investment (I) is a negatively sloped schedule plotted against the interest rate. Investment plus the exogenously determined government deficit ($G - T$), all of which we assume to be financed by selling bonds, equals the bond supply. In classical terminology, this is the *demand for loanable funds*. In the diagram, r_0 is the equilibrium interest rate, the rate of interest that equates the demand and supply for loanable funds.

The interest rate plays a stabilizing role in the classical system, as can be seen by examining the effects of a change in the expected profitability of investment. Recall that in the short run, investment depends on the interest rate and the expected future profitability of investment projects. Let us suppose that as a result of an exogenous event (e.g., fear of a future war), business managers in general lower their expectation

FIGURE 4-3 Interest Rate Determination in the Classical System

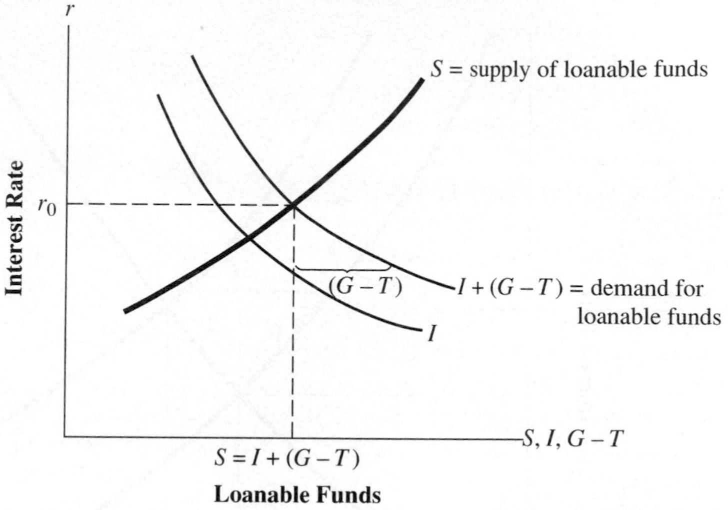

The equilibrium interest rate r_0 is the rate that equates the supply of loanable funds, which consists of saving (S), with the demand for loanable funds, which consists of investment (I) plus the bond-financed government deficit ($G - T$).

about future profits from investment. The effect would be reduced investment and, hence, a reduced demand for loanable funds *at each interest rate*.

Figure 4-4 illustrates the effect of this autonomous decline in investment demand. For simplicity, we assume that the government budget is balanced ($G = T$), so there is no government borrowing. Investment is the only source of the demand for loanable funds. The fall in expected profitability of investment projects is shown as a shift in the investment schedule downward from I_0 to I_1. At a given rate of interest, the amount of the decline in investment is measured by ΔI in Figure 4-4.

At the initial equilibrium interest rate of r_0, after the fall in investment, the supply of loanable funds exceeds demand, putting downward pressure on the rate of interest. As the rate of interest declines, two adjustments occur. First, saving declines; thus, consumption (C) increases. The amount of this decline in saving and the equal increase in current consumption is given by the distance marked A in Figure 4-4.[4] Second, investment is somewhat revived by the decline in the interest rate. This interest-rate–induced increase in investment is measured by the distance B in Figure 4-4. Equilibrium is restored at interest rate r_1, with saving (the supply of loanable funds) again equal to investment (the demand for loanable funds). At the new equilibrium, the increase in consumption (fall in saving) plus the increase in investment caused by the drop in the interest rate, the distance A + B in Figure 4-4, is just equal to the original autonomous decline in investment demand, the distance ΔI in Figure 4-4. Because of the adjustment of the interest rate, the sum of private-sector demands (C + I) is unaffected by the autonomous decline in investment demand.

This stabilizing role of the interest rate is important to the classical system. The interest-rate adjustment is the first line of defense for full employment. Shocks that affect consumption demand, investment demand, or government demand will *not* affect

[4]It is important to note that as saving declines, there is a dollar-for-dollar increase in current consumption. Real income is fixed, as are taxes, so *all* changes in saving are mirrored in changes in current consumption.

FIGURE 4-4 Autonomous Decline in Investment Demand

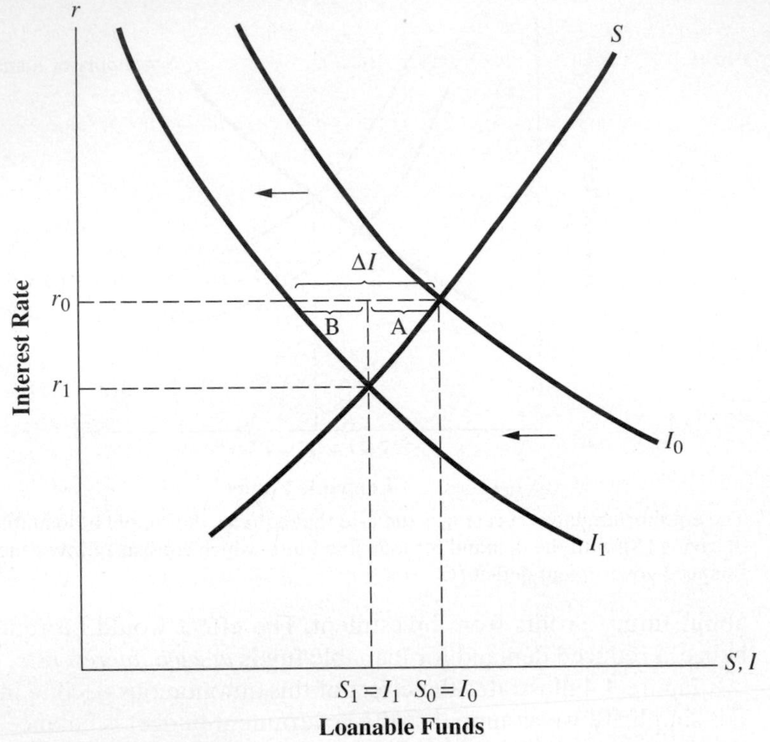

An autonomous decline in investment shifts the investment schedule to the left from I_0 to I_1—the distance ΔI. The equilibrium interest rate declines from r_0 to r_1. As the interest rate falls, there is an interest-rate–induced increase in investment—distance B. There is also an interest-rate–induced decline in saving, which is an equal increase in consumption—distance A. The interest rate–induced increases in consumption and investment just balance the autonomous decline in investment.

the demand for output as a whole. These shocks will not shift the aggregate demand curve in Figure 4-2. Even if they did, there would be no effect on output or employment because of the self-adjusting properties of the classical labor market as reflected in the vertical aggregate supply curve—the second line of defense for full employment.

4.3 POLICY IMPLICATIONS OF THE CLASSICAL EQUILIBRIUM MODEL

In this section we analyze the effects of fiscal and monetary policy actions within the classical model. We consider the effects that various policy shifts will have on output, employment, the price level, and the interest rate.

Fiscal Policy

Fiscal policy is the setting of the federal budget and thus comprises decisions on government spending and taxation. In considering the classical view of fiscal policy, it is convenient to begin with government spending.

Government Spending

Consider the effects of an increase in government spending. The question of how the increased spending is financed arises first. Like a business or household, the government has a budget constraint, the condition that all expenditures must be financed from some source. The government has three sources of funds: taxation, selling bonds to the public (borrowing funds from the public), or creating new money. The creation of new money can take several forms, but in our discussion of here, it will do no harm to assume that the government simply prints new currency to finance its spending.

To increase spending, then, the government must increase taxation, sell additional bonds to the public, or increase the money supply. For now, to avoid bringing in a monetary policy change, we assume that the money supply is fixed. We also assume that tax collections are fixed. The increased government expenditures are therefore assumed to be financed by selling bonds to the public.

It follows from our analysis to this point that a bond-financed increase in government spending will *not* affect the equilibrium values of output or the price level. This must be the case, because we constructed both the aggregate demand and aggregate supply curves, which together determine output and the price level, without reference to the level of government spending. Output is not affected by changes in government spending, so employment must also be unaffected. To understand these results, we examine how a change in government spending affects the interest rate.

Figure 4-5 shows the effect in the loanable funds market of an increase in government spending financed by a sale of bonds to the public. If government spending is greater than tax revenue, then $(G-T)$ is positive, where G is government spending, T is tax revenue, and $(G-T)$ is the government deficit. We assume that before the increase in government spending the government budget was in balance—that is, $(G=T)$. The government deficit is then equal to the increase in government spending, $(G-T)_1$. Initially, with no government deficit, the loanable funds market is in equilibrium at point E. Assuming there is no government borrowing, the equilibrium interest rate, r_0, equates the supply of loanable funds with the demand for loanable funds. Initially investment, I, is the only source of demand for loanable funds. If the increase in government spending is financed by selling bonds, then total demand for loanable funds includes both investment, I, and government borrowing, $(G-T)_1$. The increase in demand for loanable funds is shown as a rightward shift in demand, from I to $I+(G-T)_1$, moving from equilibrium point E to equilibrium point F. Note that the distance of the horizontal shift in the curve measures the amount of the increase in government deficit spending. This amount is measured by the distance $(G-T)_1$ in Figure 4-5.

The increase in government spending creates an increased demand for loanable funds as the government sells bonds to the public to finance the new spending. This creates an excess of borrowers over lenders at the initial interest rate r_0, and the interest rate is pushed up to r_1. The increase in the interest rate has two effects. Saving increases from S_0 to S_1; this is the distance A in Figure 4-5. As was explained in the preceding section, an increase in saving is mirrored by an equal decline in consumption. Second, the quantity of investment declines with the higher interest rate. At r_1, we can read the new level of investment as I_1 along the I schedule. The investment decline is the distance B in Figure 4-5.

The figure shows that the decline in consumption, which equals the amount of increased saving (distance A) plus the decline in investment (distance B), just equals the amount of the increase in government spending $(G-T)_1$. The increase in government

FIGURE 4-5 Effect of an Increase in Government Spending in the Classical Model

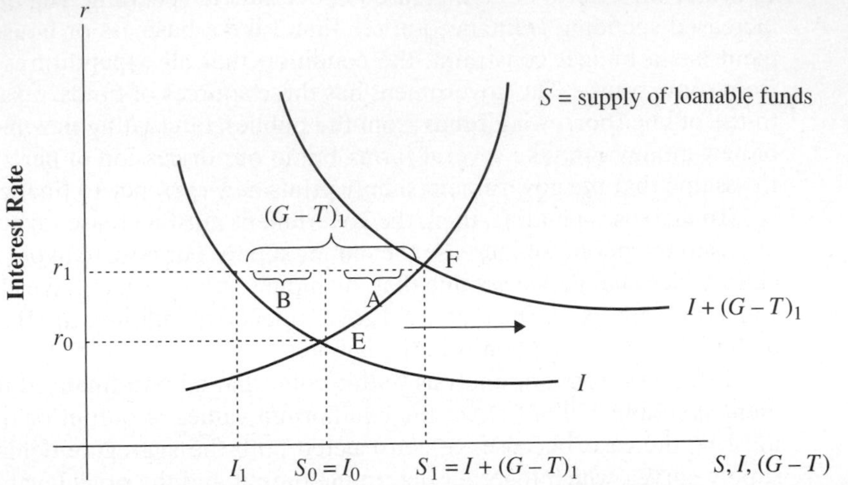

At equilibrium point E, the interest rate r_0 equates the supply of loanable funds, S, with the demand for loanable funds, I. Adding government deficit spending, $(G - T)_1$, shifts the demand for loanable funds to the right. The equilibrium interest rate rises to r_1 at point F. The increase in the interest rate causes a decline in investment from I_0 to I_1, a distance B, and an increase in saving, which is an equal decline in consumption, from S_0 to S_1, a distance A. The decline in investment and consumption just balances the increase in government spending.

spending financed by selling bonds to the public pushes the interest rate up by enough to "crowd out" an equal amount of private expenditure (consumption plus investment). Private expenditures are discouraged because the higher interest rate causes households to substitute future consumption for current consumption—in other words, to save more. Investment declines because fewer projects appear profitable with higher borrowing costs. It is this crowding out that keeps aggregate demand from increasing when the government component of demand rises. Because aggregate demand is not changed, increases in government expenditures financed by bonds do not affect the price level.

What are the effects of an increase in government spending if, alternatively, the government prints money to finance the new spending? Here, because the quantity of money is changed, the price level will change proportionately. We have previously analyzed the way an increase in the money supply shifts the aggregate demand curve up along the vertical aggregate supply curve, raising the price level (see Figure 4-2). In the classical system, the source of the increase in the money supply does not matter. A given change in the money supply has the same effect whether it enters the economy to finance an increase in government spending or in another manner. Put differently—and this is the crucial point—*the increase in government spending has no independent effect on aggregate demand.*

Tax Policy

Demand-Side Effects. As long as we consider only the effects on demand, analysis of a change in taxes produces results that are analogous to those for government spending. For example, by increasing the disposable income of households, a tax cut would stimulate consumption. If, however, the government sold bonds to the public to replace the revenues lost by the tax cut, the same crowding-out process would follow, as in the case of a bond-financed increase in government spending. The equilibrium interest rate would rise, investment would fall, and there would also be an interest-rate–induced rise in saving, meaning that consumption would fall back toward the pre–tax-cut level. In the case of a tax cut, as with an increase in spending, aggregate demand would not be affected.

If revenues lost because of the tax cut were replaced by printing new money, then, as with an increase in government spending, the money creation *would* increase aggregate demand, and the tax cut would cause the price level to rise. Again, though, it would simply be the increase in the money supply that affected the price level. The tax cut would have no *independent* effect on aggregate demand.

Supply-Side Effects. If the tax cut were a lump-sum cut, meaning, for example, that every household received a tax cut of $100, then the demand-side effects would be all that we would need to consider.[5] But suppose the tax cut was in the form of reduced income tax rates. Suppose the marginal income tax rate were cut from an initial rate of 40 percent to a new rate of 20 percent. Instead of 40 cents of every additional dollar being taken as a tax payment, only 20 cents would be taken. In the classical model, such a change would have an incentive effect on labor supply. The change would affect the supply side of the model and would affect output and employment.

Figure 4-6 illustrates the effect of a cut in the marginal income tax rate within the classical model. Part *a* shows the effects in the labor market. A cut in the tax rate would increase the labor supply at any value of the (pretax) real wage and shift the labor supply schedule out to the right. This shift follows because the worker is concerned about the *after-tax* real wage, which in this case is $(1 - t^y)\,W/P$, where t^y is the marginal income tax rate. If we had included an income tax in our classical model in Chapter 3, the labor supply function would have been

$$N^s = g\left[(1 - t^y)\frac{W}{P}\right] \tag{3.6}$$

For a given pretax real wage (W/P), a cut in the income tax represents an increase in the after-tax real wage and therefore increases labor supply.

In Figure 4-6*a*, as the marginal income tax rate falls from 0.40 to 0.20, the labor supply schedule shifts from N^s $(t^y = 0.40)$ to N^s $(t^y = 0.20)$. Equilibrium employment increases from N_0 to N_1. Part *b* of Figure 4-6 shows the aggregate production function. The increase in employment from N_0 to N_1 as a result of the increase in labor supply leads to an increase in output from Y_0 to Y_1.

In part *c* of the figure, this increase in the supply-determined level of output (from Y_0 to Y_1) is shown as a shift to the right in the aggregate supply curve from Y^s $(t^y = 0.40)$ to Y^s $(t^y = 0.20)$. Because aggregate demand is unchanged (determined by the level of the money supply), this increase in aggregate supply results in a fall in the price level.[6]

[5] Because the tax cut would affect wealth, which in turn might influence the labor–leisure choice, even a lump-sum tax cut could affect the supply side. We are neglecting wealth effects here.

[6] The aggregate demand curve is fixed as long as revenues that were lost because of the cut in the income tax rate are replaced by increased bond sales to the public. If lost revenue were instead replaced by printing money, the aggregate demand curve would shift to the right, and the price level might not fall.

FIGURE 4-6 The Supply-Side Effects of an Income Tax Cut

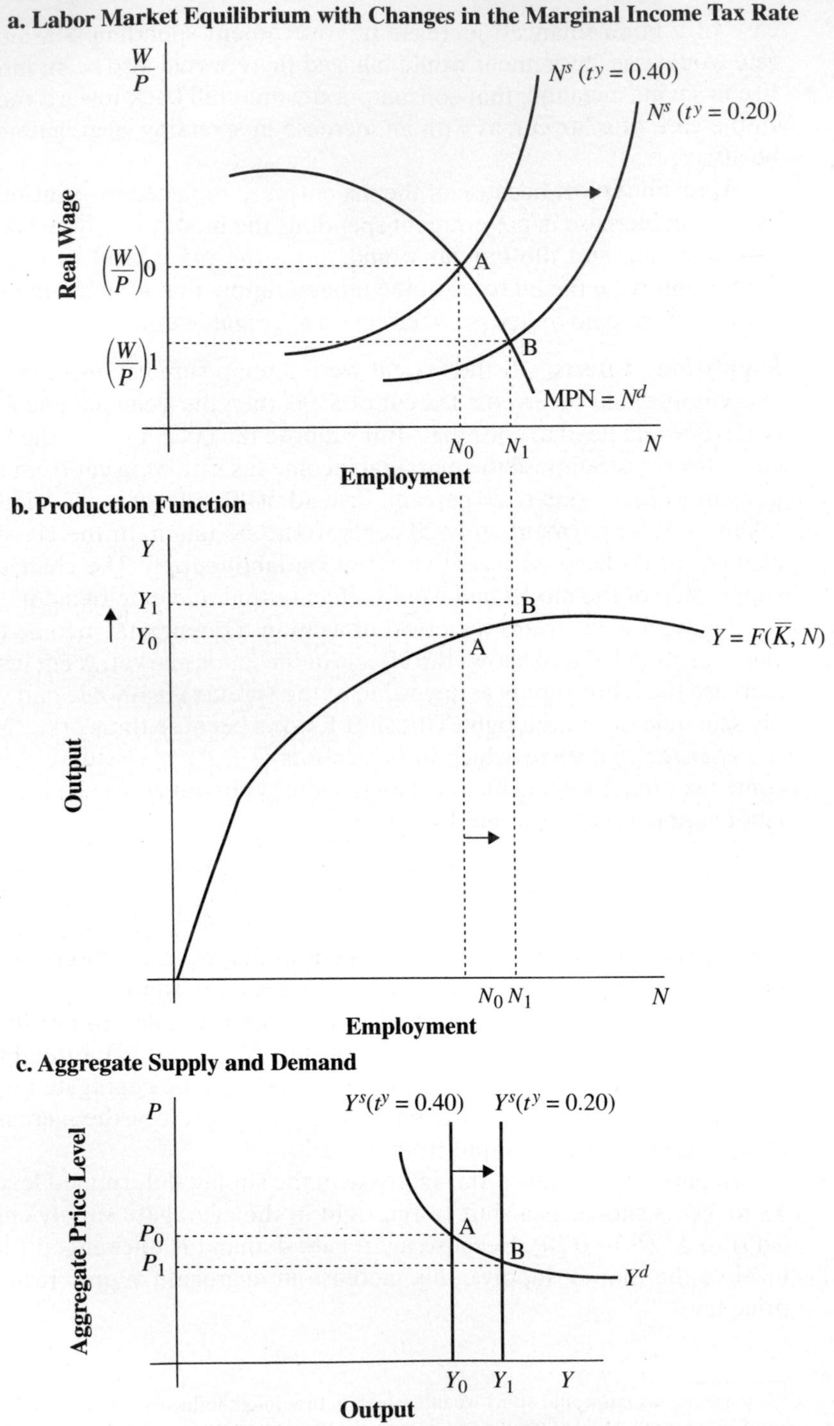

In part *a*, a reduction in the marginal income tax rate (from 0.40 to 0.20) increases the after-tax real wage for a given value of the pretax real wage. The labor supply curve shifts to the right. Equilibrium moves from point A to point B. Employment and output increase, as shown in part *b* of the graph, moving from point A to point B on the production function. This increase in output is represented by the shift to the right in the vertical aggregate supply curve in part *c*.

In summary, changes in government spending or taxes have no independent effects on aggregate demand because of the interest-rate adjustment and resulting crowding-out effects on components of private-sector demand. Changes in marginal income tax rates have additional supply-side effects. A reduction in the marginal income tax rate, for example, stimulates labor supply and leads to an increase in employment and output.

Read Perspectives 4-2.

PERSPECTIVES 4-2

SUPPLY-SIDE ECONOMICS—A MODERN CLASSICAL VIEW

Classical economists in the nineteenth and early twentieth centuries did not give much attention to the supply-side effects of changes in income tax rates. At the time, the marginal income tax rate was low and pertained only to the relatively wealthy. As can be seen from Table 4-3, in the United States, the average marginal income tax rate (averaged across each tax bracket) in 1920 was only 4.6 percent and by 1929 had declined to 3.5 percent. Moreover, in the 1920s, fewer than 15 percent of U.S. households had incomes high enough to require filing an income tax return.

As can also be seen from Table 4-3, the situation was different in the post–World War II period. By 1980, the average marginal income tax rate was above 30 percent, and a large majority of U.S. households had incomes high enough to be subject to the income tax. In the 1970s, a group that became known as the *supply-side economists* argued, much along the lines of the analysis in this subsection, that such taxes formed a "wedge" between the real wage paid by employers and that received by the worker. Reducing the size of that wedge, they argued, would increase the incentives to supply labor and result in higher output and employment, as illustrated in Figure 4-6.

By the late 1970s, economists such as Robert Mundell of Columbia University and Arthur B. Laffer, then at the University of Southern California, had popularized the idea that tax cuts would have strongly favorable supply-side effects. Then Representative Jack Kemp and Senator William Roth accepted the supply-siders' argument, and in 1977 they introduced a bill calling for across-the-board cuts of 10 percent in personal income tax rates in each of three successive years. In 1980, Ronald Reagan endorsed the Kemp–Roth proposal, and in 1981 the Reagan–Kemp–Roth tax bill, calling for a 23 percent across-the-board income tax cut over three years, was passed. Later, the Tax Reform Act of 1986 further reduced marginal income tax rates.

In general, over the three post-1980 decades, the income tax rates of most households trended down. Tax rates for social insurance (Social Security and Medicare) rose in the 1980s, then stabilized. The lowest overall tax rates occurred in 2002–7 following the tax cuts during the first George W. Bush administration. The outlook going forward is, however, for rising tax rates as increasing pressures on Social Security and Medicare spending emerge with the retirement of the baby-boom generation.

TABLE 4-3 Average Marginal Tax Rate, Selected Years (Percent)

1916	1.2	1950	19.6
1920	4.6	1970	24.3
1929	3.5	1980	30.4

SOURCE: Robert J. Barro and Chaipat Sahasakul, "Measuring the Average Marginal Tax Rate from the Individual Income Tax," *Journal of Business* 56 (October 1983), pp. 434–35, Table 2. Reprinted by permission of the University of Chicago Press.

Monetary Policy

In the classical system, the quantity of money determines the price level and the level of *nominal* income. In this sense, monetary policy was quite important to classical economists. Stable money was a requirement for stable prices.

In another sense, money was not important. The quantity of money did not affect the equilibrium values of the real variables in the system: output, employment, and the interest rate. The supply-determined nature of output and employment was the subject of Chapter 3. The theory of the equilibrium interest rate we have constructed here is a real theory that did not mention the quantity of money. Factors determining the interest rate were real investment demand, real saving, and the real value of the government deficit—what the classical economists called the forces of "productivity and thrift."

To classical economists, money was a "veil" that determined the nominal values by which we measure such variables as the level of economic activity, but had no effect on real quantities.

4.4 CONCLUSION

Classical economists stressed the *self-adjusting tendencies of the economy*. Free from destabilizing government actions, the private sector would be stable, and full employment would be achieved. The first of these self-stabilizing mechanisms is the interest rate, which adjusts to keep shocks to sectoral demands from affecting aggregate demand. The second set of stabilizers consists of freely flexible prices and money wages, which keep changes in aggregate demand from affecting output. Flexibility of prices and wages is crucial to the full-employment properties of the classical system. The inherent stability of the private sector led classical economists to *noninterventionist* policy conclusions. To be sure, many of the interventionist mercantilist policies that classical economists opposed (tariffs, trading monopolies, etc.) were a far cry from the macroeconomic stabilization policies of today, but the model itself argues for nonintervention in a very general sense.

A second central feature of the classical system is the *dichotomy between the factors determining real and nominal variables*. In the classical theory, real (supply-side) factors determine real variables. Output and employment depend primarily on population, technology, and capital formation. The interest rate depends on productivity and thrift. Money is a veil determining the nominal values by which quantities are measured, but monetary factors do not play a role in determining these real quantities.

In the next theoretical system that we consider—Keynesian theory—we will see policy conclusions that are more interventionist. We will also see that monetary and real variables are more closely interrelated in the Keynesian system.

KEY TERMS

- quantity theory of money 51
- velocity of money 51
- Cambridge approach 53

Review Questions and Problems

1. Explain the role of money in the classical system. Specifically, in the classical model, what role does money have in determining real output, employment, the price level, and the interest rate? Explain how money affects these variables; or, if money has no effect on some of them, explain why.
2. What are the differences between the Fisherian and Cambridge versions of the quantity theory of money?
3. Define the term *velocity of money*. What factors determine the velocity of money in the classical system? What is the relationship between the velocity of money and the Cambridge k?
4. Explain how aggregate demand is determined within the classical model. What would be the effects on output and the price level of an increase in aggregate demand?
5. Classical economists assumed that velocity was stable in the short run. But suppose that, because of a change in the payments mechanism—for example, greater use of credit cards—there was an exogenous rise in the velocity of money. What effect would such a change have on output, employment, and the price level within the classical model?
6. Explain how the interest rate is determined in the classical theory.
7. Explain how the interest rate works in the classical system to stabilize aggregate demand in the face of autonomous changes in components of aggregate demand such as investment or government spending.
8. Within the Cambridge form of the quantity theory, the demand for money is given by

$$M^d = kPY \tag{4.7}$$

Suppose that income (Y) is given at 300 units and the money supply (M) is fixed at 200 units. Also suppose that the value of k initially is 1/4; initially, individuals wish to hold money balances equal to one-fourth of their income. Then assume that individuals increase the money demand to one-third of their income; k rises to 1/3.

How does this increase in money demand affect the equilibrium value of the aggregate price level (P)? What was the initial equilibrium price level? What is the value after the increase in money demand? Explain the process that leads to the change in the aggregate price level.
9. In deriving the labor supply curve in Figure 3-3, we implicitly assumed that the marginal income tax rate (t^y) was equal to zero. Assume instead that $t^y = 0.20$. Redraw the figure with this modification and compare the resulting labor supply curve with the present one in Figure 3-3*b*.
10. Within the classical model, analyze the effects of an increase in the marginal income tax rate. Explain how output, employment, and the price level are affected. Consider cases in which the increased revenue produced by the tax increase results in a decline in bond sales to the public and in which it results in lower money creation.
11. What are the major policy conclusions of classical economics? Explain how these policy conclusions follow from the key assumptions of the classical theoretical system.

CHAPTER 5

The Keynesian System (I): The Role of Aggregate Demand

5.1 THE PROBLEM OF UNEMPLOYMENT

Keynesian economics developed against the background of the Great Depression of the 1930s. The effect of the Depression on the U.S. economy can be seen in Figure 5-1, which shows the annual unemployment rates for the years 1929–41. The unemployment rate rose from 3.2 percent of the labor force in 1929 to 25.2 percent in 1933, the low point for economic activity during the Depression. Unemployment remained at over 10 percent throughout the decade. Real gross national product fell by 30 percent between 1929 and 1933, and did not reach the 1929 level again until 1939.

The British economist John Maynard Keynes, whose book *The General Theory of Employment, Interest and Money* is the foundation of the Keynesian system, was more heavily influenced by events in his own country than those in the United States. In Great Britain, high unemployment began in the early 1920s and persisted into and throughout the 1930s.[1] The high unemployment in Great Britain led to a debate among economists and policymakers over the causes and the proper policy response to increased unemployment. Keynes was a participant in this debate, during the course of which he developed his revolutionary theory of macroeconomics.

According to Keynes's theory, high unemployment in Great Britain and the United States (as well as in other industrialized countries) was the result of a deficiency in *aggregate demand.* Aggregate demand was too low because of inadequate investment demand. Keynes's theory provided the basis for economic policies to combat unemployment by stimulating aggregate demand. At the time of the Depression, Keynes favored fiscal policy measures, primarily government spending on public works projects, to stimulate demand. More generally, the Keynesian theory advocates using monetary and fiscal policies to regulate aggregate demand. To understand the revolutionary nature of this theory, consider the state of macroeconomic thinking about unemployment as an economic policy question at the time Keynes's thought was developing.

Classical economists recognized the human cost of unemployment, as stated, for example, by Alfred Marshall:

> Forced interruption to labour is a grievous evil. Those, whose livelihood is secure, gain physical and mental health from happy and well-spent holidays. But want of work, with long continued anxiety, consumes a man's best strength

[1] The unemployment rate in Great Britain was above 10 percent as early as 1923 and remained above 10 percent, except for one brief fall to 9.8 percent, until 1936, the year *The General Theory* was published.

FIGURE 5-1 U.S. Unemployment Rate, 1929–41

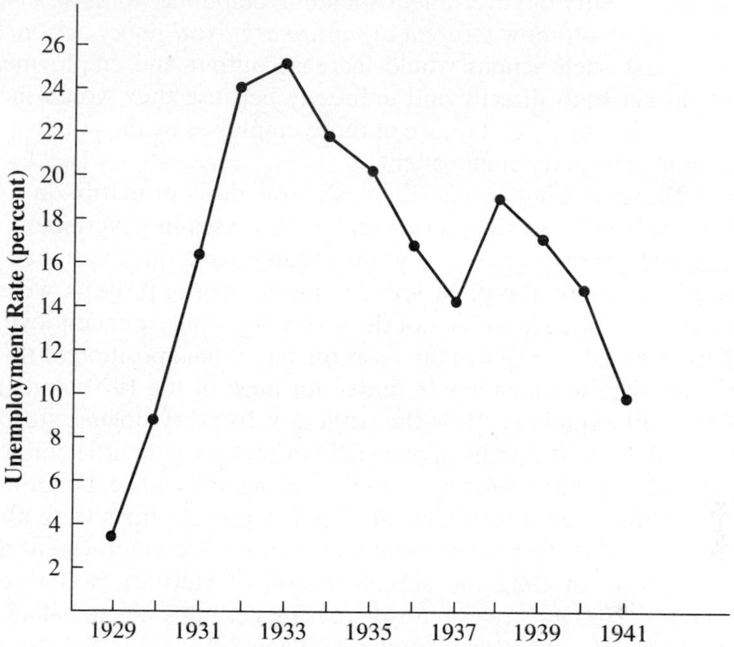

without any return. His wife becomes thin; and his children get, as it were, a nasty notch in their lives, which is perhaps never outgrown.[2]

But Marshall had little to say about the causes of unemployment. He noted that unemployment existed in early times and argued that knowledge was the cure, in that it would increase the skills of labor and also keep laborers and firms from making poor economic decisions that would result in business failures and unemployment. When Marshall suggested ways to diminish fluctuations in employment, the following was the first given:

> Those causes of discontinuity which lie within our scope, and are remediable, are chiefly connected in some way or other with the want of knowledge; but there is one which is willful: it is fashion. Until a little while ago only the rich could change their clothing at the capricious order of their dressmakers: but now all classes do it. The histories of the alpaca trade, the lace trade, the straw hat trade, the ribbon trade, and a multitude of others, tell of bursts of feverish activity alternating with deadening idleness.[3]

To the modern reader, this analysis appears quaint; it was hardly a basis for solutions to the unemployment problem of Britain in the 1920s. Marshall and the other economists relying on the classical theory had little else to offer.

---

[2]Alfred Marshall, *Money, Credit and Commerce* (London: Macmillan, 1922), p. 260.

[3]Ibid.

Much of the debate over economic policy in Great Britain at that time focused on the desirability of government spending on public works as a cure for unemployment, what we would now term an *expansionary fiscal policy* action. Keynes and others argued that such actions would increase output and employment. Such expenditures would act both directly and indirectly because they would increase the income and hence consumer expenditure of those employed by the public works projects, thus generating secondary employment.

Those arguing against Keynes's view drew primarily on the classical analysis we have presented in Chapters 3 and 4. Increases in government expenditure, unless financed by money creation and thus changes in monetary policy, would not affect either employment or the price level. If public works projects were financed by creating money, the price level but not the levels of output or unemployment would be affected. This classical theory was the basis for the official position of the Conservative Party in Great Britain, which was in power for most of the 1920s and early 1930s. As Winston Churchill explained, "It is the orthodox Treasury dogma, steadfastly held, that whatever might be the political or social advantages, very little employment can, in fact, as a general rule, be created by state borrowing and state expenditure."

In the United States, classical policy prescriptions were also influential. Far from trying to raise demand and stimulate output and employment during the height of the Depression in 1932, the administration of Herbert Hoover engineered a large tax *increase.* Hoover's reason for increasing tax rates was to balance the federal budget in the wake of falling tax revenues as income declined. Because, in the classical system, fiscal policy had no effect on income, prudent budget management had come to mean simply balancing spending with tax revenues.[4] When Franklin Roosevelt ran against Hoover for the presidency in 1932, he attacked Hoover for failing to balance the budget and argued for *cuts* in government spending. Bernard Baruch, an advisor to several presidents, expressed the conventional policy prescription as follows:

> Balance budgets, stop spending money we haven't got. Sacrifice for frugality and revenue. Cut government spending—cut it as rations are cut in a siege. Tax—tax everybody for everything.[5]

Would not the increase in taxes or the cut in government spending lower aggregate demand, output, and employment? Not in the classical system, because output and employment were supply-determined. In any case, in the classical model, fiscal policy did not affect aggregate demand. As we will see, such a tax increase or spending cut is just the opposite of the "correct" policy action indicated by the Keynesian model.

In sum, the situation in the early 1930s was one of massive unemployment that was not well explained by the classical system and for which classical economics provided no remedy. Many economists and political figures argued in favor of various policy actions, including public works projects, to try to increase aggregate demand. Such policies would not work in the classical system, where output and employment were not demand-determined. As Keynes pointed out: "The strength of the self-adjusting school

[4]This ignores the supply-side effects of a change in the tax rate, discussed in Section 4.3. As explained there, the classical economists gave little consideration to those effects, though they have become an important policy consideration in recent years.

[5]Arthur M. Schlesinger, *The Crisis of the Old Order* (New York: Houghton Mifflin, 1957), p. 457.

depends on its having behind it almost the whole body of organized economic thinking and doctrine of the last hundred years."[6] Keynes ranged himself among the "heretics" to the classical view of the self-adjusting properties of the economy. Of the heretics, he wrote: "They are deeply dissatisfied. They believe that common observation is enough to show that facts do not conform to the orthodox reasoning. They propose remedies prompted by instinct, by flair, by practical good sense, by experience of the world—half right, most of them, half wrong."[7] Keynes felt that the heretics would never prevail until the flaw in the orthodox classical theory had been found. He believed that flaw to be the lack of an explicit theory of the aggregate demand for output and, hence, of the role of aggregate demand in determining output and employment. We discuss next the theory provided by Keynes and his followers to fill this gap.

Read Perspectives 5-1.

5.2 THE SIMPLE KEYNESIAN MODEL: CONDITIONS FOR EQUILIBRIUM OUTPUT

A central notion in the Keynesian model is that an equilibrium level of output requires that *output be equal to aggregate demand.* In our model, this condition for equilibrium can be expressed as

$$Y = E \tag{5.1}$$

where Y is equal to total output (GDP) and E equals aggregate demand or desired expenditures on output. Aggregate demand (E) consists of three components: household consumption (C), desired business investment demand (I), and the government sector's demand for goods and services (G). Thus, in equilibrium we have

$$Y = E = C + I + G \tag{5.2}$$

The simple form of (5.2) and of the identities discussed later results from neglecting some complexities in the definitions of GDP and national income. These simplifications, discussed in Chapter 2, are noted here briefly again. Exports and imports do not appear in equation (5.2). For now, we are dealing with a "closed" economy, neglecting foreign trade. The roles of imports and exports in the simple Keynesian model will be considered in Section 5.7. Notice that for a closed economy we need not distinguish between GDP and GNP, the other output measure defined in Chapter 2. Depreciation is also neglected, so we do not need to distinguish between GDP and net national product. We also assume that GDP and national income are equivalent. This means that we do not include items in the model that cause a discrepancy between the two totals (primarily indirect business taxes). A final assumption relates to the units in which each of the variables is measured. For this chapter, we assume that *the aggregate price level is fixed.* All variables are *real* variables, and all changes are changes in real terms.

[6] John M. Keynes, *Collected Works,* vol. 13 (London: Macmillan, 1973), p. 489.
[7] Ibid., pp. 488–89.

PERSPECTIVES 5-1

MACROECONOMIC CONTROVERSIES

In this part we consider different schools of macroeconomics. This puts the emphasis on controversies. It should be kept in mind, though, that we are interested in fundamental differences, which are rooted in macroeconomic models, not in partisan policy disputes. The dividing line between the two is not always clearly drawn, but to see that the line exists, consider the following.

Lionel Robbins was a prominent exponent of the classical economics. Dismissing some critics of that theory he wrote:

> On this plane, not only is any real knowledge of the classical writers non-existent but further their place has been taken by a set of mythological figures, passing by the same names, but not infrequently invested with attitudes almost exactly the reverse of those which the originals adopted. These dummies are very malignant creatures indeed. . . . They can conceive of no function for the state than that of the night watchman. . . . Hence, when a popular writer of the day wishes to present his own point of view in a specially favourable setting, he has only to point the contrast with the attitude of these reprehensible people and the desired effect is produced.[a]

Robbins conceded the need to critically reexamine the writings of the classical economists to see "to what extent is their theory of the market sustained by the results of more recent analysis? How far were they justified in the hope that financial controls (about the exact nature of which they never reached agreement) were sufficient to maintain the stability of the envelope of aggregate demand? Were the Classical Economists right in their apprehensions of over-all collectivism?"[b]

That Robbins Keynes was no popular writer of the day but rather a very serious critic can be seen from a description he provided in a different context:

> Keynes was in his most lucid and persuasive mood; and the effect was irresistible. At such moments, I often find myself thinking that Keynes must be one of the most remarkable men that ever lived—the quick logic, the bird-like swoop of intuition, the vivid fancy, the wide vision, above all the incomparable sense of the fitness of words, all combine to make something several degrees beyond the limit of ordinary human achievement. . . . He uses the classical style of our life and language, it is true, but it is shot through with something which is not traditional, a unique unearthly quality of which one can only say that it is pure genius.[c]

The quote shows the awe in which Keynes was held (at least at times) even by those he attacked. I also use it to indicate that Keynes's arguments with the classical economists and the later criticisms of Keynes's theory by economists such as Milton Friedman and Robert Lucas are contributions by some of the major intellectual figures of our age.

[a] Lionel Robbins, *The Theory of Economic Policy* (London: Macmillan, 1952), p. 5.

[b] Ibid., p. 206.

[c] Quoted from Robert Skidelsky, *John Maynard Keynes, Fighting For Freedom, 1937–1946* (New York: Viking, 2001), p. 341.

With national product Y also measuring national income, we can write

$$Y \equiv C + S + T \tag{5.3}$$

Equation (5.3) is an accounting definition, or identity, stating that national income, all of which is assumed to be paid to households in return for factor services (wages, interest, rents, dividends), is either consumed (C), paid out in taxes (T), or saved (S).[8] In addition, from the fact that Y is national product, we can write

$$Y \equiv C + I_r + G \tag{5.4}$$

Equation (5.4) defines national product as consumption plus *realized* investment (I_r) plus government spending.[9]

Using the definitions given in equations (5.3) and (5.4), we can rewrite the condition for equilibrium income given in equation (5.2) in two alternative ways, which will help us understand the nature of equilibrium in the model. By (5.2), Y must equal ($C + I + G$) in equilibrium, and from (5.3), Y is defined as ($C + S + T$); *in equilibrium*, therefore,

$$C + S + T \equiv Y = C + I + G$$

or, equivalently,

$$S + T = I + G \tag{5.5}$$

In similar fashion, from equations (5.2) and (5.4) we can see that in equilibrium

$$C + I_r + G \equiv Y = C + I + G$$

or, by canceling terms,

$$I_r = I \tag{5.6}$$

There are then three equivalent ways to state the condition for equilibrium in the model:

$$Y = E = C + I + G \tag{5.2}$$

$$S + T = I + G \tag{5.5}$$

$$I_r = I \tag{5.6}$$

To help interpret these conditions, we turn to the flowchart in Figure 5-2. Each magnitude in the chart (each of the variables in our model) is a *flow* variable. The magnitudes are measured in dollars per period. In the national income accounts, they are measured as billions of dollars per quarter or year. The flow marked with the uppermost arrow in the diagram is the flow of national income from the business sector to the household sector. This flow consists of payments for factor services. Such payments sum to national income, which is equal to national product. There is a corresponding flow from the household sector to the business sector, consisting of the factor services supplied by the household sector. This flow and similar flows are not shown in the diagram because they are not money flows.

National income is distributed by households into three flows. One is a flow of consumption expenditures that goes back to the business sector as a demand for the output. Thus the inner loop of our diagram depicts a process whereby firms produce

[8] The model does not allow for retained earnings. All profits are paid out as dividends. Also, firms are assumed to make no tax payments; all taxes are paid by households.

[9] Recall from Chapter 2 that *realized* investment is the total that appears in the national income accounts, whether or not that investment was desired by firms.

FIGURE 5-2 Circular Flow of Income and Output

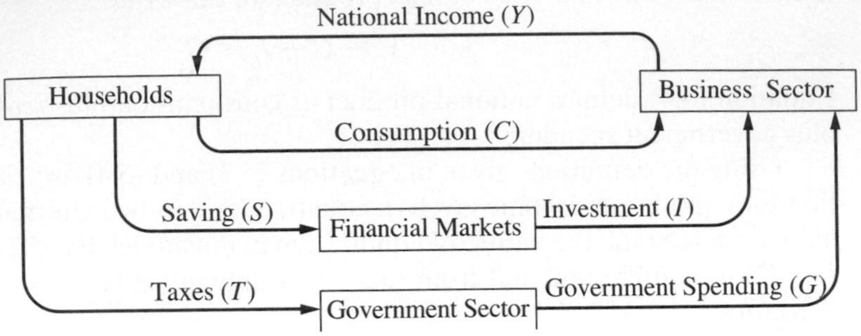

output (Y), which generates an equal amount of income to the household sector, which in turn generates a demand for the output (C).

Not all national income returns directly to the firms as a demand for output. There are two flows out of the household sector in addition to consumption expenditure—the saving flow and the flow of tax payments. If we regard the inner loop of our diagram, linking the households (as suppliers of factor services and demanders of output) and the business sector (as suppliers of output and demanders of factor services) as the central income- and output-generating mechanism, the saving and tax flows are *leakages* from this central loop.

The saving leakage flows into financial markets, which means that the part of income that is saved is held in the form of some financial asset (currency, bank deposits, bonds, equities, etc.). The tax flow is paid to the government sector. The tax flow in the diagram is *net* taxes—that is, gross tax payments minus transfer payments from the government to the household sector (Social Security benefits, welfare payments, unemployment compensation, etc.). Consequently, in later discussions, a tax increase or a tax cut can be interpreted equivalently as a change in the opposite direction in the level of transfer payments.

Although each dollar of output and, hence, national income does not directly generate one dollar of demand for output on the part of the household sector, this does not mean that total demand must fall short of output. There are additional demands for output on the part of the business sector itself for investment and from the government sector. In terms of the circular flow, these are *injections* into the central loop of our diagram. The investment injection is shown as a flow from financial markets to the business sector. The purchasers of the investment goods are the firms in the business sector themselves. These purchases must, however, be financed by borrowing. Thus the dollar amount of investment represents an equivalent flow of funds lent to the business sector. Government spending is a demand for the output of the business sector and is shown as a money flow from the government to the business sector.

We can now examine the three equivalent expressions for equilibrium given by equations (5.2), (5.5), and (5.6). Production of a level of output, Y, generates an equivalent amount of income to households. A portion of this income, equal to consumption demand (C), returns directly to the firms as a demand for output. The level of output will be at equilibrium if this directly generated demand (C), when added to desired investment expenditures of firms (I) and government spending (G), produces a total demand equal to Y—that is, if

$$Y = E = C + I + G \tag{5.2}$$

From the second version of the condition for equilibrium income

$$S + T = I + G \tag{5.5}$$

we see that a flow rate of output will be an equilibrium rate if the leakages ($S + T$) from the central loop of our diagram are just balanced by injections ($I + G$) into this central income and output circular flow. This rate ensures that the amount of income households do not spend on output ($S + T$), and therefore the amount of output that is produced but not sold to households ($Y - C \equiv S + T$), is just equal to the amount the other two sectors wish to buy ($I + G$). This is equivalent to saying that total output equals aggregate demand and is thus also equivalent to the first way of stating the condition for equilibrium.

The third way of expressing the condition for equilibrium, equation (5.6) ($I = I_r$), states that in equilibrium desired investment must equal realized investment. What does it mean for desired investment to differ from realized investment? The GDP accountant computes investment as the total volume of business spending on plant and equipment, plus inventory investment, the increase (or decline) in inventories.[10] We assume that desired spending on plant and equipment equals actual spending as recorded by the GDP accountant. It is in the last category, inventory investment, that desired and realized totals may differ. The GDP accountant will record all goods that are produced by a firm and not sold as inventory investment—*whether such investment was intended or not.*

To see how realized and intended inventory investment can differ, consider what happens when a level of output ($Y \equiv C + I_r + G$) is produced that exceeds aggregate demand ($E = C + I + G$). In this case,

$$\begin{gathered} Y > E \\ C + I_r + G > C + I + G \\ I_r > I \end{gathered} \tag{5.7}$$

whcrc I_r I is thc *unintended inventory accumulation.* Thc amount by which output exceeds aggregate demand ($I_r - I$) will be unsold output over and above the amount of inventory investment the firm desired. This excess is unintended inventory accumulation.

In the reverse situation, in which aggregate demand exceeds output, we have

$$\begin{gathered} E > Y \\ C + I + G > C + I_r + G \\ I > I_r \end{gathered} \tag{5.8}$$

where $I - I_r$, is the *unintended inventory shortfall.* Demand is greater than output, and firms sell more than was planned. Inventories end up at less than the desired level. The

[10] Here, to keep the discussion simple, we ignore residential construction. In Chapter 6, the investment concept will be broadened.

equilibrium point ($I = I_r$) is a level of production that, after all sales are made, leaves inventory investment at the level desired by firms. As can be seen from equation (5.7) or (5.8), this is the level at which output equals aggregate demand and hence is equivalent to the other two ways of expressing the condition for equilibrium.

This third way of expressing the condition for equilibrium in the model shows clearly why there cannot be an equilibrium at any other point. If, at a given level of output, firms are accumulating undesired inventories or are seeing their inventories depleted, there is a tendency for output to change. If production exceeds demand ($Y > E$), firms are accumulating unwanted inventories ($I_r > I$), and there is a tendency for output to fall as firms cut production to reduce inventories. If, alternatively, demand is outstripping production ($E > Y$), there is an inventory shortfall ($I_r < I$) and a tendency for output to rise as firms try to prevent further falls in inventories. Only when aggregate demand equals output will firms be satisfied with their current level of output. There is neither an unintended inventory buildup nor a shortfall and, therefore, no tendency for output to change.

5.3 THE COMPONENTS OF AGGREGATE DEMAND

We have expressed the condition for equilibrium in the simple Keynesian model in terms of the components of aggregate demand. To see the factors that determine the level of income, we consider the factors that affect the components of aggregate demand: consumption, investment, and government spending. Saving and taxes also enter into our discussion.

Consumption

Consumer expenditure is the largest component of aggregate demand, amounting to between 60 and 70 percent of GDP in recent years.

Keynes believed that the level of consumer expenditure was a stable function of disposable income, where disposable income (Y_D) in our simple model is national income minus net tax payments ($Y_D = Y - T$).[11] Keynes did not deny that variables other than income affect consumption, but he believed that income was the dominant factor determining consumption. In a first approximation, other influences could be neglected.

consumption function the Keynesian relationship between income and consumption

The specific form of the consumption–income relationship, termed the **consumption function**, proposed by Keynes was as follows:

$$C = a + bY_D, \qquad a > 0, \qquad 0 < b < 1 \tag{5.9}$$

Figure 5-3 graphs this relationship. The intercept term a, which is assumed to be positive, is the value of consumption when disposable income equals zero. As such, a can be thought of as a measure of the effect on consumption of variables other than income, variables not explicitly included in this simple model. The

[11] Recall here that T is net taxes (i.e., gross tax payments minus transfer payments). Disposable income ($Y_D = Y - T$) is therefore national income minus gross taxes plus transfer payments.

FIGURE 5-3 Keynesian Consumption Function

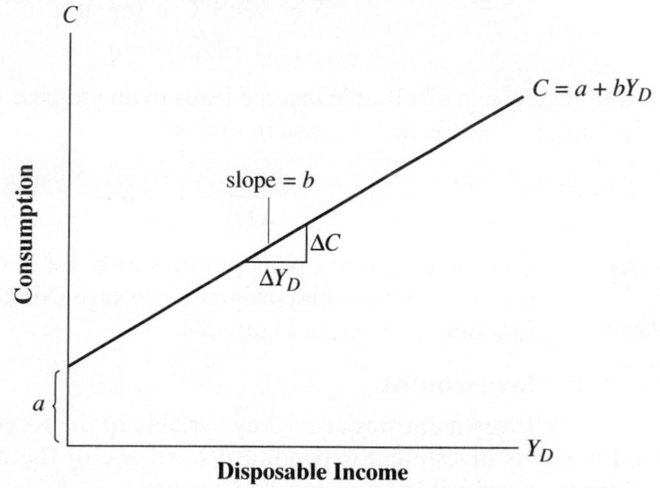

The consumption function shows the level of consumption (C) corresponding to each level of disposable income (Y_D). The slope of the consumption function ($\Delta C/\Delta Y_D$) is the marginal propensity to consume (b), the increase in consumption per unit increase in disposable income. The intercept for the consumption function (a) is the (positive) level of consumption at a zero level of disposable income.

parameter b, the slope of the function, gives the increase in consumer expenditure per unit increase in disposable income. In notation, we frequently use

$$b = \frac{\Delta C}{\Delta Y_D} \tag{5.10}$$

where, as in Chapter 3, the differencing symbol, Δ, indicates the change in the variable it precedes. The value of the increment to consumer expenditure per unit increment to income (b) is termed the **marginal propensity to consume (MPC)**. The Keynesian assumption is that consumption will increase with an increase in disposable income ($b > 0$) but that the increase in consumption will be less than the increase in disposable income ($b < 1$).

marginal propensity to consume (MPC) the increase in consumption per unit increase in disposable income

From the definition of national income,

$$Y \equiv C + S + T \tag{5.3}$$

we can write

$$Y_D \equiv Y - T \equiv C + S \tag{5.11}$$

which shows that disposable income is, by definition, consumption plus saving. Thus a theory of the consumption–income relationship also implicitly determines the saving–income relationship. In the case of the Keynesian theory, we have

$$S = -a + (1 - b)Y_D \tag{5.12}$$

If consumption is a units with Y_D equal to 0, then *at that point*

$$S \equiv Y_D - C = 0 - a$$
$$= -a$$

If a 1-unit increase in disposable income leads to an increase of b units in consumption, the remainder $(1 - b)$ is the increase in saving:

$$\frac{\Delta S}{\Delta Y_D} = 1 - b \tag{5.13}$$

marginal propensity to save (MPS) the increase in saving per unit increase in disposable income

This increment to saving per unit increase in disposable income $(1 - b)$ is called the **marginal propensity to save (MPS)**. The graph of the saving function is shown in Figure 5-4.

Investment

Investment was also a key variable in the Keynesian system. Changes in desired business investment expenditure were one of the major factors that Keynes thought were responsible for changes in income.

As noted previously, Keynes believed that consumption was a stable function of disposable income. This view did not imply that consumption expenditures would be stable over time. It did imply that, in the absence of other factors that caused income to change, consumption expenditures would not be an important independent source of variability in income. Consumption was primarily *induced* expenditure, meaning expenditure that depends directly on income.

To explain the underlying causes of movements in aggregate demand and, hence, income, Keynes looked to the *autonomous* components of aggregate demand. These components were determined, in large part, independently of current income. When these expenditure components varied, they caused income to vary. Keynes believed that investment was the most highly variable of the autonomous components of aggregate demand. He believed that variable investment spending was primarily responsible for income instability.

Table 5-1 contains figures for investment and consumption as percentages of GNP in selected years. The data contrast investment and consumption spending in

FIGURE 5-4 Keynesian Saving Function

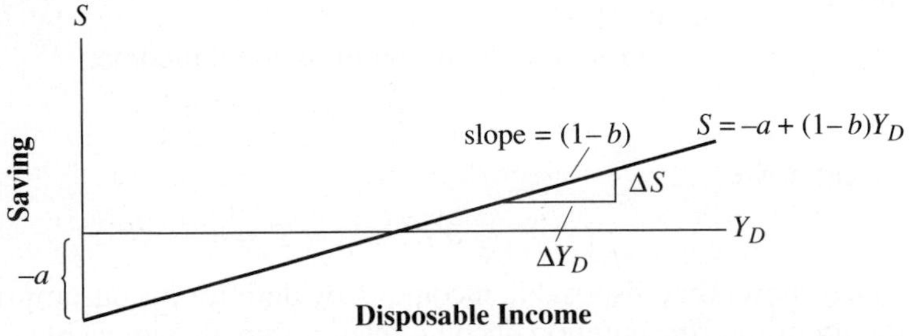

The saving function shows the level of saving (S) at each level of disposable income (Y_D). The slope of the saving function is the MPS $(1 - b)$, the increase in saving per unit increase in disposable income. The intercept for the saving function ($-a$) is the (negative) level of saving at a zero level of disposable income.

TABLE 5-1 Consumption and Investment as a Percentage of GNP, Selected Years

Year	*Investment*	*Consumption*
1929	15.7	74.8
1933	2.5	82.1
1955	17.1	63.5
1958	13.8	64.5
1973	16.1	62.6
1975	12.5	64.0
1979	16.0	62.7
1982	13.1	65.3
1989	11.0	67.1
1991	9.6	68.5
2000	17.7	68.7
2001	16.0	69.8

prosperous years (1929, 1955, 1973, 1979, 1989, 2000) with corresponding spending in subsequent depression or recession years (1933, 1958, 1975, 1982, 1991, 2001). Investment spending does appear to be more volatile and is a logical choice as a factor explaining income variability. The question remains: What determines investment?

Keynes suggested two variables as primary determinants of investment expenditures in the short run: the interest rate and the state of business expectations.

In explaining the relationship between investment and the rate of interest, Keynes's analysis did not differ from the classical view. The level of investment is assumed to be inversely related to the level of the interest rate. At higher interest rates, fewer investment projects have a prospective return high enough to justify borrowing to finance them. This link will be important in Chapter 6. For now, because we have not explained how the interest rate is determined in the Keynesian model, we neglect the effect of the interest rate on investment. We focus on the second factor determining investment, the expected yield on investment projects.

Business managers' expectations about the future profitability of investment projects are a central element in Keynes's analysis. Keynes emphasized the "uncertain knowledge" upon which expectations of the future must be based. To predict the profitability of a project that will produce output over 20 or 30 years, a manager needs a great deal of knowledge about the future. He needs to know the future demand for the product, which requires knowledge about future consumer tastes and the state of aggregate demand. He needs knowledge about future costs, including money wages, interest rates, and tax rates; a well-grounded forecast of such variables cannot be made for 20 or 30 years into the future.

Nevertheless, investment decisions are made. Keynes felt that rational managers faced with the need to make decisions under extreme uncertainty formed expectations using the following techniques:

1. They tended to extrapolate past trends into the future, ignoring possible future changes, unless there was specific information about a prospective change.
2. "Knowing that our own individual judgment is worthless, we endeavor to fall back on the judgment of the rest of the world, which is perhaps better informed.

That is, we endeavor to conform with the behavior of the majority or the average. The psychology of a society of individuals each of whom is endeavoring to copy the others leads to what we may strictly term a *conventional* judgment."[12]

Keynes believed that an expectation formed in this manner would have the following property.

In particular, being based on so flimsy a foundation, it is subject to sudden and violent changes. The practice of calmness and immobility, of certainty and security, suddenly breaks down. New fears and hopes will, without warning, take charge of human conduct. The forces of disillusion may suddenly impose a new conventional basis of valuation. All these pretty, polite techniques, made for a well-panelled board room, are liable to collapse. At all times the vague panic fears and equally vague and unreasoned hopes are not really lulled, and lie but a little way below the surface.[13]

In summary, expectations of the future profitability of investment projects rested on a precarious base of knowledge, and Keynes felt that such expectations could shift frequently, at times drastically, in response to new information and events. Consequently, investment demand was unstable.

Government Spending and Taxes

Government spending (G) is a second element of autonomous expenditures. Government spending is assumed to be controlled by the policymaker and therefore does not depend directly on the level of income.

We assume that the level of tax receipts (T) is also controlled by the policymaker and is a policy variable. A more realistic assumption is that the policymaker sets the tax rate, and tax receipts vary with income. This assumption would complicate our calculations but would not change the essential conclusions (more complex tax structures are discussed in Chapter 18, where we consider fiscal policy in more detail).

5.4 DETERMINING EQUILIBRIUM INCOME

We now have all the elements needed to determine equilibrium income (output).[14] The first form of the condition for an equilibrium level of income is

$$Y = E = C + I + G \quad \textbf{(5.2)}$$

Equilibrium income (Y) is the *endogenous* variable to be determined. The *autonomous* expenditure terms I and G are given, as is the level of T; these are the *exogenous* variables determined by factors outside the model. Consumption is, for the most part, *induced* expenditure determined *endogenously* by the consumption function

[12]John M. Keynes, "The General Theory of Employment," *Quarterly Journal of Economics* (February 1937), p. 214.

[13]Ibid., pp. 214–15.

[14]Recall that *national output* and *income* are identical under the assumptions we have made. These terms are used interchangeably in our discussion.

$$C = a + bY_D = a + bY - bT \tag{5.9}$$

where the second equality uses the definition of disposable income ($Y_D \equiv Y - T$).

Substituting the equation for consumption given by equation (5.9) into the equilibrium condition (5.2), we can solve for $\overline{Y}$, the equilibrium level of income, as follows:

$$\begin{aligned} Y &= C + I + G \\ Y &= a + bY - bT + I + G \\ Y - bY &= a - bT + I + G \\ Y(1 - b) &= a - bT + I + G \\ \overline{Y} &= \frac{1}{1 - b}(a - bT + I + G) \end{aligned} \tag{5.14}$$

Figure 5-5 depicts the determination of equilibrium income. Income is measured along the horizontal axis, and the components of aggregate demand are measured along the

FIGURE 5-5 Determination of Equilibrium Income

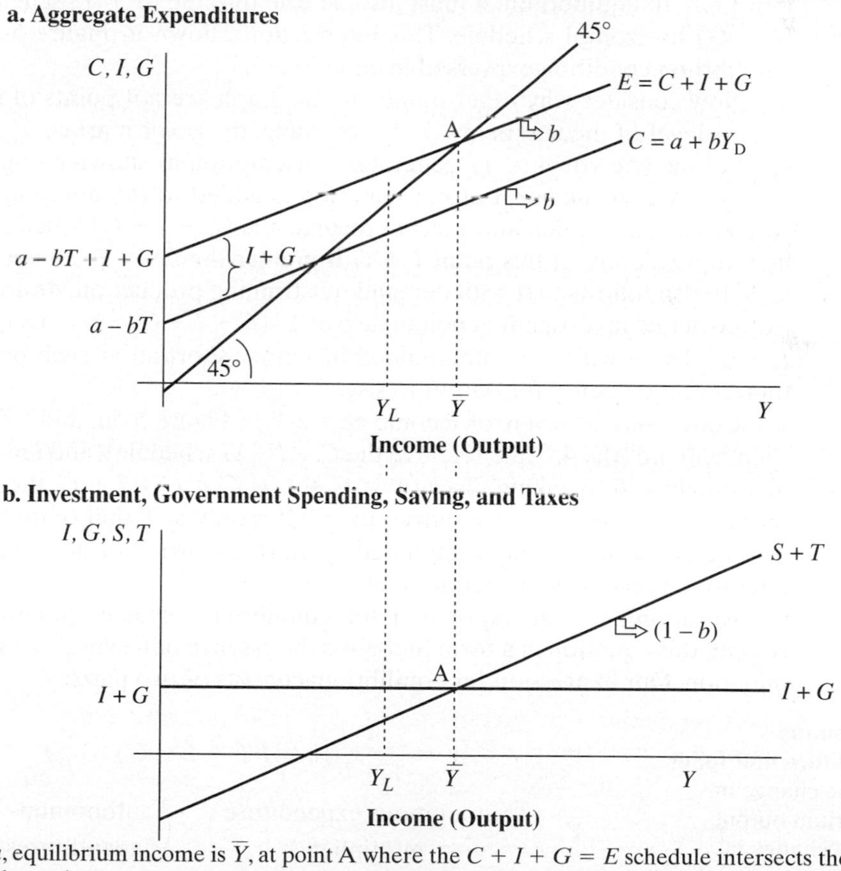

In part a, equilibrium income is $\overline{Y}$, at point A where the $C + I + G = E$ schedule intersects the 45° line. At that point, aggregate expenditures equal output, $(C + I + G) = Y$. At point A in part b, at the equilibrium level of output, $\overline{Y}$, the $S + T$ and $I + G$ schedules intersect, so $S + T = I + G$. At the level of income Y_L, which is less than equilibrium output $\overline{Y}$, aggregate demand exceeds output, $(C + I + G) > Y$. At points greater than equilibrium output $\overline{Y}$, output exceeds aggregate demand.

vertical axis. The 45° line is drawn to split the positive quadrant of the graph. All points along this line indicate that aggregate expenditures equal aggregate output. The value of the variables measured on the vertical axis, $(C + I + G)$, is equal to the value of the variable measured on the horizontal axis, (Y). The consumption function $(C = a + bY_D)$ is shown on the graph, and we have also plotted the $(C + I + G)$ or aggregate expenditure (E) schedule, which is obtained by adding the autonomous expenditure components, investment and government spending, to consumption spending at each level of income. Because the autonomous expenditure components (I, G) do not depend directly on income, the $(C + I + G)$ schedule lies above the consumption function by a constant amount.

As shown in Figure 5-5*b*, the line plotting these autonomous expenditure components alone, the $I + G$ line, is horizontal because their level does not depend on Y. The upward-sloping line, marked $S + T$ in the graph, plots the value of saving plus taxes. This schedule slopes upward because saving varies positively with income.

In Figure 5-5*a*, the equilibrium level of income is shown at the point where the $(C + I + G)$ schedule crosses the 45° line, and aggregate demand is therefore equal to income (Y). This intersection illustrates the equilibrium condition expressed in equation (5.2). In equilibrium, it must also be true that the $(S + T)$ schedule intersects the $(I + G)$ horizontal schedule. This intersection, shown in Figure 5-5*b*, illustrates the equilibrium condition expressed in equation (5.5).

Now consider why other points on the graph are not points of equilibrium. Consider a level of income below $\bar{Y}$, for example, the point marked Y_L in Figure 5-5*a*. A level of income equal to Y_L generates consumption as shown along the consumption function. When this level of consumption is added to the autonomous expenditures $(I + G)$, aggregate demand exceeds income; the $(C + I + G)$ schedule is above the 45° line. Equivalently, at this point $I + G$ is greater than $S + T$, as can be seen in Figure 5.5*b*. It also follows that with demand outstripping production, desired investment will exceed actual investment at points such as $Y_L (C + I + G > Y \equiv C + I_r + G$; therefore, $I > I_r)$. There will be an unintended inventory shortfall at such points below $\bar{Y}$ and therefore a tendency for output to rise.

Conversely, at levels of income above $\bar{Y}$ in Figure 5-5*a*, and 5-5*b*, output will exceed demand (the 45° line is above the $C + I + G$ schedule), and unintended inventory investment will be taking place $(Y \equiv C + I_r + G > C + I + G$; therefore, $I_r > I)$, and there will be a tendency for output to fall. It is only at $\bar{Y}$ that output is equal to aggregate demand; there is no unintended inventory shortfall or accumulation and, consequently, no tendency for output to change.

Returning to our expression for equilibrium income, equation (5.14), we can rewrite this equation in a form that gives the essence of Keynes's view of income determination. Our expression for equilibrium consists of two parts:

autonomous expenditure multiplier gives the change in equilibrium output per unit change in autonomous expenditures (e.g., government spending)

$$\bar{Y} = \frac{1}{1 - b}(a - bT + I + G)$$

$$\bar{Y} = \begin{pmatrix}\text{autonomous expenditure}\\ \text{multiplier}\end{pmatrix} \times \begin{pmatrix}\text{autonomous}\\ \text{expenditures}\end{pmatrix} \qquad \textbf{(5.15)}$$

The first term, $1/(1 - b)$, is called the **autonomous expenditure multiplier**. Note that b is the fraction of any increment to disposable income that goes to consumption—the marginal propensity to consume (MPC). The term $1/(1-b)$ or $1/(1-\text{MPC})$ is then 1 divided by a fraction and, hence, some number greater than 1. Some examples are as follows:

$$b = 0.5: \quad \frac{1}{1-b} = \frac{1}{1-0.5} = \frac{1}{0.5} = 2$$

$$b = 0.8: \quad \frac{1}{1-b} = \frac{1}{1-0.8} = \frac{1}{0.2} = 5$$

$$b = 0.9: \quad \frac{1}{1-b} = \frac{1}{1-0.9} = \frac{1}{0.1} = 10$$

We call this term the *autonomous expenditure multiplier* because every dollar of autonomous expenditure is multiplied by this factor to get its contribution to equilibrium income.

autonomous expenditures are expenditures that are largely determined by factors other than current income

The second term in the expression is the level of **autonomous expenditures**. We have already discussed two elements of autonomous expenditures, investment (I) and government spending (G). The first two terms (a and $-bT$) require a few words of explanation. These terms measure the autonomous component of consumption expenditures (a) and the autonomous effect of tax collections on aggregate demand ($-bT$), which also works through consumption. Consumption is, for the most part, induced expenditures, as explained previously. The two terms (a and $-bT$), however, affect the amount of consumption *for a given level of income* (Y). In terms of Figure 5-5, they determine the height of the consumption function. Like G and I, they affect the amount of aggregate demand for a given level of income rather than being themselves directly determined by income. They are thus appropriately included as autonomous factors affecting aggregate demand.

Keynes's theory in its simplest form can be stated as follows. Consumption is a stable function of income; that is, the MPC is stable. Changes in income come primarily from changes in the autonomous components of aggregate demand, especially from changes in the unstable investment component. A given change in an autonomous component of aggregate demand causes a larger change in equilibrium income because of the multiplier, for reasons we explain later. Equation (5.15) makes it clear that, in the absence of government policies to stabilize the economy, income will be unstable because of the instability of investment. From equation (5.15) one can also see that by appropriate changes in government spending (G) and taxes (T), the government could counteract the effects of shifts in investment. Appropriate changes in G and T could keep the sum of the terms in parentheses (autonomous expenditures) constant even in the face of undesirable changes in the I term.

5.5 CHANGES IN EQUILIBRIUM INCOME

Consider the effect on equilibrium income of a change in autonomous investment demand. We assume that the other determinants of autonomous expenditures, the other items in parentheses in equation (5.15), are fixed. We solve for the change in equilibrium income from equation (5.15) as follows:

$$\Delta \bar{Y} = \frac{1}{1-b} \Delta I \tag{5.16}$$

or

$$\frac{\Delta Y}{\Delta \bar{I}} = \frac{1}{1-b} \tag{5.17}$$

A 1-unit change in investment causes a change in income of $1/(1-b)$ units. If b is 0.8, for example, Y changes by 5 units for each 1-unit change in investment. Why does income change by a multiple of the change in investment and why by the precise amount $1/(1-b)$?

One analogy to the process behind the multiplier is the "ripple effect" of a stone dropped in a pond. There is the initial effect as the stone disturbs the water. Added to this is the effect on the rest of the surface as the water displaced by the stone spreads out to the adjoining water, with intensity that diminishes with the distance from the initial point of impact. The investment change is the initial disturbance; let us assume that this equals 100 units. As some firms experience increased demand as a result of this increased investment, their output increases. In consequence, their payments to factors of production (wages, rents, interest, dividends) increase. To the households, this is an increase in income and, because taxes are fixed, an equal increase in disposable income. Consumption will then increase, although by less than the increase in income. This is the beginning of the indirect effects of the shock. With ΔI equal to 100 as assumed, if the MPC were 0.8, for example, there would now be an additional 80 units of consumer demand.

The process does not stop here; the 80 units of new consumer expenditure, with the resulting increase in production, generate a second-round increase in income for households of 80 units. There will be a further increase in consumer demand (64 units if the MPC is 0.8). Thus, the reason that income rises by more than the autonomous rise in investment is that the rise in investment leads to induced increases in consumer demand as income increases.

Why is the increase in income per dollar increase in investment just equal to $1/(1-b)$? With the other elements of autonomous expenditures fixed, we can write the change in equilibrium income as investment varies as

$$\Delta Y = \Delta I + \Delta C \tag{5.18}$$

Restoring the equality of income and aggregate demand requires that equilibrium income rise by an amount equal to the increase in investment (ΔI) plus the income-induced increase in consumer demand. Rearranging terms in equation (5.18), we have

$$\Delta Y - \Delta C = \Delta I$$

or[15]

$$\Delta S = \Delta I \tag{5.19}$$

Equation (5.19) also follows from our second way of expressing the condition for equilibrium income:

$$S + T = I + G \tag{5.5}$$

[15]Note that tax collections are fixed, so $\Delta Y = \Delta Y_D$. Thus, $\Delta Y = \Delta Y_D \equiv \Delta C + \Delta S$ and, therefore, $\Delta Y - \Delta C = \Delta S$.

With T and G fixed, to restore equilibrium, S must rise by the amount of the increase in I, as required by equation (5.19). Restoring equilibrium requires that income rise by enough to generate new saving equal to the new investment.

Because ΔS is equal to $(1 - b)\Delta Y$, we have, from equation (5.19),

$$(1 - b)\Delta Y = \Delta I$$

$$\frac{\Delta \overline{Y}}{\Delta I} = \frac{1}{1 - b} = \frac{1}{1 - \text{MPC}} = \frac{1}{\text{MPS}} \quad \textbf{(5.20)}$$

For example, if b equals 0.8, the marginal propensity to save (MPS $= 1 - b$) is equal to 0.2. Each dollar increase in income will generate 20 cents worth of new saving, and a 5-dollar increase in income will be required to generate the 1 dollar of new saving to balance a 1-dollar increase in investment. The value of the multiplier in this case is 5.

The effect of an increase in autonomous investment is illustrated in Figure 5-6. Initially, with investment at I_0 and government spending and taxes at G_0 and T_0, equilibrium income is at $\overline{Y}_0$. Now let investment increase to the higher level, I_1. The aggregate demand (E) schedule shifts up by the amount ($\Delta I = I_1 - I_0$), from E_0 ($= C + I_0 + G_0$) to E_1 ($= C + I_1 + G_0$). The ($I + G$) schedule shifts up by the same amount. Equilibrium is restored at $\overline{Y}_1$, where income is now equal to the higher value of aggregate demand. Note that the increase in income is equal to the initial increase in investment plus an induced increase in consumption (ΔC), as shown in the graph. Note also that at the new equilibrium, saving has increased by the same amount as investment ($\Delta S = \Delta I$).

The multiplier concept is central to Keynes's theory because it explains how shifts in investment caused by changes in business expectations set off a process that causes not only investment but also consumption to vary. The multiplier shows how shocks to one sector are transmitted throughout the economy. Keynes's theory also implies that other components of autonomous expenditure affect the overall level of equilibrium income. The effect on equilibrium income of a change in each of the policy-controlled elements of autonomous expenditures, government spending and taxes, can be calculated from equation (5.15).

We proceed just as we did in considering the effects of a change in investment and let one component of autonomous expenditures change while each of the others is held constant. For a change in government spending (G), we have

$$\Delta \overline{Y} = \frac{1}{1 - b}\Delta G$$

$$\frac{\Delta \overline{Y}}{\Delta G} = \frac{1}{1 - b} \quad \textbf{(5.21)}$$

For a change in taxes, we have

$$\Delta \overline{Y} = \frac{1}{1 - b}(-b)\Delta T$$

$$\frac{\Delta \overline{Y}}{\Delta T} = \frac{-b}{1 - b} \quad \textbf{(5.22)}$$

For government spending, a 1-dollar increase has the same effect as a 1-dollar increase in investment. Both are 1-dollar increases in autonomous expenditures.

FIGURE 5-6 Effect of an Increase in Autonomous Investment on Equilibrium Income

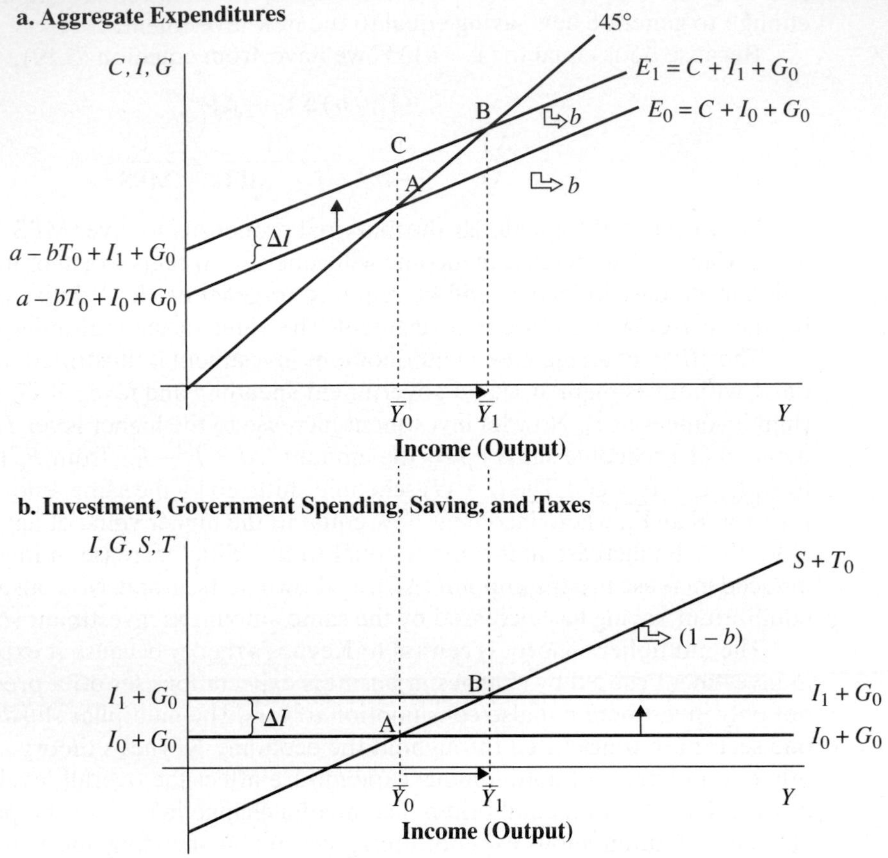

In part *a*, beginning at equilibrium A, an increase in autonomous investment, from I_0 to I_1, shifts the aggregate expenditure schedule upward from $E_0 = C + I_0 + G_0$ to $E_1 = C + I_1 + G_0$. Equilibrium income increases from point A to point B, $\overline{Y}_0$, to $\overline{Y}_1$. The increase in income is equal to the initial increase in investment (shown as an increase in the intercept), I_0 to I_1, *plus* an income-induced increase in consumption. This increase in consumption is shown as we move along the higher expenditure function, E_1, from point C to point B. In part *b*, beginning at equilibrium A, the $I + G$ schedule shifts up from $I_0 + G_0$ to $I_1 + G_0$. Equilibrium income increases from point A to point B, $\overline{Y}_0$, to $\overline{Y}_1$.

The multiplier process, whereby the initial increase in income generates induced increases in consumption, is the same for an increase in government spending as for investment.

In terms of Figure 5-6, in part *a*, an increase in government spending of ΔG would shift up the expenditure schedule by the same amount as an *equal* increase in investment. In this case, the intercept would shift up due to an increase in government spending. In part *b*, an increase in government spending of ΔG would shift up the $I + G$ schedule from $I_0 + G_0$ to $I_0 + G_1$, the same amount as an *equal* increase in investment. In both figures, ΔY will be the same; $\overline{Y}_0$ to $\overline{Y}_1$.

From equation (5.22) we see that the effect of an increase in taxes is in the opposite direction to that of increased government spending or investment. A tax

FIGURE 5-7 Effect of an Increase in Taxes on Equilibrium Income

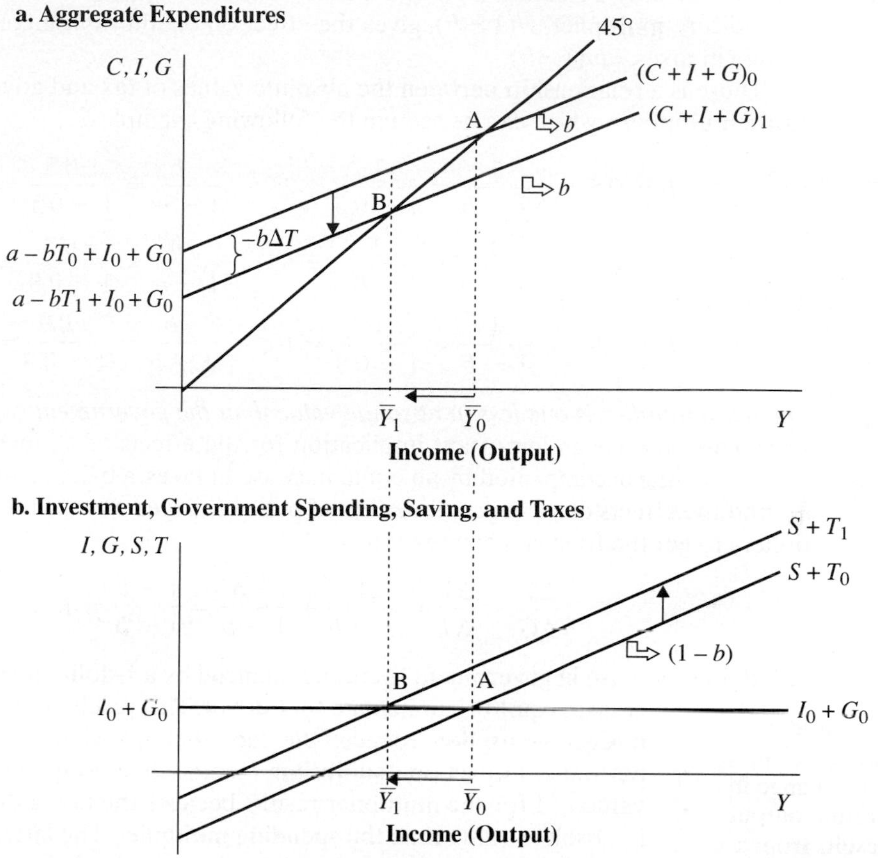

An increase in taxes from T_0 to T_1 shifts the aggregate expenditure schedule downward in part *a*, from $(C + I + G)_0$ to $(C + I + G)_1$ to equilibrium point B, since taxes are in the intercept. Equilibrium income falls from $\overline{Y}_0$, to $\overline{Y}_1$. In part *b*, starting at equilibrium point A, the saving plus taxes schedule shifts up, from $S + T_0$ to $S + T_1$. Equilibrium moves from A to B.

increase lowers the level of disposable income $(Y - T)$ for any level of national income (Y). This effect shifts the aggregate demand schedule down because it reduces consumption spending *for any level of national income*. The effect on equilibrium income from a tax increase is illustrated in Figure 5-7. We assume that taxes rise by ΔT from T_0 to T_1. The aggregate demand schedule shifts from $(C + I + G)_0$ down to $(C + I + G)_1$. This is the consequence of the downward shift in the consumption function caused by the rise in taxes from T_0 to T_1. Equilibrium income falls from $\overline{Y}_0$ to $\overline{Y}_1$.

Notice that the aggregate demand schedule shifts down by $(-b\Delta T)$, that is, by only a fraction (b) of the increase in taxes. The reason is that, at a given level of income, a 1-dollar increase in taxes reduces disposable income by 1 dollar but lowers the consumption component of aggregate demand by only b dollars. The rest of the decline in disposable income is absorbed by a fall of $(1 - b)$ dollars in saving. Unlike changes in government expenditures and investment, which have a dollar-for-dollar effect on autonomous aggregate demand, a 1-dollar change in taxes shifts the aggregate demand schedule by only a fraction $(-b)$ of 1 dollar. This fraction $(-b)$ times the autonomous expenditure multiplier, $1/(1-b)$, gives the effect on equilibrium income of a 1-dollar change in taxes, $-b/(1-b)$.

There is a relationship between the absolute values of tax and government expenditure multipliers, which can be seen in the following examples:

$$b = 0.5: \quad \frac{1}{1-b} = \frac{1}{1-0.5} = 2; \quad \frac{-b}{1-b} = \frac{-0.5}{1-0.5} = -1$$

$$b = 0.8: \quad \frac{1}{1-b} = \frac{1}{1-0.8} = 5; \quad \frac{-b}{1-b} = \frac{-0.8}{1-0.8} = -4$$

$$b = 0.9: \quad \frac{1}{1-b} = \frac{1}{1-0.9} = 10; \quad \frac{-b}{1-b} = \frac{-0.9}{1-0.9} = -9$$

The tax multiplier is one less in absolute value than the government expenditure multiplier. This fact has an important implication for the effects of an increase in government spending accompanied by an equal increase in taxes, a balanced-budget increase. To find the effects of such a combination of policy changes, we add the two policy multipliers to get the following expression:

$$\frac{\Delta\overline{Y}}{\Delta G} + \frac{\Delta\overline{Y}}{\Delta T} = \frac{1}{1-b} + \frac{-b}{1-b} = \frac{1-b}{1-b} = 1$$

A 1-dollar increase in government spending financed by a 1-dollar increase in taxes increases equilibrium income by 1 dollar. This result, termed the **balanced-budget multiplier**, reflects the fact that tax changes have a smaller per-dollar impact on equilibrium income than do spending changes. The value of 1 for the multiplier results because the tax multiplier is one less in absolute value than the spending multiplier. The latter result does not carry through in many more complex models, but the result that tax changes affect aggregate demand by less per dollar than changes in government spending is quite general.

balanced-budget multiplier
gives the change in equilibrium output that results from a 1-unit increase or decrease in *both* taxes and government spending

5.6 FISCAL STABILIZATION POLICY

Because equilibrium income is affected by changes in government spending and taxes, these fiscal policy instruments can be varied to stabilize the total of autonomous expenditures and, therefore, equilibrium income, even if the investment component is unstable.

An example of fiscal stabilization policy is illustrated in Figure 5-8. The economy is assumed to be in equilibrium at a potential level $\overline{Y}_P$, with aggregate demand at E_P equal to $(C + I_0 + G_0)$. We assume that from this point autonomous investment declines from I_0 to I_1, as a result of an unfavorable change in business expectations. In the absence of a policy action, aggregate demand declines to E_L, equal to $(C + I_1 + G_0)$. The new level of equilibrium income is below potential output at $\overline{Y}_L$.

FIGURE 5-8 An Example of Fiscal Stabilization Policy

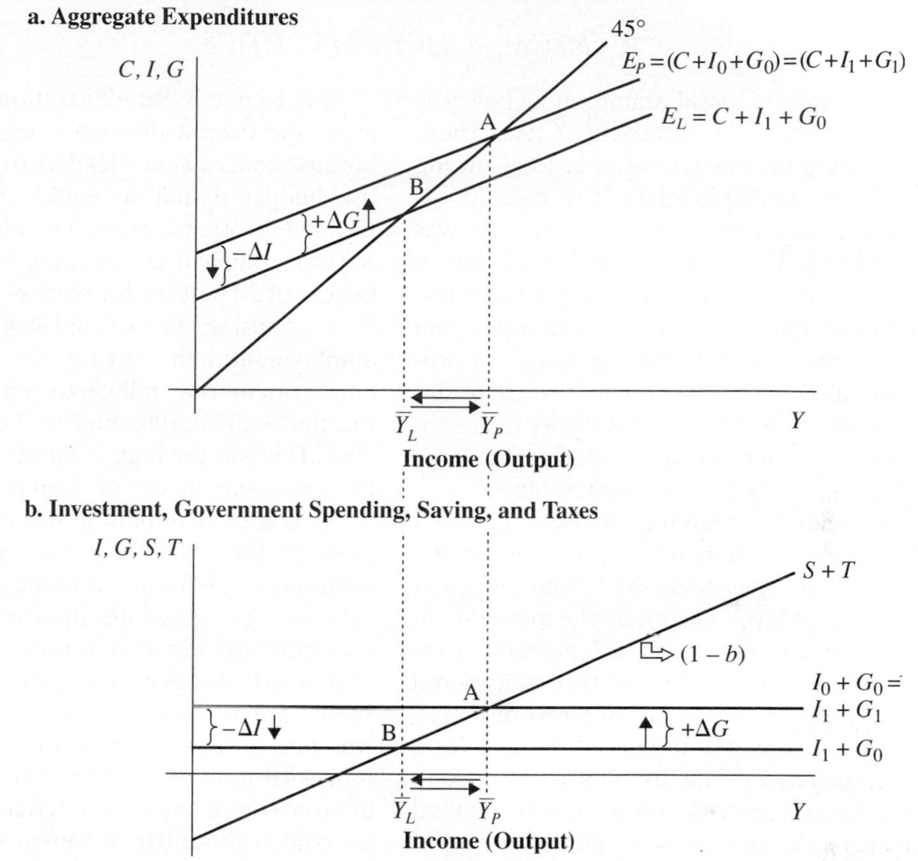

Beginning at equilibrium point A in part *a*, a decline in autonomous investment expenditure from I_0 to I_1 shifts the aggregate expenditure schedule downward from $E_P = (C + I_0 + G_0)$ to $E_L = (C + I_1 + G_0)$, moving to equilibrium point B. A compensating increase in discretionary government spending from G_0 to G_1 shifts the aggregate expenditure schedule back to equilibrium point A, where $(C + I_1 + G_1) = E_P = (C + I_0 + G_0)$. Equilibrium income is again at $\overline{Y}_P$. In part *b*, starting at equilibrium point A, the decline in autonomous investment expenditure shifts the $I + G$ schedule downward, from $I_0 + G_0$ to $I_1 + G_0$, moving to equilibrium point B, decreasing income from $\overline{Y}_P$ to $\overline{Y}_L$. A compensating increase in discretionary government spending from G_0 to G_1 shifts the $I + G$ schedule upward, to $I_1 + G_1$, moving back to equilibrium point A, and increasing income back to $\overline{Y}_P$.

Within the model, an appropriate fiscal policy response would be to increase government spending by an amount sufficient to restore equilibrium at $\overline{Y}_P$. In the graph, a rise in government spending from G_0 to G_1 shifts the aggregate demand curve back up to E_P, now equal to $(C + I_1 + G_1)$. Alternatively, a tax cut could be used to restore the initial level of aggregate demand. Because the tax multiplier is smaller, the appropriate tax cut would be larger than the required spending increase.

Read Perspectives 5-2.

PERSPECTIVES 5-2

FISCAL POLICY IN PRACTICE

An example of fiscal stabilization policy is the Kennedy–Johnson tax cut of 1964. There had been a serious recession in 1958, during which the unemployment rate rose to 6.8 percent. Recovery from this recession was short-lived. The economy sank back into a recession in 1960. The Kennedy administration came into office in 1961 with a program to "get the economy moving again"—a program called the *new economics*—which meant the application of Keynesian theory to macroeconomic policy. Kennedy proposed a large cut in both personal and business taxes.

Kennedy's economic advisers believed that aggregate demand was too low for the economy to operate at the full-employment or potential level. The unemployment rate in 1961, for example, was 6.7 percent, compared with the 4.0 percent then considered to be "full" employment. In terms of Figure 5-8, the economy in the early 1960s was at a point such as $\overline{Y}_L$. The tax cut was intended to shift the aggregate demand schedule upward to move the economy to potential output ($\overline{Y}_P$ in Figure 5-8).

The Kennedy administration could not move the tax cut through Congress, mainly because congressional leaders worried about the budget deficit it would create. After Kennedy's assassination, President Lyndon Johnson persuaded Congress to enact the tax cut of 20 percent for persons and 10 percent for businesses early in 1964. Output and employment then grew rapidly, with the unemployment rate falling to 4.8 percent by the first half of 1965 and to 3.8 percent in 1966. This was the high point of influence for the Keynesian theory of fiscal policy.

As U.S. involvement in the Vietnam War grew in the 1966–68 period, government spending on defense increased rapidly. This increase in aggregate demand, with the economy already at potential output, generated inflationary pressures. In terms of Figure 5-8, the aggregate demand schedule was being pushed above the level consistent with potential output (Y_P). The 1960s demonstrated that, in practice, fiscal policy could destabilize as well as stabilize the economy.

5.7 EXPORTS AND IMPORTS IN THE SIMPLE KEYNESIAN MODEL

Both imports and exports have been growing as shares of GDP over recent decades. In 1960, U.S. imports of goods and services totaled 4.4 percent of GDP. By 2006, this figure was 16.6 percent of GDP. Exports rose from 4.9 percent of GDP in 1960 to 10.8 percent in 2006. Overall, the U.S. economy has become much more closely linked to those of other nations over the past 40 years. This section focuses on the roles of imports and exports in determining equilibrium income in the simple Keynesian model. Recall from Chapter 2 that GDP (Y) consists of consumption, investment, and government spending *plus* net exports. Net exports are exports minus imports. The condition for equilibrium output in the *open* economy (including exports and imports) is

$$Y = E = C + I + G + X - Z \qquad \textbf{(5.23)}$$

Compared with equation (5.2), the condition for equilibrium in the *closed* economy, we have added exports (X) to aggregate demand and subtracted imports (Z). Exports are the foreign demand for domestic output and therefore part of aggregate demand. Also, because imports are included in C, I, and G but are *not* demands for domestic goods, we must subtract them from aggregate demand.

To find an expression for equilibrium GDP in the open-economy model, we follow the same procedure as for the closed-economy case; we take investment and government spending as exogenous—that is, as autonomous expenditure components. Consumption is given by the consumption function

$$C = a + bY \tag{5.24}$$

where, because they play no essential role in our discussion here, we have left out taxes, and therefore do not need to distinguish between GDP (Y) and disposable income ($Y_D = Y - T$). To compute equilibrium output for the open-economy case, we need to specify the determinants of imports and exports.

To simplify our analysis, we assume that imports consist solely of consumption goods. The demand for imports is assumed to depend on income and to have an autonomous component.

$$Z = u + vY \qquad u > 0, \qquad 0 < v < 1 \tag{5.25}$$

The parameter u represents the autonomous component of imports. The parameter v is the marginal propensity to import, the increase in import demand per unit increase in GDP, a concept analogous to the MPC (b) in (5.24).[16]

The demand for U.S. exports is a part of the *foreign* demand for imports. The foreign demand for imports depends on the level of *foreign* income, being determined by an import demand function analogous to equation (5.25). From the U.S. point of view, foreign income and, hence, the demand for our exports are exogenous.

Additional variables that we would expect to influence both U.S. demand for imports and foreign demand for U.S. exports are the relative price levels in the two countries and the level of the exchange rate. These variables determine the relative costs of the two countries' products to residents of either country. Note that we are assuming that price levels and the exchange rate are fixed. The effects on imports and exports of changes in the price level or exchange rate are examined in Part IV.

With imports given by equation (5.25) and exports assumed to be exogenous, we can compute equilibrium income from equation (5.23) as follows:

$$Y = C + I + G + X - Z \tag{5.23}$$

$$= \overbrace{a + bY}^{C} + I + G + X \overbrace{- u - vY}^{-Z}$$

$$Y - bY + vY = a + I + G + X - u$$

$$(1 - b + v)Y = a + I + G + X - u$$

$$\overline{Y} = \frac{1}{1 - b + v}(a + I + G + X - u) \tag{5.26}$$

To examine the effects of foreign trade in the model, we compare equation (5.26) with the equivalent expression for equilibrium income from the closed-economy

[16] Note that, because consumption includes imports, b is the MPC for both domestic and imported goods. Because v is the marginal propensity to import (consumption goods), $b - v$ is the MPC for domestic goods.

model, equation (5.14). This expression, omitting the tax variable (T), can be written as

$$\bar{Y} = \frac{1}{1 - b}(a + I + G) \tag{5.27}$$

In both equations (5.26) and (5.27), equilibrium income is expressed as the product of two terms: the autonomous expenditure multiplier and the level of autonomous expenditures. Consider how each of these is changed by adding imports and exports to the model.

Take first the autonomous expenditure multiplier, $1/(1 - b + v)$ in equation (5.26) as opposed to $1/(1 - b)$ in equation (5.27) for the closed-economy model. Because v, the marginal propensity to import, is greater than zero, the multiplier in (5.26), $1/(1 - b + v)$, will be *smaller* than the multiplier in (5.27), $1/(1 - b)$. For example, if $b = 0.8$ and $v = 0.3$, we would then have

$$\frac{1}{1 - b} = \frac{1}{1 - .08} = \frac{1}{0.2} = 5$$

and

$$\frac{1}{1 - b + v} = \frac{1}{1 - 0.8 + 0.3} = \frac{1}{0.5} = 2$$

From these expressions, it can be seen that the more open an economy is to foreign trade (the higher v is), the lower will be the autonomous expenditure multiplier.

The autonomous expenditure multiplier gives the change in equilibrium income per unit change in autonomous expenditures. It follows, therefore, that the more open an economy is (the higher v is), the smaller will be the response of income to aggregate demand shocks, such as changes in government spending or autonomous changes in investment demand. The decline in the value of the autonomous expenditure multiplier with a rise in v can be explained with reference to the multiplier process (Section 5.5). A change in autonomous expenditures—a change in government spending, for example—will have a direct effect on income and an induced effect on consumption with a further effect on income. The higher the value of v, the larger the proportion of this induced effect that will be a change in demand for *foreign*, not domestic, consumer goods. Consequently, the induced effect on demand for domestic goods and, hence, on domestic income will be smaller.[17] The increase in imports per unit of income constitutes an additional *leakage* from the circular flow of (domestic) income at each round of the multiplier process and reduces the value of the autonomous expenditure multiplier.

Now consider the second term in the expression for equilibrium income in the open-economy case [equation (5.26)], the level of autonomous expenditures. In addition to the elements for a closed economy ($a + I + G$), autonomous expenditures for the open economy include exports and the autonomous component of imports. Recall

[17] Recall from footnote 16 that $b - v$ is the MPC for domestic goods. A higher v (given b) therefore means a lower MPC for domestic goods and a lower value for the multiplier.

that the autonomous components of aggregate demand are not directly determined by income. Rather, shifts in the components of autonomous expenditures affect the level of aggregate demand *for a given level of income* and result in changes in equilibrium income. Thus, changes in exports and autonomous changes in import demand are additional shocks that will change equilibrium income.

From equation (5.26) we can compute the multiplier effects of changes in X and u.

$$\frac{\Delta \overline{Y}}{\Delta X} = \frac{1}{1 - b + v} \tag{5.28}$$

$$\frac{\Delta \overline{Y}}{\Delta u} = \frac{-1}{1 - b + v} \tag{5.29}$$

An increase in the demand for our exports is an increase in demand for domestically produced output and will increase equilibrium income just as would an increase in government spending or an autonomous increase in investment.[18]

In contrast, an autonomous increase in import demand, an increase in u, will cause a decline in equilibrium income. An autonomous increase in import demand represents a shift from demand for domestic goods to demand for foreign goods. For example, because of the large rise in gasoline prices in the 1970s, U.S. consumers shifted demand from domestic to (smaller) foreign automobiles. As such, the autonomous increase in import demand is a *decline* in demand for domestic output and causes equilibrium income to decline.

In summary, an increase in the demand for our exports has an expansionary effect on equilibrium income, whereas an autonomous increase in imports has a contractionary effect on equilibrium income. This outcome should not be interpreted to mean that exports are good and imports harmful in their economic effects. Countries import goods that can be more efficiently produced abroad, and trade increases the overall efficiency of the worldwide allocation of resources. However, the expansionary effect of increases in exports and the contractionary effect of increases in imports do explain why at times nations have tried to stimulate the domestic economy by promoting exports and restricting imports.

5.8 Conclusion

The model in this chapter is incomplete. We need to consider money and interest rates and to explain the behavior of prices and wages before we complete our analysis of the Keynesian system. However, this simple model highlights several features of the Keynesian system.

The simple model clearly illustrates the role of aggregate demand in determining income in the Keynesian system. As we will see later, it *overstates* the role of aggregate demand. Still, a key feature of all Keynesian models is that demand plays a

[18]Note that from equation (5.26) we can also compute $\frac{\Delta \overline{Y}}{\Delta G} = \frac{\Delta \overline{Y}}{\Delta I} = \frac{1}{1 - b + v}$.

crucial role in income determination. In the Keynesian view, changes in the autonomous elements of aggregate demand, especially investment demand, are key factors causing changes in the equilibrium level of income. By means of the multiplier process, such changes in autonomous expenditures also induce changes in consumption spending. Inadequate investment, and a consequent low level of aggregate demand, was the Keynesian explanation for massive unemployment in the Depression of the 1930s.

The model also illustrates the role of fiscal stabilization policy in managing aggregate demand to cushion equilibrium output from shifts in the unstable investment demand. Although the simple expressions we derive for the government expenditure and tax multipliers require modification, the principles behind them remain intact.

In addition, this chapter has considered the role of imports and exports within the simple Keynesian model. Exogenous changes in these components of aggregate demand are additional factors that alter equilibrium income. Moreover, we have seen that the openness of the economy affects the value of the autonomous expenditure multiplier and thus the vulnerability of the economy to both foreign and domestic changes in autonomous expenditures.

KEY TERMS

- consumption function 75
- marginal propensity to consume (MPC) 76
- marginal propensity to save (MPS) 77
- autonomous expenditure multiplier 82
- autonomous expenditures 82
- balanced-budget multiplier 87

REVIEW QUESTIONS AND PROBLEMS

1. Explain how the origins of the Keynesian revolution can be found in the problem of unemployment.
2. Interpret each of the three ways of writing the condition for equilibrium income in the simple Keynesian model [equations (5.2), (5.5.), and (5.6)]. Explain why the three ways are equivalent.
3. Explain the difference between realized and desired investment. In which component of investment does the discrepancy between the two totals occur?
4. Explain Keynes's theory of how expectations affect investment demand. How is this theory related to Keynes's view that aggregate demand would be unstable in the absence of government stabilization policies?
5. Consider the numbers in Table 5-1 giving consumption as a percentage of income in prosperous years (1929, 1955, 1973, 1979, 1989, 2000) compared with recession years (1933, 1958, 1975, 1982, 1991, 2001). Notice that in each case consumption is higher as a percentage of income in the recession years. Is this outcome what you would predict on the basis of Keynes's consumption function given by equation (5.9)? Explain.

6. In the simple Keynesian model, an increase of 1 dollar in autonomous expenditure will cause equilibrium income to increase by a multiple of this 1-dollar increase. Explain the process by which this happens.
7. Explain carefully why the tax multiplier $[\Delta Y/\Delta T = -b/(1-b)]$ is negative and why it is smaller in absolute value than the government expenditure multiplier $[\Delta Y/\Delta G = 1/(1-b)]$.
8. Suppose that for a particular economy and period, investment was equal to 100, government expenditure was equal to 75, net taxes were fixed at 100, and consumption (C) was given by the consumption function

$$C = 25 + 0.8Y_D$$

where Y_D is disposable income and Y is GDP.

a. What is the level of equilibrium income ($\bar{Y}$)?
b. What is the value of the government expenditure multiplier ($\Delta Y/\Delta G$)? Of the tax multiplier ($\Delta Y/\Delta T$)?
c. Suppose that investment declined by 40 units to a level of 60. What will be the new level of equilibrium income?

9. Suppose that initially equilibrium income was 200 units and that this was also the full-employment level of income. Assume that the consumption function is

$$C = 25 + 0.8Y_D$$

and that, from this initial equilibrium level, we now have a decline in investment of 8 units. What will be the new equilibrium level of income? What increase in government spending would be required to restore income to the initial level of 200? Alternatively, what reduction in tax collections would be sufficient to restore an income level of 200?

10. Suppose that government spending was increased by 10 units and that this increase was financed by a 10-unit increase in taxes. Would equilibrium income change or remain the same as a result of these two policy actions? If equilibrium income changed, in which direction would it move, and by how much? Explain.
11. Suppose that, instead of a fixed level of taxes, we had an income tax so that

$$T = t_1 Y$$

where t_1 was the income tax rate. Following the procedure of Section 5.4, derive an expression for equilibrium income $\bar{Y}$ analogous to equation (5.14) for this case in which the level of tax collections depends on income. What is the expression equivalent to the autonomous expenditure multiplier $[1/(1-b)]$ for this case of an income tax?

12. In question 8, assume that, beginning from the initial equilibrium position (investment equal to 100, government expenditure equal to 75, and net taxes fixed at 100), there was an autonomous fall in consumption and an increase in saving such that the consumption function shifted from

$$C = 25 + 0.8Y_D$$

to

$$C = 5 + 0.8Y_D$$

a. Find the change in equilibrium income resulting from this autonomous increase in saving.
b. Calculate the level of saving before and after the shift in the consumption and, therefore, the saving function. How do you explain this result?

13. Suppose that within the open-economy version of the Keynesian model in Section 5.7, we now include taxes. Disposable income ($Y_D = Y - T$) therefore replaces GDP (Y) in the

consumption function (5.24). Compute the expression for equilibrium income for this version of the open-economy model. Compute an expression for the tax multiplier ($\Delta Y/\Delta T$) in the model.

14. Within the open-economy version of the Keynesian model, including taxes (see question 13), suppose there is an autonomous increase in imports of 20 units [u in equation (5.25) rises by 20]. To counteract the effects of this contraction in domestic aggregate demand, assume that the government cuts taxes by 20 units. Will equilibrium income rise or fall? By how much? Explain.

CHAPTER 6

The Keynesian System (II): Money, Interest, and Income

In Chapter 5, we ignored the interest rate and monetary policy. Here we explain the role of the interest rate and money in the Keynesian system and construct a model that shows how the interest rate and income are jointly determined. In Chapter 7, we use this model to provide a more realistic view of how income depends on aggregate demand and to make clear how monetary policy can affect income by having an effect on aggregate demand. We also see how the results in Chapter 5 concerning fiscal policy are modified by including a money market in the model.

6.1 MONEY IN THE KEYNESIAN SYSTEM

Fundamental to Keynes's theory of money was the view that money affects income via the interest rate. An increase in the money supply, for example, lowers the interest rate, and the lower interest rate, in turn, increases aggregate demand and income. We need to examine two links in the chain of events connecting changes in the money supply and changes in income. The first is the relationship between money and the interest rate. The second is the effect of the interest rate on aggregate demand. We begin with the latter one.

Interest Rates and Aggregate Demand

We have already considered the reasons why business investment depends on the interest rate. Briefly, an investment project will be pursued only if its expected profitability exceeds the cost of borrowing to finance the project by an amount sufficient to justify the risks of the project. At a high interest rate (borrowing cost), fewer projects satisfy this criterion.

When considering the possible influences of the interest rate, we also consider components of aggregate demand other than business investment. The first of these is residential construction investment. Residential construction is a component of investment in the national income accounts, but the reason such investment is affected by the interest-rate level requires further explanation. The value of newly constructed houses enters the GDP accounts as the houses are built. One element of building cost is the cost of short-term borrowing to finance construction of a house. Higher interest rates mean higher costs to the builder and, other things equal, these higher costs discourage housing starts. Moreover, an important factor determining the rate of new housing construction is the overall state of demand for houses, existing and newly constructed. Most home purchases are financed by long-term borrowing in the mortgage market, and high interest rates include high rates of mortgage interest. High mortgage rates increase the cost of buying a house and reduce the demand for new and existing homes. This reduced demand in the housing market lowers the volume of new residential construction.

Additional components of aggregate demand are not counted as investment by the national income accounts but may be affected by interest-rate changes. The first of these is consumer expenditures on durable goods. Such expenditures are counted as current-quarter consumption in the national income accounts, but to the consumer the purchase of a car or an appliance such as a personal computer or television set is a form of investment. Such purchases are often financed by borrowing, especially car purchases. Higher interest rates raise the cost of such purchases and should lower this component of aggregate demand.

A final component of aggregate demand that may be affected by interest rates is a subcomponent of government spending. Government spending in the national income accounts includes state and local government spending for services, consumption goods, and investment goods. In the models constructed here, we take government spending to be exogenously fixed by the policymaker. The actual policymaker would be the federal government, and the appropriate policy variable is federal government expenditures. State and local government spending can more properly be considered with private consumption and investment spending. Much state and local government investment spending is financed by borrowing through bond issues. High interest rates should, in theory, increase such borrowing costs and discourage this part of state and local government expenditures. There are, however, many determinants of the level and timing of such state and local government spending projects, and the importance of interest rates in practice remains uncertain.

Within the simple model of Chapter 5, the effects on aggregate demand and equilibrium income as a result of a change in the interest rate are illustrated in Figure 6-1. Initially, we assume that the economy is in equilibrium at Y_0 with aggregate demand at E_0 equal to $(C + I_0 + G_0)$, corresponding to an interest rate of r_0. A decline in the interest rate to r_1 shifts the aggregate demand curve up to E_1, equal to $(C + I_1 + G_0)$. This shift represents the combined effects of the interest rate on business investment, residential construction investment, consumer expenditures on durable goods, and state and local government investment spending. Equilibrium income rises to Y_1.

One important factor determining the change in equilibrium income $(Y_1 - Y_0)$ that will occur for a given change in the interest rate is the size of the shift in aggregate demand caused by the change in the interest rate. The more sensitive the components of aggregate demand are to interest-rate changes, the larger will be the shift in the aggregate demand function in Figure 6-1 and the greater the effect on equilibrium income. The interest sensitivity of aggregate demand will therefore be important in determining how effective monetary policy will be in affecting equilibrium income.

Figure 6-1*a* illustrates the idea that investment is negatively related to the interest rate. At interest rate r_0, investment is I_0 at point A on the investment schedule. If the interest rate decreases to r_1, investment increases to I_1 at point B. Looking at Figure 6-1*b*, since investment is a component of aggregate expenditures, the expenditure schedule shifts up, from equilibrium point A to equilibrium point B, and equilibrium income increases from Y_0 to Y_1.

In our models, we represent the effect of interest rates on aggregate expenditures as an effect on I, the investment component of aggregate expenditures. The discussion in this section should, however, be kept in mind. To account fully for the

FIGURE 6-1 Effect of a Decrease in the Interest Rate on Investment and Equilibrium Income

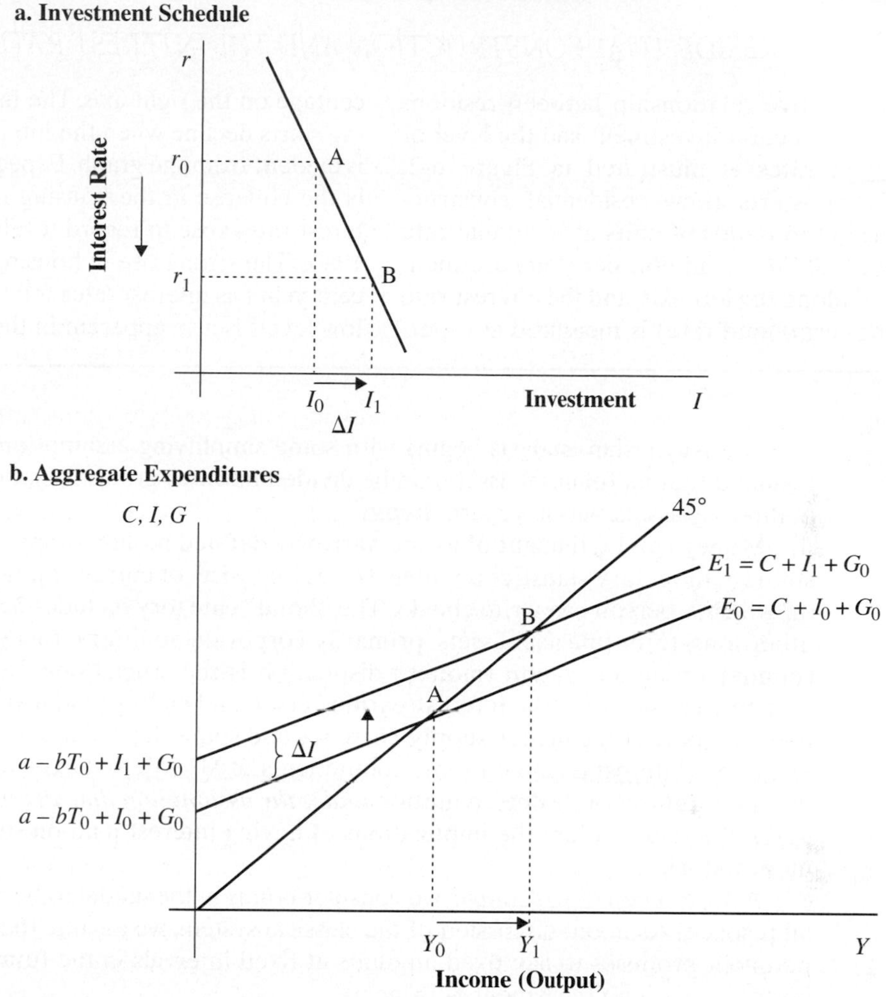

In part *a*, as the interest rate decreases from r_0 to r_1, investment increases from I_0 to I_1. In part *b*, this increase in investment, ΔI, shifts the aggregate expenditure schedule up since the intercept is larger, from $E_0 = C + I_0 + G_0$ to $E_1 = C + I_1 + G_0$. Income increases from Y_0 to Y_1.

effects of interest rates on aggregate expenditures, we must define investment broadly as including the other components of aggregate expenditure discussed here.

Read Perspectives 6-1.

The Keynesian Theory of the Interest Rate

The next relationship we consider is that between the quantity of money and the rate of interest. Keynes believed that the quantity of money played a key role in determining the rate of interest, and he structured his theory to highlight that role.

PERSPECTIVES 6-1

RESIDENTIAL CONSTRUCTION AND THE INTEREST RATE

The negative relationship between residential construction investment and the level of interest rates is illustrated in Figure 6-2. Housing starts (new residential construction) in thousands of units at an annual rate (e.g., 1,200 = 1.2 million per year) are measured along the left axis, and the interest rate (long-term bond rate) is measured as a percentage on the right axis. The fact that housing starts decline when the interest rate rises is evident from the graph. Especially notable is the collapse in the housing market as interest rates rose to record levels in the early 1980s. The strong rise in housing starts in recent years as interest rates fell to historically low levels is also apparent in the figure.

The Keynesian analysis begins with some simplifying assumptions. First, Keynes assumed that all financial assets can be divided into two groups: (1) money and (2) all nonmoney assets, which we term *bonds*.

Money can be thought of as the narrowly defined money supply that in the official U.S. monetary statistics is called *M1*. M1 consists of currency plus bank accounts on which a person can write checks. The "bond" category includes actual bonds plus other long-term financial assets, primarily corporate equities (stock). The *long-term* (bonds) versus *short-term* (money) distinction is the crucial one. In addition, for a long time, bonds were the interest-earning asset, and money paid no interest. It is still true that part of the money supply, currency and some checkable accounts, pay no interest, but interest is paid on some components of M1. We first explain the Keynesian theory of interest-rate determination *under the assumption that all money pays no interest*. We then explore the implications of having interest paid on some parts of the money stock.

Also, to keep things simple, we consider bonds in the model to be homogeneous in all respects. As in our discussion of the classical system, we assume that bonds are perpetuities, promises to pay fixed amounts at fixed intervals in the future (e.g., 1 dollar per year), with no repayment of principal.

Within this simplified framework, Keynes considers the way in which individuals allocate their financial wealth between the two assets, money (M) and bonds (B). At a point in time, wealth (Wh) is fixed at some level, and because bonds and money are the only stores of wealth, we have

$$Wh \equiv B + M \tag{6.1}$$

The equilibrium interest rate on bonds is that rate at which the demand for bonds is equal to the existing stock of bonds. It might seem most natural to develop a theory of the equilibrium interest rate by studying the factors that directly determine the supply of and demand for bonds. Keynes did not proceed in this manner. Note that given equation (6.1), there is only one independent portfolio decision, the split between money and bonds. If, for an individual, wealth is equal to \$50,000, the decision to hold \$10,000 in the form of money implicitly determines that bond holdings will be the remainder, \$40,000. In terms of equilibrium positions, this means that a person

FIGURE 6-2 Housing Starts and the Interest Rate, 1972–2005

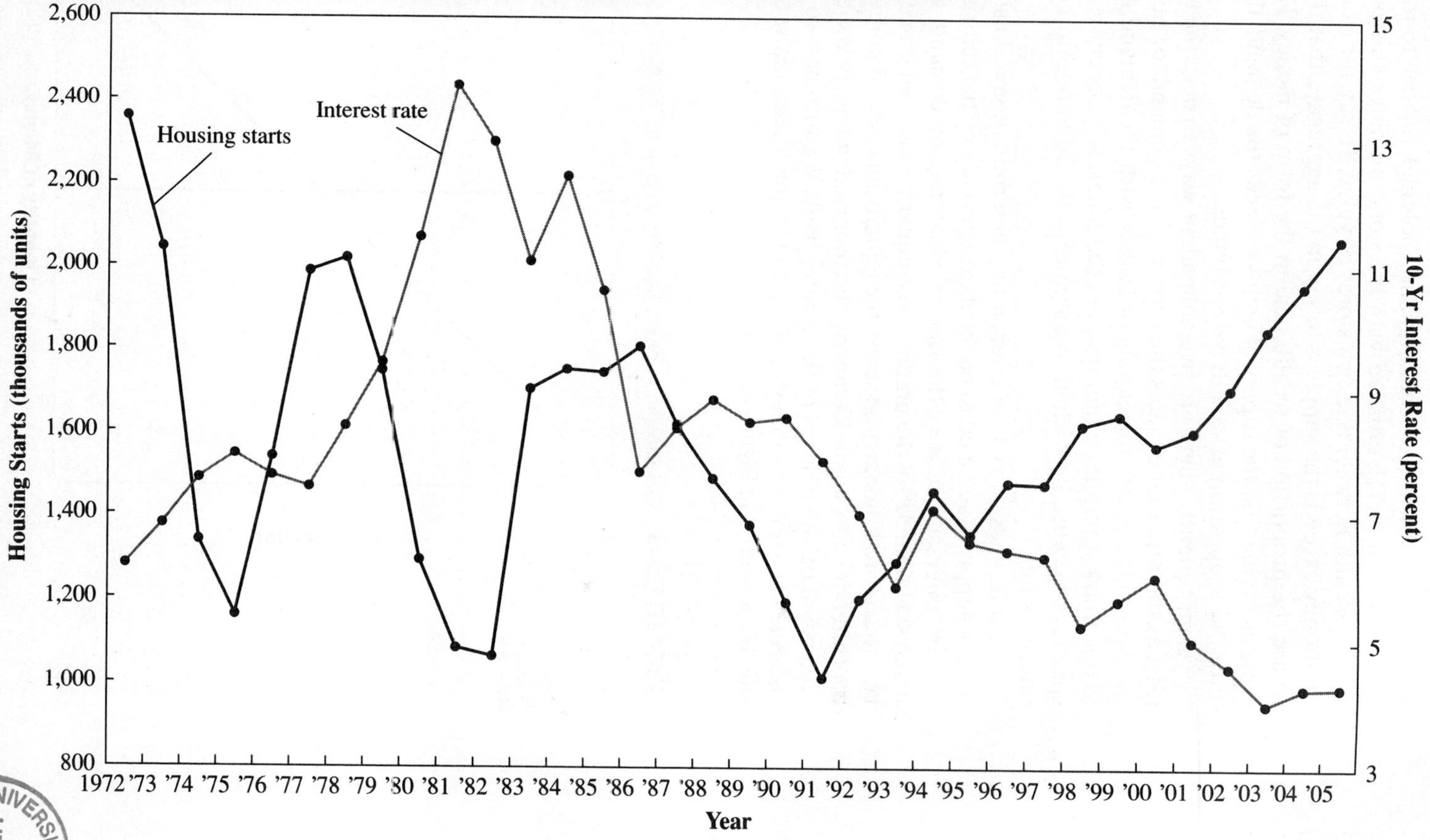

who is satisfied with the level of money holdings relative to total wealth is, by definition [equation (6.1)], satisfied with the bond holdings; this person is at the optimal split of wealth between the two stores of value. To say, for example, that the demand for money exceeds the supply is to say, in the aggregate, that the public is trying to increase the proportion of wealth held in the form of money. This is definitionally the same as saying that the supply of bonds exceeds the demand; the public is trying to reduce the proportion of wealth held as bonds.

Consequently, there are two equivalent ways to describe the equilibrium interest rate: as the rate that equates the supply of and demand for bonds or, alternatively, as the rate that equates the supply of money with the demand for money. Equilibrium in one market implies equilibrium in the other. Keynes chose the latter of these perspectives because he wished to emphasize the relationship between money and the interest rate.

This Keynesian view of interest rate determination is illustrated in Figure 6-3. The money supply is assumed to be fixed exogenously by the central bank at M_0^s. The equilibrium interest rate is r_0, the rate at which money demand, given by the money demand schedule M^d in the graph, is just equal to the fixed money supply.

In a more fundamental sense, the equilibrium rate of interest is determined by factors affecting the supply of money and money demand. In the case of supply, the major factor will be the policies of the central bank. We turn now to the factors that Keynes believed determined money demand, the factors determining the position and slope of the M^d schedule in Figure 6-3.

FIGURE 6-3 Determination of the Equilibrium Interest Rate

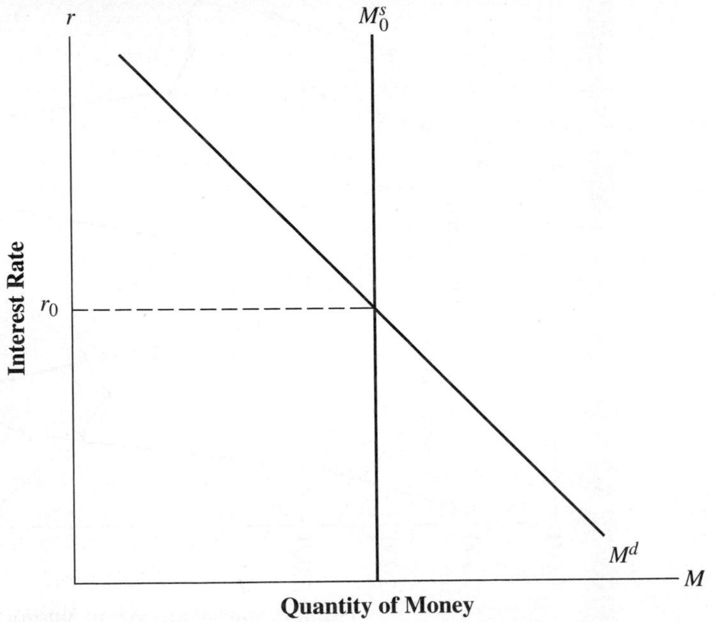

In the Keynesian system, the equilibrium interest rate (r_0) is the interest rate that equates money supply and money demand.

The Keynesian Theory of Money Demand

Keynes considered three motives for holding money.

Transactions Demand

The first motive is the transactions motive. Money is a medium of exchange, and individuals hold money for use in transactions. Money bridges the gap between the receipt of income and expenditures. The amount of money held for transactions would vary positively with the volume of transactions in which the individual engaged. Income is assumed to be a good measure of the volume of transactions, and thus the transactions demand for money is assumed to depend positively on income.

Money received in one transaction can be used to buy bonds, which can then be sold to get money again when the time came for an expenditure. The gain from doing so is the interest earned for the time the bonds were held. Brokerage fees involved in buying bonds and the inconveniences of a great number of such transactions would make it unprofitable to purchase bonds for small amounts to be held for short periods. Some money would be held for transactions. Still, there is room to *economize* on transaction balances by such bond purchases. Because the return to be gained is interest earnings on bonds, we would expect the incentive to economize on transaction balances to increase as the interest rate increases. Consequently, in addition to depending positively on income, the transactions demand for money would be expected to be negatively related to the rate of interest.

Keynes did not emphasize the interest rate when discussing the transactions motive for holding money, but it has proved to be important, especially for the business sector. Firms with a high volume of transactions can, by cash management practices, reduce their average money holdings. The incentive to make the expenditures required for cash management depends on the rate of interest.

Precautionary Demand

Keynes believed that, beyond money held for planned transactions, additional money balances were held in case of unexpected expenditures such as medical or repair bills. Keynes termed money held for this motive the *precautionary demand* for money. He believed that the amount held for this purpose depends positively on income. Again, the interest rate might be a factor if people tended to economize on the amount of money held for the precautionary motive as interest rates rose. Because the motives for holding precautionary balances are similar to those for transactions demand, we simplify our discussion here by subsuming the precautionary demand under the transactions demand category, transactions being expected or unexpected ones.

Speculative Demand

The final motive for holding money that Keynes considered was the speculative motive. Keynes began by asking why an individual would hold any money above that needed for the transactions and precautionary motives when bonds pay interest and money does not. Such an additional demand for money did exist, Keynes believed, because of the uncertainty about future interest rates and the relationship between changes in the interest rate and the price of bonds. If interest rates were expected to move in such a way as to cause capital losses on bonds, it was possible that these expected losses would outweigh the interest earnings on the bonds and cause an investor to hold money instead. Such money would be held by those speculating on future changes in the interest rate. To see how such speculation works, we analyze the relationship between the interest rate and bond prices.

Consider the case of a perpetuity, which is what we have been assuming the bonds in our model to be. Suppose that at some point in the past you paid the then prevailing market price of $1,000 to buy a government bond that entitles you to payment of $50 per year, termed the *coupon payment*. You bought a perpetual bond at a price of $1,000, at a market interest rate of 5 percent (50/1,000 = 0.05, or 5 percent). How much would this bond be worth if you tried to sell it today? The value of a financial asset that entitles the owner to a coupon payment of $50 per year depends on the *current* market rate of interest. First, suppose the current market rate of interest is 5 percent, the same as the interest rate that prevailed when you bought the bond. In this case, the bond would still sell for $1,000; at that price, it would yield the current interest rate of 5 percent.

Next, consider the case in which the market interest rate has risen to 10 percent over the time since you purchased the bond. The going price today for a bond with a coupon payment of $50 per year is $500 (50/500 = 0.10, or 10 percent). Your bond has no feature that will enable you to sell it for more. Even though you paid $1,000, given the rise in interest rates, you will be able to sell it only at a *capital loss* for $500, the price that makes it competitive at *current* market rates. *A rise in the market interest rate results in a capital loss on previously existing bonds.*

If, instead, from the time you purchased the bond, the market interest rate had fallen; then the value of your bond would have increased. If the interest rate had declined from 5 percent to 2 percent, the bond price would have increased from the $1,000 you paid to $2,500. At that price, your bond, which has a coupon of $50 per year, will pay 2 percent (50/2,500 = 0.02, or 2 percent). Thus, *a decline in interest rates results in a capital gain on previously existing bonds*. With this relationship between bond prices and interest-rate changes in mind, we return to the question of the relative desirability of money and bonds.

The expected returns on the two assets can be expressed as follows:

$$\text{return on money} = 0$$

$$\text{expected return on bonds} = \left.\begin{matrix}\text{interest}\\ \text{earnings}\\ (=r)\end{matrix}\right\} \begin{matrix}(+)\ \text{expected capital gain}\\ \text{or}\\ (-)\ \text{expectecd capital loss}\end{matrix}$$

The return on money is zero, because it earns no interest (our assumption so far) and because its value is not subject to capital gains or losses as the interest rate changes.[1] The bond will pay an interest rate of r. The *expected* return on bonds will equal this interest return plus or minus any expected capital gain or loss. For reasons just discussed, an investor who expected interest rates to fall would expect a capital gain, and one who expected interest rates to rise would expect a capital loss. This uncertainty about the future course of interest rates is crucial to Keynes's analysis.

Suppose that an investor believes interest rates will fall. Bonds then have the higher expected return. They pay interest and are expected to yield a capital gain. If interest rates are expected to rise, however, it is possible that the expected capital loss on bonds

[1] Notice that we are not allowing for the effect of commodity price changes. The *real* value of money declines proportionately with increases in the aggregate price level. However, so does the real value of bonds; therefore, the relative returns are not directly affected by commodity price changes.

will outweigh the interest earnings. The expected return on bonds would be negative in such a case, and money would be the preferred asset. Money held in anticipation of a fall in bond prices (a rise in interest rates) is Keynes's speculative demand for money.

To this point, we have a relationship between the amount of money demanded and expected future *changes* in interest rates. Keynes converts this to a relationship between money demand and the *level* of the interest rate by an assumption about how people form expectations about future interest-rate changes. He assumes that investors have a relatively fixed conception of the normal interest rate. When the actual interest rate is above the normal rate, investors expect the interest rate to fall. When the interest rate is below the normal rate, they expect it to rise. Given this assumption about how expectations about interest rates are formed, we can develop a relationship between the level of the speculative demand for money and the interest rate. We do so first for an individual investor and then consider the corresponding aggregate relationship.

For the individual investor, the demand curve for speculative balances is shown in Figure 6-4*a*. Here M_i^2 represents the speculative demand for money by the *i*th individual, and M_i^1 is the person's transactions demand. We have then

$$M_i^1 + M_i^2 \equiv M_i$$

and

$$M_i + B_i \equiv Wh_i \tag{6.2}$$

where M_i, B_i, and Wh_i are the individual's total money holdings, bond holdings, and wealth, respectively.

Following Keynes's theory, the individual is assumed to have a preconceived view of the normal interest rate. This rate is shown as r_i^n in Figure 6-4*a*. Because at rates of interest above r_i^n interest rates are expected to fall, at those rates bonds will be preferred to money as an asset. The speculative demand for money will be zero, and bond holdings will equal $(Wh_i - M_i^1)$. The speculative demand for money will also be zero for interest rates over a certain range below r_i^n. If the interest rate is not too far below r_i^n, the interest earnings on the bond will be greater than the small expected capital loss. The expected capital loss will be small because only a small rise in r will be expected as r returns to r_i^n.

There is a level of the interest rate below r_i^n, however, at which the expected capital loss on bonds, which increases as the interest rate declines below r_i^n, will come to just equal the interest earnings on the bond. We term this value the individual's *critical interest rate* (r_i^c). Below this rate, money will be preferred. The individual will sell bonds and hold speculative balances of $(Wh_i - M_i^1)$, which means that all of this person's wealth will be held in money.

Keynes assumed that different individuals had different views as to what was a normal interest rate. As the interest rate fell, beginning, for example, at a very high rate where there was very little speculative demand, the rate would move successively below the critical rates of different investors. The lower the interest rate, the more investors would find that, given their view of the normal rate, money was the preferred asset. At a very low interest rate, almost all investors would come to expect the interest rate to rise substantially in the future $(r < r_i^c)$, and money would be almost universally preferred as an asset. Proceeding in this manner, we construct the aggregate demand for speculative balances shown in Figure 6-4*b*.

FIGURE 6-4 Individual and Aggregate Speculative Demand Schedules for Money

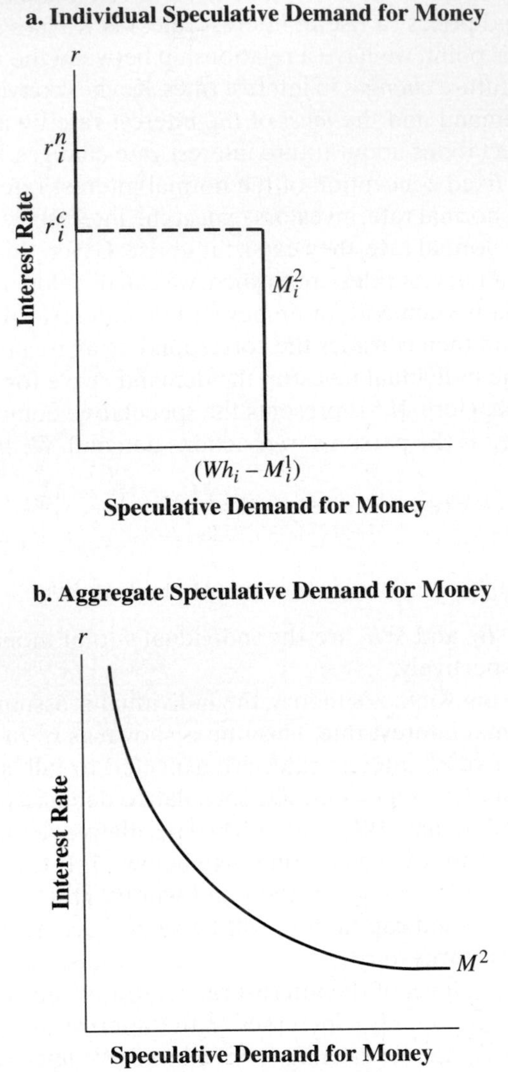

The individual's speculative demand for money is shown in part *a*. At any interest rate above the critical rate (r_i^c), the speculative demand for money is zero. Below the critical interest rate, the individual shifts to money. Part *b* shows the aggregate speculative demand for money schedule (M^2). As the interest rate becomes lower, it falls below the critical rate for more individuals, and the speculative demand for money rises.

liquidity trap
a situation at a very low interest rate where the speculative demand for money schedule becomes nearly horizontal

The schedule is smooth, reflecting the gradual increase in the speculative demand for money at successively lower interest rates. The schedule flattens out at a very low rate of interest, showing that at this low rate, there is a general expectation of capital losses on bonds that outweigh interest earnings. At this rate, increments to wealth would be held in the form of money, with no further drop in the interest rate. Keynes termed this situation the **liquidity trap**. For the most part, however, we assume that we are on the downward-sloping portion of the speculative demand for money schedule.

The Total Demand for Money

We have looked at the three motives for holding money in the Keynesian system and can now put these together to construct the total money demand function. The transactions demand and the precautionary demand vary positively with income and negatively with the interest rate. The speculative demand for money is negatively related to the interest rate. Taking those factors together, we can write total money demand as

$$M^d = L(Y, r) \tag{6.3}$$

where Y is income and r is the interest rate. A rise in income increases money demand; a rise in the interest rate decreases money demand. In the following analysis, we sometimes make the simplifying assumption that the money demand function is linear:

$$M^d = c_0 + c_1 Y - c_2 r \quad c_1 > 0; \quad c_2 > 0 \tag{6.4}$$

Equation (6.4) assumes that we can plot the money demand function as a straight line on our graphs. The parameter c_1 gives the increase in money demand per unit increase in income, and c_2 gives the amount by which money demand declines per unit increase in the interest rate.

The Effects of an Increase in the Money Supply

In Figure 6-5, we plot this linear Keynesian money demand schedule [equation (6.4)] as a function of the interest rate and illustrate the effect of an increase in the money supply on the money market. The money demand function, M^d, is downward-sloping; a decline in the interest rate, for example, increases the demand for money. To fix the position of the money demand function, we must fix the level of income. The schedule in Figure 6-5 is drawn for a level of income Y_0. An increase in income shifts the schedule to the right, reflecting the fact that, for a given interest rate, money demand increases with income. The money supply is assumed to be an exogenously controlled policy variable set initially at $M_0{}^s$.

Now consider the effects of an increase in the money supply to the level shown by the $M_1{}^s$ schedule in Figure 6-5. At the initial equilibrium interest rate r_0, after the money supply increases, there is an excess supply of money. At r_0 people are not content to hold the new money. They attempt to decrease their money holdings by buying bonds. The increase in the demand for bonds decreases the rate of interest suppliers of bonds (borrowers) offer to sell their bonds. The fall in the interest rate causes the demand for money to rise, and a new equilibrium is reached at interest rate r_1.

Some Implications of Interest on Money

In recent years, some components of the money supply have begun to pay market-determined interest rates. This development is contrary to our assumption that bonds are the only interest-bearing asset. What implications does interest-bearing money have for the Keynesian theory?

In Chapter 16, we discuss different definitions of money. Here we consider only one: M1. In the official U.S. monetary statistics, M1 consists of currency, travelers checks (a relatively minor item), demand deposits (regular checking accounts), and a

FIGURE 6-5 Equilibrium in the Money Market

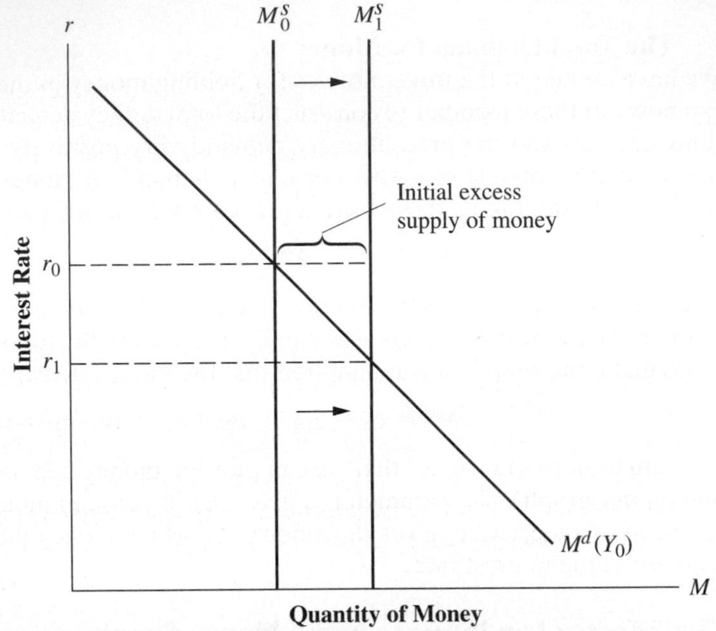

An increase in the money supply from $M_0{}^s$ to $M_1{}^s$ causes an initial excess supply of money. The interest rate falls from r_0 to r_1 to restore equilibrium in the money market.

category called *other checkable deposits*. Currency, travelers checks, and demand deposits, which together accounted for approximately three-quarters of M1 in 2007, do not pay interest; the other checkable deposits do. Moreover, following a period of deregulation of deposit interest rates in the 1980s, banks and other depository institutions can pay whatever interest rate they wish on these deposits.[2]

The question of interest-bearing money comes into our analysis when we consider the Keynesian theory of money demand and the relationship of money demand to the interest rate. Suppose the interest rate on bonds rises. From equation (6.4) or Figure 6-5, the Keynesian theory predicts a decline in money demand as individuals shift into bonds. But this analysis was based on the assumption that money earned no interest.

From the previous discussion, we see that for the majority of the assets in M1, this assumption is valid. For other checkable deposits accounts, we would expect the rate paid on deposits to rise as the rate of interest on bonds rises. But we would not expect the rate paid on those deposits to increase by as much as the rise in the interest rate paid on bonds. Banks have costs associated with providing checkable deposits; an important cost results from the requirement that banks set aside a certain percentage of such deposits (currently 10 percent) as reserves, on which the bank itself will not be able to earn any interest. Therefore, if the interest rate on bonds rises by 1 percent, the interest rate on other checkable deposits will rise by *less* than 1 percent. The *relative*

[2]The types of other checkable deposits have varied over time. Currently, most of these deposits are NOW (negotiated order of withdrawal) accounts.

interest rate on bonds will be higher, and there will still be an incentive for individuals to shift from money to bonds.

Thus, some components of M1 pay no interest, and even for those that do pay interest, the rate adjusts only partially to changes in the interest rate on bonds. Therefore, we continue to assume that the Keynesian money demand function will be downward-sloping, as drawn in Figure 6-5. Money demand depends negatively on the rate of interest, which in our discussion always means the interest rate on bonds. None of this means that the emergence of interest-paying money, one of several financial-sector innovations in recent years, does not have important implications, especially for monetary policy. These implications are discussed in Chapter 17.

Going Forward

We have seen how changes in the money supply affect the interest rate. We have also seen how a change in the interest rate affects aggregate demand. Can we not combine Figure 6-5 with Figure 6-1 to examine sequentially the effect on income of a change in the money supply? Unfortunately, we cannot.

In Figure 6-5, we analyzed the effects of a change in the money supply in the money market not allowing effects in other markets. Specifically, we held income constant (at Y_0) to fix the position of the money demand function. Now, as the interest rate drops from r_0 to r_1, we can see from Figure 6-1 (assuming the subscripts have the same meaning in the two diagrams) that income increases from Y_0 to Y_1. This rise in income will shift the money demand schedule in Figure 6-5 to the right. There will be a further change in the interest rate back toward r_0 and consequently a further change in income. What we need to find is the effect of changes in the money supply on the equilibrium values of the interest rate and income, equilibrium values for *both* the money and commodity markets. We have all the relationships required, but we need a new framework in which to fit them together. This new framework is the *IS–LM* model.

6.2 THE *IS–LM* MODEL

Our task in this section is to find the values of the interest rate and income that simultaneously equilibrate the commodity market and the money market. Because equilibrium in the money market implies equilibrium in the bond market, such a combination will equilibrate all three markets (commodities, money, and bonds). First, we identify combinations of income and the interest rate that equilibrate the money market, neglecting the commodity market. Next, we identify combinations of income and the interest rate that are equilibrium values for the commodity market. These two sets of equilibrium combinations of interest rate and income levels are then shown to contain one combination that equilibrates both markets. To find a unique point of equilibrium, we have to assume that policy variables, including the money supply, government spending, and taxes, are fixed at some levels. Other autonomous influences on income and interest rates (e.g., the state of business expectations that affects investment) must also be assumed to be fixed. We see that these policy variables and other exogenous influences determine the positions of the equilibrium schedules for the money and product markets, termed below the *LM* and *IS schedules*. In Chapter 7, we see how changes in these policy variables and other exogenous influences affect the equilibrium values of income and the interest rate.

Money Market Equilibrium: The *LM* Schedule

Construction of the *LM* Schedule

Money demand in the Keynesian model depends positively on income because of the transactions demand. Money demand also varies inversely with the rate of interest, owing to the speculative demand for money and because the amount of transaction balances held at any income level declines as the interest rate (the opportunity cost of holding such balances) increases. We expressed this relationship as

$$M^d = L(Y, r) \tag{6.3}$$

or, in linear form

$$M^d = c_0 + c_1 Y - c_2 r \quad c_1 > 0, \quad c_2 > 0 \tag{6.4}$$

Now we wish to find all the combinations of r and Y that equilibrate money demand with a fixed money supply, denoted M_0^s. The schedule of such points is termed the *LM schedule* because, along this schedule, money demand, for which we use the symbol L [equation (6.3)], is equal to the money supply (M). For simplicity, we discuss the case in which money demand is given by the linear form (6.4). For this case, the condition that must be satisfied for money market equilibrium, the *LM* schedule equation, can be written as

$$M_0^s = M^d = c_0 + c_1 Y - c_2 r \tag{6.5}$$

We have already considered the nature of equilibrium in the money market. In Figure 6-6*a*, for example, three separate demand-for-money schedules are drawn, corresponding to three successively higher levels of income, Y_0, Y_1, and Y_2. As income increases from Y_0 to Y_1 and then from Y_1 to Y_2, the money demand schedule shifts to the right when plotted against the interest rate. The points where these money demand schedules intersect the vertical line, giving the value of the fixed money supply, are points of equilibrium for the money market. Income–interest-rate combinations at which equilibrium occurs, (Y_0, r_0), (Y_1, r_1), and (Y_2, r_2), are points along the *LM*, or money market equilibrium, schedule. These points are plotted in Figure 6-6*b*. Proceeding in this manner, we can find the equilibrium value of the interest rate for each level of income and construct the complete *LM* schedule shown in Figure 6-6*b*.

The *LM* schedule slopes upward to the right. At higher levels of income, equilibrium in the money market occurs at higher interest rates. The reason for the positive slope for the *LM* schedule is the following. An increase in income (e.g., from Y_0 to Y_1 in Figures 6-6*a* and *b*) increases money demand at a given interest rate, because the transactions demand for money varies positively with income. Restoring demand to a level equal to the fixed money supply requires that the interest rate be higher (r_1 instead of r_0 in Figures 6-6*a* and *b*). The higher interest rate results in a lower speculative demand for money and lowers the transactions component *corresponding to any level of income*. The interest rate must rise until this decline in money demand is just equal to the initial income-induced increase in transactions demand.

To complete our discussion of the *LM* schedule, we consider two questions. First, we want to know what determines the value of the slope of the *LM* schedule. We know that the schedule is upward-sloping, but is it steep or relatively flat? The slope of the *LM* schedule is important for our later discussion of policy effects. The second question concerns the position of the *LM* schedule: What factors shift the schedule?

FIGURE 6-6 Equilibrium in the Money Market and the *LM* Schedule

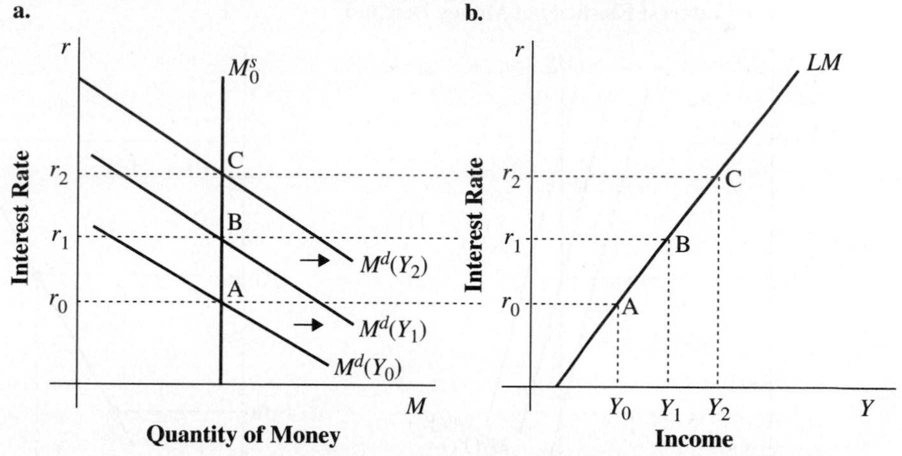

(a) Increases in income from Y_0 to Y_1 to Y_2 shift the money demand schedule from $M^d(Y_0)$ to $M^d(Y_1)$, then to $M^d(Y_2)$. Equilibrium in the money market requires successively higher interest rates $r_0, r_1\ r_2$ at higher levels of income $Y_0, Y_1\ Y_2$. (b) The *LM* schedule shows combinations of income (Y) and the interest rate (r) that equilibrate the money market. Equilibrium combinations such as (r_0, Y_0), ($r_1\ Y_1$), and (r_2, Y_2) from part *a* are points along the *LM* schedule (A, B, C). As we see in part *a*, at higher levels of income, higher interest rates are required for money market equilibrium; the *LM* schedule slopes upward to the right.

Factors That Determine the Slope of the *LM* Schedule

To see which factors determine the slope of the *LM* schedule, we begin by considering the effect on money market equilibrium of an increase in income, ΔY, for example, from Y_0 to Y_1 in Figures 6-6*a* and *b*. The income-induced increase in money demand as a result of this change will equal $c_1 \Delta Y$, where c_1 is the parameter giving the increase in money demand per unit increase in income from equation (6.4). The interest rate will have to rise by enough to offset this income-induced increase in money demand. The higher the value of c_1, the larger the increase in money demand per unit increase in income, and hence, the larger the upward adjustment in the interest rate required to restore total money demand to the level of the fixed money supply. The higher the value of c_1, the steeper will be the *LM* schedule. The value of c_1 is, however, not a subject of much debate. Controversy on this subject centers on the second factor that determines the slope of the *LM* schedule.

For a given income-induced increase in money demand (a given c_1), the amount by which the interest rate has to rise to restore total money demand to the value of the fixed money supply depends on how *elastic* (sensitive) money demand is with respect to changes in the rate of interest.[3] In equation (6.4), the interest elasticity of money demand depends on the value of c_2, which determines the change in money demand for a

[3]The concept of *elasticity* refers to the percentage change in one variable that results from a 1 percent change in another variable. In the case of the interest elasticity of money demand, the elasticity is negative. A 1 percent increase in the interest rate will cause money demand to decline. In the text, the term *high elasticity* refers to the absolute value of the elasticity. If money demand is very responsive to changes in the interest rate, we say that money demand is highly elastic. If money demand is not very responsive to interest rate changes, we term this a *low interest elasticity* of money demand.

FIGURE 6-7 Interest Elasticity of Money Demand and the Slope of the *LM* Schedule

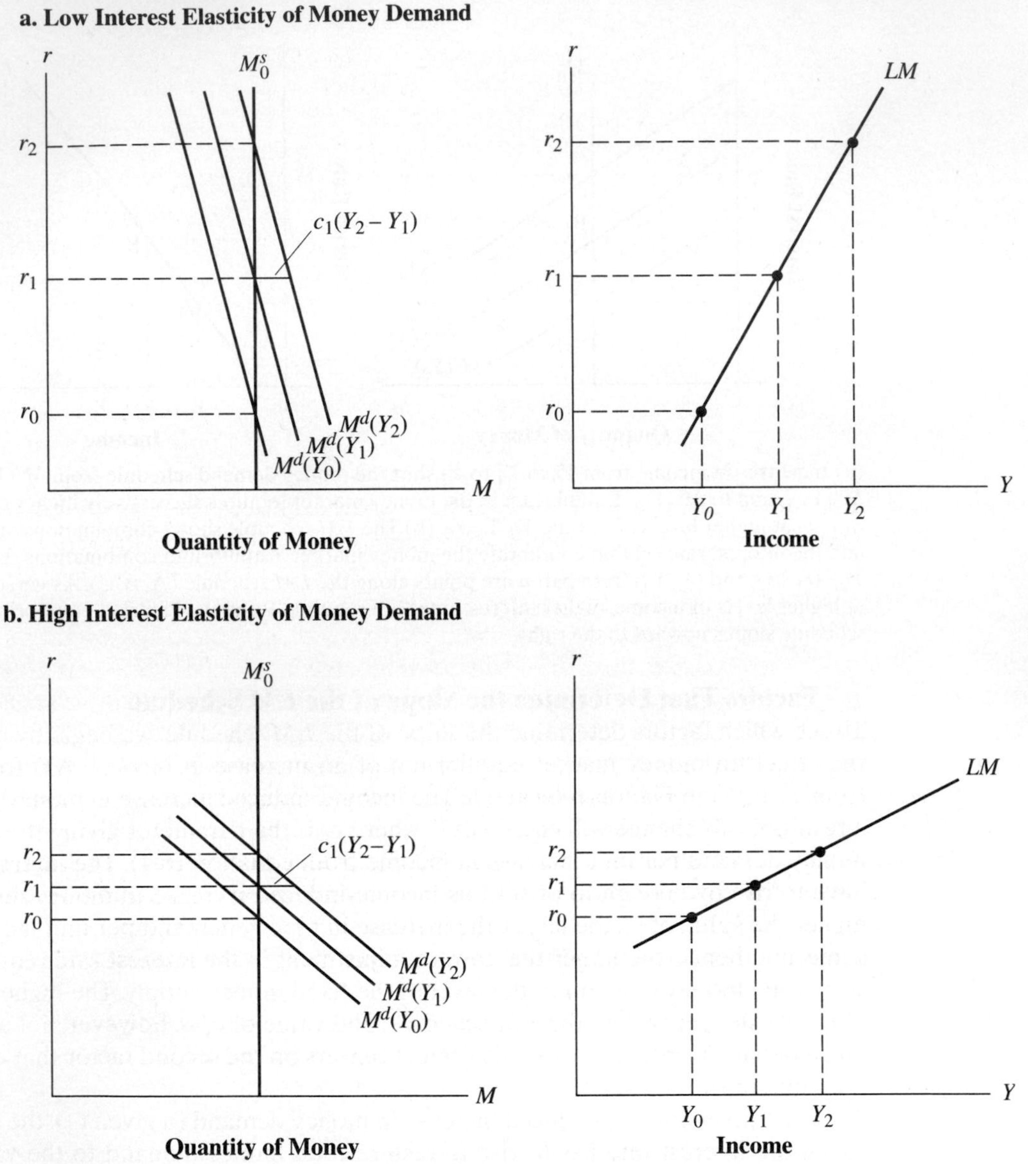

The steep money demand schedule in part *a* reflects the assumption that the interest elasticity of money demand is low (in absolute value). With a low interest elasticity of money demand, the *LM* schedule is relatively steep. In part *b*, money demand is assumed to be highly interest-elastic and, as a result, the money demand schedule is relatively flat. The *LM* schedule in this case is also relatively flat.

given change in the interest rate ($-c_2 = \Delta M^d/\Delta r$). The relationship between the interest elasticity of money demand and the slope of the *LM* schedule is illustrated in Figure 6-7.

Part *a* of the figure shows the case of a low interest elasticity of money demand. The money demand schedule is steep, indicating that large changes in the interest rate will not significantly change the level of money demand. To see how the slope of the *LM* schedule is related to the interest elasticity of money demand, consider how money market equilibrium changes at progressively higher income levels. Increases in income from Y_0 to Y_1 and then to Y_2 will shift the money demand schedule to the right in Figure 6-7*a*, from $M^d(Y_0)$ to $M^d(Y_1)$ and then to $M^d(Y_2)$. These increases in income raise the transactions demand for money by $c_1\,(Y_1 - Y_0)$ and $c_1\,(Y_2 - Y_1)$, respectively. Because a given increase in the interest rate will not reduce money demand by much (c_2 is small), the interest rate will have to rise by a large amount to reduce money demand back to the fixed M_0^s level. This fact is reflected in the *LM* curve in Figure 6-7*a*, which is quite steep.

The case in which money demand is highly interest-elastic is shown in Figure 6-7*b*. Here the money demand schedule is quite flat. A small drop in the interest rate, for example, increases money demand significantly. Here again, the money demand schedule shifts to the right as income increases from Y_0 to Y_1 and then to Y_2. The graph is constructed such that the increase in income and the value of c_1 from equation (6.4) are the same as in Figure 6-7*a*. Thus, the income-induced increases in money demand are the same in Figures 6-7*a* and *b*. Notice that in Figure 6-7*b* the interest rate must rise by a relatively small amount to restore equilibrium in the money market. As a consequence, the *LM* schedule in Figure 6-7*b* is relatively flat. If money demand is highly responsive to changes in the interest rate (c_2 is large), a relatively small rise in the interest rate will offset the income-induced increases in transactions balances as income rises from Y_0 to Y_1 and then to Y_2.

Two special cases for the slope of the *LM* schedule result from the interest elasticity of money demand taking on the value of zero or, alternatively, becoming extremely high.

First, consider the case in which money demand is completely interest-insensitive [c_2 equals zero in equation (6.4)]. Beginning at some initial equilibrium, consider the rise in the interest rate required to reequilibrate the money market if income increased. To have income at a higher level would mean increased transactions demand for money. With money demand completely unresponsive to changes in the interest rate, there is *no* possible rise in the interest rate that would reduce money demand back to the level of the fixed money supply. In this case, a rise in the interest rate is assumed not to cause people either to reduce the speculative demand for money or to economize on transactions balances. Consequently, only one level of income can be an equilibrium level. To see this, notice that with c_2 equal to zero, equation (6.4) becomes

$$M^d = c_0 + c_1 Y$$

and the *LM* schedule equation (6.5) is given by

$$M_0^s = c_0 + c_1 Y$$

Consequently, with M fixed at M_0^s for equilibrium, we must have

$$Y = \frac{M_0^s - c_0}{c_1} \tag{6.6}$$

Only one level of income can be an equilibrium level for the money market.

The *LM* schedule for this case is shown in Figure 6-8. We refer to this case as the *classical case* because the Keynesian money demand function *when c_2 equals zero* does not differ substantively from the classical money demand function. As in the classical theory (see Section 4.1), money demand depends only on income. The distinguishing feature of the Keynesian theory of money demand is the negative relationship between money demand and the interest rate.

FIGURE 6-8 *LM* Schedule: The Classical Case

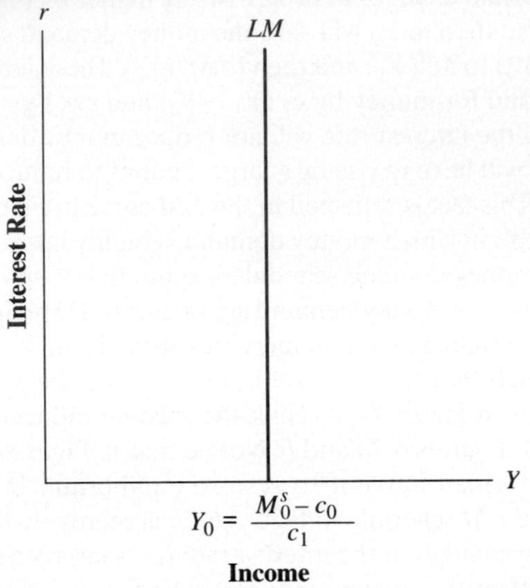

The *LM* schedule is vertical if money demand is completely interest-insensitive.

The alternative extreme case occurs when the interest elasticity of money demand becomes extremely large, approaching infinity. What causes this? Our discussion of Keynes's theory of the speculative demand for money showed that as the interest rate becomes very low, relative to what is considered normal, a consensus develops considering future interest-rate increases as likely. In this situation, with expected future capital losses outweighing the small interest earnings on bonds, the public would hold any increase in money balances with only a negligible fall in the interest rate. In this range of the money demand schedule, the interest elasticity of money demand becomes extremely high. This case, which Keynes termed the *liquidity trap*, is illustrated in Figure 6-9. Notice that here we have to abandon the linear form of the money demand function. In the liquidity trap case, we are considering a change in the slope of the money demand function. The function becomes very flat at low interest rates.

In Figure 6-9*a*, consider first the money demand schedules $M^d(Y_0)$ and $M^d(Y_1)$ corresponding to the income levels Y_0 and Y_1 shown in Figure 6-9*b*. Relative to income levels Y_2 and Y_3, these are low levels of income. Consequently, $M^d(Y_0)$ and $M^d(Y_1)$ are to the left of $M^d(Y_2)$ and $M^d(Y_3)$ in Figure 6-9*a*.

At these low income levels, with the money supply at M_0^s, the equilibrium interest rate is so low that we are on the flat portion of the money demand schedule. Within this range, a rise in income, from Y_0 to Y_1, for example, requires only a slight rise in the interest rate to restore equilibrium in the money market; money demand is highly responsive to changes in the interest rate. In this range, the *LM* schedule in Figure 6-9 is nearly horizontal.

At higher levels of income, between Y_2 and Y_3, for example, an increase in income would require a larger increase in the interest rate to restore equilibrium in the money market. Here the equilibrium interest rates are such that we are not in the liquidity trap. The interest elasticity of money demand is lower over this portion of the money demand schedule.

FIGURE 6-9 Liquidity Trap

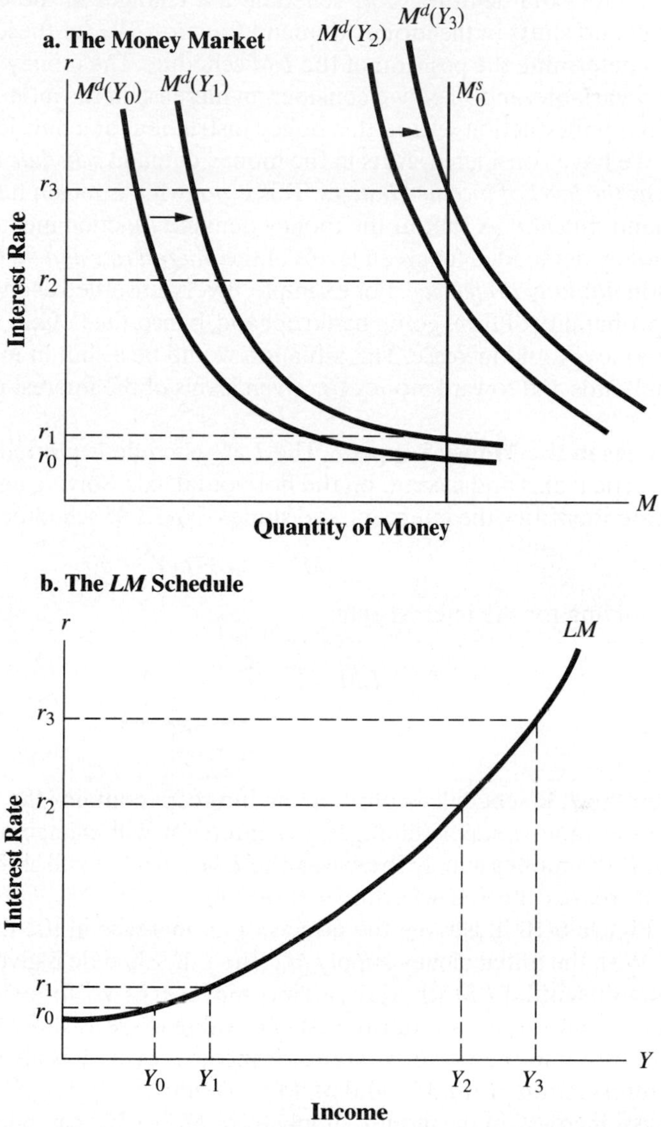

At very low levels of income, Y_0 and Y_1, equilibrium in the money market in part *a* occurs at points along the flat portion of the money demand schedule where the elasticity of money demand is extremely high. Consequently, the *LM* schedule in part *b* is nearly horizontal over this range. At higher income levels, such as Y_2 and Y_3, money market equilibrium is at steeper points along the money demand schedules M^d (Y_2), $M^d(Y_3)$, and the *LM* schedule becomes steeper.

Factors That Shift the *LM* Schedule

Two factors that shift the *LM* schedule are changes in the exogenously fixed money supply and shifts in the money demand function. We set these two factors at given levels to determine the position of the *LM* schedule. The money supply is assumed to be a policy variable, and when we consider an increase in the money supply, for example, we mean a policy action setting this policy instrument at a new level.

We have considered shifts in the money demand *schedule* drawn against the interest rate *as the level of income changes*. This is *not* what is meant here by a shift in the money demand *function*. A shift in the money demand function means a change in the amount of money demanded for given levels of the *interest rate and income*, what Keynes called a shift in *liquidity preference*. For example, if very unsettled economic conditions increased the probability of firms going bankrupt and, hence, the default risk on bonds, the demand for money would increase. This situation would be a shift in individuals' portfolios away from bonds and toward money for given levels of the interest rate and income.

Changes in the Money Supply. The *LM* schedule is plotted with the interest rate on the vertical axis and income on the horizontal axis. Solving equation (6.5) for the interest rate identifies the intercept and slope of the *LM* schedule.

$$M_0^s = c_0 + c_1Y - c_2r$$

Solving for the interest rate:

$$LM:\quad r = \underbrace{\frac{c_0}{c_2} - \frac{1}{c_2}(M_0^s)}_{\text{intercept}} + \underbrace{\frac{c_1Y}{c_2}}_{\text{slope}} \tag{6.5a}$$

When the *LM* schedule is plotted, the intercept contains the money supply (M_0^s). Any time the money supply changes, the intercept will change and the *LM* schedule will shift. If the money supply increases, the *LM* schedule will shift down. If the money supply decreases, the *LM* schedule will shift up.

Figure 6-10 illustrates the effects of an increase in the money supply from M_0^s to M_1^s. With the initial money supply M_0^s, the *LM* schedule is given by LM_0 in Figure 6-10*b*. Along this initial *LM* schedule, an income level of Y_0, for example, is a point of money market equilibrium for an interest-rate value of r_0, as shown at point A on the graph. Equilibrium in the money market for income level Y_0 is also shown in Figure 6-10*a* at the intersection of the M_0^s and $M^d(Y_0)$ schedules.

An increase in the money supply from M_0^s to M_1^s can be seen in Figure 6-10*a* to reduce the equilibrium interest rate to r_1 for a given level of income Y_0. With income fixed, in order for the new higher money supply to be equal to the money demand, the interest rate must be lower to increase the speculative demand for money and transactions demand for a given income level. In terms of the *LM* schedule in Figure 6-10*b*, the point on the new *LM* schedule (for money supply $M^s{}_1$) that gives the equilibrium interest rate for income level Y_0 will be at interest rate r_1. This income–interest-rate combination (Y_0, r_1) is a point on the new *LM* schedule, LM_1, as shown at point B on the graph.

In general, with a higher money supply for a given level of income, the interest rate that equilibrates the money market will be lower. The new *LM* schedule, LM_1, will lie below the initial schedule LM_0, as shown in Figure 6-10*b*.

FIGURE 6-10 Shift in the *LM* Schedule with an Increase in the Quantity of Money

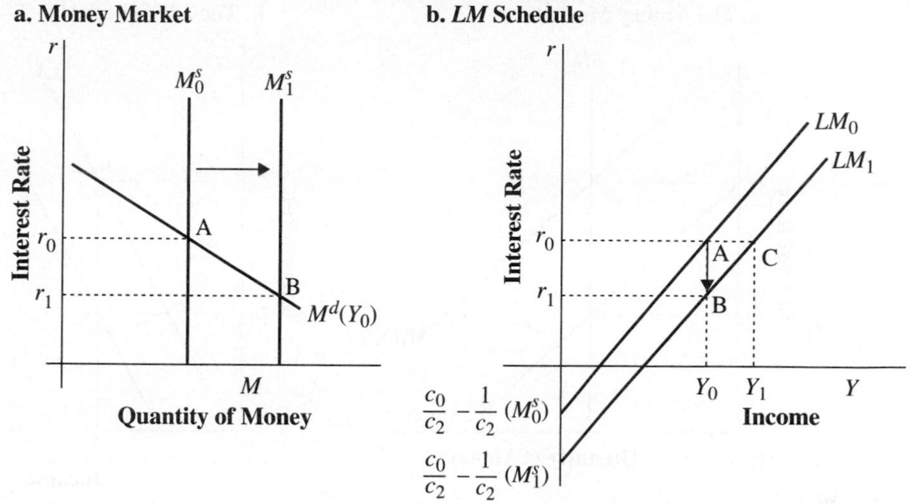

Beginning at point A in the money market, with money supply (M_0^s), the equilibrium interest rate is r_0. This is the combination Y_0, r_0, at point (A) on the *LM* schedule. When the money supply increases, from (M_0^s) to (M_1^s), *given the money demand at income level*, Y_0, the money supply schedule shifts to the right. Equilibrium in the money market changes from point A to point B, and the interest rate decreases from r_0 to r_1.

Alternatively, consider the point on the new *LM* schedule that gives the equilibrium level of income corresponding to interest rate r_0. At M_0^s the income level Y_0 was an equilibrium level for interest rate r_0 (point A). With the money supply M^s_1, in order for r_0 to be an equilibrium value in the money market, income would have to be higher at Y_1. With a higher money supply and a given interest rate, in order for there to be equilibrium in the money market, income must be at a higher level. The point on the new *LM* schedule LM_1, corresponding to r_0, must lie to the right of point A. This point is shown as point C in Figure 6-10*b*. The new *LM* schedule, LM_1, with the higher money supply M^s_1 will lie to the right of the original *LM* schedule in Figure 6-10*b*.

In sum, *an increase in the money supply shifts the LM schedule downward and to the right*. By reversing the foregoing analysis, a decline in the money supply shifts the *LM* schedule upward and to the left.

Shifts in the Money Demand Function. Consider next the effect on the *LM* schedule of a shift in the money demand function. Assume that there is an increase in money demand for a given level of income and the interest rate. A possible reason for such a shift, as suggested previously, is a loss of confidence in bonds.

Figure 6-11*a* shows an initial equilibrium in the money market corresponding to income level Y_0. Initially, money demand is given by $M_0^d(Y_0)$. The equilibrium interest rate is r_0, as shown at point A on the initial *LM* schedule, LM_0 in Figure 6-11*b*. Now assume that the money demand function shifts to $M_1^d(Y_0)$, an increase in money demand for a given level of income. Note here that it is the *function* that shifts, from $M_0^d(Y_0)$ to $M_1^d(Y_0)$. At the unchanged level of income, Y_0, equilibrium in the money market requires an interest rate of r_1. The point on the new *LM* schedule, LM_1 in Figure 6-11*b*,

FIGURE 6-11 Shift in the *LM* Schedule with a Shift in the Money Demand Function

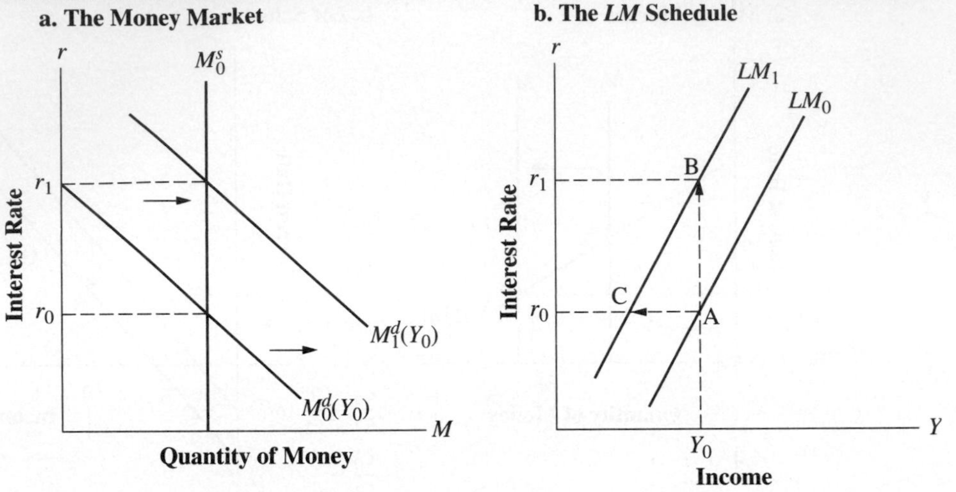

A shift in the money demand function upward from $M_0{}^d$ (Y_0) to $M_1{}^d(Y_0)$ in part *a* raises the equilibrium interest rate for a given income level. The *LM* schedule in part *b* shifts upward to the left from LM_0 to LM_1.

for a given level of income Y_0 will be above the old *LM* schedule. This point is shown as point B in Figure 6-11*b*.

Similarly, maintaining equilibrium in the money market at r_0 after the shift in the money demand schedule would require a fall in income to a level below Y_0, which would shift the schedule in Figure 6-11*a* down to the level of the original $M_0{}^d(Y_0)$ line. Thus the point on LM_1 at r_0 is to the left of LM_0. This is shown as point C in Figure 6-11*b*.

A shift in the money demand function that increases the demand for money at a given level of both the interest rate and income shifts the *LM* schedule upward and to the left. A reverse change in money demand (lowering the amount of money demanded at given levels of income and the interest rate) shifts the *LM* schedule downward to the right.

The *LM* Schedule: Summary

The essentials about the *LM* schedule are:

1. The *LM* schedule is the schedule giving the combinations of values of income and the interest rate that produce equilibrium in the money market.
2. The *LM* schedule slopes upward to the right.
3. The *LM* schedule will be relatively flat (steep) if the interest elasticity of money demand is relatively high (low).
4. The *LM* schedule will shift downward (upward) to the right (left) with an increase (decrease) in the quantity of money.
5. The *LM* schedule will shift upward (downward) to the left (right) with a shift in the money demand function that increases (decreases) the amount of money demanded at given levels of income and the interest rate.

Product Market Equilibrium: The *IS* Schedule

Construction of the *IS* Schedule

The condition for equilibrium in the product market is

$$Y = C + I + G \tag{6.7}$$

An equivalent statement of this equilibrium condition is

$$I + G = S + T \tag{6.8}$$

We construct the product market equilibrium schedule, termed the *IS schedule*, from this second form of the equilibrium condition, although the same results could be derived from equation (6.7).

We proceed by finding the set of interest-rate and income combinations that produces equilibrium for the product market. Next, we examine the factors that determine the slope and position of this product market equilibrium schedule.

To begin, we consider a simplified case that omits the government sector (i.e., G and T equal zero). For this simple case, we can rewrite (6.8) as[4]

$$I(r) = S(Y) \tag{6.9}$$

Equation (6.9) also indicates that investment depends on the interest rate and saving depends on income. Our task is to find combinations of the interest rate and income that equate investment with saving.

Figure 6-12 illustrates the construction of the *IS* schedule for this case. In Figure 6-12*a* investment is plotted as a negatively sloped function of the interest rate; a decline in the interest rate will increase investment expenditures. Saving is depicted as a positively sloped function of income, the slope being the positive marginal propensity to save (MPS).

Consider an interest rate of r_0. For this level of the interest rate, investment is the amount I_0, as shown along the investment schedule. An amount of saving just equal to I_0 is shown as S_0 along the saving function. This level of saving results if income is at Y_0. Thus, for the interest rate r_0, a point of product market equilibrium will be at Y_0. This interest-rate–income combination (r_0, Y_0) is one point on the *IS* schedule, shown as point A in Figure 6-12*b*.

Now consider a higher value of the interest rate, such as r_1. At interest rate r_1, investment will be I_1, a smaller amount than at r_0. For equilibrium, saving must be at S_1, lower than S_0. This saving level is generated by income level Y_1, which is lower than Y_0. Thus a second point on the *IS* schedule will be at r_1 and Y_1, point B on Figure 6-12*b*. Notice that for the higher interest rate, the corresponding equilibrium income level is lower. *The IS schedule has a negative slope.* By choosing additional interest rate values such as r_2 in Figure 6-12*a* and finding the corresponding income level for equilibrium Y_2, where $I_2 = S_2$, we can find additional points on the *IS* schedule in Figure 6-12*b*, such as point C. In this way we trace the complete set of combinations of income and interest-rate levels that equilibrate the product market.

[4]The label *IS* comes from this simple version of the product market equilibrium curve, an equality between investment (I) and saving (S).

FIGURE 6-12 Construction of the *IS* Schedule ($T = G = 0$)

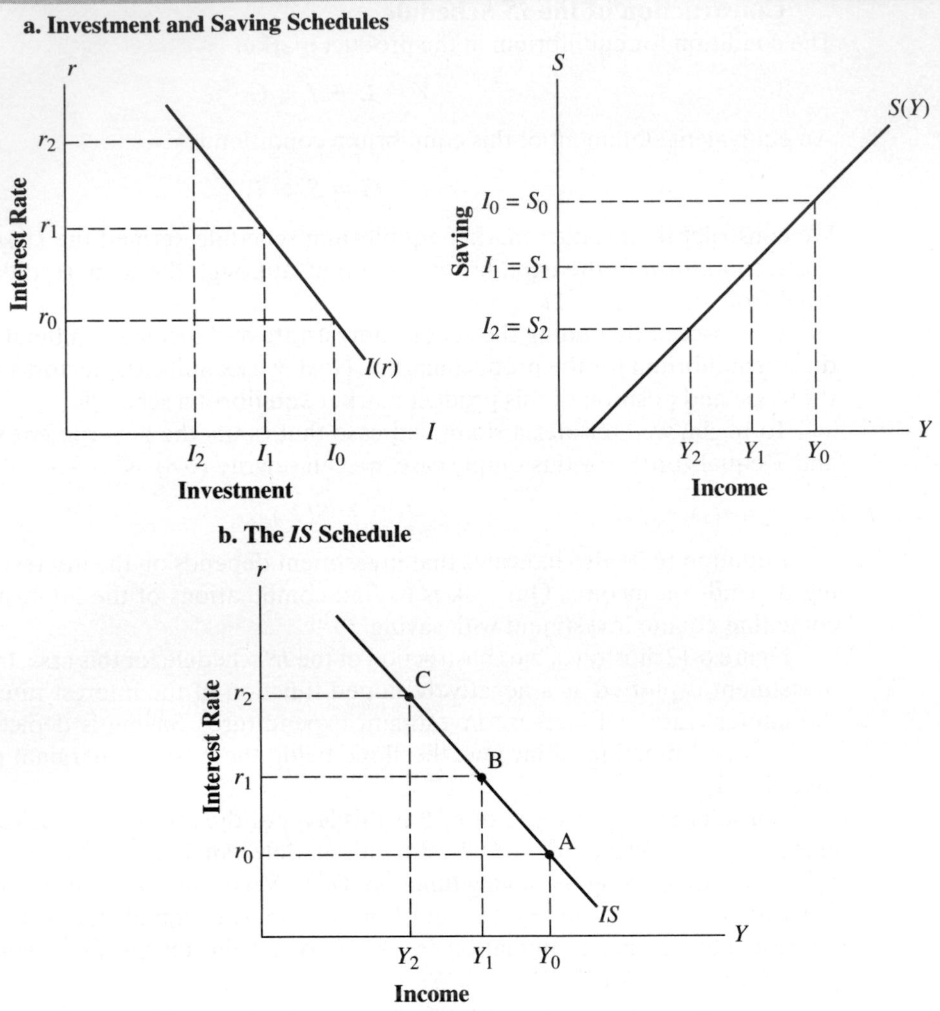

At interest rates r_0, r_1, r_2, investment levels will be I_0, I_1, and I_2 in part *a*. To generate saving S_0, S_1, and S_2 equal to these levels of investment, income must be at Y_0, Y_1, and Y_2, respectively. Therefore, interest-rate–income combinations (r_0, Y_0), (r_1, Y_1), and (r_2, Y_2) are points (A, B, C) along the *IS* schedule in part *b*.

Factors That Determine the Slope of the *IS* Schedule

Next, we consider the factors that determine the degree of the slope of the *IS* schedule. We know that the schedule will be negatively sloped, but will it be steep or flat? As with the *LM* schedule, the question is of interest because we will see that the steepness of the *IS* schedule is a factor determining the relative effectiveness of monetary and fiscal stabilization policies.

In constructing the *IS* schedule, we have looked at how investment changes as we vary the interest rate and then at the required change in income to move saving to equal the new investment level. In considering the steepness of the *IS* schedule, we

FIGURE 6-13 Interest Elasticity of Investment and the Slope of the *IS* Schedule

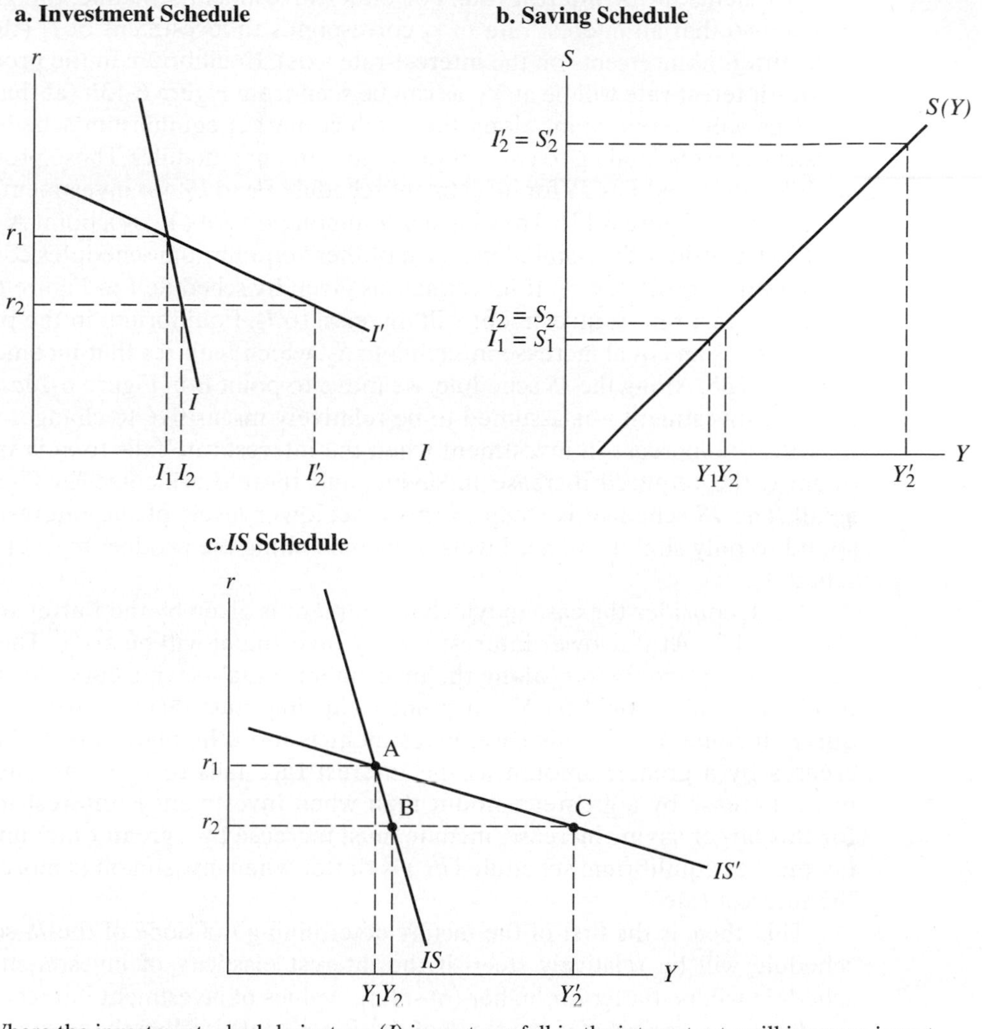

Where the investment schedule is steep (I) in part a, a fall in the interest rate will increase investment by a small amount. In part b, therefore, only a small increase in saving and, hence, income is required to restore product market equilibrium. Therefore, the IS schedule in part c (IS in this case) will be steep. Where the investment schedule is relatively flat (I'), investment will increase by a greater amount with a fall in the interest rate. Saving, and therefore income, must then increase by a greater amount; the IS schedule for this case (IS') will be relatively flat.

are asking whether, at progressively lower interest rates, for example, equilibrium in the product market requires *much* higher income levels (the schedule is relatively flat) or only *slightly* increased income levels (the schedule is steep). The answer depends on the slopes of the investment and saving functions. Figure 6-13 illustrates how the slope of the *IS* schedule is related to the slope of the investment function. Two investment schedules are depicted. Schedule I is very steep, indicating that investment is not very sensitive to changes in the interest rate; the interest elasticity of investment demand is low.[5] Schedule I' is drawn for the case in which investment is more sensitive to movements in the interest rate. For either investment schedule, the graph is constructed so that an interest rate of r_1 corresponds to investment of I_1 (the schedules have different intercepts on the interest-rate axis). Equilibrium in the product market for this interest rate will be at Y_1, as can be seen from Figure 6-13*b* (at that point, $I_1 = S_1$). This will be one point along the product market equilibrium schedules that we construct corresponding to each of these investment schedules. These product market equilibrium schedules, *IS* for investment schedule I and IS' for investment schedule I', are shown in Figure 6-13*c*. They have a common point at (Y_1, r_1), point A.

Now consider the point along each of these equilibrium schedules corresponding to a lower interest rate r_2. If investment is given by schedule I in Figure 6-13*a*, at the lower interest rate r_2 investment will increase to I_2. Equilibrium in the product market requires an equal increase in saving to S_2, which requires that income be at Y_2 in Figure 6-13*b*. Along the *IS* schedule, we move to point B in Figure 6-13*c*. Notice that, because investment was assumed to be relatively insensitive to changes in the interest rate, the increase in investment when the interest rate falls to r_2 is small. Consequently, the required increase in saving, and therefore income, in Figure 6-13*b* is small. The *IS* schedule is steep in this case; lower levels of the interest rate correspond to only slightly higher levels of income along the product market equilibrium schedule.

Next, consider the case in which investment is given by the flatter schedule I' in Figure 6-13*a*. At the lower interest rate r_2, investment will be at I_2'. The level of income corresponding to r_2 along the investment-equals-saving curve for this case, IS' in Figure 6-13*c*, would be Y_2' at point C. Saving must increase to S_2', and this requires income Y_2'. In this case, investment is more highly interest-elastic and increases by a greater amount as the interest rate falls to r_2. Consequently, saving must increase by a greater amount than when investment is interest-inelastic, and for this larger saving increase, income must increase by a greater amount. The product market equilibrium schedule (IS') is flatter when investment is more sensitive to the interest rate.

This, then, is the first of the factors determining the slope of the *IS* schedule. The schedule will be relatively steep if the interest elasticity of investment is low. The schedule will be flatter for higher (absolute) values of investment interest elasticity.

One extreme case for the slope of the *IS* schedule is when the interest elasticity of investment demand is zero; investment is completely insensitive to the interest rate. In this case, the investment schedule in Figure 6-13*a* will be vertical and the *IS* schedule will also be vertical. For this case, a fall in the interest rate from r_1 to r_2 would not increase investment at all. Consequently, equilibrium in the product market requires the same level of saving, and hence income, at r_2 as at r_1.

The second factor affecting the slope of the *IS* schedule is the saving function. Until we consider more elaborate theories of consumption, we do not encounter controversy over the slope of the saving function in Figure 6-13*b*, which is equal to the MPS. Consequently, in this section the value of the MPS does not play much of a role

[5]The concept of elasticity is defined in footnote 3. Here, as in the case of money demand, the interest elasticity is negative; an increase in the interest rate lowers investment. By saying that elasticity is low, we refer to the absolute value of elasticity.

in our discussion of the factors determining the slope of the *IS* schedule. It can be shown, however, that the *IS* curve will be relatively steeper the higher the MPS.

To see this relationship, first note that the higher the value of the MPS, the steeper is the saving function in Figure 6-13*b* (saving increases by more per unit of income). Once we have determined the slope of the investment schedule, we fix the change in investment for a given change in the interest rate. A given decline in the interest rate, for example, then leads to a given increase in investment, and for product market equilibrium along the *IS* schedule, saving must be higher by the same amount. If the MPS is relatively high, then a smaller increase in income will generate this new saving than if the MPS were low. Thus, for a given fall in the interest rate, the amount by which income would have to be increased for a new point of equilibrium in the product market is smaller (larger) the higher (lower) the value of the MPS. This means that the *IS* schedule is relatively steeper, other factors as given, the higher the MPS.

Factors That Shift the *IS* Schedule

Next, consider the factors that determine the position of the *IS* schedule and changes that shift the schedule. Here we drop the assumption that government expenditures and taxes are zero; we bring the government sector back into the model. The *IS* schedule will shift when any or all of the components of autonomous expenditures change: *a*, *T*, *I*, and *G*. With the government sector in the model, the condition for product market equilibrium is given by (6.8), which we rewrite as

$$I(r) + G = S(Y - T) + T \tag{6.10}$$

Notice that saving must now be written as a function of *disposable income* ($Y_D = Y - T$), which differs from income by the amount of tax collections.

Construction of the *IS* schedule for this more general case is illustrated in Figure 6-14. In part *a*, we plot both the investment function and the level of investment plus government spending. Note that the $I + G$ schedule is downward-sloping only because investment depends on the rate of interest. The $I + G$ schedule lies to the right of the I schedule by the fixed amount of government spending. In Figure 6-14*b*, the saving schedule is plotted against the level of income. Saving plus taxes $[S(Y - T) + T]$ is also plotted. We assume that tax collections are fixed exogenously, so the saving-plus-taxes schedule lies above the saving schedule by a fixed distance (equal to T).

Consider the interest rate r_0 in Figure 6-14. At this interest rate, the level of investment [which can be read from the $I(r)$ schedule] plus the fixed level of government spending equals $I_0 + G$. For equilibrium, this must be balanced by an equal total of saving plus tax collections, given by $S_0 + T$ in Figure 6-14*b*. The level of income that generates this level of saving plus tax collections is given by Y_0. Thus, one point along the *IS* schedule is point A in Figure 6-14*c*, corresponding to interest rate r_0 and income level Y_0. If we considered a higher interest rate, such as r_1, investment would be less; hence, with government spending unchanged, investment plus government spending would be at the lower level $I_1 + G$. For equilibrium, a lower level of saving plus taxes is required. This level is shown as $S_1 + T$ in Figure 6-14*b*, where it should be noted that the change is only in the saving component, because taxes are fixed. For this lower level of saving, income must be at Y_1, below Y_0 in Figure 6-14*b*. The corresponding point on the *IS* schedule is point B in Figure 6-14*c*.

FIGURE 6-14 *IS* Schedule with the Addition of a Government Sector

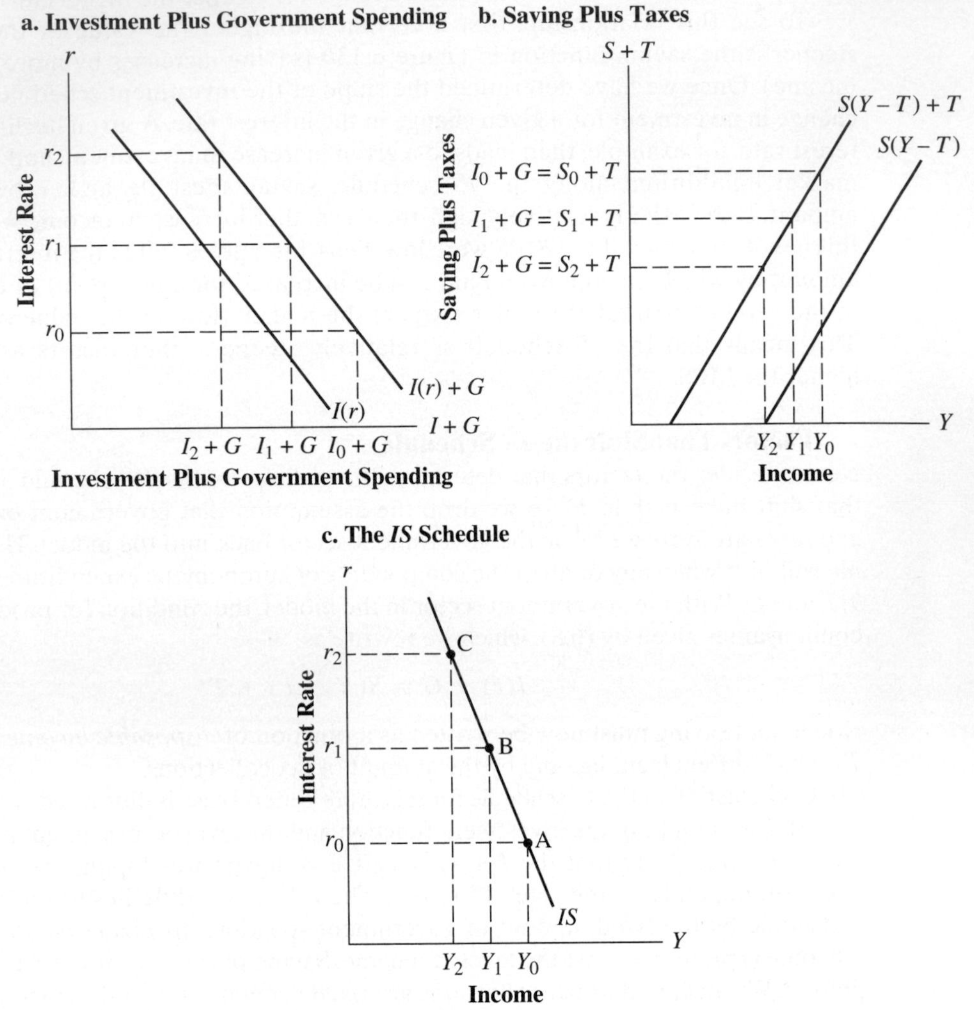

With the inclusion of the government sector, the condition for equilibrium in the goods market becomes $I + G = S + T$. At an interest rate of r_1 in part *a*, investment plus government spending will be equal to $I_1 + G$. Therefore, equilibrium in the goods market requires that saving plus taxes, as shown in part *b*, equal $S_1 + T (= I_1 + G)$, which will be the case at an income level Y_1. Thus, the combination r_1, Y_1 is one point (B) along the *IS* schedule in part *c*.

By similar reasoning, we can establish that an interest rate of r_2 will require an income level of Y_2 for equilibrium in the product market (point C in Figure 6-14*c*). The complete *IS* schedule is constructed by proceeding in this manner.

We can now look at factors that would cause a shift in the *IS* schedule. The equilibrium condition given by (6.10) shows that a change in either the level of government spending (G) or the level of taxes (T) will disturb an initial product market equilibrium position—this will be a shift in the *IS* schedule. In addition, an autonomous investment change that shifts the investment function will shift the *IS* schedule. Note that, in general,

FIGURE 6-15 Shift in the *IS* Schedule with an Increase in Government Spending

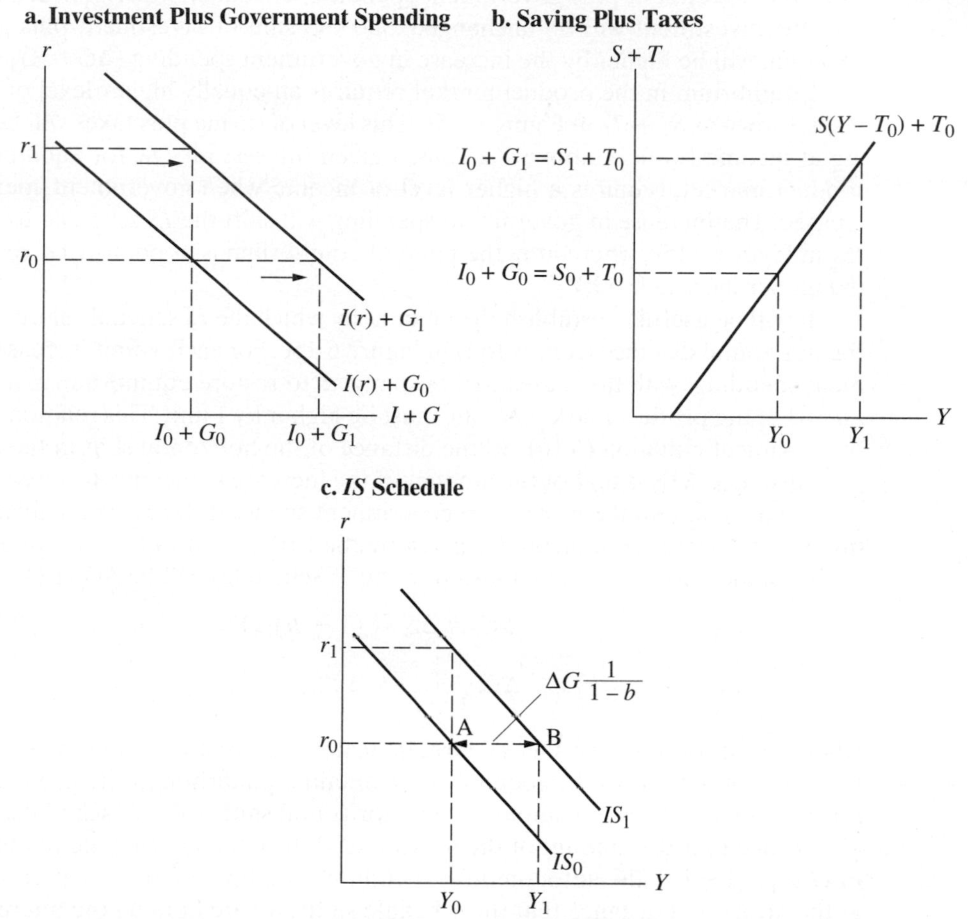

At interest rate r_0, an increase in government spending increases the total of investment plus government spending from $I_0 + G_0$ to $I_0 + G_1$ in part *a*. To maintain the condition $I + G = S + T$, with a fixed level of taxes, saving must rise from S_0 to S_1, which requires income to be Y_1 instead of Y_0 in part *b*. At interest rate r_0, the equilibrium point in the product market is point B instead of point A. An increase in government spending shifts the *IS* schedule to the right from IS_0 to IS_1 in part *c*.

the factors that shift the *IS* schedule are those that determined autonomous expenditures in the simple Keynesian model of Chapter 5.

Changes in Government Spending. Consider first the effects of a change in government spending. The shift in the *IS* schedule when government spending increases from an initial level G_0 to a higher level G_1 is illustrated in Figure 6-15. For the initial level of government spending, the *IS* schedule is given by IS_0 in Figure 6-15*c*. An interest rate of r_0, for example, will be an equilibrium level for the product market if income is at Y_0, as shown at point A on IS_0. At interest rate r_0, investment plus government spending will be $I_0 + G_0$, as shown in Figure 6-15*a*. As shown in Figure 6-15*b*, an income level of Y_0 generates saving plus taxes just equal to this amount of government spending plus investment ($S_0 + T_0 = I_0 + G_0$).

Now let government spending increase to G_1 Figure 6-15*a* shows that this increase shifts the investment-plus-government-spending schedule to the right. At a given interest rate, investment will be unchanged, and the sum of investment plus government spending will be higher by the increase in government spending ($\Delta G = G_1 - G_0$).

Equilibrium in the product market requires an equally higher level of saving plus taxes, shown as $S_1 + T_0$ in Figure 6-15*b*. This level of saving plus taxes will be forthcoming at income level Y_1 above Y_0. Thus, a given interest rate r_0, for equilibrium in the product market, requires a higher level of income when government spending is increased. The increase in government spending will shift the *IS* schedule to the right to IS_1 in Figure 6-15*c*, where at r_0 the point of equilibrium is at point B, corresponding to the higher income level Y_1.

It will be useful to establish the amount by which the *IS* schedule shifts to the right, the horizontal distance from A to B in Figure 6-15*c*. For each 1-unit increase in government spending, with taxes assumed unchanged, to restore equilibrium *at a given interest rate* in the product market, saving must be higher by 1 unit. This relation can be seen by looking at equation (6.10). So the distance of the horizontal shift in the *IS* schedule (e.g., distance AB) is that of the amount of the increase in income required to generate new saving equal to the increase in government spending. Because the increase in saving per unit increase in income is given by the MPS equal to $(1 - b)$, the required increase in income (the horizontal shift in the *IS* schedule) will be $\Delta G\,[1/(1 - b)]$,

$$\Delta G = \Delta S = (1 - b)\Delta Y|_{r_0}$$

$$\Delta G\frac{1}{1 - b} = \Delta Y|_{r_0} \tag{6.11}$$

where the subscript r_0 on the ΔY term indicates that we are computing the increase in the value of Y that will be required to maintain equilibrium in the product market *at interest rate* r_0. This is the amount of the horizontal shift in the *IS* schedule.

Notice that the amount of the horizontal shift in the *IS* schedule per unit increase in G is $[1/(1 - b)]$, the autonomous expenditure multiplier from Chapter 5. In looking at the horizontal distance that the schedule shifts, we are holding the interest rate constant and therefore fixing investment. Once investment is assumed given, our model is identical to that in Chapter 5. We are looking for the increase in income that will come with investment fixed, government spending rising, and a consequent induced increase in consumption. This is the same question analyzed in Chapter 5, and we get the same answer.

Changes in Taxes. Next, consider the shift in the *IS* schedule with a change in taxes. The effect on the position of the *IS* schedule of a tax increase from T_0 to T_1 is depicted in Figure 6-16. For each 1-dollar increase in taxes *at a given income level*, taxes are higher by 1 dollar and saving is less by $(1 - b)$ dollars. The latter effect follows because an increase of 1 dollar in taxes lowers disposable income by 1 dollar and reduces saving by the MPS $(1 - b)$. For a given income level, the decline in saving is less than the increase in taxes, so an increase in taxes will shift the $S + T$ schedule upward. In Figure 6-16*b*, an increase in taxes from T_0 to T_1 shifts the schedule from $[S(Y - T_0) + T_0]$ to $[S(Y - T_1) + T_1]$.

At an interest rate such as r_0 in Figure 6-16*a*, we can find the level of government expenditures plus investment along the $I(r) + G$ schedule at $I_0 + G_0$. Equilibrium in

FIGURE 6-16 Shift in the *IS* Schedule with an Increase in Taxes

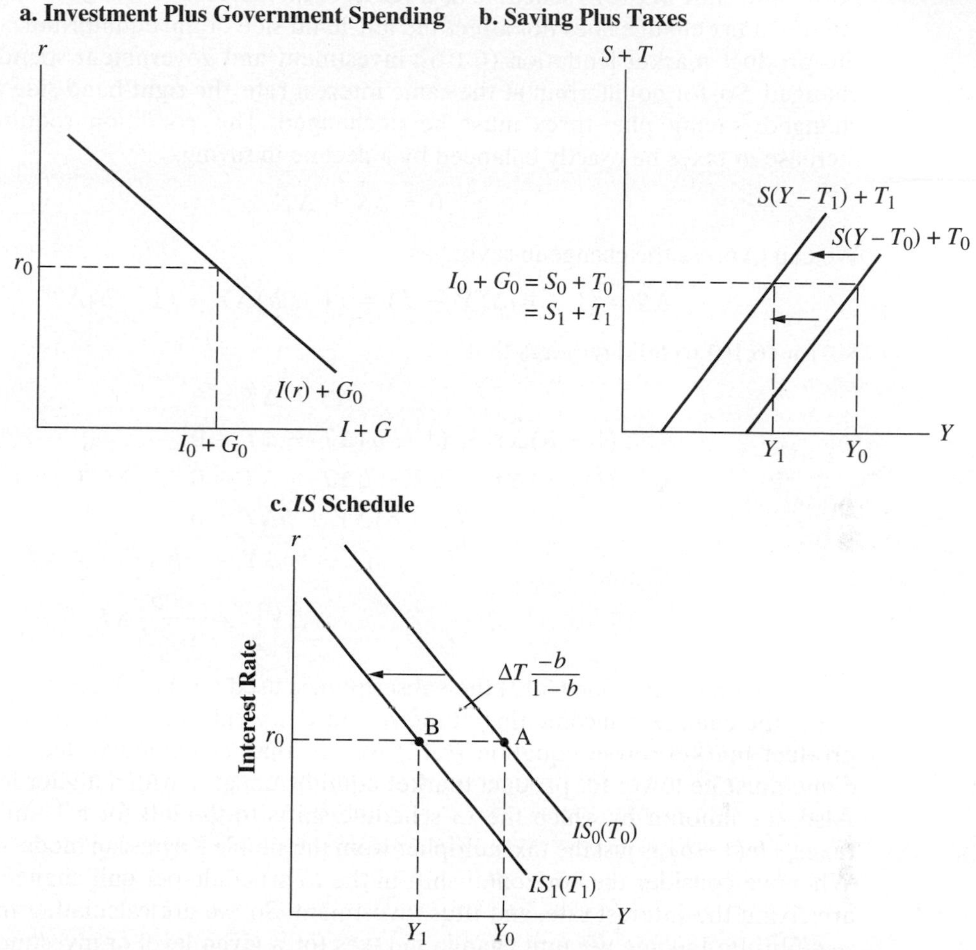

An increase in taxes shifts the $S + T$ schedule to the left in part *b*. At interest rate r_0, which fixes $I_0 + G_0$, with higher taxes, saving, and therefore income must be lower to maintain the condition $I + G = S + T$. After the tax increase, an income level of Y_1 (point B) rather than Y_0 (point A) clears the product market for interest rate r_0. The *IS* schedule shifts leftward from IS_0 to IS_1 in part *c*.

the product market requires an equal amount of saving plus taxes. Initially, with taxes at T_0, the equilibrium level of saving plus taxes is $S_0 + T_0$, and this requires income to be at Y_0. This combination of (r_0, Y_0) is a point on the initial *IS* schedule IS_0, point A in Figure 6-16*c*.

After the tax increase, for equilibrium in the product market at r_0, we must still have the same total of saving plus taxes. This is because there has been no change in investment plus government spending. With the higher level of taxes, in order for saving plus taxes to be unchanged, saving and therefore income must be lower. The new level of income required for product market equilibrium is given by Y_1 in Figure 6-16*b*. The corresponding point on the new *IS* schedule is point B in Figure 6-16*c*. The increase in taxes shifts the *IS* schedule to the left.

As with the change in government spending, we can calculate the magnitude of the horizontal shift in the *IS* schedule as a result of an increase in taxes. *For a given rate of interest*, a tax change does not affect the left-hand side of the equilibrium condition for the product market [equation (6.10)]; investment and government spending are unchanged. So, for equilibrium at the same interest rate, the right-hand side must be unchanged; saving plus taxes must be unchanged. This condition requires that the increase in taxes be exactly balanced by a decline in saving,

$$0 = \Delta S + \Delta T$$

We can express the change in saving as

$$\Delta S = (1 - b)\Delta(Y - T) = (1 - b)\Delta Y - (1 - b)\Delta T$$

So, for (6.10) to hold requires that

$$\begin{aligned} \Delta S + \Delta T &= 0 \\ (1 - b)\Delta Y - (1 - b)\Delta T + \Delta T &= 0 \\ (1 - b)\Delta Y - \Delta T + b\Delta T + \Delta T &= 0 \\ (1 - b)\Delta Y + b\Delta T &= 0 \\ (1 - b)\Delta Y &= -b\Delta T \\ \Delta Y\Big|_{r_0} &= \frac{-b}{1 - b}\Delta T \end{aligned} \tag{6.12}$$

where again in equation (6.12) the subscript r_0 is used on the ΔY term to indicate that this is the change in income that at interest rate r_0 will be an equilibrium value for the product market. From equation (6.12) we see that, as demonstrated previously, income must be lower for product market equilibrium at r_0 with a higher level of taxes. Also, the amount by which the *IS* schedule shifts to the left for a 1-unit increase in taxes, $-b/(1-b)$, is just the tax multiplier from the simple Keynesian model of Chapter 5. When we consider the horizontal shift in the *IS* schedule per unit change in taxes, we are fixing the interest rate, and thus investment. So, we are calculating the change in equilibrium income per unit change in taxes for a given level of investment. This was given in Chapter 5 by the tax multiplier $-b/(1-b)$.

Autonomous Changes in Investment. The last factor we consider that shifts the *IS* schedule is an autonomous change in investment. By this we mean a shift in the investment schedule as drawn against the interest rate. For example, a favorable shift in expectations about the future profitability of investment projects increases investment demand *corresponding to each interest rate*, shifting the $I(r)$ schedule and hence the investment-plus-government-spending schedule to the right in Figure 6-15*a*. This rightward shift in the $I(r)$ schedule, by the amount of the autonomous increase in investment, has exactly the same effect on the *IS* schedule as an equal increase in government spending, analyzed in Figure 6-15. Both changes shift the investment plus government spending schedule and, as was seen in the previous discussion, this shift, in turn, shifts the *IS* schedule to the right by $1/(1 - b)$ units per unit increase in government spending, or in this case, autonomous investment expenditures.

In this section we have considered the various factors that shift the *IS* schedule. We have also generalized the analysis to allow for a government sector and hence to enable us to see how fiscal policy variables affect the position of the *IS* schedule. Because the new variables, government spending and taxes, were exogenous, the slopes of the investment-plus-government-spending schedule and of the saving-plus-taxes schedule were the same as those for the investment and saving schedules considered in the preceding section. Because the slopes of these functions were shown to determine the slope of the *IS* schedule and because they are unchanged, adding the government sector to the model requires no revision of the previous discussion of the slope of the *IS* schedule.

The *IS* Schedule: Summary

We have derived the following results concerning the *IS* schedule, the equilibrium schedule for the product market:

1. The *IS* schedule slopes downward to the right.
2. The *IS* schedule will be relatively flat (steep) if the interest elasticity of investment is relatively high (low).
3. The *IS* schedule will shift to the right (left) when there is an increase (decrease) in government expenditures.
4. The *IS* schedule will shift to the left (right) when taxes increase (decline).
5. An autonomous increase (decrease) in investment expenditures will shift the *IS* schedule to the right (left).

The *IS* and *LM* Schedules Combined

In Figure 6-17, we combine the *LM* and *IS* schedules. The upward-sloping *LM* schedule shows the points of equilibrium for the money market. The downward-sloping *IS* schedule shows the points of equilibrium for the product market. The point of intersection between the two schedules, point E in the figure, is the (only) point of general

FIGURE 6-17 *IS* and *LM* Schedules Combined

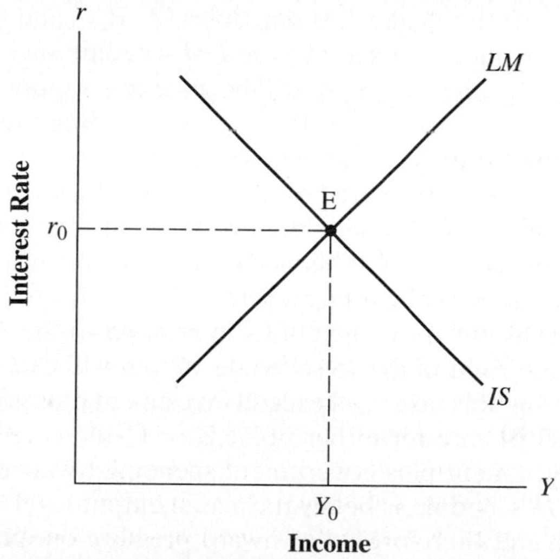

The point of intersection of the *IS* and *LM* schedules gives the combination of the interest rate and income (r_0, Y_0) that produces equilibrium for the money and product markets.

FIGURE 6-18 Adjustment to Equilibrium in the *IS–LM* Model

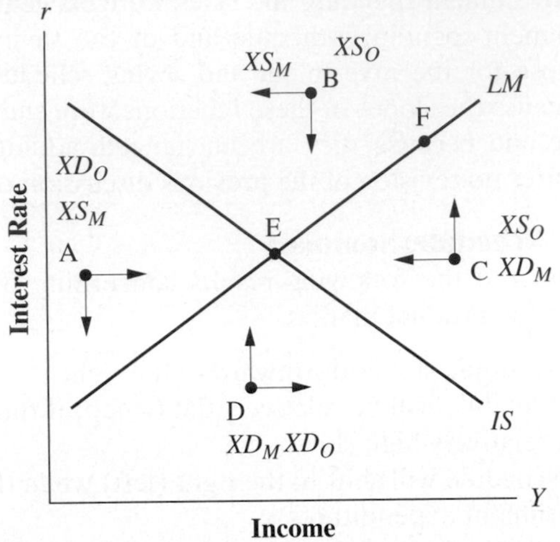

At points such as A, B, C, and D, there are either excess supplies or demands in the money and product markets and therefore pressures for the interest rate and output to change. At point F, the product market is out of equilibrium, and there is pressure for output to change. Only at point E are both the money and product markets in equilibrium.

equilibrium for the two markets. As pointed out at the beginning of our discussion, if the money market is in equilibrium, the bond market must also be in equilibrium. Thus, the interest rate and income level at the intersection of the *IS* and *LM* schedules in Figure 6-17, denoted r_0 and Y_0, are values that produce a simultaneous equilibrium for the money market, product market, and bond market. The nature of equilibrium in the *IS–LM* model can be better understood by considering why points other than the point of intersection of the two schedules are not points of equilibrium. Figure 6-18 shows four points off the *IS* and *LM* schedules (A, B, C, and D).

First, consider points above the *LM* schedule such as points A and B. At all points above the *LM* schedule, there will be an excess supply of money (XS_M). At the level of income for either point A or B, the corresponding interest rate is too high for money market equilibrium. With an excess supply of money, there is downward pressure on the interest rate, as indicated by the downward-direction arrow. There is a tendency to move toward the *LM* schedule. Conversely, at points below the *LM* schedule, such as points C and D, there will be an excess *demand* for money (XD_M) and consequently upward pressure on the interest rate.

Now consider the same points in relation to the *IS* schedule. At points such as B and C, to the right of the *IS* schedule, output will exceed aggregate demand or, analogously, saving plus taxes will exceed investment plus government spending. At the level of the interest rate for either point B or C, the corresponding output level that will equate investment plus government spending to saving plus taxes, given by the point along the *IS* schedule, is below the actual output level. There is an excess supply of output (XS_0), and therefore a downward pressure on output, as indicated by the arrows pointing to the left. Conversely, at points to the left of this *IS* schedule, such as points A and D, actual output is below the level that will clear the product market. There is an excess demand for output (XD_0), and there will be upward pressure on output, as indicated by the rightward-directed arrows at these points.

Finally, note that points on one schedule but not on the other are *disequilibrium* points relative to one of the two markets. A point such as F, for example, is a point of equilibrium for the money market but a point of excess supply for the product market. Similarly, any point along the *IS* schedule other than point E would result in disequilibrium in the money market. Only at point E are both the money and product markets in equilibrium. There is no excess demand or supply in either the money or product market, and therefore there are no pressures for the interest rate or output to change.

6.3 Conclusion

In this chapter, we have added the money market to our Keynesian model. The role of money and monetary policy in the Keynesian system was considered. We then analyzed how the equilibrium level of income and the interest rate are simultaneously determined in the *IS–LM* schedule model. The next task is to see how these equilibrium values are affected by monetary and fiscal policy variables as well as by other shocks to the model.

Key Terms

- liquidity trap

Review Questions and Problems

1. Explain the Keynesian theory of interest-rate determination. What differences do you see between this theory and the classical theory of the interest rate?
2. How would the level of aggregate demand be affected by a rise in the interest rate in the Keynesian theory? Which components would be affected most strongly?
3. What are the three motives for holding money according to Keynes's theory of money demand? Explain each motive.
4. What property is shared by all points along the *LM* schedule? Along the *IS* schedule?
5. Explain why the *IS* schedule in the *IS–LM* model is negatively sloped and the *LM* schedule is positively sloped.
6. What factors determine the magnitude of the slope of the *IS* schedule? That is, what factors determine whether the schedule is steep or flat?
7. What variables will shift the position of the *IS* schedule? Explain how a change in each variable will shift the schedule (to the left or to the right).
8. What factors determine the magnitude of the slope of the *LM* schedule? That is, what factors determine whether the schedule is steep or flat?
9. Trace the procedure for deriving the *IS* schedule, as was done in Figure 6-14, for the case in which, rather than a fixed level of taxes (T), we have taxes depending on income

$$T = t_1 Y$$

   where t_1 is the marginal income tax rate. Will the *IS* schedule for this case be steeper or flatter than when the level of taxes is fixed?
10. Suppose that the interest elasticity of investment demand is zero. What will be the resulting slope of the *IS* schedule. Explain.

11. If the level of government spending were to increase by 50 units in the *IS–LM* schedule model, how would this affect the position of the *IS* schedule? In which direction would the schedule shift and by how many units?
12. What variables will shift the position of the *LM* schedule? Explain how a change in each variable will shift the schedule (to the left or to the right).
13. What condition is required for the *LM* schedule to be vertical? What condition is required for the alternative extreme case, in which the *LM* schedule becomes nearly horizontal over a range?
14. Why are we assured that when the money and product markets are in equilibrium, the bond market will also be in equilibrium?
15. Explain why at a point such as B in Figure 6-18, there is downward pressure on both the level of output and the interest rate.

APPENDIX

The Algebra of the *IS–LM* Model

In this appendix, the *IS–LM* model is presented in algebraic form. This algebraic presentation is a supplement to the verbal and graphical explanation given in the chapter.

For simplicity, we deal with a linear form of the *IS* and *LM* equations. We have already written out a linear form of the *LM* equation

$$M^s = M^d = c_0 + c_1 Y - c_2 r \qquad c_1; c_2 > 0 \quad \textbf{(6.5)}$$

Equation (6.5) states that the fixed money supply (M^s) is equal to the demand for money (M^d), which depends positively on the level of income (Y) and negatively on the interest rate (r).

The condition met for each point on the *IS* schedule is

$$I + G = S + T \qquad \textbf{(6.8)}$$

Investment (I) plus government spending (G) is equal to saving (S) plus taxes (T). Let us derive a linear form of this condition.

In Chapter 5, saving was represented by the saving function

$$\begin{aligned} S &= -a + (1 - b)Y_D \\ &= -a + (1 - b)(Y - T) \qquad \textbf{(5.12)} \end{aligned}$$

Investment is assumed to have an autonomous component and to depend negatively on the interest rate. In linear form, we can write an *investment function* as follows:

$$I = \bar{I} - i_1 r \qquad i_1 > 0 \qquad \textbf{(A.1)}$$

where $\bar{I}$ is the autonomous component of investment and i_1 is a parameter that measures the interest sensitivity of investment (i.e., $-i_1 = \Delta I / \Delta r$).[1] The levels of government spending (G) and taxes (T) are assumed to be fixed exogenously by policymakers.

Substituting equation (5.12) for S and equation (A.1) for I into the *IS* equation (6.8), we can write a linear *IS* equation

$$\bar{I} - i_1 r + G = -a + (1 - b)(Y - T) + T \qquad \textbf{(A.2)}$$

If we rearrange terms so that income appears alone on the left-hand side, we have

$$Y = \frac{1}{1 - b}[a + \bar{I} + G - bT] - \frac{i_1 r}{1 - b} \qquad \textbf{(A.3)}$$

We can also rearrange the terms in our *LM* equation (6.5) so that the interest rate (r) is alone on the left-hand side, as follows:

$$r = \frac{c_0}{c_2} - \frac{M^s}{c_2} + \frac{c_1 Y}{c_2} \qquad \textbf{(A.4)}$$

[1] A parameter is a given or known value. An example of a parameter in our previous analysis is the MPS $(1 - b)$ in (5.12).

Equations (A.3) and (A.4) are linear *IS* and *LM* schedules. These two equations determine the two endogenous variables in the model, income (Y) and the interest rate (r). From here we consider the properties of the *LM* schedule and then the *IS* schedule, deriving in algebraic form the graphical results in section 6.2. We then examine the solution of these two equations for the equilibrium levels of income and the interest rate, the analog to the graphical representation of equilibrium in Figure 6-17.

A.1 The *LM* Schedule

The Slope of the *LM* Schedule

The slope of the *LM* schedule is the change in r (movement up the vertical axis in the *IS–LM* graph) per unit change in Y (movement along the horizontal axis), holding constant the factors that fix the position of the schedule. From equation (A.4) we compute this slope as $\Delta r/\Delta Y$ for fixed values of (c_0/c_2) and $(-M^s/c_2)$, which gives

$$\Delta r = \frac{c_1}{c_2}\Delta Y$$

$$\text{Slope of } LM = \left.\frac{\Delta r}{\Delta Y}\right|_{LM} = \frac{c_1}{c_2} \qquad \textbf{(A.5)}$$

The *LM* schedule has a positive slope. If the expression for the slope of the schedule is large (small), then the schedule will be steep (flat). From equation (A.5) it can be seen that the schedule will be steeper the higher the value of c_1 and the lower the value of c_2. This means that the more money demand increases per unit increase in income (the higher c_1) and the *less* sensitive money demand is to the interest rate (the lower c_2), the steeper will be the *LM* schedule.[2]

Factors That Shift the *LM* Schedule

Now consider factors that shift the *LM* schedule. One way to look at such shifts mathematically is the change in r for one right-hand-side variable in the *LM* schedule equation (A.4), *holding income and the other right-hand-side variables constant*. This is the vertical displacement of the schedule. For example, if the money supply changes, all other variables remaining the same, then

$$\Delta r = \frac{-1}{c_2}\Delta M^s \qquad \textbf{(A.6)}$$

$$\left.\frac{\Delta r}{\Delta M^s}\right|_{LM} = \frac{-1}{c_2} < 0$$

An increase in the money supply (M^s) causes a downward shift in the *LM* schedule; $\Delta r/\Delta M^s$ is negative. This is what we found in Figure 6-10.

The other factor we considered that would shift the *LM* schedule was a shift in the money demand *function*, a change in the level of money demand for given levels of income and the interest rate. In our linear version of the *IS–LM* model, such a shift in the money demand function is represented as a change in the c_0 term in equation (6.5) and therefore in (c_0/c_2) in equation (A.4). For example, an increase in c_0 would mean that more money was demanded for given levels of income and the interest rate. From equation (A.4) we can see that if c_0 rises, then holding constant the other terms on the right-hand side of the equation, the interest rate will rise. This means that, as illustrated in Figure 6-11, an upward shift in the money demand function will shift the *LM* schedule upward to the left.

A.2 The *IS* Schedule

The Slope of the *IS* Schedule

To compute an expression for the slope of the *IS* schedule, we again consider the relationship between r and Y given the values of the terms that fix the position of the schedule [the terms in brackets in equation (A.3)]. From equation (A.3), holding these terms constant, we can write

$$\Delta Y = \frac{-i_1}{1-b}\Delta r$$

[2]Notice also from equation (A.5) that, as c_2 approaches zero, the expression becomes extremely large, indicating that the *LM* schedule becomes vertical. This is the so-called classical case illustrated in Figure 6-8. Alternatively, as c_2 becomes extremely large, the expression for the slope of the *LM* schedule approaches zero, indicating that the *LM* schedule becomes flat. This is the liquidity trap illustrated in Figure 6-9.

or, after rearranging terms

$$\text{slope of } IS = \left.\frac{\Delta r}{\Delta Y}\right|_{IS} = -\frac{(1-b)}{i_1} < 0 \quad \textbf{(A.7)}$$

As discussed in Section 6.2, the *IS* slope is negative. The larger the absolute value of the slope of the *IS* schedule, the steeper the schedule will be. From equation (A.7), it follows that the *IS* schedule will be steeper the larger is $(1-b)$, the higher the marginal propensity to save, and the smaller the value i_1, the parameter measuring the interest sensitivity of investment.[3]

Factors That Shift the *IS* Schedule

When we use equation (A.3), it is most convenient to examine the horizontal shift in the *IS* schedule as the result of changes in the factors that determine the position of the curve. To do this, we examine how Y changes in equation (A.3) as one of the right-hand-side variables changes, *holding constant the interest rate and the other right-hand-side variables*. If, these other things being equal, an increase in a variable raises (lowers) Y, this represents a shift to the right (left) in the *IS* schedule.

For example, if the level of government expenditure changes, from equation (A.3) we compute

$$\Delta Y = \frac{1}{1-b}\Delta G \quad \textbf{(A.8)}$$

$$\left.\frac{\Delta Y}{\Delta G}\right|_{IS} = \frac{1}{1-b} > 0$$

This is the same result we found in equation (6.11); an increase in government spending shifts the *IS* schedule to the right. From equation (A.3) we can see that the analogous expression for the horizontal shift in the *IS* schedule as the result of a change in autonomous expenditure ($\bar{I}$) or in the intercept of the consumption function (a) would be identical to equation (A.8). An increase of 1 unit in each of these would be an increase in autonomous expenditure of 1 unit, and the two would have identical effects in the *IS–LM* model.

Finally, consider the effect on the *IS* schedule of a change in taxes (T). From equation (A.3) we compute

$$\Delta Y = \frac{1}{1-b}(-b\Delta T)$$

or

$$\left.\frac{\Delta Y}{\Delta T}\right|_{IS} = \frac{-b}{1-b} < 0 \quad \textbf{(A.9)}$$

As in the chapter [see equation (6.12)], we see that an increase in taxes lowers income (other things being equal), shifting the *IS* schedule to the left.

A.3 Equilibrium in the *IS–LM* Model

An equilibrium point in the *IS–LM* model is a combination of income and the interest rate that satisfies both the *IS* and *LM* conditions. In terms of our linear *IS* and *LM* schedules, the equilibrium values of Y and r are the values that satisfy equations (A.3) and (A.4).

To find these values, we solve the two equations. First, substitute the value of r from equation (A.4) into equation (A.3). Solving the resulting equation for Y yields the equilibrium value for income (Y_0):

$$Y_0 = \left[\frac{1}{(1-b) + i_1c_1/c_2}\right] \times \left[a + \bar{I} + G - bT + \frac{i_1}{c_2}(M^s - c_0)\right] \quad \textbf{(A.10)}$$

We can then find the equilibrium value of the interest rate (r_0) by substituting equation (A.10) or alternatively equation (A.3) into the *LM* equation (A.4). The resulting expression is

$$r_0 = \left[\frac{1}{(1-b) + i_1c_1/c_2}\right] \times \left[\frac{(1-b)}{c_2}(c_0 - M^s) + \frac{c_1}{c_2}(a + \bar{I} + G - bT)\right] \quad \textbf{(A.11)}$$

[3] A special case for the *IS* schedule is where i_1 approaches zero; investment is almost completely interest-insensitive. Here the slope of the *IS* schedule, given by equation (A.7), becomes extremely large; the schedule becomes nearly vertical.

Notice the difference between the *IS* and *LM* equations (A.3 and A.4) and the solutions for the equilibrium values of Y and r (equations A.10 and A.11). The former equations are relationships that must hold between the two variables, with both Y and r appearing in each equation. The solution for equilibrium Y and r expresses these endogenous variables as depending on the exogenous variables of the model. In Chapter 7, we examine how these equilibrium values of Y and r change with changes in the exogenous variables. The appendix to Chapter 7 extends this analysis to the linear model considered here.

REVIEW PROBLEMS

1. Suppose that

$$C = 60 + 0.8Y_D$$
$$I = 150 - 10r$$
$$G = 250$$
$$T = 200$$
$$M^s = 100$$
$$M^d = 40 + 0.1Y - 10r$$

   a. Write the equations for the *IS* and *LM* schedules.
   b. Find the equilibrium values for income (Y_0) and the interest rate (r_0).
2. Suppose we change the model in problem 1 such that investment is assumed to be completely interest inelastic; investment does not depend on the rate of interest and we have $I = 150$.
   a. Write the new equations for the *IS* and *LM* schedules. Show the schedules graphically.
   b. Find the new equilibrium values for income and the interest rate.

CHAPTER 7

The Keynesian System (III): Policy Effects in the IS–LM Model

In this chapter, we use the *IS–LM* model to analyze the effects of policy actions on income and the interest rate. We also consider other factors that affect income and the interest rate. The groundwork for this analysis was established in Chapter 6. Equilibrium levels of income and the interest rate are given by the intersection of the *IS* and *LM* schedules. The factors that change these equilibrium levels are those that shift either the *IS* or the *LM* schedule. In Section 7.1, we see how such shifts affect income and the interest rate when we consider the two schedules jointly. In Section 7.2, we see how the magnitude of the effects of different policies depends on the slopes of the *IS* and *LM* schedules. The slopes of the *IS–LM* schedules were shown in Chapter 6 to depend on various features of the economic system, the most important being the interest sensitivity of investment and of money demand. Section 7.2 shows how policy effectiveness depends on these factors.

7.1 FACTORS THAT AFFECT EQUILIBRIUM INCOME AND THE INTEREST RATE

Monetary Influences: Shifts in the *LM* Schedule

Consider the effects on income and the interest rate of changes in the money supply. Figure 7-1 illustrates the effects of an increase in the money supply from M_0 to M_1. Initially, assume that the *IS* and *LM* schedules are IS_0 and $LM(M_0)$. Income and the interest rate are at Y_0 and r_0, respectively. As we saw in Chapter 6, an increase in the money supply shifts the *LM* schedule to the right to a position such as $LM(M_1)$ in Figure 7-1. Consequently, the interest rate falls from r_0 to r_1 and income rises from Y_0 to Y_1.

The process producing these results is straightforward. The increase in the money supply creates an excess supply of money, which causes the interest rate to fall. As the interest rate falls, investment is increased, and this increase causes income to rise, with a further income-induced increase in consumption. A new equilibrium is achieved when the fall in the interest rate and the rise in income jointly increase money demand by an amount equal to the increase in the money supply. This equivalence occurs at the point where the new *LM* schedule intersects the *IS* schedule.

A decline in the money supply has the opposite effects. The *LM* schedule shifts to the left; equilibrium income falls; and the equilibrium interest rate rises.

The other factor that shifts the *LM* schedule is a shift in the money demand function. Consider, for example, an increase in money demand *for given levels of income and the interest rate*. Such a portfolio shift away from bonds to money will shift the *LM*

FIGURE 7-1 Effects of an Increase in the Quantity of Money

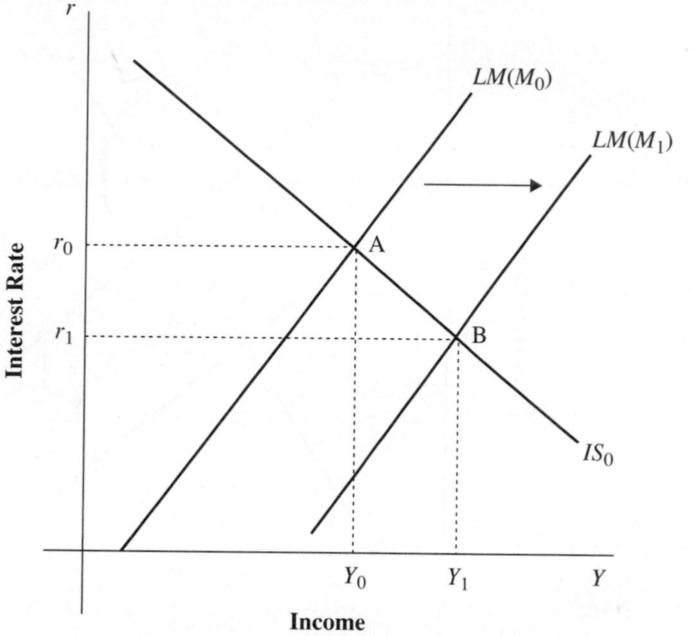

The initial equilibrium is at interest rate r_0 and income level Y_0. An increase in the money supply from M_0 to M_1 shifts the LM schedule to the right from $LM(M_0)$ to $LM(M_1)$. The interest rate falls from r_0 to r_1, and income rises from Y_0 to Y_1.

schedule to the left. As people try to reduce their bond holdings in order to increase their money holdings, the interest rate will rise. The higher interest rate will cause income to decline. An increase in money demand, in the sense of a shift in the function such that more money is demanded at a given level of income and interest rate, has the same effect as a decline in the money supply. Equilibrium income falls and the interest rate rises. A reverse portfolio shift toward holding more bonds and less money has the opposite effects.

Real Influences: Shifts in the *IS* Schedule

Fiscal policy variables are one set of factors that shift the *IS* schedule and hence affect equilibrium income and the interest rate. Figure 7-2 illustrates the effects of one fiscal policy shift, an increase in government spending from G_0 to G_1. The initial positions of the *IS* and *LM* schedules are given by $IS(G_0)$ and LM_0. The increase in government spending to G_1, as shown in Chapter 6, shifts the *IS* schedule to the right to a position such as $IS(G_1)$ in Figure 7-2. The equilibrium level of income rises, as does the equilibrium interest rate.

The force pushing up income is the increase in aggregate demand both directly as government demand rises and then indirectly as a result of an income-induced increase in consumer expenditures. The forces pushing up the interest rate require some explanation. Notice that the *LM* schedule does not shift. At a given level of income, equilibrium in the money market, and therefore in the bond market, is undisturbed by the

FIGURE 7-2 Effects of an Increase in Government Spending

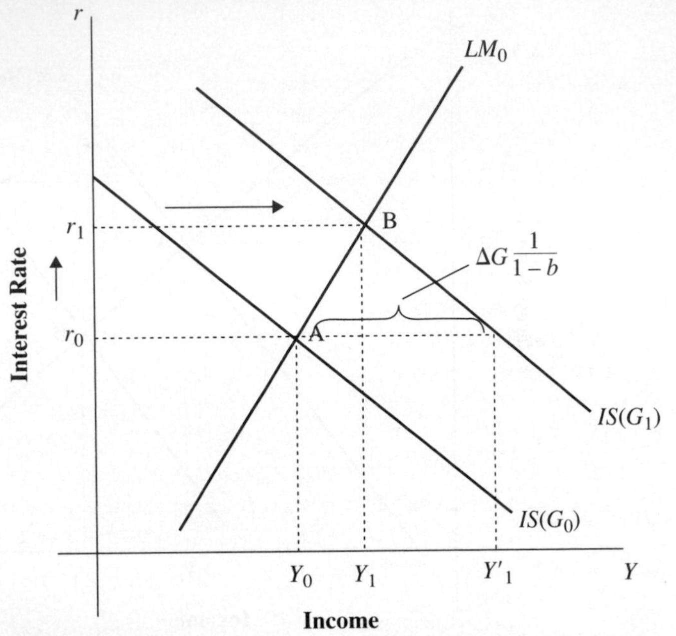

An increase in government spending shifts the *IS* schedule to the right from $IS(G_0)$ to $IS(G_1)$. Income rises from Y_0 to Y_1; the interest rate rises from r_0 to r_1.

government spending change. It is the rise in income in response to the fiscal policy shift that necessitates the interest-rate adjustment. As income increases, the transactions demand for money rises. The attempt to increase transactions balances requires a decline in the demand for bonds. This income-induced increase in money demand and decline in bond demand cause the interest rate to rise.

In the aggregate, the public cannot increase money holdings; the money supply is fixed. The attempt to do so, however, will push up the interest rate, reducing the speculative demand for money and causing individuals to economize on the amount of transactions balances held for any level of income. At the new equilibrium, the interest rate must rise sufficiently that money demand is unchanged even though income is higher.

As shown in Chapter 6, the horizontal distance by which the *IS* schedule shifts when government spending increases is equal to $\Delta G\ [1/(1-b)]$ where ΔG equals $(G_1 - G_0)$. The distance of the shift in the *IS* schedule is the increase in government spending times the autonomous expenditure multiplier from the simple (no money market) Keynesian model. This distance equals the amount by which income would have increased in that simple model. In Figure 7-2, this increase in equilibrium income would have been to Y_1'. When we take into account the required adjustment in the money market, it can be seen that income rises by less than this amount, to Y_1 in Figure 7-2. Why?

FIGURE 7-3 Effects of an Increase in Taxes

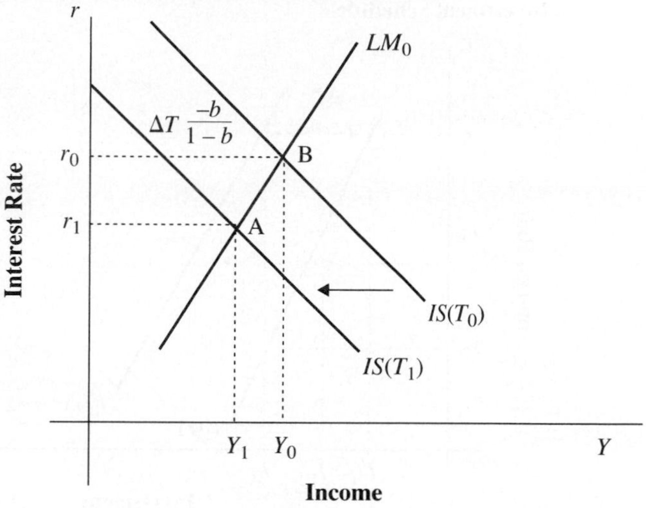

An increase in taxes shifts the *IS* schedule to the left from $IS(T_0)$ to $IS(T_1)$. Income falls from Y_0 to Y_1, and the interest rate falls from r_0 to r_1.

The difference between the simple Keynesian model and the *IS–LM* model is that the latter includes a money market. When government spending increases, as we have just seen, the rate of interest must rise to maintain equilibrium in the money market. The increase in the interest rate will cause a decline in investment spending. The decline in investment will partially offset the increase in aggregate demand resulting from the increase in government spending. Consequently, the increase in income will be less than that in the simple Keynesian model, where investment was taken as completely autonomous.

Next, consider the effects of an increase in tax collections (T) as illustrated in Figure 7-3. An increase in tax collections from T_0 to T_1 will, as shown in Chapter 6, shift the *IS* schedule to the left. In the figure, this situation is shown as a shift in the *IS* schedule from its initial position, $IS(T_0)$ to $IS(T_1)$. As can be seen, income declines from Y_0 to Y_1. The interest rate declines, from r_0 to r_1.

Income falls as taxes rise because the tax increase lowers disposable income $(Y - T)$ and causes consumption to decline. The reason for the drop in the interest rate parallels that for the income-induced interest-rate increase when government spending was increased. As income declines due to the tax increase, money demand declines and bond demand increases. This shift causes the interest rate to fall.

Figure 7-3 indicates that, as was the case with a change in government spending, income falls by less than the horizontal distance of the shift in the *IS* schedule. As explained in Chapter 6, the horizontal distance by which the *IS* schedule shifts with a change in taxes is equal to $\Delta T\,[-b/(1-b)]$, the tax multiplier from the simple Keynesian model times the change in taxes. Thus it is again true that in the *IS–LM* model, fiscal policy multipliers are reduced relative to our results for the simple Keynesian model.

FIGURE 7-4 Effects of an Autonomous Decline in Investment

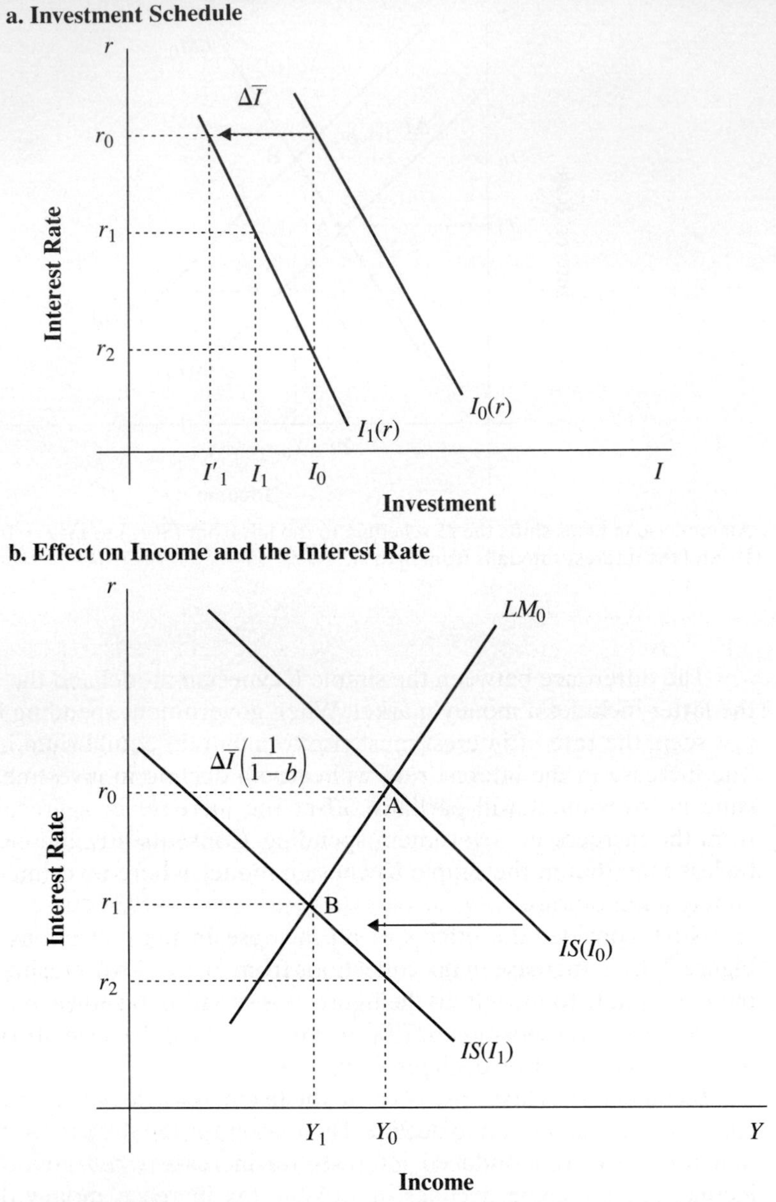

An autonomous decline in investment shifts the investment schedule to the left in part *a*. At the initial interest rate r_0 investment falls from I_0 to I_1'. The shift in the investment function causes the *IS* schedule in part *b* to shift to the left from IS_0 to IS_1. Equilibrium income falls from Y_0 to Y_1, and the equilibrium interest rate falls from r_0 to r_1. As a result of the fall in the interest rate, investment is revived somewhat to I_1 in part *a*.

For a tax increase, the reason is that the decline in the interest rate discussed previously will cause investment to rise, partially offsetting the decline in consumption caused by the tax increase.

A decrease in taxes has the opposite effects of a tax increase. The *IS* schedule shifts to the right, and both income and the interest rate rise. Similarly, a decline in government spending has effects just opposite of those for an increase in government spending.

Fiscal policy variables are not the only factors that shift the *IS* schedule. Any autonomous change in aggregate demand will have this effect. One such change is an autonomous change in investment demand, meaning a shift in the function giving the level of investment for each level of the interest rate. For example, such a change would occur if, as a result of some exogenous event, the expected profitability of investment projects changed.

Figure 7-4 illustrates the effects of an autonomous decline in investment. In part *a*, the investment schedule is plotted. The initial schedule is $I_0(r)$. The autonomous decline in investment of $\Delta\bar{I}$ shifts the schedule to the left to $I_1(r)$, reducing investment at each rate of interest. In Figure 7-4*b*, this autonomous decline in investment shifts the *IS* schedule to the left, from $IS(I_0)$ to $IS(I_1)$. Income falls from Y_0 to Y_1. The interest rate declines from r_0 to r_1. Income declines because investment at the initial interest rate has fallen (from I_0 to I_1' in Figure 7-4*a*). As income falls, an income-induced decline in consumption also occurs. The interest-rate decline is also income-induced, as was the case when we considered the effects of fiscal policy changes. The decline in income causes money demand to fall and bond demand to rise; consequently, the interest rate falls.

Notice that the decline in the interest rate causes investment to return toward its initial level. At the new equilibrium, investment is at I_1 in Figure 7-4*a*, having increased from I_1' to I_1 as a result of the decline in the interest rate.

It is interesting to compare the effects of an autonomous decline in investment in the *IS–LM* version of the Keynesian model with the effect of the same shift within the classical model analyzed in Section 4.2. There, the interest rate played a stabilizing role such that a change in investment did not affect aggregate demand. The interest rate fell sufficiently to restore aggregate demand to its initial level. In the *IS–LM* model, the interest-rate adjustment is stabilizing but incomplete. For income to be unchanged with an autonomous decline in investment, the interest rate would have to fall to the level r_2 in Figure 7-4*b*. At that level of the interest rate, income would be at the original level Y_0 along the new *IS* schedule, $IS(I_1)$. Figure 7-4*a* shows that, at level r_2, the interest rate has fallen sufficiently to return investment to its initial level, I_0. The interest rate falls only to r_1, however; the offset to the initial autonomous drop in investment is incomplete.

In one case, the offset is complete. This is where the *LM* schedule is vertical. In that case, when the *IS* schedule shifts from $IS(I_0)$ to $IS(I_1)$, we simply move down the vertical *LM* schedule to a new equilibrium at the initial income level Y_0 and with the interest rate declining to r_2. The vertical *LM* schedule was termed a classical case, so it should not be surprising that classical conclusions result from that assumption. An explanation of these results for the vertical *LM* curve case is provided in the next section.

Read Perspectives 7-1.

PERSPECTIVES 7-1

THE MONETARY–FISCAL POLICY MIX: SOME HISTORICAL EXAMPLES

We have seen that either monetary or fiscal policy can affect income in the Keynesian view. But the effects of the two on the interest rate, and therefore on investment, are different. In the case of expansionary monetary policy, the interest rate declines and investment increases. With an expansionary fiscal policy action—an income tax cut, for example—the interest rate rises and investment declines. This is a significant difference because the level of investment determines the rate of capital formation and is important to long-term growth of the economy.

Our analysis, then, suggests that within a Keynesian framework there is a preference for a policy *mix* of relatively "tight" fiscal policy and "easy" monetary policy in order to keep the interest rate low and to encourage investment. Moreover, whenever fiscal policy actions such as income tax cuts are used to expand the economy, the Keynesians would like to see an *accommodating* monetary policy—an accompanying increase in the money supply that will prevent the interest rate from rising and thus prevent the crowding out of investment. Such a monetary–fiscal policy combination is illustrated in Figure 7-5. At the same time that the *IS* schedule is shifted to the right by a tax cut, the money supply is increased sufficiently so that the *LM* schedule shifts far enough to the right to prevent a rise in the interest rate.

As an example of a coordinated expansion, Keynesians point to the tax cut of 1964 and the accompanying increase in money supply. As explained in Perspectives 5.2, the tax cut was 20 percent for individuals and 10 percent for businesses. Growth in the money supply increased to 4.7 percent over the 1964–65 period, compared with 3.7 percent in 1963. The result was a GNP growth of 5.4 percent in 1964 and 5.5 percent in 1965 (rates well above growth in potential output). As a result of the accommodating monetary policy, the interest rate (corporate bond rate) rose only slightly, from 4.0 percent in 1963 to 4.3 percent in 1965. The business tax reductions included in the 1964 tax cut were also aimed at preventing any decline in investment. In fact, fixed business investment increased from 9.0 to 10.5 percent of GNP between 1963 and 1965.

Later, Keynesian economists were critical of the monetary–fiscal policy mix in the first Reagan administration. They interpreted this mix as one of tight monetary policy, as growth in the money supply slowed, and easy fiscal policy, primarily the large cuts in personal and business taxes. The Keynesians saw the two policy moves as canceling each other out in terms of their effects on GNP. Keynesian economist James Tobin compared the Reagan policy to putting a train in New Haven, Connecticut, with an engine on the front headed for Boston and one in the back headed for New York. In graphical terms, the Keynesians saw the Reagan administration's monetary policy shifting the *LM* schedule to the left to lower income while fiscal policy shifted the *IS* schedule to the right to increase income. They believed that both policies would increase the interest rate (both schedules shift upward), with unfavorable effects on investment.

During the Clinton administration, efforts to eliminate the federal deficit (and, in fact, generate budget surpluses) were aimed in part at permitting monetary policy to be more expansionary than would otherwise be the case. *Rubinomics,* named after Treasury Secretary Robert Rubin, replaced *Reaganomics.*

FIGURE 7-5 Monetary–Fiscal Policy Combination

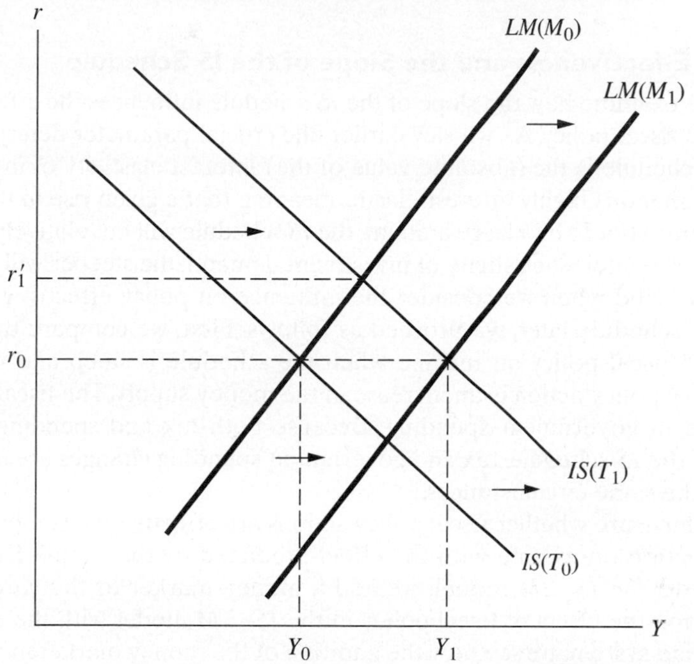

A tax cut from T_0 to T_1 shifts the *IS* schedule from $IS(T_0)$ to $IS(T_1)$. By itself, this fiscal policy shift would push the interest rate up to r_1'. If the tax cut were accompanied by an increase in the money supply from M_0 to M_1, the *LM* schedule would shift to the right from $LM(M_0)$ to $LM(M_1)$. Together, the two policy actions would increase output to Y_1, with the interest rate remaining at r_0.

7.2 THE RELATIVE EFFECTIVENESS OF MONETARY AND FISCAL POLICY

In Section 7.1, we examined the qualitative effects of monetary and fiscal policy actions within the *IS–LM* model, as summarized in Table 7-1. As the table shows, both monetary and fiscal policy instruments can affect the level of income. In this section, we examine the relative effectiveness of the two types of policy actions. By *effectiveness* we mean the size of the effect on income of a given change in the policy variable. The effectiveness of each type of policy (monetary and fiscal) will be shown to depend on the

TABLE 7-1 Effects of Monetary and Fiscal Policy Variables

Effect of:	*M*	*G*	*T*
on *Y*	+	+	−
r	−	+	−

Note: M, money stock; G, level of government spending; T, taxes. A (+) sign indicates that a change in the policy instrument causes the variable in that row (Y, income, or r, the interest rate) to move in the same direction. A (−) sign indicates the reverse.

slopes of the *IS* and *LM* schedules, which in turn are determined by certain behavioral parameters of our model.

Policy Effectiveness and the Slope of the *IS* Schedule

First, we examine how the slope of the *IS* schedule influences the effectiveness of monetary and fiscal policy. As we saw earlier, the crucial parameter determining the slope of the *IS* schedule is the (absolute value of the) interest elasticity of investment. If investment demand is highly interest-elastic, meaning that a given rise in the interest rate will reduce investment by a large amount, the *IS* schedule will be relatively flat. The lower the value of the interest elasticity of investment demand, the steeper will be the *IS* schedule.

Here, and when we consider the influence on policy effectiveness of the slope of the *LM* schedule later, we proceed as follows. First, we compare the effects of monetary and fiscal policy on income when the schedule is steep and when it is flat. The monetary policy action is an increase in the money supply. The fiscal policy action is an increase in government spending. Because both tax and spending changes work by shifting the *IS* schedule, tax and government spending changes are effective or ineffective in the same circumstances.

To measure whether fiscal policy actions are effective, we compare the effect of the policy action on income with the effect predicted by the simple Keynesian model. In moving to the *IS–LM* model, we add a money market to the Keynesian system. By comparing the effect of fiscal policy in the *IS–LM* model with the effect in the simple Keynesian system, we see how the addition of the money market modifies our previous results. The distance of the horizontal shift in the *IS* schedule for a given fiscal policy action equals the effect on income in the simple Keynesian model: for example, $\Delta Y = \Delta G\,[1/(1-b)]$, for a government spending change. Consequently, to evaluate the effectiveness of fiscal policy on the following graphs, we compare the change in income with the horizontal shift in the *IS* schedule.

To evaluate the effectiveness of monetary policy, we compare the effect on income of the change in the money supply with the horizontal distance of the shift in the *LM* schedule. The horizontal shift in the *LM* schedule when the money supply changes is equal to $\Delta M(1/c_1)$ where c_1 is the coefficient on income in the money demand function [equation (6.4)]. The coefficient c_1 gives the amount of the increase in money demand per unit of income; therefore, $\Delta M(1/c_1)$ gives the increase in income that could occur for an increase in the money supply if *all* new money balances went to support increased transactions demand for money due to increased income. This distance measures the maximum possible increase in income for a given increase in the money supply.

Monetary Policy Effectiveness and the Slope of the *IS* Schedule

Parts *a* and *b* of Figure 7-6 show the effects of an increase in the money supply for two differently sloped *IS* schedules. In each case, the increase in the money supply shifts the *LM* schedule from LM_0 to LM_1. In Figure 7-6*a*, the *IS* schedule is steep, reflecting a low interest elasticity of investment. As can be seen from the graph, monetary policy is relatively ineffective in this case. Income rises very little as a result of the increase in the money supply.

In Figure 7-6*b*, the slope of the *LM* schedule has been kept the same as in Figure 7-6*a*. The size of the horizontal shift in the *LM* schedule, $\Delta M(1/c_1)$, which fixes the size of the

FIGURE 7-6 Monetary Policy Effects and the Slope of the *IS* Schedule

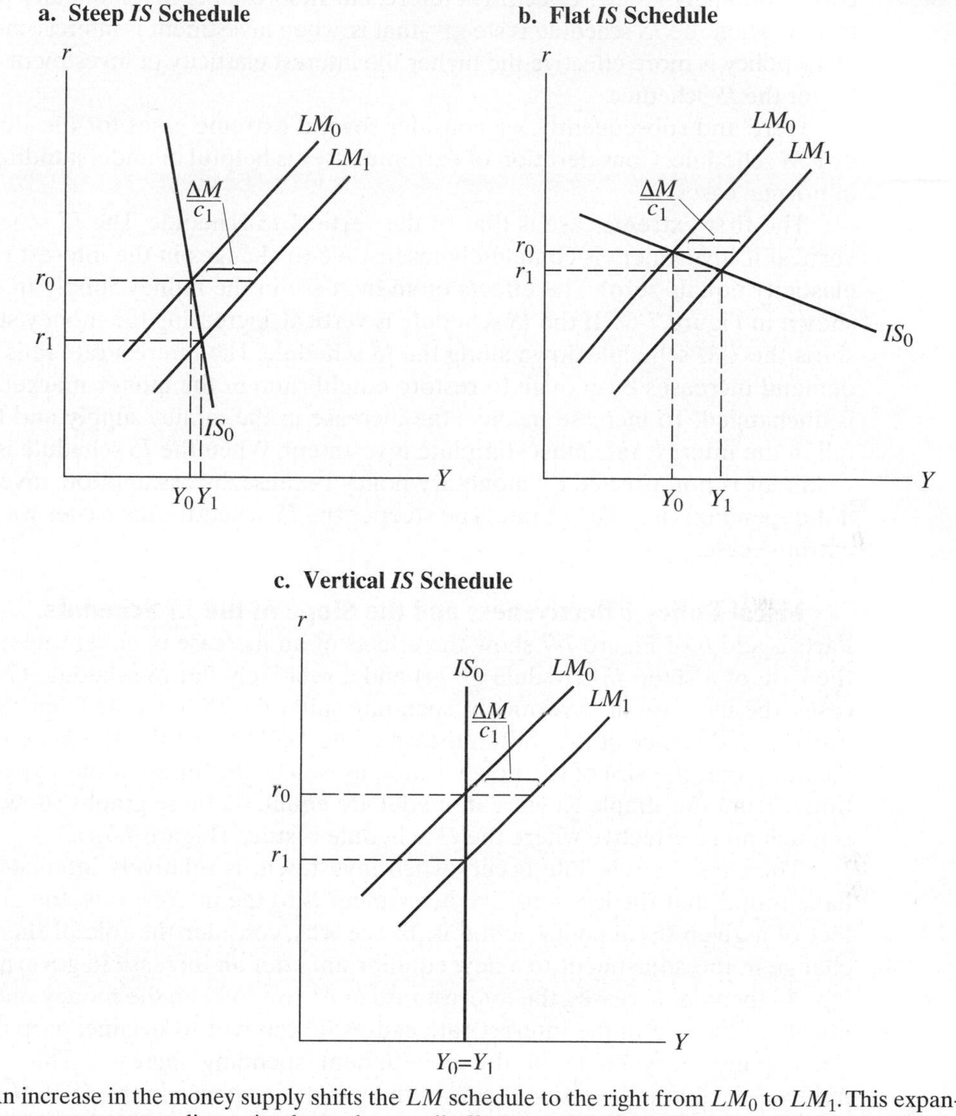

An increase in the money supply shifts the *LM* schedule to the right from LM_0 to LM_1. This expansionary monetary policy action has only a small effect on output in part *a*, where the *IS* schedule is steep. It has a much larger effect in part *b*, where the *IS* schedule is relatively flat. In part *c*, where the *IS* schedule is vertical, the increase in the money supply has no effect on equilibrium income.

policy action, has also been kept the same. The difference is in the slope of the *IS* schedule. In Figure 7-6*b*, that schedule is drawn much flatter, reflecting a higher interest elasticity of investment. As can be seen, monetary policy becomes more effective when the *IS* schedule is flatter.

Within the *IS–LM* model, monetary policy affects income by lowering the interest rate and stimulating investment. If investment is little affected by interest-rate changes, which is the assumption in Figure 7-6*a*, monetary policy will be ineffective. In Figure 7-6*b*, where the interest sensitivity of investment is substantially greater, monetary policy has correspondingly greater effects. Therefore, our first result is that monetary policy is ineffective when the *IS* schedule is steep—that is, when investment is interest-inelastic. Monetary policy is more effective the higher the interest elasticity of investment and thus the flatter the *IS* schedule.

Here and subsequently, we consider several extreme cases for the slope of the *IS* or *LM* schedule. Consideration of extreme cases is helpful in understanding our results in normal cases.

The first extreme case is that of the vertical *IS* schedule. The *IS* schedule will be vertical if investment is completely insensitive to changes in the interest rate (interest elasticity equals zero). The effects of an increase in the money supply in this case are shown in Figure 7-6*c*. If the *IS* schedule is vertical, increasing the money supply simply shifts the *LM* schedule down along the *IS* schedule. The interest rate falls until money demand increases by enough to restore equilibrium in the money market, but income is unchanged. To increase income, the increase in the money supply and the resulting fall in the interest rate must stimulate investment. When the *IS* schedule is vertical, investment is not affected by monetary policy because, by assumption, investment does not depend on the interest rate. The steeper the *IS* schedule, the closer we come to this extreme case.

Fiscal Policy Effectiveness and the Slope of the *IS* Schedule

Parts *a* and *b* of Figure 7-7 show the effects of an increase in government spending in the case of a steep *IS* schedule (7-7*a*) and a relatively flat *IS* schedule (7-7*b*). In both cases, the increase in government spending shifts the *IS* schedule from IS_0 to IS_1. The horizontal distance of the shift in the schedule $\Delta G\,[1/(1-b)]$ is the same in both cases, meaning that the size of the policy action as well as the autonomous expenditure multiplier from the simple Keynesian model are equal. As these graphs show, fiscal policy is much more effective where the *IS* schedule is steep (Figure 7-7*a*).

The steep *IS* schedule occurs when investment is relatively interest-inelastic. We have found that the less sensitive investment is to the interest rate, the greater the effect of a given fiscal policy action is. To see why, consider the role of the interest-rate change in the adjustment to a new equilibrium after an increase in government spending. As income increases, the interest rate must rise to keep the money market in equilibrium. This rise in the interest rate causes investment to decline, partially offsetting the expansionary effect of the government spending increase. This interest-rate–induced decline in investment causes the income response in the *IS–LM* model to fall short of the response given by the multiplier from the simple Keynesian system; that is, income rises by less than the horizontal shift in the *IS* schedule.

How important is this effect on investment, which is often referred to as *crowding out*? One factor determining the importance of such crowding out of private investment is the slope of the *IS* schedule. If investment is not very sensitive to changes in the interest rate, the assumption in Figure 7-7*a*, then the interest-rate increase will cause only a slight drop in investment, and income will rise by almost the full amount of the horizontal shift in the *IS* schedule. Alternatively, if investment is highly interest-sensitive, the assumption in Figure 7-7*b*, then the rise in the interest rate will reduce investment substantially, and the increase in income will be reduced significantly relative to the prediction of the simple Keynesian model.

FIGURE 7-7 Fiscal Policy Effects and the Slope of the *IS* Schedule

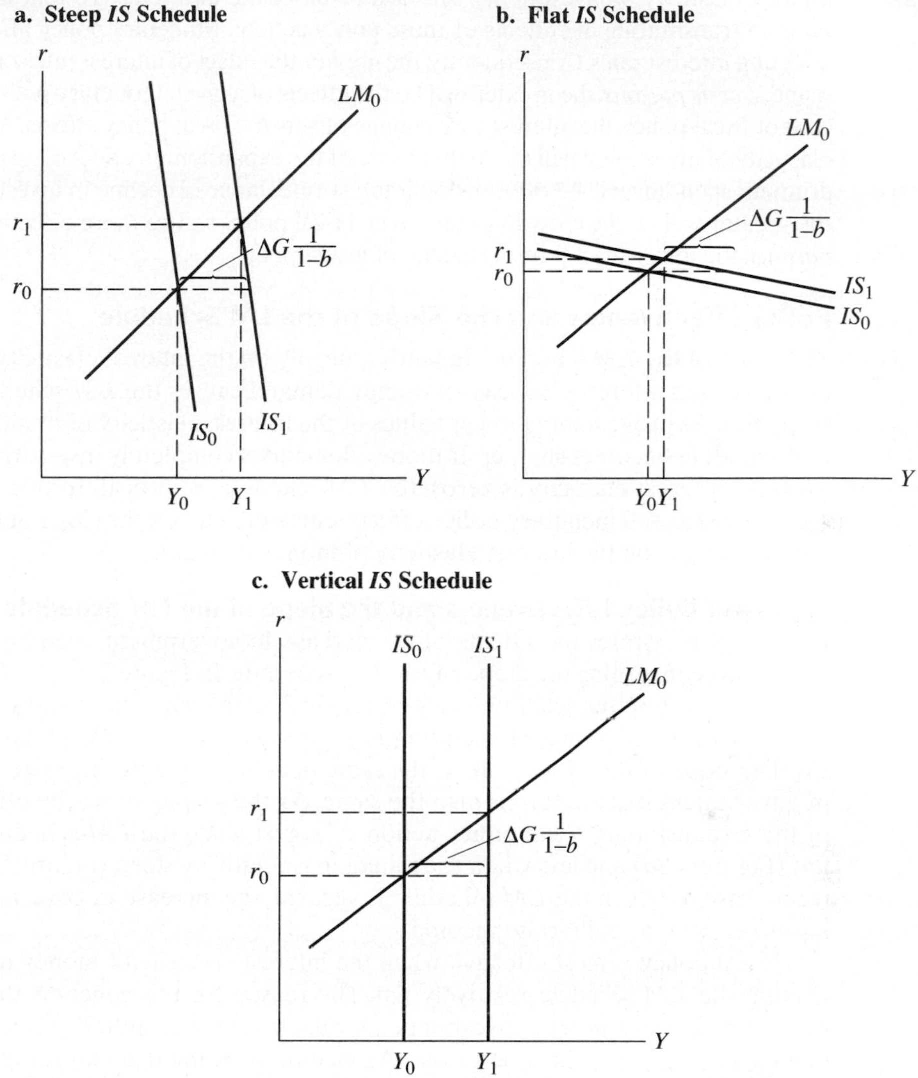

In each part of the figure, an increase in government spending shifts the *IS* schedule to the right from IS_0 to IS_1. In part *a*, where the *IS* schedule is steep, this expansionary fiscal policy action results in a relatively large increase in income. This fiscal policy action is much less effective in part *b*, where the *IS* schedule is relatively flat. Fiscal policy is most effective in part *c*, where the *IS* schedule is vertical.

The case of the vertical *IS* schedule is shown in Figure 7-7*c*. Here investment is completely interest-insensitive. The increase in government spending causes the interest rate to rise, but this rise does not result in any decline in investment. Income increases by the full amount of the distance of the horizontal shift in the *IS* schedule; there is no crowding out of investment.

A comparison of the results in this subsection with those in the preceding subsection shows that fiscal policy is most effective when the *IS* schedule is steep (low interest elasticity of investment), whereas monetary policy is most effective when the *IS* schedule is flat (high interest elasticity of investment). This is a result of the different role that the interest rate plays in transmitting the effects of these policy actions. Monetary policy affects income by affecting interest rates. Consequently, the greater the effect of interest rates on aggregate demand, *ceteris paribus*, the greater will be the effects of a given monetary policy action. In the case of fiscal policy, the interest-rate change offsets the fiscal policy effects. A larger interest elasticity of investment will mean that more of the expansionary effect of an increase in government spending will be offset by an interest-rate–induced decline in investment, and thus the greater will be the crowding-out effect. Fiscal policy will be more effective, again *ceteris paribus*, the lower the interest elasticity of investment.

Policy Effectiveness and the Slope of the *LM* Schedule

The slope of the *LM* schedule depends crucially on the interest elasticity of money demand. A high interest elasticity of money demand causes the *LM* schedule to be relatively flat. At progressively lower values of the interest elasticity of money demand, the *LM* schedule becomes steeper. If money demand is completely insensitive to the interest rate (interest elasticity is zero), the *LM* schedule is vertical. In this subsection, we see how fiscal and monetary policy effectiveness depend on the slope of the *LM* schedule and, hence, on the interest elasticity of money demand.

Fiscal Policy Effectiveness and the Slope of the *LM* Schedule

Figure 7-8 illustrates the effects of an increase in government spending for three assumptions concerning the slope of the *LM* schedule. In Figure 7-8*a* the *LM* schedule is rather flat, in 7-8*b* the schedule is steep, and in 7-8*c* the schedule is vertical. In each case the increase in government spending is assumed to shift the *IS* schedule from IS_0 to IS_1. The slope of the *IS* schedule is the same in all three graphs. The size of the increase in government expenditure is also the same. As the graphs show, the effect on income of this expansionary fiscal policy action is largest when the *LM* schedule is relatively flat (Figure 7-8*a*) and less when the schedule is relatively steep (Figure 7-8*b*). In the extreme case in which the *LM* schedule is vertical, the increase in government spending has no effect on equilibrium income.

Fiscal policy is most effective when the interest elasticity of money demand is high, making the *LM* schedule relatively flat. The reason for this concerns the effect of the interest-rate adjustment on investment after the fiscal policy shift. The increase in government spending causes income to rise. As income rises, the demand for transactions balances increases, and to reequilibrate the money market with an unchanged supply of money requires a rise in the interest rate. The rise in the interest rate must lower the speculative demand for money and cause individuals and corporations to economize on transactions balances. If money demand is highly sensitive to changes in the interest rate, only a small rise in the interest rate is required to restore equilibrium in the money market. This is the case in Figure 7-8*a*, where the interest rate rises by a small amount, from r_0 to r_1.

Because in this case there is a small increase in the interest rate, other things being equal, the decline in investment will be small.[1] With little crowding out of private investment, income rises by nearly the full amount of the horizontal shift in the *IS* schedule.

[1]The primary "other thing" being held equal in this case is the amount by which a given increase in the interest rate will cause investment to decline—the interest elasticity of investment.

FIGURE 7-8 Fiscal Policy Effects and the Slope of the *LM* Schedule

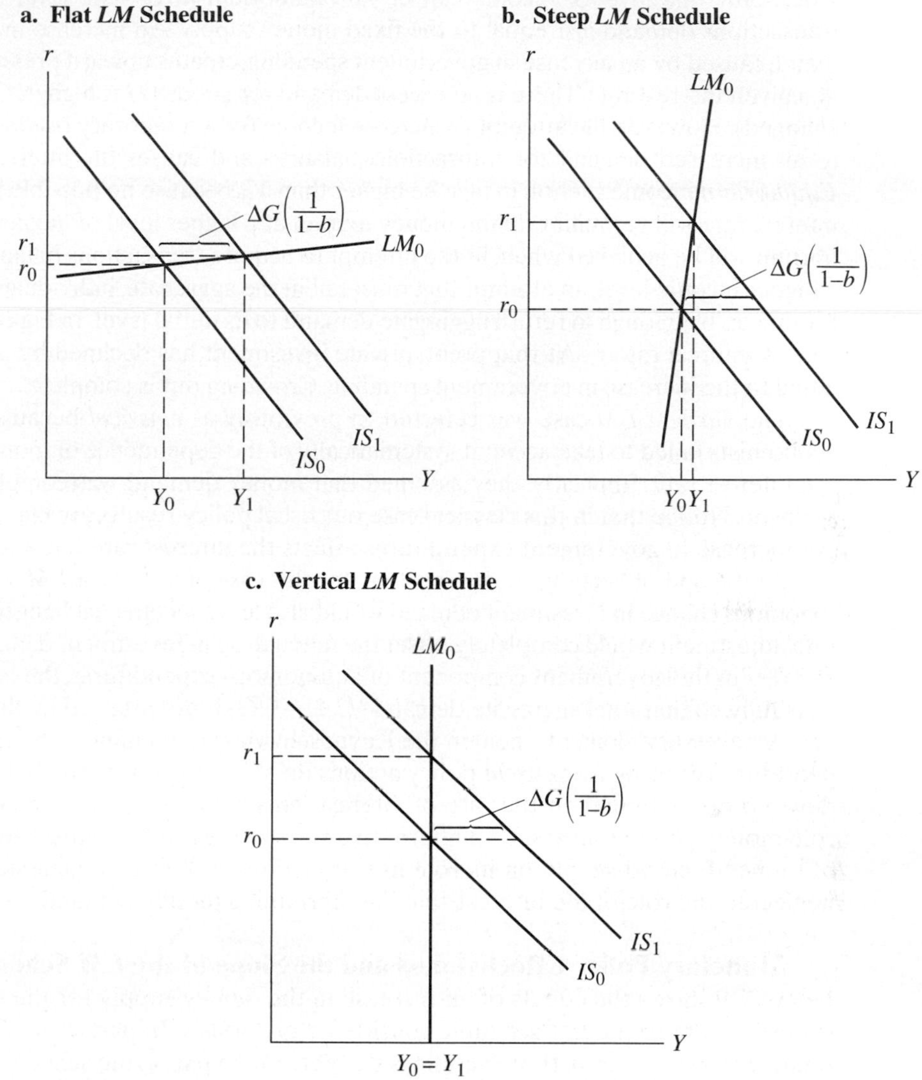

In each part of the figure, an increase in government spending shifts the *IS* schedule to the right from IS_0 to IS_1. Fiscal policy is most effective in part *a*, where the *LM* schedule is relatively flat; less effective in part *b*, where the *LM* schedule is steeper; and completely ineffective in part *c*, where the *LM* schedule is vertical.

When money demand is relatively interest-inelastic (Figure 7-8*b*), a greater increase in the interest rate (from r_0 to r_1 in Figure 7-8*b*) is required to reequilibrate the money market as income rises. The larger increase in the interest rate leads to a larger decline in investment, offsetting more of the expansionary effect of the increase in government spending. Consequently, the increase in income for the steeper *LM* schedule (Figure 7-8*b*) is smaller.

If money demand is completely insensitive to changes in the interest rate (Figure 7-8*c*), only one level of income can be an equilibrium level—the level that generates transactions demand just equal to the fixed money supply. An increase in aggregate demand, caused by an increase in government spending, creates upward pressure on income at a given interest rate. There is an excess demand for goods (G is higher, C and I are unchanged). However, the attempt to increase income (or a temporary rise in income) leads to an increased demand for transactions balances and causes the interest rate to rise. *Equilibrium* income cannot, in fact, be higher than Y_0, because no possible increase in the interest rate will reequilibrate the money market at a higher level of income. A new equilibrium will be achieved when, in the attempt to acquire transactions balances to support a higher income level, an attempt that must fail in the aggregate, individuals bid the interest rate up by enough to return aggregate demand to its initial level. In Figure 7-8*c*, this occurs at interest rate r_1. At that point, private investment has declined by an amount just equal to the increase in government spending. Crowding out is complete.

The vertical LM case was referred to previously as *classical* because the classical economists failed to take account systematically of the dependence of money demand on the interest rate. Implicitly, they assumed that money demand was completely interest-inelastic. Notice that in this classical case our fiscal policy results are classical in nature. An increase in government expenditures affects the interest rate but not income.

At the end of Section 7.1, we saw that, for this case of a vertical LM schedule, an autonomous change in investment demand would also leave income unchanged. The interest-rate adjustment would completely offset the initial drop in investment demand. Again, for changes in the government component of autonomous expenditures, the interest rate adjusts fully, so that total aggregate demand ($C + I + G$) is not affected by the shift.

A necessary element, then, in the Keynesian view that changes in autonomous expenditure resulting from fiscal policy actions do affect income is the belief that money demand does depend on the rate of interest. This belief follows from considering the role money plays as an asset, an alternative store of wealth to bonds. The classical view of money focused simply on its role in transactions, and thus the classical economists neglected the role of the interest rate in determining money demand.

Monetary Policy Effectiveness and the Slope of the *LM* Schedule

Figure 7-9 shows the effects of an increase in the money supply for the same three assumptions about the LM schedule considered previously. In part *a*, the LM schedule is relatively flat. In part *b*, the schedule is steeper; and in part *c*, the schedule is vertical. In each case, the increase in the money stock shifts the LM schedule by an equal amount from LM_0 to LM_1.

As can be seen from the figure, monetary policy is least effective in Figure 7-9*a*, where the LM schedule is relatively flat (the interest elasticity of money demand is high). The effect on income of the increase in the money supply is successively greater as we consider Figure 7-9*b*, where the interest elasticity of money demand is lower, and then Figure 7-9*c*, where the interest elasticity of money demand is zero and the LM schedule is vertical.

The reason can be seen by comparing the fall in the interest rate that results from the money supply increase in each case. At the initial level of income and interest rate, the increase in the money supply will create an excess supply of money, causing the interest rate to fall. This fall will stimulate investment and, hence, income. The interest

FIGURE 7-9 Monetary Policy Effects and the Slope of the *LM* Schedule

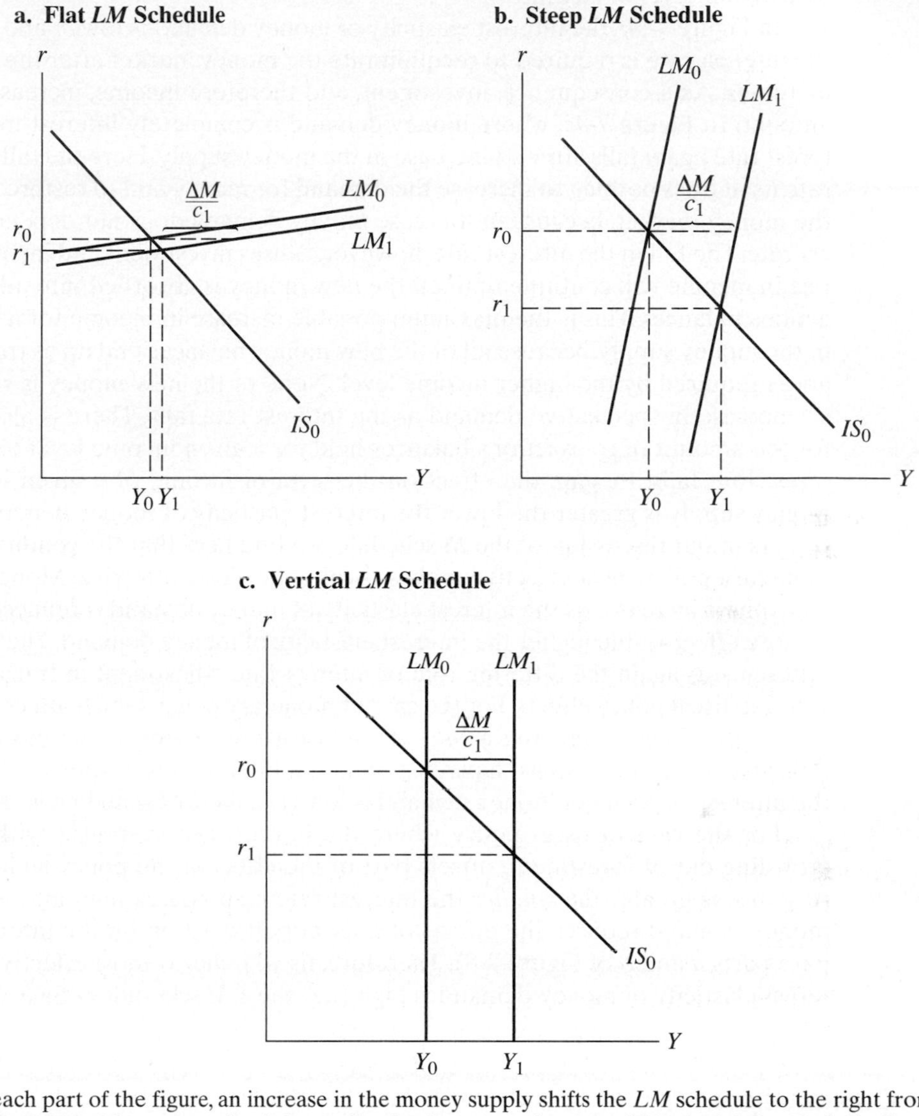

In each part of the figure, an increase in the money supply shifts the *LM* schedule to the right from LM_0 to LM_1. Monetary policy is least effective in part *a*, where the *LM* schedule is relatively flat; more effective in part *b*, where the *LM* schedule is steeper; and most effective in part *c*, where the *LM* schedule is vertical.

rate must decline to a point where the lower interest rate and higher income level have increased money demand by an amount equal to the increase in the money supply. In Figure 7-9*a*, where money demand is very interest-sensitive, a small drop in the interest rate is all that is required for this purpose. Consequently, the increase in investment, and hence income, will be small in this case. With a highly interest-elastic demand for money, as the interest rate falls, individuals substantially increase their speculative balances and economize less on transactions balances. Most of the newly created money is used for these purposes, and relatively little ends up as transactions balances required by a higher level of income.

In Figure 7-9*b*, the interest elasticity of money demand is lower, and a larger fall in the interest rate is required to reequilibrate the money market after the money supply increases. As a consequence, investment, and therefore income, increase by a greater amount. In Figure 7-9*c*, where money demand is completely interest-inelastic, the interest rate again falls after an increase in the money supply. Here the fall in the interest rate itself does nothing to increase the demand for money and to restore equilibrium in the money market, because in this case money demand does not depend on the interest rate. The fall in the interest rate, however, causes investment and income to rise. The rise in income will continue until all the new money is absorbed into additional transactions balances. This is the maximum possible increase in income for a given increase in the money supply, because all of the new money balances end up as transactions balances required by the higher income level. None of the new money is siphoned off as an increase in speculative demand as the interest rate falls. There is also no tendency for the amount of transactions balances held for a given income level to rise as the interest rate falls. In sum, the effect on the level of income of a given increase in the money supply is greater the lower the interest elasticity of money demand.

As in our discussion of the *IS* schedule, we find here that the condition that makes monetary policy most effective makes fiscal policy least effective. Monetary policy effectiveness increases as the interest elasticity of money demand is reduced. Fiscal policy is more effective the higher the interest elasticity of money demand. The reason for this difference is again the differing role of interest-rate adjustment in transmitting monetary and fiscal policy effects. For the case of monetary policy, which affects income by affecting the interest rate, the *greater* the interest-rate response, the more effective the policy action will be. As we have just seen, the interest-rate response is greatest when the interest elasticity of money demand is low (i.e., the *LM* schedule is steep).

For the case of fiscal policy where the interest-rate response, with the resulting crowding out of investment, offsets part of the effect of the policy action, the income response is greater the *smaller* the interest rate response. A high interest elasticity of money demand reduces the effects of a fiscal policy action on the interest rate (compare parts *a* and *b* of Figure 7-8). Therefore, fiscal policy is most effective when the interest elasticity of money demand is high (i.e., the *LM* schedule is flat).

7.3 CONCLUSION

In Section 7.1, we examined the effects of monetary and fiscal policy actions on income and the interest rate, assuming that the *IS–LM* schedules had normal slopes; that is, the slopes of both the *IS* and *LM* schedules were in an intermediate range—neither so steep nor so flat as to make either monetary or fiscal policy impotent. In Section 7.2, the relationships between the slopes of the *IS* and *LM* schedules and the relative effectiveness of monetary and fiscal policies were examined. The results of that analysis are summarized in Table 7-2.

A relevant question at this point is, Which of the cases in Table 7-2 actually characterizes the economy? What are the actual slopes of the relationships in our economy that correspond to the model's *IS* and *LM* schedules?

TABLE 7-2 Monetary and Fiscal Policy Effectiveness and the Slopes of the *IS* and *LM* Schedules

	Monetary Policy	
	IS Schedule	***LM Schedule***
Steep	Ineffective	Effective
Flat	Effective	Ineffective
	Fiscal Policy	
	IS Schedule	***LM Schedule***
Steep	Effective	Ineffective
Flat	Ineffective	Effective

Issues concerning the slopes of the *IS* and *LM* schedules form part of the controversy between the Keynesians and the next group of macroeconomists we will analyze, the monetarists. There is also some divergence between the positions of some of the earlier Keynesians and modern Keynesians concerning the slopes of these schedules. Here we confine ourselves to the position of the modern Keynesians, who believe that both the *IS* and *LM* schedule slopes are in the intermediate or normal range, where both monetary and fiscal policies are effective. Our results in Section 7.1—summarized in Table 7.1—characterize this modern Keynesian position.

Read Perspectives 7-2.

PERSPECTIVES 7-2

JAPAN IN A SLUMP AND THE LIQUIDITY TRAP

A qualification to the Keynesian view that both monetary and fiscal policy will be effective concerns monetary policy in periods when the interest rate becomes very low, approaching or hitting the "zero bound." In such situations the economy may sink into a liquidity trap, as discussed in Chapter 6 and illustrated in Figure 6-9.

Many economists believe that the U.S. economy was in a liquidity trap during the Great Depression of the 1930s, when short-term interest rates fell to below 1 percent. Discussion of the liquidity trap almost disappeared in the 1970s and early 1980s, when interest rates in the major economies were often at double-digit levels. There has been revived interest in the liquidity trap as interest rates have fallen to very low levels in some countries in recent years. Japan is a case in point.

In the mid-1980s the Japanese economy was growing rapidly. In the United States, the discussion of Japan then mirrored that of China today. Commentators feared that "Japan Incorporated" would outdistance the U.S. economy. The United States had a large trade deficit with Japan, and Japanese products such as automobiles and appliances were replacing their U.S. counterparts. Then in the 1990s, after a boom-and-bust cycle in Japanese property and financial markets, the Japanese economy fell into a prolonged slump from which it has yet to recover fully. The slump in economic activity was accompanied by deflation.

These trends can be seen in Figure 7-10, which shows the percentage rate of growth in Japanese GDP and in the GDP deflator as a measure of inflation. Following real GDP growth averaging 4.8 percent from 1981 to 1990, growth after 1992 slowed markedly, with GDP actually declining in 3 of those years. The GDP deflator fell during most of the post-1992 period. Japan was in a deflationary slump. As Figure 7-11 shows, the short-term interest rate fell rapidly, hit the zero bound, and remained there after 2003. This was the result of the economic slump and of the Bank of Japan's following an expansionary policy to revive the economy. Not until late 2006 did the Bank raise the interest rate, and then only to 0.25 percent.

Figure 7-12 illustrates the ineffectiveness of monetary policy in a liquidity trap. At the current low level of interest rates in Japan, the *LM* schedule would be very flat, reflecting a high interest elasticity of money demand. This follows because at such a low level of the interest rate, the speculative demand curve for money would become very flat; a consensus would develop that future increases in interest rates were likely with expected capital losses on bonds. An increase in the money supply would be absorbed with only a very slight fall in the interest rate and therefore little stimulus to investment. In the recent Japanese situation, where the short-term interest rate has hit zero, we would expect no further decline to be possible.

Before leaving the experience of Japan, a few more points should be noted. Our analysis in this chapter would lead us to believe that in a liquidity trap, fiscal policy should be highly effective. The case of a flat *LM* schedule means that there is little crowding out. The Japanese government did follow an expansionary fiscal policy for most of the post-1992 period. The budget deficit rose to over 6 percent of GDP due to increased government spending and some tax reductions. Still, Japan remained in a slump. This and much else about the Japanese experience in the years since 1992 is puzzling. What caused such a prolonged slump even with policy actions to stimulate the economy? Economists

FIGURE 7-10 Japan's GDP and GPD Deflator

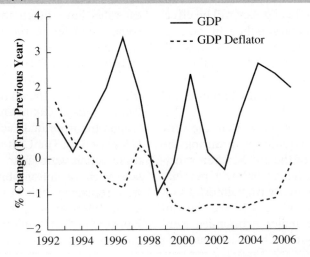

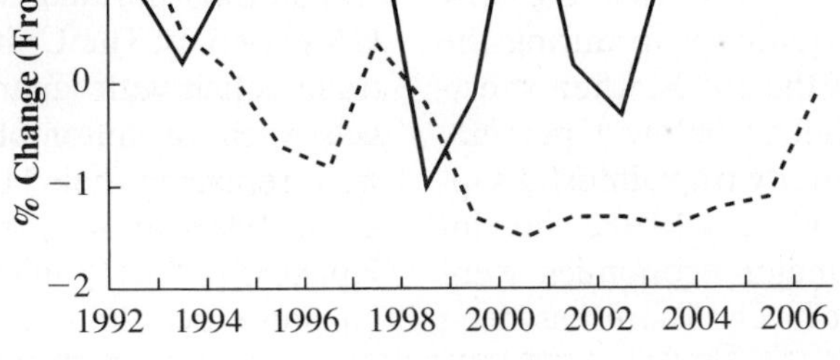

FIGURE 7-11 Japan's Short-Term Interest Rate (1992–2006)

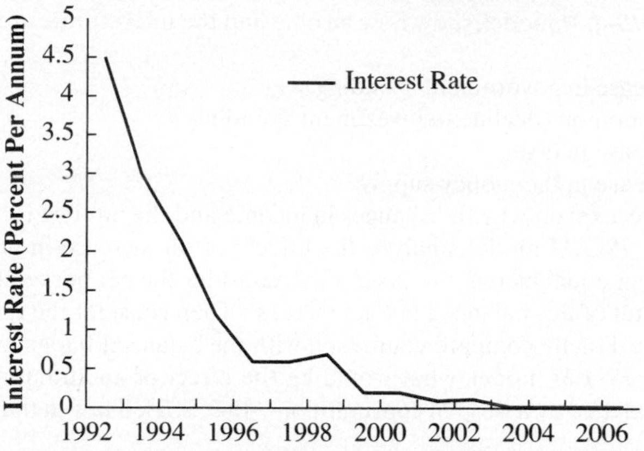

FIGURE 7.12 Monetary Policy Ineffectiveness in a Liquidity Trap

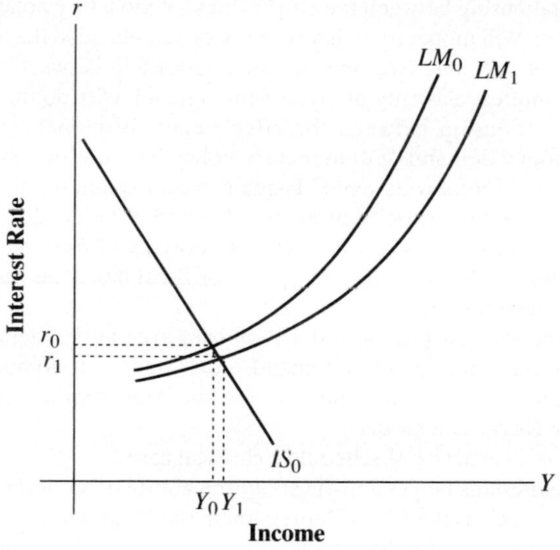

At the low levels of the interest rate that would prevail in a liquidity trap, Keynesians expect the economy to be on the nearly horizontal range of the *LM* schedule. Monetary policy is ineffective in this situation.

have been led to look at structural problems in the Japanese economy such as an inefficient banking system, poor regulatory oversight, insufficient infrastructure, low labor mobility, and overreliance on export demand. Fiscal policies have been criticized as governed more by politics than economic concerns and as delayed and inefficient. Generally, institutions that served Japan well in the recovery and rapid expansion of the post–World War II years were inadequate to the stage the economy had reached by 1990.[a]

[a]On these issues, see the papers in Takatoshi Ito, Hugh Patrick, and David Weinstein, eds, *Reviving Japan's Economy: Problems and Prescriptions*. (Cambridge, MA: MIT Press, 2005)

REVIEW QUESTIONS AND PROBLEMS

1. Within the *IS–LM* model, show how income and the interest rate are affected by each of the following:
   a. An increase in government spending.
   b. An autonomous decline in investment spending.
   c. An increase in taxes.
   d. An increase in the money supply.
   In each case, explain why the changes in income and the interest rate occur.
2. Within the *IS–LM* model, analyze the effects of an increase in government spending financed by an equal increase in taxes. First, consider the net horizontal shift in the *IS* schedule as a result of this balanced budget increase. Then consider the effects on income and the interest rate. Finally, compare your result with the balanced-budget multiplier in Section 5.5.
3. Within the *IS–LM* model, what would be the effect of an autonomous increase in saving that was matched by a drop in consumption—that is, a fall in a in the consumption function?
   $$C = a + b(Y - T)$$
   Which schedule would shift? How would income and the interest rate be affected?
4. Explain the relationship between the effectiveness of monetary policy and the interest elasticity of investment. Will monetary policy be more or less effective the higher the interest elasticity of investment demand? Now explain the relationship between the effectiveness of fiscal policy and the interest elasticity of investment demand. Why do the two relationships differ?
5. Explain the relationship between the effectiveness of monetary policy and the interest elasticity of money demand. Will monetary policy be more or less effective the higher the interest elasticity of money demand? Explain. Now explain the relationship between fiscal policy and the interest elasticity of money demand. Why do the two relationships differ?
6. Suppose we had a case in which the interest elasticity of *both* money demand and investment were quite low. Would either monetary or fiscal policy be very effective? How would you interpret such a situation?
7. We saw that the interest rate played a stabilizing role in the classical system, adjusting so that a shock to one component of demand, a decline in autonomous investment, for example, would not affect aggregate demand. Does the interest rate perform a similar stabilizing function in the Keynesian model?
8. In what sense is a vertical *LM* schedule a classical case?
9. Why might Keynesians be pessimistic about the ability of monetary policy to stimulate output in situations such as the 1930s Depression in the United States or the recessions in Japan in the 1990s? What type of policy would Keynesian economists expect to be effective in such situations?
10. Consider the case in which the *LM* schedule is vertical. Suppose there is a shock that increases the demand for money for given levels of income and the interest rate. Illustrate the effect of the shock graphically and explain how income and the interest rate are affected.

APPENDIX

Monetary and Fiscal Policy Multipliers in the *IS–LM* Model

Here we extend the algebraic treatment of the *IS–LM* model given in the appendix to Chapter 6. We examine how the equilibrium value of income, which was derived there, changes as monetary and fiscal policy variables are changed. In doing so, we establish algebraically the graphical results in Section 7.1. We then consider the same question taken up in Section 7.2, the relative effectiveness of monetary and fiscal policy, within the linear version of the *IS–LM* model.

A.1 The Effects of Monetary and Fiscal Policy on Income

In the appendix to Chapter 6, we derived the following expressions[1] for the equilibrium values of income (Y_0) and the interest rate (r_0) in the *IS–LM* model:

$$Y_0 = \left[\frac{1}{(1-b) + i_1c_1/c_2}\right] \times \left[a + \bar{I} + G - bT + \frac{i_1}{c_2}(M^s - c_0)\right] \qquad \textbf{(A.10)}$$

$$r_0 = \left[\frac{1}{(1-b) + i_1c_1/c_2}\right] \times \left[\frac{(1-b)}{c_2}(c_0 - M^s) + \frac{c_1}{c_2}(a + \bar{I} + G - bT)\right] \qquad \textbf{(A.11)}$$

We can use these two equations to see how the interest rate and income change when any of the exogenous variables in the model change. This is the mathematical equivalent to seeing how these equilibrium values changed on the graphs in Section 7.1 with a shift in the *IS* or *LM* schedules. In this section, we compute expressions that show how income changes with changes in policy variables using equation (A.10). Finding the effects on the interest rate of changes in these variables is left as an exercise (see review problem 1).

[1]Because we return to equations in the appendix to Chapter 6, to avoid confusion, we number equations here consecutively with those equations.

Fiscal Policy

Consider first how equilibrium income changes with a change in government spending. From equation (A.10), letting G vary but holding constant all other exogenous variables, and for given values of the parameters, we compute

$$\Delta Y = \frac{1}{(1-b) + i_1c_1/c_2}\Delta G \qquad \textbf{(A.12)}$$

$$\frac{\Delta Y}{\Delta G} = \frac{1}{(1-b) + i_1c_1/c_2} > 0$$

Equation (A.12) indicates that, as we saw graphically (Figure 7-2), an increase in government spending will lead to an increase in equilibrium income within the *IS–LM* model. Moreover, the increase in equilibrium income per unit increase in government spending, as given by equation (A.12), is *smaller* than in the simple Keynesian model. Within the simple Keynesian model analyzed in Chapter 5, the increase in equilibrium income per unit increase in government spending was given by the autonomous expenditure multiplier $1/(1-b)$. The *multiplier* in equation (A.12) contains an additional positive term in the denominator (i_1c_1/c_2) and is therefore smaller.

Notice also, looking back at equation (A.10), that the change in equilibrium income per unit change in autonomous investment

$(\Delta Y/\Delta \bar{I})$ would be exactly the same as with a change in government spending.

The effect on income from a change in taxes is

$$\Delta Y = \frac{1}{(1-b) + i_1 c_1/c_2}(-b\Delta T) \qquad \textbf{(A.13)}$$

$$\frac{\Delta Y}{\Delta T} = \frac{-b}{(1-b) + i_1 c_1/c_2} < 0$$

This *tax multiplier* is opposite in sign to the government spending multiplier and smaller in absolute value, because $-b$ rather than 1 appears in the numerator.

Monetary Policy

From equation (A.10) we compute the effects on income from a change in the money supply as

$$\Delta Y = \left(\frac{1}{(1-b) + i_1 c_1/c_2}\right)\frac{i_1}{c_2}\Delta M^s$$

or

$$\frac{\Delta Y}{\Delta M^s} = \left(\frac{1}{(1-b) + i_1 c_1/c_2}\right)\frac{i_1}{c_2} > 0$$

which simplifies to

$$\frac{\Delta Y}{\Delta M^s} = \frac{i_1}{(1-b)c_2 + i_1 c_1} \qquad \textbf{(A.14)}$$

An increase in the money supply causes equilibrium income to rise, as was illustrated in Figure 7-1.

A.2 Policy Effectiveness and the Slopes of the *IS* and *LM* Curves

The expressions given by equations (A.12) and (A.14) are, respectively, fiscal and monetary policy *multipliers*. They give the change in equilibrium income per unit change in the policy variables G and M^s. In this section, we examine the relationship between the magnitude of these multipliers and the slopes of the *IS* and *LM* schedules. Our results parallel those of Section 7.2.[2]

The *IS* Curve and Policy Effectiveness

In the appendix to Chapter 6, we found that the slope of the *IS* schedule was given by

$$\left.\frac{\Delta r}{\Delta Y}\right|_{IS} = -\frac{(1-b)}{i_1} \qquad \textbf{(A.7)}$$

The crucial parameter, over which there is dispute, is i_1, which measures the interest sensitivity of investment demand. If i_1 is large (small), investment demand is interest-sensitive (-insensitive), and the *IS* schedule is flat (steep).

Now examine the role i_1 plays in the two multiplier expressions. We see from equation (A.12) that as i_1 becomes smaller, $\Delta Y/\Delta G$ becomes larger. That is, as investment becomes less sensitive to the interest rate and the *IS* schedule becomes steeper, fiscal policy becomes more effective (see Figure 7-7). If i_1 goes to zero, equation (A.12) reduces to $1/(1-b)$, the multiplier from the simple Keynesian model in Chapter 5.

We next consider equation (A.14), the monetary policy multiplier. As i_1 gets smaller (the *IS* schedule becomes steeper), the numerator in equation (A.14) becomes proportionately smaller, whereas only one term in the denominator falls. Therefore, the value of the expression declines.[3] The lower the interest elasticity of investment, the steeper the *IS* schedule, and the less effective is monetary policy (see Figure 7-6). In the extreme case, where i_1 is zero (vertical *IS* schedule), the value of equation (A.14) goes to zero, and monetary policy becomes completely ineffective.

The *LM* Curve and Policy Effectiveness

The expression in the appendix to Chapter 6 for the slope of the *LM* schedule was

$$\left.\frac{\Delta r}{\Delta Y}\right|_{LM} = \frac{c_1}{c_2} \qquad \textbf{(A.5)}$$

The crucial parameter (the one subject to dispute) determining whether the schedule is

[2] As in the chapter, we do not need to consider separately the effectiveness of tax policy. The same factors that influence the effectiveness of changes in G determine the effectiveness of changes in T.

[3] To see this clearly, rewrite the right-hand side of equation (A.14) as $1/[(1-b)c_2/i_1 + c_1]$. As i_1 falls, the denominator increases in value and the size of the multiplier declines.

steep or flat is c_2, which measures the interest sensitivity of money demand. If c_2 is large (small), meaning that money demand is interest-sensitive (insensitive), the *LM* schedule will be relatively flat (steep). This outcome follows because the expression in equation (A.5) decreases in value as c_2 becomes larger.

Now examine the way c_2 affects the fiscal policy multiplier given by equation (A.12). As c_2 becomes smaller, the second term in the denominator of equation (A.12) becomes larger. No other terms are affected, so the whole expression becomes smaller. The lower the interest sensitivity of money demand, the steeper is the *LM* schedule and the less effective is fiscal policy (see Figure 7-8). In the extreme case in which c_2 approaches zero, the denominator of equation (A.12) becomes extremely large, and the whole expression goes toward zero. As the *LM* schedule becomes vertical, fiscal policy becomes completely ineffective.

Finally, consider the relationship between c_2 and the effectiveness of monetary policy as measured by equation (A.14). As c_2 becomes smaller, the denominator of equation (A.14) becomes smaller, and the expression becomes larger. The less sensitive money demand is to the interest rate, the steeper is the *LM* schedule and the more effective is monetary policy (see Figure 7-9). If c_2 is zero, equation (A.14) reduces to $1/c_1$. The *LM* schedule is vertical, and equilibrium income will increase by the full amount of the horizontal shift in the *LM* schedule as the money supply increases (Figure 7-9*c*).

REVIEW PROBLEMS

1. Using equation (A.11), show how the equilibrium value of the interest rate (r) will be affected by
   a. An increase in the money supply (M^s).
   b. An increase in government spending (G).
   c. An increase in taxes (T).
2. Start with the solution for the equilibrium values of Y and r from review question 1 in the appendix to Chapter 6. Show how these values would change if government spending rose from 250 to 310.

CHAPTER 8

The Keynesian System (IV): Aggregate Supply and Demand

Chapters 5, 6, and 7 analyzed income determination assuming that the price level and money wage were fixed. The fixed-price–fixed-wage version of the Keynesian system highlights the role of aggregate demand. The demand-determined nature of output in this Keynesian model stands in sharp contrast to the supply-determined nature of output in the classical system. In this chapter, we examine the Keynesian system when prices and wages are not held constant and see that demand as well as supply factors play a role in determining output. In this sense, the models in this chapter are a synthesis of the classical and Keynesian systems.

In section 8.1, we illustrate the demand-determined nature of output in the Keynesian models considered so far. We construct a Keynesian aggregate demand schedule. In Section 8.2, this Keynesian aggregate demand schedule is put together with the classical supply side. It will be seen that as long as we retain the classical assumptions of perfect information in the labor market and perfect price and wage flexibility, the substitution of the Keynesian aggregate demand schedule does not change the classical nature of the model. As long as the supply schedule remains vertical, as it does if the foregoing labor market assumptions are made, aggregate output will be determined independently of demand. For aggregate demand to play a role in output determination, the classical labor market assumptions must be modified.

Alternative Keynesian assumptions about the supply side of the economy are analyzed in Sections 8.3 and 8.4. In these sections, we develop the Keynesian aggregate supply function. In Section 8.5, we see how shifts in this aggregate supply function play a role in determining price and output in the Keynesian model. The final section of the chapter compares the classical and Keynesian systems.

8.1 THE KEYNESIAN AGGREGATE DEMAND SCHEDULE

The model of Chapter 5 presented Keynes's theory of the aggregate demand for output. The essential notion embodied in that simple Keynesian model was that for output to be at an equilibrium level, aggregate demand must equal output. In Chapters 6 and 7, the effect of the interest rate on investment, and hence on aggregate demand, was considered. It was shown that in order for an output (Y) and interest-rate (r) combination to be an equilibrium point, output must equal aggregate demand and money demand must equal money supply.

What guarantees that this level of output will be equal to aggregate supply—equal to the amount the business sector will choose to produce? Our implicit assumption about the aggregate supply schedule is depicted in Figure 8-1. We assumed that any

FIGURE 8-1 Aggregate Supply Schedule in the Fixed-Price Keynesian Model

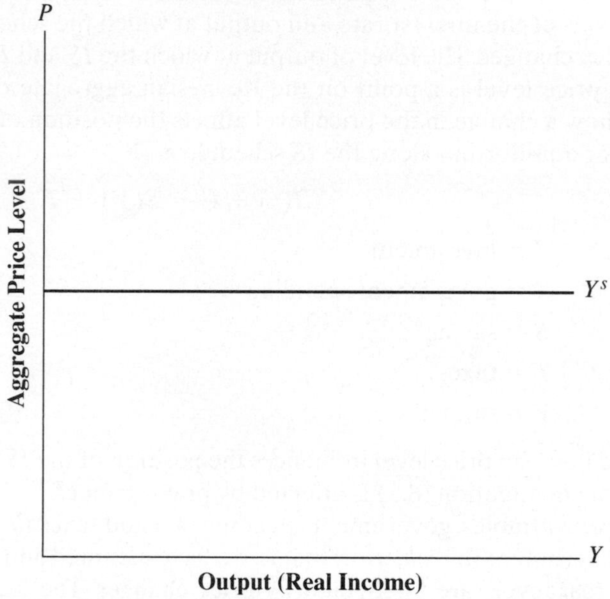

In previous chapters on the Keynesian model, where the price level was fixed and output was determined by aggregate demand, we assumed that the aggregate supply schedule was horizontal.

level of output demanded would be forthcoming at the given price level. Supply was assumed to be no constraint on output.

Such an assumption could be plausible when output is far below the capacity of the economy. In these conditions—for example, during the Depression of the 1930s—increases in output might not put upward pressure on the level of the money wage, given the high level of unemployment. Also, the marginal product of labor (MPN) might not fall as more labor is employed when we begin at a low level of employment (see Figure 3-1). As a consequence, the cost of producing additional units of output *W*/MPN might remain constant even with increases in output. In more normal conditions, an increase in output would put upward pressure on both the wage and price levels. We would expect the supply schedule to be upward-sloping.

In the more general case of the upward-sloping aggregate supply schedule, we cannot assume that price is given (supply is no constraint) and determine output simply by determining aggregate demand. Output and price will be jointly determined by supply and demand factors. The Keynesian aggregate supply schedule is discussed in Sections 8.3 and 8.4. First, we construct the Keynesian aggregate demand schedule, the relationship between aggregate demand and the price level in the Keynesian model.

The factors that determine aggregate demand in the Keynesian system have been analyzed in detail. These factors determine the positions of the *IS* and *LM* schedules and, therefore, the income–interest-rate combination that equilibrates the money market and causes output to equal aggregate demand. In constructing an aggregate demand schedule, we want to find the output demanded for each price level. To do this, we examine how the position of the *IS* and *LM* schedules, and consequently how the levels of the interest rate and output at which the schedules intersect, are affected by price changes. The level of output at which the *IS* and *LM* schedules intersect for a given price level is a point on the Keynesian aggregate demand schedule. Consider, first, how a change in the price level affects the position of the *IS* schedule. The condition for equilibrium along the *IS* schedule is

$$I(r) + G = S(Y) + T \tag{8.1}$$

where I = investment
G = government spending
S = saving
T = taxes
Y = output

To see how the price level influences the position of the *IS* schedule, consider how each variable in equation (8.1) is affected by price changes.

Two variables, government spending (G) and taxes (T), are assumed to be fixed by the government in *real terms*; that is, we have assumed and will continue to assume that their real levels are unaffected by price changes. The level of investment is also assumed to be determined in real terms; a given interest rate determines a level of real investment. Changes in the price level do not *directly* affect investment.

Similarly, *real* saving is assumed to depend on real income and is not directly affected by changes in the price level. None of the four terms in equation (8.1), the *IS* schedule equilibrium condition, depends directly on the price level, so a change in the price level does not shift the *IS* schedule.

What about the *LM* schedule? The equilibrium condition for the money market, the *LM* schedule, is

$$\frac{M}{P} = L(Y, r) \tag{8.2}$$

The condition equates the real supply of money (M/P) with the demand for money in real terms. The real money supply is equal to the exogenously fixed *nominal* money supply (M) divided by the price level (P).

The Keynesian theory of the demand for money considered in Chapter 8 related the demand for money in *real* terms to the level of *real* income and to the interest rate, although as long as prices were held constant, there was no need to distinguish between changes in real and nominal values. People wish to hold a certain amount of real money balances for a given volume of transactions measured in real (constant-dollar) terms, where real income is a proxy for the real volume of transactions. Consequently, equilibrium in the money market occurs when the demand for real money balances is just equal to the real money supply. It is the nominal money supply—not the real money supply—that can be exogenously fixed by the monetary authority. Any change in the price level will affect the real money supply and consequently will shift the *LM* schedule.

Figure 8-2*a* illustrates the effect of changes in the price level on the real money supply and, therefore, on the position of the *LM* schedule. Holding the nominal money

FIGURE 8-2 Construction of the Aggregate Demand Schedule

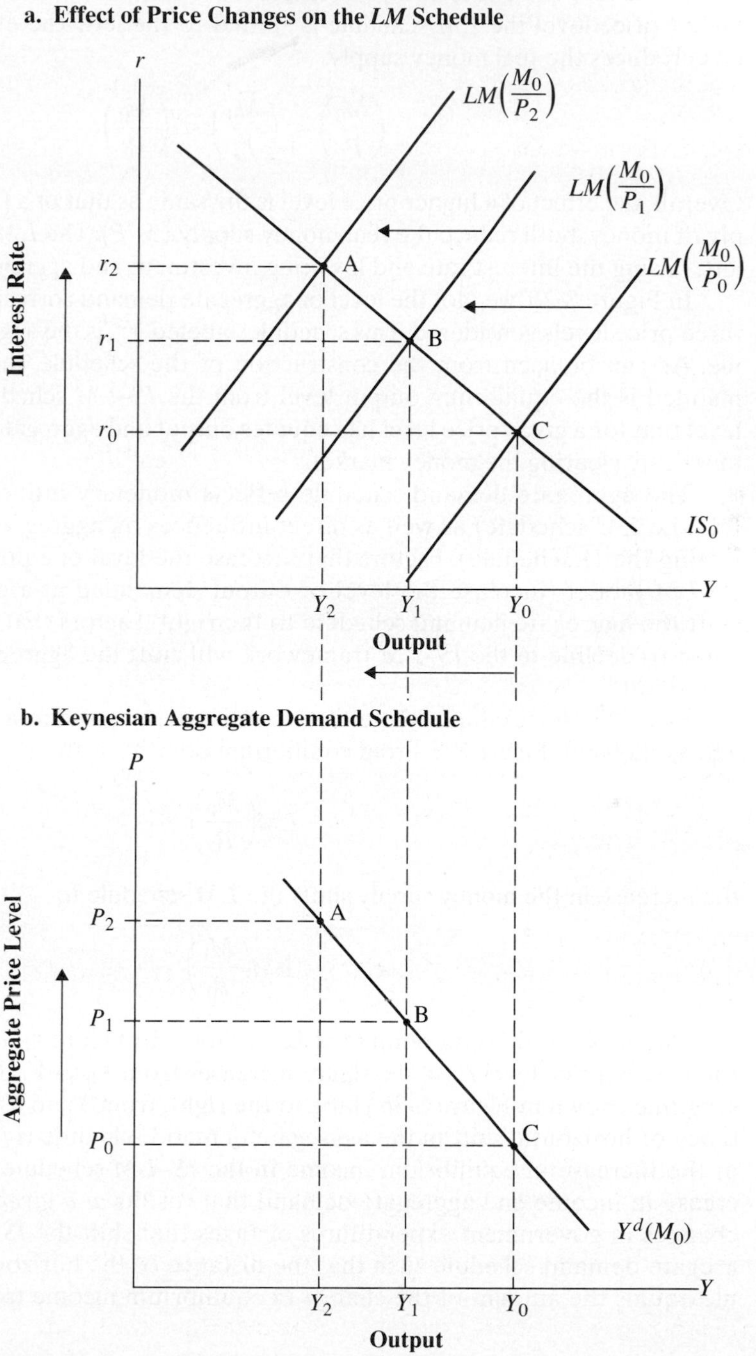

At successively higher price levels, P_0, P_1, P_2, the *LM* schedule in part *a* is shifted farther to the left. This shift results in successively lower levels of aggregate demand Y_0, Y_1, Y_2. These combinations of price and aggregate demand are plotted to give the negatively sloped aggregate demand schedule in part *b*.

supply fixed at M_0, three price levels are considered, where $P_2 > P_1 > P_0$. Notice that as we consider the effect of a price increase from P_0 to P_1, then from P_1 to P_2, at the higher price level the LM schedule is shifted to the left. The effect of a higher price level reduces the real money supply,

$$\left(\frac{M_0}{P_2}\right) < \left(\frac{M_0}{P_1}\right) < \left(\frac{M_0}{P_0}\right)$$

Overall, the effect of a higher price level is the same as that of a fall in the nominal supply of money; both reduce the real money supply (M/P). The LM schedule shifts to the left, raising the interest rate and lowering investment and aggregate demand.

In Figure 8-2*b*, we plot the level of aggregate demand corresponding to each of the three price levels considered. This schedule, labeled Y^d, is the aggregate demand schedule. As can be seen from the construction of the schedule, this level of output demanded is the equilibrium output level from the IS–LM schedule model, the output level that for a given price level just equates output and aggregate demand while simultaneously clearing the money market.

The aggregate demand schedule reflects monetary influences (factors that affect the LM schedule) as well as direct influences on aggregate demand (factors affecting the IS schedule). Factors that increase the level of equilibrium income in the IS–LM model (increase the level of output demanded at a given price level) will shift the aggregate demand schedule to the right. Factors that cause equilibrium income to decline in the IS–LM framework will shift the aggregate demand schedule to the left.

Consider, for example, the effect of an increase in the money supply, from M_0 to M_1, as shown in Figure 8-3. From equilibrium point A, with

$$LM\left(\frac{M_0}{P_0}\right),$$

the increase in the money supply shifts the LM schedule to

$$LM\left(\frac{M_1}{P_0}\right)$$

The new equilibrium point is at B, as shown in Figure 8-3*a*. Equilibrium income for a given price level P_0 in the figure increases from Y_0 to Y_1. The aggregate demand schedule shown in Figure 8-3*b* shifts to the right, from Y_0^d to Y_1^d.[1] Notice that the distance of horizontal shift in the aggregate demand schedule is $(Y_1 - Y_0)$, the amount of the increase in equilibrium income in the IS–LM schedule model. This is the increase in income and aggregate demand that results *at a given price level*. Similarly, changes in government expenditures or taxes that shift the IS schedule shift the aggregate demand schedule such that the distance of the horizontal shift in the schedule equals the amount of the change in equilibrium income from the IS–LM model.

[1]For simplicity, the Keynesian aggregate demand schedule here and in later graphs is drawn as a straight line. The curvature of the aggregate demand schedule is not important for our analysis.

FIGURE 8-3 Effect on Aggregate Demand of an Increase in the Money Supply

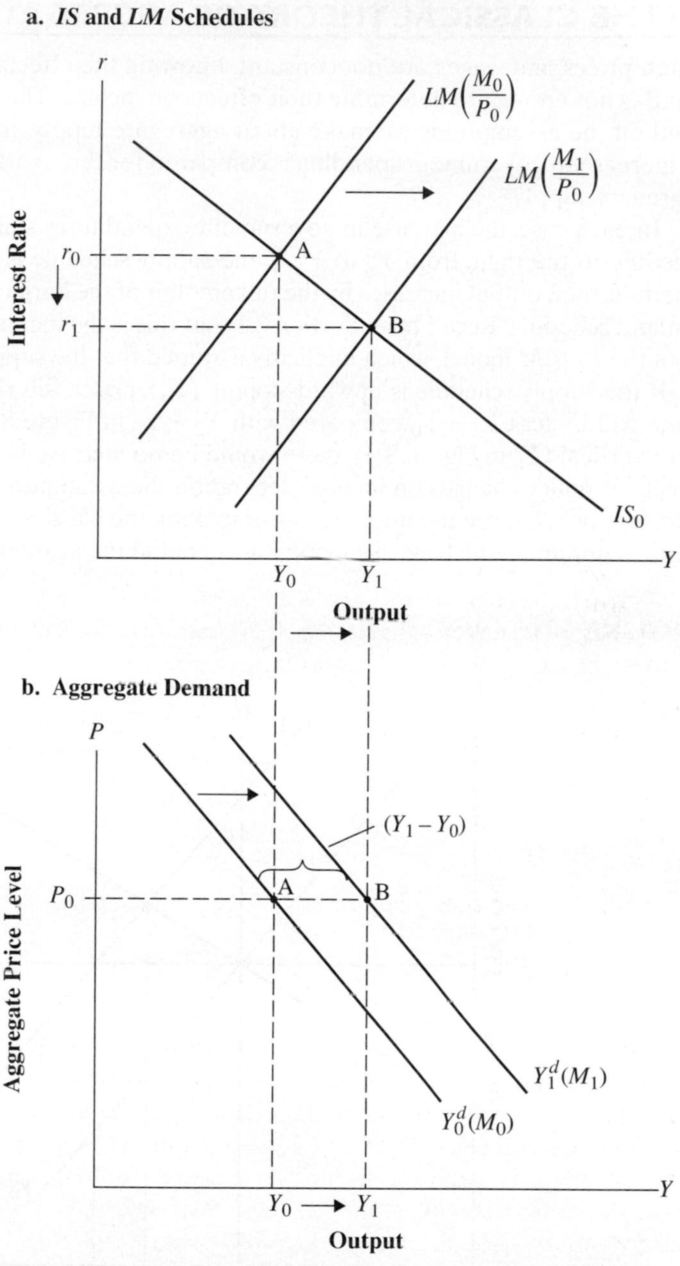

An increase in the money supply shifts the *LM* schedule in part *a* to the right, from $LM(M_0/P_0)$ to $LM(M_1/P_0)$, and shifts the aggregate demand schedule to the right from Y_0^d to Y_1^d in part *b*.

8.2 THE KEYNESIAN AGGREGATE DEMAND SCHEDULE COMBINED WITH THE CLASSICAL THEORY OF AGGREGATE SUPPLY

When prices and wages are not constant, knowing the effects of policy actions on demand is not enough to determine their effects on income. The effect on income will depend on the assumptions we make about aggregate supply. In Figure 8-4, the effect of an increase in government spending is compared for three different assumptions about aggregate supply.

In each case, the increase in government expenditures shifts the aggregate demand schedule to the right, from Y_0^d to Y_1^d. If the supply schedule is given by Y_2^s, a horizontal schedule, then output increases by the full amount of the horizontal shift in the aggregate demand schedule. Recall from Section 8.1 that this is the increase in equilibrium income from the *IS–LM* model, which implicitly assumed that the supply schedule was horizontal. If the supply schedule is upward-sloping (Y_1^s), prices will rise and the increase in income will be less, $Y_1 - Y_0$ compared with $Y_2 - Y_0$ in Figure 8-4. If the supply schedule were vertical (Y_0^s in Figure 8-4), there would be no increase in income. Clearly, then, the effects of policy changes on income depend on the assumption made concerning aggregate supply. What are the implications of making the classical assumptions about supply while maintaining the Keynesian apparatus behind the aggregate demand schedule?

FIGURE 8-4 Role of Aggregate Supply in Determining the Output Response to a Policy Shock

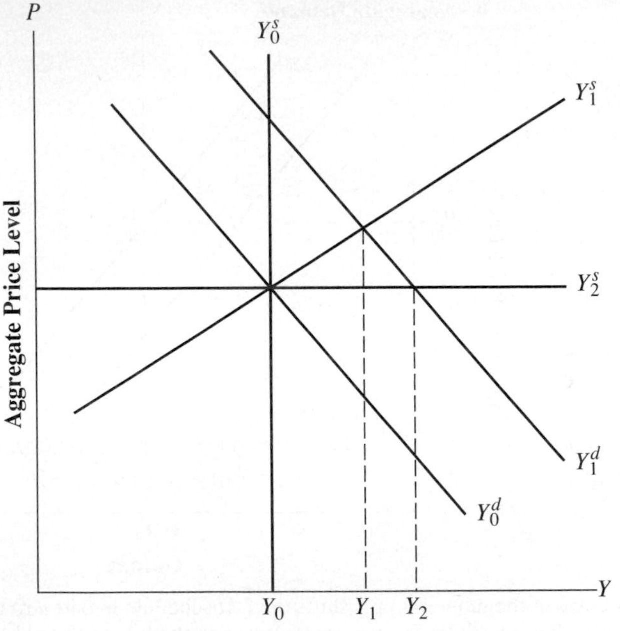

An increase in government spending shifts the aggregate demand schedule from Y_0^d to Y_1^d. If the aggregate supply schedule is horizontal (Y_2^s), output increases from Y_0 to Y_2. If the aggregate supply schedule slopes upward (Y_1^s), output increases only to Y_1. If the supply schedule is vertical (Y_0^s), output is unchanged at Y_0.

The classical analysis of aggregate supply was explained in Chapter 3. The central elements of this analysis are that in the labor market, both supply and demand depend solely on the real wage (*W*/*P*), which is assumed to be known to all. Further, the labor market is assumed always to be in equilibrium with a perfectly flexible money wage, adjusting to equate supply and demand.

These classical assumptions result in a vertical aggregate supply schedule (see Section 3.5). With the classical assumptions, the aggregate supply schedule would be given Y_0^s by in Figure 8-4; output would be supply-determined. Factors such as changes in government spending, taxes, and the money supply, which shift the demand schedule, would not affect the equilibrium output.[2]

This analysis shows that *the classical theory of aggregate supply based on the classical auction market characterization of the labor market is fundamentally incompatible with the Keynesian system.* The central feature of Keynesian analysis is the theory of aggregate demand. With classical assumptions about aggregate supply, leading to the vertical supply schedule, there is *no* role for aggregate demand in determining output and employment. It was necessary for Keynes and his followers to attack the classical assumptions and to develop a Keynesian theory of the supply side.

8.3 A CONTRACTUAL VIEW OF THE LABOR MARKET

Keynes believed that the money wage would not adjust sufficiently to keep the economy at full employment. In the classical system, both labor supply and demand are functions of the real wage, and the intersection of the labor supply and demand schedules determines an equilibrium real wage and level of employment. Wage bargains are, however, set in terms of money wages, and one assumption crucial to the classical model is that the money wage is perfectly flexible.

Sources of Wage Rigidity

The Keynesian theory offers a number of reasons why the money wage will *not* quickly adjust, especially in the downward direction, to maintain equilibrium in the labor market. The most important of these explanations for the *rigidity* of money wages are as follows.

1. Keynes argued that workers are interested in their relative as well as absolute wage. There exists in any labor market a set of wage differentials between workers with different trades and skills. Much of the work of wage bargaining is done to arrive at a relative wage structure that is acceptable to both labor and management. Wage differentials can be measured by relative money wages, because price-level changes affect all wages symmetrically.

Keynes believed that workers would resist money wage cuts even as the demand for labor fell. They would see the wage cuts as unfair changes in the structure of relative wages. Workers in one firm or industry would have no assurance that if they accepted a cut in money wages, workers in other sectors of the labor market would do the

[2]Some fiscal policy changes, such as a change in the marginal tax rate, have supply-side effects in the classical system, as explained in Section 4.3. These are being ignored here.

same. A decline in the real wage as a result of a rise in prices would not be seen by labor as affecting the structure of relative wages. For this reason, Keynes believed that declines in real wages caused by price-level increases would meet much less resistance from labor than an equivalent fall in the real wage from a money wage cut.

2. Another factor leading to stickiness in the money wage level is an institutional one. In the unionized sector of the labor market, wages are set by labor contracts, most often of 2 or 3 years' duration. Such contracts typically fix money wage levels for the life of the contract. The money wage will not respond to events, such as a decline in labor demand, over the life of the contract. Indexation of the money wage set in the contract (i.e., provisions that tie changes in the money wage to changes in the price level) provides some flexibility in the money wage over the length of the contract. In the United States, however, when any indexation of labor contracts exists, it is generally incomplete. Thus fixed-money-wage contracts impart stickiness to the money wage. Once such a labor contract is signed, the decision of how much labor to hire is left to the employer. The labor supply function no longer plays a role in determining employment. The firm hires the profit-maximizing amount of labor at the fixed money wage.

3. Even in segments of the labor market in which no explicit contract fixes the money wage, there is often an implicit agreement between employer and employee that fixes the money wage over some time period. In particular, such implicit contracts keep employers from cutting money wages in the face of a fall in the demand for their products and a consequent decline in labor demand. The incentive for employers to refrain from attempting to achieve such wage cuts, or alternatively from hiring workers from among the pool of the unemployed who might be willing to work for a lower wage, is their desire to maintain a reputation as a good employer. Firms might achieve a temporary gain by forcing a money wage cut to reduce labor costs, but this gain could be more than counter-balanced by the effect of poor labor relations with existing employees and difficulties in recruiting new employees. Keynesians believe that the conventions of labor markets are such that firms find it in their interest to cut the length of the work week or to have layoffs in response to falls in demand rather than to seek money wage cuts.

Keynesians believe that contractual arrangements are central to understanding how modern labor markets function. The *contractual* view of the labor market stands in contrast to the frictionless *auction* market view of the classical economists. In the Keynesian view, as expressed by Arthur Okun,

> [W]ages are not set to clear markets in the short run, but rather are strongly conditioned by longer-term considerations involving . . . employer worker relations. These factors insulate wages . . . to a significant degree from the impact of shifts in demand so that the adjustment must be made in employment and output.[3]
>
> *Read Perspectives 8-1.*

[3]Arthur Okun, *Prices and Quantities* (Washington, DC: The Brookings Institution, 1981), p. 233.

PERSPECTIVES 8-1

PRICE AND QUANTITY ADJUSTMENT IN GREAT BRITAIN, 1929–36

Keynes's view that the money wage would not adjust quickly to clear the labor market was in part a result of his observation of events in Great Britain. Table 8.1 provides data for the money wage, price level, real wage, and unemployment rate in Britain for the years 1929–36.

The money wage fell over the first part of the period, but only 5 percent by 1933. After 1933, the money wage rose slowly despite the exceptionally high unemployment rate. Data for the price level, real wage, and unemployment rate clearly indicate that no downward adjustment in the real wage to clear the labor market—the classical labor market adjustment—occurred.

TABLE 8-1 Wages, Prices, and Unemployment in Great Britain, 1929–36

Year	*Money Wage (W) (Index 1914 = 100)*	*Price Level (P) (Index 1914 = 100)*	*Real Wage (W/P × 100)*	*Unemployment Rate (Percent)*
1929	193	164	118	11.0
1930	191	157	122	14.6
1931	189	147	129	21.5
1932	185	143	129	22.5
1933	183	140	129	21.3
1934	183	141	130	17.7
1935	185	143	130	16.4
1936	190	147	129	14.3

SOURCE: B. P. Mitchell and P. Deane, *Abstract of British Historical Statistics* (Cambridge: Cambridge University Press, 1962), pp. 67, 345.

A Flexible Price–Fixed Money Wage Model

To model this contractual view of the labor market, we assume that, although prices are free to vary, the money wage is *fixed*.[4] A fixed money wage is an extreme version of a sticky wage, and Keynesian economists do not believe that the money wage is completely rigid. Still, if the response of the money wage to labor market conditions is slow to materialize, as the contractual approach to the labor market suggests, results based on the assumption of a fixed money wage will be approximately correct for the short run.

Finally, before we analyze this flexible price fixed money wage model, we should point out that Keynes's concern was with the downward rigidity of the money wage—the failure of the money wage to fall sufficiently to restore full employment. The main situations to which we would want to apply the fixed-wage model are those in which there is an excess supply of labor.

With the money wage fixed and labor supply greater than labor demand, actual employment will be determined by demand. Firms will be able to hire the amount of labor

[4]The models in this chapter focus on the traditional Keynesian view that money wage rigidity is the key explanation of why output and employment must respond to changes in aggregate demand. In Section 12.2, we consider *new Keynesian models* in which the key rigidities are, instead, in product prices and real wage rates.

FIGURE 8-5 Employment with a Fixed Money Wage

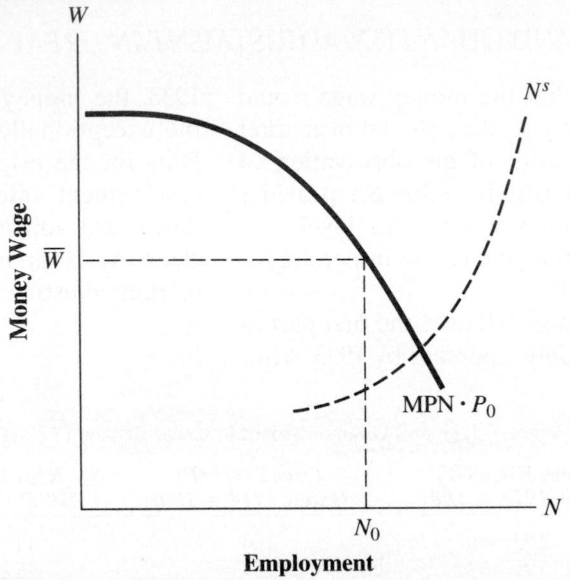

With the money wage fixed at $\overline{W}$, employment will be at N_0, the amount of labor demanded.

they demand at the going wage. Keynes did not object to the classical theory of labor demand. According to this theory, the profit-maximizing firm demands labor up to the point at which the real wage (W/P) is equal to the MPN or, equivalently, to the point at which

$$W = \text{MPN} \cdot P \quad \textbf{(8.3)}$$

The money wage is equal to the money value of the marginal product (the marginal revenue product) of labor. Because, with an excess supply of labor and a fixed money wage, employment depends only on labor demand, the determination of employment is as depicted in Figure 8-5. At a fixed money wage $\overline{W}$, labor demand, and therefore employment, will be N_0.

The labor supply schedule is shown in Figure 8-5 as a dashed line. Notice that at the fixed money wage ($\overline{W}$), the labor supply schedule is to the right of N_0, indicating an excess supply of labor. Demand, not supply, is the factor constraining employment. The labor supply schedule plays *no* role and is not shown in the subsequent figures in this section. The properties of the Keynesian labor supply function are explained in the next section, where we analyze a Keynesian model in which the money wage is allowed to vary.

The position of the labor demand schedule, the schedule giving the money value of the MPN corresponding to each level of employment (the MPN · P_0 schedule in Figure 8-5), depends on the price level. The number of workers firms will hire, and as a consequence the amount of output they will supply, depend on the price level. This relationship between output supplied and the price level is developed in Figure 8-6.

Figure 8-6*a* shows the level of employment that will result at three successively higher price levels, P_0, P_1, and P_2, with the money wage fixed at $\overline{W}$. An increase in the price level (from P_0 to P_1, then from P_1 to P_2) will increase the money value of the MPN corresponding to any level of employment and therefore will increase labor demand for a given money wage. The labor demand (MPN · P) schedule shifts to the

FIGURE 8-6 The Keynesian Aggregate Supply Schedule When the Money Wage Is Fixed

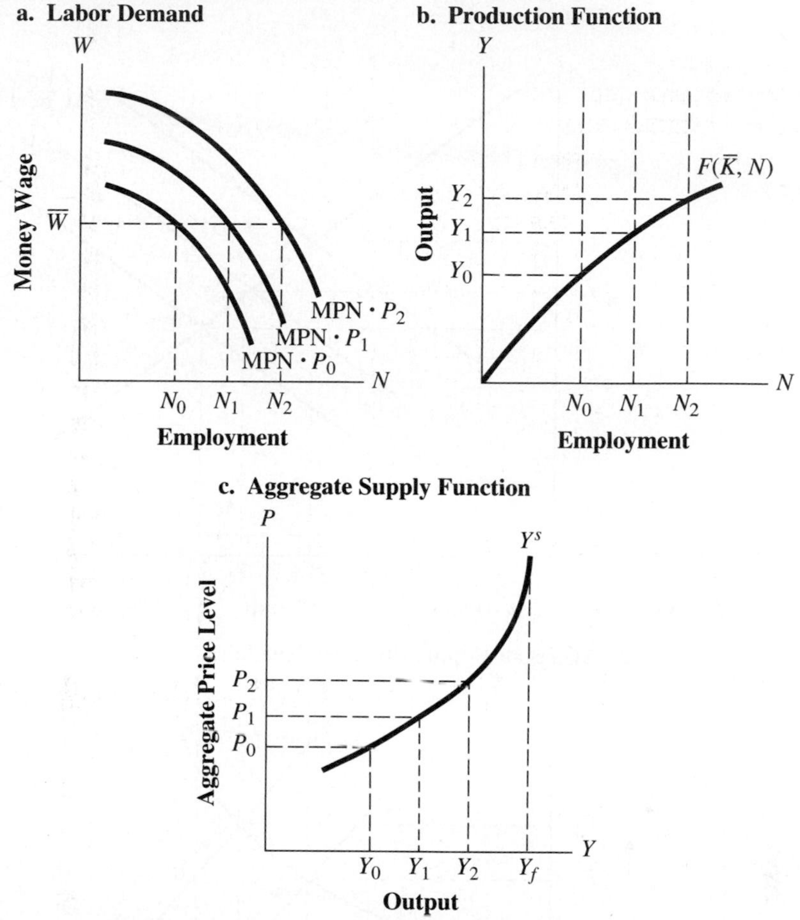

Part *a* shows the levels of employment N_0, N_1, N_2 for three successively higher price levels, P_0, P_1, P_2. Part *b* shows the levels of output, Y_0, Y_1, Y_2 that will be produced at these three levels of employment. In part *c*, we put together the information in *a* and *b* to show output supplied at each of the three price levels. Notice that at higher price levels, employment, and hence output supplied, increase; *the aggregate supply curve* (Y^s) *is upward-sloping.*

right, and employment increases. As employment increases, output is shown to rise in Figure 8-6*b*, where we have plotted the aggregate production function giving the level of output for each level of employment.

Figure 8-6*c* combines the information from Figures 8.6*a* and 8.6*b* to show output supplied for each price level. Higher prices result in higher supply; the aggregate supply function is upward-sloping. At some level of output (Y_f in Figure 8.6*c*), full employment would be reached and further increases in price would have no effect on output. The aggregate supply schedule becomes vertical at this level.

Below full employment, the supply schedule will not be vertical; shifts in the aggregate demand schedule will change the level of output. The effects of an increase in the money supply and the effects of an increase in government spending are illustrated in Figures 8-7 and 8-8, respectively.

FIGURE 8-7 Effects of an Increase in the Money Supply When the Price Level Is Flexible

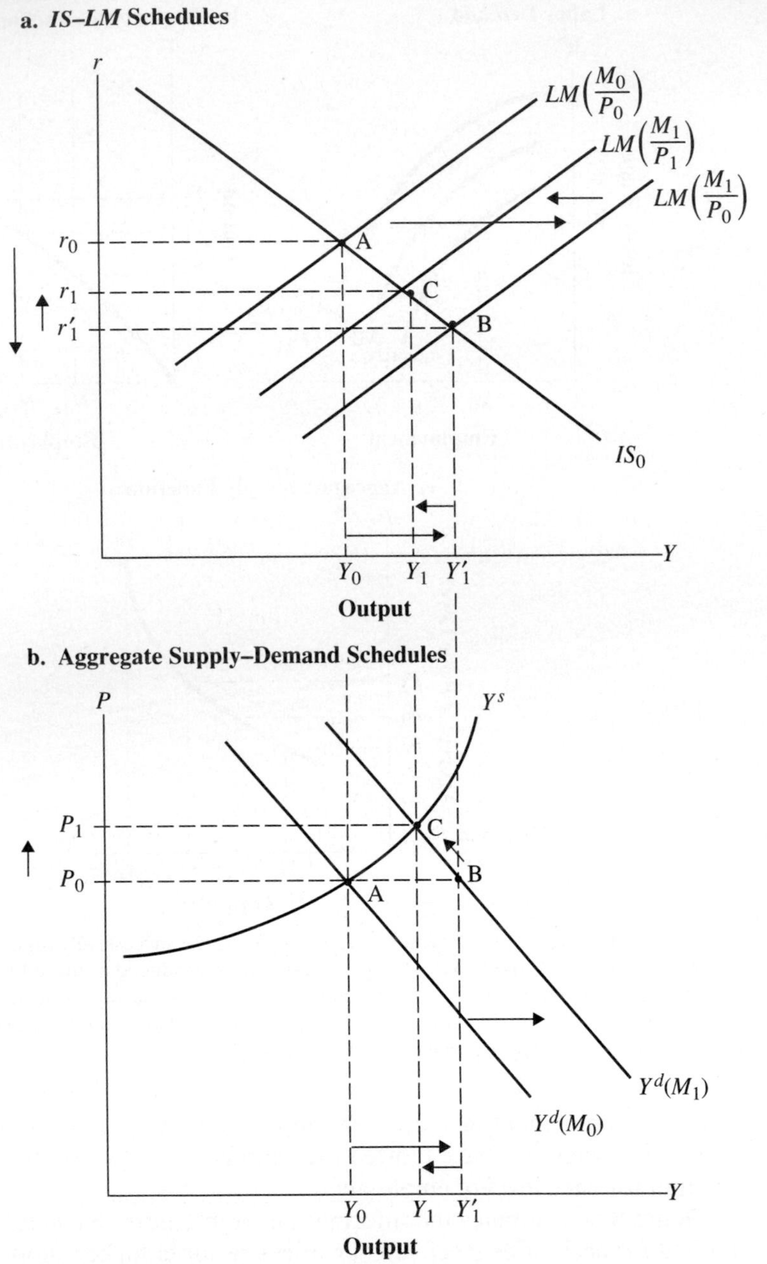

An increase in the money supply shifts the LM schedule from $LM(M_0/P_0)$ to $LM(M_1/P_0)$ (part a) and shifts the aggregate demand schedule from $Y^d(M_0)$ to $Y^d(M_1)$ (part b). The increase in aggregate demand causes output to rise from Y_0 to Y_1 and the price level to rise from P_0 to P_1. The increase in the price level shifts the LM schedule from $LM(M_1/P_0)$ to $LM(M_1/P_1)$.

FIGURE 8-8 Effects of an Increase in Government Spending When the Price Level Is Flexible

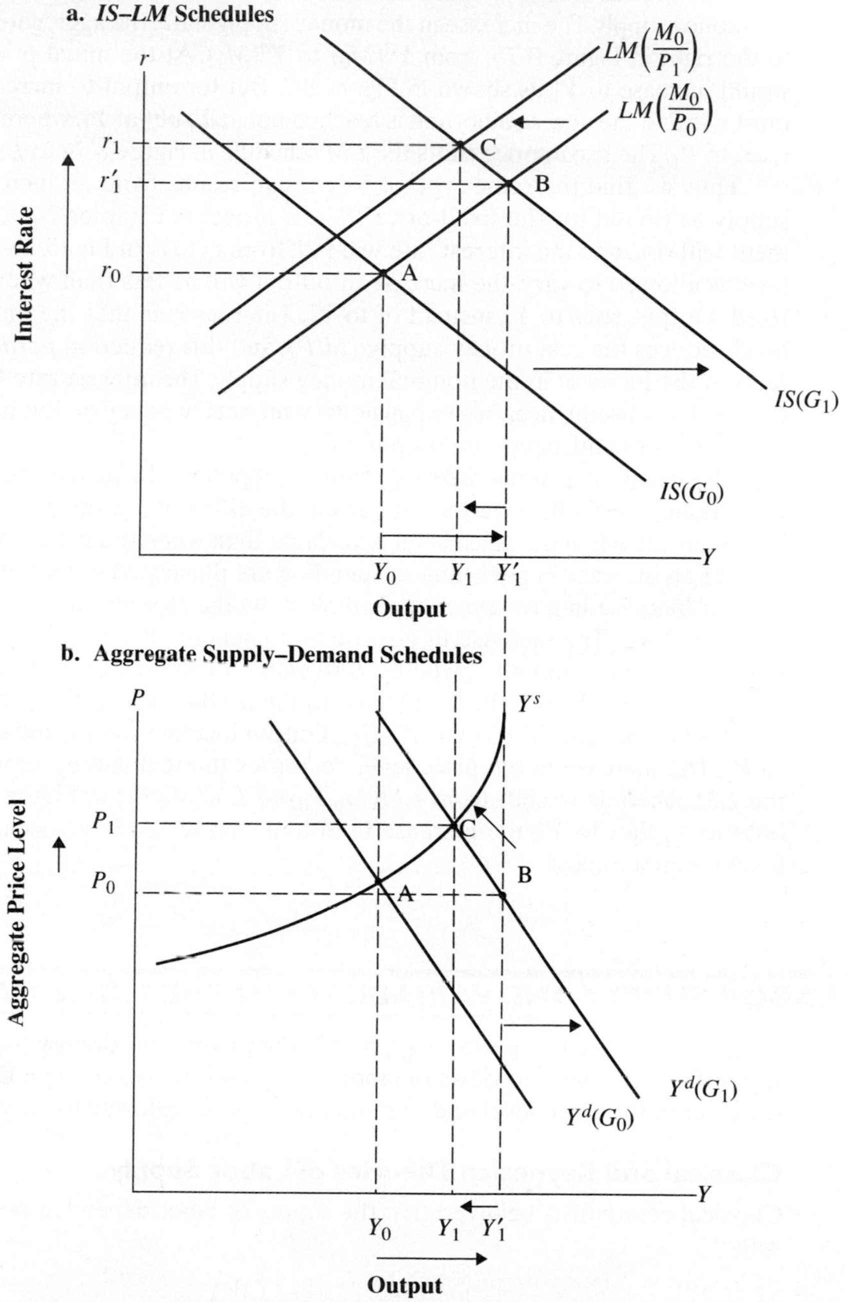

An increase in government spending shifts the IS schedule from $IS(G_0)$ to $IS(G_1)$ (part *a*) and shifts the aggregate demand schedule from $Y^d(G_0)$ to $Y^d(G_1)$ (part *b*). The increase in aggregate demand causes output to rise from Y_0 to Y_1 and the price level to rise from P_0 to P_1. The increase in the price level shifts the LM schedule from $LM(M_0/P_0)$ to $LM(M_0/P_1)$.

In Figure 8-7*a*, an increase in the money supply shifts the *LM* schedule from $LM(M_0/P_0)$ to $LM(M_1/P_0)$. This shift in the *LM* schedule is a direct result of the change in the money supply. The increase in the money supply shifts the aggregate demand schedule to the right in Figure 8-7*b*, from $Y^d(M_0)$ to $Y^d(M_1)$. At the initial price level P_0, output would increase to Y_1' as shown in Figure 8-7. But for output to increase, the price level must rise and the new equilibrium is reached not at Y_1' but at Y_1, where the price level has risen to P_1. The rise in price shifts the *LM* schedule in Figure 8-7*a* to $LM(M_1/P_1)$.

Thus we find the same type of Keynesian results from an increase in the money supply as we did for the fixed-price *IS–LM* model in Chapter 7. Output and employment will rise, and the interest rate will fall, from r_0 to r_1 in Figure 8-7*a*. When the price level is allowed to vary, the increase in output will be less than when the price level is fixed. Output rises to Y_1 instead of to Y_1'. The reason is that the increase in the price level reduces the real money supply (M/P), and this reduction *partially* offsets the effects of the increase in the nominal money supply. The interest rate falls only to r_1, not to r_1'. As a consequence, this expansionary monetary policy action has a smaller effect on investment and, hence, on output.

The situation is much the same with fiscal policy. The results are Keynesian in that fiscal policy does affect output, but again, the effect of a given policy action is smaller in magnitude when the price level is variable than when the price level is fixed. The effects of an increase in government spending are illustrated in Figure 8-8.

An increase in government spending shifts the *IS* schedule from $IS(G_0)$ to $IS(G_1)$ in Figure 8-8*a*. The increase in government spending has no direct effect on the *LM* schedule, which is initially given by $LM(M_0/P_0)$. The increase in aggregate demand as the *IS* schedule shifts right is reflected in Figure 8-8*b* in the shift of the aggregate demand schedule from $Y^d(G_0)$ to $Y^d(G_1)$. Output increases to Y_1, and the price level rises to P_1. The increase in the price level decreases the real money supply (M/P), causing the *LM* schedule to shift from $LM(M_0/P_0)$ to $LM(M_0/P_1)$ in Figure 8-8*a*. Output rises only to Y_1, not to Y_1', the increase in output that would have occurred had the price level remained fixed.

8.4 LABOR SUPPLY AND VARIABILITY IN THE MONEY WAGE

In this section, we bring labor supply into the picture. We discuss the differences in the Keynesian and classical views of labor supply and then examine a Keynesian model in which both the price level and that money wage are allowed to vary.

Classical and Keynesian Theories of Labor Supply

Classical economists believed that the supply of labor depended positively on the real wage,

$$N^S = g\left(\frac{W}{P}\right) \tag{8.4}$$

A rise in the real wage increases the income that can be gained from an hour's labor or, looked at in reverse, increases the opportunity cost of taking 1 hour of leisure. Consequently, an increase in the real wage increases labor supply.

The Keynesian theory of labor supply begins with the observation that the wage bargain is struck in terms of the *money* wage, not the real wage. The classical theory assumes that suppliers of labor (workers) know the price level (P) and money wage (W) and therefore know the real wage (W/P). Keynesians argue that, because the labor bargain is in terms of the money wage, we can assume that workers know the money wage but not the price level. As explained previously, through implicit or explicit contracts, workers agree to provide labor services over some period, let us say for a year. They have no way of knowing the value that the aggregate price level will take on over the coming year. It is this aggregate price level that will determine the purchasing power of any money wage they agree to in a current wage bargain. As a consequence, the Keynesians believe that decisions about labor supply depend on the current money wage and the *expectation* of the aggregate price level. Further, the Keynesian view has been that workers' expectations about the price level depend for the most part on the past behavior of prices.

To see the implications of the Keynesian view of workers' bargaining for a known money wage with only imperfect information about prices, we construct a Keynesian labor supply schedule, which we compare with the classical labor supply schedule [equation (8.4)]. We then consider a model in which the money wage is perfectly flexible but labor supply is given by the Keynesian labor supply function. In this analysis, we neglect the factors enumerated previously, which Keynesians believe cause the money wage to be sticky. One purpose of this analysis is to show that *even if the money wage were perfectly flexible*, with the Keynesian labor supply schedule, the aggregate supply schedule would not be vertical. Output and employment would not be completely supply-determined; aggregate demand would also play a role. In reality, the Keynesians believe that the money wage *is* sticky in the downward direction and that much unemployment is the result of the failure of the money wage to clear the labor market. Imperfect information about prices is, however, an additional factor that the Keynesians believe explains fluctuations in output and employment.

The Keynesian labor supply function can be written as

$$N^S = t(W/P^e) \tag{8.5}$$

An increase in the money wage (W) for a given value of the expected price level (P^e) would increase labor supply, because it would be viewed by workers as an increase in the real wage. An increase in the expected price level would cause labor supply to decline. Fundamentally, workers are interested in the real wage, not the money wage, and they reduce their supply of labor when they perceive that the real wage has declined. The difference between the Keynesian and classical labor supply functions is that in the Keynesian version workers must form an expectation of the price level. Labor supply therefore depends on the *expected* real wage. In the classical system, workers know the real wage; labor supply depends on the *actual* real wage.

The Keynesian theory of labor supply is incomplete without an assumption about how workers form an expectation of the price level (P^e). The Keynesian assumption is that such price expectations are based primarily on the past behavior of the price level. Thus

$$P^e = a_1P_{-1} + a_2P_{-2} + a_3P_{-3} + \cdots + a_nP_{-n} \tag{8.6}$$

where P_{-i} ($i = 1, 2, 3, \ldots$) is the price level from i periods back and $a_1, a_2, \ldots, a_n$ are the weights given to a number of past observations on the price level in forming the expectation of the current price level. Clearly, there is additional information that might prove useful in accurately predicting the behavior of prices. The Keynesian assumption is that the cost of gathering and processing such additional information is high enough that the price expectations of labor suppliers are reasonably accurately represented by a simple formulation such as equation (8.6). As we will see later, this assumption has not gone unchallenged.

According to equation (8.6), price expectations are essentially *backward-looking*, adjusting to the past behavior of the price level. Moreover, in the Keynesian view, there is considerable inertia in this adjustment process; price expectations adjust only *slowly* to the past behavior of the price level. If this is the case, then price expectations do not change as a result of current economic conditions. In analyzing the effects of various policy changes, for example, we can take P^e as constant. In the longer run (after many short periods have passed), we will need to take account of how stabilization policies affect P^e.

The Keynesian Aggregate Supply Schedule with a Variable Money Wage

Figure 8-9 illustrates the construction of the aggregate supply schedule, where labor supply is given by equation (8.5) and the money wage is assumed to adjust to equate labor supply and labor demand. In Figure 8-9*a*, labor supply (N^s) and labor demand are plotted as functions of the money wage. As in the previous analysis, labor demand depends on the real wage; firms are assumed to know the price level at which they will be able to sell their products. The labor demand schedule will shift to the right with an increase in the price level. Figure 8-9*a* shows labor demand schedules for three successively higher price levels: P_0, P_1, and P_2, respectively.

The labor supply schedule is drawn for a given value of the *expected* aggregate price level. As just explained, this expected price level is assumed to be fixed in the short run. With the fixed labor supply schedule, increases in the price level shift the labor demand schedule along the supply schedule, so that for a higher price level the equilibrium levels of employment and the money wage are increased. The process at work here is as follows. The increase in price (from P_0 to P_1, for example) causes an excess demand for labor at the old money wage (W_0). The money wage is bid up, and for a given value of P^e, an increase in the money wage causes more workers to accept jobs (or to increase the number of hours worked in existing jobs); employment rises.

At the higher levels of employment N_1 and N_2, corresponding to the higher price levels P_1 and P_2, output is higher at the levels shown by Y_1 and Y_2 in Figure 8-9*b*. Thus, a higher price level corresponds to a higher level of output supplied. This information is reflected in the upward-sloping aggregate supply schedule in Figure 8-9*c*, plotting output supplied for each price level.

Policy Effects in the Variable-Wage Keynesian Model

Because the variable-wage Keynesian aggregate supply schedule is still upward-sloping (nonvertical), changes in aggregate demand that shift the aggregate demand schedule will affect output. Increases in the money supply or level of government expenditures will shift the aggregate demand schedule to the right, increasing both output and the aggregate price level. Graphical illustrations of such policy shifts are *qualitatively* the same as Figures 8-7 and 8-8.

FIGURE 8-9 The Keynesian Aggregate Supply Schedule When the Money Wage Is Variable

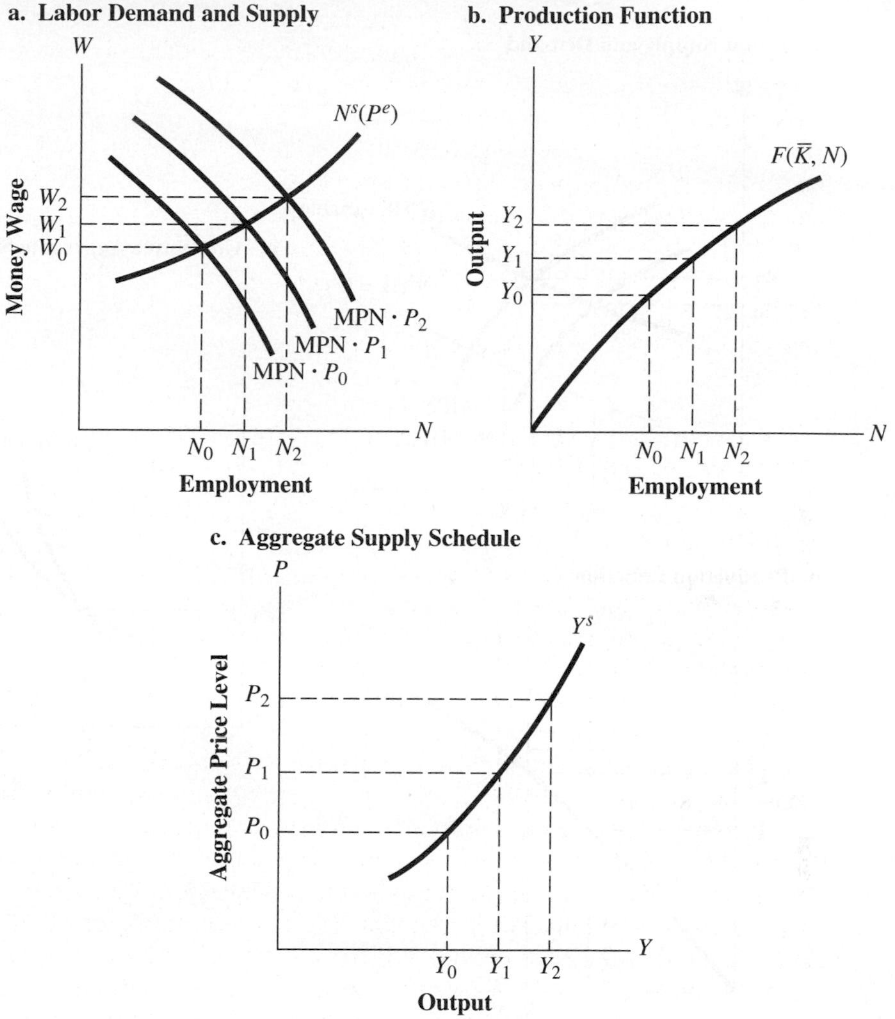

Part *a* shows equilibrium levels of employment N_0, N_1, N_2, corresponding to successively higher values of the price level, P_0, P_1, P_2. Part *b* gives the level of output, Y_0, Y_1, Y_2 that will be produced at each of these employment levels. Part *c* combines the information in parts *a* and *b* to show the relationship between the price level and output supplied. At higher values of the price level, output supplied increases; as in the fixed-wage case, *the aggregate supply curve* (Y^s) *is upward-sloping.*

Suppose that we compare the effects on price and output of a given change in aggregate demand when the money wage is variable with the effects for the case in which the money wage is fixed. Is there a predictable *quantitative* difference? The answer is yes. When the money wage is variable, a given increase in aggregate demand will cause output to increase by less than when the money wage is fixed. When the money wage is variable, an increase in aggregate demand will cause the price level to rise by more than when the money wage is fixed. The reason for these results is that the aggregate

FIGURE 8-10 Keynesian Aggregate Supply Schedules for the Fixed- and Variable-Money-Wage Cases

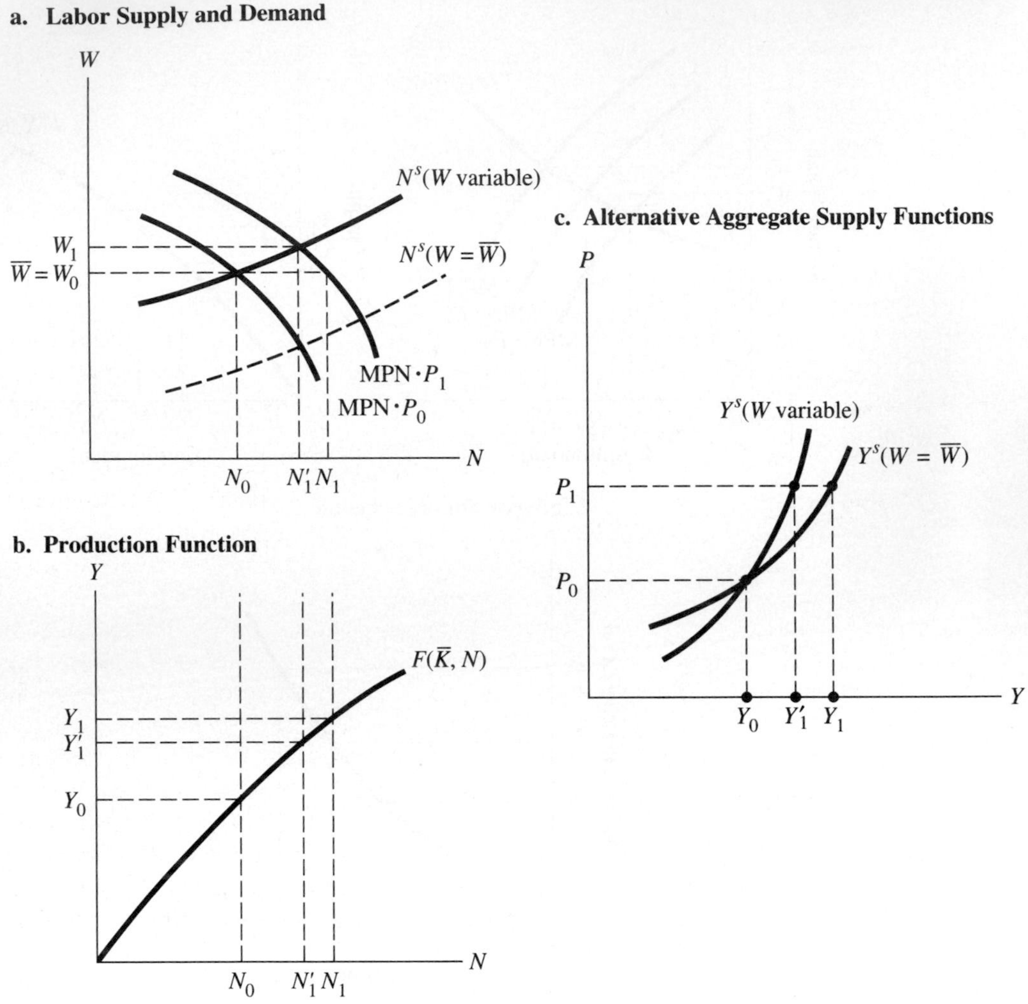

The aggregate supply schedule in part *c* for the case when the money wage is variable [Y^s(*W* variable)] is steeper than when the money wage is fixed [$Y^s(W = \overline{W})$] because the increase in employment (part *a*) with a rise in price and therefore the increase in output (part *b*) are smaller when the money wage is variable than when it is fixed. This outcome follows because the rise in the money wage in the variable-wage case dampens the effect on employment and output from an increase in the price level.

supply schedule when the money wage varies is steeper than when the money wage is fixed. As the aggregate demand schedule is shifted to the right along the steeper aggregate supply schedule, the increased demand results less in increased output and more in increased price.

The reason the aggregate supply schedule is steeper in the variable-money-wage case is illustrated in Figure 8-10. In Figure 8-10*a*, the labor market response to an increase in the price level is illustrated for the fixed- and variable-money-wage cases. If the money wage is fixed at $\overline{W} = W_0$ an increase in the price level from P_0 to P_1 shifts the labor demand schedule from MPN · P_0 to MPN · P_1, and employment rises from N_0 to N_1. Recall from the previous section that in the fixed-money-wage case, we assume there is an excess supply of labor. The labor supply schedule in this case, N^s $(W = \overline{W})$, is to the right of N_0 at $\overline{W}$ (as in Figure 8-5). Labor supply is no constraint on employment, which is determined solely by labor demand. For this case of $(W = \overline{W})$, output supplied can be seen from Figure 8-10*b* to rise from Y_0 to Y_1. The aggregate supply schedule is given by $Y^s(W = \overline{W})$ in Figure 8-10*c*.

With a variable money wage, when the labor demand schedule shifts from MPN · P_0 to MPN · P_1, as a result of the increase in price, employment rises only to N_1'. Here we are assuming that there is no initial excess supply of labor. At W_0, labor demand equals supply along the labor supply schedule N^s (*W* variable). The money wage must rise from W_0 to W_1 to increase labor supply. This increase in the money wage dampens the effect of the increase in labor demand. Because employment increases by less than in the fixed-wage case, output supplied also increases by less, rising only to Y_1', as shown in Figure 8-10*b*. The increase in the price level leads to a smaller rise in output supplied, and this relationship is reflected in the steeper aggregate supply schedule for the variable-money-wage case, as shown in Figure 8-10*c*, the Y^s (*W* variable) schedule.

At this point, it is useful to draw some conclusions from the preceding two sections concerning how allowing price and wage flexibility affects the policy implications of the Keynesian system. In Section 8.3, we saw that when the price level was assumed to vary (the money wage still fixed), policy multipliers were reduced relative to their values in the simple *IS–LM* model of Chapter 7, where both the price level and the money wage had been fixed. In that simple *IS–LM* model, the assumption was that the aggregate supply schedule was horizontal. Supply was no barrier to an increase in output. In the model in Section 8.3, we were taking account of the fact that in normal circumstances, as output increases, the MPN declines. Because the unit cost of producing additional units of output is the money wage divided by the MPN, firms will supply a greater output only at a higher price—even if the money wage is fixed. The aggregate supply schedule was upward-sloping, and increases in aggregate demand consequently had smaller output effects than with the horizontal aggregate supply schedule.

When the money wage is also assumed to be variable, the implied aggregate supply schedule becomes steeper. Now as output is increased, not only does the MPN decline, causing an increase in unit costs (*W*/MPN), but the rise in the money wage required to induce workers to supply more labor will also push up the unit cost. As a result, any increase in output supplied requires a larger increase in price; the aggregate supply schedule is steeper. Aggregate demand changes have still smaller output effects.

In the classical system, the aggregate supply schedule was vertical; output was completely supply-determined. The price and wage were perfectly flexible. In the simple *IS–LM* model, output was completely demand-determined. Prices and wages were completely rigid. The models in these two sections, by introducing price and wage flexibility in the Keynesian system, have brought the Keynesian results closer to those of the classical model.

8.5 THE EFFECTS OF SHIFTS IN THE AGGREGATE SUPPLY SCHEDULE

So far in our development of the Keynesian theory of aggregate supply, we have focused on how taking account of supply factors changes the role of aggregate demand in determining output. The output and employment effects of changes in aggregate demand—shifts in the aggregate demand schedule—depend on the slope of the aggregate supply schedule. In addition, supply factors have an independent role in determining output and employment. Shifts can occur in the aggregate supply schedule, and such shifts will affect output, employment, and the price level.

Shifts in the aggregate supply schedule have at times played an important part in the Keynesian explanation of movements in price, output, and employment. In fact, if shifts in the aggregate supply schedule are not taken into account, the behavior of price, output, and unemployment over the decade of the 1970s cannot be explained within a Keynesian framework. To see why, consider the data in Table 8-2. Notice that while the GNP deflator increased substantially in each year between 1973 and 1981, real output fell in 3 of those years. In fact, output fell in 3 of the 4 most inflationary years.

This pattern of price and output changes is inconsistent with the Keynesian model unless shifts in the aggregate supply schedule are taken into account. Consider Figure 8-11. In part *a*, movements in output and price are caused by shifts in the aggregate demand schedule (from Y_0^d to Y_1^d, then to Y_2^d). In this case, increases in price (from P_0 to P_1, then to P_2) would be accompanied by increases in output (from Y_0 to Y_1, then to Y_2). The demand schedule shifts to the right along the fixed upward-sloping supply schedule, increasing both price and output. Shifts to the left in the aggregate demand schedule cause *both* output and price to fall. Therefore, shifts in the aggregate demand schedule do not explain the behavior of price and output in years such as 1974, 1975, and 1980, when output fell but price rose.

TABLE 8-2 Percentage Growth Rates in Real GNP and the GNP Price Deflator, 1973–81

Year	*Growth in Real GNP*	*Increase in GNP Deflator*
1973	5.8	5.8
1974	–0.6	8.8
1975	–1.2	9.3
1976	5.4	5.2
1977	5.5	5.8
1978	5.0	7.4
1979	2.8	8.6
1980	–0.3	9.2
1981	2.5	9.6

FIGURE 8-11 Price and Output Variations with Shifts in Aggregate Demand and Supply

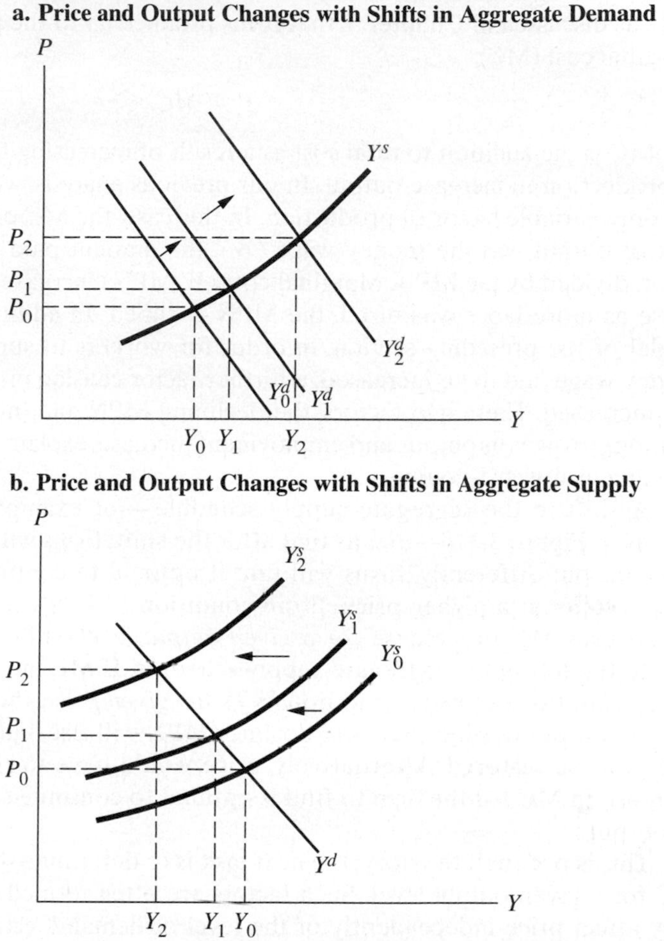

If changes in output were the result of shifts in the aggregate demand schedule along a fixed supply schedule, as in part *a*, we would expect a positive relationship between price and output changes. On the other hand, if output changes resulted from shifts in the aggregate supply schedule along a fixed demand schedule, as in part *b*, we would expect a negative association between price and output changes.

In Figure 8-11*b*, we can see that shifts to the left in the aggregate supply schedule (from Y_0^s to Y_1^s and to Y_2^s) would result in price increases (from P_0 to P_1, then to P_2) associated with declines in output (from Y_0 to Y_1, then to Y_2). Such "supply shocks" could explain the U.S. economy's inflationary recessions over the 1970s—periods when output declined and prices increased.

Factors That Shift the Aggregate Supply Schedule

The question remains of the causes of shifts in the aggregate supply schedule—the nature of supply shocks. Recall that points on the aggregate supply schedule give the desired output of the firms for each aggregate price level. Each firm, and therefore firms in the aggregate, will choose the level of output that maximizes profits. This implies, as discussed in Chapter 3, that firms produce up to the point where P is equal to marginal cost (MC):

$$P = MC \tag{8.7}$$

MC is the addition to total cost as a result of increasing the use of variable factors of production to increase output. In our previous analysis, we assumed that labor was the only variable factor of production. In this case, the MC of producing an additional unit of output was the money wage (W), the amount paid for an additional unit of labor, divided by the MPN. Marginal cost (W/MPN) increased as output increased because as more labor was hired, the MPN declined. In addition, in the variable-wage model of the preceding section, in order for workers to supply additional labor, the money wage had to be increased, a further factor causing marginal cost to rise as output increased. These two factors, the declining MPN and increasing upward pressure on money wages as output and employment increase, explain why the aggregate supply schedule is upward-sloping.

A shift in the aggregate supply schedule—for example, a shift upward to the left, as in Figure 8-11*b*—means that after the shift, firms will produce less for a given price or, put differently, firms will find it optimal to continue to produce the same output, only at a higher price. From condition (8.7) it can be seen that any factor that causes MC to increase *for a given output level* will cause such a shift upward and to the left in the aggregate supply schedule. If MC increases for a given output, then to continue to meet condition (8.7) *at a given price*, the firm must decrease output. As output declines, MC will decline (MPN will rise and W will fall) and equality (8.7) can be restored. Alternatively, price would have to rise by the amount of the increase in MC for the firm to find it optimal to continue to produce the same level of output.

This is only half the story; the next task is to determine the factors that will change MC for a given output level. Such factors are often termed *cost push factors* because they affect price independently of the level of demand, acting by shifting the supply schedule. One set of cost push factors affects the money wage demands on the part of labor at a given level of employment; these are factors that shift the labor supply schedule as drawn, for example, in Figure 8-9. So far, we have considered one factor that shifts the labor supply schedule, a change in workers' expectation about the aggregate level of price (P^e).

In the preceding section, we assumed that workers' expected price level depended on the past behavior of prices and, hence, was given in the short run. Over time, however, as new information is received, workers will adjust their price expectation. Figure 8-12 shows the effect on labor supply and on the aggregate supply schedule of an increase in workers' expectations concerning the aggregate price level.

Suppose that as a result of observed past increases in the aggregate price level, workers' expectation of the current price level rose from P_0^e to P_1^e. The labor supply schedule would then shift to the left in Figure 8-12*a*, from $N^s(P_0^e)$ to $N^s(P_1^e)$. Less labor would be supplied at each money wage because with the higher expectation about the aggregate price level, a given money wage would correspond to a lower real wage. At

FIGURE 8-12 Shift in the Aggregate Supply Schedule with an Increase in the Expected Price Level

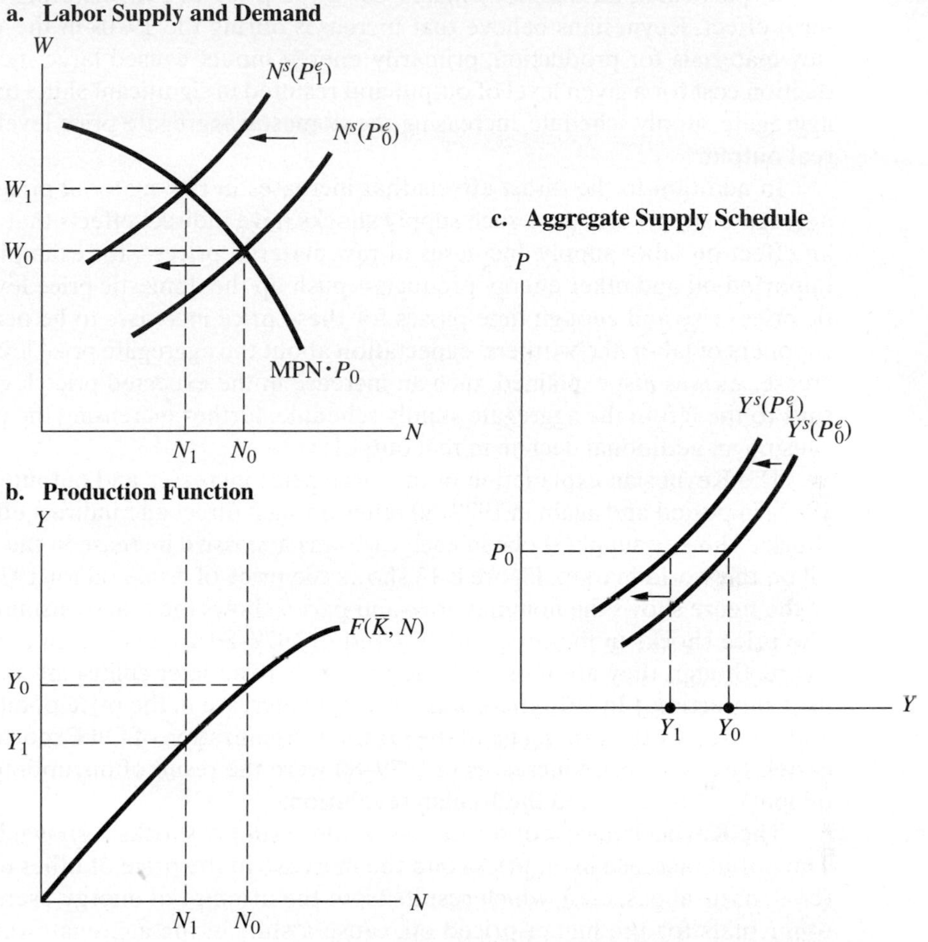

An increase in the expected price level shifts the labor supply schedule to the left from $N^s(P_0^e)$ to $N^s(P_1^e)$ in part *a*. At a given price level, P_0, employment declines from N_0 to N_1, and output falls from Y_0 to Y_1 (part *b*). This decline in output for a given price level is reflected in a shift to the left in the aggregate supply schedule from $Y^s(P_0^e)$ to $Y^s(P_1^e)$ in part *c*.

the initial price level P_0, the shift in the labor supply schedule would reduce employment (from N_0 to N_1). Consequently, output at price level P_0 would fall (from Y_0 to Y_1), as can be seen in Figure 8-12*b*. The aggregate supply schedule would shift to the left in Figure 8-12*c* [from $Y^s(P_0^e)$ to $Y^s(P_1^e)$].

Thus, any factor that shifts the labor supply schedule upward to the left, lowering labor supply for a given money wage or, what amounts to the same thing, increasing the money wage at which a given amount of labor will be supplied shifts the aggregate supply schedule to the left. If we broaden our analysis to allow for variable factors of production other than labor, it follows that an autonomous increase in the price of *any* variable factor of production will increase MC for a given output level and shift the aggregate supply schedule to the left.

In particular, autonomous increases in the price of raw materials have this cost push effect. Keynesians believe that increases during the 1970s in the world price of raw materials for production, primarily energy inputs, caused large increases in production cost for a given level of output and resulted in significant shifts to the left in the aggregate supply schedule, increasing the domestic aggregate price level and reducing real output.

In addition to the direct effects that increases in raw material prices have on the aggregate supply schedule, such supply shocks have indirect effects that come through an effect on labor supply. Increases in raw material prices—for example, the price of imported oil and other energy products—push up the domestic price level. As domestic prices rise and enough time passes for these price increases to be perceived by the suppliers of labor, the workers' expectation about the aggregate price level (P^e) will increase. As was just explained, such an increase in the expected price level will cause a shift to the left in the aggregate supply schedule, further increasing the price level and causing an additional decline in real output.

The Keynesian explanation of the large price increases and output declines in the 1973–75 period and again in 1979–80 relies on such direct and indirect effects of supply shocks. The key supply shock in each case was a massive increase in the price of crude oil on the world market. Figure 8-13 shows the price of crude oil for 1970–2006. Part *a* of the figure shows the nominal price and part *b* shows the real (constant-dollar) price. The price shocks in the series in 1974 and in 1979–80 are evident in both parts of the figure, though they are most notable in part *b*. (The later spikes are discussed in the next subsection.) In 1974 there was a fourfold increase in the price of oil (nominal and real) caused by the firming up of the OPEC (Organization of Oil Exporting Countries) cartel. The large price increases in 1979–80 were the result of disruptions in the world oil market that followed the Iranian revolution.

The Keynesian view of the effects of these supply shocks is shown in Figure 8-14. The initial increase in oil prices and the increase in the price of other energy sources (coal, natural gas, etc.), which results from the attempt of energy users to substitute other fuels for the higher-priced oil, cause a shift in the aggregate supply schedule from $Y_0^s(P_0^e)$ to $Y_1^s(P_0^e)$. Output declines from Y_0 to Y_1, and price rises from P_0 to P_1. This is the direct effect of the supply shock. As prices of energy-related products and of all products that use such energy in the production process—a virtually all-inclusive category—rise, labor suppliers in time perceive the increase in price; the expected price level rises (from P_0^e to P_1^e). There is a further shift to the left in the aggregate supply schedule, from $Y_1^s(P_0^e)$ to $Y_1^s(P_1^e)$. Price increases further to P_2, and output declines to Y_2.

More Recent Supply Shocks

Figure 8-13 shows that the price of oil remained volatile during the post-1980 period. Oil prices fell sharply in the years from 1981 to 1986 as new sources became available and the OPEC cartel weakened. This was in effect a favorable supply shock. By simply reversing the graphical analysis in Figure 8-14, we can see that such a favorable shock would, in the absence of other changes, reduce the aggregate price level and increase output. In fact, during the first half of this period, there was

FIGURE 8-13 Oil Prices, 1970–2006

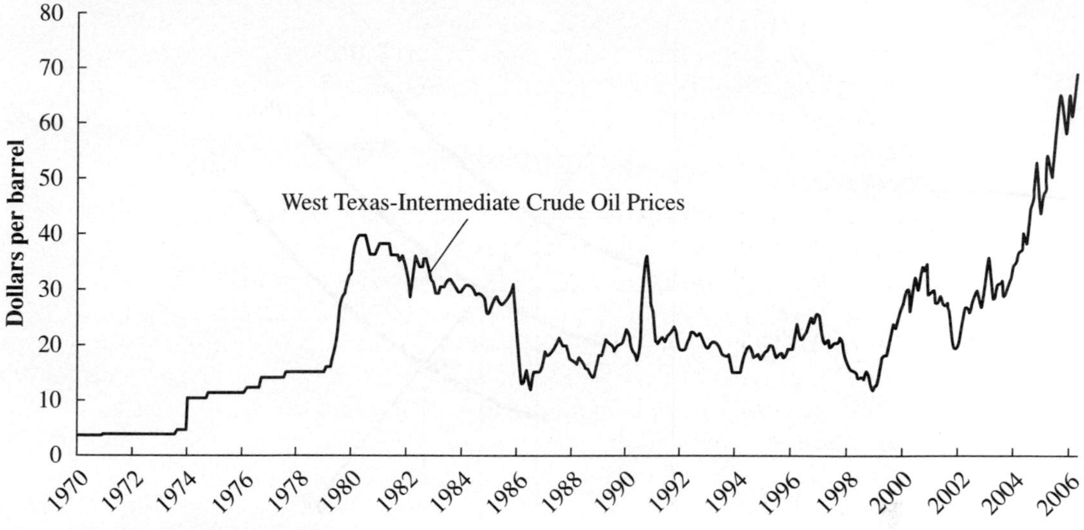

a. The Nominal Price of Oil

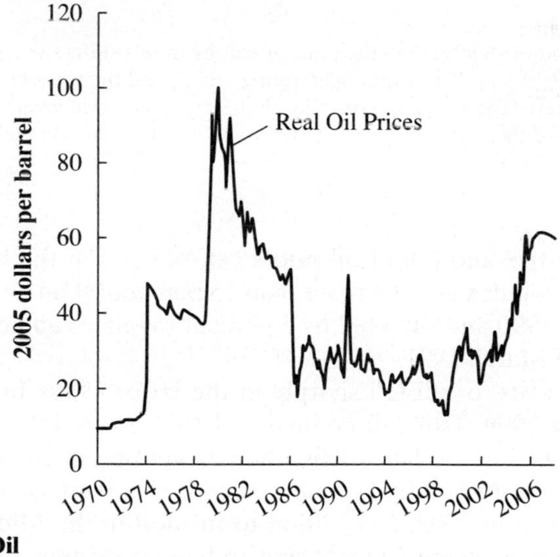

b. The Real Price of Oil

a severe recession, which in the Keynesian view was caused by demand-side factors. The decline in the price of oil did contribute to the dramatic fall in the inflation rate during these years.

The next large change in oil prices came in August 1990, following Iraq's invasion of Kuwait. The price of oil shot up as Kuwaiti oil production was halted and the United Nations placed an embargo on Iraqi oil exports. The price of oil declined as rapidly as it had risen once a swift victory of UN forces was evident in early 1991. The effects of

FIGURE 8-14 Effects of an Autonomous Increase in the World Price of Energy Inputs

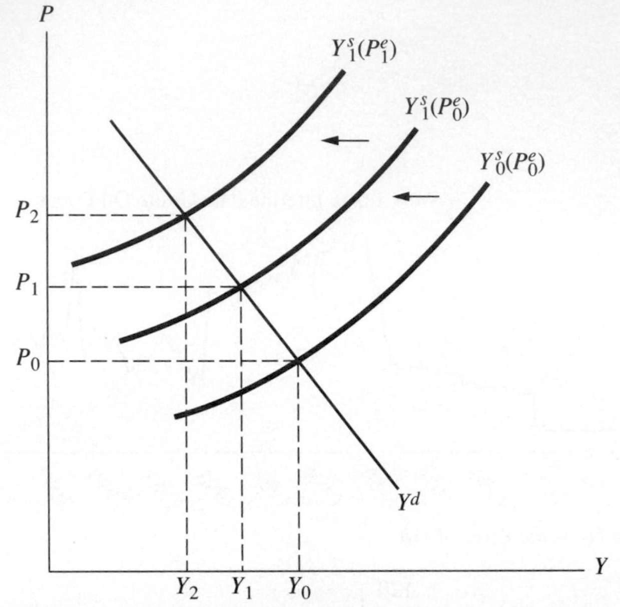

An autonomous increase in the price of energy inputs shifts the aggregate supply schedule to the left from $Y_0^s(P_0^e)$ to $Y_1^s(P_0^e)$; output falls from Y_0 to Y_1 and the price level rises from P_0 to P_1. As labor suppliers perceive the rise in the price level, the expected price level rises from P_0^e to P_1^e. The aggregate supply schedule shifts farther to the left to $Y_1^s(P_1^e)$. Output falls to Y_2, and the price level rises to P_2.

both the rise and fall of oil prices can be seen in the behavior of the producer price index. The index rose by more than 15 percent (at an annual rate) between August and October 1990 and then fell by 5 percent (again at an annual rate) between December 1990 and March 1991.

The price of oil fell sharply in the latter 1990s, bottoming out at about $10 per barrel in 1999. This fall contributed to the low inflation in the United States and Europe during the late 1990s. Then, beginning in 2000, the price of oil began to rise rapidly in both real and nominal terms. This increase accelerated with the U.S. invasion of Iraq in 2003. In addition to turmoil in the Mideast, rising demand for oil by the rapidly growing Chinese and Indian economies pushed up oil prices. This latest period of rapidly rising oil prices has had only modest effects on the industrialized economies. One reason is that these economies have reduced their dependence on oil to some extent. Oil input per dollar of GDP in industrialized countries has fallen by approximately 50 percent in the years since 1972. This has been partly due to the increased share of services relative to goods in GDP. Moveover, as Figure 8-13*b* shows, the large rises in nominal oil prices in recent years have still left the real price of oil lower than it was in the late 1970s.

Still, the recent rise in the price of oil and other sources of energy poses a threat to the economies of the oil-importing countries and a challenge to their policymakers. Another surge in the price of oil in 2007 pushed its real price nearly up to the late 1970s

FIGURE 8-15 Classical and Keynesian Aggregate Supply and Demand Schedules

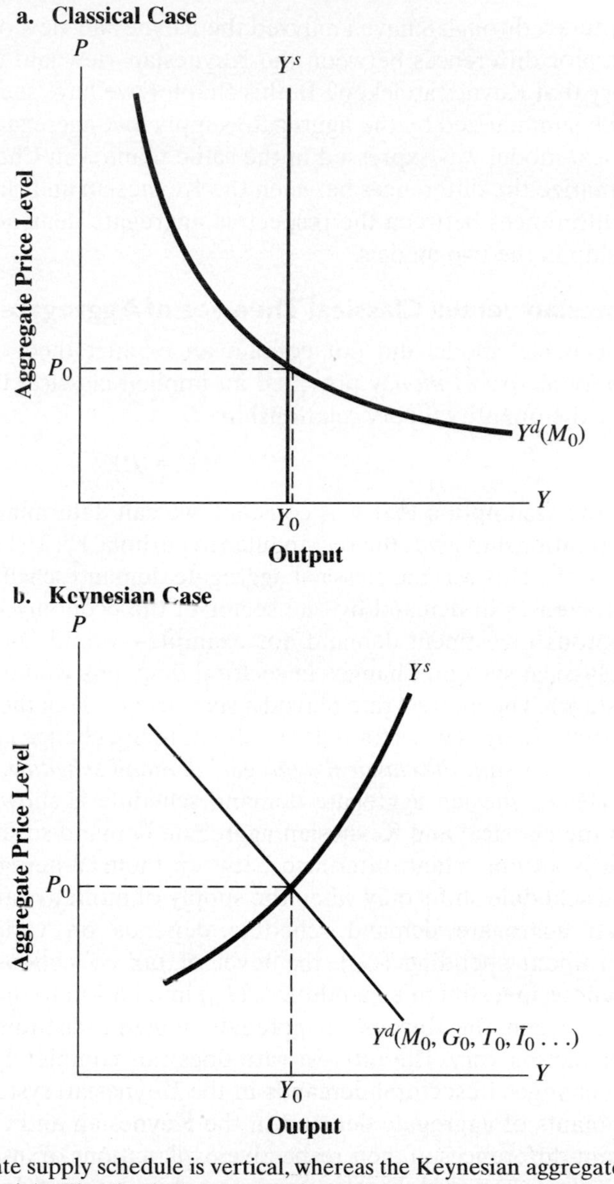

The classical aggregate supply schedule is vertical, whereas the Keynesian aggregate supply schedule slopes upward to the right. The classical aggregate demand schedule depends only on the level of the money supply (M_0); in the Keynesian system, aggregate demand depends also on fiscal variables (G_0, T_0), autonomous investment (I_0), and other variables.

peak. Moreover, the prices of many agricultural products have been rising rapidly. This is related to the rise in energy prices, as some agricultural products, such as corn in the United States and sugar in Brazil, have been diverted from food production for use in producing ethanol. The resilience of the U.S. and other industrialized economies to these further supply shocks has yet to be tested.

8.6 CONCLUSION: KEYNES VERSUS THE CLASSICS

Chapters 5 through 8 have analyzed the Keynesian view of macroeconomics. What are the major differences between the Keynesian view and the classical macroeconomic theory that Keynes attacked? In this chapter, we have seen how the Keynesian system can be summarized by the aggregate supply and aggregate demand relationships. The classical model was expressed in the same manner in Chapter 4. A convenient way to summarize the differences between the Keynesian and classical theories is to examine the differences between the respective aggregate demand and aggregate supply relationship in the two models.

Keynesian versus Classical Theories of Aggregate Demand

The classical model did not contain an explicit theory of aggregate demand. The *quantity theory of money* provided an implicit classical theory of aggregate demand. Using the quantity theory relationship

$$MV = PY \tag{8.8}$$

with the assumption that V is constant, we can determine PY for a given value of M. This relationship gives the rectangular hyperbola $Y^d(M_0)$ plotted in Figure 8-15*a* for M equals M_0. This was the classical aggregate demand schedule.

Increases in demand by one sector of the economy—government demand or autonomous investment demand, for example—would not affect aggregate demand in the classical system. Changes in sectoral demands would cause adjustments in the interest rate. The interest rate played a stabilizing role in the classical system and ensured that such changes in sectoral demands could not change aggregate demand. *Only monetary factors shift the classical aggregate demand schedule.*

The Keynesian aggregate demand schedule is shown in Figure 8-15*b*. Although both the classical and Keynesian aggregate demand schedules are downward-sloping, there is an important difference between them. Whereas the classical aggregate demand schedule shifts only when the supply of money changes, the position of the Keynesian aggregate demand schedule depends on variables such as the level of government spending (G_0), the level of tax collections (T_0), and the level of autonomous investment expenditures ($\bar{I}_0$) in addition to the quantity of money (M_0). As we have seen, the Keynesian aggregate demand schedule will shift when any of these other factors vary. The interest rate does not completely insulate aggregate demand from changes in sectoral demands in the Keynesian system. This difference in the determinants of aggregate demand in the Keynesian and classical models produces important differences in their respective explanations of instability in the economy.

Keynes believed that the instability of investment demand was the major cause of cyclical fluctuations in income. Autonomous changes in investment demand caused by changes in expectations cause shifts in the aggregate demand schedule and consequently instability in price and output.

Keynesian versus Classical Theories of Aggregate Supply

The classical aggregate supply schedule, shown in Figure 8-15*a*, is vertical, resulting from the classical assumptions about the labor market. Labor supply and demand are assumed to depend only on the real wage, which is known to all. The money wage is assumed to be perfectly flexible, adjusting quickly to equate supply and demand. Because the aggregate supply schedule is vertical, output and employment are completely supply-determined.

In the short run, the Keynesian aggregate supply schedule slopes upward to the right. We would expect the schedule to be quite flat at levels of output well below full capacity and to become steeper as full-capacity output is approached. The Keynesian view of aggregate supply (Sections 8.3 and 8.4) emphasizes the stickiness of the money wage and the failure of market participants to perceive the real wage correctly. As a consequence, the labor market will not be in continual equilibrium at full employment. Actual output and employment will not be completely determined by the supply factors. Shifts in the aggregate demand function will move the economy along the upward-sloping supply schedule, causing output to change. In the Keynesian system, the level of aggregate demand is important in determining the level of output and employment.

The Keynesian aggregate supply schedule in Figure 8-15*b* was termed a *short-run supply schedule*, to emphasize that it pertained to a short period of time, not to a long-run equilibrium situation. Factors such as explicit long-term labor contracts, implicit contracts, and resistance to wage cuts seen as cuts in the relative wage would slow but not permanently prevent the necessary wage adjustment to return the economy to a full-employment level. Imperfect information about the real wage on the part of labor suppliers would also be a short-run phenomenon. Eventually, expectations would approach the actual value of the price level and, hence, of the real wage. The Keynesians do not deny that eventually the economy would approach full employment. But to the Keynesians, such long-run classical properties of the economy are unimportant. They agree with Keynes that "this *long run* is a misleading guide to current affairs. *In the long run* we are all dead. Economists set themselves too easy, too useless a task if in tempestuous seasons they can only tell us that when the storm is long past the ocean is flat again."[5]

Keynesian versus Classical Policy Conclusions

Classical economists stressed the self-adjusting tendencies of the economy. If left free from destabilizing government policies, the economy would achieve full employment. Classical economists were noninterventionist in that they did not favor active monetary and fiscal policies to stabilize the economy. Such policies, to affect aggregate demand, would have no effects on output or employment given the supply-determined nature of those variables in the classical system.

Keynesians view the economy as unstable as a result of the instability of aggregate demand, primarily its private-investment component. Aggregate demand does affect output and employment in the Keynesian view. Consequently, swings in aggregate demand will cause undesirable fluctuations in output and employment in the short run. These fluctuations can be prevented by using monetary and fiscal policies to offset undesirable changes in aggregate demand.

[5]John M. Keynes, *A Tract on Monetary Reform* (London: Macmillan, 1923), p. 80.

REVIEW QUESTIONS AND PROBLEMS

1. Explain why the Keynesian aggregate demand schedule is downward-sloping when plotted against the price level.
2. Derive the Keynesian aggregate demand schedule for the case in which investment is completely interest-inelastic and therefore the *IS* schedule is vertical (follow the procedure in Figure 8-2). Explain the resulting slope of the aggregate demand-schedule for this case.
3. In what sense is the classical theory of aggregate supply "fundamentally incompatible" with the Keynesian system?
4. Why are fiscal policy multipliers smaller in magnitude in the variable price–fixed wage version of the Keynesian model than in the fixed-price *IS–LM* model? Why are these multipliers still smaller when we allow the money wage as well as the price level to be variable?
5. Return to the case considered in question 2, where investment is completely interest-inelastic and the *IS* schedule is vertical. Analyze the effects of an increase in government spending in this case within the variable price–fixed wage version of the Keynesian model. Compare the effects with those in the fixed price version of the model.
6. Analyze the effects of an increase in the money supply within the Keynesian model where both the price level and money wage are assumed to be variable. Include in your answer the effects on the level of real income, the price level, the interest rate, and the money wage.
7. In the Keynesian system, increases in aggregate demand lead to increases in output because the money wage rises less than proportionately with the price level in response to such increases in demand. This condition is necessary because firms will hire more workers only if the real wage (W/P) falls. Explain the possible reasons why the money wage does not adjust proportionately with the price level in the short-run Keynesian model.
8. Assume that there is an exogenous decline in the price of imported oil. Using the graphical analysis in this chapter, explain how such a shock would affect output and the price level. Explain the role inflationary expectations play in this adjustment.
9. "Money is more important in the Keynesian system than in the classical system." Do you agree? Or would you maintain that the opposite is true?
10. What do you see as the essential differences between the classical and Keynesian theories of aggregate supply?
11. What do you see as the essential differences between the classical and Keynesian theories of aggregate demand?
12. Compare the effects of an expansionary fiscal policy action—an increase in government spending financed by government bond sales to the public, for example—in the Keynesian and classical models. Include in your answer the effects of this policy shift on the level of real income, employment, the price level, and the rate of interest.
13. Within the variable price–variable wage version of the Keynesian model, analyze the effects that an unfavorable supply shock, such as a rise in the price of oil, would have on the rate of interest. Would the equilibrium rate of interest rise or fall?

PART THREE

Macroeconomic Theory After Keynes

The Keynesian revolution created a new framework in which macroeconomic questions were addressed. Little time passed, however, before there were challenges to the new orthodoxy, challenges that had roots in the classical model. In this part, we consider these challenges and the Keynesian responses to them.

CHAPTER 9

The Monetarist Counterrevolution

The British news magazine *The Economist* defined a monetarist as someone "who thinks it more important to regulate the supply of money in an economy than to influence other economic instruments. This is thought very wicked by those who can't be bothered to find out what it means." In this chapter we examine the monetarist position.

The Keynesian attack on the classical orthodoxy was successful. After Keynes died in 1946, his successors took up the task of refining his theories and applying them to the policy questions facing Western nations as they converted to peacetime economies in the aftermath of World War II. As we have seen, one aspect of the Keynesian revolution was an attack on the classical quantity theory of money. In fact, *early* Keynesian economists attached very little importance to the money supply. Monetarism began as an attempt to reassert the importance of money and therefore of monetary policy.

Milton Friedman, who died at age 94 in November 2006, was the major intellectual force in the early development of monetarism. Friedman was a longtime professor at the University of Chicago. After his retirement in 1977, he became a senior fellow at the Hoover Institution at Stanford University. Friedman published articles in professional economics journals as late a 2005. At the time of his death, many publications wrote of him as one of the two most influential economists of the twentieth century. The other was Keynes.

9.1 MONETARIST PROPOSITIONS

Rather than give a definition of monetarism, we list four propositions that characterize the monetarist position:

1. The supply of money is the dominant influence on nominal income.
2. In the long run, the influence of money is primarily on the price level and other *nominal* magnitudes. In the long run, *real* variables, such as output and employment, are determined by real, not monetary, factors.
3. In the short run, the supply of money does influence real variables. Money is the dominant factor causing cyclical movements in output and employment.
4. The private sector is inherently stable. Instability in the economy is primarily the result of government policies.

The central policy conclusion that follows from these propositions is that stability in the growth of the money supply is crucial for a stable economy. Monetarists believe that such stability is best achieved by adopting a rule for monetary policy. Milton Friedman long proposed a constant money growth rate rule. In hindsight, though, the crucial element of Friedman's view is the preference for monetary policy by a rule, not by discretion. Monetary policy, he often said, was "too important to be left to central bankers."

The first monetarist proposition is that the level of economic activity in current dollars is determined primarily by the supply of money. An important element in this proposition is that causation is assumed to be primarily from money to income. For the most part, changes in the money supply are assumed to *cause* changes in nominal income. The level and rate of growth of the money supply are assumed to be determined primarily by the central bank.

The second monetarist proposition asserts that, in the long run, economic activity measured in real dollars does not depend on the quantity of money. In the long run, real output is determined by real factors such as the stock of capital goods, the size and quality of the labor force, and the state of technology. If, in the long run, the level of real economic activity is not affected by the quantity of money, while the level of economic activity in nominal terms is almost completely determined by the supply of money, it follows that the long-run effect of money is on the price level.

The third proposition states that, in the short run, output and employment *are* strongly influenced by changes in the supply of money. Prices are influenced as well, but in the short run, prices, including wage rates (the price of labor), are not perfectly flexible. Thus, when the quantity of money changes, in the short-run prices do not make the full adjustment. Output and employment are also affected.

The fourth monetarist proposition asserts that the private sector (businesses and households) is not the source of instability in the economy. As one monetarist, Karl Brunner, put it, the private sector is "essentially a shock-absorbing, stabilizing and self-adjusting process. Instability is produced dominantly by the operation of the government sector." The government causes instability in the economy primarily by allowing instability in the growth of the money supply, the major determinant of economic activity. In the monetarist view, the government can also destabilize the economy by interfering with the normal adjustment mechanisms in the private economy. Mandatory controls on prices and wages are an obvious example of government interference with such adjustment properties. Other examples are usury ceilings on interest rates, rent controls, and minimum wage laws.

In considering these propositions and monetarist policy conclusions, it is convenient to divide the analysis into two parts. First, we examine the reasons why the monetarists ascribe such predominance to money (i.e., the basis of propositions 1 and 3). We postpone until Chapter 10 the question of what monetary policy cannot do, the basis for proposition 2. Although proposition 4 is not given separate consideration, it will be important in our discussion.

9.2 THE REFORMULATION OF THE QUANTITY THEORY OF MONEY

The early development of monetarism centered on redefining the quantity theory of money in light of Keynes's attack. Milton Friedman described the classical quantity theory as follows:

> In monetary theory, that analysis was taken to mean that in the quantity equation $MV = PT$ the term for velocity could be regarded as highly stable, that it could be taken as determined independently of the other terms in the equation, and that as a result changes in the quantity of money would be reflected either in prices or in output.[1]

[1]Milton Friedman, *The Counter-revolution in Monetary Theory* (London: Institute of Economic Affairs, 1970), p. 12

This is proposition 1 of monetarism, (Notice that stable velocity means not only that changes in M will cause changes in PT but also that *only* changes in M can change PT.)

The quantity theory had come into disrepute, together with the rest of classical economics, as a result of the Great Depression of the 1930s. Friedman believed that the events of the 1930s had been improperly assessed and did not, in fact, offer evidence against the quantity theory of money. He did, however, see the need to restate the quantity theory in terms that took account of Keynes's contribution. His purpose was to reassert the importance of money. The reasons he felt this reassertion was needed can be seen best by first considering the role (or lack of a role) that some early Keynesians attributed to money as a determinant of economic activity.

Money and the Early Keynesians

Our analysis of the Keynesian system made it clear that within that framework money was one important determinant of economic activity. But velocity was not constant or independently determined; it was systematically determined within the system. Factors other than money could also affect the level of economic activity. Consider, for example, the response of the system to an increase in government spending, as depicted in Figure 9-1.

The increase in government spending from G_0 to G_1 shifts the IS schedule from $IS(G_0)$ to $IS(G_1)$. Income rises from Y_0 to Y_1, and the interest rate increases from r_0 to r_1.

FIGURE 9-1 Effects of an Increase in Government Spending: The Keynesian View

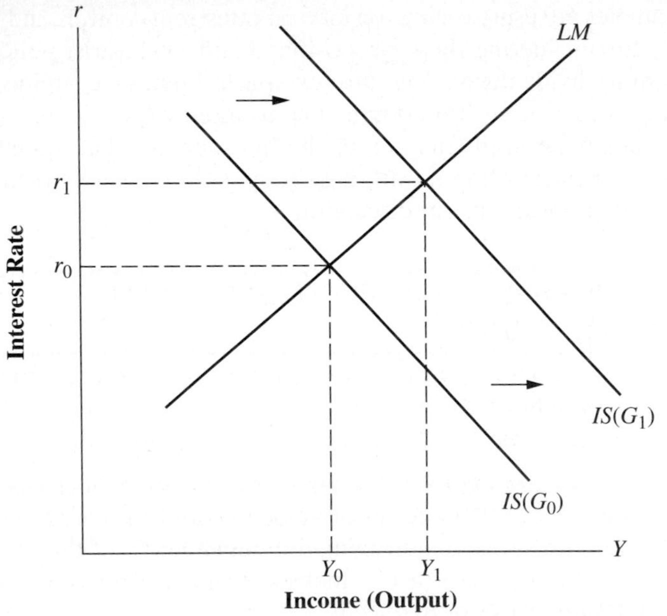

An increase in government spending shifts the IS schedule to the right. Both the interest rate and equilibrium level of income rise. Because the money supply is unchanged and income has risen, the velocity of money, the ratio of income to money, has increased.

The money supply is held constant here, with the increased government spending assumed to be financed by selling bonds to the public. The higher level of income causes a higher transactions demand for money. Bringing money demand back to equality with the unchanged money supply requires a rise in the interest rate. At the higher interest rate the speculative demand for money will have declined, and the demand for transactions balances *at a given level of income* will also have fallen. Thus, the same money supply can support a higher income level. Another way to express this finding is to say that velocity varies positively with the interest rate.

Because velocity is variable in the Keynesian system, there is no one level of income corresponding to a given money supply. It is not even an approximately accurate statement of the Keynesian view that in the short run nominal or real income is determined solely by the level of the money supply. This is not to say that Keynesians believe that money is unimportant; they do not. The quantity of money is *one* key determinant of income in the Keynesian system.

Many *early* Keynesian economists (circa 1945–50) did, however, believe that money was of little importance. Their view was based on empirical judgments about the slopes of the *IS–LM* schedules, which, as we saw in our analysis of the Keynesian system, are important in determining the relative effectiveness of monetary and fiscal policy. Influenced by the Depression, they believed that the *LM* schedule was quite flat and the *IS* schedule quite steep—the configuration that would be characteristic of depression conditions such as those of the 1930s. The Depression was characterized by low levels of income and a low interest rate. At such a low level of the interest rate, the elasticity of money demand would be high, for reasons discussed in Chapter 6. Such a situation approaches the liquidity trap; the *LM* schedule becomes very flat. Further, in depression conditions, the early Keynesian economists believed that investment would be relatively interest-inelastic, making the *IS* schedule steep. The Depression was a period with a very low utilization rate of existing plant and equipment. Early Keynesian economists thought that, with massive excess capacity, investment would be unlikely to respond much to changes in the interest rate.

Figure 9-2 shows this configuration of the *IS* and *LM* schedules and illustrates the ineffectiveness of an increase in the quantity of money that shifts the *LM* schedule from LM_0 to LM_1. With the *LM* schedule flat around the point of equilibrium, a given change in the money supply does very little to lower the interest rate, the first link in the chain connecting money and income in the Keynesian model. Further, with a steep *IS* schedule, a drop in the interest rate would not increase investment very much. This combination of an assumed high interest elasticity of money demand and low interest elasticity of investment led early Keynesian economists to conclude that money was unimportant.

What role was there for monetary policy? During World War II, much of the war expenditure had been financed by selling bonds to the public at relatively low interest rates. Keeping the interest rate on bonds low and stable would have the desirable effects of keeping the cost of interest payments on the debt low and protecting the capital value of the bonds for the investors (recall that bond prices and interest rates vary inversely). Low interest rates also meant that monetary policy would make whatever limited contribution it could to strengthening aggregate demand. Because early Keynesian economists feared a return to the depression conditions of the 1930s, this was another desirable feature of low interest rates. Thus, low and stable interest rates

FIGURE 9-2 Early Keynesian View of Monetary Policy Ineffectiveness

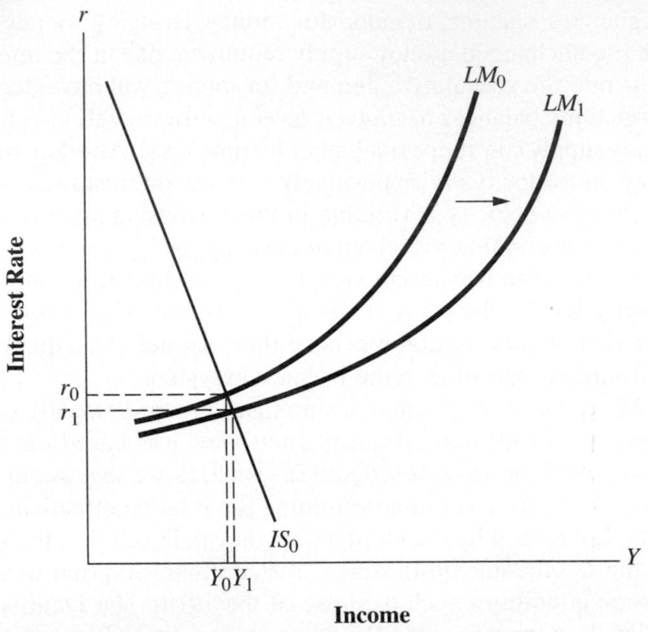

With the *IS* schedule quite steep and over the range where the *LM* schedule is nearly horizontal, an increase in the quantity of money, which shifts the *LM* schedule from LM_0 to LM_1, has little effect on income.

became the goal of monetary policy. To achieve this goal, the monetary authority cooperated with the U.S. Treasury to "peg" or fix the level of interest rates.

A further element in the view of the early Keynesians made pegging the interest rate desirable. Following Keynes, they felt that the demand for money was highly unstable. The *LM* schedule was not only flat (in the relevant range) but shifted around in an unpredictable way. These shifts would lead to instability in financial markets that could be avoided by pegging the interest rate.

In Chapter 17, we will consider the process by which the monetary authority can "peg" or fix the interest rate. For our purposes here, the key point is that, in doing so, the monetary authority loses control of the money supply. The monetary authority must supply whatever quantity of money it takes to produce equilibrium in the money (and therefore bond) market at the desired interest rate. To the early Keynesians, this loss of control of the money supply was not important because the quantity of money was not important.

Read Perspectives 9-1.

Friedman's Restatement of the Quantity Theory

Contrary to the view of early Keynesians, Friedman argued that the demand for money was stable. Contrary to the near-liquidity-trap characterization, Friedman maintained that the interest elasticity of money demand was certainly not infinite and was in fact

PERSPECTIVES 9.1

THE MONETARIST VIEW OF THE GREAT DEPRESSION

Both Friedman and the Keynesians agree that the Great Depression of the 1930s put the classical theories, including the quantity theory of money, in disrepute. Friedman, however, believes that the Keynesians misread the evidence from the Depression.

Friedman does not deny that the experience of the United States and other industrialized countries in the 1930s contradicts the classical view of the labor market, where the money wage adjusts quickly to maintain full employment. Friedman does believe that Keynesians wrongly concluded that the Depression disproved the quantity theory of money.

Table 9-1 shows the level of several macroeconomic aggregates in 1929, at the start of the Depression, compared with their level in 1933, at the low point of the slump. The table shows that nominal GNP fell 46.0 percent and real GNP fell 29.6 percent. The rest of the drop in nominal GNP is accounted for by a fall in the aggregate price level. Column 3 shows that the narrowly defined money supply, M1 (currency plus checkable deposits), fell by 26.5 percent between 1929 and 1933. The M2 measure of the money supply, a broader measure that includes other bank deposits, fell by 33.3 percent.

We see that there *was* a large decline in the money supply as we fell into the Great Depression, which is consistent with the quantity theory. Velocity also fell, as evidenced by the larger percentage decline in nominal income relative to the fall in either money supply measure. But quantity theorists would expect this outcome because, during the deflation of the Depression, the value of money (in terms of purchasing power) was rising. This rise would be likely to increase the demand for money for a given nominal income and therefore to lower velocity.

Keynesians dispute the monetary explanation of the Depression. They do believe that if the Federal Reserve had been able to prevent a decline in the money supply during the 1929–33 period, the Depression would have been less severe than it was. They believe, however, that the primary causes of the Depression were autonomous declines in several components of aggregate demand: consumption, investment, and exports, caused in turn by factors such as the stock market crash in 1929, overbuilding in the construction sector by the late 1920s, and the breakdown of the international monetary system. This has been called the *spending hypothesis*, in contrast to the *money hypothesis* advanced by Friedman and other monetarists.[a]

TABLE 9-1 Selected Macroeconomic Aggregates (1929, 1933)

	Nominal GNP($P \times Y$)	*Real GNP(Y) (1982 Dollars)*	*M1*	*M2*
1929	\$103.9 billion	\$708.6 billion	\$26.4 billion	\$46.2 billion
1933	\$56.0 billion	\$498.5 billion	\$19.4 billion	\$30.8 billion
Percentage decline	46.0%	29.6%	26.5%	33.3%

[a]For Friedman's analysis, see Milton Friedman and Anna J. Schwartz, *The Great Contraction* (Princeton, N.J.: Princeton University Press, 1965). Also on the subject of the causes of the Great Depression, see Peter Temin, *Did Monetary Forces Cause the Great Depression?* (New York: Norton, 1976), and *Lessons from the Great Depression* (Cambridge, Mass.: MIT Press, 1990).

"rather small." The quantity of money, far from being unimportant, was the dominant influence on the level of economic activity.

Friedman's conclusions rest on a restatement of the classical quantity theory of money. Friedman's version of the quantity theory is closest to the Cambridge approach we considered previously. That approach focused on the demand for money. The central relationship was

$$M^d = \bar{k}PY \tag{9.1}$$

expressing a proportional relationship between money demand (M^d) and the level of nominal income [price (P) times real income (Y)]. The factor of proportionality (k) was taken as constant in the short run.

Friedman emphasizes that the quantity theory was, as can be seen from equation (9.1), a theory of money demand. Because k was treated as a constant by the Cambridge economists and the *nominal* supply of money (M) was treated as being set exogenously by the monetary authority, the Cambridge equation can be transformed into a theory of nominal income,

$$M = M^d = \bar{k}PY$$

$$M\frac{1}{\bar{k}} = PY \tag{9.2}$$

or the alternative form (where V, the velocity of money, equals $1/k$)

$$M\bar{V} = PY \tag{9.3}$$

where the bar over k or V indicates that these magnitudes do not vary. Friedman examined the changes in the Cambridge theory of money demand that must be made in the light of Keynes's theory of money demand.

Keynes's theory of money demand stressed the role of money as an asset in addition to its role in transactions. In studying the factors that determined how much money people would hold, Keynes considered factors that determined the desirability of money relative to other assets. He made the simplifying assumption that other assets were a homogeneous enough group to be lumped together under the category "bonds." He then considered how an individual allocated wealth between money and bonds. The key factors that he thought determined the split were the level of income and the level of the interest rate. Put in terms of the Cambridge equation, Keynes focused on the interest rate as the primary determinant of k, the amount of money balances a person would hold for a given level of income. A rise in the interest rate led to a fall in k or, equivalently, a rise in velocity, as we saw in the preceding subsection. Because k was a variable, not a constant, the Cambridge equation could not by itself provide a theory of nominal income.

Friedman accepted Keynes's emphasis on the role of money as an asset. With this as a basis, he sets out his own theory of the demand for money. Again income is one determinant of money demand and, as with Keynes's analysis, we can view Friedman's analysis as providing a theory of what determines the Cambridge k, money holdings as a proportion of nominal income. Friedman's money demand function can be written as follows:

$$M^d = L(P, Y, r_B, r_E, r_D) \tag{9.4}$$

where P = price level

Y = real income

r_B = nominal interest rate on bonds

r_E = nominal return on equities

r_D = nominal return on durable goods

Money demand is assumed to depend on nominal income, the product of the first two arguments in the demand function. An increase in nominal income would increase money demand. For a given level of nominal income, Friedman assumes, as did Keynes, that the amount of money demanded depends on the rate of return offered on alternative assets. These are bonds (the asset Keynes focused on), equities (shares of stock in corporations), and durable goods such as consumer durables, land, and houses. Durable goods do not pay an explicit interest rate. Their return is the expected increase in the price of the good over the period for which it is held. Thus, the expected rate of inflation is also a determinant of money demand. An increase in the rate of return on any of these alternative assets causes the demand for money to decline.

Friedman's theory differs from Keynes's in several respects. First, Friedman views the money demand function as stable. Keynes's view was that the demand-for-money function was unstable, shifting with changes in the public confidence in the economy.

Second, Friedman does not segment money demand into components representing transaction balances, speculative demand, and a precautionary demand. Money, like other "goods," has attributes that make it useful, but Friedman does not find it helpful to specify separate demands based on each of the uses of money.

The third difference between Keynes's and Friedman's money demand theories is that Friedman includes separate yields for bonds, equities, and durable goods. Keynes focused on the choice of money versus bonds. It is not clear how substantive this difference is, since what Keynes termed *bonds* can be considered more broadly as at least including equities. Often this has not been done, however, and Keynesian analysis has focused narrowly on the choice between money and bonds. Friedman makes explicit the possibility of other substitutions and also allows for a shift from money directly into commodities (durable goods) as rates of return change.

Friedman's money demand theory can be used to restate the Cambridge equation as follows:

$$M^d = k(r_B, r_E, r_D)PY \qquad \textbf{(9.1')}$$

where instead of a constant k we now have k expressed as a function of the rates of return on the assets that are alternatives to holding money. A rise in the rate of return on any one of these alternative assets would cause k to fall, reflecting the increased desirability of the alternative asset. In these terms, we see that Friedman restated the quantity theory, providing a systematic explanation of k that takes into account the Keynesian analysis of money's role as an asset.

If this is the restated quantity theory, how would we characterize a modern quantity theorist? How would this person differ from a Keynesian? In Friedman's view, a quantity theorist believes the following:

1. The money demand function is stable.
2. This demand function plays an important role in determining the level of economic activity.
3. The quantity of money is strongly affected by money supply factors.

In Friedman's version of the Cambridge equation, the equilibrium condition in the money market is

$$M = M^d = k(r_B, r_E, r_D)PY \tag{9.5}$$

With a stable money demand function, an exogenous increase in the money supply must either lead to a rise in PY or cause declines in $r_B, r_E,$ and r_D (*which will cause k to rise*), *with indirect effects on PY*. A quantity theorist believes that the money demand function is in fact stable; that changes in the money supply come mostly from the supply side as a result of central bank policies; and finally, that changes in the quantity of money are important in determining nominal income (that much of the effect of a change in M comes in the form of a change in PY).

In what way does a quantity theorist differ from a Keynesian? Friedman's theory is antithetical to the early Keynesian position. The early Keynesians believed that the money demand function was unstable; that the interest elasticity of money demand was extremely high; and that, as a consequence, changes in the quantity of money did not have important predictable effects on the level of economic activity. In Friedman's view, the quantity theorist believes that the money demand function is stable and that the quantity of money is an important determinant of the level of economic activity. Further, Friedman believes, as we will see shortly, that the interest elasticity of money demand is low.

What about the differences between the quantity theory as outlined so far and the modern Keynesian position? Keynesians today believe that monetary policy is important. They believe that innovations in the financial sector during recent years have cast doubt on the stability of the money demand function. The problem is partly a matter of how to define money as new types of deposits become available. The monetarists recognize these definitional problems as well. On the interest elasticity of money demand, recent estimates by Keynesians are higher than suggested by Friedman's own research, but certainly not so high as to indicate the presence of a liquidity trap in most countries. Overall, if a quantity theorist or monetarist need only subscribe to the three propositions listed by Friedman, the modern Keynesian and modern quantity theory positions would differ but not be extremely far apart.

Friedman's Monetarist Position

Friedman, however, used his restatement of the quantity theory to develop a strong monetarist position that does produce sharp differences with the Keynesian position.

Friedman's monetarist position extends the quantity theory from a theory of money demand to one of nominal income. We have seen how the Cambridge quantity theorists extended the quantity theory with the assumption of a constant k [see equation (9.1) or (9.3)]. Friedman points out that his version of the quantity theory can also be turned into a theory of nominal income if the variables in his money demand function [equation (9.4)] other than nominal income (r_B, r_E, r_D) have little effect on money demand. This being the case, these variables will have little effect on k. Money holdings as a proportion of income (k) will be nearly constant. Friedman does not believe that money demand is completely independent of these rates of return, so the theory of nominal income that results from assuming that k is a constant will only be an approximation. But *any* theory will hold only approximately. Friedman and others have done empirical work that convinces them that such a strong monetarist position, which can be written as

FIGURE 9-3 *IS–LM*: A Monetarist Version

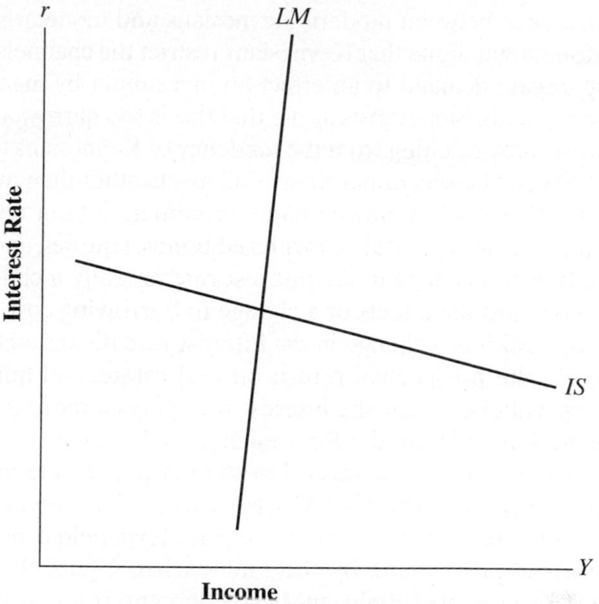

In the monetarist view, the *IS* schedule is quite flat, reflecting a high interest elasticity of aggregate demand. The *LM* schedule is nearly vertical, reflecting a very low interest elasticity of money demand.

$$PY = \frac{1}{k}M \tag{9.6}$$

is a better approximation than that given by simple representations of the Keynesian view. This monetarist position is required for statements by Friedman such as "I regard the description of our position as 'money is all that matters for changes in *nominal* income and for *short-run* changes in real income' as an exaggeration but one that gives the right flavor to our conclusions" or "appreciable changes in the rate of growth of the stock of money are a necessary and sufficient condition for appreciable changes in the rate of growth of money income."[2]

It is useful to represent the monetarist position in terms of the *IS–LM* diagram and the aggregate supply–aggregate demand framework used to explain the Keynesian position. In Figure 9-3, we have drawn *IS–LM* schedules as monetarists would. The *LM* schedule is nearly, but not quite, vertical, reflecting Friedman's view that the interest elasticity of money demand is low.

Another divergence from the Keynesian position concerns the slope of the *IS* schedule. Here a flatter *IS* schedule is consistent with the monetarist position that aggregate demand is quite sensitive to changes in the interest rate. Modern Keynesians also believe

[2]These two quotations are from Milton Friedman, "A Theoretical Framework for Monetary Analysis," in Robert Gordon, ed., *Milton Friedman's Monetary Framework* (Chicago: University of Chicago Press, 1974), p. 27; and Milton Friedman and Anna Schwartz, "Money and Business Cycles," *Review of Economics and Statistics*, 45, Suppl. (February 1963), pp. 32–64, respectively.

that the interest rate affects aggregate demand and would not argue that the *IS* schedule should be as nearly vertical as we drew it for the model of the early Keynesians (Figure 9-2). The difference between modern Keynesians and monetarists on this point is one of degree. Monetarists argue that Keynesians restrict the channels by which the interest rate affects aggregate demand to an effect on investment by means of a change in the cost of borrowing funds. Monetarists argue that this is too narrow an interpretation of the effects of interest rates, resulting from the tendency of Keynesians to think of "bonds" as just one class of financial assets rather than as all assets other than money.

In his theory of money demand, Friedman did not lump all nonmoney assets into one category. He separately considered bonds, equities, and durable goods. Monetarists believe that if a change in *the* interest rate is really a change in all these yields, its effects go beyond the effects of a change in borrowing cost to firms that buy investment goods. In addition, a change in *the* interest rate means a change in the prices of corporate stock, the prospective return on real estate, and holding durable goods as well. Monetarists believe that the interest rate plays a more important role in determining aggregate demand than the Keynesian model allowed.

Figure 9-3 brings out several of the features of the monetarist view, but it is deficient in one respect. The *IS–LM* schedules by themselves show how real GNP and the interest rate are determined, with the price level held constant. A constant price level is *not* an assumption made by the monetarists. Figure 9-4 shows the monetarist view within the aggregate supply–aggregate demand framework of previous chapters.

FIGURE 9-4 Aggregate Supply and Demand: The Monetarist View

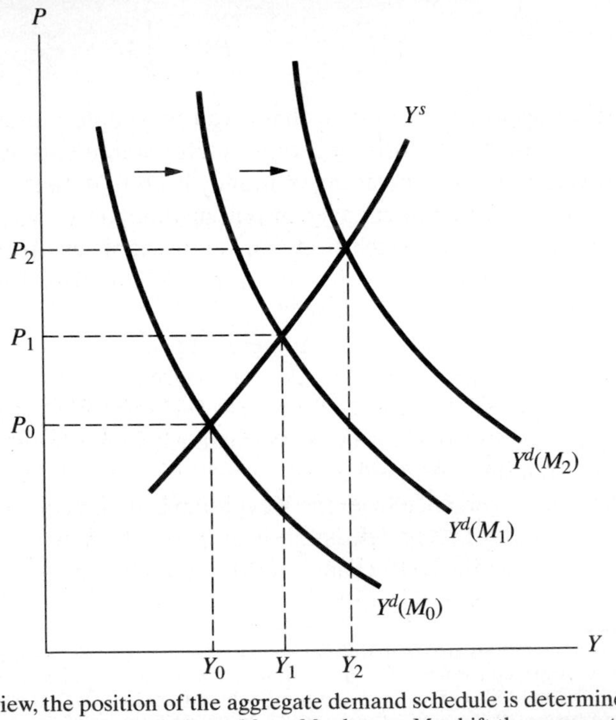

In the monetarist view, the position of the aggregate demand schedule is determined by the money supply. Increases in the money supply from M_0 to M_1, then to M_2, shift the aggregate demand schedule from $Y^d(M_0)$ to $Y^d(M_1)$, then $Y^d(M_2)$.

Three positions for the aggregate demand schedule are shown in the graph, $Y^d(M_0)$, $Y^d(M_1)$, and $Y^d(M_2)$, corresponding to three values of the money supply, M_0, M_1, and M_2. The monetarist position can be represented as asserting that changes in M are *required* for significant shifts in the aggregate demand schedule. Money is the only important systematic influence on aggregate demand.

Left unanswered is the question of what determines aggregate supply. The real variables that determine the position of the aggregate supply schedule will, in the monetarist view, determine the level of real output *in the long run* (see proposition 2). There is also the question of the slope of the aggregate supply schedule and, consequently, the proportions of a money-induced rise in nominal income that go to increase output and price, respectively. Those are the central questions of the next chapter. In the following section, we analyze the differing views of monetarists and Keynesians on the relative effectiveness of fiscal and monetary policies. Here the issue is the effect of these policies on aggregate demand, and we revert to the *IS–LM* graph to illustrate these policy differences.

9.3 FISCAL AND MONETARY POLICY

Fiscal Policy

The monetarist and Keynesian frameworks produce quite different views about the effectiveness of fiscal policy changes. The monetarist view on the effectiveness of fiscal policy has been expressed by Milton Friedman as follows: "I come to the main point—in my opinion, the state of the budget by itself has no significant effect on the course of nominal income, on deflation, or on cyclical fluctuations."[3] In reference to the Keynesian proposition that fiscal policy was effective, Friedman wrote: "The 'monetarists' rejected this proposition and maintained that fiscal policy by itself is largely ineffective, that what matters is what happens to the quantity of money."[4]

When Friedman discusses the independent effects of fiscal policy, the question at issue, he means the effects of changes in the government budget *holding constant the quantity of money*. Consider an increase in government spending. If tax rates are not changed, which has been our usual assumption when we consider one policy change at a time, the new spending must be financed by printing money or by selling bonds. Similarly for a tax cut, if spending is to be unchanged, lost tax revenues must be replaced by sales of bonds to the public or by printing new money.

If a tax cut or spending increase is financed by printing new money, we have both a monetary policy action (M increases) and a fiscal policy action (G increases or T falls). In terms of the *IS–LM* framework, both the *IS* and *LM* schedules shift. Monetarists *do not* argue that this type of policy change will be ineffective. They do argue that the policy effect will come mainly because the supply of money changes. The controversy is over what Friedman refers to as the effect of a change in the federal budget *by itself*, meaning without an accompanying change in the quantity of money. This means, in the case of a tax cut or spending increase, that the deficit created by these actions would be financed completely by sales of bonds to the public. The monetarist position is that such policy actions will have little systematic effect on nominal income (prices or real output).

[3]Milton Friedman and Walter Heller, *Monetary versus Fiscal Policy* (New York: Norton, 1969), p. 51.

[4]Friedman, *The Counter-revolution in Monetary Theory*, p. 18.

FIGURE 9-5 Effects of an Increase in Government Spending: The Monetarist Case

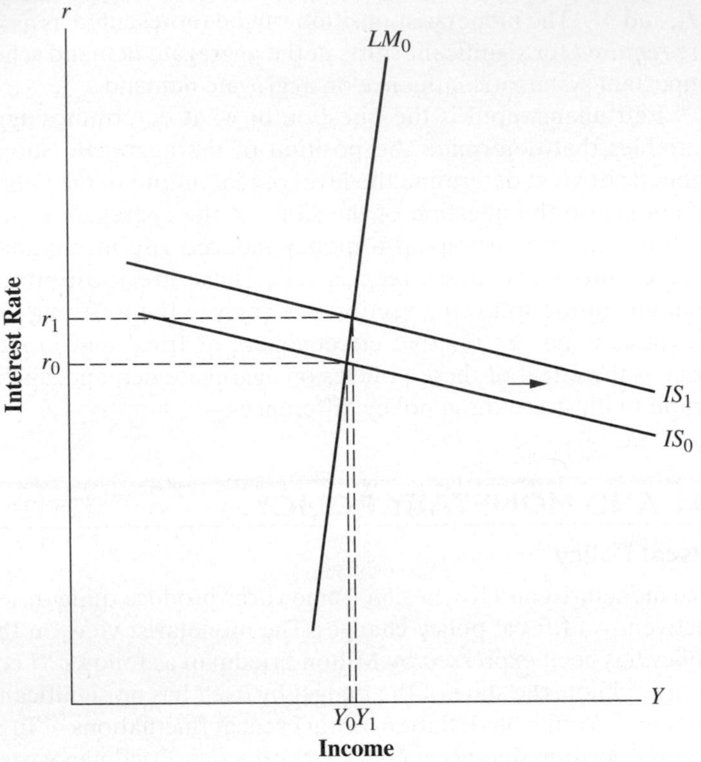

An increase in government spending shifts the *IS* schedule from IS_0 to IS_1. With the relatively flat *IS* schedule and the nearly vertical *LM* schedule, this fiscal policy action has little effect on income (Y rises only from Y_0 to Y_1).

The reasons monetarists reach this conclusion can be seen from Figure 9-5. There we consider the effects of an increase in government spending when we accept the monetarist assumptions about the slopes of the *IS* and *LM* schedules. An increase in government spending from G_0 to G_1 shifts the *IS* schedule to the right, from IS_0 to IS_1. The effect of the increase in government spending in the monetarist case is to cause the interest rate to rise (from r_0 to r_1). Income is changed only slightly (from Y_0 to Y_1). Why?

The explanation has already been supplied in the discussion about the dependence of the relative effectiveness of monetary and fiscal policy on the slopes of the *IS* and *LM* schedules, in particular on the assumed magnitudes of the interest elasticities of money demand and of investment demand. Monetarists assume that the interest elasticity of money demand is small; the *LM* schedule is steep. The increase in government spending increases aggregate demand initially. As income begins to rise, the demand for transactions balances increases. With the money supply fixed, this increase puts upward pressure on the interest rate, which rises until money supply and demand are again equal. If money demand is interest-inelastic, a large increase in the interest rate is required to reequilibrate money demand with the fixed money supply.

The *IS* schedule is relatively flat in the monetarist view. Investment demand is highly sensitive to changes in the interest rate. Therefore, the rise in the interest rate required to keep the money market in equilibrium will cause private-sector aggregate demand to decline substantially as government spending begins to stimulate income. This reduction in private-sector aggregate demand is what we referred to in Chapter 4 as *crowding out*. In the monetarist model, crowding out occurs almost dollar for dollar with an increase in government spending.

Monetary Policy

Both monetarists and modern Keynesians believe that monetary policy actions have substantial and sustained effects on nominal income. The early Keynesians did, as we have seen, doubt the effectiveness of monetary policy. The difference today between Keynesians and monetarists over monetary policy concerns not *whether* monetary policy can affect income but *how* monetary policy should be used to stabilize income.

The Monetarist Position

Monetarists believe that changes in the quantity of money are the dominant influence on changes in nominal income and, for the short run, on changes in real income as well. It follows that stability in the behavior of the money supply would go a long way toward producing stability in income growth. Friedman traces most past instability in income growth to unstable money growth. Because of the importance of money and because of what Friedman regards as past mistakes in money management, his position on monetary policy was for a long time as follows:

> My own prescription is still that the monetary authority go all the way in avoiding such swings by adopting publicly the policy of achieving a specified rate of growth in a specified monetary total. The precise rate of growth, like the precise monetary total, is less important than the adoption of some stated and known rate.[5]

Today some monetarists propose alternative rules for monetary policy that are less inflexible than Friedman's constant money growth rate rule. Reasons for these alternatives are considered in Section 9.4. The common element in the monetarist proposals, however, is that monetary policy should be determined by a rule, not left to the discretion of policymakers.

If we accept the reasoning that one will do pretty well with a monetary policy rule, the question still remains: Why not the best? Why not use monetary policy to offset even minor shocks that affect income? Why not "fine-tune" the economy? Friedman's answer is, "We simply do not know enough to be able to recognize minor disturbances when they occur or to be able to predict either what their effects will be with any precision or what monetary policy is required to offset their effects."[6] Friedman and other monetarists believe that changes in the money supply will have a strong effect on income, but that there is a lag, with the bulk of the effect occurring only after 6 to 18 months. Thus, to offset a minor shock, we must be able to predict its size and when it

[5]Milton Friedman, "The Role of Monetary Policy," *American Economic Review*, 58 (March 1968), p. 16.

[6]Ibid., p. 14.

will affect the economy several quarters in advance. Friedman and other monetarists do not think we know enough to do this. To again quote Friedman: "There is a saying that the best is often the enemy of the good, which seems highly relevant. The goal of an extremely high degree of economic stability is certainly a splendid one; our ability to attain it, however, is limited."[7]

Contrast with the Keynesians

Keynesians believe that both monetary and fiscal policy should be *actively* adjusted to offset shocks to the economy. Franco Modigliani, a leading Keynesian, expressed this view (which he characterized as nonmonetarist) as follows:

> Nonmonetarists accept what I regard to be the fundamental practical message of *The General Theory*: that a private enterprise economy using an intangible money *needs* to be stabilized, *can* be stabilized, and, therefore, *should* be stabilized by appropriate monetary and fiscal policies.[8]

Keynesians favor active discretionary monetary as well as fiscal policy actions. They oppose money growth rate rules espoused by Friedman and other monetarists.

The first explanation for these differing views is the disagreement between monetarists and Keynesians concerning the need for active stabilization policies. Whereas monetarists view the private sector as stable and shock-absorbing, Keynesians see the private sector as shock-producing and unstable. This is not to say that Keynesians believe that without government stabilization policies we would constantly experience depressions and hyperinflations, but rather that shocks would result in substantial prolonged deviations from conditions of full employment and price stability.

A second source of the differing views of monetarists and Keynesians is also evident from Modigliani's statement. He believes that we *can* stabilize the economy. We can predict shocks that will hit the economy and design policies to combat them. To be sure, there will be errors, but overall such policies will result in more stable economic performance than we would have with simple policy rules.

9.4 UNSTABLE VELOCITY AND THE DECLINING POLICY INFLUENCE OF MONETARISM

The peak in monetarist influence on policy came at the end of the 1970s. In October 1979, the U.S. Federal Reserve began what has been called its *monetarist experiment*—an attempt to get control of the money supply to rein in an accelerating inflation rate. Also in 1979, the Thatcher government came to power in the United Kingdom and adopted a monetary policy along monetarist lines. In the post-1980 period, however, the influence of the monetarists eroded as the money–income relationship showed increasing instability.

[7]Milton Friedman, *The Optimum Quantity of Money and Other Essays* (Chicago: Aldine, 1969), p. 187.

[8]*The General Theory* was Keynes's major work. Franco Modigliani, "The Monetarist Controversy, or Should We Forsake Stabilization Policies?" *American Economic Review*, 67 (March 1977), p. 1.

FIGURE 9-6 M1 Velocity, (1979–2005)

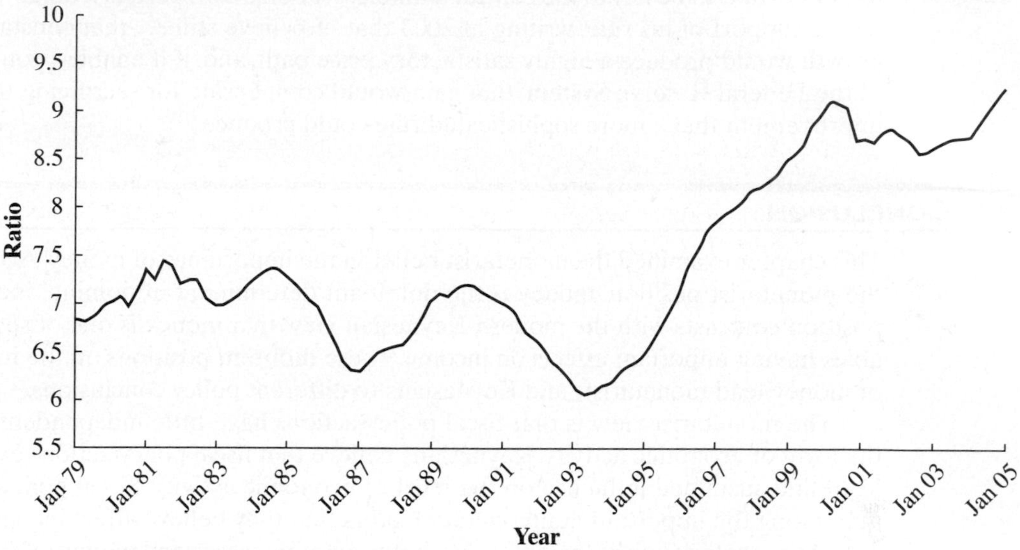

Recent Instability in the Money–Income Relationship

Figure 9-6 shows the velocity of the M1 measure of the money supply for each year from 1979 through 2005. In the monetarist view, changes in velocity should be a minor factor in explaining the cyclical behavior of nominal GDP. If the money supply and nominal GDP move closely together, then velocity, which is the ratio of the two (PY/M), should be stable. Figure 9-6 indicates, however, that velocity was subject to considerable instability after 1980. Especially notable are the sharp declines in velocity during 1985–87 and 1989–93 and then a sharp rise in velocity between 1994 and 2001.

Monetarist Reaction

Because of the instability in the money–income relationship, *The Economist* was led to ask in 1986, "Is this the year monetarism vanishes?" The data from the post-1980 period have led monetarists to reconsider their position in some areas but not to change their fundamental views.

Friedman and other monetarists have a number of explanations for the instability of velocity in the post-1980 period. They believe that lower interest rates and lower inflation rates in the 1980s reduced the opportunity cost of holding money. This led to a general increase in the demand for money relative to income (fall in velocity) for much of that decade. There was also substantial deregulation of deposit markets in the 1980s, leading to innovations in deposit markets that caused instability in money demand and therefore velocity. These innovations continue to the present day.

Still, as noted previously, the instability in velocity has led many monetarists to favor more flexible rules for money growth than Friedman's constant money growth rate rule. Some have moved away from support of money growth rate rules to rules that directly target the inflation rate. Such rules will be discussed in Chapter 17. Monetarists, however, continue to support Friedman, who concludes that "the long and the short of it is that I remain convinced of a fundamental tenet of monetarism: Money is too important to be left to the central bankers."[9] For his own part, Friedman was steadfast in support of his rule, writing in 2003 that "I believe still . . . that constant money growth would produce a highly satisfactory price path, and, if it enabled you to get rid of the Federal Reserve System, that gain would compensate for sacrificing the further improvement that a more sophisticated rule could produce."[10]

9.5 CONCLUSION

This chapter examined the monetarist belief in the importance of money. According to the monetarist position, money is the dominant determinant of nominal income. This position contrasts with the modern Keynesian view that money is one of several variables having important effects on income. These different positions on the importance of money lead monetarists and Keynesians to different policy conclusions.

The monetarist view is that fiscal policy actions have little independent effect on the level of economic activity. Keynesians believe that fiscal policy actions exert significant and sustained influence on the level of economic activity. Fiscal policy variables are among the important nonmonetary factors that they believe affect income.

On monetary policy, the difference between monetarists and modern Keynesians is not about the potential of monetary policy to significantly affect economic activity; both believe monetary policy has strong effects. They differ on what they view as the proper role for monetary policy. Monetarists are *noninterventionists*. They favor a rule for monetary policy that creates an environment in which a stable private sector of the economy can function effectively. Keynesians are *interventionists*. They see the need for active discretionary monetary and fiscal policies to keep an unstable private economy on track.

Given the erosion in the policy influence of monetarism, it might be surprising that a nonmonetarist economist, Bradford De Long, would in 2000 entitle an article "The Triumph of Monetarism." Also surprising would be that Ben Bernanke, another nonmonetarist and at the time a member of the Board of Governors of the Federal Reserve, would write in 2003, "Friedman's monetary framework has been so influential that, in its broad outlines at least, it has nearly become identical with modern monetary theory and practice."[11]

But central features of Milton Friedman's framework *have* become part of the common wisdom concerning monetary policy even as specific policy recommendations of the monetarists have lost influence. Rule-based monetary policies have gained popularity among academic economists and central bankers. The dominant role of monetary policy in determining inflation has been widely accepted. Friedman's views on the limitations of stabilization policy also remain highly influential. It is to one of these limitations to which we now turn our attention.

[9]Milton Friedman, "M1's Hot Streak Gave Keynesians a Bad Idea," in Peter McClelland, ed., *Readings in Introductory Macroeconomics* (New York: McGraw-Hill, 1988), p. 78, reprinted from the *Wall Street Journal*.

[10]Quoted in Edward Nelson, "Milton Friedman and U.S. Monetary History: 1961–2006," Federal Reserve Bank of St. Louis *Review*, 89 (May–June 2007), p. 172.

[11]References here are to Bradford De Long, "The Triumph of Monetarism," *Journal of Economic Perspectives*, 14 (Winter 2000), pp. 83–94; and Ben Bernanke, "Remarks," Federal Reserve Bank of Dallas Conference (October 2003).

REVIEW QUESTIONS AND PROBLEMS

1. Compare Keynesian and monetarist views on how the velocity of money is determined. How do their differing views on velocity affect their respective policy conclusions?
2. Why were early Keynesian economists so pessimistic about the effectiveness of monetary policy?
3. Compare Milton Friedman's formulation of the money demand function with the Keynesian specification in previous chapters.
4. Show how the *IS* and *LM* schedules look in the monetarist view. Use these schedules to illustrate the monetarist conclusions about the relative effectiveness of monetary and fiscal policy.
5. Compare monetarist and Keynesian views on the proper conduct of fiscal policy. For both monetarists and Keynesians, explain not only their conclusions concerning fiscal policy but also how those conclusions are related to their respective theories.
6. Compare monetarist and modern Keynesian views on the proper conduct of monetary policy. For both monetarists and Keynesians, explain not only their conclusions concerning monetary policy but also how those conclusions are related to their respective theories.
7. Analyze the effects of a decrease in taxes from T_0 to T_1 in the monetarist framework. In your answer, be sure to take account of the financing of the deficit that results from the tax cut. How are the equilibrium levels of income and the interest rate affected by the tax cut?

CHAPTER 10

Output, Inflation, and Unemployment: Alternative Views

This chapter examines alternative views of the relationship between the levels of output and unemployment and the rate of inflation. In Chapter 1, we saw that for the 1953–69 period there was a negative relationship between unemployment and inflation (Figure 1-5*a*), but the post-1970 relationship between these two variables was much less clear (Figure 1-5*b*). Some explanations for the shift in this relationship are provided in this chapter, beginning with Milton Friedman's theory of the natural rate of unemployment. We also examine Keynesian views on the output-inflation trade-off, including Friedman's natural rate concept. Finally, we consider how thinking about the natural rate of unemployment has varied over the 40 years since Friedman introduced the concept and evaluate the current relevance of the concept.

10.1 THE NATURAL RATE THEORY

The theory of the natural rates of unemployment and output was developed by Milton Friedman as a part of the monetarist system. The theory was developed independently by Edmund Phelps apart from monetarism.[1] Today the natural rate theory is central to the question of the long-run relationships among output, unemployment, and inflation—questions that must be addressed by any macroeconomic system. We begin with Friedman's formulation.

In Chapter 9, we analyzed the monetarist proposition that *short-run* changes in the money supply are the primary determinant of fluctuations in output and employment. However, the monetarists place a limitation on the real effects of changes in the money supply, as expressed in the second of the monetarist propositions given in Chapter 9.

> In the long run the influence of money is primarily on the price level and other *nominal* magnitudes. In the long run, *real* variables, such as real output and employment, are determined by real, not monetary, factors.

The basis of this proposition is Milton Friedman's theory of the **natural rates of unemployment and output**.

natural rates of unemployment and output in the monetarist model are determined by *real* supply-side factors: the capital stock, the size of the labor force, and the level of technology.

According to the natural rate theory, there exists an equilibrium level of output and an accompanying rate of unemployment determined

[1]See, for example, the contributions by Phelps and others in Edmund Phelps, ed., *Employment and Inflation Theory* (New York: Norton, 1970).

by the supply of factors of production, technology, and institutions of the economy (i.e., determined by real factors). This is Friedman's natural rate. Changes in aggregate demand, which Friedman believes are dominated by changes in the supply of money, cause temporary movements of the economy away from the natural rate. Expansionary monetary policies, for example, move output above the natural rate and move the unemployment rate below the natural rate for a time. The increased demand resulting from such an expansionary policy would also cause prices to rise. In the short run, the price adjustment would not be complete, as in the classical theory, where increases in demand cause prices to rise but do not affect output.

Friedman does believe that equilibrating forces cause output and employment to return to their natural rate over a longer period. It is not possible, in Friedman's view, for the government to use monetary policy to maintain the economy permanently at a level of output that holds the unemployment rate below the natural rate, at least it is not possible for the policymakers to do so unless they are willing to accept an ever-accelerating rate of inflation. The natural rate of unemployment is defined by Friedman as the rate "which has the property that it is consistent with equilibrium in the structure of *real* wage rates."[2] Thus, the natural rate of unemployment, or the corresponding natural rate of employment, will be such that labor demand equals labor supply at an equilibrium real wage, as depicted in Figure 10-1*a*.

The labor demand schedule in part *a* of the figure is the familiar marginal product of labor (MPN) schedule. At N^*, the natural rate of employment, labor demand is equated with labor supply, where in drawing the labor supply schedule, $N^s[W/(P^e = P)]$, we stipulate that the price level expected by labor suppliers is equal to the actual price level ($P^e = P$). Only at this level of employment is there no tendency for the real wage to change. Labor demand and supply are equated. Moreover, labor suppliers have a correct expectation of the price level. If such were not the case, labor supply would tend to change as workers perceived that their expectations were in error.

The natural rate of unemployment can be found simply by subtracting those employed from the total labor force to find the number unemployed and then expressing this number as a percentage of the total labor force. Using the production function in Figure 10-1*b*, we can find the level of output that will result from an employment level N^*. This is the natural level of output, Y^*.

Figure 10-1 shows that the natural rates of output and employment depend on the supply of factors of production and the technology of the economy—supply-side factors. The natural rates of output and employment do *not* depend on aggregate demand. All this is much the same as in the classical system; the difference between the monetarists and the classical economists is that the monetarists do not assume that the economy is necessarily at these natural levels of employment and output in the short run.

Like the Keynesians, the monetarists assume that labor suppliers do not have perfect information about the real wage. They must base their labor supply decisions on the expected real wage (W/P^e). Therefore, in the short run, labor supply may not be given by the supply schedule in Figure 10-1*a*; P^e may not equal P. In this case, employment and hence output will not be at their natural rates.

[2]Milton Friedman, "The Role of Monetary Policy," *American Economic Review*, 58 (March 1968), p. 8.

FIGURE 10-1 Natural Rates of Employment and Output

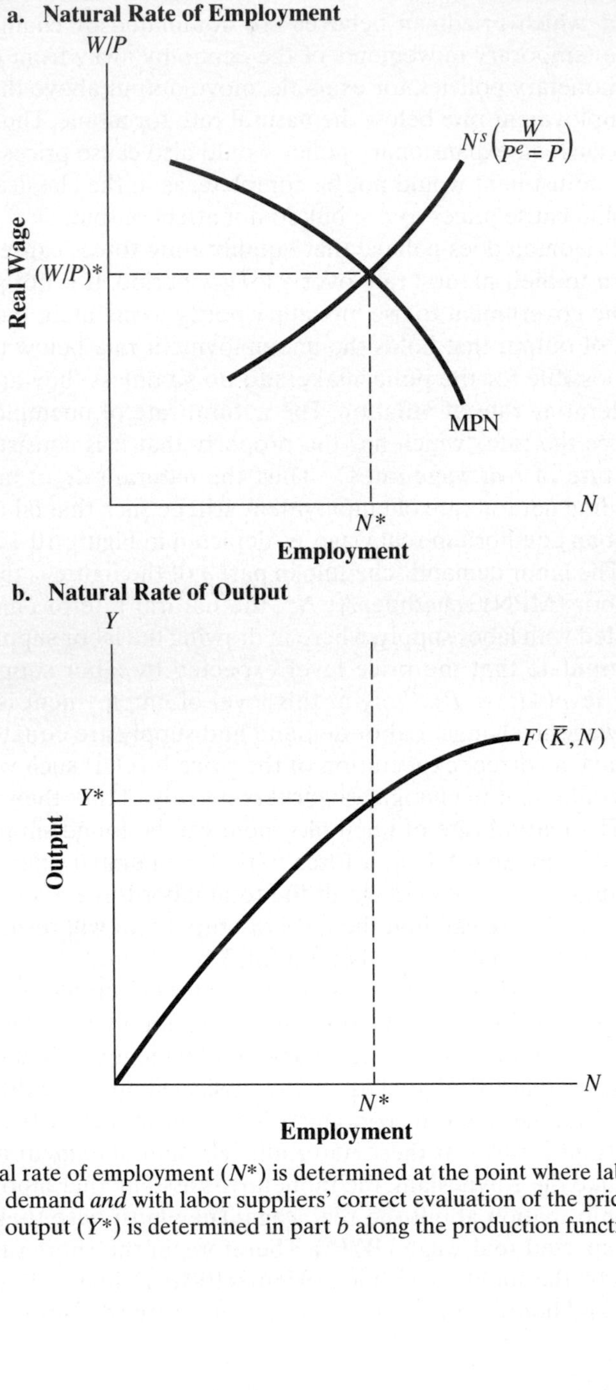

In part *a*, the natural rate of employment (N^*) is determined at the point where labor supply is equated with labor demand *and* with labor suppliers' correct evaluation of the price level ($P^e = P$). The natural rate of output (Y^*) is determined in part *b* along the production function.

10.2 MONETARY POLICY, OUTPUT, AND INFLATION: FRIEDMAN'S MONETARIST VIEW

To see why Friedman believes that output and employment diverge from their natural rates temporarily, but will eventually be drawn to these rates, we examine Friedman's analysis of the short-run and long-run consequences of an increase in the rate of growth in the money supply.

Monetary Policy in the Short Run

Let us begin with a situation in which the economy is at the natural rate of unemployment and output. Also suppose that the money supply (and hence nominal income) has been growing at a rate equal to the rate of growth of real output. Thus, the price level is assumed to have been stable for some time. Suppose now that the rate of growth in the money supply is increased above the rate consistent with price stability. For concreteness, assume that the rate of growth in the money supply rises from 3 percent to 5 percent.

The increase in the growth rate of the money supply will stimulate aggregate demand and, as a consequence, nominal income. The *short-run* consequences of this increase in aggregate demand are described by Friedman as follows:

> To begin with, much or most of the rise in income will take the form of an increase in output and employment rather than in prices. People have been expecting prices to be stable, and prices and wages have been set for some time in the future on that basis. It takes time for people to adjust to a new state of demand. Producers will tend to react to the initial expansion in aggregate demand by increasing output, employees by working longer hours, and the unemployed by taking jobs now offered at former nominal wages. This much is pretty standard doctrine.[3]

Phillips curve is the schedule showing the relationship between the unemployment and inflation rates

The *standard doctrine* to which Friedman refers is the **Phillips curve**. The Phillips curve is a negative relationship between the unemployment rate (U) and the inflation rate ($\dot{P}$), such as that plotted in Figure 10-2. High rates of growth in aggregate demand stimulate output and hence lower the unemployment rate. Such high rates of growth in demand also cause an increase in the rate at which prices rise (i.e., raise the inflation rate). Thus, the Phillips curve postulates a trade-off between inflation and unemployment; lower rates of unemployment can be achieved, but only at the cost of higher inflation rates.[4] Friedman is agreeing with this notion of a trade-off between inflation and unemployment *in the short run.*

Monetary Policy in the Long Run

The distinctive element in Friedman's analysis is his view of the long-run effects of monetary policy. Here the notion of the natural rate of unemployment comes into play. We have just considered the short-run effects of an increase in the rate of growth of the money supply from 3 percent to 5 percent. In terms of Figure 10-2, the original equilibrium was with stable prices ($\dot{P} = 0$) and unemployment equal to the natural rate assumed to be 6 percent (point A in Figure 10-2). We assume that, as a result of the increase in the

[3] Ibid., p. 10.

[4] The Phillips curve derives its name from the New Zealand economist A. W. H. Phillips, who studied the trade-off between unemployment and wage inflation in the British economy.

FIGURE 10-2 The Phillips Curve

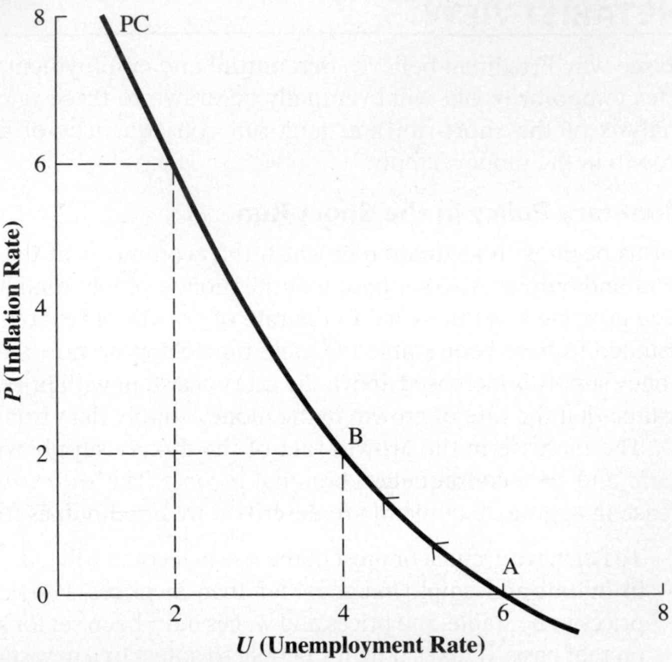

In the short run, an increase in the rate of growth in the money supply moves the economy from point A to point B along the short-run Phillips curve (PC). Unemployment declines, and inflation rises.

rate of growth in the money supply, the economy moves to a new *short-run* equilibrium, with unemployment reduced to 4 percent and an inflation rate at 2 percent (point B in Figure 10-2). The expansionary aggregate demand policy lowers the unemployment rate below the natural rate.

Friedman accepts this outcome:

> But it describes only the initial effects. Because selling prices of products typically respond to an unanticipated rise in nominal demand faster than prices of factors of production, real wages received have gone down—though real wages anticipated by employees went up, since employees implicitly evaluated the wages offered at the earlier price level. Indeed, the simultaneous fall *ex post* in real wages to employers and rise *ex ante* to employees is what enabled employment to increase. But the decline *ex post* in real wages will soon come to affect anticipations. Employees will start to reckon on rising prices of the things they buy and to demand higher nominal wages for the future. "Market" unemployment is below the natural level. There is an excess demand for labor so real wages will tend to rise toward their initial level.[5]

Friedman points out that in the short run, product prices increase faster than factor prices, the crucial factor price being the money wage. Thus, the real wage (*W*/*P*) falls. This is necessary for output to increase, because firms must be on the labor demand

[5]Friedman, "The Role of Monetary Policy," p. 10.

schedule shown in Figure 10-1. Firms expand employment and output only with a decline in the real wage.

Friedman does not argue that workers are always on the labor supply schedule shown in Figure 10-1. That schedule expresses labor supply as a function of the *actual* real wage, and Friedman does not assume that workers know the real wage. In the short run, after a period of stable prices, workers are assumed to evaluate nominal wage offers "at the earlier price level." Prices have risen, but workers have not yet seen this rise, and they will increase the labor supply if offered a higher money wage *even if this increase in the money wage is less than the increase in the price level, even if the real wage is lower*. In the short run, labor supply increases because the *ex ante* (or expected) real wage is higher as a result of the higher nominal wage and unchanged view about the behavior of prices. Labor demand increases because of the fall in the *ex post* (actual) real wage paid by the employer. Consequently, unemployment can be pushed below the natural rate.

This situation is temporary, for workers eventually observe the higher price level and demand higher money wages. In terms of Figure 10-1, the real wage has been pushed below $(W/P)^*$, the wage that clears the labor market once labor suppliers correctly perceive the price level and, hence, the real wage. At a lower real wage, an excess demand for labor pushes the real wage back up to its equilibrium level, and this rise in the real wage causes employment to return to the natural rate shown in Figure 10-1.

The implications for the Phillips curve of this long-run adjustment back to the natural rate are illustrated in Figure 10-3. The schedule labeled PC ($\dot{P}^e = 0$) is the short-run Phillips curve from Figure 10-2. Here the schedule is explicitly drawn for a given expected rate of inflation on the part of the suppliers of labor, in this case stable prices ($\dot{P}^e = 0$, where $\dot{P}^e$ is the expected rate of inflation). We have already analyzed the

FIGURE 10-3 Short-Run and Long-Run Phillips Curves

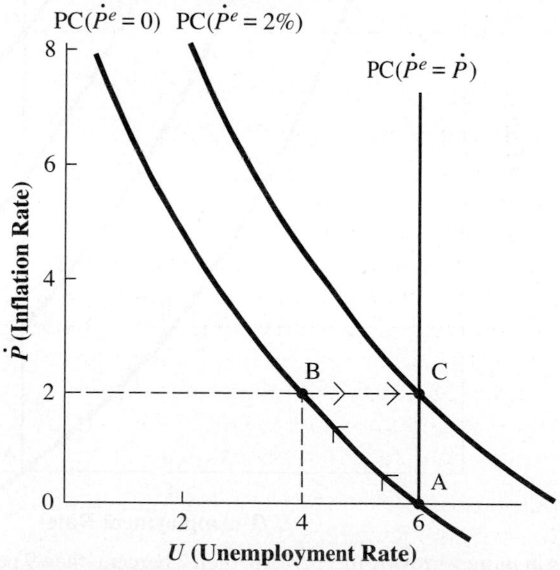

As labor suppliers come to anticipate higher inflation the short-run Phillips curve shifts from PC ($\dot{P}^e = 0$) to PC ($\dot{P}^e = 2\%$) The unemployment rate returns to the natural rate of 6 percent; the inflation rate remains higher at 2 percent (we move from point B to point C).

process whereby an increased rate of growth of the money supply from 3 percent to 5 percent moves the economy in the short run from point A to point B.

As suppliers of labor anticipate that prices are rising, the Phillips curve will shift upward to the right. Suppliers of labor will demand a higher rate of increase in money wages and, as a consequence, a higher rate of inflation will now correspond to any given unemployment rate. If money growth is continued at 5 percent, the economy will return to the natural 6 percent rate of unemployment, but now with an inflation rate of 2 percent instead of the initial stable price level. In terms of Figure 10-3, this longer-run adjustment moves the economy from point B to point C.

A policymaker who is not content with this return to 6 percent unemployment (the natural rate) may still pursue a target unemployment rate below the natural rate by again increasing the rate of growth in the money supply. Let us suppose that this time the policymaker increases money supply growth from 5 percent to 7 percent. The effects of this further expansion of aggregate demand are illustrated in Figure 10-4. Until the suppliers of labor come to anticipate the further increase in the inflation rate, employment will expand. The economy will move to a point, such as D in Figure 10-4, with unemployment below the natural rate of unemployment.

FIGURE 10-4 Effect of an Attempt to "Peg" the Unemployment Rate

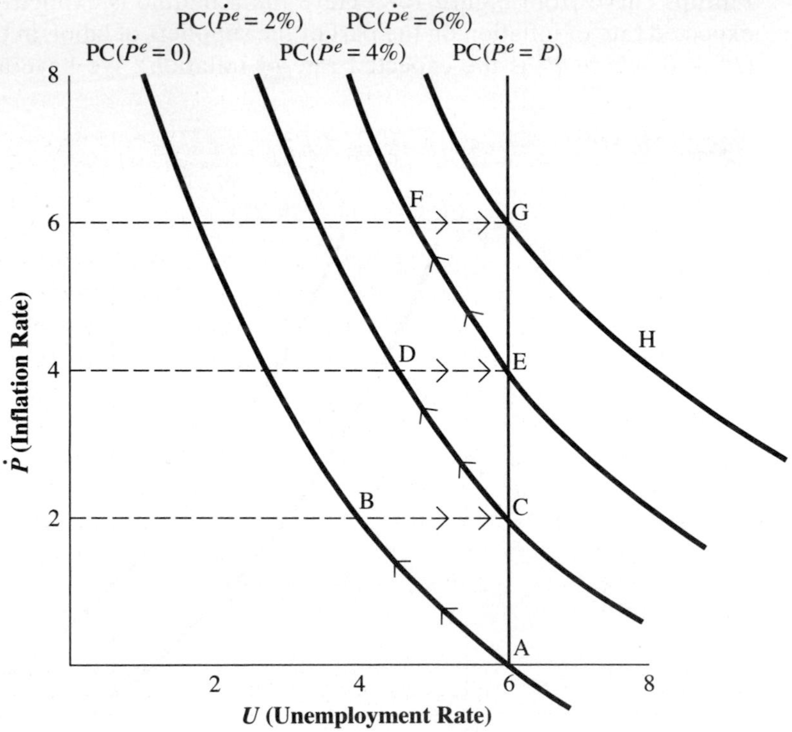

Increases in money growth, to 5 percent, then 7 percent, then 9 percent, result in temporary reductions in unemployment (movements from C to D and from E to F, for example). But in the longer run, we simply move up the vertical Phillips curve (to points E and G, for example).

Suppliers of labor, after a time, will come to anticipate the higher inflation that corresponds to a 7 percent growth in the money supply. The short-run Phillips curve will shift to the schedule labeled PC ($\dot{P}^e = 4\%$), and the economy will return to the natural rate of unemployment, with the inflation rate increased to 4 percent (7 percent money growth minus 3 percent growth in real income). In terms of Figure 10-4, we move from point D to point E. If the policymaker persists in attempting to "peg" the unemployment rate, money supply growth will again increase, for example, to 9 percent. This increase will move the economy in the short run to point F, but in the long run to point G, with a still higher rate of inflation.

Eventually, the policymaker will conclude that inflation has become a more serious problem than unemployment (or will be replaced by a policymaker who has this view), and the acceleration of inflation will stop. Notice, however, that when inflation has persisted for a long time, inflationary expectations become built into the system. At a point such as point G in Figure 10-4, expansionary aggregate demand policies have increased the expected (and actual) inflation rate to 6 percent (9 percent money growth minus 3 percent growth in real income). An attempt to lower inflation by slowing the rate of growth in the money supply, let us suppose all the way back to the initial noninflationary 3 percent, will *not* immediately move the economy back to a point such as the initial point A. In the short run, we would move along the short-run Phillips curve that corresponds to an expected inflation rate of 6 percent, to a point such as H in Figure 10-4, with high inflation and unemployment above the natural rate. Just as it took time for suppliers of labor to recognize that the rate of inflation had increased and, hence, to demand a faster rate of growth in money wages, it will take time for them to recognize that the inflation rate has slowed and to modify their money wage demands to a level compatible with price stability. In the meantime, in the monetarist view, the economy must suffer from high inflation and high unemployment.

Friedman believes that an expansionary monetary policy can only temporarily move the unemployment rate below the natural rate. There is a trade-off between unemployment and inflation only in the short run. In terms of Figures 10-3 and 10-4, the downward-sloping short-run Phillips curves *that are drawn for given expected inflation rates* illustrate the short-run trade-off between unemployment and inflation. The long-run Phillips curve showing the relationship between inflation and unemployment *when expected inflation has time to adjust to the actual inflation rate* ($\dot{P} = \dot{P}^e$)—*when inflation is fully anticipated*—is vertical, as shown in Figures 10-3 and 10-4.

Friedman's theory of the natural rate of unemployment and output is the theoretical foundation for the monetarist belief that in the long run the influence of the money supply is primarily on the price level and other nominal variables. Real variables such as output and employment have time to adjust to their natural rates in the long run. Those natural rates of output and employment depend on real variables such as factor supplies (labor and capital) and technology.

10.3 A KEYNESIAN VIEW OF THE OUTPUT–INFLATION TRADE-OFF

Friedman's theory of the natural rate of unemployment explains both the short-run and long-run relationship between inflation and unemployment. What is the Keynesian view of the Phillips curve, and how does it differ from the natural rate view? How can

Keynesians defend activist policies to affect output and employment if the natural rate theory is correct and such policies have only a temporary effect on output and employment? These questions are considered in this section.

To anticipate our conclusions, we find the following:

1. Traditional Keynesian models, such as those considered in Chapter 8, also imply that once the economy has fully adjusted to a change in inflation (caused, for example, by a change in money supply growth), output and employment will be unaffected. These Keynesian models also imply a vertical long-run Phillips curve.
2. Keynesians, however, draw different policy conclusions from this absence of a long-run trade-off between inflation and unemployment.

The Phillips Curve: A Keynesian Interpretation

Keynesians' view of the relationship between the rate of inflation and the levels of employment and output follows directly from their theory of how price and output are determined. Here we relate that theory to the Phillips curve.

The Short-Run Phillips Curve

Figure 10-5 shows the effect on price, output, and employment of a sequence of expansionary policy actions increasing aggregate demand. The version of the Keynesian model here is the same as in Section 8.4. The money wage is flexible, and labor supply is assumed to depend on the expected real wage (W/P^e), the money wage divided by the expected price level.

In the Keynesian system, an expansionary aggregate demand policy might be a monetary policy action, such as the increase in the rate of growth in the money supply

FIGURE 10-5 Short-Run Effects of Increases in Aggregate Demand in the Keynesian Model

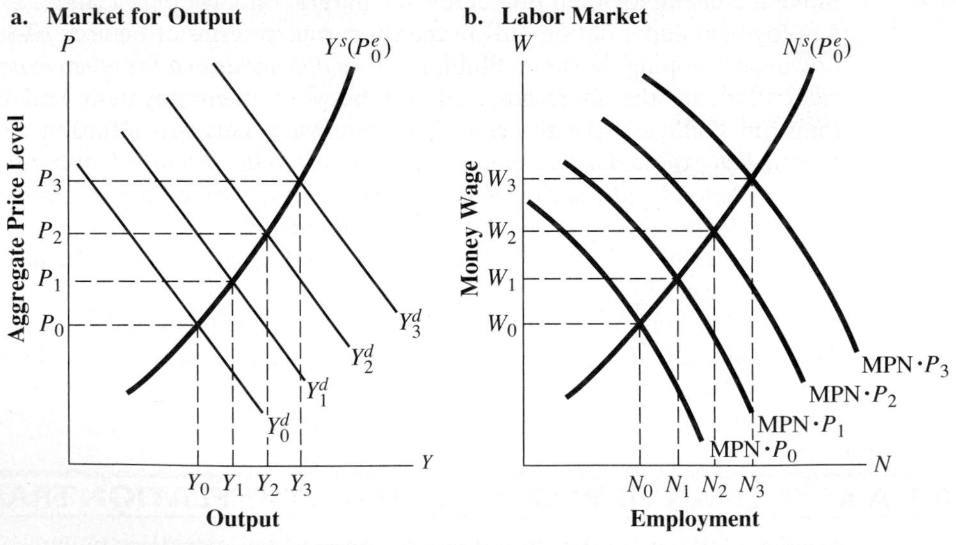

An expansionary aggregate demand policy, such as an increase in the rate of growth in the money supply, will cause a series of shifts to the right in the aggregate demand schedule (from Y_0^d to Y_1^d, to Y_2^d, to Y_3^d). In the short run, output, the price level, and employment all rise.

analyzed in the preceding section, or it might be a fiscal policy action, such as a series of increases in government spending. In either case, policy will produce a series of shifts in the aggregate demand schedule, as shown in Figure 10-5*a*. As can be seen, these increases in aggregate demand will increase output (from Y_0 to Y_1, to Y_2, then to Y_3) and employment (from N_0 to N_1, to N_2, then to N_3), as well as the price level (from P_0 to P_1, to P_2, then to P_3). As employment increases, the unemployment rate will decline. The level of the money wage will increase.

These results can be interpreted in terms of a Phillips curve relationship. The more quickly aggregate demand grows, the larger will be the rightward shifts in the aggregate demand schedule, and, other things being equal, the faster will be the rate of growth in output and employment. For a given growth in the labor force, this means that the unemployment rate will be lower the faster the rate of growth in aggregate demand. As can also be seen from Figure 10-5*a*, increases in aggregate demand cause the price level to rise, so again, other things being equal, the faster the growth of aggregate demand is, the higher the rate of inflation will be.

The Keynesian model, then, implies a trade-off between inflation and unemployment. High rates of growth in demand correspond to low levels of unemployment and high rates of inflation. Slower growth in aggregate demand means a lower inflation rate but a higher rate of unemployment. The Phillips curve implied by the Keynesian model is downward-sloping.

But is this a short-run or a long-run relationship? Notice that so far we have held the expected price level constant. We are considering the effects of increases in demand in the short run. As explained in Chapter 8, Keynesians view the expected price level as depending primarily on the past behavior of prices. Thus, as successive periods go by with increases in the actual price level, the expected price level will rise. In the long run, we must take account of the effects of such increases in the expected price level. Because we did not do so in Figure 10-5, our results there, and the Phillips curve relationship derived from them, pertain to the short run. To emphasize their short-run relevance, we have labeled the labor supply schedule $N^s(P_0^e)$ and the aggregate supply schedule $Y^s(P_0^e)$ to indicate that these schedules are drawn for the initial value of the expected price level. In Figure 10-6, we label the Phillips curve implied by the example in Figure 10.5 as the short-run Phillips curve, $PC_{\text{short-run}}$.[6]

The Long-Run Phillips Curve

In the long run, the expected price adjusts to the actual price. Suppliers of labor perceive the inflation that has resulted from the expansionary aggregate demand policy.

The longer-run adjustment of output and employment following an increase in aggregate demand is illustrated in Figure 10-7. Recall that, in the Keynesian system, labor supply depends on the expected real wage:

$$N^s = t\left(\frac{W}{P^e}\right) \tag{10.1}$$

[6]The short-run nature of the downward-sloping Phillips curve was recognized before Friedman's work. Paul Samuelson and Robert Solow wrote in this context:

> All of our discussions has been phrased in short-run terms, dealing with what might happen in the next few years. . . . What we do in a policy way during the next few years might cause it [the Phillips curve] to shift in a definite way. [Paul Samuelson and Robert Solow, "Analytical Aspects of Anti-Inflation Policy," *American Economic Review*, 50 (May 1960), pp. 177–94.]

FIGURE 10-6 The Phillips Curve: The Keynesian Perspective

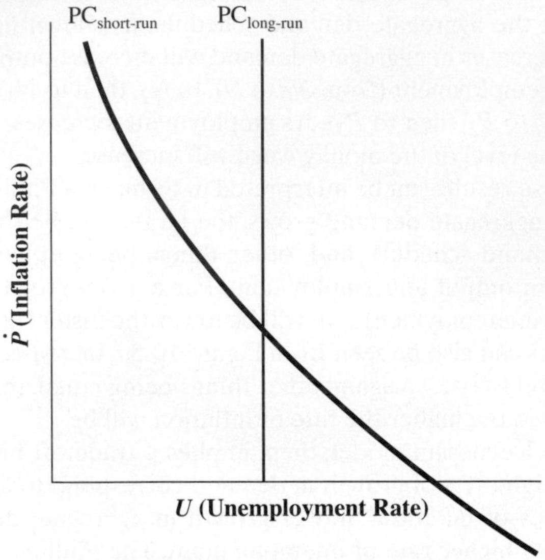

In the short run, the Phillips curve implied by the Keynesian model is downward-sloping. In the long run in the Keynesian model, as in Friedman's analysis, the Phillips curve is vertical.

where the effect of the money wage on labor supply is positive and the effect of an increase in expected price is negative. As the expected price rises, the labor supply schedule in Figure 10-5*b* shifts to the left. Less labor will be supplied at any money wage (W) because a given money wage corresponds to a lower expected real wage (W/P^e) after an increase in the expected price level. This shift in the labor supply schedule is shown in Figure 10-7*b*. As the expected price level rises to P_1^e, to P_2^e, and then to P_3^e, the labor supply schedule shifts to $N^s(P_1^e)$, to $N^s(P_2^e)$, then to $N^s(P_3^e = P_3)$.

As the labor supply schedule shifts to the left, the level of employment for any given price level declines. We move back up on a given labor demand schedule (which is drawn for a given price level). The increase in expected price lowers employment for any price level and, therefore, lowers output supplied at any price level. The aggregate supply schedule also shifts upward to the left with each increase in expected price, reflecting this decline in output supplied at a given price level. These shifts in the supply schedule are illustrated in Figure 10-7*a*.

The labor supply and aggregate supply schedules continue to shift to the left until expected price and actual price are equal. The *long-run* equilibrium position is shown in Figure 10-7, where the labor supply schedule is $N^s(P_3^e = P_3)$ and the aggregate supply schedule is $Y^s(P_3^e = P_3)$. Notice that at this point income and employment have returned to their initial levels, Y_0 and N_0. This must be the case, because output and employment can be maintained above Y_0 and N_0 only as long as the expected price is below the actual price—that is, only as long as labor suppliers underestimate inflation. Once the suppliers of labor correctly perceive the increases in the price level, they will demand increases in the money wage proportionate to the increase in the price level. At this point, the real wage will have returned to its initial level ($W_3/P_3 = W_0/P_0$). Both

FIGURE 10-7 Long-Run Effects of Increases in Aggregate Demand in the Keynesian Model

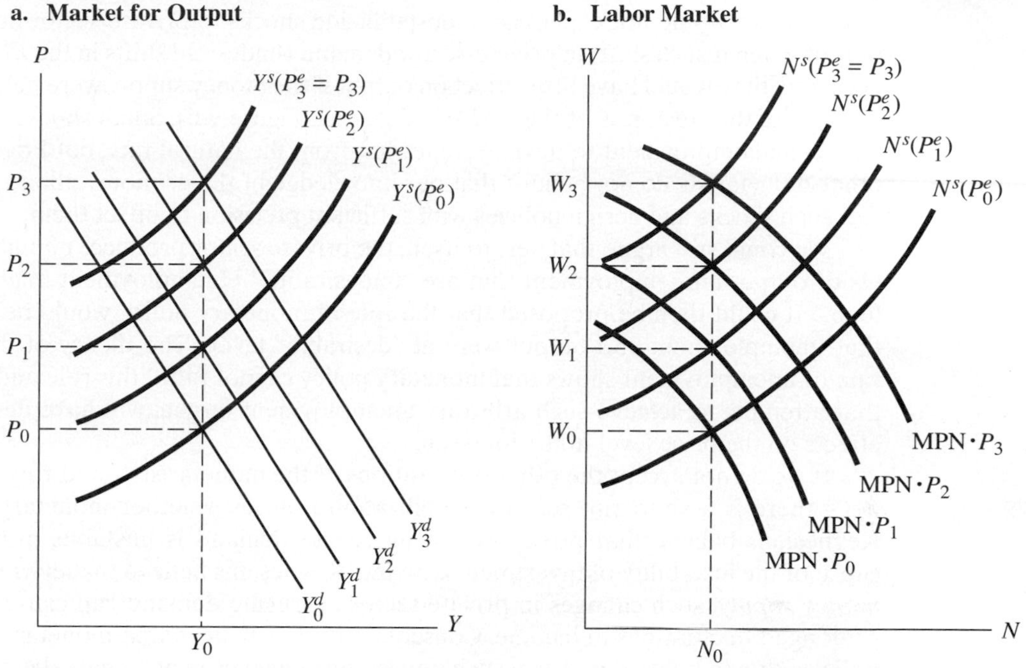

In the long run, leftward shifts in the labor supply and the aggregate supply schedules reverse the increases in output and employment that result from the expansionary aggregate demand policy. Output and employment return to their initial levels, Y_0 and N_0.

labor supply and labor demand will have returned to their initial levels. Consequently, employment and output will be at their initial levels of N_0 and Y_0.[7] An increase in aggregate demand increases output and employment and, as a consequence, lowers the unemployment rate only in the short run. As shown in Figure 10-6, the long-run Phillips curve is vertical in the Keynesian as well as the monetarist view.

Stabilization Policies for Output and Employment: The Keynesian View

Why does the absence of a long-run effect of aggregate demand on output and employment not lead the Keynesians to accept the monetarist noninterventionist policy position? The reason is that in the Keynesian view, aggregate demand policies are aimed at stabilizing output and employment in the *short run*.

The goal of such stabilization policies is to keep the economy at its equilibrium level in the face of shocks to aggregate demand or supply. In other words, the aim of *stabilization* policies is, as the name implies, to offset what would otherwise be destabilizing influences on output and employment.

[7]In this discussion, we are ignoring elements of the Keynesian theory that explain why the money wage is sticky in the *short run* (see Section 8.3). We are not, for example, allowing for the effects of implicit or explicit labor contracts that prevent the money wage from adjusting to changes in demand conditions. Such factors can slow but not ultimately prevent adjustment to the long-run equilibrium position.

The monetarist noninterventionist policy conclusion is based, to a large extent, on the propositions discussed in Chapter 9. The private sector is basically stable if left to itself. Thus we would not expect large destabilizing shocks to private-sector demand for output. Even if such shifts in private-sector demand (undesired shifts in the *IS* schedule) occurred, they would have little effect on output if the money supply were held constant because of the steepness of the *LM* schedule (see Figure 9-6). Small shocks may cause output and employment to deviate somewhat from the natural rate, but Friedman and other monetarists do not believe that our knowledge of the economy allows us to predict such shocks and design policies with sufficient precision to offset them.

We could still argue that, left to itself, the private sector produces equilibrium levels of output and employment that are "undesirable." Unemployment might be "too high." It could then be proposed that the role of monetary policy would be to ensure that unemployment and output were at "desirable" levels. The theory of the natural rate of unemployment shows that monetary policy cannot fulfill this role and indicates that attempts to achieve such arbitrary unemployment targets will have destabilizing effects on the price level in the long run.

If we do not accept the other propositions of the monetarists—and Keynesians do not—there is a short-run role for stabilization policies, whether monetary or fiscal. Keynesians believe that private-sector aggregate demand is unstable, primarily because of the instability of investment demand. Keynesians believe that *even for a given money supply*, such changes in private-sector aggregate demand can cause large and prolonged fluctuations in income. Consequently, they believe that monetary and fiscal policies should be used to offset such undesirable changes in aggregate demand and to stabilize income.

10.4 EVOLUTION OF THE NATURAL RATE CONCEPT

Milton Friedman's purpose in advancing the concept of natural rates of output and unemployment was to illustrate a limitation on monetary policy. Monetary policy could not permanently lower unemployment below the natural rate, not without causing an ever-accelerating inflation rate. Over the three decades since Friedman introduced the concept, however, much attention has also been focused on what determines the natural rate and what that value is for different countries.[8] If, for example, it is important for policymakers to avoid driving the unemployment rate below the natural rate and thereby setting off inflationary pressures, how do they know how by much they can safely reduce the unemployment rate? In the late 1990s this became a crucial question in the United States as the unemployment rate fell to a 30-year low.

Determinants of the Natural Rate of Unemployment

Friedman did address the question of what determines the natural rate of unemployment. As we have seen, the natural rate is the rate that is consistent with an equilibrium real wage. Within our model of the labor market, this is simply an equilibrium between labor supply and demand subject to the condition that labor suppliers correctly esti-

[8]In this subsequent literature, the term *nonaccelerating inflation rate of unemployment* (*NAIRU*) is often used in place of *natural rate of unemployment*.

mate the price level. Friedman argued that, in the real world, the natural rate would be the rate "ground out" by an equilibrating process that would also be affected by "the actual structural characteristics of labor and commodity markets, including market imperfections, stochastic variability in demands and supplies, the cost of gathering information about job vacancies and labor availabilities, the cost of mobility, and so on."[9] These additional characteristics are ones we think of as determining the levels of *frictional* and *structural* unemployment. Low labor mobility in a country, for example, might be expected to lead to a higher natural rate of unemployment because, as demand shifted from one region of the country to another, workers would not be quick to follow. Poor information about job vacancies might also lead to a higher natural rate of unemployment, as workers take longer to find initial jobs or to move between jobs. In Friedman's view, then, the natural rate in each country will be determined by the structural characteristics of that country's commodity and labor markets.

Time-Varying Natural Rates of Unemployment

One observer commented that "when Milton Friedman first proposed the natural rate hypothesis . . . in 1968, it sounded like a royal edict had established the natural rate as another one of the universe's invariant constants."[10] If, as Friedman argued, the natural rate of unemployment depends on the structural characteristics of a country's commodity and labor markets, there is no reason why it need be constant over time, though we would expect changes to be gradual rather than abrupt. In fact, the behavior of unemployment over the past three decades indicates that if the natural rate of unemployment is a useful concept, it *must* be time-varying.

To see why, consider the unemployment figures for selected European countries in Table 10.1. The first five columns show average unemployment rates in eight countries for five periods ranging in length from 6 to 10 years (ignore the last column for the moment.) Averages over periods of this length should give reasonable approximations of the natural rate. If there is a tendency for unemployment to move to one rate, as suggested by the natural rate hypothesis, then actual unemployment should fluctuate

TABLE 10.1 European Unemployment Rates, Selected Periods (percent)

	1960–67	*1968–73*	*1974–79*	*1980–89*	*1990–98*	*2005–07*
Belgium	2.1	2.3	5.7	11.1	11.5	12.2
Germany	0.8	0.8	3.5	6.8	8.8	10.3
Spain	2.3	2.7	5.3	17.5	20.5	8.6
France	1.5	2.6	4.5	9.0	11.2	8.9
Italy	4.9	5.7	6.6	9.9	11.7	7.1
Ireland	4.9	5.6	7.6	14.0	13.6	4.7
United Kingdom	1.5	2.4	4.2	9.5	7.9	5.3
Denmark	1.6	1.0	5.8	9.0	9.6	4.5

SOURCE: *Historical Statistics, 1960–89, 1990–2006 (Paris: Organization for Economic Cooperation and Development) and Economic Outlook (December 2007).*

[9] Friedman, "The Role of Monetary Policy," p. 11.

[10] Joseph Stiglitz, "Reflections on the Natural Rate Hypothesis," *Journal of Economic Perspectives*, 11 (Winter 1997), p. 3.

around that rate—sometimes above it, sometimes below it. If averaging the unemployment rate over these periods does provide an estimate of the natural rate, then the natural rate of unemployment in the countries in the table has been rising over the past three decades. Almost all reached extremely high levels in the 1990s.[11]

In the United States, there is also evidence of a time-varying natural rate of unemployment. As in Europe, the unemployment rate trended upward in the United States in the 1970s and 1980s, though less sharply. In the 1990s, however, the behavior of the U.S. unemployment rate was quite different from unemployment rates in most European economies. The U.S. unemployment rate fell steadily throughout the 1990s to below 4 percent in 2000 before rising as a recession began in 2001.

Explaining Changing Natural Rates of Unemployment

If the natural rate of unemployment changes over time, is it still a useful concept? To use a changing natural rate as a guide for monetary policy, for example, policymakers would need to know what it was and where it was going. Policymakers would want to understand the factors that cause changes in the natural rate.

There is a large amount of literature on the apparent increase in the natural rate of unemployment in European countries.[12] One possible cause researchers have pointed to is rigidity in European labor markets, especially among nations that are members of the European Union. Labor market regulations in European Union countries include limitations on plant closings and provisions for mandatory severance pay that may discourage firms from expanding employment. European countries also have high degrees of unionization, which may result in wage rigidity. Moreover, European countries typically have generous unemployment compensation and other social benefits that make unemployment less painful.

hysteresis is the property that, when a variable is shocked away from an initial value, it shows no tendency to return even when the shock is over. Persistently high unemployment rates in many European countries have led economists to argue that unemployment exhibits hysteresis

Rising European unemployment may not be the result of *increases* in rigidities and the generosity of the social safety net, but may be the result of growing competition from lower-wage countries, in particular the rapidly growing Asian economies, given the existing rigidity of labor markets and benefit levels. In other words, growing competition, instead of pulling down European real wages, raises European unemployment.

An alternative explanation for high European unemployment focuses on the idea that the current value of the unemployment rate may be strongly influenced by its past values, a property called **hysteresis**. From this perspective, high unemployment in the recessions of the 1970s and 1980s, which was *cyclical* in nature, had long-lasting effects on unemployment in later years. The economic processes that result in unemployment having the hysteresis property are considered in Chapter 12, which examines recent directions in Keynesian research.

---

[11] There are other, more sophisticated methods of estimating the natural rate of unemployment. These other estimates also indicate sharp increases in the natural rate for the countries in the table, as well as for some other European nations.

[12] Two useful surveys of this literature are Olivier Blanchard and Lawrence F. Katz, "What We Know and Do Not Know About the Natural Rate of Unemployment," *Journal of Economic Perspectives*, 11 (Winter 1997), pp. 51–72; and Charles Bean, "European Unemployment: A Survey," *Journal of Economic Literature*, 32 (June 1994), pp. 573–619.

The divergent behavior of unemployment in the United States and Europe, especially in the 1990s, has been attributed to different structural characteristics of labor markets in the two regions. According to this view, greater flexibility in the U.S. labor market, due to less regulation and lower unionization, has meant that increased global competition and skill-biased technological change have caused stagnant real wages in the United States (especially for low-skilled workers) instead of slower job growth and higher unemployment. Moreover, in the post-1990 years, any hysteresis effects have been favorable in the United States, as a low-unemployment environment has been maintained for a long period.

Recent Trends

Now consider the rightmost column in Table 10.1. The column gives the average unemployment rate over the past 3 years for each of the countries in the table. High unemployment continued in the large continental European economies (first five rows). This reflects the high unemployment in the overall Euro (European common currency) area, which averaged 7.8 percent over this period. In contrast, in the United States after recovery from the 2001 recession, unemployment settled in the 4–5 percent range during these years.

But the unemployment picture did improve markedly in several countries. Rapid economic growth in Ireland, which came to be called the *Celtic tiger*, reversed a 30-year upward trend in unemployment. In the United Kingdom, the downward trend in the unemployment rate that began in the 1990s continued. Denmark instituted a comprehensive (and expensive) program of job retraining and placement. The result was a dramatic fall in unemployment.

The varied experience of these countries is representative of broader trends. Clearly, the natural rate (or *equilibrium rate*) of unemployment varies across countries and through time.

10.5 Conclusion

Friedman's theory of the natural rates of unemployment and output has been highly influential. It demonstrates the limits of the trade-off between inflation and unemployment. However, the apparent large variations of the natural rate of unemployment in Europe have caused some to doubt the usefulness of the concept to the conduct of macroeconomic policy. Robert Solow, for example, argues that "a natural rate that hops around . . . under the influence of unspecified forces, *including past unemployment rates*, is not 'natural' at all."[13]

In contrast, Joseph Stiglitz, chairman of the Counsel of Economic Advisors in the Clinton administration, defends the concept, believing that "the natural rate provides a useful framework for thinking about policy questions even if there is considerable uncertainty about its exact magnitude."[14]

[13] Robert Solow, "Unemployment: Getting the Questions Right," *Economica*, 33, Suppl. (1986), p. S.33. See also James K. Galbraith, "Time to Ditch the NAIRU," *Journal of Economic Perspectives*, 11 (Winter 1997), pp. 93–108.

[14] Stiglitz, "Reflections on the Natural Rate Hypothesis," p. 10.

KEY TERMS

- natural rates of unemployment and output 210
- Phillips curve 213
- hysteresis 224

REVIEW QUESTIONS AND PROBLEMS

1. Explain the concept of the natural rate of unemployment. What are the implications of Milton Friedman's theory of the natural rate of unemployment for the effectiveness of economic stabilization policies?
2. Explain why monetarists believe that monetary policy affects output and employment in the short run but not in the long run. What is the crucial difference between the short run and the long run?
3. Contrast Friedman's and the Keynesian views of the relationship between real output (or employment) and aggregate demand in both the short run and the long run. Contrast the conclusions that Friedman and Keynesians draw from this analysis of the aggregate demand–output relationship for the usefulness of activist policies to stabilize output and employment. To what degree do differences in the theoretical analysis explain the differences in policy conclusions?
4. Explain the concept of the Phillips curve. Is there any difference between monetarist and Keynesian views of the Phillips curve?
5. At the end of the inflationary decade of the 1970s, the Federal Reserve is widely perceived to have moved to a much more restrictive monetary policy. Use the Phillips curve framework of Figures 10-2 and 10-3 to provide a monetarist analysis of the effects this policy shift would have on inflation and unemployment.
6. "A supply shock such as the exogenous increase in the price of oil analyzed in Section 8.5 would have no effect on real or nominal income within the monetarist model. This follows because such a supply shock would not affect the quantity of money, which is the dominant factor determining nominal income and, in the short run, real income." Do you agree or disagree with this statement? Explain.
7. Contrast the monetarist and classical views on the short-run effects of an increase in the quantity of money.
8. Beginning in the late 1960s, the number of entrants to the labor market increased as the baby boom generation reached working age. In addition, labor force participation rates for women began to increase in the mid-1960s. What effect do you think these demographic factors had on the U.S. natural rate of unemployment at the time? What effect did they have on the natural rate of output?
9. Are the data in Table 10.1 for European unemployment consistent with the existence of a natural rate of unemployment in these countries? Explain why or why not.

CHAPTER 11

New Classical Economics

The next theoretical system we consider, the *new classical economics*, developed against the background of the high inflation and unemployment of the 1970s and the accompanying dissatisfaction with the prevailing Keynesian orthodoxy. Both monetarism and the new classical economics have their origins in classical economics, and the two schools of economists reach similar noninterventionist policy conclusions. Robert Lucas, the central figure in the development of the new classical economics, basically agrees with Milton Friedman's proposal for noninterventionist policy rules.[1] Much in the spirit of Friedman, Lucas says, "As an advice giving profession we are in way over our heads."[2] In fact, new classical economists are even more skeptical than monetarists about the usefulness of activist stabilization policies.

The new classical economics, however, is a more fundamental attack on the Keynesian *theoretical* system than is monetarism. Monetarists and Keynesians reach different policy conclusions and differ on a number of empirical questions, but in Chapter 9 we presented no distinct monetarist theoretical model. New classical economists have been motivated by a belief that the Keynesian structure is fundamentally flawed. They have attacked not just the usefulness of Keynesian analysis for understanding economic events and designing useful policies but also its internal consistency. The alternative way new classical economists propose to address macroeconomic questions is important not only to their own theory, as set out in this chapter, but also to the *real business cycle* theory and to the *new* Keynesian analysis we consider in Chapter 12.

This chapter first presents the new classical economists' critique of Keynesian macroeconomics, focusing especially on the differences in the policy conclusions of the two groups (Section 11.1). Next, we take a broader look at the new classical economics (Section 11.2). We then consider the Keynesian response to the new classical economics (Section 11.3). The final section (11.4) contains concluding comments on the current state of the controversy between Keynesian and new classical economists.

11.1 THE NEW CLASSICAL POSITION

We have already quoted Franco Modigliani's Keynesian view that a private-enterprise economy needs to be, can be, and should be stabilized by active government aggregate demand management. The central policy tenet of the new classical economics is that stabilization of *real* variables, such as output and employment, cannot be achieved by aggregate demand management. The values of such variables *in both the short run and the long run* are insensitive to *systematic* aggregate demand management policies. In

[1] Robert Lucas, "Rules, Discretion, and the Role of the Economic Advisor," in Stanley Fischer, ed., *Rational Expectations and Economic Policy* (Chicago: University of Chicago Press, 1980), p. 259.

[2] Ibid., p. 259.

new classical policy ineffectiveness proposition asserts that systematic monetary and fiscal policy actions that change aggregate demand will *not* affect output and employment even in the short run

other words, in the new classical view, systematic monetary and fiscal policy actions that change aggregate demand will not affect output and employment, even in the short run. This has been termed the **new classical policy ineffectiveness proposition**.

A Review of the Keynesian Position

To see the basis for this new classical position, we first consider the new classical economists' critique of Keynesian macroeconomics. A good starting place is a review of the Keynesian analysis of the relationships among output, employment, and aggregate demand, as discussed in Section 10.3. Consider the effects in the Keynesian model of an expansionary policy action—for example, an increase in the money supply. In the short run, such a policy action would increase aggregate demand. The aggregate demand schedule would shift to the right along the upward-sloping aggregate supply schedule (as illustrated, for example, in Figure 10-5*a*). The price level and level of output would rise. Parallel to the increase in output is a rise in employment as labor demand increases, with the rise in prices shifting the labor demand schedule to the right along the upward-sloping (drawn against the money wage) labor supply schedule (as illustrated, for example, in Figure 10-5*b*).

Crucial to these results is the fact that the positions of both the aggregate supply schedule and labor supply schedule are fixed in the short run. The position of both of these schedules depends on the value of the expected price level (P^e), which is assumed to depend primarily on past prices and not to change with current policy actions.

In the long run, the expected price level converges to the actual price level, and both the aggregate supply schedule and the labor supply schedule shift to the left. The initial levels of employment and output are restored, with only the price level and the money wage left permanently higher as a result of the increase in the money supply (see Figure 10-7). Output and employment remain above their long-run equilibrium levels only as long as it takes labor suppliers to perceive correctly the change in the price level that results from the expansionary policy action. As long as our attention is confined to monetary policy actions, monetarists would agree with the foregoing analysis.

The Rational Expectations Concept and Its Implications

New classical economists do not agree. In particular, they do not accept the difference between the short-run and long-run results in the Keynesian or monetarist analysis of the effects of aggregate demand on output and employment. The focal point of their criticism is the Keynesian (and monetarist) assumption concerning price expectations. This formulation assumes that labor suppliers form an expectation of the current aggregate price level (or inflation rate) on the basis of the past behavior of prices. In practice, Keynesians and monetarists have assumed that such price expectations adjust slowly and can be fixed for the analysis of policy effects over short periods.

New classical economists criticize such formulations of expectations as naive in the extreme. Why, they ask, would rational economic agents forming an expectation of the price level rely only on past values of the price level? Why especially would they do so when in general such behavior results in their being *systematically* wrong when aggregate demand shifts? We have been assuming that after changes in aggregate demand—for example, the increase in the money supply considered in the preceding subsection—labor suppliers fail to perceive that the demand shift will affect price.

rational expectations expectations formed on the basis of all available relevant information concerning the variable being predicted. Moreover, economic agents are assumed to use available information intelligently; that is, they understand the relationships between the variables they observe and the variables they are trying to predict.

New classical economists propose that economic agents will form **rational expectations**, rational in that they will not make systematic errors. According to the hypothesis of rational expectations, *expectations are formed on the basis of all available relevant information concerning the variable being predicted*. Furthermore, the hypothesis maintains that individuals use available information intelligently; that is, they understand the way in which the variables they observe will affect the variable they are trying to predict. Thus, according to the rational expectations hypothesis, expectations are, as the originator of the concept, John Muth, suggested, "essentially the same as the predictions of the relevant economic theory,"[3] based on available information.

If expectations are rational, then in forming a prediction of the value of the aggregate price level, labor suppliers will use all relevant past information, not just information about the past behavior of prices. In addition, they will use any information they have about the current values of variables that play a role in the price level. Most important from the standpoint of aggregate demand management policy, labor suppliers will take account of any anticipated (expected) policy actions. Further, they are assumed to understand the relationship between such policies and the price level.

A useful contrast can be made between the *backward-looking* nature of expectations in the Keynesian model and the *forward-looking* nature of rational expectations. In the Keynesian model, expectations are backward-looking. The expectation of a variable such as the price level adjusts (slowly) to the past behavior of the variable. According to the rational expectations hypothesis, economic agents instead use all available relevant information and intelligently assess the implication of that information for the future behavior of a variable.

If labor suppliers make forward-looking rational forecasts of the price level, then the preceding analysis must be modified. To see this modification, we analyze the effects of an expansionary policy action previously considered: a one-time increase in the money supply. To analyze this change with the assumption that expectations are rational, we must begin by specifying whether the policy change was anticipated.[4] Anticipated and unanticipated policy changes have very different effects when expectations are assumed to be rational. First, we assume that the policy change is anticipated, perhaps because the policymaker announced the policy change. Alternatively, the public may anticipate the change because the policymaker is known to act in certain ways. For example, if the policymaker systematically responds to an increase in unemployment in one period by increasing the money supply in the next period

[3]John Muth, "Rational Expectations and the Theory of Price Movements," *Econometrica*, 29 (July 1961), p. 316.

[4]The terms *expected* and *anticipated* or *unexpected* and *unanticipated* are used interchangeably here. Policy shifts are referred to as either *anticipated* or *unanticipated*, whereas we refer to *expected* levels of variables, including policy variables.

FIGURE 11-1 Output and Employment in the New Classical Model

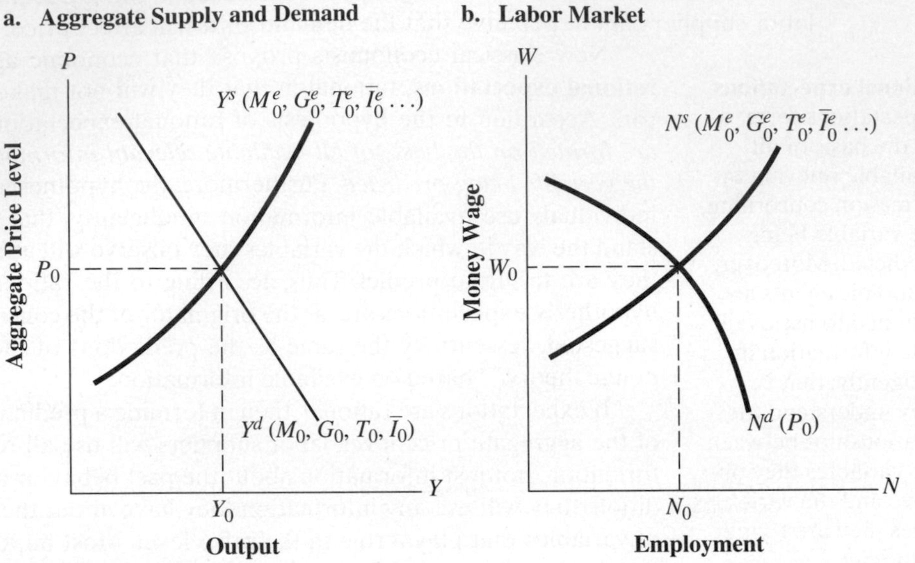

In the new classical model, the aggregate supply and labor supply schedules depend on the rationally formed expectations of current variables, including monetary and fiscal policy variables (M_0^e, G_0^e, T_0^e).

(to counteract unemployment), the public will come to anticipate an increase in the money supply for period t when they observe an increase in the unemployment rate of period $t-1$.

To begin, consider the characterization of equilibrium output and employment in the new classical analysis, as illustrated in Figure 11-1. The crucial difference between the new classical case and the Keynesian case concerns the variables that determine the positions of the labor supply and aggregate supply schedules. As in the Keynesian theory, we assume here that labor supply depends on the expected real wage, the known money wage divided by the expected price level:

$$N^S = t\left(\frac{W}{P^e}\right) \tag{11.1}$$

Consequently, the position of the labor supply schedule, and therefore that of the aggregate supply schedule, depends on the expected price level. Increases in the expected price level will shift both schedules to the left.

In the new classical model, with the assumption of rational expectations, the expected price level depends on the expected levels of the variables in the model that actually determine the price level. These include the *expected* levels of the money supply (M^e), government spending (G^e) and tax collections (T^e), autonomous investment ($\bar{I}^e$) and possibly other variables.[5] The dependence of the expected price level, and hence the positions of the labor supply and aggregate supply schedules on these variables, are

[5]Expected changes in oil prices or other supply-side factors, for example, would affect the expected price level.

FIGURE 11-2 Effects of an Increase in the Money Supply: The New Classical View

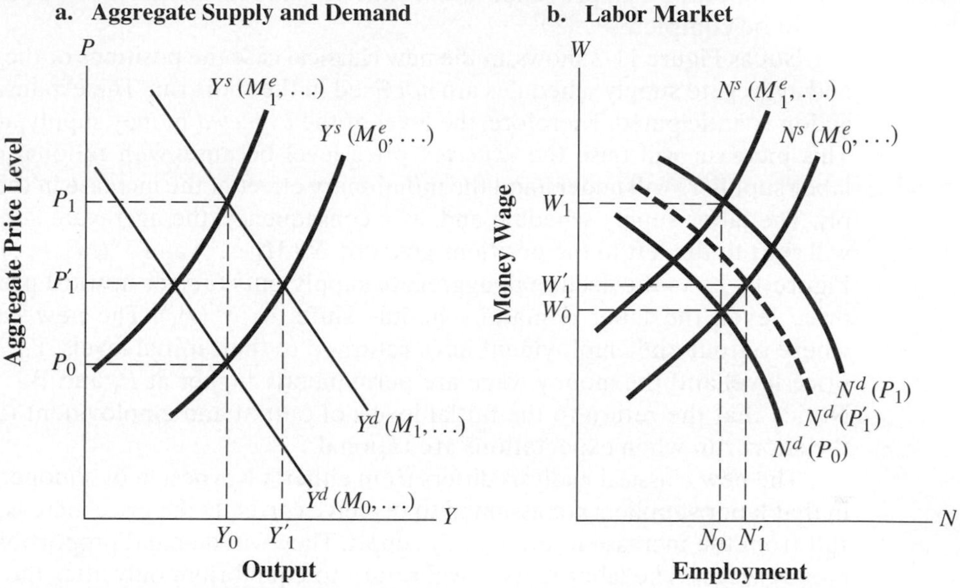

The increase in the money supply shifts the aggregate demand schedule from $Y^d(M_0, \ldots)$ to $Y^d(M_1, \ldots)$. By itself, this change would increase output to Y'_1 and the price level to P'_1. The increase in the price level would shift the labor demand schedule from $N^d(P_0)$ to $N^d(P'_1)$, and employment would rise to N'_1. However, because the increase in the money supply was anticipated, there is also an increase in the *expected* money supply. This increase shifts the aggregate supply schedule to the left from $Y^s(M^e_0, \ldots)$ to $Y^s(M^e_1, \ldots)$ and shifts the labor supply schedule to the left from $N^s(M^e_0, \ldots)$ to $N^s(M^e_1, \ldots)$. These shifts cause employment and output to fall back to their initial levels, N_0 and Y_0.

indicated by the labeling of these curves in Figure 11-1. Especially important is the fact that the positions of the labor supply and aggregate supply schedules depend on the expected levels of the policy variables (M^e, G^e, T^e).

Consider the effect of a fully anticipated increase in the money supply from M_0 to M_1, as depicted in Figure 11-2.[6] Initially, assume that the aggregate demand, aggregate supply, and labor supply and demand schedules are at the same positions as in Figure 11-1, with actual and expected variables subscripted zero (0). The increase in the money supply will shift the aggregate demand schedule to $Y^d(M_1, \ldots)$. If the supply schedule did not shift, output would rise from Y_0 to Y'_1 and the price level would increase from P_0 to P'_1. With the rise in the price level, the labor demand schedule shifts to the right [to the dashed schedule $N^d(P'_1)$ in Figure 11-2*b*. *If the labor supply schedule did not also shift*, employment would rise (from N_0 to N'_1). In the Keynesian or monetarist frameworks, with the expected price level

[6] The positions of the aggregate demand schedule and other schedules continue to depend on all the variables discussed previously, including policy variables, but for notational simplicity the labels on the schedules in the graph contain only the variables that are assumed to change.

unrelated to the current level of policy variables, the positions of the aggregate supply and labor supply schedules *would* be fixed in the short run and our analysis would be complete.

But as Figure 11-2 shows, in the new classical case the positions of the labor supply and aggregate supply schedules are *not* fixed in the short run. The expansionary policy action is anticipated. Therefore, the level of the *expected* money supply also increases. This increase will raise the *expected* price level because, with rational expectations, labor suppliers will understand the inflationary effect of the increase in the money supply. The labor supply schedule and, as a consequence, the aggregate supply schedule will shift to the left to the positions given by $N^s(M_1^e, \ldots)$ and $Y^s(M_1^e, \ldots)$, as shown in Figure 11-2. As the decline in aggregate supply puts further upward pressure on the price level, the labor demand schedule shifts to $N^d(P_1)$. The new equilibrium is where output and employment have returned to their initial levels, Y_0, N_0, while the price level and the money wage are permanently higher at P_1 and W_1, respectively. Notice that the return to the initial levels of output and employment takes place in the short run when expectations are rational.

The new classical analysis differs from either a Keynesian or a monetarist analysis in that labor suppliers are assumed to perceive correctly the price increase that will result from the increase in the money supply. They will demand proportionately higher money wages. The labor market will return to equilibrium only after the money wage and price level have increased in the same proportion, the real wage is unchanged, and consequently employment and output are back at their initial levels. Put differently, in the Keynesian or monetarist analysis, the increase in the money supply leads to an increase in employment and output in the short run—that is, until labor suppliers correctly perceive the increase in the price level that results from the expansionary monetary policy action. In the Keynesian or monetarist view, because expectations about prices are backward-looking, this short-run period in which the increase in the money supply affects output and employment can be of considerable length. If expectations are rational, forward-looking labor suppliers cannot be systematically fooled by anticipated changes in aggregate demand policy.

If expectations are formed rationally, anticipated aggregate demand policy actions will not affect real output or employment, even in the short run. Notice that, because the public will learn any systematic rules of policy action, such as the hypothetical response of the money supply to unemployment mentioned previously, any such set of systematic policy actions will be anticipated and will not affect the behavior of output or employment.[7] The values of real variables such as output and employment will be insensitive to systematic changes in aggregate demand management policies.

Thus far, we have been assuming that the increase in the money supply was anticipated either because it was announced or because it was a systematic policy response that could be predicted. Now consider the effects of an *unanticipated* increase in aggregate demand. We again consider the effects of an increase in the money supply from M_0 to M_1, but the analysis would be similar for an unanticipated increase in aggregate

[7]That the public would learn systematic policy rules follows from the assumption of rational expectations. Estimates of such rules could be based on past policy behavior. Such estimates would be helpful in predicting policy actions and consequently in predicting the behavior of prices and other variables, so the rational economic agent would use the information.

demand from another source. The short-run effects of this unanticipated increase in the money supply—what can be termed a *monetary surprise*—can also be explained with reference to Figure 11-2. As before, the increase in the money supply shifts the aggregate demand schedule from $Y^d(M_0, \ldots)$ to $Y^d(M_1, \ldots)$. As the price level rises to P'_1, the labor demand schedule also shifts to the right, to $N^d(P'_1)$. If the increase in the money supply is unanticipated, these are the only schedules that shift in the short run. The additional shift to the left in the labor supply schedule and consequently the shift to the left in the aggregate supply schedule shown in Figure 11-2, where the increase in the money supply was anticipated, do *not* occur for an unanticipated increase in the money supply. When the increase in the money supply is not anticipated, it does not affect the labor suppliers' expectation of the value the aggregate price level will take on over the current period, so the labor supply schedule does not shift.

When the increase in the money supply is unanticipated, the new classical model indicates that output and employment will be affected. In Figure 11-2, output will rise from Y_0 to Y'_1 and employment will increase from N_0 to N'_1, results identical to those of the Keynesian or monetarist analysis of such an increase in aggregate demand. For the short run, even assuming rational expectations, labor suppliers do not perceive the inflationary effect of the increase in aggregate demand. This was the assumption in both the Keynesian and monetarist views for any change in aggregate demand. New classical economists deny that anticipated changes in aggregate demand can affect output and employment, but their view of the effects of unanticipated changes in aggregate demand does not differ from that of Keynesians and monetarists.

This analysis of the effects of an unanticipated monetary policy action illustrates an important difference between the new classical theory and the classical theory explained in Chapters 3 and 4. In the new classical model, economic agents form rational expectations but they do not have perfect information; they make mistakes in predicting the price level, and such mistakes cause short-run deviations of output and employment from their long-run equilibrium rates. In the classical model, economic agents were assumed to have perfect information. Labor suppliers knew the real wage; there were no monetary (or other) surprises and no deviations from the supply-determined rates of output and employment.

New Classical Policy Conclusions

The new classical view that unanticipated aggregate demand changes affect output and employment still does not provide a meaningful role for macroeconomic stabilization policy. To see this, consider the new classical economists' view of the proper policy response to a decline in private-sector demand—for example, an autonomous decline in investment. We have already analyzed the Keynesian view of the proper policy response to shocks of this type. Keynesians argue that a decline in private-sector demand should be offset by an expansionary monetary or fiscal policy action to stabilize aggregate demand, output, and employment.

The effects of the decline in investment are depicted in Figure 11-3. The decline in investment demand shifts the aggregate demand schedule from $Y^d(\bar{I}_0)$ to $Y^d(\bar{I}_1)$ in Figure 11-3*a*. This shift causes output to decline from Y_0 to Y'_1. The price level will fall from P_0 to P'_1 and as a result, the labor demand schedule in Figure 11-3*b* will shift

FIGURE 11-3 Effects of an Autonomous Decline in Investment: A New Classical View

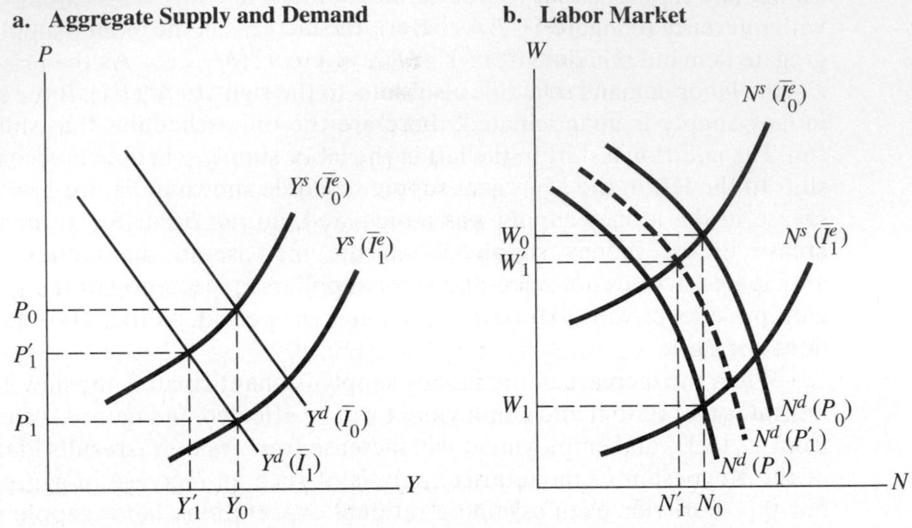

An autonomous decline in investment shifts the aggregate demand schedule from $Y^d(\bar{I}_0)$ to $Y^d(\bar{I}_1)$. This shift would reduce output from Y_0 to Y'_1 and lower the price level from P_0 to P'_1. The fall in the price level shifts the labor demand schedule from $N^d(P_0)$ to $N^d(P'_1)$, and as a result employment falls from N_0 to N'_1. These are the only effects if the decline in investment was not anticipated. If the decline in investment was anticipated, the expected level of autonomous investment (I^e) will also fall (from $\bar{I}_0^e$ to $\bar{I}_1^e$). The aggregate supply schedule will shift from $Y^s(\bar{I}_0^e)$ to $Y^s(\bar{I}_1^e)$, and the labor supply schedule will shift from $N^s(\bar{I}_0^e)$ to $N^s(\bar{I}_1^e)$. Those shifts cause output and employment to return to their initial levels.

downward from $N^d(P_0)$ to $N^d(P'_1)$. Whether there are additional effects from the decline in investment depends, in the new classical view, on whether the decline was or was not anticipated. To begin, we assume that it was anticipated.

In that case, labor suppliers will anticipate the decline in the price level that will result from the decline in aggregate demand. Labor suppliers, now expecting the price level to be lower, will supply more labor at a given money wage, because with the lower expected price level, a given money wage corresponds to a higher expected real wage. This fall in the expected price level shifts the labor supply schedule to the right in Figure 11-3*b* [from $N^s(\bar{I}_0^e)$ to $N^s(\bar{I}_1^e)$]. As a consequence, the aggregate supply schedule shifts to the right in Figure 11-3*a* [from $Y^s(\bar{I}_0^e)$ to $Y^s(\bar{I}_1^e)$]. There is a further decline in the price level to P_1 and therefore a further downward shift in the labor demand schedule to $N^d(P_1)$. At the new *short-run* equilibrium, the money wage and price level have fallen sufficiently to restore employment and output to their initial levels, N_0 and Y_0.

This analysis is just the reverse of our analysis of an anticipated increase in aggregate demand resulting from an increase in the money supply. In the new classical system, output and employment are not affected by anticipated changes in aggregate demand, even in the short run. Consequently, there is no need for a stabilization policy response to an anticipated demand change such as a decline in investment.

But what if the decline in investment had not been anticipated? In that case, the labor suppliers would not have foreseen the price decline that resulted from the decline in aggregate demand. The labor supply schedule (Figure 11-3*b*) and the aggregate supply schedule (Figure 11-3*a*) would have remained at $N^s(\bar{I}_0^e)$ and $Y^s(\bar{I}_0^e)$, respectively. The decline in investment would have caused output and employment to decline to the levels given by Y'_1 and N'_1. Would not an offsetting policy action to raise aggregate demand back to its initial level be called for?

The answer is that such a policy response would be desirable but not feasible. The decline in investment was by definition unanticipated. That is, assuming rational expectations, the decline could not have been predicted on the basis of *any* available information. Policymakers, like any other economic agents, would have been unable to foresee the investment decline in advance. They could not have acted to raise aggregate demand to offset the decline. Once the investment decline has occurred and had its effect on output, policymakers could act to raise aggregate demand if the low investment level was expected to be repeated in future periods. If low investment was *expected* to continue, however, there would be no need for a policy response because private agents would also hold this expectation. At this point, the shift in the labor supply and aggregate supply schedules would take place. In other words, as long as the shock is unanticipated, policymakers lack the knowledge needed to offset the shock. Once the shock is anticipated by policymakers, it is also anticipated by other economic agents, including labor suppliers, and there is no need to offset the shock.

The foregoing analysis indicates that the new classical view includes no useful role for aggregate demand policies aimed at stabilizing output and employment. New classical economists' policy conclusions are noninterventionist, just as were those of classical economists. In this respect, new classical economists agree with the monetarists. Concerning monetary policy, many new classical economists favor a policy rule. A policy rule targeting money growth or inflation would reduce unanticipated policy changes, which have no stabilization value and cause economic agents to make price forecast errors.

In the case of fiscal policy, new classical economists favor stability and the avoidance of excessive and inflationary stimuli. New classical economists Thomas Sargent and Neil Wallace, for example, were critical of the large deficits that resulted from the Reagan administration's fiscal policy of the 1980s.[8]

Instability in fiscal policy causes uncertainty, making it difficult for agents forming rational expectations to correctly anticipate the course of the economy. Moreover, Sargent and others believe that a *credible* noninflationary monetary policy cannot coexist with a fiscal policy that generates large deficits. Huge deficits put great pressure on the monetary authority to increase money growth in order to help finance the deficit. Sargent and other new classical economists believe that control of the government budget deficit is necessary for a credible, noninflationary monetary policy.

Read Perspectives 11-1.

---

[8]Thomas Sargent and Neil Wallace, "Some Unpleasant Monetarist Arithmetic," Federal Reserve Bank of Minneapolis *Review* (Fall 1981).

PERSPECTIVES 11.1

U.S. STOCK PRICES: RATIONAL EXPECTATIONS OR IRRATIONAL EXUBERANCE?

We have been considering the implications of the rational expectations assumption for macroeconomic stabilization policies. The assumption of rational expectations also has implications for other economic questions, an important one being determining the prices of financial assets. Here we consider the rational expectations assumption applied to the theory of stock price determination.

If agents form rational expectations, then in deciding how much a given stock (e.g., General Electric) is worth, they will use all information and use it intelligently. The relevant information in this context would be anything known about the future earnings prospects of the corporation, what are called *market fundamentals*. In a market populated by such agents, stock prices will move very quickly in response to new information about a corporation's earning prospects. In fact, prices will move so quickly that the current price of a corporation's stock is assumed to already reflect all currently available information. Such a market is termed an *efficient market*.[a]

Just as in the case of stabilization policy, the application of the rational expectations assumption to prices in the stock market is controversial. Many doubt that investors in the stock market are so rational. These doubters believe that decisions to buy and sell stock are in large part made independently of new information about market fundamentals. Among the early doubters was John Maynard Keynes. Keynes described the stock market as "a game of Snap, of Old Maid, of Musical Chairs—a pastime in which he is victor who says Snap neither too soon nor too late, who passes the Old Maid to his neighbor before the game is over, who secures a chair for himself when the music stops." Keynes and later doubters believe that *herd instincts, momentum investing*, and *feedback trading* are better descriptions of the motives for buying and selling stock than decisions motivated by rational expectations. According to these doubters, investors are strongly conditioned by what other investors are doing.

As opposed to the behavior of stock prices in an efficient market, stock prices in a market driven by the type of investors described by Keynes might be excessively volatile as investors feed off one another's actions and drive prices either up or down. In 1996, Federal Reserve Board Chairman Alan Greenspan questioned whether the rapid rise in stock prices at that time was not being driven by "irrational exuberance" rather than rational expectations.[b]

Figure 11-4 plots the values of two stock price indices, the broad Standard and Poors 500 and the NASDAQ, which contains many high-tech companies, for the period 1987–2007. The sharp run-up in stock prices in the late 1990s and the subsequent sharp decline in 2000–02 lent support to believers in irrational exuberance. The boom and collapse in NASDAQ seemed especially to be more consistent with the idea of a speculative bubble as opposed to an efficient stock market.

Defenders of the efficient market were not convinced. Burton Malkiel, in an article in 2003, argued that while market pricing was not always "perfect," deviations from market efficiency were more the "exception than the rule."[c] Malkiel argued that any serious market inefficiency should present

FIGURE 11-4 The NASDAQ and the S&P 500 (February 2, 1987–February 2, 2007)

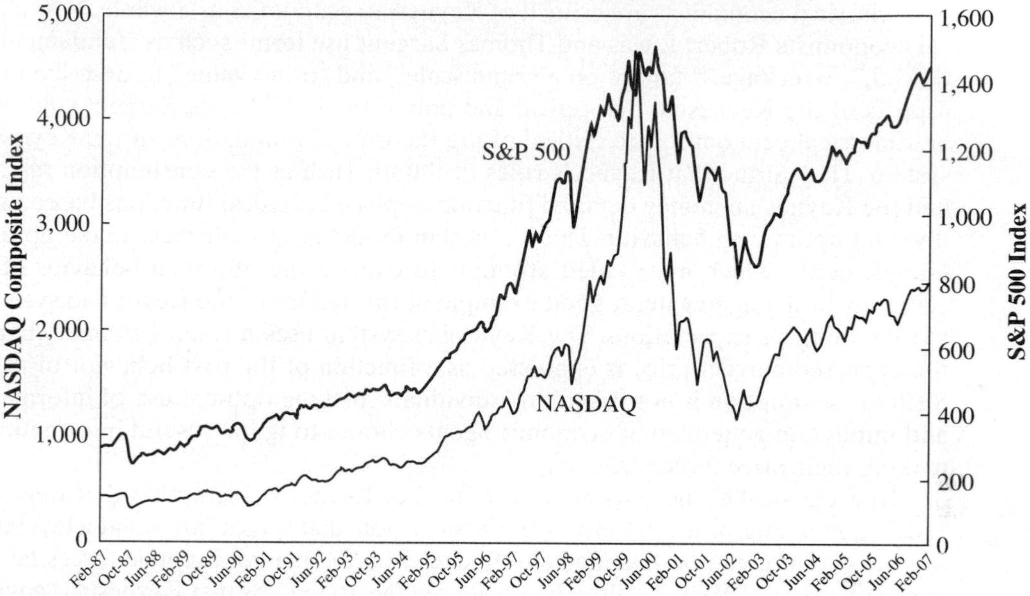

SOURCE: Yahoo Finance.

an exploitable profit opportunity. If information is not efficiently incorporated into stock prices, there should be potential profit in its use. On this point he quoted Richard Roll, a finance theorist and a portfolio manager, as follows: "I have personally tried to invest money, my clients' money and my own, in every single anomaly and predictive device that academics have dreamed up. . . . And I have yet to make a nickel on any of these supposed market inefficiencies."[d]

Whether the stock market is driven by rational expectations or irrational exuberance has important implications for the economy. Excessive volatility is costly in that it may drive investors away from the market and increase firms' costs of obtaining funds. A market made up of mainly irrational investors would be a more likely target for regulation than one in which prices were determined by investors with rational expectations responding to market fundamentals.

---

[a]A classic statement of the efficient markets hypothesis is in Eugene F. Fama, "Efficient Capital Markets: A Review of Theory and Empirical Work," *Journal of Finance* (1970), pp. 383–416.

[b]Robert Shiller has used Greenspan's phrase as the title of his book *Irrational Exuberance* (Princeton, N.J.: Princeton University Press, 2000), which questions the validity of the efficient markets hypothesis.

[c]Burton Malkiel, "The Efficient Market Hypothesis and Its Critics," *Journal of Economic Perspectives*, 17 (Winter 2003), pp. 59–82.

[d]Ibid., p. 72.

11.2 A BROADER VIEW OF THE NEW CLASSICAL POSITION

New classical economists are critical of Keynesian economics as a whole. New classical economists Robert Lucas and Thomas Sargent use terms such as "fundamentally flawed," "wreckage," "failure on a grand scale," and "of no value" to describe major aspects of the Keynesian theoretical and policy analysis.[9] Lucas, Sargent, and other new classical economists are critical of the theoretical foundations of the Keynesian system. They argue that Keynes's rules of thumb, such as the consumption function and the Keynesian money demand function, replaced classical functions based on individual optimizing behavior. The Keynesian model is, in their view, made up of *ad hoc* elements, which were failed attempts to explain the observed behavior of the economy in the aggregate. A good example of this failure of the Keynesian system is the handling of expectations. The Keynesian system uses a rule of thumb whereby the expected current price is expressed as a function of the past behavior of prices. Such an assumption is not based on individuals' making optimal use of information and implies, in general, that economic agents choose to ignore useful information in making their price forecasts.

New classical economists are also critical of Keynes's assumption that wages are "sticky," meaning, as they interpret this assumption, that wages "are set at a level or by a process that could be taken as uninfluenced by the macroeconomic forces he proposed to analyze." We have already considered the arguments that Keynesians advance to support the assumption of wage rigidity. New classical economists do not find these arguments convincing. They favor the classical view that markets, including the labor market, *clear*; that is, prices, including the money wage rate, move to equate supply and demand.

New classical economists argue that fruitful macroeconomic models should rectify the failures of Keynesian economics by consistently adhering to the following assumptions:

1. Agents optimize; that is, they act in their own self-interest.
2. Markets clear.

Why, then, did Keynes dispense with those assumptions? Keynesian economics was a response to the failure of classical economics to explain the problem of unemployment and the relationship between unemployment and aggregate demand. Recall that the classical aggregate supply schedule was vertical. With supply schedule, aggregate output was totally dependent on supply factors. The classical model was abandoned by Keynes because it did not explain prolonged deviations of output and employment from full-employment levels.

New classical economists argue that a model in the classical tradition can explain the deviations from full employment if the assumption of rational expectations is incorporated into the classical system. Recall that the classical theory of the labor market, which was the basis for the classical vertical aggregate supply function, assumed that labor suppliers knew the real wage, implying that labor suppliers had *perfect information*

[9] Robert Lucas and Thomas Sargent, "After Keynesian Macroeconomics," in *After the Phillips Curve: Persistence of High Inflation and High Unemployment* (Boston: Federal Reserve Bank of Boston, 1978).

about the value that the aggregate price level would take on over the short run. New classical economists substitute the assumption that labor suppliers make a rational forecast of the aggregate price level. In this case, as we have seen, systematic, and hence anticipated, changes in aggregate demand will not affect output and employment, but unanticipated changes in aggregate demand will. Such unanticipated changes in aggregate demand can explain deviations from full employment.

This substitution of the assumption of rational expectations for the classical assumption of perfect information does not require substantive changes in the noninterventionist classical policy conclusions, for as we saw earlier in this chapter, meaningful aggregate demand management policies involve *systematic* variations in aggregate demand, and these have no effect on output and employment in the new classical view.

11.3 THE KEYNESIAN COUNTERCRITIQUE

The theme that runs through the Keynesian response to the new classical criticisms is that, although they raise valid points, especially concerning the weakness of the Keynesian treatment of expectations formation, it is still, as the Keynesian Robert Solow puts it, "much too early to tear up the *IS–LM* chapters in the textbooks of your possibly misspent youth."[10] Keynesians continue to believe that Keynes provided the basis for a useful framework in which to analyze the determinants of output and employment. They continue to believe in the usefulness of activist policies to stabilize output and employment. Major areas in which the Keynesians have raised objections to the new classical view are as follows.

The Question of Persistence

In the preceding section, we saw that the new classical model, with the concept of rational expectations, could explain deviations from potential output. Unanticipated declines in aggregate demand would move output and employment below their potential levels. Keynesians argue that although such an explanation might be plausible for brief departures from potential output and employment, it is not adequate to explain the persistent and substantial deviations that we have experienced. An unanticipated decline in investment, such as we considered previously (Figure 11-3), might well cause output and employment to decline over a short period, say one year. By the next year, however, this decline in aggregate demand would be apparent; it would no longer be unanticipated. Labor suppliers would recognize that the price level had declined. Consequently, the shifts to the right in the labor supply schedule and the aggregate supply schedule discussed previously (see Figure 11-3) would restore employment and output to their initial levels.

This being the case, how can the new classical model explain unemployment rates of 10 percent or more in Great Britain for the entire period 1923–39 or during the Great Depression of the 1930s in the United States, when the unemployment rate exceeded 14 percent for 10 consecutive years? How can the model explain the movement

[10] Robert Solow, "Alternative Approaches to Macroeconomic Theory: A Partial View," *The Canadian Journal of Economics, 12* (August 1979), p. 354.

of the unemployment rate during the deep and prolonged recessions of the mid-1970s and early 1980s?

New classical economists respond that although the source of the unemployment, the unanticipated change in aggregate demand, will be of short duration, the effects of the shock will persist. Consider, for example, the response to an unanticipated decline in demand. Assume that after one year or so, everyone recognizes that demand has fallen, so the change is no longer unanticipated. Declines in output and employment will have occurred. New classical economists argue that it will take time before such declines are reversed. Firms that have already cut output will not find it optimal to restore production immediately to preshock levels because of the cost of adjusting output. Moreover, firms will have accumulated excess inventory stocks over the period during which output was in decline. It will take time to run off such stocks; in the meantime, production and employment will remain depressed. On the labor supply side, workers who have become unemployed will not find it optimal to take the first job offer that comes along but will search for the best opportunity. New classical economists argue that, as a consequence of these adjustment lags, lengthy deviations from full employment, such as the United States experienced during the mid-1970s and early 1980s, can be explained even though the shocks that cause such deviations are short-lived.

What about the depression in Great Britain and the United States in the 1930s? One proponent of the new classical position, Robert Barro, has explained the severity of the U.S. experience by the extent of the largely unanticipated monetary collapse during the early years of the Depression, when the money supply fell by one-third. The slow recovery is viewed as a result of the massive government intervention during the New Deal period that subverted the normal adjustment mechanisms of the private sector.[11] Other new classical economists, such as Sargent and Lucas, agree with Keynesians that the Great Depression is not well explained by their theory, but they do not find the Keynesian explanation convincing.

On this question of persistence, Keynesians remain unconvinced that adjustment lags sufficiently explain prolonged and severe unemployment. They believe that accepting the classical or new classical framework can explain episodes such as the Great Depression only as a result of factors on the supply side, which in their view are the only factors in these models that could cause prolonged unemployment. If markets clear and there is no involuntary unemployment, then, as Modigliani puts it, to the classical or new classical economists "what happened to the United States in the 1930s was a severe attack of contagious laziness."[12]

The Extreme Informational Assumptions of Rational Expectations

Keynesians accept the new classical economists' criticism of price expectations formulations based only on information about past prices. Such rules are naive because they assume that economic agents neglect available and potentially useful information in

[11]See Robert Barro, "Second Thoughts on Keynesian Economics," *American Economic Review*, 69 (May 1979), p. 57. Examples of such New Deal interventions include National Recovery Administration codes to fix prices and wages, agricultural policies to restrict output and raise prices, and increased regulation of the banking and securities industries, which might have hindered the raising of funds for investment. (See Perspectives 11.2.)

[12]Franco Modigliani, "The Monetarist Controversy, or Should We Forsake Stabilization Policies?" *American Economic Review*, 67 (March 1977), p. 6.

making their forecasts. Such naive assumptions about expectations came into use in the 1950s and early 1960s, when the inflation rate was both low and stable. In these circumstances, such rules might have been reasonable approximations of the way people made forecasts, because good forecasts could, in fact, have been based on the past behavior of prices. With the volatile and, at times, high inflation of the post-1970 period, it is harder to believe that economic agents did not find it worthwhile to make more sophisticated forecasts.

Still, many Keynesians argue that the rational expectations assumption errs in assuming that economic agents are unrealistically sophisticated forecasters, especially when rational expectations are assumed for individual suppliers of labor. Keynesians criticize the assumption that individuals use *all* available relevant information in making their forecasts. Such an assumption ignores the costs of gathering information.

The rational expectations theory also presumes that individuals use available information intelligently. They know the relationships that link observed variables with variables they are trying to predict. They are also able to understand the systematic response pattern of policymakers. For example, if the monetary policymaker typically responds to rising unemployment by increasing the money supply, the public will come to anticipate such policy actions. Moreover, they will be able to predict the effects of such anticipated monetary policy actions. If the economy, including the behavior of policymakers, had been subject to little change for a long period of time, Keynesians believe, it is perhaps reasonable to believe that economic agents would come to know the underlying relationships that govern policy variables and economic aggregates. The rational expectations assumption might be realistic in a long-run equilibrium model, but Keynesians argue that it is not realistic in the short run. In the short run, the cost of gathering and processing information may be high enough that labor suppliers making forecasts of the aggregate price level or inflation rate do not find it worthwhile to use much information over and above the past behavior of prices.

If expectations are not rational, there is a role for aggregate demand management aimed at stabilizing output and employment. Even systematic changes in aggregate demand will affect output and employment because they will not be predicted by economic agents. If private-sector aggregate demand is unstable, as Keynesians believe it is, a stabilization policy is needed. Further, the monetary and fiscal policymaking authorities should be able to forecast systematic changes in private-sector aggregate demand. These policymaking authorities *do* gather what they consider to be all the available and important information on variables they wish to forecast and control. They also invest considerable resources in trying to estimate the relationships that characterize the economy. Keynesians regard the rational expectations assumption as reasonably correct when applied to the policymakers. The policymakers can design policy changes to offset what to the public are unanticipated changes in private-sector aggregate demand. In essence, this role for stabilization policy stems from an *information advantage* on the part of the policymaker.

Keynesians conclude:

> Macroeconomic models based on the assumptions of the rational expectations hypothesis do not demonstrate the short-run ineffectiveness of policy, therefore, because they are not really short-run models. The information availability

> assumption of the rational expectations hypothesis implicitly places such models in a long-run equilibrium context in which their classical properties . . . are not surprising.[13]

New classical economists defend the rational expectations assumptions. They admit that the rational expectations hypothesis is unrealistic, but as Bennett McCallum argues, "All theories or models are 'unrealistic' in the sense of being extremely simplified descriptions of reality. . . . So the true issue is: of all the simple expectational assumptions conceivable, which one should be embodied in a macroeconomic model to be used for stabilization analysis?"[14] New classical economists favor the rational expectations assumption over the assumption that individuals form price expectations based only on the past history of prices.

Auction Market versus Contractual Views of the Labor Market

In the new classical view, as in the original classical theory, the money wage is assumed to adjust quickly to clear the labor market—to equate labor supply and demand. This is an *auction market* characterization. In contrast, in the Keynesian *contractual* view of the labor market, "wages are not set to clear markets in the short run, but rather are strongly conditioned by longer-term considerations involving . . . employer–worker relations."[15] The money wage is sticky in the downward direction. In Arthur Okun's phrase, the labor market functions more by the *invisible handshake* than by the *invisible hand* of a competitive market mechanism. Most of the response to a decline in aggregate demand and, consequently, the demand for labor comes in the form of a reduction in employment rather than in a fall in the money wage.

Keynesians view the labor market as one in which long-term arrangements are made between buyers and sellers. In general, such relationships fix the money wage while leaving the employer free to adjust hours worked over the course of the explicit or implicit contract. Layoffs or reduced hours are considered an acceptable response on the part of the employer to a fall in demand. Applying pressure for wage cuts or replacing current workers with unemployed workers who will work for lower wages is not acceptable. This contractual Keynesian view explains wage stickiness on the basis of the institutional mechanisms that characterize the labor market. Much work is underway to investigate the theoretical reasons such labor market institutions have developed. Even without such theoretical foundations, the Keynesians argue that institutional mechanisms of this nature *do exist*, and they criticize new classical economists for ignoring these elements of reality that their model cannot explain.

[13]Benjamin Friedman, "Optimal Expectations and the Extreme Informational Assumptions of 'Rational Expectations' Macromodels," *Journal of Monetary Economics,* 5 (January 1979), pp. 39–40.

[14]Bennett McCallum, "The Significance of Rational Expectations Theory," *Challenge Magazine* (January–February 1980), p. 39.

[15]Arthur Okun, *Price and Quantities* (Washington, D.C.: The Brookings Institution, 1981), extends this contractual view to product markets, with resulting price stickiness. New Keynesian models of this type are examined in Chapter 12.

New classical economists agree that the labor market is, at least in part, characterized by long-term contracts. They deny, however, that the existence of such contracts has, of itself, any implication for whether the labor market will clear—that is, for whether there will be involuntary unemployment. They deny that the terms of labor contracts are so rigid that employers and employees cannot effect changes desirable to both parties. For example, if the money wage specified is too high to maintain the market-clearing level of employment, workers could give up other provisions in the contract, increase the work done per hour, or in extreme cases allow revision of the wage in some fashion. New classical economists do not deny that labor contracts cause some deviation of employment from the market-clearing levels, but they do not believe this deviation is significant.

Read Perspectives 11-2.

PERSPECTIVES 11.2

THE GREAT DEPRESSION: NEW CLASSICAL VIEWS

The Great Depression of the 1930s was a pivotal event in the development of our thinking about macroeconomic questions. Consequently, it is of interest to examine how each of the theories we consider explains this phenomenon.

Let us examine what several leading proponents of the new classical view have had to say about the Depression. First, Robert Lucas:

> If you look back at the '29 to '33 episode, there were a lot of decisions made that, after the fact, people wished that they had not made. There were a lot of jobs people quit that they wished they had hung onto; there were job offers that people turned down because they thought the wage offer was crappy. Then three months later they wished they had grabbed [them]. Accountants who lost their accounting jobs passed over a cab driver job, and now they're sitting on the street while their pal's driving a cab. So they wish they'd taken the cab driver job. People are making this kind of mistake all the time. Anybody can look back over the '30's and think of decisions he could have taken to make a million. Stocks I would have bought. All kinds of things. I don't see what's *hard* about this question of people making mistakes in the business cycle.[a]

Lucas points to misperceptions—unanticipated changes in prices—having real effects. Lucas sees unanticipated declines in the price level as the result of the sharp decline in the money supply, as Milton Friedman suggests (see Perspectives 9.1).[b]

Robert Barro also sees monetary and other government policies as key factors in the 1929–33 experience: "The unprecedented monetary collapse over this period accords quantitatively with the drastic decline in economic activity."[c] In addition to the effects that the rapid decline in the money supply may have had, Barro points to a real (or supply-side) effect from the collapse of much of the banking system during this period. (Nine thousand banks failed between 1923 and 1933.) As banks failed, for example, crops might not be produced because farmers could not get loans to buy farm machinery. In general, a decline in the availability of financial services may have reduced overall output supply in the 1929–33 period.[d]

As a further alternative to Keynesian explanations of the Depression, Barro suggests that "the government interventions associated with the New Deal, including the volume of public expenditures and direct price regulations, retarded the recovery of the economy, which was nevertheless rapid after 1933."[e]

But both Barro and Lucas still find parts of the Depression phenomenon puzzling and would, at least in some respects, agree with new classical economist Thomas Sargent that

> I do not have a theory, nor do I know somebody else's theory that constitutes a satisfactory explanation of the Great Depression. It's really a very important, unexplained event and process, which I would be very interested in and would like to see explained.[f]

[a]Arjo Klamer, *The New Classical Macroeconomics: Conversations with the New Classical Economists and Their Opponents* (Totowa, N.J.: Rowman and Allanheld, 1983), p. 41.

[b]Ibid., p. 42.

[c]Robert J. Barro, "Second Thoughts on Keynesian Economics," *American Economic Review*, 69 (May 1979), p. 58.

[d]Robert J. Barro, "Rational Expectations and Macroeconomics in 1984," *American Economic Review*, 74 (May 1984), p. 180.

[e]Barro, "Second Thoughts on Keynesian Economics," p. 57.

[f]Klamer, *The New Classical Macroeconomics*, p. 69.

11.4 CONCLUSION

The new classical economics presents a fundamental challenge to Keynesian orthodoxy. On the theoretical level, new classical economists question the soundness of the Keynesian model, arguing that many of its relationships are not firmly based on individual optimizing behavior. New classical economists point to the naive treatment of price expectations in the Keynesian model as an example. Further, they criticize what they consider Keynesians' arbitrary assumptions concerning wage stickiness and consequent involuntary unemployment.

On policy questions, new classical economists maintain that output and employment are independent of systematic and, therefore, anticipated changes in aggregate demand. This is the new classical policy ineffectiveness postulate. Because meaningful aggregate demand management policies to stabilize output and employment consist of systematic changes in aggregate demand, new classical economists see no role for these policies. They arrive at noninterventionist policy conclusions similar to those of the classical economists.

Keynesians criticize the new classical theory on several grounds. They argue that the new classical model cannot explain the prolonged and severe unemployment experienced by the United States and other industrialized countries. They claim that the rational expectations assumption ascribes an extreme and unrealistic availability of information to market participants. Finally, and most important, they criticize the auction market characterization of the labor market in the new classical model. Keynesians believe that the labor market is a contractual market and that the nature of these contractual arrangements leads to wage rigidities and consequent involuntary unemployment.

The new classical critique has, however, stimulated new avenues of Keynesian research on the causes of unemployment. The new Keynesian models emerging from this research are considered in Chapter 12, in which we also examine the development of a second generation of new classical models—the so-called real business cycle models.

KEY TERMS

- new classical policy ineffectiveness proposition 228
- rational expectations 229

REVIEW QUESTIONS AND PROBLEMS

1. Explain the concept of *rational expectations*. How does this view of how expectations are formed differ from the assumption made in previous chapters that workers form expectations of current and future price levels based on past information about prices?
2. Explain the implications of the rational expectations assumption for the effectiveness of economic stabilization policy.
3. Contrast the new classical and Keynesian views of the way labor markets function.
4. Within the new classical framework, how could you explain a sustained departure from potential output such as that experienced by the United States beginning in 2001?
5. Compare the new classical and monetarist positions concerning the effectiveness of aggregate demand management policies to stabilize output.
6. Even within the new classical model, anticipated policy actions such as an increase in the money supply will affect *nominal* income. Explain why the adjustment of economic agents' expectations, which offsets the real effects of such a policy change, does not offset the nominal effects as well.
7. Why attach the adjective *new* to *classical* to describe the model in this chapter? How does this analysis differ from the classical model presented in Chapters 3 and 4?
8. Comment on the following statement. Do you agree or disagree with this view concerning the effectiveness of systematic or anticipated fiscal policy actions within a new classical economic framework? Explain.

   > The new classical economics or rational expectations theory provides a convincing explanation of the inability of systematic monetary policy to affect real income or employment. The situation is quite different, however, with fiscal policy actions such as increases in government spending, which will affect real output and employment whether they are anticipated or not—the difference between monetary and fiscal policy being that monetary policy affects aggregate demand and, hence, output by *inducing* private economic agents to change their demands for output. With rational expectations this effect will be offset. An increase in government spending affects aggregate demand directly, and there is no way for the private sector to offset its effects on income and employment.

9. How would a supply shock, such as the exogenous increase in the price of oil analyzed in Section 8.5, affect the aggregate price level and the level of real output in the new classical model?
10. During the administration of George W. Bush, reductions in the tax rates on labor income, dividends, and capital gains were the centerpiece of fiscal policy. Analyze the macroeconomic effects of such tax cuts within the new classical model.

CHAPTER 12

Real Business Cycles and New Keynesian Economics

Concerning the debate between Keynesians and new classical economists, one observer commented that the most impressive feature of the position of each side was its criticism of the other. Whether this is the case or not, the debate did leave some in each camp feeling that further research was needed to bolster their fundamental position. These feelings spawned two new directions in macroeconomic research. One, strongly rooted in the classical tradition, is the *real business cycle theory*. The second, the *new Keynesian theory*, as its name suggests, follows in the Keynesian tradition. The real business cycle theory is discussed in Section 12.1. We then turn to the new Keynesian theory in Section 12.2.

12.1 REAL BUSINESS CYCLE MODELS

Real business cycle theory is an outgrowth of the new classical theory, which in turn built on the original classical economics. In fact, real business cycle models are sometimes referred to as the *second generation* of new classical models.

Central Features of Real Business Cycle Models

Recall that new classical economists believe macroeconomic models should have two characteristics:

1. Agents optimize.
2. Markets clear.

Real business cycle theorists agree. A hallmark of real business cycle models is their careful attention to microeconomic foundations—the individuals' optimizing decisions. Real business cycle theorists also believe that the business cycle is an *equilibrium* phenomenon in the sense that all markets clear. This belief contrasts with the Keynesian view that the labor market does not clear. The Keynesian model includes involuntary unemployment. In real business cycle models, as in new classical models, all unemployment is voluntary.

Where real business cycle theorists part company with new classical economists is on the causes of fluctuations in output and employment. Real business cycle theorists see these fluctuations as "arising from variations in the real opportunities of the private economy."[1] Factors that cause such changes include shocks to technology, variations

[1]Robert G. King and Charles Plosser, "Money, Credit and Prices in a Real Business Cycle Model," *American Economic Review*, 74 (June 1984), p. 363.

in environmental conditions, changes in the real (relative) prices of imported raw materials (e.g., crude oil), and changes in tax rates. Fluctuations in output also occur with changes in individuals' preferences—for example, a change in the preference for goods relative to leisure. These are the same factors that determined output in the classical model. But classical economists believed that for the most part these factors changed only slowly over time. In the short run, they were taken as given.[2] They were the factors that would determine long-run growth. The real business cycle theorists argue that these supply-side variables are also the source of short-run fluctuations in output and employment.

This view distinguishes the real business cycle theorists from new classical economists, who regarded unanticipated changes in aggregate demand, resulting, for instance, from "monetary surprises," as the main source of fluctuations in output and employment. Nothing in the new classical framework precludes an important role for supply-side variables, such as the oil price shocks of the 1970s or changes in tax rates, in the short run. Still, unanticipated changes in demand were viewed as the major source of cyclical fluctuations in output. Factors such as technology shocks or changes in individual preferences received less attention.

The view that changes in real supply-side factors determine short-run fluctuations in output and employment also differentiates real business cycle models from Keynesian models. As we saw in Chapter 8, Keynesian models can incorporate the effects of supply-side shocks, but a central tenet of the Keynesian theory is the importance of aggregate demand in determining output and employment in the short run.

Before we consider a real business cycle model, there are two more general points to make. First is the question of why real business cycle theorists reject the new classical explanation of the source of short-run fluctuations in output, while in other respects the two approaches are so similar. One reason is that the empirical evidence on the role of unanticipated changes in aggregate demand in determining output is mixed. Probably more importantly, real business cycle theorists believe that the view that errors in predicting aggregate demand can explain large and costly fluctuations in output ultimately violates the postulate that agents optimize. As Robert Barro expresses this view, "If information about money and the general price level mattered much for economic decisions, people could expend relatively few resources to find out quickly about money and prices."[3] If they do not, they are not optimizing.

Finally, note that there are two possible interpretations of the real business cycle theory. One views it as proposing that real supply-side factors are simply more important than nominal demand-side influences. In this interpretation, however, real business cycle models are just versions of the new classical model that, as explained previously, can also incorporate supply-side shocks. When real business cycle theorists differentiate their models from new classical models, such as the one considered in Chapter 11, they assert a much stronger position—that is, that monetary and other nominal demand-side shocks have *no* significant effect on output and employment.

[2]Tax rates could change in the short run, with effects that we considered in Section 4.3. As noted there, however, classical economists gave little attention to the effect of changes in tax rates because of the low level of tax rates at the time they wrote.

[3]Robert J. Barro, *Modern Business Cycle Theory* (Cambridge, Mass.: Harvard University Press, 1989), p. 2.

A Simple Real Business Cycle Model

Real business cycle models, in the words of one of their developers,

> view aggregate economic variables as the outcomes of the decisions made by many individual agents acting to maximize their utility subject to production possibilities and resource constraints. As such the models have an explicit and firm foundation in microeconomics.[4]

In this section, we construct a simple real business cycle model. Having constructed the model, we consider how optimizing economic agents respond to changes in economic conditions and the implications of their responses for aggregate economic variables.

A usual assumption in real business cycle models is that the economy is populated by a group of identical individuals. The behavior of the group can then be explained in terms of the behavior of one individual, called a *representative agent*. We will call the agent Robinson Crusoe.

Robinson's goal is to maximize his utility in each period of his life. He gets utility from two sources: consumption and leisure. We assume that he has the following utility function (U):

$$U_t = U(C_t, le_t) \qquad \textbf{(12.1)}$$

where C is consumption and le is leisure. To consume, Robinson must first produce output. In doing so, he forgoes leisure. Thus, as in the earlier models, there is a labor–leisure trade-off. Output in the model is generated by the production function

$$Y_t = z_t F(K_t, N_t) \qquad \textbf{(12.2)}$$

Equation (12.2) is similar to the aggregate production function in the classical model in Chapter 3. The production function specifies the amount of output (Y) that will result from employing given amounts of capital (K) and labor (N) in time period t.

There are two differences between equation (12.2) and our earlier production function. Equation (12.2) contains the additional term z_t, which represents shocks to the production process. By *shocks* we mean events that change the level of output forthcoming for given levels of labor and capital. Real business cycle theorists include a number of factors in this category. Among the important ones are shocks to technology, environmental factors, changes in government regulations that affect productivity, and changes in the availability of raw materials.

The second difference between equation (12.2) and our earlier version of the production function is the absence of a bar over the K in equation (12.2). In the real business cycle, the capital stock is not taken as given but rather is chosen for each period by the representative agent, in a manner discussed presently.

Robinson does not have to consume all the output he produces in each period. The young Robinson might want to save for when he is an old Robinson or for a future generation of Crusoe Jrs. What is required is that

$$Y_t = C_t + S_t \qquad \textbf{(12.3)}$$

Saving (S) plus consumption (C) must equal income, ignoring the existence of taxes. Equation (12.3) indicates that, in addition to a labor–leisure trade-off, the representative

[4]Charles Plosser, "Understanding Real Business Cycles," *Journal of Economic Perspectives*, 3 (Summer 1989), p. 53.

agent faces a trade-off between consumption today and saving for future consumption. Saving today will increase consumption in the future because saving is assumed to be invested to increase the capital stock in the next period:

$$K_{t+1} = S_t + (1 - \delta)K_t \qquad \textbf{(12.4)}$$

The capital stock in period $t + 1$ is equal to saving in period t plus the portion of the capital stock $(1 - \delta)$ left over from period t, where δ is the depreciation rate for capital (the fraction of the capital stock that wears out in each period).

In this representative agent framework, the behavior of aggregate output, employment, consumption, and saving is described in terms of the choices made by Robinson Crusoe. We now consider how those choices are affected by a change in the economic environment Robinson confronts.

Effects of a Positive Technology Shock

Suppose that in a given time period there is a favorable shock to technology. For now, we will assume that the shock is temporary, lasting only one period; later, we will consider shocks that are more long-lived. This shock is assumed to occur exogenously and is represented in our model by a rise in the z_t term in equation (12.2), say from an initial level z_{0t}, to a higher value z_{1t}. Given K_t and N_t, there is an exogenous rise in Y_t.

The effect of this shock is illustrated in Figure 12-1. Initially, with z_t equal to z_{0t}, the production function is given by $z_{0t}F(K_t, N_t)$. Suppose that, faced with this set of production

FIGURE 12-1 The Effect of a Positive Technology Shock in a Real Business Cycle Model

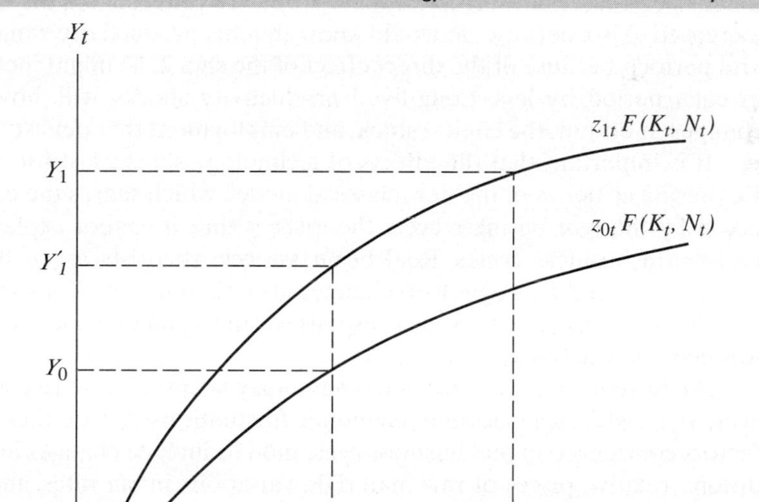

A positive technology shock shifts the production function up from $z_{0t}F(K_t, N_t)$ to $z_{1t}F(K_t, N_t)$. Robinson responds to this rise in his productivity by increasing his labor input from N_0 to N_1. Because of the increase in productivity and increase in the labor input, output rises from Y_0 to Y_1.

possibilities, Robinson chooses N_0 as the optimal amount of work to perform, and as a result, output is at Y_0. The positive technology shock shifts the production function upward to $z_{1t}F(K_t, N_t)$. In addition to this shift, the nature of the shock is assumed to be such that the production function becomes steeper for any level of the labor input. Recall from Chapter 3 that the slope of the production function is the marginal product of labor. We are assuming that the shock increases Robinson's marginal productivity.

Even at the same level of labor input (N_0), this increase in productivity would cause a rise in output, to Y'_1 in Figure 12-1. The favorable shock has, however, changed the production possibilities facing Robinson. If he observes the change, which we will assume to be the case, he will react. In the figure, we assume that he reacts to the increase in his productivity by working more. The level of the labor input rises to N_1 in Figure 12-1, and output rises to Y_1.

Robinson must decide what to do with the increased output. Equation (12.3) tells us that the increase in output will go to consumption or saving. He could just consume it all. But, particularly in the case of a temporary shock, it is likely that he will save a portion of the increase in output to allow consumption to also be higher throughout the future. If this is the case, then equation (12.4) tells us that the higher saving, which in turn means higher investment, will cause the capital stock to be higher in the next period than it otherwise would be. Because of a higher capital stock, output in the next period as well as other future periods will also be higher than it would have been in the absence of the technology shock. This is true even though the *direct* effect of the shock lasted for only one period.

Had the shock lasted for several periods or been permanent, Robinson's responses would have been somewhat different. He would know that output would be high for a longer period, so his incentive to save would be reduced and his incentive to consume increased. Also, because he would know that his productivity would be higher for several periods, because of the direct effect of the shock, he might increase his work effort in each period by less. Long-lived productivity shocks will, however, also result in changes in output, the capital stock, and employment that persist for many periods.

It is important that the effects of technology shocks last for many periods. A key Keynesian criticism of the new classical model, which shares the equilibrium approach taken by the real business cycle theorists, is that it cannot explain the *persistence* of real-world business cycles. Real business cycle theorists argue that the dynamic responses of optimizing agents to changes in economic conditions will, as just explained, have long-lasting effects. These responses can explain periods of persistently high or low economic activity.

We have focused on shocks to technology because they are central to real business cycle theorists' explanation of economic fluctuations. As noted earlier, however, other factors considered in real business cycle models include changes in environmental conditions, relative prices of raw materials, variations in tax rates, and changes in preferences. All these shocks are additional potential causes of cyclical movements in output and employment.

Macroeconomic Policy in a Real Business Cycle Model

In a real business cycle model, fluctuations arise from individuals' responses to changes in the economic environment. These responses are the result of optimizing behavior.

In these models, it would be suboptimal for policymakers to eliminate the business cycle if they could actually do so. What role is there, then, for macroeconomic policy in a real business cycle model? Let us start with monetary policy and then turn to fiscal policy.

Monetary Policy

The defining feature of real business cycle models is that real, not monetary, factors are responsible for fluctuations in output and employment. In real business cycle models, the role of money is to determine the price level, much the same as in the original classical model. Changes in the quantity of money result in proportionate changes in the price level with no change in output or employment.[5]

It follows, then, that monetary policy should focus on controlling the price level. A desirable monetary policy would result in slow, steady growth in the money supply and thus stable prices, or at least a low rate of inflation. When we consider fiscal policy, however, we will see that an alternative view of the optimal conduct of monetary policy emerges from the real business cycle theory. In any case, there is certainly no role for activist monetary stabilization policy of a Keynesian type. Monetary policy cannot affect output and employment, and even if it could, it would be suboptimal to try to eliminate the business cycle.

Fiscal Policy

Many fiscal policy actions *will* affect output and employment in a real business cycle model. The effect will not be caused by an effect on aggregate demand, as in the Keynesian model, but by supply-side effects. Changes in tax rates on labor income or the return to capital will affect the choices of optimizing agents. Moreover, these effects will be distortionary. A tax on labor income, for example, will cause an individual to choose too much leisure in relation to employment (with resulting lower consumption). Even a lump-sum tax will affect individual behavior by affecting wealth over the planning horizon.

The task of fiscal policy in the real business cycle framework is to minimize these tax distortions subject to providing needed government services (e.g., defense). This is where an alternative role for monetary policy emerges (alternative to simply keeping inflation low through slow, steady money growth). Recall from our previous discussion of the government budget constraint (Section 4.3) that an alternative to financing government spending by taxation is to finance it by printing money.[6] Policymakers can reduce the distortion due to taxation by financing a portion of government spending with

---

[5]Here we are considering a model in which all money is issued by the government: a world of only currency. Were we to consider bank deposits as well, the role of money in a real business cycle model would become considerably more complex because banks that issue deposits also provide credit and other services to firms. These services can affect the productivity of firms. Thus, changes in the banking industry—bank failures, for example—have real effects in a real business cycle model. For a real business cycle model that includes both currency and bank deposits, see King and Plosser, "Money, Credit and Prices in a Real Business Cycle Model."

[6]Borrowing from the public by selling government bonds is another way to pay for government spending. In real business cycle models, however, the government is constrained to repay all borrowing at some point. Thus bond sales can affect only the timing of taxation or money financing, not their amount.

seigniorage is the amount of real resources bought by the government with newly created money

newly created money. The term economists use for this practice in which the government gets real resources through money creation is **seigniorage**. However, seigniorage also has costs because the faster the money supply grows, the higher will be the inflation rate. In the real business cycle model, it follows that the optimal use of monetary and fiscal policies is to combine them so as to minimize the total costs from inflation and tax distortion. This is far different from the Keynesian view of optimal monetary and fiscal *stabilization* policy.

Read Perspectives 12-1.

PERSPECTIVES 12-1

ROBERT LUCAS AND REAL BUSINESS CYCLE THEORY

As noted at the beginning of the chapter, real business cycle models and the new classical models described in the previous chapter share important features. Moreover, one interpretation of the real business cycle theory is simply that real supply-side factors are quantitatively much more important than nominal demand-side influences. With that interpretation, real business cycle theories are simply extensions of new classical models that focus attention on these real supply-side variables. In a recent paper, Robert Lucas, the central figure in the development of the new classical models, concludes that this type of model is characteristic of the United States economy.

Lucas therefore argues that "Taking U.S. performance over the past 50 years as a benchmark, the potential for welfare gains from better long-run, supply-side policies exceeds *by far* the potential from further improvements in short-run demand management."[a] Lucas accepts that "the stability of monetary aggregates and nominal spending in the postwar United States is a major reason for the stability of aggregate production and consumption during these years, relative to the experience of the inter-war period and the contemporary experience of other economies."[b] But he argues that important welfare gains from further improvement in such demand-side policies are unrealistic. His estimate of such potential gains is less than one-tenth of 1 percent of aggregate consumption.

This estimate is based on consideration of optimizing agents functioning in an environment such as the Robinson Crusoe economy of Section 12.1 and subject to uncertainty about their consumption streams. Within such an economy, Lucas estimates the welfare gain that could be generated by reducing consumption risk via improved aggregate demand stabilization.

While the estimated gain from this source is tiny, Lucas cites other studies indicating that much larger welfare gains would result from fiscal policy changes that improved incentives to work and save—*supply-side* policies that will be analyzed in Chapter 19.

[a]Robert Lucas, "Macroeconomic Priorities," *American Economic Review*, 93 (March 2003), p. 1.

[b]Ibid., p. 11.

Questions About Real Business Cycle Models

Real business cycles have been an active research area in recent years, but the approach is not without its critics. These critics argue that "real business cycle theory does not provide an empirically plausible explanation of economic fluctuations."[7] Critics have raised several issues concerning the realism of the theory's explanation of economic fluctuations. We consider two that appear to be central: the question of whether technology shocks are of sufficient magnitude to explain observed business cycles and the related question of whether observed changes in employment can be explained as the voluntary choices of economic agents facing changing production possibilities (or with changing tastes).

The Importance of Technology Shocks

Critics of the real business cycle approach question whether technology shocks are large enough to cause economic fluctuations of the type and size we observe. These critics point out that many technology shocks are likely to be specific to individual industries. In any given year, while some industries might be experiencing negative shocks, others will have positive shocks. But in a real-world recession, for example, the decline in output is widespread across industries of diverse structure. Although the critics do not deny that some technology shocks affect many industries (e.g., the information transmission revolution), they do not believe there are enough of these to explain recessions in which output falls to as much as 10 percent below potential output.

Technology shocks are, of course, only one type of shock considered in the real business cycle theory, though they have received the most emphasis. Concerning the other shocks (and technology shocks as well) included in real business cycle models, critics allow that real supply-side shocks are important but argue that they are not all-important. Many economists who do not accept the real business cycle explanation of economic fluctuations do believe that the sharp rise in the relative price of imported oil was the central cause of the deep recession in the United States and other industrialized nations in the mid-1970s. Other recessions, such as the one in the United States in the early 1980s, the critics believe are better explained by changes in aggregate demand—in this case, by a restrictive Federal Reserve monetary policy.

Voluntary Employment Changes

In real business cycle models, changes in employment come as economic agents respond to changes in economic conditions. In our discussion of the effects of a positive shock to technology, we saw that Robinson Crusoe became more productive and responded by working more. Output rose because of both the direct effect of the shock and the increase in Crusoe's labor input. A negative technology shock would have the opposite effect; both output and employment would decline. In each case, the changes in employment would be voluntary and desirable (agents are optimizing).

[7] N. Gregory Mankiw, "Real Business Cycles: A New Keynesian Perspective," *Journal of Economic Perspectives*, 3 (Summer 1989), p. 79. Additional surveys of the real business cycle literature, from several viewpoints, include Bennett T. McCallum, "Real Business Cycle Models," in Barro, ed., *Modern Business Cycle Theory*; Lawrence H. Summers, "Some Skeptical Observations on Real Business Cycle Theory," Federal Reserve Bank of Minneapolis *Quarterly Review*, 10 (Fall 1986), pp. 23–27; George Stadler, "Real Business Cycles," *Journal of Economic Literature*, 32 (December 1994), pp. 1750–83; Robert G. King and Sergio T. Rebelo, "Resuscitating Real Business Cycles," in John B. Taylor and Michael Woodford, eds., *Handbook of Macroeconomics* (Amsterdam: North Holland, 1999), pp. 927–1007.

Another way of putting this concept is that individuals are moving along their labor supply schedules in response to changes in their marginal productivity and, therefore, their real wage. This was the analysis of employment changes in the classical model presented in Chapter 3. Critics of the real business cycle approach argue that to explain real-world fluctuations in this manner requires an implausibly high response of labor supply to changes in the real wage—a very flat labor supply schedule. This outcome follows because, although swings in employment over the business cycle are large, changes in the real wage are small. Critics argue that studies show only small responses of hours worked to changes in the real wage (a steep labor supply schedule).[8] They argue that the data are more consistent with the Keynesian explanation in which workers are assumed to be thrown off of their labor supply schedules; unemployment is involuntary.

Read Perspectives 12-2.

Concluding Comment

Real business cycle theorists are convinced that the business cycle can be explained as an equilibrium phenomenon. Fluctuations in output come as optimizing economic agents respond to real shocks that affect production possibilities. Policies that try to prevent these fluctuations are unnecessary and misguided. Critics of the real business cycle approach, many of whom view the business cycle from a Keynesian perspective, find this explanation implausible. They see business cycles as the result of changes in nominal aggregate demand as well as changes in real supply-side variables. Economists who view the business cycle from this Keynesian perspective believe that the policy prescription of the real business cycle theory wrongfully calls for inaction in the face of costly deviations from potential output.

12.2 NEW KEYNESIAN ECONOMICS

Keynes sought to explain involuntary unemployment—at times, mass involuntary unemployment. He set out to show how aggregate demand affected output and employment. The Keynesian models can explain unemployment and a role for aggregate demand in determining output and employment. A key element in these models is money wage rigidity. A fall in aggregate commodity demand, for example, leads to a fall in labor demand. As a result of fixed-wage labor contracts and workers' backward-looking price expectations, the money wage will not fall sufficiently in the short run to maintain the initial employment level. Employment and output will fall. Unemployment will rise.

Over the past two decades, economists working within the Keynesian tradition have pursued additional explanations of involuntary unemployment. The models that have resulted from this research effort are called *new Keynesian models*. In part, this new research is a response to the new classical critique of the older Keynesian models. N. Gregory Mankiw and David Romer, both of whom have made important contributions to the new Keynesian economics, state that "the new classical economists argued persuasively that Keynesian economics was theoretically inadequate, that macroeconomics

[8]See, for example, Joseph G. Altongi, "Intertemporal Substitution in Labor Supply: Evidence from Micro Data," *Journal of Political Economy*, 94 (June 1986), part 2, pp. S176–S215.

PERSPECTIVES 12-2

LABOR MARKET FLOWS

Critics of the real business cycle approach argue that the nature of labor market flows is inconsistent with a theory in which cyclical unemployment is voluntary. Figure 12-2 shows the share of total unemployment accounted for by job leavers and job losers for the years 1984–96. Job leavers are those who quit their jobs; these workers would be classified as voluntarily unemployed. Job losers are those who were laid off or fired.

Notice that during the long recovery following the 1981–82 recession the proportion of job losers fell and that of job leavers rose. This trend is consistent with a pattern: As economic activity picked up, layoffs fell, and as other job opportunities were created, the number of job leavers rose. Then, in the recession that began in 1990, the proportion of job losers rose sharply, while fewer workers quit their jobs. Later in the 1990s, with improving conditions in the labor market, the proportion of job losers fell and that of job leavers rose.

The pattern of labor market flows in Figure 12-2 is not, however, easily explained from a real business cycle perspective. If cyclical unemployment is voluntary, then the number of job leavers should rise, not fall, during a recession. Moreover, a real business cycle explanation of Figure 12-2 must somehow account for job losers. Did they voluntarily lose their jobs? On the face of it, these data seem more consistent with an explanation of cyclical unemployment as involuntary.

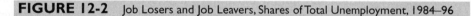

FIGURE 12-2 Job Losers and Job Leavers, Shares of Total Unemployment, 1984–96

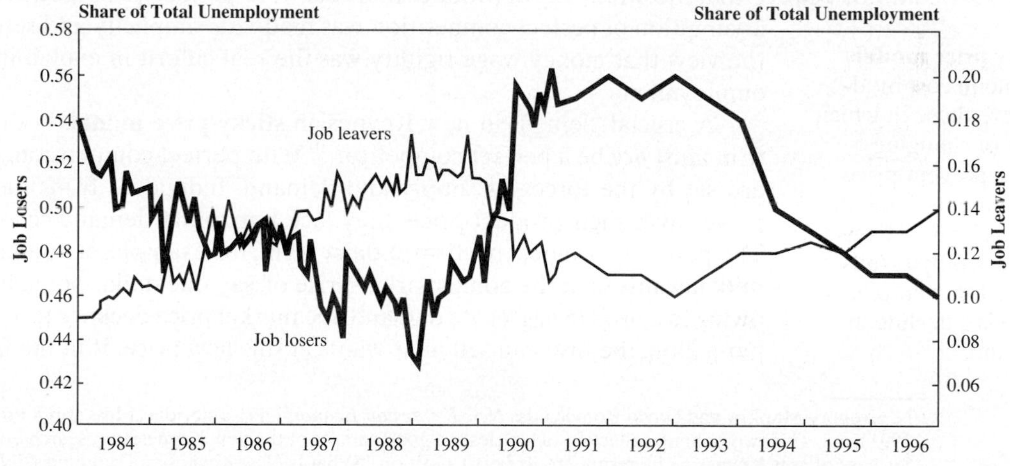

must be built on a firm microeconomic foundation."[9] Not all new Keynesians are this critical of the earlier Keynesian models, but their main task has been to improve the microeconomic foundations of the Keynesian system. Because they see wage and price rigidities as central to Keynes's explanation of involuntary unemployment, much effort has gone to show that these rigidities can arise from the behavior of optimizing agents.

New Keynesian economists have not tried to develop one rationale for all price and wage rigidities. Rather, they believe that a number of features of the wage- and price-setting process explain such rigidities. In fact, the new Keynesian literature is characterized by what has been called a "dizzying diversity" of approaches. These approaches have, however, the following common elements:

1. In new Keynesian models, imperfect competition is assumed for the product market. This assumption contrasts with the earlier Keynesian models that assumed perfect competition.
2. Whereas the key nominal rigidity in earlier Keynesian models was the money wage, new Keynesian models also focus on product price rigidity.
3. In addition to factors that cause nominal variables (e.g., the money wage) to be rigid, new Keynesian models introduce real rigidities—factors that make the real wage or firm's relative price rigid in the face of changes in aggregate demand.

We consider three types of new Keynesian models: sticky price (menu cost) models, efficiency wage models, and insider–outsider models.

Sticky Price (Menu Cost) Models

Keynesian models viewed the money wage as the variable that failed to adjust to changes in aggregate demand; output and employment had to adjust. The product market in those models was characterized by perfect competition. Keynesian economists did not believe that most real-world product markets were perfectly competitive. The assumption of perfect competition was made for simplicity and reflected the view that money wage rigidity was the real culprit in explaining unemployment.

sticky price models (or menu cost models) are those in which costs of changing prices prevent price adjustments when demand changes. Consequently, output falls when, for example, there is a decline in demand.

A crucial element in new Keynesian **sticky price models** is that the firm must *not* be a perfect competitor.[10] With perfect competition, prices are set by the forces of supply and demand. Individual firms have no power over their product price; they face horizontal demand schedules. The perfectly competitive firm, a dairy farm, for example, can sell all the milk it wants to at the going market price of, say, one dollar per gallon. If, owing to a drop in aggregate demand, the market price declines to 80 cents per gallon, the firm can sell all it wants at this new price. If in the face of

[9] N. Gregory Mankiw and David Romer, eds., *New Keynesian Economics* (Cambridge, Mass.: MIT Press, 1991), p. 1. This two-volume collection of articles is a good sample of the new Keynesian research effort. Surveys of new Keynesian literature are Robert J. Gordon, "What Is New Keynesian Economics?" *Journal of Economic Literature*, 28 (September 1990), pp. 1115–71; David Romer, "The New Keynesian Synthesis," *Journal of Economic Perspectives*, 7 (Winter 1993), pp. 5–22; and John B. Taylor, "Staggered Price and Wage Setting in Macroeconomics," in Taylor and Woodford, eds., *Handbook of Macroeconomics*, pp. 1009–50.

[10] Examples of sticky price models are N. Gregory Mankiw, "Small Menu Costs and Large Business Cycles: A Macroeconomic Model of Monopoly," *Quarterly Journal of Economics*, 100 (May 1985), pp. 529–38; and George Akerlof and Janet Yellin, "A Near Rational Model of the Business Cycle with Wage and Price Inertia," *Quarterly Journal of Economics*, 100, Suppl. (1985), pp. 823–38.

the fall in demand the perfectly competitive firm maintained its original product price, it would sell no output. There is no room for sticky prices in this market.

However, in the case of a monopolistic competitor or oligopolistic firm, the situation is different.[11] If La Residence, a Chapel Hill restaurant, did not lower prices in the face of a general fall in the demand for restaurant meals, it would lose some, but not all, of its customers. Similarly, during a recession, when the demand for automobiles declines, Ford Motor Company can continue to sell cars even if its prices remain unchanged. Monopolistic competitors and oligopolies have some control over the price of their products. In fact, the incentive to lower prices may be fairly weak for these types of firms. If they hold to their initial price when demand falls, they will lose sales, but the sales they retain will still be at the relatively high initial price. Also, if all firms hold to the initial price, no individual firm will lose sales to its competitors.

Still, in the face of a fall in demand, the profit-maximizing price will decline even for a firm in a setting of imperfect competition. Though the gain in profits from lowering the price may be small, there is some gain. Why, then, might firms still not lower prices? Firms would hold product prices constant even as demand fell if there was a perceived cost to changing prices that outweighed the benefit of the price cut. Such costs of price changes are called **menu costs**.

menu costs refer to any type of cost that a firm incurs if it changes its product price

The name stems from the fact that if restaurants change prices, they must print new menus. More generally, when firms change prices, they incur direct and indirect cost of several types.

One type is called *managerial costs*. These include the costs of gathering the information required to decide on the optimal price change, the cost of communicating to customers the logic for the change, and perhaps negotiating with customers who resist the change. Each of these activities takes management time away from other activities.

A second cost is loss of consumer goodwill. Consumer goodwill would be lost only through price increases, but firms that cut prices in recessions must raise them in recoveries. Firms may instead find it optimal to change prices when their costs change, the necessity of which customers will understand, but not to vary prices with changes in demand. They will thus not be considered "price gougers" in periods of high demand and will not lower prices when demand falls off.

A second possible perceived cost of a price reduction in a recession is that it may set off competitive rounds of price cuts or even lead to a price war as other firms respond. This potential cost is relevant for oligopolistic markets, where firms are cognizant of other firms' reactions to their pricing decisions.

If these perceived costs of price changes are high enough, price stickiness will exist. Declines in aggregate demand will result in falls in output and employment, not price reductions. Of course, not all prices need to be sticky. As long as the number of industries in which prices are rigid constitutes a significant segment of the economy, the declines in output and employment will be substantial.

Read Perspectives 12-3.

[11]Recall from microeconomics that *monopolistic competition* is a situation in which many firms provide differentiated products, for example, different types of food at different restaurants. *Oligopoly* refers to situations in which, owing to substantial costs to enter the market, there are only a few firms. The product may be standardized or differentiated (e.g., aluminum or automobiles).

PERSPECTIVES 12-3

ARE PRICES STICKY?

New Keynesian economists have examined whether real-world prices are in fact sticky. In one study, Stephen Cecchetti found considerable rigidity in the newsstand prices of magazines.[a] *Readers Digest*, for example, changed its newsstand price only six times between 1950 and 1980. In many years, only a few of the 38 magazines in the study had price changes.

In a broader study, Alan Blinder supervised interviews of corporate executives on the frequency with which their firms change prices.[b] A summary of some of his findings is given in Table 12-1. The survey data indicate that 49.5 percent of firms change prices once a year or less. This finding indicates a considerable departure from auction-market behavior.

TABLE 12-1 Frequency of Price Changes

Number of Price Changes Per Year	*Percent of Companies*
More than 12	14.5
4 to 12	7.5
2 to 4	12.9
1 to 2	15.6
1	39.3
Less than 1	10.2

[a]Stephen Cecchetti, "The Frequency of Price Adjustment: A Study of the Newsstand Prices of Magazines," *Journal of Econometrics*, 31 (April 1986) pp. 255–74

[b]Alan Blinder, "On Sticky Prices," in N. Gregory Mankiw, ed., *Monetary Policy* (Chicago: University of Chicago Press, 1994), pp. 117–50.

efficiency wage models are models in which labor productivity depends on the real wage workers are paid. In such models, the real wage is set to maximize the efficiency units of labor per dollar of expenditure, not to clear the labor market.

Efficiency Wage Models

In 1914, Henry Ford instituted the five-dollar day for his workers. At the time, the going competitive wage rate was between two and three dollars a day. Ford decided to pay this above-market wage because he thought it would discourage absenteeism, reduce turnover in Ford's labor force, and improve worker morale; productivity would therefore increase. Modern **efficiency wage models** have the same premise: The efficiency of workers depends positively on the real wage they are paid.[12]

The efficiency wage idea can be formalized by defining an index of worker efficiency, or productivity (e), such that

$$e = e\left(\frac{W}{P}\right) \qquad \textbf{(12.5)}$$

[12]Ford's experiment with the five-dollar day is analyzed from the viewpoint of the modern efficiency wage theory in Daniel M. G. Ruff and Lawrence H. Summers, "Did Henry Ford Pay Efficiency Wages?" *Journal of Labor Economics*, 5 (October 1987), part 2, pp. S57–S86. Examples of efficiency wage models are Akerlof and Yellin, "A Near Rational Model of the Business Cycle with Wage and Price Inertia"; and Lawrence Katz, "Efficiency Wage Theories: A Partial Evaluation," *NBER Macroeconomics Annual*, (Cambridge, Mass.: MIT Press, 1986), pp. 235–76.

Worker efficiency is a positive function of the real wage. This being the case, we now write the aggregate production function as

$$Y = F[\bar{K}, eN] \tag{12.6}$$

As before, output (Y) depends on the amount of capital (K).[13] Output also depends on the amount of the labor input, which we now measure in efficiency units. The number of efficiency units of labor equals the number of physical units (N), measured in man-hours per period, for example, multiplied by the index of efficiency (e). Output increases either when more units of labor are hired (N increases) or when the efficiency of the existing labor force improves (e is increased by a rise in W/P).

With the production function as given by equation (12.6), the goal of the firm is to set the real wage so that the cost of an efficiency unit of labor is minimized or, to say the same thing in reverse, to maximize the number of efficiency units of labor bought with each dollar of the wage bill. This goal is accomplished by increasing the real wage to the point where the elasticity of the efficiency index $[e(W/P)]$ with respect to the real wage is equal to 1.

Let's use an example to see why this is the case. First, recall that elasticity is the percentage change in one variable (here the efficiency of labor) per 1 percent change in another (here the real wage). So, we are saying that the condition that determines the optimal level of the real wage, which in the literature is called the *efficiency wage*, $(W/P)^*$, is

$$\frac{\text{percentage change in } e\left(\dfrac{W}{P}\right)}{\text{percentage change in}\left(\dfrac{W}{P}\right)} = 1 \tag{12.7}$$

Suppose that, beginning at a low level, a 1 percent increase in the real wage leads to a 2 percent increase in the efficiency of labor. The firm will benefit from this increase because each dollar of the wage bill will buy more efficiency units of labor (wage bill up 1 percent, number of efficiency units up 2 percent). With further increases in the wage bill, efficiency gains begin to decline. At the point where a 1 percent increase in the real wage produces only a 1 percent increase in efficiency, the firm will not find it optimal to increase the real wage any further; the efficiency wage has been reached.

Proponents of the efficiency wage theory argue that in many industries real wages are set on efficiency grounds. Real wages do not adjust to clear labor markets. In fact, the rationales that underlie efficiency wage models imply that firms will set the real wage *above* the market-clearing level. Persistent, involuntary unemployment will result. Our next task is to examine these rationales for efficiency wages, some of which were anticipated by Henry Ford.

Several rationales have been offered for the payment of efficiency wages:

1. The shirking model. By setting the real wage above going market levels (i.e., a worker's next best opportunity), a firm gives a worker an incentive not

[13] Here we have gone back to the specification of the aggregate production function in earlier chapters, where the stock of capital is fixed, as indicated by the bar over K. We also ignore the technology shock introduced in the previous section on real business cycle models and, for simplicity, omit the time (t) subscripts used earlier in the chapter.

to shirk or loaf on the job. If he does, he may be fired, and he knows it would be hard to get another job at such a high wage. If firms can monitor job performance only imperfectly and with some cost, such a high-wage strategy may be profitable.

2. ***Turnover cost models.*** By paying an above-market wage, firms can reduce quit rates and, thus, recruiting and training costs. The high wage also allows them to develop a more experienced, and therefore more productive, workforce.
3. ***Gift exchange models.*** Another explanation of why efficiency depends on the real wage centers on the morale of a firm's workers. According to this argument, if the firm pays a real wage above the market-clearing wage, this higher wage improves morale, and workers put forth more effort. The firm pays the workers a *gift* of the above-market wage, and the workers reciprocate with higher efficiency.[14]

None of these rationales is intended to apply to all parts of the labor market. If, however, efficiency wage considerations are important and therefore real wage rates are set above market-clearing levels in many sectors, substantial involuntary unemployment may result. Workers will continue to seek jobs in the high-wage sector, working, for example, when demand is high, rather than take low-paying jobs.

Notice that the real wage is fixed on efficiency grounds [to meet condition (12.7)]. Efficiency wage models explain a *real* rigidity. We have just seen how this real rigidity can explain involuntary unemployment. By itself, however, the rigidity of the *real* wage due to the payment of efficiency wages does not explain why changes in aggregate demand affect output and employment and therefore the level of involuntary unemployment. If there was a fall in nominal aggregate demand, resulting, for example, from a decline in the money supply, firms could lower their prices sufficiently to keep output (sales) unchanged and lower the *money* wage by the same amount to keep the real wage at the efficiency wage, $(W/P)^*$. If, however, firms do not lower prices because of menu costs, as explained in the previous section, then to keep the real wage at the efficiency wage requires the money wage also to be fixed. In this case, when aggregate demand declines, output and employment will fall and involuntary unemployment will rise. Thus, a nominal rigidity, the menu cost, and the real wage rigidity due to efficiency wages combine to explain involuntary unemployment.

Insider–Outsider Models and Hysteresis

The last direction in new Keynesian research that we consider is the one most closely related to persistent high unemployment rates in Europe since 1980 (see Table 10-2). Such persistent high unemployment contrasts sharply with the low unemployment for the same countries from the late 1950s to the early 1970s. These patterns have led to the hypothesis that present unemployment is strongly influenced by past unemployment. Economies can, as it were, get stuck in *unemployment traps*. The term for this condition

[14] A different argument for the positive relationship between worker efficiency and the real wage is applicable to developing countries. A higher real wage allows for a higher consumption level, which provides better nutrition and health. These factors, in turn, reduce absenteeism and make workers more energetic and productive. An early model of this relationship is given by Harvey Leibenstein, "The Theory of Underemployment in Densely Populated Backward Areas," in *Economic Backwardness and Economic Growth* (New York: Wiley, 1963), though a similar argument can be found in the work of Alfred Marshall in the nineteenth century.

that we used in Chapter 10 is **hysteresis**. A variable exhibits hysteresis if, when shocked away from an initial value, it shows no tendency to return even when the shock is over. In terms of unemployment, hysteresis models try to explain why high unemployment persists even after its initial cause is long past.

There are a number of explanations for hysteresis in the unemployment process. This discussion here is limited to one model that has received considerable attention—the **insider–outsider model**.[15] Rather than present the model formally, we will explain it with an example.

insider–outsider models provide one explanation of hysteresis in unemployment. Insiders (e.g., union members) are the only group that affects the real wage bargain. Outsiders (e.g., those who want jobs) do not. Recessions cause insiders to become outsiders. After the recession, with fewer insiders, the real wage rises and unemployment persists.

Like sticky price models, versions of the insider–outsider model require imperfect competition. In the case of the insider–outsider model, it is assumed that both the product and the labor market are imperfectly competitive. So, we will consider a situation with a labor union on the employee side and a few firms as employers—for example, the German steel industry. The union members, whom we will call *insiders*, are assumed to have bargaining power with employers because it is costly to replace them with *outsiders* (nonunion members). The cost of replacing them is a recruiting and training cost for new workers. Union members may also impose costs on outsiders who attempt to underbid them for jobs—for example, by setting up picket lines.

The insiders are assumed to use their bargaining power to push the real wage above the market-clearing level, resulting in an unemployed group of outsiders. Insiders will push the real wage only up to a certain point, however, because the higher the real wage, the fewer insiders will be employed. This relationship follows because employment is equal to the firms' demand for labor, which depends negatively on the real wage. If in our example the insiders number 200,000, we will assume that they bargain for a real wage that they *believe* will result in all (or almost all) of them being employed. They may not, however, end up being employed, because if economywide aggregate demand slackens unexpectedly, output and employment will fall. A percentage of the insiders will be laid off.

Thus, in the insider–outsider model, unemployment results from a real wage set above the market-clearing level (outsider unemployment) as well as from a cyclical response to changes in aggregate demand. A novel feature of these models is the interrelationship of these two types of unemployment.

To see this interrelationship, consider the effect of several prolonged recessions such as those in the 1970s, early 1980s, and 1990s. During the recessions, some layoffs are permanent, and some workers drift out of the union. *Some insiders become outsiders.* How quickly this happens depends on union rules. With the pool of insiders reduced, say to 160,000 workers, when an economic recovery takes place, the union will bargain for a higher real wage than previously (before the recessions, when there were 200,000 insiders). There are now fewer insiders whose employment

[15] An early version of the insider–outsider model is provided by Olivier J. Blanchard and Lawrence Summers, "Hysteresis and the European Unemployment Problem," in Stanley Fischer, ed., *NBER Macroeconomics Annual* (Cambridge, Mass.: MIT Press, 1986). See also Assar Lindbeck and Dennis Snower, "Wage Setting Unemployment and Insider–Outsider Relations," *American Economic Review*, 76 (May 1986), pp. 235–39; and Robert M. Solow, "Insiders and Outsiders in Wage Determination," *Scandinavian Journal of Economics*, 87 (1985), pp. 411–28.

prospects matter. (Notice here the assumption that insiders are unconcerned about outsiders.) With a higher real wage, employment will remain lower than in the pre-recession period.

Past unemployment, then, causes current unemployment by turning insiders into outsiders; this is the hysteresis phenomenon. Once insiders have become outsiders, a sort of unemployment trap occurs. The outsiders do not exert downward pressure on real wages because they are irrelevant to the wage-bargaining process.[16] Insider–outsider models thus explain why high unemployment has persisted in some European countries for such long periods—periods too long to be the result of fixed money wage contracts or backward-looking price expectations.

12.3 CONCLUSION

Real business cycle theory and the new Keynesian economics are extensions of two conflicting traditions in macroeconomics. The real business cycle theory is a modern version of classical economics. The business cycle is an equilibrium phenomenon. It is the result of the actions of optimizing agents in the face of changes in the economic environment (e.g., productivity shocks) or in preferences. Macroeconomic stabilization policies are counterproductive. The real business cycle theorists therefore reach noninterventionist policy conclusions, as did the original classical economists.

The new Keynesian economics is set firmly in the tradition of John Maynard Keynes. New Keynesian economists believe that much unemployment is involuntary. They believe that the deviations of output below potential output during recessions are socially costly. There is a potential role for stabilization policy in preventing such output shortfalls and alleviating the personal costs of involuntary unemployment. New Keynesian economics is an attempt to improve the microeconomic foundations of the traditional Keynesian models, not to challenge their major premises.

Notice that real business cycle theorists and new Keynesian economists share a desire to put macroeconomics on a sound microeconomic basis. In recent years, this has led to considerable convergence between the two schools. As we will see in the chapters in Part V, much modern policy analysis is carried out in models that combine elements of these two schools. These are models where agents optimize but some type of rigidity (often a menu cost) is incorporated. A role for policy is created, namely, causing the economy to behave as it would in the absence of the rigidity. For some Keynesians, these models go too far in incorporating other elements of the real business cycle theory (e.g., rational expectations), but for many economists they form a happy middle ground.

[16]There are extensions of the basic insider–outsider model in which the unemployed outsiders do have some influence on the wage bargain. In these extended models, the higher the rate of unemployment, the less bargaining power the insiders are able to exert. Their fear of becoming unemployed is greater, because they know that their prospect of finding another job is poorer and the employers' threat to replace them with unemployed workers is more credible. In these extended models, however, there is still persistent unemployment. See the discussion in Olivier J. Blanchard, "Wage Bargaining and Unemployment Persistence," *Journal of Money, Credit, and Banking*, 23 (August 1991), pp. 278–92.

KEY TERMS

- seigniorage 252
- sticky price models 256
- menu costs 257
- efficiency wage models 258
- insider–outsider models 264

REVIEW QUESTIONS AND PROBLEMS

1. Compare the real business cycle theorists' view of the causes of fluctuations of output and employment with the view of new classical economists.
2. Within the simple real business cycle model presented in Section 12.1, analyze the effect of a negative shock to technology (a negative shock to z_t) that lasts for one period.
3. Explain the real business cycle theorists' views on the proper conduct of monetary and fiscal policies.
4. Suppose there was a change in preferences in a real business cycle model such that the representative agent valued leisure more and consumption goods less. How would output and employment be affected by the change?
5. Explain why the assumption of imperfect competition is important within each of the new Keynesian models considered in Section 12.2.
6. Suppose wage data show that workers with identical skills are paid very different wage rates in different industries. Is this difference consistent with the assumption that the labor market is competitive? Is it consistent with the efficiency wage model?
7. Explain how the insider–outsider model accounts for the persistent high unemployment in European countries during the post-1980 period.
8. New classical economists believe that in useful macroeconomic models (a) agents optimize and (b) markets clear. Do the models that emerge from the new Keynesian research effort have either or both of these properties? Explain.
9. Explain the relationship of the new Keynesian models to the Keynesian models considered in Chapters 5 through 8.
10. During the administration of George W. Bush, reductions in the tax rates on labor income, dividends, and capital gains were the centerpiece of fiscal policy. Analyze the effects of these tax cuts within the real business cycle theory.

CHAPTER 13

Macroeconomic Models: A Summary

This chapter summarizes the theories considered in earlier chapters and clarifies areas of agreement and controversy among the various schools.

13.1 THEORETICAL ISSUES

It is convenient to center our discussion on the aggregate supply–aggregate demand framework used previously to characterize the economic models. The first model we considered, the classical model, views output as completely determined by supply factors. This view is embodied in the *vertical aggregate supply schedule* shown in Figure 13-1*a*.

Central to the classical theory are the classical labor market assumptions. Both labor supply and demand depend only on the real wage, which is known to all market participants. The money wage is perfectly flexible and moves to equate demand and supply in the labor market. Increases in aggregate demand cause the price level to rise. The price rise, other things being equal, spurs production. To clear the labor market, however, the money wage has to rise proportionately with the price level. The real wage is then unchanged, and consequently employment and output are unchanged in the new equilibrium.

In the classical system, the role of aggregate demand is to determine the price level. The classical theory of aggregate demand is an implicit theory based on the quantity theory of money. The quantity theory provides a proportional relationship between the exogenous quantity of money and nominal income. In the Cambridge form, this relationship is

$$M = kPY \tag{13.1}$$

With k treated as a constant, changes in the quantity of money result in proportional changes in nominal income (PY). With real income (Y) fixed, the full adjustment comes in prices.

This relationship provides the classical aggregate demand schedule in Figure 13.1*a*. The economic process behind this theory is that if, for example, there is an excess supply of money ($M > kPY$), a corresponding excess demand for commodities will drive up the aggregate price level. The classical model has a *monetary theory of aggregate demand*.

The real business cycle theory is a modern version of the classical theory. As in the classical model, output and employment in the real business cycle model are determined

FIGURE 13-1 Theories of Aggregate Demand and Supply

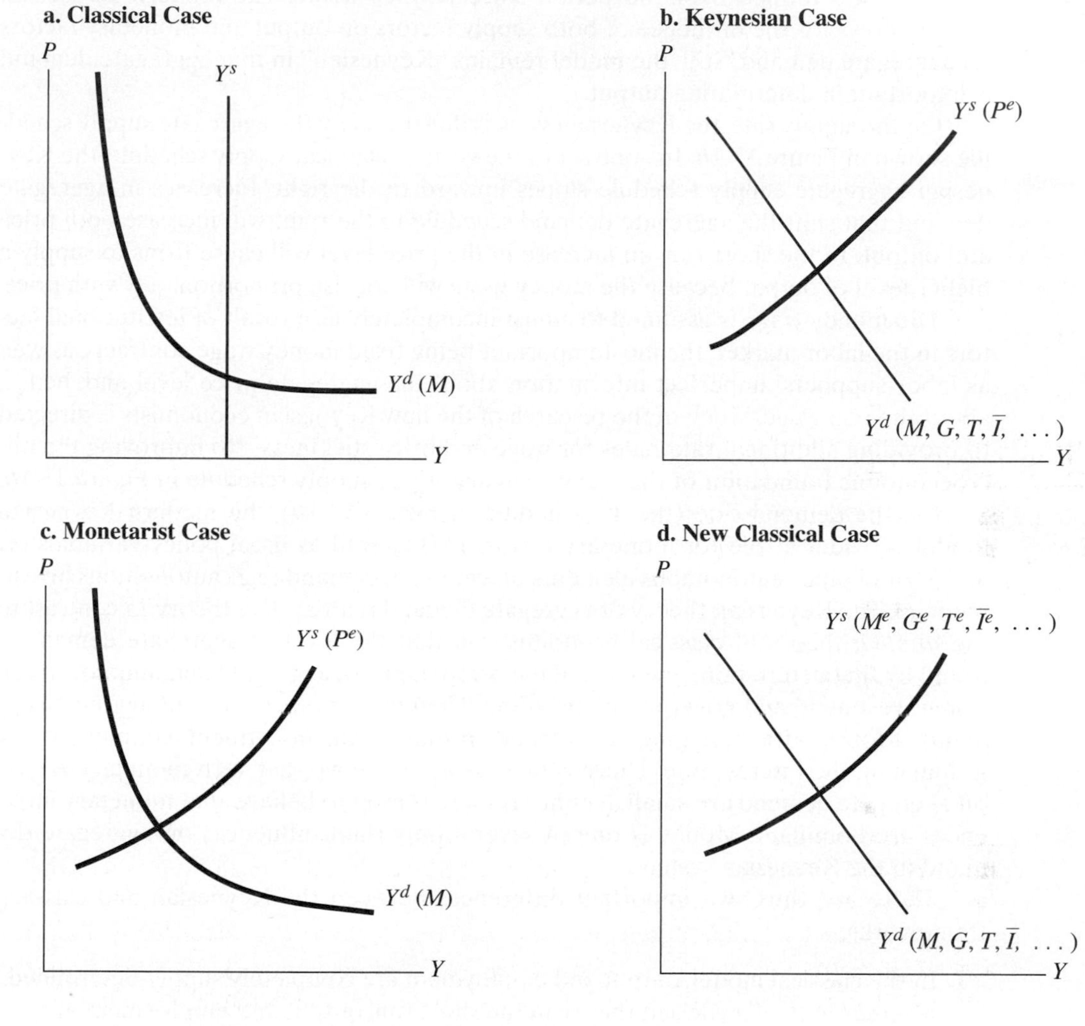

by real variables. The labor market is always in equilibrium; all unemployment is voluntary. The role of money in the real business cycle model, as in the classical model, is solely to determine the price level.

In its simplest form, the Keynesian model is the antithesis of the classical and real business cycle theories. In a simple Keynesian model, such as that discussed in Chapter 5, supply plays no role in output determination. The aggregate supply schedule implied by such simple Keynesian models is horizontal, indicating that supply is no constraint on the level of production, an assumption appropriate, if ever, only to situations in which production is well below capacity levels. On the demand side, the simple Keynesian model concentrates on the determinants of autonomous expenditures: government spending, taxes, and autonomous investment demand. Monetary factors are neglected. This simple model highlights a central notion in Keynesian economics—the importance of aggregate demand in determining output and employment.

But this simple Keynesian model is incomplete. The Keynesian theory has been modified and refined over the period since Keynes wrote. The modern Keynesian model allows for the influence of both supply factors on output and monetary factors on aggregate demand. Still, the model remains "Keynesian" in that aggregate demand is important in determining output.

On the supply side, the Keynesian view is illustrated by the aggregate supply schedule shown in Figure 13-1*b*. In contrast to the vertical classical supply schedule, the Keynesian aggregate supply schedule slopes upward to the right. Increases in aggregate demand that shift the aggregate demand schedule to the right will increase both price and output. In the short run, an increase in the price level will cause firms to supply a higher level of output because the money wage will not rise proportionately with price.

The money wage is assumed to adjust incompletely as a result of institutional factors in the labor market, the most important being fixed money wage contracts, as well as labor suppliers' imperfect information about the aggregate price level and, hence, about the real wage. Much of the research of the new Keynesian economists is directed to providing additional rationales for wage and price stickiness—to improving the microeconomic foundation of the Keynesian aggregate supply schedule in Figure 13-1*b*.

On the demand side (the Y^d schedule in Figure 13-1*b*), the modern Keynesian model provides a role for monetary factors (M) as well as fiscal policy variables (G and T) and other autonomous elements of aggregate demand (e.g., autonomous investment, $\bar{I}$). The Keynesian theory of aggregate demand is an *explicit* theory, in contrast to the *implicit* theory of classical economists, in that the level of aggregate demand is found by first determining the level of the components of aggregate demand: consumption, investment, and government spending. Then we sum these to find aggregate demand. Money affects aggregate demand, primarily its investment component, by influencing the interest rate. There is no reason to believe that such monetary effects on aggregate demand are small. Neither is there reason to believe that monetary influences are dominant. Money is one of several important influences on aggregate demand in the Keynesian system.

There are, thus, two important differences between the Keynesian and classical frameworks:

1. In the classical model, output and employment are completely supply-determined, whereas in the Keynesian theory in the short run, output and employment are determined jointly by aggregate supply and demand. In the Keynesian system, aggregate demand is an important determinant of output and employment.
2. Aggregate demand in the classical model is determined solely by the quantity of money. In the Keynesian system, money is only one of several factors that determine aggregate demand.

These two issues, the role of aggregate demand in determining output and employment and the relative importance of monetary and other factors as determinants of aggregate demand, are also the ones that divide the Keynesians from monetarists and new classical economists.

The major controversy between monetarists, whose view of aggregate supply and demand is represented in Figure 13-1*c*, and Keynesians has centered on point 2, the degree to which monetary forces dominate the determination of aggregate demand.

Monetarists have taken the Cambridge version of the quantity equation [equation (13.1)] as the basis for their own quantity theory view that money is the dominant influence on aggregate demand and, therefore, on nominal income. On the supply side, there is no fundamental difference between the monetarist and Keynesian theories. In both monetarist and Keynesian models, the aggregate supply schedule slopes upward to the right in the short run and approaches the vertical classical formulation only in the long run. In both models, changes in aggregate demand affect output in the short run.

The new classical view of aggregate supply and demand is illustrated in Figure 13-1*d*. The issue dividing new classical economists and Keynesians concerns point 1, the degree to which aggregate demand plays a role in determining real output. New classical economists believe that systematic, and therefore predictable, changes in aggregate demand will not affect real output. Such changes will be anticipated by rational economic agents. The aggregate demand schedule and the aggregate supply schedule will shift symmetrically, changing the price level but leaving real output unchanged. To reflect this dependence of the aggregate supply schedule on expected changes in the determinants of aggregate demand and consequently in the rational expectation of the price level, the aggregate supply schedule in Figure 13-1*d* is shown as depending on the expected level of the money supply (M^e) as well as expected values of fiscal policy variables and other possible determinants of aggregate demand ($G^e, T^e, \bar{I}^e, \ldots$).

Unanticipated changes in aggregate demand—for example, an increase in the money supply (M) that could not have been predicted (M^e is unchanged)—will shift the aggregate demand schedule without shifting the aggregate supply schedule. Unanticipated changes in aggregate demand will cause labor suppliers to make price forecast errors and will therefore affect output and employment. In this respect, the new classical model is a modification of the original classical model, in which aggregate demand had *no* role in determining output and employment. The modification is the substitution of the rational expectations assumption in the new classical analysis for the classical assumption of perfect information. In the classical analysis, there were no price forecast errors on the part of labor suppliers. Labor suppliers had perfect information about the price level. No unanticipated changes in aggregate demand were assumed. On the demand side, there are no obvious differences between the new classical and Keynesian positions. (Compare the Y^d schedules in Figure 13-1*b* and *d*.) This is not to say, however, that new classical economists agree with all aspects of the Keynesian theory of aggregate demand. In fact, they do not believe that much of the Keynesian theory rests on strong microeconomic foundations.

From the foregoing it should be clear that the monetarist–Keynesian dispute and the Keynesian–new classical dispute revolve around the same issues that separate Keynesians from classical economists and real business cycle theorists. The Keynesian revolution attacked the classical supply-determined, full-employment theory of output and employment, as well as the quantity theory of money. New classical economists and monetarists have modified these two aspects of classical economics and used the modified versions to attack the Keynesian system. Points 1 and 2, which in terms of Figure 13-1 concern the slope of the short-run aggregate supply function and the determinants of the aggregate demand function, have been the central issues in macroeconomic controversies for 70 years.

13.2 POLICY ISSUES

Given the classical roots of the real business cycle, monetarist, and new classical theories, it is not surprising that these theories share the noninterventionist policy conclusions of the original classical model. In contrast, Keynesians are policy interventionists who favor managing aggregate demand to stabilize output and employment.

In the classical system, output and employment are self-adjusting to the supply-determined level of full employment. There is no role for aggregate demand stabilization policies. This is also the case in real business cycle models, where fluctuations in output and employment result from optimal responses of economic agents to changes in the economic environment. In the new classical model, unanticipated shifts in aggregate demand do affect output and employment. Sensible stabilization policies, however, would have to consist of systematic reaction patterns to the state of the economy. Such systematic shifts in aggregate demand would be anticipated by the public and, therefore, would not affect output or employment. Consequently, new classical economists also view aggregate demand stabilization policies as ineffective.

Monetarists believe that *monetary* policy actions, whether anticipated or not, affect output and employment in the short run. Still, they arrive at the same noninterventionist policy conclusions as classical and new classical economists. Like classical economists, monetarists believe that the private sector is stable if left free from destabilizing government policy actions. Further, because monetarists view aggregate demand as determined predominantly by the money supply, the best way to stabilize aggregate demand is to provide stable growth in the money supply.

Against this noninterventionist view is the Keynesian position that a private-enterprise monetary economy is unstable without government policies to regulate aggregate demand. Keynesians favor monetary and fiscal policies to offset shocks to private aggregate demand.

Thus, although we have considered several schools of macroeconomic theory, the major policy controversy is between two positions—the noninterventionist position, with roots in the original classical system, and the Keynesian interventionist position. On this issue, as with the theoretical issues discussed previously, the controversy is long-standing. In modern form, it extends back to the Keynesian attack on the classical orthodoxy. But there were heretics before Keynes, and the origins of the policy and theoretical controversies discussed here date back to the early 1800s.

How can such controversies proceed for so long without resolution? In economics, we have no way to conduct controlled laboratory experiments. We cannot, for example, construct an economy, let the money supply grow for 10 years at a constant rate, and then see if the monetarist predictions are verified. As Milton Friedman has written on this issue,

> Controlled experiments permitting near isolation of one or a few forces are virtually impossible. We must test our propositions by observing uncontrolled experience that involves a large number of people, numerous economic variables, frequent changes in other circumstances, and, at that, is imperfectly recorded. The interpretation of the experience is further complicated because the experience affects directly many of the observers, often

giving them reasons, irrelevant from a scientific view, to prefer one rather than another interpretation of the complex and ever-changing course of events.[1]

Or as Keynes wrote earlier, "In economics you cannot *convict* your opponent of error—you can only convince him of it."[2]

13.3 CONSENSUS AS WELL AS CONTROVERSY

Discussing alternative macroeconomic theories tends to place emphasis on the differences between them. This obscures areas of agreement. Before leaving the discussion of alternative theories, it is good, then, to look at some areas of agreement, of near consensus, among the different schools.

At the heart of the classical quantity theory of money is the equation of exchange. This statement of the quantity theory was written earlier in this chapter in the form used by the Cambridge economists as equation (13.1). In its Fisherian version it takes the form

$$MV = PY \tag{13.2}$$

Based on equation (13.2), we can state what may be called the *valid core of the quantity theory:* Sustained high inflation requires sustained high money growth. The original quantity theorists, as well as Milton Friedman, would have made a more precise statement about the relationship of money growth and inflation, but as just stated, the relationship is not controversial. The growth of real output (Y) is limited to a fairly narrow range by physical constraints. The velocity of money (V) has varied historically within a relatively narrow range. Thus, if money growth is very high (e.g., double-digit rates for several years), high inflation must result.

In another area, Keynesian and new classical economists today are less far apart than they were in the 1980s concerning the specification of expectations. Few Keynesian economists today would use simple backward-looking formulations of inflationary expectations. Conversely, new classical economists today are exploring learning models that make less extreme informational assumptions than the early formulations of rational expectations. Moreover, most Keynesian economists today would acknowledge that policy effects depend to an extent on whether policy changes are predictable or not and, more broadly, on the environment in which policy is formed. For example, as we will see in our later discussion of monetary policy, credibility matters.

Finally, while there are differences between real business cycle theorists and Keynesians concerning the relative importance of productivity shocks and aggregate demand in determining output, most macroeconomists today accept some role for demand. This may be called the *valid core of Keynes's economics.*

[1]Milton Friedman, "Why Economists Disagree," in Milton Friedman, *Dollars and Deficits* (Upper Saddle River, N.J.: Prentice Hall, 1968), pp. 15–16.

[2]Quoted from Paul Davidson, *Money and the Real World* (New York: Wiley, 1978), p. ix.

REVIEW QUESTIONS AND PROBLEMS

1. Suppose that investment demand in a given economy is predicted to be weak next year, say 10 percent below this year's level, because of an exogenous shock. All other components of aggregate demand are predicted to be at levels comparable to this year's. These levels were consistent with high employment and relatively stable prices. For each of the following macroeconomic systems, explain the effects of this exogenous fall in aggregate demand and explain the proper policy response implied by the model; that is, what action should the policymaker take?
   a. Classical model
   b. Keynesian model
   c. New classical model
2. The question of what information market participants possess at any point in time and how quickly they learn—in other words, the information structure of the model—is a distinguishing feature of the different macroeconomic systems discussed. With reference to the classical, Keynesian, monetarist, and new classical models, explain the differing assumptions about the information that market participants possess and the degree to which these differing assumptions account for the different policy conclusions derived from these models.
3. Within the classical, real business cycle, Keynesian, monetarist, and new classical models, analyze the effect of an autonomous fall in the price of imported oil. Explain the effect of this change on output, employment, and the aggregate price level within each framework.
4. One rule that has been proposed for fiscal policy is that the government budget should be balanced each year—no budget deficits. What position do you think each of the following groups of economists would take on this proposal?
   a. New classical economists
   b. Keynesians
   c. Real business cycle theorists
5. Which of the frameworks that we have considered do you view as the most useful in explaining the behavior of the economy and in providing proper policy prescriptions? Defend your choice.

PART FOUR

Open Economy Macroeconomics

CHAPTER 14

Exchange Rates and the International Monetary System

CHAPTER 15

Monetary and Fiscal Policy in the Open Economy

Part IV examines U.S. international economic relations, including both trade flows and capital movements. Chapter 14 analyzes how exchange rates are determined in different international monetary systems and considers the relative merits of these systems. In Chapter 15, we develop an open economy version of the *IS–LM* model. We then use this model to study the effects of monetary and fiscal policies in the open economy under fixed and flexible exchange rates.

CHAPTER 14

Exchange Rates and the International Monetary System

In 1960, U.S. imports of goods and services totaled 4.4 percent of GDP; by 2006, this figure was 16.6 percent. Exports rose from 4.9 percent of GDP in 1960 to 10.8 percent in 2006. Financial markets in the United States and other nations have also become much more closely linked over the past three decades. The U.S. economy has become much more *open* in the sense of having more extensive trade and financial dealings with other economies.

In other chapters, examples and Perspectives emphasize the interrelations of the U.S. economy and the economies of other nations. The chapters in this part focus explicitly on the macroeconomics of open economies, which brings these interrelations to center stage. This chapter considers the determination of exchange rates, the current international monetary system as well as the system it replaced, and the interactions between the domestic economy and our international economic transactions.

balance of payments accounts
the Balance of Payments Accounts record economic transactions between U.S. and foreign residents both in goods and assets

We begin by examining the U.S. **balance of payments accounts**, which summarize our foreign economic transactions (Section 14.1). Next, we explain how exchange rates are determined in currency markets under differing exchange rate systems (Section 14.2). The actual exchange rate arrangements that make up the current international monetary system are examined (Section 14.3). The relative merits of pegged versus flexible exchange rate systems are assessed (Section 14.4). We then review the U.S. experience with a system of at least partially flexible exchange rates over the years since 1973 (Section 14.5). Finally, the risks from some growing imbalances in world trade are evaluated (Section 14.6).

Exchange rates are central to the focus of this chapter. An exchange rate between two currencies is the price of one currency in terms of the other. The price of the British pound in terms of the U.S. dollar on May, 17, 2007, was $1.98 ($1.98 = 1 pound); the price of a Canadian dollar was 92 U.S. cents; the price of a euro (the common currency of 13 European countries) was $1.35. Exchanges between the U.S. dollar and other currencies take place when U.S. residents want to purchase foreign goods or assets, as well as when foreign residents want to purchase U.S. goods and assets. A look at these transactions between the United States and other countries is the starting point for our study of how exchange rates are determined.

14.1 THE U.S. BALANCE OF PAYMENTS ACCOUNTS

The U.S. Department of Commerce records foreign economic transactions in the balance of payments accounts. On one side of the accounts, all earnings from the foreign activities of U.S. residents and the U.S. government are recorded as credits; on the other side, expenditures abroad are reported as debits. A point to notice is that, by the usual principles of double-entry bookkeeping, each credit must be matched by an equal debit, and vice versa. Each expenditure on foreign goods, for example, must be financed somehow; the source of financing is recorded as a credit. A first conclusion, then, before we even look at the numbers, is that if *all* transactions are counted, the balance of payments always balances.

We will, however, want to consider subcategories of our foreign transactions, and for such subcategories there is no reason to believe that receipts from abroad will equal earnings from abroad. In recent years, for example, expenditures on our merchandise exports by foreign residents (a credit in our balance of payments) have fallen far short of our expenditures on imported goods (a debit in our balance of payments). This *deficit* in our **merchandise trade balance** has been a matter of concern, for reasons to be discussed.

merchandise trade balance measures exports minus imports in the U.S. balance of payments

Table 14-1 summarizes the U.S. balance of payments accounts for 2006.

The Current Account

current account in the U.S. balance of payments is a record of U.S. merchandise exports and imports as well as trade in services and foreign transfer payments

The first group of items in the table are **current account** transactions. Among these, the first items listed are *merchandise exports and imports*, to which we have just referred. Examples of merchandise exports are the sale of a U.S. computer system to a British firm or the sale of U.S. grain to Russia. Purchases of Japanese cars, German cameras, or Honduran bananas by U.S. residents are examples of U.S. imports. In 2006, U.S. merchandise imports exceeded exports by $836.0 billion. We had a merchandise trade deficit of that amount.

TABLE 14-1 U.S. Balance of Payments, 2006 (billions of dollars)

	Credit (+)	*Debit (−)*	*Balance (−) Deficit (+)Surplus*
Current account			
Merchandise exports (+) and imports (−)	1,023.7	−1,859.7	−836.0
Service transactions (net)	63.4		
Transfers (net)		−84.1	
Current account balance			−856.7
Capital account			
Capital inflows (+) and outflows (−)[a]	1,465.8	−1,053.4	
Capital account subbalance			412.4
Statistical discrepancy			141.4
Official reserve transactions			
Reduction in U.S. official reserve assets			2.4
Increase in foreign official assets in the United States			300.5
Total official reserve transactions			302.9

[a]Includes increases in U.S. government foreign assets other than official reserve assets.

SOURCE: *Survey of Current Business*, April 2007. Data are on a slightly different basis (coverage and timing) from U.S. census data shown elsewhere in the book.

The next category in the table is imports and exports of *services*, entered only in terms of their net value. Examples of transactions in the service category are financial, insurance, and shipping services. Also in this category are dividends and interest earned by U.S. residents from their assets abroad (a credit) and interest and dividends paid to foreign residents who hold U.S. assets (a debit). The net item in the table, $63.4 billion, indicates that in 2006 we exported more of such services than we imported. The last transactions in the current account are *net transfers*. Recorded here are private and government transfer payments made between the United States and other countries. Such payments include U.S. foreign aid payments (a debit) and private or government pension payments to persons living abroad (a debit). Any such transfer to a U.S. resident from abroad would be a credit on this line.

If we stop or draw the line at this point, we can compute the *current account balance*. The table indicates that in 2006 the current account was in deficit by $856.7 billion.

Overall, just considering current account transactions, U.S. residents spent over $856.7 billion more abroad than was earned.

capital account
in the balance of payments is a record of purchases of U.S. assets by foreign residents (capital inflows) and purchases of foreign assets by U.S. residents (capital outflows)

The Capital Account

The next entries in the table record **capital account** transactions.[1] Capital inflows (credits) are purchases of U.S. assets by foreign residents. Capital inflows include purchases by foreigners of U.S. private or government bonds, stocks, and bank deposits. In addition, foreign direct investments in the United States, such as Honda's building of a plant in Ohio, are capital inflows in the balance of payments. Purchases by U.S. residents of financial assets or direct investments in foreign countries are capital outflows (debits) in the balance of payments. During the 1980s, the United States began to run large surpluses in the capital account that partly balanced out large deficits in the current account. In 2006, this surplus was $412.4 billion.

An important point concerning the U.S. capital account is that foreign purchases of our assets largely represent U.S. borrowing from foreign residents. The large capital inflows of 1982–2006 included $2,000 billion of foreign purchases of U.S. government securities and an even larger amount of foreign loans or purchases of private U.S. securities. During this period, large excesses of merchandise imports over exports (trade deficits) were, in effect, financed by borrowing from abroad. Between 1983 and 2006, as a result of this borrowing, the United States went from being a net creditor nation to a nation with a *net* foreign debt in excess of $2,900 billion.

Statistical Discrepancy

The next item in the table is the *statistical discrepancy*. Because not all international economic transactions are properly recorded, the statistical discrepancy (or errors and omissions term) is the amount that must be added to make the total balance of payments balance. As can be seen from the table, the statistical discrepancy for 2006 was $141.4 billion.

[1]In previous chapters, the term *investment* was used exclusively to refer to purchases of physical capital goods. The term *capital* referred to those physical goods themselves. In the discussion of international economic relations, the term *capital flows* refers to exchanges of financial assets involving individuals in different countries, as well as direct investment such as the purchase of a plant in another country.

Official Reserve Transactions

Let us stop and examine the point we have now reached in considering U.S. foreign economic transactions. Suppose we draw a line below the statistical discrepancy. All the items above the line represent international economic transactions undertaken by private U.S. residents or the U.S. government for some independent motive. By this we mean a motive other than the effect the transaction will have on the balance of payments or, as we will see presently, on the value of the U.S. dollar relative to other currencies. A U.S. resident buys a Japanese car or a share of stock in a German company because of a preference for it over its domestic counterpart. The U.S. government may give foreign aid to another government to stabilize the political situation in that country. All the items above the line, from the point of view of the balance of payments accounts, can be termed *autonomous*, or independently motivated, transactions.

In contrast, the official reserve transactions below this line are carried out by central banks, either the U.S. Federal Reserve System or foreign central banks (e.g., the Bank of England or the Bank of Japan) in pursuit of international economic policy objectives. Here we simply explain the nature of these transactions. The motivation for them is explained later in the chapter.

The first item below the statistical discrepancy in Table 14-1 is the *reduction in U.S. official reserve assets*. Official reserve assets are holdings of gold, special drawing rights (a reserve asset created by the International Monetary Fund),[2] and foreign currency holdings. From Table 14-1 we see that, in 2006, U.S. official reserve assets declined by $2.4 billion. That amount of our reserve assets was used to finance expenditures abroad. Reductions in official reserve assets are a credit in the balance of payments.

The next and last item in the balance of payments table is the *increase in foreign official assets in the United States*. Foreign central banks hold a portion of their reserve assets in the form of dollars. Dollars are an important reserve asset because the dollar is commonly used in international transactions. If foreign central banks buy dollars, that is a credit in our balance of payments (a capital inflow), because they are investing in the United States.[3] In 2006, foreign central banks increased the amount of official reserve assets held in the United States by $300.5 billion, hence the positive item in this line of our balance of payments accounts.

Read Perspectives 14-1.

14.2 EXCHANGE RATES AND THE MARKET FOR FOREIGN EXCHANGE

foreign exchange a general term to refer to an aggregate of foreign currencies

The demand for foreign currencies by domestic residents is called the demand for **foreign exchange**. The foreign exchange market is the market in which national currencies are traded for one another. It is in this market, for example, that U.S. residents sell dollars to purchase foreign exchange

[2]The International Monetary Fund (IMF) is an agency that was set up at the end of World War II to administer the international monetary agreements signed at that time. These agreements, the Bretton Woods agreements, are discussed in Sections 14.3 and 14.4. Special drawing rights (SDRs) are sometimes referred to as "paper gold." They are a type of deposit at the IMF that can be exchanged between nations to settle payment imbalances.

[3]They need not hold U.S. currency. After buying dollars, they can use them to purchase U.S. government or private securities.

PERSPECTIVES 14-1

U.S. CURRENT ACCOUNT DEFICITS—ARE THEY SUSTAINABLE?

From Table 14-1 it can be seen that the U.S. current account deficit was $856.7 billion in 2006, approximately 6.5 percent of GDP. As of mid-2007 the current account deficit continued to run at nearly $75 billion per month. Are current account deficits of this magnitude something we should be concerned about? How concerned?

Many argue that we should worry about these deficits. In 2004 the International Monetary Fund (IMF) warned that the U.S. current account deficit posed serious risks for both the U.S. and the world economy. Domestically, many have warned that, at least eventually, such current account deficits will result in a crisis where the value of the U.S. dollar will fall precipitously, the demand for U.S. financial assets will fall, and U.S. interest rates will shoot up.

Other observers, including Alan Greenspan, chairman of the Federal Reserve Board from 1987 to 2006, see no impending crisis. They believe that the current account deficit is likely to be reversed by market forces in a benign fashion. Let's look at the issues.

Table 14-1 shows that the U.S. deficit on the current account is balanced for the most part by a surplus in the capital account and an increase in foreign official assets in the United States. The United States finances its current account deficit by borrowing abroad: from private investors (the capital account surplus) and from foreign central banks (the increase in foreign official assets). As the United States has run repeated large current account deficits, our foreign debt grew to approximately $3 trillion by 2007.

Those who are worried about current account deficits believe that at a not too distant point in the future, foreign investors, including foreign central banks, will no longer be willing to buy such large amounts of U.S. financial assets. At this point, the dollar will fall sharply and U.S. interest rates will rise. In particular, these observers point to the huge purchases of dollars by Asian central banks over the past few years, an unsustainable flow of capital to the United States. Moreover, as the IMF has pointed out, the U.S. borrowing to finance the current account deficit has, by increasing overall borrowing, led to an increase in world interest rates, making it harder for other countries, including emerging economies, to borrow to finance their investment needs.

Those who do not see the current account deficit as an immediate serious problem point to increasing globalization of the world capital markets. As other countries have liberalized their capital markets, investors in those countries have increased their demand for foreign assets, in large part U.S. assets. Even in countries that had for a long time allowed capital mobility, investors have made more cross-border investments in recent years. Economists have referred to this tendency as a decline in *home bias*. These observers see the increased demand for dollar-denominated assets by Asian central banks as due to the particular policies of these countries. China, for example, whose central bank has in recent years been the largest purchaser of dollars, does so to keep the value of its currency, the yuan, fixed in terms of the dollar. The factors that have led to the increased demand for U.S. assets and forces in the United States that contribute to the current account deficit will, in their view, be reversed in a gradual manner.

We will return to the question of recent U.S. current account deficits after we develop a framework for analyzing exchange rate determination and explain some other aspects of the current international monetary system. There we will be able to put the United States situation within a broader context of recent international trade imbalances.

(foreign currencies). In the United States, the central market for foreign exchange is composed of brokers and bank foreign exchange departments in New York City.

To see the link between the balance of payments accounts and transactions in the foreign exchange market, we begin by recognizing that all expenditures by U.S. residents on foreign goods, services, or assets and all foreign transfer payments (debits in the balance of payments accounts) also represent demands for foreign currencies—that is, demands for *foreign exchange*. The U.S. resident buying a Japanese car pays for it in dollars, but the Japanese exporter will expect to be paid in yen. So, dollars must be exchanged for yen in the foreign exchange market. Take another example: If a U.S. resident wants to buy a share of stock on the London stock exchange, a broker must convert the buyer's dollars into British pounds before actually making the purchase. *Thus, the total U.S. residents' expenditure abroad represents a demand for foreign exchange.* Looked at from the point of view of the dollar, we can also state that the *total foreign expenditure of U.S. residents represents an equal supply of dollars in the foreign exchange market.*

Conversely, all foreign earnings of U.S. residents reflect equal earnings of foreign exchange. American exporters, for example, will expect to be paid in dollars, and to buy our goods, foreigners must sell their currency and buy dollars. *Total credits in the balance of payments accounts are then equal to the supply of foreign exchange or, what is the same thing, the demand for dollars.*

Demand and Supply in the Foreign Exchange Market

Exchange rates between national currencies are determined in the foreign exchange market. In our discussion of this process, we make the following simplifying assumptions. Initially, we exclude official reserve transactions by central banks. In the jargon of international economics, we assume that central banks do not *intervene* in the foreign exchange market. We relax this assumption later in this section. Also for simplicity, we assume that there are only two countries: the United States, whose domestic currency is the dollar, and "Europe," whose domestic currency is the euro.[4] The *exchange rate* in this simple situation is the relative price of the two currencies, which we express as *the price of the euro in terms of dollars*. For example, if the price of the euro is 1 dollar, then 1 euro trades for 1 dollar; at 1.25 dollars, the exchange rate (price of the euro) is higher, and 1 euro equals 1.25 dollars, (0.80 euro = 1 dollar). It is important to remember that with the exchange rate expressed in this manner, a higher exchange rate means that the price of foreign currency (or foreign exchange) has risen. When the exchange rate rises, we say that the foreign currency has *appreciated* or the dollar has *depreciated*. Alternatively, a fall in the exchange rate means that the price of foreign exchange (price of the euro) has declined. The euro has *depreciated* while the dollar has *appreciated*.

Figure 14-1 shows the supply and demand schedules for foreign exchange plotted against the exchange rate (π). As was explained, foreign expenditures by U.S. residents (imports, purchases of foreign assets, and foreign transfers) are demands for

[4]Europe is, of course, not one country. We refer here to the set of European countries that have the euro as a common currency. Details are discussed in Perspectives 14-3. The fiction of a two-country world is employed to avoid the details of how the individual exchange rate with each foreign currency is determined.

FIGURE 14-1 Foreign Exchange Market

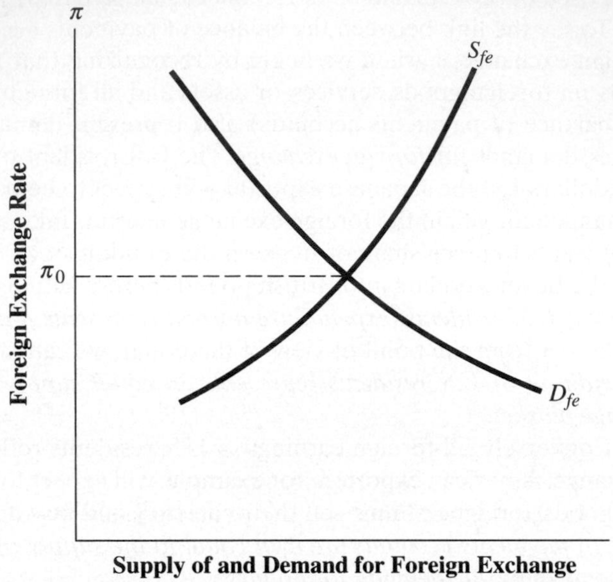

The demand schedule for foreign exchange is downward-sloping because the demand for foreign exchange to finance imports falls as the exchange rate rises, making foreign goods more expensive. The supply schedule for foreign exchange is upward-sloping, reflecting the assumption that the foreign exchange proceeds from export sales rise as the exchange rate rises, making domestic goods less expensive to foreign buyers. The equilibrium exchange rate is π_0, the rate that equates demand and supply.

foreign exchange. How will this demand for foreign exchange vary with the price of foreign exchange? In Figure 14-1, the demand curve (D_{fe}) is downward-sloping, indicating that as the price of foreign exchange (price of euros) rises, the demand for foreign falls. The reason is that a rise in the price of foreign exchange will increase the cost *in terms of dollars* of purchasing foreign goods. Imports will therefore decline, and less foreign exchange will be demanded. Note that here we are holding all prices other than the exchange rate constant. Suppose that you are considering the purchase of a German camera that costs 200 euros. If the exchange rate, the price of the euro in terms of dollars, is 1.00, the camera will cost \$200 (200 euros = \$200 at 1.00 euro to the dollar). If the exchange rate rises to 1.25, the camera will cost \$250 (200 euros = \$250 at 0.8 euro to the dollar). The higher the exchange rate, the higher the dollar cost of imported goods and the lower the demand for foreign exchange.

What about the demand for foreign exchange for the purchase of foreign assets and for foreign transfers? With respect to the latter, there is no reason for a definite relationship between the amount of foreign transfers and the exchange rate. It is not clear what effect the change in the exchange rate would have on foreign aid programs, pension payments to persons living abroad, or gifts to foreign nationals. In the case of purchases of foreign assets, an increase in the exchange rate will, as in the case of imported goods, push up the price in dollars of the foreign stocks or bonds. The rise in the exchange rate will, however, also result in a proportional increase in the interest or dividend payment on the foreign bond or stock, again as measured in dollars. For example, a French bond costing 800 euros and paying interest of 80 euros per year will cost $800 and pay interest of $80 per year at an exchange rate of 1.00 (1.00 euro = 1 dollar). At an exchange rate of 1.25 (0.80 euro = 1 dollar), the bond will cost $1,000 and pay interest of $100 per year. In either case, the bond represents an asset that pays a return of 10 percent per year. Consequently, we would not necessarily expect any effect on the demand for foreign assets as a result of a change in the exchange rate.[5] The downward slope of the demand for foreign exchange schedule results only from the fact that imports decline as the exchange rate rises.

The supply schedule for foreign exchange is drawn with a positive slope in Figure 14-1, which reflects the assumption that the supply of foreign exchange increases as the exchange rate rises. As the exchange rate (price of euros) rises, U.S. export goods become less expensive to Europeans in terms of euros. Again we are holding all other prices, including the dollar price of U.S. exports, fixed. For example, U.S. wheat that sells for $5 a bushel would cost a European 5 euros per bushel at an exchange rate of 1.00 but only 4 euros at an exchange rate of 1.25.

The demand for U.S. exports should therefore increase as the exchange rate rises. Notice, however, that a given *dollar* volume of exports earns less foreign exchange (fewer euros) at the higher exchange rate. For example, if the exchange rate rose by 10 percent and as a result the *dollar* volume of exports rose 10 percent, earnings of foreign exchange would be unchanged. The United States would be selling 10 percent more but earning 10 percent fewer euros on each sale.

For the supply of foreign exchange to increase as the exchange rate rises, the foreign demand for our exports must be more than *unit elastic*, meaning that a 1 percent increase in the exchange rate (which results in a 1 percent decline in the price of the export good to Europeans) must result in an increase in demand of more than 1 percent. If this condition is met, the dollar volume of our exports will rise more than in proportion to the rise in the exchange rate, and earnings of euros (the supply of foreign exchange) will increase as the exchange rate rises. This is the assumption we make in Figure 14-1.[6]

Exchange Rate Determination: Flexible Exchange Rates

So far, we have excluded intervention (official reserve transactions) by central banks. The supply and demand schedules in Figure 14-1 are for only autonomous transactions in the balance of payments accounts. Let us continue with this assumption and see how the exchange rate is determined in the absence of intervention. In this case, we would expect the exchange rate to move to clear the market, to equate the demand for and supply of foreign exchange. In Figure 14-1, this equilibrium exchange rate is π_0. The

[5] It is the expectation of a change in the exchange rate that would trigger changes in the demand for foreign versus domestic assets. If, for example, you expected the price of the euro to rise from 1 dollar today to 1.25 dollars next week, you could buy the French bond discussed in the text now for $800 and sell it next week for $1,000. For now, we are not allowing for *expected* changes in exchange rates.

[6] Empirical support for this assumption is provided by Hendrik Houthakker and Stephen Magee, "Income and Price Elasticities in World Trade," *Review of Economics and Statistics*, 5 (May 1969), pp. 111–25. A later estimate by Jaime Marquez, "Bilateral Trade Elasticities," *Review of Economics and Statistics*, 72 (February 1990) pp. 75–76, indicates a just unit-elastic foreign demand for U.S. exports. This implies a vertical supply of foreign exchange. To assume a vertical supply schedule would not change our analysis.

FIGURE 14-2 Effect in the Foreign Exchange Market of an Increase in the Demand for Imports

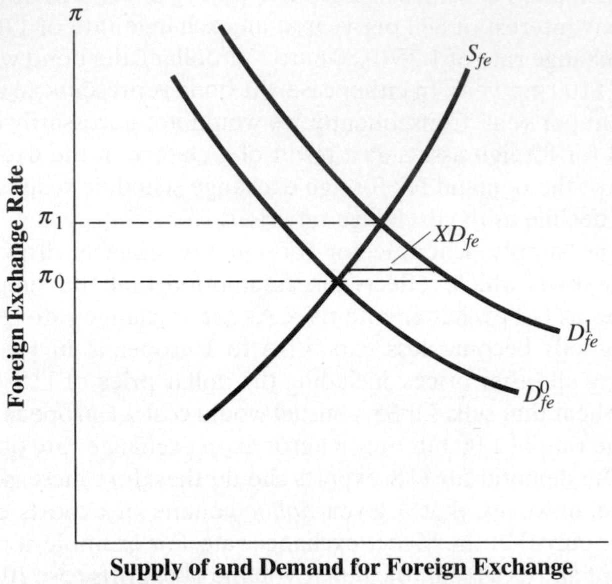

An autonomous increase in import demand shifts the demand schedule for foreign exchange from D^0_{fe} to D^1_{fe}. At the initial equilibrium exchange rate, there is an excess demand for foreign exchange (XD_{fe}). The exchange rate rises to π_1 to reequilibrate supply and demand in the foreign exchange market.

autonomous elements in the balance of payments account, those above the lines where the official reserve transactions are recorded, are equated by the adjustment of the exchange rate. Such a system of exchange rate determination, in which there is no central bank intervention, is a *flexible exchange rate system* or, as it is sometimes called, a *floating rate system*. An exchange rate system or regime is a set of international rules governing the setting of exchange rates. A completely flexible or floating rate system is a particularly simple set of rules for the central banks to follow; they do nothing to directly affect the level of their exchange rate. The exchange rate is market-determined.

To better understand the workings of a flexible exchange rate system, we examine the effect of a shock that increases the demand for foreign exchange. Suppose that the U.S. demand for imported goods increases. For example, assume that an increase in gasoline prices causes a shift from SUVs to small, fuel-efficient foreign cars. The effect of this increase in import demand would show up in the foreign exchange market as a shift to the right in the demand schedule for foreign exchange—for example, from D^0_{fe} to D^1_{fe} as illustrated in Figure 14-2. At a given exchange rate, there is a greater demand for imports in the United States and, correspondingly, a greater demand for foreign exchange. At the initial equilibrium exchange rate π_0, there is now an excess demand for foreign exchange (shown as XD_{fe} in Figure 14-2). To clear the market, the exchange rate must rise to the new equilibrium value, π_1. The rise in the exchange rate will cause the quantity of imports demanded to decline, because the dollar price of imported goods rises with the exchange rate. Also, the quantity of exports demanded will increase because the rise in the exchange rate makes U.S. exports less expensive to foreigners. At the new equilibrium with the higher exchange rate (π_1), the supply of and demand for foreign exchange are again equal. The increase in import demand leads to a depreciation of the dollar.

In 1973, the United States moved toward greater flexibility in the exchange rate, as did other industrialized countries. Over the post-1970 period, however, the United States has not had a *completely* flexible exchange rate system. To varying degrees over this period, central banks, including the U.S. central bank, have intervened in the foreign exchange market to influence the values of their currency. The features of the current international monetary system are discussed later. Before we begin this discussion, it is useful to examine the working of the foreign exchange market under the polar opposite of a completely flexible rate system, a system of *fixed*, or *pegged*, exchange rates.

Exchange Rate Determination: Fixed Exchange Rates

An international monetary system is a set of rules organizing exchange rate determination and agreeing on which assets will be official reserve assets. An example of a fixed exchange rate system is the post–World War II **Bretton Woods system**. The international monetary agreements that made up this system were negotiated near the end of the war (at Bretton Woods, New Hampshire). The IMF was set up to administer the Bretton Woods system. According to IMF rules, the United States was to set a parity, or *par value*, for its currency in terms of gold. Other nations would set parities for their currencies in terms of dollars, which with the dollar tied to gold also fixed the gold value of these other currencies. The United States agreed to maintain convertibility between the dollar and gold at the fixed price (originally $35 per ounce). Other countries agreed to maintain convertibility (after a period of postwar adjustment) with the dollar and other currencies but not with gold. The other countries agreed to maintain their exchange rates vis-à-vis the dollar within a 1 percent range on either side of the parity level. The differential responsibility of the United States compared to other IMF members concerning convertibility into gold seemed sensible because, at the time, the United States had approximately two-thirds of the official world gold reserves.

Bretton Woods system was a pegged exchange rate system set up at the end of World War II

Pegging the Exchange Rate

To see how a system of fixed exchange rates functions, we examine the way a country can "peg," or fix, the level of its exchange rate. To do so we return to our two-country example and assume that the United States wants to fix its exchange rate against the euro, which we are using to represent the currencies of the rest of the world. We ignore the 1 percent margin just mentioned and assume that the U.S. central bank wishes to fix an exact par value for the dollar, say at an exchange rate of 1 euro equals 1 dollar. The working of the foreign exchange market with this fixed exchange rate system is illustrated in Figure 14-3.

We assume that this official fixed exchange rate, 1.0, is below the equilibrium exchange rate in a flexible rate system, the equilibrium rate in Figure 14-3 being 1.25 (0.80 euro = 1 dollar). At the fixed exchange rate in such a situation, the dollar would be said to be *overvalued* and the euro *undervalued*. This terminology means that, if the

FIGURE 14-3 Foreign Exchange Market with a Fixed Exchange Rate

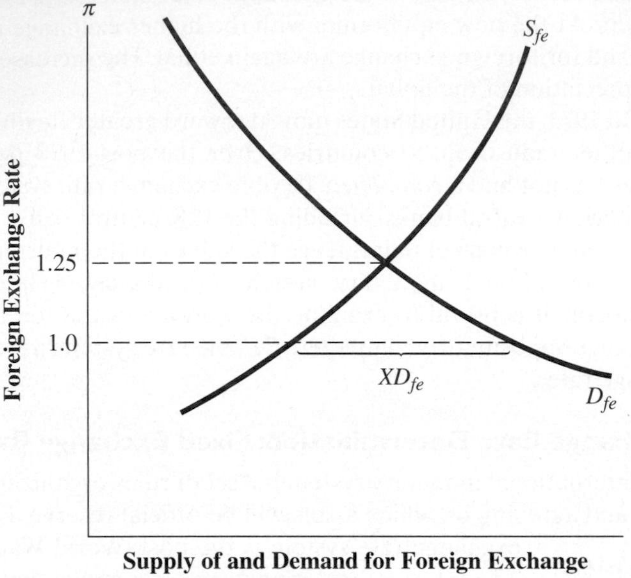

In a fixed exchange rate system, if the official exchange rate ($\pi = 1.0$) is below the market equilibrium rate ($\pi = 1.25$), there will be an excess demand for foreign exchange, XD_{fe}. To keep the exchange rate from rising, domestic or foreign central banks must supply foreign exchange.

exchange rate were market-determined, the price of the euro relative to the dollar (the exchange rate) would have to rise to clear the market. What prevents this from happening?

Recall that the demand and supply schedules we constructed for the foreign exchange market measure only *autonomous* transactions; they do not take account of accommodating transactions undertaken by central banks to finance payments imbalances. It is precisely such *intervention* by central banks that is required to peg the exchange rate at a nonequilibrium value such as 1.0 dollar in Figure 14-3. To keep the rate at 1.0, the United States must stand ready to buy and sell dollars at that exchange rate. If the U.S. central bank will buy euros for 1 dollar, the exchange rate cannot fall below that point because no one would sell elsewhere for less. Similarly, the exchange rate cannot rise above 1.0 because the central bank will be willing to sell euros at that price.

In the situation depicted in Figure 14-3, with the exchange rate below the equilibrium rate, there is an excess demand for foreign exchange (euros), shown as XD_{fe} in the figure. To keep the exchange rate from rising, the U.S. central bank can supply foreign exchange; that is, it can exchange euros for dollars in the foreign exchange market.

Alternatively, the European Central Bank might be the one to intervene. This bank would supply euros (sell euros and buy dollars) to satisfy the excess demand for euros and to keep the price of the euro at the official exchange rate.

Implications of Intervention

There are two points to note concerning central bank intervention. The first concerns the effect on the U.S. balance of payments as a result of intervention in the foreign exchange market. Suppose the U.S. central bank intervenes. Where does it get the euros that it sells to keep the exchange rate from rising? Our central bank must use up its international reserve assets to buy euros from the European Central Bank in order to sell them in the foreign exchange market. This action would show up in Table 14-1 as a reduction in U.S. official reserve assets.

Alternatively, if the European Central Bank supplied the euros directly in the foreign exchange market to satisfy the U.S. excess demand for foreign exchange, it would end up with increased holdings of dollars. In the U.S. balance of payments (Table 14-1), this action would show up as an increase in foreign official assets in the United States. The sum of these two items (a reduction in U.S. official reserve assets and an increase in foreign official assets in the United States) equals the U.S. balance of payments *deficit*. This is a deficit because it is the amount by which our spending abroad (demand for foreign exchange) exceeds our earnings from abroad (supply of foreign exchange), taking account of only autonomous transactions (those reflected in the D_{fe} and S_{fe} curves). This deficit must be financed by central bank intervention if the official exchange rate is to be maintained.

Conversely, if, at the official exchange rate, the supply of foreign exchange exceeds the demand (there is an excess supply of foreign exchange), a country will have a surplus in the balance of payments. In this case, earnings from sales to foreign residents that produce the supply of foreign exchange exceed domestic residents' expenditures abroad. When this occurs in the United States, our official reserve assets increase, or foreign official reserve assets in the United States decrease.

The second point to note about central bank intervention is that countries that must intervene continually to finance deficits will run out of official reserve assets. In our example, it is clear that if the United States financed its deficits by reducing U.S. official assets, it would eventually exhaust its reserve holdings. But what if the deficit were financed by the European Central Bank (or other central banks), increasing reserve assets in the United States by buying dollars? If foreign central banks continued to hold dollars, our reserves would not be affected. Under the Bretton Woods agreement, however, if they wished, the foreign central banks could request that the U.S. buy back dollars, using reserve assets (gold and SDRs). If they did, our reserves would then fall.

To an extent, the United States was able to run continual balance of payments deficits during the Bretton Woods period because foreign central banks did not ask us to buy back dollars they had acquired in foreign exchange market interventions. At first, they did not do so because they wanted the dollars, which served as a reserve asset for them. (Remember, they were committed to maintaining the convertibility between their currency and the dollar.) Later on, they did not ask us to redeem our dollars because they knew we could not do it; foreign dollar holdings far exceeded our reserves. This situation contributed to the collapse of the system, as we will see.

Countries other than the United States—Denmark, for example—could not run persistent deficits without losing their reserves quickly. Their currency, the Danish krone, was not used as a reserve asset, so other central banks would expect the Danish central bank to buy back the Danish krone they had obtained in foreign exchange market intervention. To do so, Denmark would have had to use up its official reserves (gold, SDRs, and U.S. dollars).

14.3 THE CURRENT EXCHANGE RATE SYSTEM

The Bretton Woods system collapsed in 1971. The current world system of exchange rate determination is best described as a *managed float* for major industrialized countries (or in the case of the countries in the euro area for a group of countries). Developing nations often have fixed exchange rate systems, although some allow exchange rate flexibility of varying degrees. A managed, or dirty, float contains elements of a flexible exchange rate system (the float part) and a fixed rate system (the managed part). For a country with a managed float, the exchange rate is allowed to move in response to market forces. However, the central bank can intervene to prevent *undesirable* or *disruptive* movements in the exchange rate. The question of how an undesirable or disruptive movement in the exchange rate has been defined in practice, and therefore when central banks have chosen to intervene in foreign exchange markets, will be considered presently. The factors that led to the breakdown of the Bretton Woods system are also discussed.

Exchange Rate Arrangements

Table 14-2 summarizes the exchange rate arrangements of the countries that are members of the IMF. As just noted, there is no one system of exchange rate determination. Some countries peg their exchange rate to one currency or a composite of currencies within a narrow margin of 1 percent or less. This is the group of 44 countries labeled "fixed peg arrangements" in the table. The group labeled "pegged arrangements within bands" also follow a fixed exchange rate policy but with a wider band. The currency group labeled "crawling pegs" adjusts the value of their currency relative to a central rate in response to a set of economic indicators (e.g., domestic versus foreign inflation rates) and thus fall partway between fixed and flexible rates. The group labeled "participate in an exchange rate mechanism" comprise the European nations that have adopted a common currency, the euro, but float as a group relative to other currencies. This exchange rate setup is described in more detail later in the chapter. The next group in the table, 77 countries, have floating rate systems, though some are managed floats. The final group, called "other," have exchange rate systems that we will describe in Perspectives 14-2.

TABLE 14-2 Exchange Rate Arrangement of IMF Member Countries

Exchange Rate Arrangement	*Number*
Fixed peg arrangements	44
Pegged arrangements within bands	14
Crawling pegs	5
Participate in an exchange rate mechanism	13
Managed floating and float independently	77
Other	34

SOURCE: IMF, *International Financial Statistics*.

Japan, Canada, the United Kingdom, and the United States are among the countries having floating exchange rates.

Read Perspectives 14-2.

How Much Managing? How Much Floating?

In a managed float, central banks intervene in foreign exchange markets to prevent undesirable or disruptive movements in their exchange rates. Otherwise, their exchange rates float. During the post-1973 period, the degree to which the industrialized countries intervened in the foreign exchange market varied significantly.

In the United States during the 1970s, the U.S. central bank frequently intervened in the foreign exchange market. For example, in November 1978, a massive support program for the price of the dollar was coordinated by the U.S. government. In 1981,

PERSPECTIVES 14-2

CURRENCY BOARDS AND DOLLARIZATION

Without a unified international monetary system such as the Bretton Woods system, individual countries have been left to choose their exchange rate arrangement as part of their overall macroeconomic policy setup. A number of emerging market countries have followed pegged exchange rate systems. Such a system aims at providing exchange rate stability to foster growth of trade and investment. In some cases the commitment to a exchange rate peg is part of a anti-inflation package.

In a world of high capital mobility, however, some countries have found that they are unable to maintain the pegs they set for their currencies. Capital outflows threaten to exhaust their reserves, and they are forced to devalue their currency. Two ways to bolster a fixed rate system are: currency boards and dollarization.

With a currency board, a country commits to fixing the value of its currency to some strong currency, such as the dollar, and being ready to convert its currency into that foreign currency on demand. It further commits itself to print more of its own currency only as it accumulates the foreign currency. This effectively takes monetary policy out of the hands of the domestic country and alleviates the fear of foreign investors that inflation will destroy the value of their holdings of the domestic currency. Currency boards therefore create credibility for the fixed exchange rate. Argentina, long plagued by high inflation, adopted a currency board in 1991 with the dollar as the foreign currency. The currency board enabled Argentina to halt inflation for a decade but collapsed in 2001. The cause of the collapse is widely believed to be continued and growing government budget deficits that eventually undermined the credibility of the fixed exchange rate.

Dollarization goes a step beyond a currency board in that a country simply adopts a strong foreign currency, again often the dollar, and eliminates its own domestic currency. Because the country's currency is, for example, the dollar, this is an extreme form of a fixed exchange rate (relative to the dollar). Again here the country gives up its ability to conduct an independent monetary policy. In the midst of high inflation and other economic difficulties, Ecuador dollarized in 2000. Panama has used the dollar as its currency since its independence in 1903.

the Reagan administration announced that central bank intervention would occur only when necessary to prevent disorder in the foreign exchange market initiated by crisis situations. Following this shift in the interpretation of what constituted a disruptive movement in the exchange rate, U.S. intervention in the foreign exchange market declined markedly.

Even in the absence of U.S. central bank intervention, the price of the dollar does not float freely with the current exchange rate system because other central banks buy or sell dollars to influence the price of their currencies relative to the dollar. For example, in 1981 and again in 1984, European central banks sold dollars from their reserve holdings to slow the rise in the price of the dollar, which would have meant a fall in the price of their currencies (a rise in their exchange rate relative to the dollar). Then, with the Plaza Accord in September 1985, central banks of the large industrialized countries began concerted intervention aimed at lowering the value of the dollar (raising the U.S. exchange rate). In 1987, for reasons that will be explained later, these central banks reversed course and intervened, again in concert, to prop up the dollar.

In recent years, the major currency market interventions have been purchases of U.S. dollars by Asian central banks. The Bank of China accumulated a massive reserve holding in order to maintain pegged value of its currency. The Bank of Japan has also bought a large amount of dollars to prevent (or limit) appreciation of the Japanese yen. Other Asian central banks have purchased hundreds of billions of dollars to add to their stocks of reserves. Overall these purchases have exceeded $2,000 billion over the past seven years.

The Breakdown of the Bretton Woods System

We see from Table 14-2 that the current international monetary system is quite disorganized. How did such a system (or lack of a system) come about? What process led to the breakdown of the Bretton Woods fixed exchange rate system?

Central to the Bretton Woods system was the set of fixed exchange rates and the key currency role of the dollar. Par values set for currencies were not assumed to be fixed for all time; the Bretton Woods system was to be one of adjustable pegs. A country was to be able to change its exchange rate if it found a "fundamental disequilibrium" in its balance of payments. Such changes were to be made in consultation with the IMF. Countries with chronic deficits would *devalue* their currencies, which means to lower the par value of the currency in terms of the dollar, and because the dollar's value in terms of gold was fixed, to also lower the currency's value in terms of gold. Countries with persistent surpluses would *revalue* their currencies at higher par values in terms of the dollar and gold.

In fact, adjustments proved extremely difficult. Countries with persistent surpluses were under no pressure to revalue their currencies. Governments of countries with persistent deficits found it politically difficult to devalue, because a decline in the value of the currency was taken as a sign of failed government economic policy. Moreover, rumors that a currency was to be devalued led to waves of speculation against the currency, as speculators sold the currency with an eye to buying it back after it had been devalued. Because of these difficulties in adjusting the par values of currencies, during the Bretton Woods period some countries (e.g., Great Britain) developed chronic balance of payments deficits, and others (e.g., Germany) developed chronic surpluses.

Most damaging to the system was the fact that the United States developed into a chronic deficit country, an indication that the dollar was overvalued. Devaluing the dollar meant a rise in the price of gold because the dollar was convertible into gold at the fixed par value. This presented special difficulties because of the key currency role played by the dollar within the system. But the growing deficits in the U.S. balance of payments were creating a glut of dollars on the market.

In the late 1960s, the U.S. balance of payments position worsened. Severe inflationary pressure developed in the United States as a result of government spending on the Vietnam War. This increased inflation worsened the U.S. balance of payments. Prices in the United States rose faster than prices in other industrial countries. With the exchange rate fixed, U.S. export goods became more expensive to foreigners, while the price of foreign imports fell relative to domestic goods prices in the United States. As a consequence, the demand for U.S. exports fell and U.S. demand for imports rose; the U.S. balance of payments deficit increased.

In 1972, the dollar was devalued, and the price of gold increased to $38 per ounce. A new set of par values for other IMF member currencies was established. However, attempts to defend the new set of par values collapsed by 1973. Again a surge of inflation in the United States and loss of confidence in the dollar were proximate causes of the problems in maintaining a set of fixed currency values. Also, beginning in 1973–74, huge increases in oil prices led to large balance of payments deficits for the industrialized oil-consuming nations and surpluses for the oil-producing countries. Exchange rate adjustments were required to restore equilibrium. The system of a managed float that emerged in the 1970s was the mechanism by which exchange rate adjustments necessitated by the declining strength of the dollar and rising oil prices were achieved.

14.4 ADVANTAGES OF ALTERNATIVE EXCHANGE RATE REGIMES

Within the current framework of exchange rate determination, each country or group of countries chooses an exchange rate regime. A key element in this decision is choosing the degree of exchange rate flexibility. A country chooses along a spectrum that at one end specifies complete flexibility of the exchange rate and at the other a rigid peg. There are other aspects of the choice of an exchange rate regime such as which currency to choose for a peg if a currency is pegged to another currency and the level and type of reserve assets to hold. Still, the choice of the degree of flexibility is central to the exchange rate regime.

The relative merits of pegged (fixed) versus flexible exchange rates have long been debated by economists and central bankers. In this section we review the major arguments that have been advanced for and against each system.

Advantages of Exchange Rate Flexibility

We begin with the arguments advanced in favor of exchange rate flexibility. Two advantages cited for greater flexibility of exchange rates are:[7]

1. Flexible exchange rates would allow policymakers to concentrate on domestic goals, free of worries about balance of payments deficits. They would remove

[7] A classic statement of the advantages of flexible exchange rates is Milton Friedman, "The Case for Flexible Exchange Rates," in *Essays in Positive Economics* (Chicago: University of Chicago Press, 1957).

potential conflicts that arise between *internal balance* (domestic goals) and *external balance* (balance of payments equilibrium).

2. Flexible exchange rates would insulate the domestic economy from economic shocks that originate abroad.

Policy Independence and Exchange Rate Flexibility

Our earlier analysis indicated that if a nation's central bank intervened in the foreign exchange market to finance a balance of payments deficit, it would lose official reserve assets. Continuing deficits would then lead, eventually, to the central bank's running out of reserves. Before the central bank ran out of reserves, it would have to take policy actions aimed at eliminating the balance of payments deficit. This is where the possible conflict occurs between domestic goals and balance of payments equilibrium.

To see the nature of the conflict more clearly, we examine how the main balance of payments items are related to the level of domestic economic activity.

The Trade Balance and the Level of Economic Activity. Figure 14-4 plots imports (Z) and exports (X) on the vertical axis and domestic national income on the horizontal axis. The import schedule is drawn sloping upward because the demand for imports depends positively on income. This relationship follows because consumption depends positively on income. As income rises, consumption of both imported and domestic goods increases. Also, as domestic national income increases, more imported inputs will be needed (e.g., imported crude oil).

In contrast, the export schedule is horizontal. The demand for U.S. exports is a part of the foreign demand for imports. The foreign demand for imports depends on *foreign* income. From the U.S. point of view, foreign income, and hence the demand for exports, are exogenous.

FIGURE 14-4 Trade Balance (TB) and the Level of Economic Activity

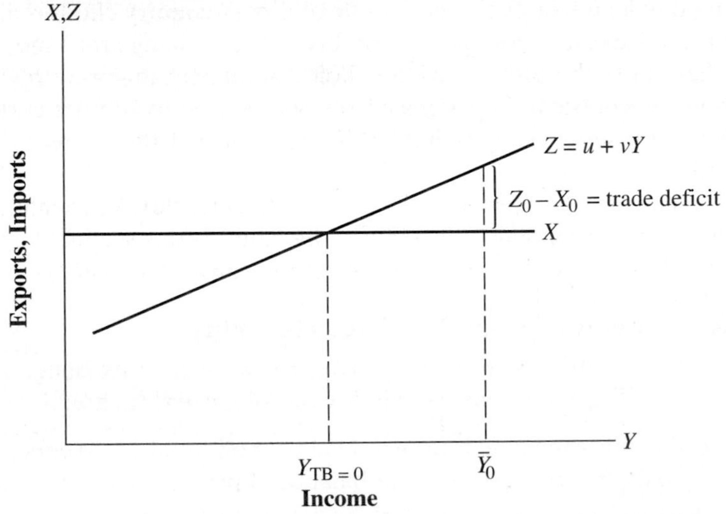

The level of income that equates imports (Z) with the exogenous level of exports (X) is $Y_{TB=0}$. There is no reason that the equilibrium level of income is equal to $Y_{TB=0}$. For example, if $\bar{Y}_0$ is the equilibrium level of income, imports will exceed exports, and there will be a deficit in the trade balance ($Z_0 - X_0$)

Additional variables that influence both U.S. demand for imports and foreign demand for U.S. exports are the relative price levels in the two countries and the level of the exchange rate. These variables determine the relative costs of the two countries' products to citizens of either country. For now, we are assuming that price levels and the exchange rate are fixed.

As shown in Figure 14-4, exports and imports will be equal if income is at $Y_{TB=0}$ (where TB, the trade balance, equals zero). This level of income generates import demand equal to the exogenous level of exports. But there is no reason to expect that $Y_{TB=0}$ will be an equilibrium level of income. Equilibrium income will be determined by aggregate demand and supply in the overall economy, not by the foreign sector alone. For example, in Figure 14-4, assume that equilibrium income is at $\overline{Y}_0$, above $Y_{TB=0}$. At $\overline{Y}_0$, imports exceed exports and there is a trade deficit.

We have seen in earlier chapters how aggregate demand management can, at least in the Keynesian view, affect equilibrium income. Such policies could then be used to move equilibrium income to the level $Y_{TB=0}$, where exports equal imports. If the other current account items and the capital account were in balance, this would be a position of *external balance* for the economy, which in a fixed exchange rate system, means balance of payments equilibrium (official reserve transactions deficit equals zero). In terms of Figure 14-4, the policymaker could, for example, use a restrictive fiscal policy such as a tax increase to reduce income from $\overline{Y}_0$ to $Y_{TB=0}$.

But policymakers also have domestic goals. Within the Keynesian framework, aggregate demand management policies are to be used to pursue unemployment and inflation goals—that is, to achieve *internal balance*. The problem is that there is no reason to believe that the level of income that produces external balance is the optimal level with regard to domestic goals. Suppose, for example, that in Figure 14-4 the optimal level from the point of view of domestic goals is $\overline{Y}_0$. If a restrictive fiscal policy were used to lower income $Y_{TB=0}$, an undesirably high unemployment rate would result, and internal balance would be disturbed. But if income is maintained at $\overline{Y}_0$, there will be a trade deficit; the economy will not have external balance.

Capital Flows and the Level of Economic Activity. The primary determinants of capital flows between nations are expected rates of return on assets in each of the countries. With a fixed exchange rate system, the effects of expected exchange rate movements on asset returns can be ignored (except at times when there is speculation that the official exchange rate is to change). Interest rates in the various countries will be measures of relative rates of return. If we take the rate of return in other countries as given, the level of the capital flow into a particular country will depend positively on the level of its interest rate (r); that is,

$$F = F(r) \tag{14.1}$$

where F is the net capital inflow (a negative value of F represents a net outflow or deficit on capital account).[8] How changes in economic activity affect the balance on

[8]Capital flows include purchases of shares of stock in other countries and direct investments as well as purchases of bonds, the asset that earns the interest rate (r). Thus, other variables that influence the expected returns on stocks and direct investments might be included in a more complex specification of the capital flow function.

the capital account will therefore depend on how the interest rate varies with the change in economic activity.

First, consider increases in economic activity caused by expansionary monetary policies. An expansionary monetary policy will stimulate aggregate demand by *lowering* the rate of interest. The effect of the lower interest rate will be unfavorable to the balance on the capital account. The amount of investment in the United States by foreigners will decline, and U.S. investment abroad will increase as foreign assets become relatively more attractive. In the preceding section, we saw that increases in income for any reason increase imports while leaving exports unchanged and therefore worsen the trade balance. If the increased income results from an expansionary monetary policy, it follows that both the trade balance and the capital account will deteriorate.

Now suppose, alternatively, that the increase in economic activity is the result of an expansionary fiscal policy. As income rises, there is a consequent increase in the demand for money, and with a fixed money supply, the interest rate will rise. In this case, the increase in income is accompanied by an increase in the interest rate. Consequently, while the balance of trade worsens, the rise in the interest rate will stimulate a capital inflow. Whether the overall effect on the balance of payments is favorable or unfavorable depends on the relative strength of these two effects of the fiscal policy–induced expansion: the favorable effect on the capital account or the unfavorable effect on the trade balance.

We therefore find that in a fixed exchange rate system, conflicts may arise between domestic goals such as low unemployment and the goal of external balance as measured by balance of payments equilibrium. The conflict is especially severe with respect to monetary policy, in which expansionary policy actions have unfavorable effects on both the trade balance and the capital account.

A final linkage between the balance of payments and economic activity is through the price level. Unless the economy is far from full employment, expansionary aggregate demand policies, whether monetary or fiscal, will cause the price level to rise. With a fixed exchange rate, an increase in the domestic price level will, for a constant foreign price level, increase imports and cause exports to decline. Foreign goods will be relatively cheaper to U.S. citizens, and U.S. exports will be more expensive to foreign buyers. This *price effect* on the balance of trade reinforces the directly unfavorable effect that an economic expansion has on the trade balance for *both* monetary and fiscal policies.

Exchange Rate Flexibility and Insulation from Foreign Shocks

A second advantage proponents suggest for flexible exchange rates is that this system will insulate an economy from certain shocks. To see the reasoning behind this claim, consider a country that is initially in a state of macroeconomic equilibrium, with an optimal level of unemployment, an optimal price level, and equilibrium in the balance of payments. Now suppose there is a recession abroad and foreign income declines. Because import demand by foreigners, which is the demand for this country's exports, depends on foreign income, it will fall with the foreign recession. In the foreign exchange market, this decline in export demand will show up as a shift to the left in the supply of foreign exchange schedule. As shown in Figure 14-5, the supply schedule will shift from S_{fe}^0 to S_{fe}^1 as a result of the foreign recession.

FIGURE 14-5 Insulation of the Domestic Economy in a Flexible Exchange Rate System

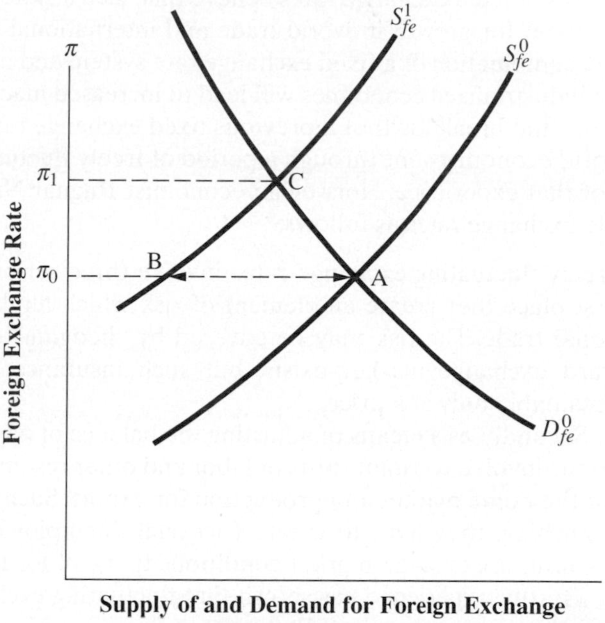

A foreign recession results in a fall in exports and a shift to the left in the supply of foreign exchange schedule from S^0_{fe} to S^1_{fe}. With a fixed exchange rate system, there will be a balance of payment deficit (distance AB). In a flexible exchange rate system, the exchange rate will rise to π_1 to clear the foreign exchange market.

In a fixed exchange rate system, the country would find itself with a balance of payments deficit equal to distance AB in Figure 14-5. Also, because export demand is a portion of aggregate demand (the foreign demand for domestic output), the recession abroad will have contractionary effects on the domestic economy; aggregate demand will fall and income will decline.

In a system of flexible exchange rates, the excess demand for foreign exchange (equal to the balance of payments deficit AB), which resulted from the foreign recession, will cause the exchange rate to rise. The new equilibrium will be at point C, with the higher exchange rate π_1. The increase in the exchange rate will eliminate the balance of payments deficit. Notice another aspect of the adjustment to a new equilibrium. As we go to point C, the increase in the exchange rate stimulates export demand and lowers import demand. This increase in exports induced by the rise in the exchange rate will have an expansionary effect on aggregate demand. The reduction in imports caused by the rise in the exchange rate will also be expansionary; domestic aggregate demand will increase as residents switch from buying imports to buying domestic goods.

In the flexible exchange rate case, we see that adjusting the exchange rate offsets the contractionary effect on the domestic economy that results from a foreign recession. In this sense, a system of flexible exchange rates works to insulate an economy from certain external shocks.

Arguments for Fixed Exchange Rates

Advocates of fixed exchange rates believe that such a system will provide a more stable environment for growth in world trade and international investment. They also argue that the combination of a fixed exchange rate system and increased policy coordination among industrialized economies will lead to increased macroeconomic stability.

After the breakdown of a previous fixed exchange rate system early in the 1930s, the world economy went through a period of freely fluctuating exchange rates. On the basis of that experience, Norwegian economist Ragnar Nurkse made the case against flexible exchange rates as follows:

> Freely fluctuating exchange rates involve three serious disadvantages. In the first place they create an element of risk which tends to discourage international trade. The risk may be covered by "hedging" operations where a forward exchange market exists; but such insurance, if obtainable at all, is obtainable only at a price. . . .
>
> Secondly, as a means of adjusting the balance of payments, exchange fluctuations involve constant shifts of labor and other resources between production for the home market and production for export. Such shifts may be costly and disturbing; they tend to create frictional unemployment, and are obviously wasteful if exchange-market conditions that call for them are temporary. . . .
>
> Thirdly, experience has shown that fluctuating exchanges cannot always be relied upon to promote adjustment. A considerable if continuous movement of the exchange rate is liable to generate anticipations of a further movement in the same direction, thus giving rise to speculative capital transfers of a disequilibrating kind.[9]

Consider each of these purported flaws of a system of fluctuating exchange rates.

Exchange Rate Risk and Trade

Exchange rates have been volatile both in the short and long run during the post–Bretton Woods period. This volatility poses a risk, for example, to a domestic exporter or an investor who plans a foreign investment, such as a plant, in another country. Some such risks can be hedged in the *forward market* for foreign exchange. A U.S. exporter who is to receive Japanese yen in three months can contract to trade those yen for dollars at a price that is set today.

But not all exchange risk in foreign trade and investment can be easily hedged. If a U.S. firm is deciding whether to enter the export market, which involves costs such as establishing foreign business contacts and foreign advertising, it must consider the future prospects of the dollar. For example, a future rise in the value of the dollar may make the firm's product noncompetitive in the export market. Fluctuations in the exchange rate are then an additional risk. Similarly, a U.S. firm planning to build a plant in a foreign country to produce for the foreign market would want to know the exchange rate to determine what the plant would earn in terms of dollars. Exchange rate risk would again be a factor.

[9]Quoted in Peter Kenen, "Macroeconomic Theory and Policy: How the Closed Economy Was Opened," in Ronald Jones and Peter Kenen, eds., *Handbook of International Economics*, vol. 2 (Amsterdam: North Holland, 1985), pp. 625–77.

Exchange Rate Swings and Adjustment Costs

Nurkse's second argument was that exchange rate fluctuations would cause resources to be shifted into and out of export industries, with consequent adjustment costs, including frictional unemployment. As the value of the U.S. dollar rose in the early 1980s, our export performance did suffer. Then as the value of the dollar fell and our export performance improved, problems arose for German and Japanese exporters. The adjustment costs that accompanied the wide swings in the value of the U.S. dollar in the 1980s were the most important source of the discontent with flexible exchange rates at that time.

Speculation and Exchange Rate Instability

Nurkse's last argument was that freely fluctuating exchange rates would lead to destabilizing speculation in foreign exchange markets. Many economists believe that this type of speculation may have been a factor in the height to which the dollar rose in 1985. Investors in financial assets saw the dollar rising, and believing it would rise even more, they demanded dollar-denominated assets. This demand put further upward pressure on the value of the dollar. To the degree that such speculation magnifies exchange rate movements, it exacerbates the problems discussed in the previous two subsections.

14.5 EXPERIENCE WITH FLOATING EXCHANGE RATES

How has the system of floating exchange rates worked during the post-1973 period? What light does evidence from this period shed on the issue of the merits of fixed versus floating rates? To consider these questions, let us look at the behavior of the U.S. exchange rate over the years of floating rates.

Figure 14-6 plots the price of the German mark measured in U.S. cents over the 1973–2000 period. The mark was the German currency unit prior to the adoption of the euro in 1999. Thus, for much of the period of floating rates, the mark is an analogue to π in previous graphs where π, the price of foreign exchange, was measured by the euro.[10] Figure 14-7 shows a more comprehensive measure of the relative price of the U.S. currency, the *effective exchange rate*, which measures the value of the U.S. dollar relative to a weighted average of other currencies. The weights given to the other currencies depend on their importance in U.S. foreign trade. Note here that what we are measuring in Figure 14-7 is the *value of the dollar*, which is the inverse of the price of foreign exchange; for example, when the value of the dollar rises, π (the price of foreign exchange) falls.

From Figures 14-6 and 14-7, we can see that the U.S. exchange rate has been quite volatile during the floating rate period. Were we to look at weekly values of the exchange rate, we would see that short-term volatility of the exchange rate was also large. This short- and medium-run volatility of exchange rates has been one cause of concern about the system of flexible exchange rates.

We can also see from either figure that there have been several sharp swings in the U.S. exchange rate over the floating rate period. Examining the causes of these swings is useful to an understanding of the functioning of the current exchange rate regime.

[10]The exchange rate between the euro and the dollar is discussed in Perspectives 14-3.

FIGURE 14-6 Price of the German Mark, 1973–2000 (in U.S. cents)

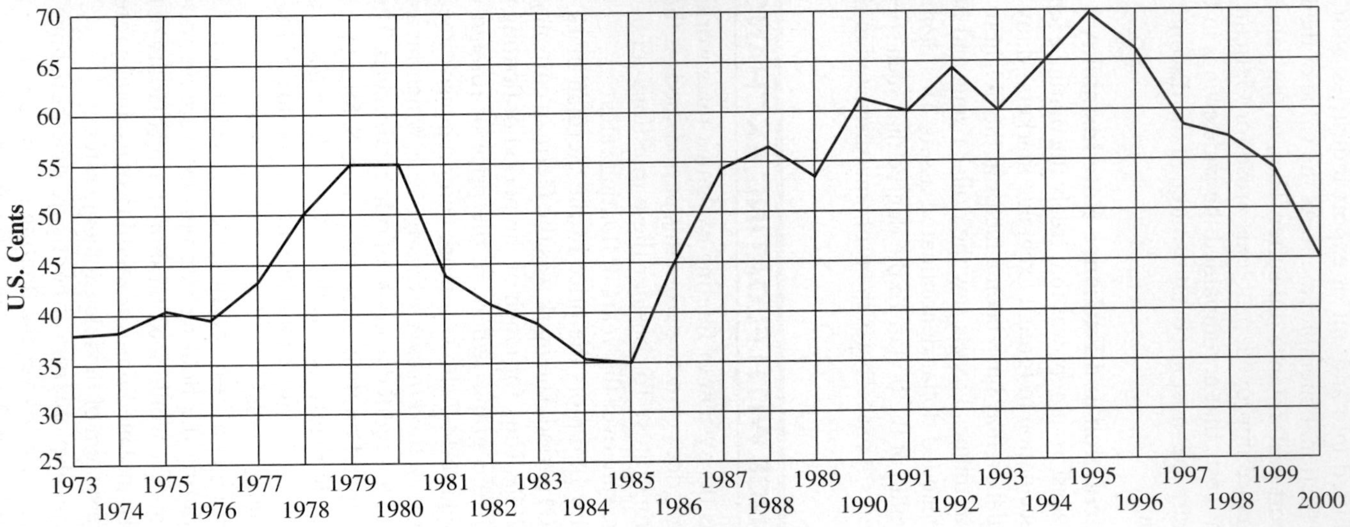

SOURCE: Federal Reserve Bulletin.

FIGURE 14-7 Value of the U.S. Dollar, 1973–2005

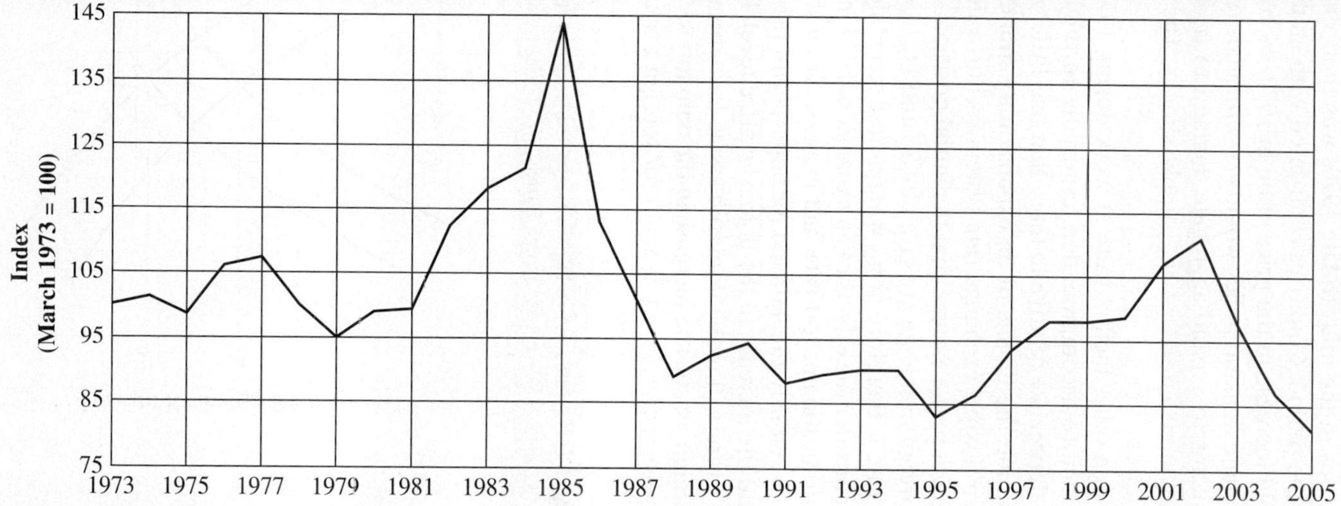

SOURCE: Board of Governors of the Federal Reserve.

The Dollar in Decline, 1976–80

An important factor determining the behavior of exchange rates among the industrialized countries in the mid- to late 1970s was their different responses to the oil price shocks of the period. Countries confronted with an unfavorable supply shock, such as the fourfold increase in the price of oil in 1973–74, had to choose the degree to which their aggregate demand policy would *accommodate* the shock. To accommodate, in this context, means to expand aggregate demand to try to offset the unfavorable output and employment effects of the supply shocks. The cost of such accommodation is higher inflation.

Although other factors were at work during 1976–80, the currencies of countries that chose more accommodation, especially through expansionary monetary policy, tended to depreciate relative to those that had little or no accommodation. To see why, let us examine the effects of an expansionary monetary policy the foreign exchange market in a flexible exchange rate system, as illustrated in Figure 14-8.

In the figure, we assume that the initial positions of the supply and demand schedules for foreign exchange are given by S_{fe}^0 and D_{fe}^0, respectively. The initial equilibrium exchange rate is therefore at π_0, where these schedules intersect.

Now consider the effects of an expansionary monetary policy. Such a policy will reduce the domestic interest rate and increase domestic income and the price level. As discussed previously, the demand for imports will rise as a result of both the increase in income and the increase in the domestic price level. Further, the decline in the domestic interest rate will make domestic assets less attractive, and domestic investors will shift to foreign assets. The increase in the demand for both imported goods and foreign assets represents increased demand for foreign exchange. In terms of Figure 14-8, the

FIGURE 14-8 Effect of an Expansionary Monetary Policy in the Foreign Exchange Market: Flexible Exchange Rates

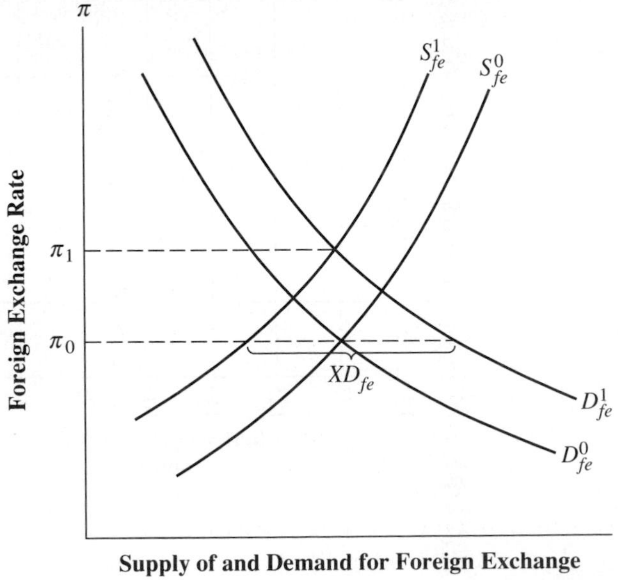

demand schedule for foreign exchange will shift from D_{fe}^0 to D_{fe}^1 as a result of the expansionary monetary policy. The expansionary monetary policy will also affect the supply of foreign exchange. The monetary policy–induced decline in the interest rate will cause foreign investors to buy fewer of the country's assets, and the rise in the domestic price level will reduce export demand. The supply of foreign exchange schedule in Figure 14-8 will shift from S_{fe}^0 to S_{fe}^1.

With a flexible exchange rate, the increase in demand and decline in supply will cause the exchange rate to rise. As the exchange rate rises, the quantity of foreign exchange demanded will fall, and the quantity of foreign exchange supplied will increase. A new equilibrium will be reached at exchange rate π_1, where the demand for and supply of foreign exchange are again equal.

Thus, we see that in a flexible exchange rate system, an expansionary monetary policy causes the exchange rate to rise (the value of the domestic currency to fall). Figure 14-8 considers the action of one country in isolation. Applied to the behavior of the major industrialized countries in the late 1970s, this analysis suggests that countries that followed more accommodative, and therefore more expansionary, monetary policies would have caused their exchange rates to rise (their currencies to depreciate). Those that accommodated less would have seen their exchange rates fall (their currencies appreciate).

The rise in the U.S. exchange rate over the 1976–80 period, measured as the price of the German mark (see Figure 14-6), can be attributed to a higher degree of accommodative aggregate demand policy in the United States relative to Germany. The fall in the value of the dollar measured more generally against the currencies of other trading partners during this period indicates that U.S. policy was among the more expansionary ones.

The Rising Dollar, 1981–85

Beginning in 1981, the dollar reversed course and began to rise sharply in value relative to other major currencies, as can be seen in Figure 14-7. This meant that our exchange rate *fell* over this period, as can be seen from Figure 14-6. Between 1980 and the peak in the dollar's value in early 1985, the mark fell from a price of 55 cents (fewer than 2 per dollar) to 31 cents (more than 3 per dollar), a drop of 44 percent. Against the trade-weighted average of foreign currencies (see Figure 14-7), the dollar rose by 64 percent.

Although there is disagreement about the factors causing the rise in the value of the dollar, one explanation sees restrictive *monetary* policy, and the resulting high interest rates, as the primary cause of the dollar's rise in value. However, especially beginning with the recovery from the 1981–82 recession in 1983, aggregate demand policy in the United States was not, on the whole, less expansionary than that of the other industrialized countries because U.S. *fiscal* policy was very expansionary. This policy *mix*, a combination of tight monetary policy and easy fiscal policy, is seen as the cause of the rising dollar at a time when the recovery in the United States was more rapid than in other major industrialized countries. How might a tight monetary–easy fiscal policy mix lead to a rising dollar even with strong U.S. expansion? The restrictive monetary policy would cause a rise in the value of the dollar (fall in the U.S. exchange rate). The analysis here is the reverse of the case depicted in Figure 14-8. High U.S. interest rates increase the net capital inflow. Moreover, the restrictive monetary policy lowers income, thereby lowering imports. Finally, other things being equal, a more restrictive monetary policy would lead to a lower domestic inflation rate, further discouraging imports and encouraging exports.

Clearly, these changes indicate that the demand for foreign exchange would fall and the supply rise; therefore, the exchange rate should fall and the value of the dollar rise. But just as clearly, other things being equal, a country with a more restrictive monetary policy than its trading partners would have less a robust rate of economic expansion.

The other factor not equal is fiscal policy. An expansionary fiscal policy will, because of positive effects on income and the domestic price level, encourage imports and discourage exports (through the price level effect). The expansionary fiscal policy will, however, result in higher interest rates and therefore increase the net *inflow* of capital. Consequently, whether an expansionary fiscal policy will, on balance, cause an excess demand for foreign exchange (through the import and export effects) or a net excess supply (through the increase in the capital inflow) is uncertain. By itself, an expansionary fiscal policy may raise or lower the exchange rate (with the opposite effect on the value of the dollar).

The U.S. experience over the first half of the 1980s is consistent with a pattern in which either the expansionary fiscal policy contributed to the rise in the value of the dollar or, if it would by itself have lowered the value of the dollar, this effect was overwhelmed by the restrictive monetary policy. Although monetary policy effects are assumed to have been predominant in pushing up the price of the dollar, fiscal policy effects were sufficiently strong domestically to have generated a robust recovery.

One additional factor that may be important in explaining the rise in the dollar's value, especially near its peak in early 1985, is *speculative buying* of U.S. financial assets. In Section 14.2, we pointed out that the demand for foreign assets does not depend on the *level* of the exchange rate. For example, if the exchange rate rose from one level to a higher level, say 10 percent higher, then the foreign asset would cost 10 percent more in domestic currency, but the interest payment on the asset would be 10 percent higher, again expressed in the domestic currency. The percentage return on the asset would be the same at either level of the exchange rate.

What would matter for asset demands, however, are *expected changes* in the exchange rate. If the U.S. exchange rate were expected to fall (the value of the dollar were expected to rise), foreign investors would want to buy U.S. financial assets now. German investors, for example, would buy U.S. financial assets because they would expect the dollar to rise relative to the mark, enabling them to sell the assets later and receive more marks. In buying dollars with which to purchase the U.S. assets, the German investors would be *speculating* on a future rise in the dollar's value.

The Dollar's Slide, 1985–88

In October 1985, the finance ministers of five of the largest market economies (the G5, or Group of Five) met at the Plaza Hotel in New York.[11] They agreed jointly to intervene in the foreign exchange market to bring down the value of the dollar. The central banks in these countries would do so by selling dollars from their reserve supplies

[11]The G5 countries are the United States, Japan, Germany, France, and the United Kingdom.

(buying their own currencies) in the foreign exchange market, thereby increasing the supply of dollars (reducing the supply of foreign currencies) and driving the price of the dollar down.

Other factors were driving down the value of the dollar as well. Just as speculative buying of dollars had contributed to the rise of the dollar, with fear of central bank intervention and other signs of weakness, speculative selling began in 1986 to contribute to the dollar's fall. In addition, as the economic expansion in the United States slowed, U.S. monetary policy became less restrictive, and the U.S. interest rate fell.

By 1987, relative to the weighted average of foreign currencies (see Figure 14-7), the value of the dollar had fallen 32 percent from its peak in 1985. In February, the finance ministers met again, this time in Paris, and reached what has been called the Louvre Accord. They decided that the dollar had fallen far enough. They agreed to use foreign exchange market intervention to try to maintain their exchange rates within ranges around their then-current values. At first these efforts were not successful, and the value of the dollar continued to fall throughout 1987. In 1988, however, as central bank intervention continued, the dollar stabilized.

The Dollar: 1990 to the Present

As can be seen from Figure 14-7, the 1990s did not bring another dramatic swing in the value of the dollar. Perhaps it is not surprising that during this period there was less pressure for change in the system of exchange rate determination.

The most recent swing in the value of the dollar consisted of a rise between 2000 and 2002 followed a by sharp fall. The swing between the dollar and the euro has been especially large, as we will presently see. This most recent swing in currency values is closely related to the growing current account imbalances in the world economy—the subject we consider next.

Read Perspectives 14-3.

PERSPECTIVES 14-3

THE EURO

A number of European countries have, among themselves, participated in some type of fixed exchange rate system since 1979. The details of the system and the number of countries participating have varied over time.

In the 1980s and until January 1999, as was the case with the Bretton Woods system, exchange rates were not set permanently within the European exchange rate mechanisms. There were periodic realignments of currency values when economic conditions warranted. Like the Bretton Woods system, this practice caused problems. When speculators expected a currency's value to be lowered, they staged a speculative attack on the currency, selling it in massive volumes. Such attacks knocked Italy and the United Kingdom out of the then-current exchange rate mechanism in 1992.

The exchange rate mechanism, with all its problems, was one step in the plan of the European Union (EU) to form a complete monetary union. In the Maastricht Treaty of 1991, the countries in the EU agreed to move, in stages, to a system with a single currency and a common European Central

Bank. Before these steps were taken, countries had to meet a set of guidelines concerning levels of interest rates, inflation rates, government budget deficits, and amounts of outstanding government debt. The purpose of these guidelines was to achieve a convergence of the countries' macroeconomic policies prior to irrevocably fixing the relative values of their currencies, which is what adopting a common currency means.

In May 1998, the countries decided to adopt a single currency, the **euro**. The currency was launched in January 1999. Initially, 11 EU members adopted the euro (Germany, the Netherlands, Luxembourg, Belgium, Finland, Spain, Portugal, France, Ireland, Italy, and Austria). Having later met the Maastricht guidelines, Greece joined the system in 2001. The United Kingdom, Denmark, and Sweden, while they are members of the EU, have not adopted the euro.

As put in effect in 1999, interbank transactions were conducted in euros and customers could set up accounts in euros. Beginning in January 2002, euro notes and coins replaced those of previous national currencies. The European Central Bank now sets monetary policy for all member countries.

Technically, the euro was introduced without major glitches. The exchange rate of the euro against the dollar is plotted in Figure 14-9. For the first three years of its existence the euro was weak against the dollar. But beginning in early 2002, the euro reversed course and rose sharply against the dollar, hitting record levels in late-2007.

Among new entrants to the EU, Slovenia joined the euro area in 2007, while Malta, Cyprus, and Estonia are scheduled for entry in 2008.

FIGURE 14-9 Euro Against the Dollar

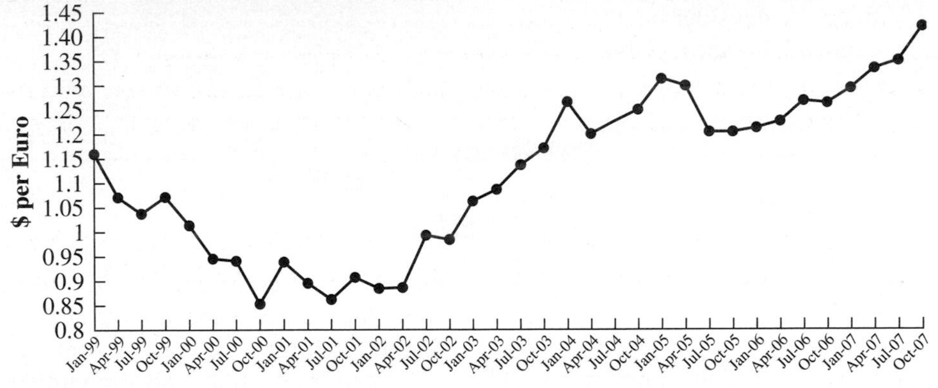

14.6 GLOBAL TRADE IMBALANCES

History is said to be "just one thing after another," with some unpleasant adjective attached to "thing." The history of international monetary systems certainly seems to be one problem after another. The system of floating rates was a response to the balance of payment problem that existed in the Bretton Woods era. The first two decades of floating rates were characterized by concern over a high degree of exchange rate

TABLE 14-3 Current Account Surplus (+) or Deficit (−) as a Percentage of GDP, 2006

China	8.1
Japan	4.0
Germany	4.9
United States	−6.1
United Kingdom	−3.0
Switzerland	15.9
Netherlands	7.6
Spain	−8.8
Saudi Arabia	20.1
Taiwan	6.7
Malaysia	13.5
Singapore	23.3
Australia	−5.5

volatility. Over the past decade, the problem receiving the most attention has been the growing trade imbalances among the major industrialized countries.

The trade imbalances show up in the current account surpluses and deficits of a number of large economies. We have already looked at the growing U.S. current account deficit. Table 14-3 shows the current account balances of some other countries as well.

The first five rows of the table show the current account balances for the economies with the largest foreign trade volumes. The U.S. deficit and Chinese surplus stand out. Japan and Germany have large surpluses, and the United Kingdom has a relatively large deficit. Note that the size of the U.S. economy results in out deficit exceeding the surpluses of China, Japan, and Germany combined by over $200 billion. The focus of attention on the U.S. current account deficit as central to global imbalances is not misplaced.

Saudi Arabia's large current account surplus reflects the high price of oil. Some other oil producers also have large surpluses. As can be seen from the table, Asian countries other than China and Japan also have significant current account surpluses.

Implication of Some Identities

So, there large current account imbalances in a number of economies, including the largest trading nations in the world. What should we make of this? Several identities will help.

First, if we sum the trade accounts of all nations, then disregarding inaccuracies in the count, trade will balance. Surpluses in some countries must be balanced by deficits in others. Where, then, should we look for the causes of the imbalances? Are U.S. policies the cause of our current account deficits? Or are Chinese and Japanese policies the cause of their surpluses, which must be reflected in deficits elsewhere?

A second identity involving the current account can be seen by going back to Table 14-1. From the fact that the overall balance of payments must balance (all expenditures are somehow financed), we can write

$$CU + CA + ORT \equiv 0 \tag{14.2}$$

If we ignore the statistical discrepancy, the sum of the current account balance (CU) plus the (private) capital account balance (CA) plus the balance for official reserve transactions (central bank interventions, *ORT*) must sum to zero. Equation (14.2) indicates that, for example, a country with a large current account surplus *must* have either a large private net capital outflow or a large increase in reserve assets as a result of central bank intervention in the foreign exchange market.

A third identity is also useful. From our discussion of national income accounting in Chapter 2, we can write the following relationship:

$$C + S + T \equiv Y = C + I + G + X - Z \qquad \textbf{(14.3)}$$

where, as defined previously, C = consumption, S = saving, T = taxes, Y = GDP, I = investment, G = government spending, X = exports, and Z = imports.

Rearranging and canceling out the *C*s, we have

$$(T - G) + (S - I) \equiv (X - Z) \qquad \textbf{(14.4)}$$

The left side of equation (14.4) can be viewed for a country as its saving-investment balance: net private $(S - I)$ plus government $(T - G)$ saving, with the surplus in the government budget measuring the saving by the public sector. This saving-investment balance is offset by the trade balance. Countries, for example, with large current account deficits, such as the United States, have investment that exceeds saving. This excess is financed by the capital inflow that must accompany the current account deficit. The situation is reversed of China, Japan, Germany, Malaysia, Singapore, and Saudi Arabia.

Causes and Effects of Global Trade Imbalances

The identities (14.2 and 14.4) tell us several things about the current global trade situation. As pointed out, seen in a global perspective, the U.S. current account deficit is very large. From equations (14.2) and (14.4), we can see that the United States saves less than it invests. Funds for investment in excess of domestic saving are provided by a capital inflow, both private (*CA*) and as a result of foreign central bank intervention (*ORT*). The current situation can be seen as the result of too little saving in the United States.

But alternatively, one can see the source of the imbalances as a *global saving glut*, a term used by U.S. Federal Reserve Board Chairman Ben Bernanke.[12] Countries such as China and Japan have capital outflows that balance their current account surpluses (equation 14.2). These reflect saving in excess of domestic investment. The same is true of oil-producing nations such as Saudi Arabia, which have had a windfall of oil revenues yet to be invested domestically.

A global perspective helps us to interpret the current trade imbalances but not necessarily to see where they will lead. One scenario is that saving in the United States will increase, perhaps with higher taxes; Japan and Germany will have sustained economic expansions that increase imports; China will allow its currency to appreciate, thus increasing imports and reducing exports; and the imbalances will gradually decline. Other, less benign scenarios are also possible.

[12] See "Remarks by Governor Ben S. Bernanke, The Global Saving Glut and the U.S. Current Account Deficit," Board of Governors of the Federal Reserve System (March 2005).

14.7 Conclusion

This chapter has dealt with the determination of exchange rates and the related question of the setup of the international monetary system. A critical question in the area is the optimal degree of flexibility in exchange rate determination. The collapse of the Bretton Woods system led to a period of a managed float for most major currencies.

The value of the U.S. dollar has been quite volatile during the period of floating exchange rates. During periods of sharply changing currency values, there have been calls for changes in the international monetary system to provide more stability of exchange rates.

As we have seen, however, swings in the value of the dollar relative to other national currencies are in large part due to divergences in the domestic monetary and fiscal policies that countries pursue. Greater exchange rate stability would most likely require greater coordination of national macroeconomic policies. There are many obstacles to effective international policy coordination, not the least of which are different preferences of policymakers and different industrial structures in major world economies. Floating exchange rates free countries from the need to coordinate policies, but at the cost of highly volatile exchange rates.

In recent years, growing current account imbalances among major world economies have also led to calls for greater policy coordination. In 2006 the IMF set up a consultation mechanism whereby deficit and surplus countries would discuss possible ways to reduce the imbalances. Efforts in this direction face the same obstacles as the previous efforts to reduce the volatility of exchange rates.

Key Terms

- balance of payments accounts 272
- merchandise trade balance 273
- current account 273
- capital account 274
- foreign exchange 275
- Bretton Woods system 281

Review Questions and Problems

1. Why do the balance of payments accounts always balance?
2. Explain how the exchange rate for a country is determined under
   a. a fixed exchange rate system.
   b. a flexible exchange rate.
   c. a managed, or dirty, float.
3. Analyze the effects of an autonomous fall in the demand for a country's exports under fixed and flexible exchange rate systems. In each case, indicate the effects on the country's balance of payments and on the exchange rate.
4. If central banks never intervened in foreign exchange markets, could there be deficits or surpluses in a country's balance of payments? Explain.
5. Describe the Bretton Woods system of exchange rate determination that was set up at the end of World War II and lasted until 1973.

6. Explain the relationship between the trade balance and the level of economic activity in a fixed exchange rate system. Why does this relationship create a potential conflict between the goals of internal and external balance?
7. Taking account of the effect on both the trade balance and the capital account, explain the relationships between balance of payments equilibrium and both expansionary monetary and fiscal policies within a fixed exchange rate system.
8. "Adoption of a system of flexible exchange rates would free monetary and fiscal policy for use in attaining domestic goals of full employment and price stability." Do you agree or disagree with this statement? Explain.
9. What are some of the relative advantages and disadvantages of fixed versus flexible exchange rates?
10. Illustrate graphically the effects in the foreign exchange market of an expansionary monetary policy carried out by the *foreign* country in our two-country framework. Consider the cases of both a fixed and a flexible exchange rate.
11. Suppose you observe that a country has a large current account surplus. From this fact, what can you determine about whether
    a. the country has a balance of payments surplus or deficit?
    b. the country has a surplus or deficit in its capital account?

CHAPTER 15

Monetary and Fiscal Policy in the Open Economy

Economies that are *open*, as all economies are to some extent, have trade and capital flows with other economies. In this chapter, we consider monetary and fiscal policy in an open economy model. How do the effects of policy actions differ in the open economy relative to the closed economy? How do they differ depending on whether exchange rates are fixed or flexible? We consider conflicts that arise between internal and external balance in a system of fixed exchange rates as discussed in Chapter 14. We illustrate why those conflicts do not arise when exchange rates are flexible.

There are several open economy macroeconomic frameworks. The one used here is the Mundell–Fleming model, often called the *workhorse model* for open economy macroeconomics.[1] The model is explained in Section 15.1. Then, in Sections 15.2 and 15.3, we consider the effects of changes in policy and other variables under two different assumptions about the mobility of capital between countries.

15.1 THE MUNDELL–FLEMING MODEL

The Mundell–Fleming model is an open economy version of the *IS–LM* model considered in Chapters 6 and 7. The closed economy *IS–LM* model consists of the following two equations:

$$M = L(Y, r) \qquad \textbf{(15.1)}$$

$$S(Y) + T = I(r) + G \qquad \textbf{(15.2)}$$

Equation (15.1) is the money market equilibrium (*LM* schedule), and equation (15.2) is the goods market equilibrium (*IS* schedule). The model simultaneously determines the nominal interest rate (r) and the level of *real* income (Y), with the aggregate price level held constant. What changes will be required to analyze an open economy?

When we consider an open economy, the *LM* schedule will not be changed. Equation (15.1) states that the *real* money supply, which we assume to be controlled by the domestic policymaker, must in equilibrium equal the real demand for money. It is the nominal supply of money that the policymaker controls, but with the assumption of a

[1]The model is named for its developers, Robert Mundell and Marcus Fleming. See Robert Mundell, "Capital Mobility and Stabilization Policy Under Fixed and Flexible Exchange Rates," *Canadian Journal of Economics and Political Science*, 29 (November 1963), pp. 475–85; and Marcus Fleming, "Domestic Financial Policies Under Fixed and Under Floating Exchange Rates," International Monetary Fund *Staff Papers*, 9 (November 1962), pp. 369–79.

fixed price level, changes in the nominal money supply are changes in the real money supply as well.

The equation for the *IS* schedule (15.2) is derived from the goods market equilibrium condition for a closed economy:

$$C + S + T \equiv Y = C + I + G \tag{15.3}$$

which, when C is subtracted from both sides, reduces to

$$S + T = I + G \tag{15.4}$$

If we add imports (Z) and exports (X) to the model, equation (15.3) is replaced by[2]

$$C + S + T \equiv Y = C + I + G + X - Z \tag{15.5}$$

and the *IS* equation becomes

$$S + T = I + G + X - Z \tag{15.6}$$

where $(X - Z)$, net exports, is the foreign sector's contribution to aggregate demand. If we bring imports over to the left-hand side and indicate the variables upon which each element in the equation depends, the open economy *IS* equation can be written as

$$S(Y) + T + Z(Y, \pi) = I(r) + G + X(Y^f, \pi) \tag{15.7}$$

Saving and investment are the same as in the closed economy model. Imports, as discussed in Chapter 14, depend positively on income. Imports also depend negatively on the exchange rate (π). And, as in Chapter 14, we are defining the exchange rate as the price of foreign currency—for example, U.S. dollars per euro. A rise in the exchange rate will, therefore, make foreign goods more expensive and cause imports to fall. U.S. exports are other countries' imports and thus depend positively on foreign income and the exchange rate. The latter relationship follows because a rise in the exchange rate lowers the cost of dollars measured in terms of the foreign currency and makes U.S. goods cheaper to foreign residents.

By a derivation analogous to that in Chapter 6, the open economy *IS* schedule can be shown to be downward-sloping, as drawn in Figure 15-1. High values of the interest rate will result in low levels of investment. To satisfy equation (15.7), at such high levels of the interest rate, income must be low so that the levels of imports and saving will be low. Alternatively, at low levels of the interest rate, which result in high levels of investment, goods market equilibrium requires that saving and imports must be high; therefore, Y must be high.

In constructing the open economy *IS* schedule in Figure 15-1, we hold four variables constant: taxes, government spending, foreign income, and the exchange rate. These are variables that shift the schedule. Expansionary shocks, such as an increase in government spending, a cut in taxes, an increase in foreign income, or a rise in the exchange rate, shift the schedule to the right. A rise in foreign income is expansionary because it increases demand for our exports. A rise in the exchange rate is expansionary both because it increases exports and because it reduces imports for a given level of

[2]Private transfer payments to foreigners should also appear on the left-hand side of equation (15.5). We ignore this minor item.

FIGURE 15-1 Open Economy *IS–LM* Model

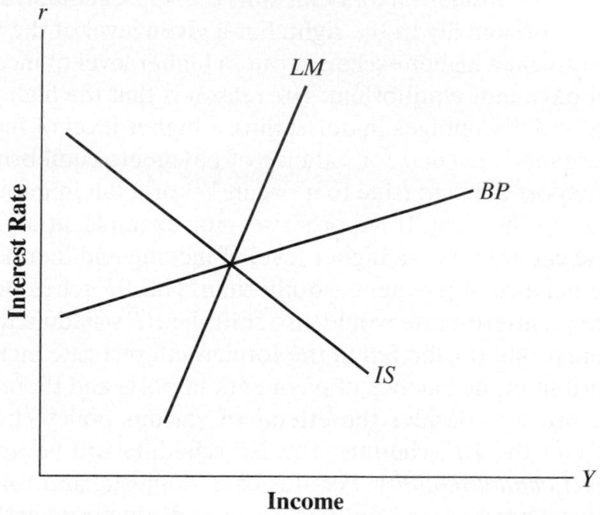

The *LM* schedule shows combinations of *r* and *Y* that are points of equilibrium for the money market, and the *IS* schedule shows combinations of *r* and *Y* that clear the goods market. The *BP* schedule shows the combinations of *r* and *Y* that will equate supply and demand in the foreign exchange market at a given exchange rate.

income; it shifts demand from foreign to domestic products. An autonomous fall in import demand is expansionary for the same reason. Changes in the opposite direction in these variables shift the *IS* schedule to the left.

In addition to the *IS* and *LM* schedules, our open economy model contains a balance of payments equilibrium schedule, the *BP* schedule in Figure 15-1. This schedule plots all interest rate–income combinations that result in balance of payments equilibrium at a given exchange rate. Balance of payments equilibrium means that the official reserve transaction balance is zero. The equation for the *BP* schedule can be written as

$$X(Y^f, \pi) - Z(Y, \pi) + F(r - r^f) = 0 \qquad \textbf{(15.8)}$$

The first two terms in equation (15.8) constitute the trade balance (net exports). The third item (*F*) is the net capital inflow (the surplus or deficit in the capital account in the balance of payments, as shown in Table 15.1). The net capital inflow depends positively on the domestic interest rate minus the foreign interest rate $(r - r^f)$, as discussed in Chapter 14. A rise in the U.S. interest rate relative to the foreign interest rate leads to an increased demand for U.S. financial assets (e.g., bonds) at the expense of foreign assets; the net capital inflow increases. A rise in the foreign interest rate has the opposite effect. The foreign interest rate is assumed to be exogenous.[3]

The *BP* schedule is positively sloped, as shown in Figure 15-1. As income rises, import demand increases whereas export demand does not. To maintain balance of payments

[3]Notice also that we did not include the foreign interest rate in the money demand function. We assume that, although investors substitute between foreign and domestic bonds on the basis of their respective yields, the demand for money depends only on the domestic interest rate.

equilibrium, the capital inflow must increase, which will happen if the interest rate is higher. Now consider factors that shift the *BP* schedule. An increase in π will shift the schedule horizontally to the right. For a given level of the interest rate, which fixes the capital flow, at a higher exchange rate, a higher level of income will be required for balance of payments equilibrium. The reason is that the higher exchange rate encourages exports and discourages imports; thus, a higher level of income that will stimulate import demand is needed for balance of payments equilibrium. Similarly, an exogenous rise in export demand (due to a rise in Y^f) or a fall in import demand will shift the *BP* schedule to the right. If exports rise—for example, at a given interest rate that again fixes the capital flow—a higher level of income and therefore of imports is required to restore balance of payments equilibrium. The *BP* schedule shifts to the right. A fall in the foreign interest rate would also shift the *BP* schedule to the right; at a given domestic interest rate (r), the fall in the foreign interest rate increases the capital inflow. For equilibrium in the balance of payments, imports and therefore income must be higher.

Before we consider the effects of various policy changes, there is one point to note about the *BP* schedule. The *BP* schedule will be upward-sloping in the case of *imperfect capital mobility*. For this case, domestic and foreign assets (e.g., bonds) are substitutes, but they are not perfect ones. If domestic and foreign assets were perfect substitutes, a situation called *perfect capital mobility*, investors would move to equalize interest rates among countries. If one type of asset had a slightly higher interest rate temporarily, investors would switch to that asset until its rate was driven down to restore equality.

In the context of our model, perfect capital mobility implies that $r = r^f$. We will see later that this equality implies a horizontal *BP* schedule. If assets are less than perfect substitutes, their interest rates need not be equal. Factors that might make assets in foreign countries less than perfect substitutes for U.S. assets include differential risk on the assets of different countries, risks due to exchange rate changes, transaction costs, and lack of information on properties of foreign assets. In Section 15.2, we assume that such factors are sufficient to make foreign and domestic assets less than perfect substitutes. Perfect capital mobility is examined in Section 15.3.

15.2 IMPERFECT CAPITAL MOBILITY

To consider monetary and fiscal policy under the assumption of imperfect capital mobility, we begin with the case of fixed exchange rates.

Policy Under Fixed Exchange Rates

Monetary Policy

Consider the effects of an increase in the money supply from M_0 to M_1, as illustrated in Figure 15-2. The increase in the money supply shifts the *LM* schedule to the right, from $LM(M_0)$ to $LM(M_1)$. The equilibrium point shifts from E_0 to E_1, with a fall in the interest rate from r_0 to r_1 and an increase in income from Y_0 to Y_1. What has happened to the balance of payments? First, note that all points below the *BP* schedule are points of balance of payments deficit, whereas all points above the schedule are points of surplus. As we move from an equilibrium point on the *BP* schedule to points below the

FIGURE 15-2 Monetary Policy with a Fixed Exchange Rate

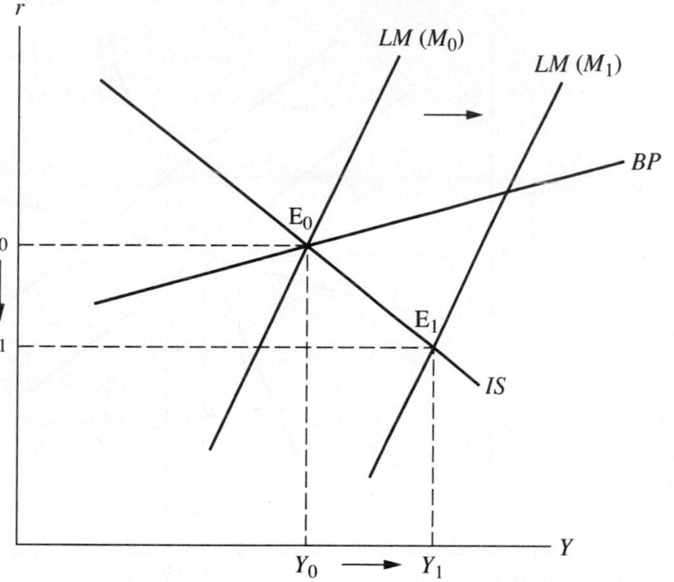

An increase in the quantity of money shifts the LM schedule from $LM(M_0)$ to $LM(M_1)$. The equilibrium point shifts from E_0 to E_1. The rate of interest falls, and the level of income rises. The new equilibrium point is below the BP schedule, indicating a deficit in the balance of payments.

schedule—for example, increasing income or reducing the interest rate, or both—we are causing a deficit in the balance of payments. Consequently, as we move from point E_0 to point E_1 after the increase in the money supply, the balance of payments also moves into deficit. As discussed in Section 14.4, the expansionary monetary policy increases income, stimulating imports and lowering the interest rate and thereby causing a capital outflow (F declines).

The fact that, beginning from a point of equilibrium, an expansionary monetary policy leads to a balance of payments deficit raises potential conflicts between domestic policy goals and external balance. If at point E_0 in Figure 15-2 the level of income, Y_0, is low relative to full employment, then the move to point E_1 and income level Y_1 may well be preferable on domestic grounds. But at point E_1 there will be a deficit in the balance of payments, and with limited foreign exchange reserves, such a situation cannot be maintained indefinitely.

Fiscal Policy

The effects of an increase in government spending from G_0 to G_1 for the fixed exchange rates case are illustrated in Figure 15-3. The increase in government spending shifts the IS schedule to the right from $IS(G_0)$ to $IS(G_1)$, moving the equilibrium point from E_0 to E_1. Income rises from Y_0 to Y_1, and the interest rate rises from r_0 to r_1. As shown in Figure 15-3, at the new equilibrium point we are above the BP schedule; there is a balance of payments surplus. We get this result because in Figure 15-3 the BP schedule is flatter than the LM schedule. Alternatively, if the BP schedule were steeper

FIGURE 15-3 Fiscal Policy with a Fixed Exchange Rate

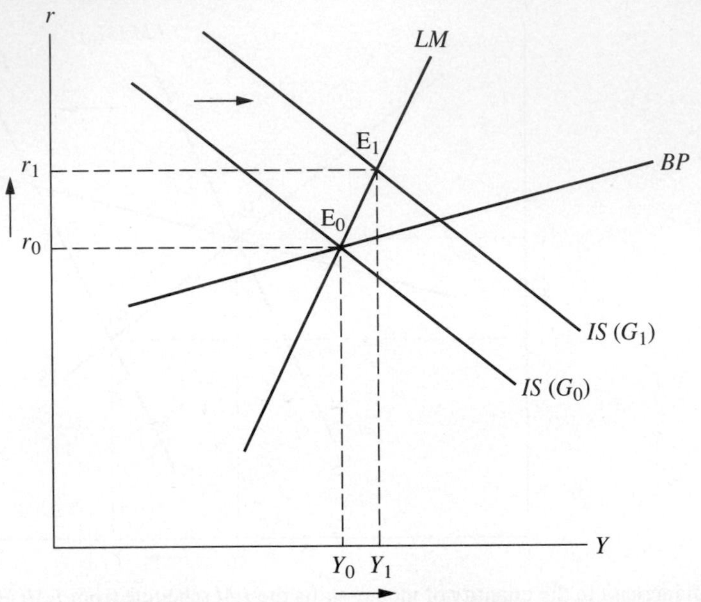

An increase in government spending shifts the *IS* schedule from $IS(G_0)$ to $IS(G_1)$. The equilibrium point shifts from E_0 to E_1. Income and the interest rate rise. The new equilibrium point is above the *BP* schedule, indicating that, with a fixed exchange rate for the case in which the *BP* schedule is flatter than the *LM* schedule, the expansionary fiscal policy results in a surplus in the balance of payments.

than the *LM* schedule, an expansionary fiscal policy action would lead to a balance of payments deficit, as can be seen in Figure 15-4.

The *BP* schedule will be steeper the less responsive capital flows are to the rate of interest. The smaller the increase in the capital inflow for a given increase in the interest rate (given the fixed value of r^f), the larger will be the rise in the interest rate required to maintain balance of payments equilibrium as we go to a higher income (and hence import) level; that is, the steeper will be the *BP* schedule. The *BP* schedule will also be steeper the larger the marginal propensity to import. With a higher marginal propensity to import, a given increase in income will produce a larger increase in imports. For equilibrium in the balance of payments, a larger compensatory increase in the capital inflow and consequently a larger rise in the interest rate will be required.

The expansionary fiscal policy action depicted in Figures 15-3 and 15-4 causes income to increase. Increased income leads to a deterioration in the trade balance and causes the interest rate to rise, resulting in an improvement in the capital account. The foregoing discussion indicates that the steeper the *BP* schedule, the larger the unfavorable effect on imports and the trade balance and the smaller the favorable effect on capital flows. Therefore, the steeper the *BP* schedule, the more likely it becomes that an expansionary fiscal policy action will lead to a balance of payments deficit.

Finally, notice that the slope of the *BP* schedule relative to the slope of the *LM* schedule determines whether an expansionary fiscal policy action will result in a balance of payments surplus or deficit. Given the slope of the *BP* schedule, the steeper the

FIGURE 15-4 Fiscal Policy with a Fixed Exchange Rate: An Alternative Outcome

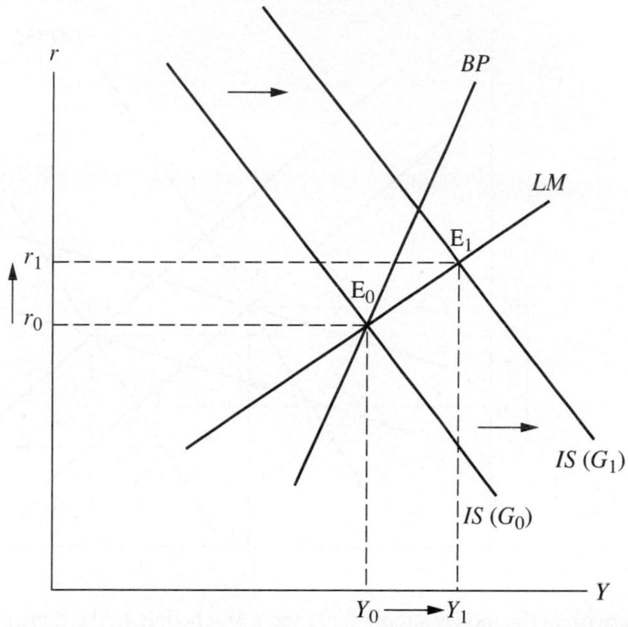

As in Figure 15-3, an increase in government spending shifts the *IS* schedule to the right, increasing both income and the rate of interest. In this case, where the *BP* schedule is steeper than the *LM* schedule, the new equilibrium point (E_1) is below the *BP* schedule. The expansionary fiscal policy results in a balance of payments deficit.

LM schedule, the more likely it is that the *LM* schedule will be steeper than the *BP* schedule, the condition required for a surplus to result from an expansionary fiscal policy action. This result follows because, other things being equal, the steeper the *LM* schedule, the larger the increase in the interest rate (which produces the favorable capital inflow) and the smaller the increase in income (which produces the unfavorable effect on the trade balance).

Policy Under Flexible Exchange Rates

Monetary Policy

We turn now to the case in which the exchange rate is completely flexible; there is no central bank intervention. The exchange rate adjusts to equate supply and demand in the foreign exchange market. First consider the same monetary policy action analyzed previously, an increase in the quantity of money from M_0 to M_1. The effects of this expansionary monetary policy action in the flexible exchange rate case are illustrated in Figure 15-5.

The initial effect of the increase in the money supply—the effect before an adjustment in the exchange rate—is to move the economy from point E_0 to point E_1. The interest rate falls from r_0 to r_1. Income rises from Y_0 to Y_1, and we move to a point below the *BP* schedule where there is an *incipient* balance of payments deficit. In a flexible exchange rate system, the exchange rate will rise (from π_0 to π_1) to clear the foreign

FIGURE 15-5 Monetary Policy with a Flexible Exchange Rate

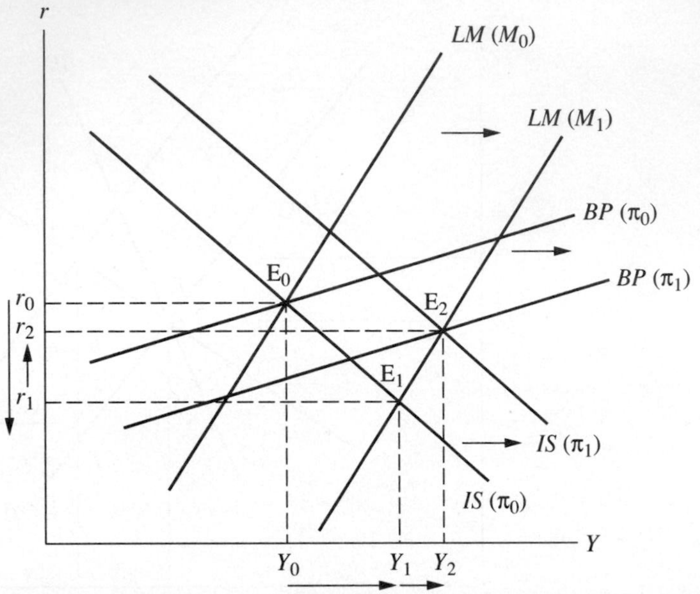

An increase in the money supply shifts the LM schedule to the right, moving the equilibrium point from E_0 to E_1. The point E_1 is below the BP schedule, where there is an incipient balance of payments deficit. In the flexible exchange rate case, the exchange rate rises, causing the BP schedule to shift to the right from $BP(\pi_0)$ to $BP(\pi_1)$ and the IS schedule to shift to the right from $IS(\pi_0)$ to $IS(\pi_1)$. The final equilibrium point is at E_2 with an income level Y_2, above Y_1, the new equilibrium for a fixed exchange rate.

exchange market. (This is the adjustment shown previously in Figure 14-8.) The rise in the exchange rate will shift the BP schedule to the right; in Figure 15-5, the schedule shifts from $BP(\pi_0)$ to $BP(\pi_1)$. The rise in the exchange rate also causes the IS schedule to shift to the right, from $IS(\pi_0)$ to $IS(\pi_1)$ in Figure 15-5, because exports rise and imports fall with an increase in the exchange rate. The new equilibrium is shown at point E_2, with the interest rate at r_2 and income at Y_2. The exchange rate adjustment reequilibrates the balance of payments after the expansionary monetary policy and eliminates the potential conflict between internal and external balance.

Notice that the rise in income as a result of the expansionary monetary policy action is greater in the flexible rate case than in the fixed rate case. With a fixed exchange rate, income would rise only to Y_1 in Figure 15-5 or Figure 15-2. With a flexible exchange rate, the rise in the exchange rate would further stimulate income by increasing exports and reducing import demand (for a given income level). Monetary policy is therefore a more potent stabilization tool in a flexible exchange rate regime than in a fixed rate regime.

Fiscal Policy

Figure 15-6 illustrates the effects of an increase in government spending from G_0 to G_1 with a flexible exchange rate. The initial effect—meaning again the effect before the adjustment in the exchange rate—is to shift the IS schedule from $IS(G_0, \pi_0)$ to $IS(G_1, \pi_0)$

FIGURE 15-6 Fiscal Policy with a Flexible Exchange Rate

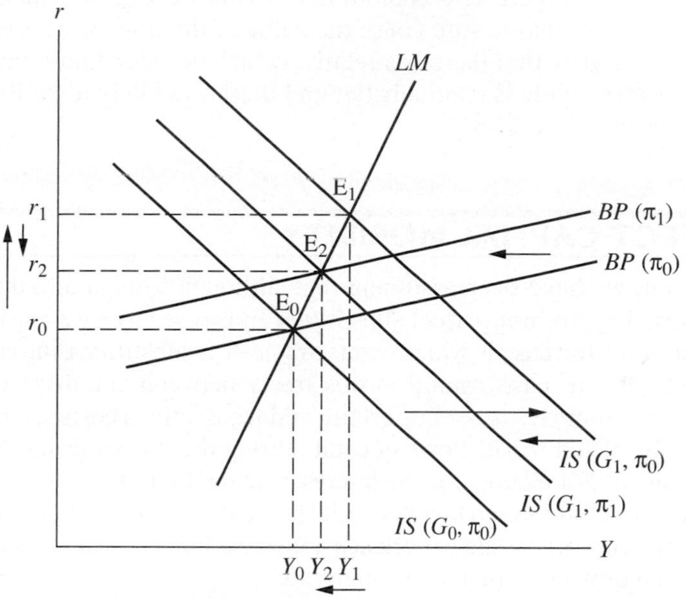

An increase in government spending shifts the *IS* schedule to the right from $IS(G_0, \pi_0)$ to $IS(G_1, \pi_0)$, moving the equilibrium point from E_0 to E_1. With the *BP* schedule flatter than the *LM* schedule, E_1 is above the initial *BP* schedule, $BP(\pi_0)$. There is an incipient balance of payments surplus and the exchange rate will fall, shifting the *BP* schedule to the left to $BP(\pi_1)$ and shifting the *IS* schedule to the left from $IS(G_1, \pi_0)$ to $IS(G_1, \pi_1)$. The final equilibrium is at E_2 with income level Y_2, below Y_1, the new equilibrium for a fixed exchange rate.

and move the economy from E_0 to E_1. The interest rate rises (from r_0 to r_1), and income increases (from Y_0 to Y_1). With the slopes of the *BP* and *LM* schedules as drawn in Figure 15-6 (with the *BP* schedule flatter than the *LM* schedule), an incipient balance of payments surplus results from this expansionary policy action. In this case, the exchange rate must *fall* (from π_0 to π_1) to clear the foreign exchange market. A fall in the exchange rate will shift the *BP* schedule to the left in Figure 15-6, from $BP(\pi_0)$ to $BP(\pi_1)$. The *IS* schedule will also shift left, from $IS(G_1, \pi_0)$ to $IS(G_1, \pi_1)$, because the fall in the exchange rate will lower exports and stimulate imports. The exchange rate adjustment will partially offset the expansionary effect of the fiscal policy action. The new equilibrium point will be at Y_2, which is above Y_0 but below Y_1, the level that would have resulted with the fixed exchange rate.

There is not, however, a definite relationship between the potency of fiscal policy and the type of exchange rate regime, as there is with monetary policy. If the *BP* schedule is steeper than the *LM* schedule, as in Figure 15-4, an expansionary fiscal policy will, for a given exchange rate, cause a balance of payments deficit. With an incipient balance of payments deficit in the flexible exchange rate regime, the exchange rate must *rise* to restore equilibrium in the foreign exchange market. The *BP* schedule and the *IS* schedule will shift to the right and reinforce the initial expansionary effect of the increase in government spending. In this case, the expansionary fiscal policy action would have a *larger* effect on income than it would in the fixed exchange rate case.

Although this alternative outcome is possible in theory, most economists think the outcome in Figure 15-6 is more likely. They believe an expansionary fiscal policy will lower the exchange rate (raise the value of the domestic currency). This belief follows from the view that there is a relatively high degree of international capital mobility, so the *BP* schedule is relatively flat and therefore likely to be flatter than the *LM* schedule, as in Figure 15-6.

15.3 PERFECT CAPITAL MOBILITY

So far, we have been assuming that, although foreign and domestic assets are substitutes, they are not perfect substitutes. In this section, we consider monetary and fiscal policy for the case in which assets are perfect substitutes, the case of perfect capital mobility. In this case, capital moves freely between countries, differential risk in assets among countries is not important, and transactions costs are negligible.

In such a world, flows of capital bring the domestic and foreign interest rates into equality.[4] For example, if the interest rate on domestic bonds was 4.1 percent and the interest rate on foreign bonds was 4.0 percent, in a world of perfect capital mobility the domestic country would experience a massive inflow of capital until the domestic rate was driven down to equal the foreign rate.

In the Mundell–Fleming model, the assumption of perfect capital mobility means that the *BP* equation (15.8) is replaced with the condition

$$r = r^f \quad \textbf{(15.9)}$$

Graphically, the assumption of perfect capital mobility makes the *BP* schedule horizontal. Because massive capital flows result from any interest-rate differential, balance of payments equilibrium can occur only when the domestic interest rate is equal to the exogenously given foreign (world) interest rate.

Before looking at policy effects in the case of perfect capital mobility, consider the assumption that the domestic interest rate must in equilibrium equal the exogenously given foreign rate. In Section 15.2, we also assumed that the foreign interest rate was exogenous, but in the case of imperfect capital mobility, the domestic interest rate could deviate from the foreign interest rate. In that case, there are two possibilities. One is that we are considering a country so small that its actions have no effect on the world economy. An expansionary monetary policy that lowers the domestic interest rate has no effect on world interest rates or income in foreign countries, which was also assumed to be exogenous. A second possible assumption is that the country is large, such as the United States, but that we were simply ignoring the effects of its actions on foreign economies and therefore ignoring possible repercussive effects. We were assuming that these were of second-order importance.

In the perfect capital mobility case, only the first assumption is plausible: The domestic country is so small that its actions cannot affect world financial market conditions, and capital is so mobile that the country's interest rate must move into line with

[4]It should be noted here that we are not taking into account possible expectations of future movements in exchange rates. As explained in Chapter 14, expected changes in exchange rates are another factor, in addition to interest-rate differentials, that influence the choice between domestic and foreign assets.

world rates. To consider the United States in the perfect capital mobility case, we would have to model the effect of U.S. policies on the world interest rate. It is unrealistic to view the U.S. interest rate as pinned down by a world interest rate completely outside its influence.

Policy Effects Under Fixed Exchange Rates

Monetary Policy

We will see that, with perfect capital mobility, monetary policy is completely ineffective when exchange rates are fixed. To understand this result, we need to consider further the relationship between intervention in the foreign exchange market and the money supply.

In Section 15.2, we found that with a fixed exchange rate, an expansionary monetary policy led to a balance of payments deficit. Suppose, for example, that at point E_1 in Figure 15-2, the balance of payments deficit is \$5 billion; there is an excess demand for foreign exchange equal to \$5 billion. As explained in Chapter 14, either the domestic or the foreign central bank must intervene to provide this amount of foreign exchange if the fixed exchange rate is to be maintained. Here we consider only the case in which intervention is by the domestic central bank.

The U.S. central bank, the Federal Reserve, then sells \$5 billion worth of foreign reserve assets (foreign currencies, SDRs, or gold). It buys \$5 billion. The direct effect of this is to reduce the U.S. money supply by \$5 billion. The money supply in circulation falls because the Federal Reserve has now increased its holdings of dollars by 5 billion and the public has reduced theirs by that amount. What we implicitly assumed in Section 15.2 was that the Federal Reserve offset this effect on the money supply by putting the dollars it purchased back into circulation. They do this by buying existing U.S. government bonds from the public. This action, called *sterilization*, prevents intervention in the foreign exchange market from affecting the domestic money supply.

With this as background, consider the effect of an expansionary monetary policy action in the case of perfect capital mobility. In line with the previous discussion, assume that a small country, such as New Zealand, increases its money supply. As illustrated in Figure 15-7, the increased money supply shifts the LM schedule to the right from $LM(M_0)$ to $LM(M_1)$. The New Zealand interest rate temporarily falls from r_0 toward r_1. The New Zealand interest rate is temporarily below the foreign (world) interest rate.

With the domestic interest rate below the foreign interest rate in the case of perfect capital mobility, there will be a massive outflow of capital. Investors will be selling New Zealand assets and therefore sell New Zealand dollars. In this case, the New Zealand central bank cannot restore equilibrium through sterilized intervention in the foreign exchange market. The massive capital outflow would continue as long as the New Zealand interest rate remained below the foreign rate. Sterilized intervention would just mean that the New Zealand central bank would soon exhaust its holdings of foreign reserve assets.

To restore equilibrium, the central bank must let its intervention reduce the money supply via the process explained at the beginning of this section. The money supply will fall until the LM schedule shifts back to the initial position, $LM(M_0)$. At this point (E_0), the New Zealand interest rate will be restored to equality with the foreign interest

FIGURE 15-7 Monetary Policy with a Fixed Exchange Rate

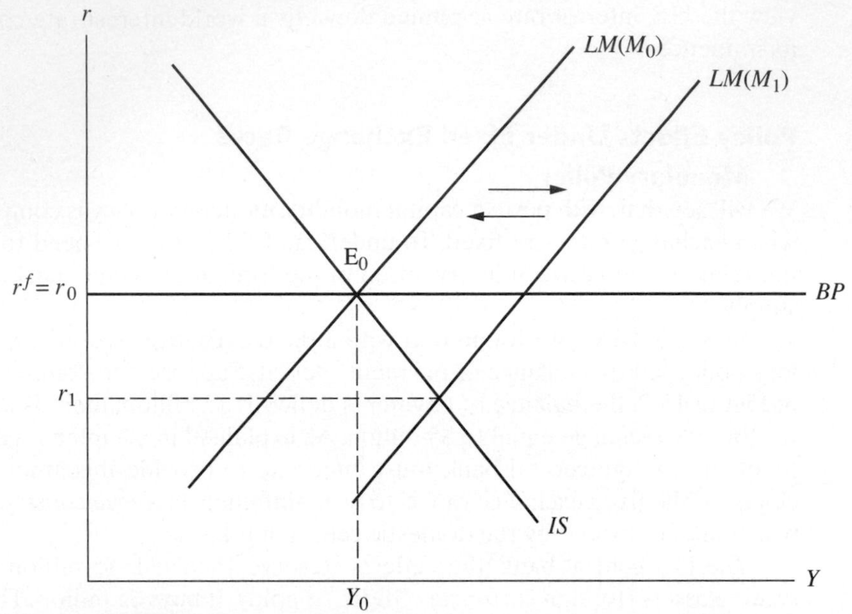

An increase in the money supply shifts the LM schedule from $LM(M_0)$ to $LM(M_1)$. The domestic interest rate falls below the foreign interest rate, triggering a massive capital outflow. Central bank intervention to maintain the fixed exchange rate causes the money supply to fall back to the initial level, M_0. The domestic interest rate is restored to equality with the foreign interest rate, and income is back at its initial level.

rate. The capital outflow, and therefore the downward movement in the money supply, will stop. But also at this point the money supply and income will be back at their initial levels. The monetary policy action will have been completely ineffective.

Fiscal Policy

The situation is quite different for fiscal policy. Figure 15-8 illustrates the effects of an increase in government spending in the perfect capital mobility case. The direct effect of the increased spending is the shift of the IS schedule to the right from $IS(G_0)$ to $IS(G_1)$. The increase in spending pushes the domestic interest rate above the foreign interest rate and sets in motion a massive capital inflow. The domestic central bank, again assume it is New Zealand's, must intervene and in this case buy foreign exchange with New Zealand dollars. This action will cause the New Zealand money supply to expand. The New Zealand central bank will have to keep buying foreign exchange until the money supply has increased enough to shift the LM schedule to $LM(M_1)$ and to restore equality between the domestic and foreign interest rates at point E_1. This endogenous increase in the money supply strengthens the expansionary effect of the increase in government spending. Output rises to Y_1 instead of to Y_1'.

In a system of fixed exchange rates, with perfect capital mobility, this expansionary fiscal policy is highly effective because there is no rise in the domestic interest rate and therefore no crowding out of private-sector spending.

FIGURE 15-8 Fiscal Policy with a Fixed Exchange Rate

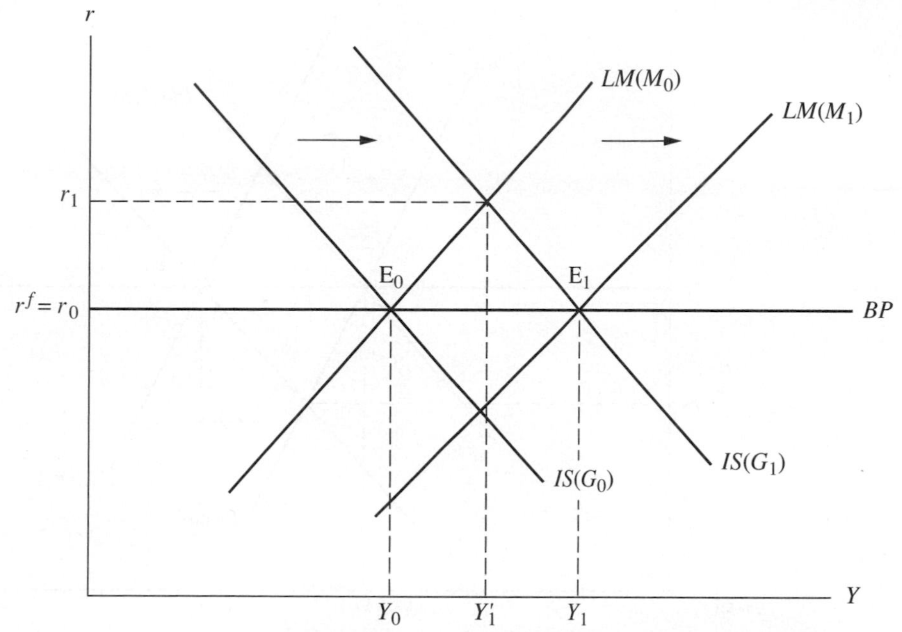

An increase in government spending shifts the *IS* schedule from $IS(G_0)$ to $IS(G_1)$. The domestic interest rate is pushed above the foreign interest rate, resulting in a massive capital inflow. Central bank intervention to maintain the fixed exchange rate causes the money supply to rise. The *LM* schedule shifts from $LM(M_0)$ to $LM(M_1)$. The domestic interest rate is brought back into equality with the foreign rate, and the increase in the money supply reinforces the expansionary effect of the increase in government spending.

Policy Effects Under Flexible Exchange Rates

In a system of flexible exchange rates, the situation is reversed. Here we find that monetary policy is highly effective and fiscal policy is completely ineffective.

Monetary Policy

Again we consider an increase in the money supply from M_0 to M_1. As shown in Figure 15-9, this increased money supply shifts the *LM* schedule from $LM(M_0)$ to $LM(M_1)$. As in the fixed exchange rate case, the increase in the money supply temporarily causes the New Zealand interest rate to fall below the foreign interest rate, triggering a massive capital outflow. But in a flexible exchange rate system, there is no resulting foreign exchange market intervention by the New Zealand central bank.

Instead, as investors sell New Zealand assets and therefore sell New Zealand dollars, the New Zealand exchange rate rises and the value of the New Zealand dollar falls. This rise in the exchange rate increases New Zealand exports, decreases New Zealand imports, and shifts the *IS* schedule to the right. The selling of New Zealand dollars continues until the exchange rate rises sufficiently, from π_0 to π_1 and shifts the *IS* schedule from $IS(\pi_0)$ to $IS(\pi_1)$. At this point (E_1), the New Zealand interest rate has been restored to equality with the foreign interest rate. Income has risen to Y_1.

FIGURE 15-9 Monetary Policy with a Flexible Exchange Rate

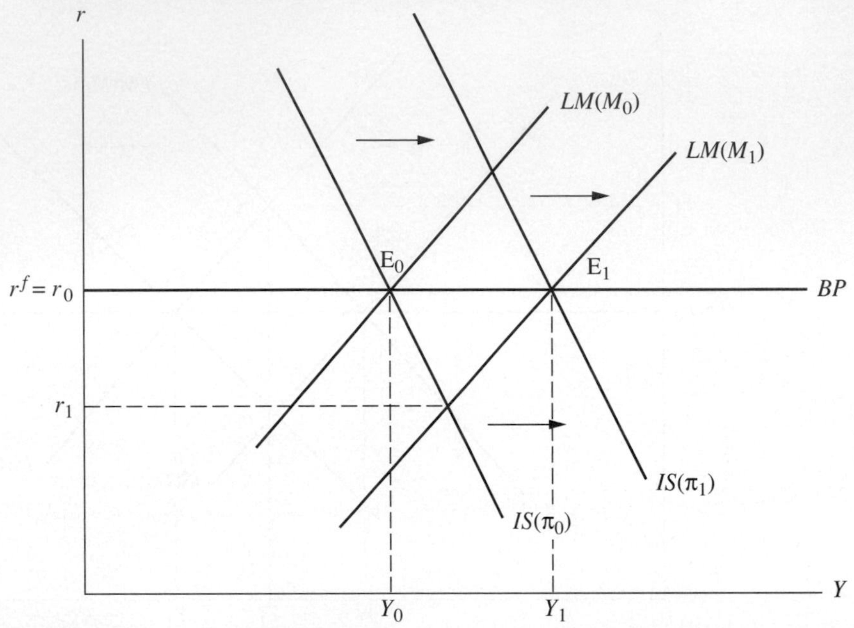

An increase in the money supply causes the *LM* schedule to shift from $LM(M_0)$ to $LM(M_1)$. The domestic interest rate falls below the foreign interest rate, triggering a massive outflow of capital. The capital outflow causes the exchange rate to rise, shifting the *IS* schedule from $IS(\pi_0)$ to $IS(\pi_1)$. The domestic interest rate is brought back into equality with the foreign interest rate, and income rises to Y_1.

Monetary policy is highly effective with perfect capital mobility and flexible exchange rates. Income rises by the full amount of the horizontal shift in the *LM* schedule. Notice that the mechanism by which monetary policy works is no longer through the interest rate, which is fixed at the foreign rate. It is instead through the exchange rate and therefore net exports.

Fiscal Policy

The effects of an increase in government spending with flexible exchange rates and perfect capital mobility are illustrated in Figure 15-10. The direct effect of increased government spending is to shift the *IS* schedule from $IS(G_0, \pi_0)$ to $IS(G_1, \pi_0)$. As a result, the domestic interest rate rises (toward r_1 in the figure) above the foreign interest rate. This movement triggers a massive capital inflow, which with a flexible exchange rate causes the exchange rate to fall (the domestic currency to appreciate). As a result, exports fall and imports rise. The *IS* schedule shifts to the left.

Equilibrium is restored only when the *IS* schedule has shifted all the way back to $IS(G_0, \pi_0) = IS(G_1, \pi_1)$ and the domestic interest rate is again equal to the foreign interest rate. At this point, the capital inflow and downward pressure on the exchange rate end. Also at this point, income is back to its initial level. Fiscal policy is completely ineffective.

Read Perspectives 15-1.

FIGURE 15-10 Fiscal Policy with a Flexible Exchange Rate

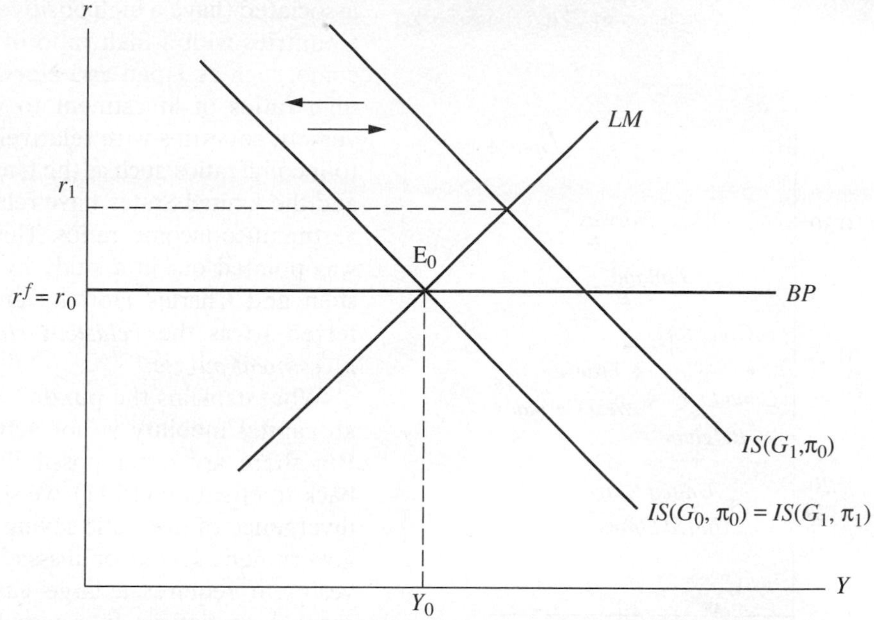

An increase in government spending causes the *IS* schedule to shift from $IS(G_0, \pi_0)$ to $IS(G_1, \pi_0)$. The domestic interest rate rises above the foreign interest rate, with a resulting massive inflow of capital. The capital inflow causes the exchange rate to fall. The fall in the exchange rate shifts the *IS* schedule back to $IS(G_0, \pi_0) = IS(G_1, \pi_1)$. The domestic interest rate is reequated with the foreign interest rate, and income returns to its initial level.

PERSPECTIVES 15-1

THE SAVING–INVESTMENT CORRELATION PUZZLE

In a closed economy, we would expect saving to have a strong positive relationship to investment. From the equation for the closed economy *IS* schedule given by (15.4), we see that

$$S + T = I + G \qquad \textbf{(15.4)}$$

or

$$S + (T - G) = I \qquad \textbf{(15.10)}$$

Private domestic saving (S) plus government saving ($T - G$) (or dissaving if there is a deficit) must equal domestic investment (I).

In an open economy, equation (15.10) is modified to include imports and exports and becomes

$$S + (T - G) + (Z - X) = I \qquad \textbf{(15.11)}$$

Domestic saving (again adjusted for government saving or dissaving) plus the trade deficit ($Z - X$) must equal domestic investment. Countries could therefore have large deviations of saving from investment if there were large current account surpluses or deficits. A country could, for example, have a large current account deficit ($Z - X$), which in the balance of payments accounts was

FIGURE 15-11 Saving (S) and Investment (I): Ratio to GNP (Y), 1965–86

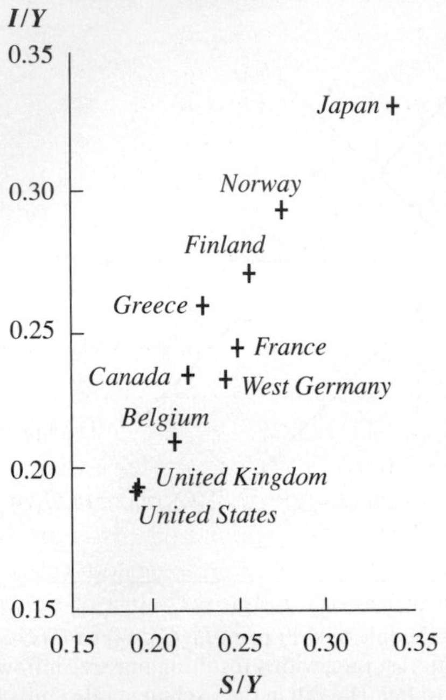

SOURCE: Tamin Bayoumi, "Saving–Investment Correlations," International Monetary Fund *Staff Papers*, 37 (June 1990), p. 364.

financed by a surplus in the capital account, which in turn financed investment in excess of domestic saving. This was the case for the United States over much of the 1980s and 1990s.

In a world of high capital mobility, we would not expect saving and investment in a particular country to be closely related. Saving would flow to the country where the return to investment was greatest. If residents of one country saved a great deal but the return to investment was low, that country would invest abroad and would have a capital account deficit and a trade surplus.

In fact, however, as can be seen from Figure 15-11, saving and investment in a sample of developed countries are closely associated (have a high positive correlation). Countries with a high ratio of saving to income, such as Japan and Norway, also have high ratios of investment to income. Conversely, countries with relatively low saving-to-income ratios, such as the United Kingdom and the United States, have relatively low investment-to-income ratios. This relationship was pointed out in a study by Martin Feldstein and Charles Horioka and is thus referred to as the *Feldstein–Horioka saving investment puzzle.*[a]

What explains the puzzle? Perhaps overall capital mobility is not actually so high. But there are other possibilities. If we go back to equation (15.11), we see that a large divergence of domestic saving (adjusted for government saving or disssaving) from investment requires a large current account surplus or deficit. If governments initiate policies to limit the extent of such current account imbalances, they force a convergence of domestic saving and investment. Certainly some countries do have substantial current account imbalances at times. The United States in recent years is an example, but limits on such imbalances could still be great enough to explain the relationship in Figure 15-11, which covers 10 countries over two decades.

A second explanation for the positive saving–investment correlation is related to limits on many firms' access to capital markets in general. If firms have limited access to capital markets, they must finance investment out of retained earnings, which are part of domestic saving.

Although these explanations of the positive saving–investment correlation are consistent with a high degree of international capital mobility, there is little empirical evidence on their importance. The puzzle remains.

---

[a]Martin Feldstein and Charles Horioka, "Domestic Saving and International Capital Flows," *Economic Journal*, 90 (June 1980), pp. 314–29.

Before leaving the puzzle of the high saving–investment correlation, it should be noted that, while still high, this correlation has declined somewhat over the past decade. This is partly due to the record high U.S. current account deficit, which has been accompanied by relatively high domestic investment and low domestic saving. But even leaving the United States out, the correlation has declined. The most likely cause for the decline is the increasing globalization of capital markets, which has raised capital mobility. Another way this shows up is that in their portfolios investors are including more foreign assets. This has been a decline in what economists call *home bias*, the preference of investors to hold domestic financial assets. This increasing capital mobility is one factor that has made financing the U.S. current account deficit easier.

15.4 Conclusion

In this chapter we have analyzed monetary and fiscal policy within an open economy version of the *IS–LM* model for the cases of both imperfect and perfect capital mobility. We have seen significant differences between the two cases. In particular, the assumption of perfect capital mobility produces some striking results: Monetary policy is completely ineffective if the exchange rate is fixed, and fiscal policy is completely ineffective if the exchange rate is flexible. With imperfect capital mobility, our results are more in line with those for the closed economy *IS–LM* model, as summarized in Table 7.1, though there are some quantitative differences.

Given these differences, which case is relevant to the real world? Few things are perfect in the world, and capital mobility is not one of them. But is the degree of capital mobility high enough that perfect capital mobility is not a bad approximation? On the basis of the situation in the mid-1980s, one study concluded that world capital markets were probably "two-thirds or three-fourths of the way but no further than that" toward perfect capital mobility.[5] Capital markets have moved further in that direction over the past 20 years. This trend might lead to a preference for the model with imperfect capital mobility but a relatively flat BP schedule.

It is hard, however, to make a blanket statement that is relevant for all countries. Some countries, though the number is diminishing, have government controls on capital movements that severely restrict capital mobility. For other countries whose capital markets are closely integrated with those of a large neighbor, such as Canada and Austria, the assumption of perfect capital mobility is preferable.

Review Questions and Problems

1. Explain why the *BP* schedule in Figure 15-1 is upward-sloping. What factors cause a shift in the *BP* schedule? Explain.
2. Within the Mundell–Fleming model assuming *imperfect* capital mobility, analyze the effects of the following policy actions for both the fixed and flexible exchange rate cases:
   a. A decline in the money supply from M_0 to M_1.
   b. A decrease in government spending from G_0 to G_1.

[5]Ralph Bryant, *International Financial Intermediation* (Washington, D.C.: The Brookings Institution, 1987), p. 86.

Include in your answer the effects of the policy action on both income and the interest rate, as well as on the balance of payments and the exchange rate.

3. Explain what it means to say that we have perfect capital mobility. Why is the *BP* schedule horizontal in the case of perfect capital mobility?
4. Consider the effects of a lump-sum tax cut, from T_0 to T_1, in a fixed exchange rate system. Consider both imperfect and perfect capital mobility. In which case will the tax cut have a larger effect on income?
5. What is meant by *sterilization* of the effects of foreign exchange market intervention? Explain how sterilization works in the case of imperfect capital mobility.
6. Within the Mundell–Fleming model assuming perfect capital mobility, analyze the effects of a positive shock to money demand (i.e., an increase in the demand for money for given levels of income and the interest rate). Consider the effect of the shock on income when the exchange rate is fixed and when it is flexible.
7. Within the Mundell–Fleming model assuming perfect capital mobility, analyze the effect of a lump-sum tax increase for the case of a flexible exchange rate. Will the tax cut be effective? Explain.

PART FIVE

Economic Policy

The chapters in this part extend the discussion of macroeconomic policy. Although monetary and fiscal policies were analyzed in previous chapters, the policy actions we considered were simple policy shifts such as a lump-sum change in tax collections or an exogenous change in the money supply. Consideration of such simple policy shifts was useful to an understanding of the properties of the models we considered. In the next three chapters we take a more detailed and realistic look at macroeconomic policymaking.

Chapters 16 and 17 deal with monetary policy. Chapter 18 considers fiscal policies aimed at stabilizing the economy.

CHAPTER 16

Money, the Banking System, and Interest Rates

So far, we have represented monetary policy actions by exogenous changes in the money supply. In this chapter and in Chapter 17 we take a more realistic look at monetary policy. We discuss the structure of the central bank in the United States, the **Federal Reserve System**, which conducts monetary policy. Part of our analysis in this chapter will be an examination of how the Federal Reserve can control the money supply. We will see that the realism of our previous assumption that the money supply is exogenous depends on the behavior of the Federal Reserve.

Federal Reserve System (Federal Reserve, or the Fed, for short) is composed of 12 regional Federal Reserve banks and the Board of Governors located in Washington

The Federal Reserve is in fact concerned about variables in addition to the money supply. This is not in conflict with our previous analysis. In that analysis, the central bank changed the money supply to influence the interest rate. Increases in the money supply, for example, caused the interest rate to decline. In recent years, however, the emphasis on the interest rate has grown and the importance of the money supply had declined. Thus, we will pay more attention to the linkages between central bank action and interest rates in this chapter and the next. We will also go into more detail about interest rates and financial assets other than money.

The banking system plays an important role in transmitting the effects of Federal Reserve action to the rest of the economy. So, we will examine the way monetary policy affects the balance sheets and behavior of banks. The behavior of the nonbank public also will enter our analysis.

In this chapter, the focus is on what the Federal Reserve actually does. In Chapter 17, the focus shifts to what the Federal Reserve and other central banks *should* do—the question of optimal monetary policy.

We begin in Section 16.1 with a definition of money. Section 16.2 explains some interest rate concepts and the associated financial assets. Section 16.3 discusses the structure of the Federal Reserve System and the tools the Federal Reserve uses for monetary control. In Section 16.4, we explain the relationship between bank reserves and deposits, a vital link in the process of Federal Reserve control over the money supply and the level of interest rates. In Section 16.5, we examine the relative roles of the nonbank public, the banking system, and the Federal Reserve in determining the money supply. Section 16.6 concludes our analysis of the money supply process and its relationship to interest-rate determination.

16.1 THE DEFINITION OF MONEY

The Functions of Money

The standard definition of *money* is whatever performs monetary functions. The three widely accepted functions of money are (1) a means of exchange, (2) a store of value, and (3) a unit of account.

Means of Exchange

Money serves as a means of exchange. You buy goods or services with money. You receive money for selling goods or services. We do not often think about it, but this function of money contributes greatly to economic efficiency. Exchange without money would require swaps of goods for goods—what is called *barter.* Some barter transactions exist even in a monetary economy.

But barter as the predominant means of trade is inefficient because barter transactions require a *double coincidence of wants.* Suppose that Ms. Jones wants to buy shoes and sell jewelry, while Ms. Smith wants to sell shoes but buy a computer. No trade takes place, and both must take time to look for trading partners whose buying *and* selling desires coincide with theirs. In a monetary economy, Ms. Jones buys the shoes from Ms. Smith with money. Ms. Smith can then use the money to buy a computer from *anyone* selling one. Ms. Jones needs only to find someone who wants to buy jewelry (without necessarily wanting to sell shoes).

Store of Value

Money functions as a store for wealth, a way to save for future spending. Money is one type of financial asset. Other stores of value (e.g., a corporate or government bond) are not money because they do not perform the other monetary functions. They cannot be used as a means of exchange or as a unit of account, the third central function of money.

Unit of Account

Prices are measured in terms of money. In Albania, prices (and debts) are measured in terms of the lek, in Poland the zloty, in Britain the pound. In the United States, as you already know, prices and debts are measured in dollars and cents. As with the means-of-exchange function, money provides conveniences as a unit of account. Merchants simply post one price in dollars, not in terms of each commodity that might be traded for their goods.

M1 is the narrower of the two money supply measures in the United States. It consists of currency plus checkable deposits. A second measure, **M2,** is broader. M2 includes all the components of M1 plus some additional bank deposits that have no or only limited provisions for checks

Components of the Money Supply

The money supply is composed of financial assets that serve the preceding functions. Which assets are these in the United States? There are two official measures of the U.S. money supply. Each is composed of currency and deposits at commercial banks and other depository institutions (e.g., savings and loan associations).

One measure, called **M1**, is the narrower of the two money measures in the United States. It consists of currency plus *checkable* deposits. Checkable deposits are those on which you can write checks—that is, those on which you can direct the bank in writing to make payments to another party.[1] Currency fulfills the three monetary functions previously discussed. So do bank deposits, as long as you can write checks on them. Checks on deposits can be used to buy things (means-of-exchange function), deposits are a store of value, and currency or deposits are a unit of account.

The other measure, **M2**, is broader. It includes the components of Ml plus additional bank deposits that have no or only limited provisions for

[1] Another small item included in Ml is travelers checks. Our discussion here ignores a number of small items in the different definitions of money. For detailed definitions, see Table 16-1.

TABLE 16-1 Money Supply Measures, April 2007 (billions of dollars)

M1	$1,376.9	Averages of daily figures for (1) currency outside the Treasury, Federal Reserve banks, and the vaults of commercial banks; (2) travelers checks on nonbank issuers; (3) demand deposits at all commercial banks other than those due to domestic banks, the U.S. government, and foreign banks and official institutions less cash items in the process of collection and Federal Reserve float; and (4) negotiable order of withdrawal (NOW) and automatic transfer service (ATS) accounts at banks and thrift institutions, credit union share draft (CUSD) accounts, and demand deposits at mutual savings banks
M2	7,218.9	M1 plus savings and small-denomination time deposits at all depository institutions, overnight repurchase agreements at commercial banks, overnight Eurodollars held by U.S. residents other than banks at Caribbean branches of member banks, money market mutual fund shares, and money market deposit accounts (MMDAs)

SOURCE: Board of Governors of the Federal Reserve.

checks. M2 includes money market mutual fund accounts, which often allow only checks for amounts above some minimum, and regular savings and time deposits on which no checks can be written.[2] Details of the composition of each of these measures of money, as well as figures for the level of these measures for April 2007, are given in Table 16-1.

The rationale for the broader money measure is that the additional deposit categories included in M2 relative to Ml are very similar to checkable deposits or are easily converted to checkable deposits. Balances in savings accounts, for example, can be converted into checkable deposits (or currency) simply by going to the bank (or using an ATM machine). If these additional deposit types are sufficiently close substitutes for checkable deposits and currency, we may want to consider them as money.

16.2 INTEREST RATES AND FINANCIAL ASSETS

In previous chapters we restricted our analysis to two financial assets: money and bonds. We have just defined money more carefully than before. Now we delve deeper into bonds.

In our previous analysis, money was the short-term asset and bonds were the long-term one. By this we mean that money is immediately available; it has no term to maturity. An example of a bond is the 10-year U.S. Treasury bond. Its term to maturity is 10 years, meaning that you receive repayment of the principal (face value) of the bond after 10 years.

In U.S. financial markets there are many types of financial assets that are stores of wealth. We don't need to go into great detail, but going a little further than the

[2]Balances in savings accounts are, in practice, available on demand. Time deposits, however, are for a specified time period (e.g., one year), and there may be penalties for early withdrawal.

bond–money distinction will help us understand how monetary policy works. One distinction in financial markets is between the capital markets and the money markets.[3] The capital markets are those for financial assets with a term to maturity of over one year. The money markets are for assets with term to maturity of less than one year. The 10-year U.S. Treasury bond and other bonds are traded in capital markets. Other types of bonds include corporate bonds and state and local government bonds. The interest rates on these types of bonds are examples of long-term interest rates.

The money market assets, which are distinct from money itself, have not previously entered our discussion. One example of an asset traded in a money market is a U.S. Treasury bill. Like the Treasury bond, it is a debt instrument issued by the U.S. Treasury, but it is short-term, with a maturity of three or six months. Another example of a money market asset is commercial paper, a short-term debt instrument issued by major corporations and large banks. A money market that is important for the conduct of monetary policy is the federal funds market. Federal funds are overnight loans between banks. Like bonds, each money market asset has an interest rate. So, we have the Treasury bill rate, the commercial paper rate, and the federal funds rate. These are examples of short-term interest rates. The **federal funds rate** is especially important because it is the rate that the Federal Reserve most closely controlls. In terminology we use in Chapter 17, the federal funds rate is the *operating target* of the Federal Reserve.

federal funds rate is the rate at which banks make loans to one another

Another set of interest rates is loan rates. In bank lending, there are interest rates for consumer loans, industrial loans (to businesses), and mortgage loans. With the additional background from this and the previous subsection, we are ready to move on to the Federal Reserve and the conduct of monetary policy.

16.3 THE FEDERAL RESERVE SYSTEM

The Structure of the Central Bank

The U.S. system of central banking was established by the Federal Reserve Act of 1913. Unlike many other countries, which have a single central bank, the United States has a system of Federal Reserve banks, one for each of 12 Federal Reserve districts. Each Federal Reserve bank is named for the city in which it is located: the Federal Reserve Bank of New York, the Federal Reserve Bank of Chicago, the Federal Reserve Bank of San Francisco, and so forth. For some of the functions of central banking the regional character of our system is important, but the making of macroeconomic policy has become centralized in Washington in two policymaking groups.

Board of Governors of the Federal Reserve is composed of seven members (governors) appointed by the president of the United States with the advice and consent of the Senate for a term of 14 years. One member of the board is appointed chairman.

The first group is the **Board of Governors of the Federal Reserve**. The board is composed of seven members (governors) appointed by the president of the United States with the advice and consent of the Senate for a term of 14 years. One member of the board is appointed by the president as chairman for a 4-year term. When this post has

[3]In our models, *capital* referred to physical capital goods. Here the term *capital markets* refers to a subset of financial markets.

Federal Open Market Committee
is composed of 12 voting members: the 7 members of the Board of Governors and 5 of the presidents of regional Federal Reserve banks. Presidents of the regional banks serve on a rotating basis, with the exception of the president of the Federal Reserve Bank of New York, who is vice chairman and a permanent voting member of the committee.

open-market operations
are purchases and sales of government securities in the open market by the Federal Reserve

been held by forceful individuals, the chairman has been the dominant figure in monetary policy formation.

The second monetary policymaking group is the **Federal Open Market Committee**. The most important method by which the Federal Reserve controls the money supply is the purchase and sale of government securities in the open market—that is, in the market of dealers in government securities located in New York City. We will see how the Federal Reserve uses open-market purchases or sales of securities to increase or decrease the *legal reserves* of the banking system. Because banks are required to hold fixed proportions of their deposits in the form of legal reserves, such **open-market operations** can control the deposit component of the money supply. The Open Market Committee controls open-market operations. This committee is composed of 12 voting members: the 7 members of the Board of Governors and 5 of the presidents of the regional Federal Reserve banks. The presidents of the regional banks serve on a rotating basis, except for the president of the New York Bank, the bank charged with carrying out open-market operations, who is always a voting member of the Open Market Committee.

Federal Reserve Control of the Money Supply

Recall that the monetary aggregates discussed in Section 16.1 consist of currency held by the public plus various classes of bank deposits. To simplify our discussion, assume that only one type of deposit represents all the different types of deposits on which checks can be written—what we will refer to as *checkable deposits*. These include demand deposits, NOW accounts, and credit union share drafts. Savings and time deposits are brought into our discussion at a later point. Currency in the United States consists primarily of Federal Reserve notes, paper money issued by the Federal Reserve.

To control the deposit component of the money supply, the Federal Reserve sets legal reserve requirements on deposits. These requirements specify that banks must hold a certain percentage of their deposit liabilities either in the form of vault cash (currency) or as deposits at regional Federal Reserve banks. Given the existence of legal reserve requirements, the Federal Reserve can control the money supply by regulating the supply of legal reserves. Technically, setting reserve requirements and fixing the level of reserves sets a ceiling only on the level of deposits. For example, if the required reserve ratio was 10 percent and reserves were set at $60 billion, the maximum amount of deposits would be $600 billion. In fact, because legal reserves (currency or deposits at regional Federal Reserve banks) do not pay interest, banks hold few reserves beyond those required by Federal Reserve regulations. Thus, the actual level of deposits remains close to the maximum value supportable by a given reserve level.

A convenient starting point for analyzing Federal Reserve control of bank deposits is the balance sheet summarizing the assets and liabilities of the Federal Reserve System. This balance sheet is shown in Table 16-2. The primary assets held by the Federal Reserve are U.S. government securities. A much smaller item on the asset side of the balance sheet, but one that we return to later in the discussion, is the amount of loans to banks; these are the *borrowed reserves* of the banking system. On the liability

TABLE 16-2 Balance Sheet of Federal Reserve Banks, February 2007 (billions of dollars)

Assets		*Liabilities*	
U.S. government securities	780.8	Federal Reserve notes	770.9
Loans to banks	0.2	Bank reserve deposits	22.9
Other assets	100.3	Other liabilities and capital	87.5
Total assets	881.3	Total liabilities and capital	881.3

SOURCE: Board of Governors of the Federal Reserve.

side, the two important items are Federal Reserve notes outstanding, which make up the bulk of U.S. paper currency, and bank reserve deposits. This latter item consists of the deposits held at the Federal Reserve banks by the banking system to satisfy legal reserve requirements.[4]

monetary base is equal to currency plus bank reserve deposits

These two items on the liability side of the Federal Reserve balance sheet (currency plus bank reserve deposits) form what is termed the **monetary base**, because together they provide the foundation for the money supply. Currency is directly included in the money supply if held by the nonbank public. The portion of currency held as bank reserves plus bank reserve deposits provides the reserves supporting the deposit component of the money supply. The Federal Reserve controls the quantity of its liabilities, which means that it can control the monetary base and therefore control bank reserves and the money supply.

The Tools of Federal Reserve Control

The Federal Reserve uses several tools to control bank reserves. In Section 16.4, we explain the process by which changes in bank reserves affect the level of bank deposits. One point should be noted before proceeding. When the Federal Reserve takes some action changing the monetary base—an action increasing the base, for example—the net effect on bank reserves depends on how much of the increase in the base goes into increased currency holding by the (nonbank) public. The behavior of the public's currency holdings, then, influences the ultimate effect of Federal Reserve actions on the level of bank reserves and, hence, deposits. This influence is explained in the next section, but for now we assume that the public's holding of currency is fixed. With this assumption, changes in the monetary base produce dollar-for-dollar changes in the quantity of bank reserves. The Federal Reserve can use three tools to control the reserve position of banks: open-market operations, the discount rate, and the required reserve ratio. In practice open-market operations are the dominant means by which the Federal Reserve controls bank reserves. We discuss the other two tools because they are used by other central banks and have been used by the Federal Reserve in the past.

Open-Market Operations

The first tool, open-market operations, was referred to previously. For an example of how an open-market action by the Federal Reserve affects bank reserves, consider an open-market purchase of a government security worth $1,000.

[4]Hereafter we drop the adjective *legal* when referring to reserve assets that satisfy reserve requirements.

TABLE 16-3 Effect on the Federal Reserve's Balance Sheet of a $1,000 Open-Market Purchase

Assets		*Liabilities*	
Government securities	+1,000	Bank reserve deposits	+1,000

Government securities constitute the major part of Federal Reserve assets, as can be seen from Table 16-2. The purchase of the additional security increases the government security item on the asset side of the Federal Reserve's balance sheet by $1,000. To pay for this security, the Federal Reserve writes a check on itself, drawn on the New York Federal Reserve Bank. A key point to note here is that the Federal Reserve, by writing this check, does not reduce the balance in *any* account. The Federal Reserve simply creates a new liability against itself. What happens to the check? Suppose that an individual investor sold the security to the Federal Reserve. That individual will take the check received and deposit it at a bank, Citibank in New York, for example.

Citibank will then present the check to the New York Federal Reserve Bank for payment. The Federal Reserve will credit the Citibank account balance at the New York Federal Reserve Bank by $1,000. The open-market purchase results in an increase of an equal amount in bank reserve deposits with the Federal Reserve. The effects of the open-market purchase on the balance sheet of the Federal Reserve are summarized in Table 16-3.

In a similar manner, a sale of government securities in the open market will reduce bank reserve deposits by an equal amount. In this case, the Federal Reserve receives a check drawn on a bank by the individual who purchased the security. The Federal Reserve lowers that bank's deposit balance at a regional Federal Reserve bank by the amount of the check. Such open-market purchases and sales of securities provide a flexible means of controlling bank reserves. Open-market operations are by far the most important of the Federal Reserve's tools of monetary control.

The Discount Rate

The Federal Reserve Open Market Committee oversees open-market operations. The remaining tools of monetary control are administered by the Board of Governors of the Federal Reserve System. One of these is the Federal Reserve **discount rate**, the interest rate charged by the Federal Reserve on its loans to banks. The Federal Reserve can raise or lower this rate to regulate the volume of such loans to banks. To see the effect on bank reserve deposits of changes in the volume of loans from the Federal Reserve, consider a loan of $1,000 from the Federal Reserve to a bank. The effects on the Federal Reserve's balance sheet are shown in Table 16-4.

discount rate the interest rate charged by the Federal Reserve on its loans to banks

The asset item "loans to banks" increases by $1,000. The proceeds from the loan are credited to the account of the borrowing bank at the Federal Reserve. At this point,

TABLE 16-4 Effect on the Federal Reserve's Balance Sheet of a $1,000 Loan to a Bank

Assets		*Liabilities*	
Loans to banks	+1,000	Bank reserve deposits	+1,000

bank reserve deposits increase by $1,000. By lowering the discount rate, the Federal Reserve encourages banks to borrow and increase the borrowed component of bank reserve deposits. Raising the discount rate has the reverse effect.

From Table 16-2 it can be seen that loans to banks by the Federal Reserve were a very small balance sheet item in 2007. These discount loans declined dramatically in the 1990s for a variety of reasons. One was that if it was found that a bank had borrowed from the Federal Reserve, it would be interpreted as a sign of possible financial problems at the bank, with adverse consequences for the bank's stock price.

In some countries, manipulation of the discount rate and of borrowed reserves is an important tool for monetary control. At present, this is not the case in the United States. Still, such lending does have a role in monetary policy. The Federal Reserve plays the role of "lender of last resort" to banks, an important role for a central bank. The Federal Reserve will lend to a bank and provide liquidity at times of crisis when other lending channels have been shut down. To keep the discount channel operative and continue to act as lender of last resort, the Federal Reserve has recently made a number of changes in the way in which it makes loans to banks. It now, for example, charges different rates to institutions based on their financial status. Thus, institutions that can borrow at a low rate because they are financially stable should not hesitate to do so for fear that such borrowing would signal otherwise.

The Required Reserve Ratio

required reserve ratio is the percentage of deposits banks must hold as reserves

A potential third tool that the Federal Reserve can use to control banks' reserve positions is the **required reserve ratio**, the percentage of deposits banks must hold as reserves. Changes in this policy instrument do not change total bank reserves, but by changing the required reserve ratio on deposits, the Federal Reserve changes the quantity of deposits that can be supported by a given level of reserves. Increases in the required reserve ratio reduce the quantity of deposits that can be supported by a given amount of reserves. Consider our previous example, where reserves were set at $60 billion, so that with a 10 percent reserve requirement, the maximum level for checkable deposits was $600 billion. If the required reserve ratio were increased to 12 percent, the maximum level of deposits, with reserves unchanged at $60 billion, would be $500 billion.

Although we have included them in our discussion, changes in reserve requirements are not currently being used in the United States to affect banks' reserve positions. One reason is that increases in reserve requirements are very unpopular with banks; being forced to hold more non-interest-paying reserves lowers bank profits. Reserve requirements are, however, a major tool in monetary policy in China.

16.4 BANK RESERVES AND BANK DEPOSITS

Thus far, we have seen how the Federal Reserve can use open-market operations, changes in the discount rate, and changes in the required reserve ratio on deposits to affect the reserve position of banks. In this section we examine the process whereby changes in reserves affect the level of deposits in the banking system. Again a convenient starting point is a balance sheet, in this case one for the commercial banking system.

TABLE 16-5 Consolidated Balance Sheet for the Commercial Banking System, April 2007 (billions of dollars)

Assets		*Liabilities*	
Cash assets, including reserves	305.4	Checkable deposits	698.8
Loans	6,192.1	Time and savings deposits	5,750.0
U.S. Treasury securities	1,175.3	Other liabilities and capital	3,468.5
Other securities	1,097.2		
Interbank loans	365.0		
Other assets	782.4		
Total assets	9,917.3	Total liabilities and capital	9,917.3

SOURCE: Board of Governors of the Federal Reserve.

A simplified consolidated balance sheet for all commercial banks is shown in Table 16-5. On the asset side, the first item is cash assets of commercial banks. Reserves (vault cash plus deposits at the Federal Reserve) come under this category, but other items are included as well (e.g., bank deposits at other banks). Reserves as of the time period for which the table was compiled (April 2007) totaled $42.7 billion, of which all but $1.5 billion were required reserves. As explained previously, banks hold few excess reserves, because reserve assets do not pay interest. The other major items on the asset side of the ledger are loans by the commercial banks, which include loans to consumers and businesses and the banks' holdings of both government and private securities. Also broken out as a separate item is "Interbank loans." These are loans in the federal funds market described in the previous section.

The major liabilities of commercial banks are deposits, both checkable deposits and saving plus time deposits. There is also a substantial "Other liabilities and capital" category. This includes other borrowing by banking corporations and bank capital that in April 2007 totaled $875 billion.

A Model of Deposit Creation

Now consider the effects on the bank of an increase in reserves. Let us return to our example of Citibank. Recall our assumption that the Federal Reserve has purchased a $1,000 security from an individual, using a check drawn on the New York Federal Reserve Bank. The individual had deposited the check at Citibank. When the check is presented for payment at the New York Federal Reserve Bank, Citibank's reserve deposits at the New York Federal Reserve increase by $1,000. To this point, the effects on Citibank's balance sheet as a result of this open-market purchase by the Federal Reserve are as shown in Table 16-6. Checkable deposits and reserves have both increased

TABLE 16-6 Initial Effect on Citibank's Balance Sheet from a $1,000 Open-Market Purchase

Assets			*Liabilities*	
Reserves		+1,000	Checkable deposits	+1,000
Required reserves	+100			
Excess reserves	+900			
Total assets		+1,000	Total liabilities	+1,000

by $1,000. For simplicity, we continue to assume that there is a uniform reserve requirement of 10 percent. In that case, the increase in reserves will consist of an increase of $100 in required reserves and of $900 in excess reserves, as shown in Table 16-6.

Table 16-6, however, shows only the initial effects of the open-market purchase on Citibank's balance sheet. The position described in Table 16-6 will *not* be an equilibrium for Citibank because the bank will not, in general, wish to increase *excess* reserves. Because reserves do not pay interest, the bank will convert the excess reserves, which are in the form of deposits at the New York Federal Reserve, into interest-earning assets. This conversion sets in motion a process of deposit creation whereby the initial increase in reserves of $1,000 causes bank deposits to increase by a multiple of that increase.

In describing this process, it is convenient to make some simplifying assumptions. First, we continue to assume that the public's holdings of currency remain unchanged. None of the initial increase in the monetary base, which was in the form of bank reserves, is siphoned off into increased currency holdings by the public. Second, we assume that the quantities of time and savings deposits are fixed. We continue to focus only on checkable deposits. Finally, we assume that the banking system's *desired* level of excess reserves is constant. The effect of altering these assumptions is examined later.

Citibank has $900 in excess reserves, which it wants to convert into interest-earning assets. The bank can make this conversion by either increasing loans or purchasing additional securities. Neither of these actions will produce any lasting effect on the liability side of the ledger; there is no effect on the *equilibrium* level of Citibank's deposits. Citibank's purchase of a security does not change deposits. If the bank makes a loan, temporarily it may credit the amount of the loan to the checking account of the customer, and this action would increase deposits. But customers do not borrow just to increase their checking account balance. Suppose that the loan was to a consumer who used the proceeds to buy a new boat. The consumer pays for the boat with a check drawn on Citibank, and when this transaction is completed, deposits at Citibank will have returned to their initial level (before the loan).

The consumer's check will be deposited in the account of the firm that sold the boat. This firm's checking account balance, suppose at Bank of America, increases by $900. Bank of America presents the check to Citibank for payment—the check clears through the Federal Reserve System—and the result is a transfer of funds from Citibank's account at the New York Federal Reserve Bank to the account of Bank of America at that Federal Reserve Bank. At this point, the $900 in excess reserves is eliminated from Citibank's balance sheet; the bank's reserve deposits have declined by $900. Citibank's balance sheet is now at its final position, where the effects of the open-market operation are shown in Table 16-7. On the liability side, deposits are higher by the $1,000 deposit of the original individual who sold a government security to the Federal

TABLE 16-7 Final Effects on Citibank's Balance Sheet from a $1,000 Open-Market Purchase

Assets			*Liabilities*	
Reserves		+100	Checkable deposits	+1,000
Required reserves	+100			
Loans		+900		
Total assets		+1,000	Total liabilities	+1,000

TABLE 16-8 Initial Effects on Bank of America's Balance Sheet

Assets			*Liabilities*	
Reserves		+900	Checkable deposits	+900
Required reserves	+90			
Excess reserves	+810			
Total assets		+900	Total liabilities	+900

Reserve. Required reserves are higher by \$100 (0.10 × 1,000). Earning assets of the bank, loans in our example, have risen by \$900.

Although we are now finished with Citibank's balance sheet, the process of deposit creation is not complete. Table 16-8 shows the effects on Bank of America's balance sheet to this point. Because of the deposit by the boat manufacturer, checkable deposits are up by \$900. After the check has cleared through the Federal Reserve System, \$900 has been transferred to Bank of America's reserve account. Thus, reserves are increased by \$900, of which only \$90 (0.10 × 900) is required to back the increase in deposits. Bank of America, finding itself with \$810 of excess reserves, will convert them into interest-earning assets by proceeding in the same manner as did Citibank. The bank will increase loans or buy additional securities.

Suppose that the bank uses the \$810 of excess reserves to purchase a security, a corporate bond, for example. The final position of Bank of America will be as shown in Table 16-9. Deposits remain up by \$900, increasing required reserves by \$90. As soon as Bank of America pays for the security with a check drawn upon itself and that check clears the Federal Reserve System, the bank's excess reserves are zero. Earning assets have increased by \$810, and the bank is in equilibrium.

The process of deposit creation continues beyond this point, however, because the individual who sold the corporate bond to Bank of America deposits the proceeds of the check for \$810 into an account at some other commercial bank. That bank now has excess reserves of \$729, the \$810 minus the \$81 of reserves required to back the deposit. Another round of deposit creation will ensue.

The initial increase of \$1,000 in reserves began a process of deposit creation whereby deposits of \$1,000, then \$900, then \$810, then \$729 resulted from the banking system's attempts to convert what were initially excess reserves into earning assets. The individual bank's attempt to rid itself of excess reserves, under the assumptions made to this point, simply transfers the reserves to another bank, together with creating a deposit at that bank. The newly created deposits increase required reserves by 10 percent of the increase in deposits; thus, at each round in the process, the newly created deposit is 10 percent smaller than the previous round. The process will stop when all the new reserves have been

TABLE 16-9 Final Effects on Bank of America's Balance Sheet

Assets			*Liabilities*	
Reserves		+90	Checkable deposits	+900
Required reserves	+90			
Securities		+810		
Total assets		+900	Total liabilities	+900

absorbed in required reserves. With a \$1,000 increase in reserves and a required reserve ratio of 10 percent, the new equilibrium will be reached when the quantity of deposits has increased by \$10,000 (\$1,000 = 0.10 × \$10,000). At this point, required reserves have increased by \$1,000. There are no longer any excess reserves in the system. The expansion of bank credit and the resulting creation of new bank deposits will come to an end.

More generally, an increase in reserves (R) of ΔR causes deposits to increase until required reserves have increased by an equal amount. The increase in required reserves is equal to the increase in checkable deposits times the required reserve ratio on checkable deposits; that is,

$$\text{increase in required reserves} = \text{rr}_d \Delta D \tag{16.1}$$

where rr_d is the required reserve ratio and ΔD is the increase in deposits. Thus, for equilibrium,

$$\text{increase in reserves} = \text{increase in required reserves} \tag{16.2}$$

$$\Delta R = \text{rr}_d \Delta D \tag{16.3}$$

Therefore,

$$\Delta D = \frac{1}{\text{rr}_d} \Delta R \tag{16.4}$$

The increase in deposits will be a multiple ($1/\text{rr}_d$) of the increase in reserves. In our previous example, with ΔR equal to 1,000 and rr_d equal to 0.1 (a 10 percent reserve requirement), we have, from equation (16.4),

$$\Delta D = \frac{1}{0.1}(1{,}000) = 10{,}000 \tag{16.5}$$

the result reached previously.

From equation (16.4) we can also define a *deposit multiplier*, giving the increase in deposits per unit increase in bank reserves:

$$\frac{\Delta D}{\Delta R} = \frac{1}{\text{rr}_d} \tag{17.6}$$

The deposit multiplier for the simple case considered so far is equal to the reciprocal of the required reserve ratio on checkable deposits. For rr_d equal to 0.1 in our example, the deposit multiplier would be 10.

This form of the deposit multiplier results from the simplifying assumptions made previously and will have to be modified when we relax those assumptions. What follows generally is that, given the system of fractional legal reserve requirements, an increase in reserves causes deposits to increase by a multiple of the reserve increase. All of our analysis can be reversed to consider the effects of an open-market sale of securities, which lowers bank reserves and begins a process of deposit contraction. Also note that a similar process of deposit creation results from a reduction in the Federal Reserve discount rate, which would increase borrowed reserves, or from a lowering of reserve requirements, which, although it would not change total reserves, would create excess reserves in the banking system at the initial level of deposits. The balance sheet changes for such policy actions would be somewhat different from those shown in

Tables 16-6 to 16-9, but the general effect would be the same. Both of these alternative expansionary policies would cause both bank credit and bank deposits to increase.

The relationship just derived between reserves and deposits can be restated as a relationship between the monetary base (MB) and the money supply (M^s). The monetary base is equal to currency held by the public plus bank reserves. Thus far, we have assumed that the public's currency holdings are constant so that the change in the monetary base equals the change in reserves ($\Delta\text{MB} = \Delta R$). In this case, the change in the *money supply* will be equal to the change in bank deposits, again because currency held by the public is held constant ($\Delta D = \Delta M^s$). As a consequence, we can write a **money multiplier**, giving the increase in the money supply per unit increase in the monetary base:

money multiplier gives the increase in the money supply per unit increase in the monetary base

$$\frac{\Delta M^s}{\Delta \text{MB}} = \frac{\Delta D}{\Delta R} = \frac{1}{\text{rr}_d} \qquad \textbf{(16.7)}$$

which in this simple case is just equal to the deposit multiplier. This expression will also require modification when we relax our simplifying assumptions, and the money multiplier will usually not be equal in value to the deposit multiplier. In general, however, a given increase in the monetary base will cause the money supply to rise by a multiple of the increase in the base.

As described so far, the process of deposit or money creation must seem mechanical. New doses of reserves are converted by simple multipliers into new deposits, and the money supply increases. Such simple models are helpful in explaining the relationship between bank deposits and bank reserves, but they tell us little about the economic processes behind deposit and money creation. Before we go on to more complex models of deposit creation, it is worthwhile to stop and consider these processes.

When banks find themselves with excess reserves after a Federal Reserve open-market purchase of securities, they attempt to convert those excess reserves into interest-earning assets. They expand bank credit by making more loans and purchasing securities. To increase its lending, a bank offers lower interest rates on loans and perhaps adopts lower standards of creditworthiness. In buying securities, banks bid up the prices of such securities; they bid down the interest rate on securities. Among the earning assets banks buy are mortgages; thus, in times of credit expansion, mortgage interest rates fall. Federal Reserve open-market purchases, as well as other expansionary policy actions that increase bank reserves, therefore lead to credit expansion and a general decline in interest rates. This is the other side of the process of deposit and money creation.

Deposit Creation: More General Cases

In addition to obscuring the economic process involved, simple models such as the one just discussed overstate the degree of precision in the relationship between Federal Reserve actions and resulting changes in the supply of deposits or money. In this subsection, we note some of the complexities involved in this relationship.

First, consider the effect of modifying the assumption that the public's currency holdings are constant throughout the process of deposit creation. Instead assume, as seems likely, that as the quantity of deposits grows, the public also chooses to hold an increased amount of currency. In this case, some of the increase that occurs in the monetary base as a result of an open-market purchase ends up not as increased bank reserves, but as an increase in the public's holding of currency.

Suppose for simplicity that the public holds a fixed ratio of currency to checkable deposits—for example, \$1 in currency per \$4 in checkable deposits ($CU/D = 0.25$, where CU denotes currency). Now, the individual who in our previous example sold the \$1,000 bond to the Federal Reserve will not deposit the full \$1,000 in a checking account but only \$800, keeping the remaining \$200 as currency ($200/800 = 0.25 = CU/D$). Bank reserves will increase by only \$800 as a result of the \$1,000 open-market operation. Further, at each stage in deposit creation, as checkable deposits rise, the public's demand for currency increases in order to maintain a constant currency/checkable deposit ratio. At each stage, there will be a further leakage from bank reserves into currency.

As a consequence of the fact that reserves will increase by less, the increase in deposits for a given increase in the monetary base will be lower when the public's holding of currency rises than when it is fixed. The increase in the money supply will also be lower. This effect follows because each dollar of the base that is part of bank reserves backs a multiple number of dollars in deposits—10 in our example of a 10 percent reserve requirement—whereas each dollar of the monetary base that ends up as currency held by the public is simply \$1 of the money supply. The more of the increase in the base that goes into bank reserves, the higher is the money multiplier.

Relaxing the assumption that banks do not change their desired holdings of excess reserves provides an additional reason that the expression derived in the preceding subsection ($1/rr_d$) is an overstatement of the true money multiplier. It appears likely that as deposits rise, banks increase their excess reserves. Excess reserves are held as a buffer against unexpected deposit flows, and as deposits increase, so does the potential volume of deposit flows. In addition, as we have discussed, the process of deposit expansion leads to a drop in the level of interest rates. The cost of holding excess reserves is the interest forgone by not using these funds to purchase interest-bearing assets. As the interest rate falls, this cost becomes lower. Banks are likely to respond by holding more excess reserves.

If some of the increase in bank reserves ends up as new excess reserves, the quantity of deposits created by a given increase in reserves is smaller than when excess reserves are constant. In general, the higher the bank's desired excess reserve/checkable deposit ratio (ER/D), the lower is the money multiplier.

Next, consider the effect of modifying the assumption that the public's holdings of time and savings deposits are fixed. A more realistic assumption would be that the public increases its time and savings deposits together with its holdings of checkable deposits. How the increase in time and savings deposits affects the money multiplier depends on whether there are legal reserve requirements on these deposits and which monetary aggregates we are considering.

In the United States, legal reserve requirements on time and savings deposits were in effect during most of the post–World War II period. In this case, the money multiplier for the Ml definition was smaller when time and savings deposits increased than when they were assumed to be fixed. With some reserves going to satisfy reserve requirements on new time and savings deposits, fewer were available to support an increase in checking deposits—the only deposits included in the Ml aggregate. Thus, the larger the increase in time and savings deposits, the smaller is the Ml multiplier.

Reserve requirements on time and savings deposits were phased out in the early 1990s. Currently, because these deposits absorb no required reserves, the M1 money multiplier is unaffected by increases in time and savings deposits. The amount of the increase does affect the size of the money multiplier for M2, which includes these deposits, but here we confine our attention to M1.

This discussion leads to the conclusion that the expression for the money multiplier will be more complex than the one derived in the preceding subsection. We would instead expect the money multiplier (*m*) *for the narrowly defined money supply* (M1) to be a function of the following form:

$$m = \frac{\Delta M^s}{\Delta(\text{MB})} = m\left(rr_d, \frac{\text{CU}}{D}, \frac{\text{ER}}{D}\right) \tag{16.8}$$

The money multiplier (m) depends on:

1. The required reserve ratio on checkable deposits (rr_d); the higher the required reserve ratio, the lower the money multiplier.
2. The public's desired currency/checkable deposit ratio (CU/D); the higher the currency/checkable deposit ratio, the lower the money multiplier.
3. The excess reserve /checkable deposit ratio (ER/D); the higher the bank's desired excess reserve/checkable deposit ratio, the lower the money multiplier.

If the value of the money multiplier (m) in (16.8) were known, the Federal Reserve could predict the change in the money supply that would result from a given change in the monetary base:

$$\Delta M^s = m\Delta\text{MB} \tag{16.9}$$

The same information can be expressed slightly differently by defining a *money supply function* giving the supply of money corresponding to a given level of the monetary base:

$$M^s = m \cdot \text{MB} \tag{16.10}$$

Equation (16.10) replaces our previous assumption that the money supply was given exogenously. Before the complications discussed in this subsection are introduced, a money supply function in the form of equation (16.10) would still imply that the money supply was exogenously set by the Federal Reserve as long as the monetary base was controlled by the Federal Reserve; the money multiplier (m) depended only on the required reserve ratio on checkable deposits, which was set exogenously by the Federal Reserve. With both the monetary base and money multiplier set by the Federal Reserve, the public or the banking system would have no role in determining the money supply. The more complicated expression for the money multiplier given by equation (16.8) contains variables determined by the nonbank public (CU/D) and by the banking system (ER/D), implying that even if the Federal Reserve set the monetary base exogenously, the level of the money supply would not be exogenous; it depends to a degree on the behavior of the public and the banking system.

Open-Market Operations and the Federal Funds Rate

As noted previously, the other side of the process of deposit and money creation is a process whereby credit expands and interest rates decline. Consider this aspect of the effect of open-market operations more closely. As banks find themselves with excess reserves, they convert them into interest-earning assets. If they buy securities, they bid down interest rates on those securities. To increase their volume of lending to consumers and businesses, they lower loan rates.

Another channel for lending is to other banks, the "Interbank loans" item in Table 16-5. This lending takes place in the federal funds market. As banks find themselves with more reserves, some increase their lending in the federal funds market. Some banks that were borrowers in the market borrow less, stop borrowing, or become lenders in the market.[5] With more lending and less borrowing in the market, the federal funds rate (the interest rate on Interbank loans) with fall.

In conducting monetary policy, the Federal Reserve and other central banks can choose to focus on the money supply, credit, or interest rates. All are affected by their actions. In regard to interest rates, there is the decision of which one (or ones) to emphasize. In Chapter 17 we will see that the Federal Reserve focuses on the federal funds rate for reasons that will be explained. In the next section, we consider the more general question of focusing on the money supply or "the" interest rate.

16.5 WHO CONTROLS THE MONEY SUPPLY?

What, then, can be said about the relative importance of the Federal Reserve, the banking system, and the nonbank public in determining the money supply? To begin with, continue to assume that the monetary base is set exogenously by the Federal Reserve. In that case, the reason the Federal Reserve would not have perfect control over the money supply is that, as just explained, the value of the money multiplier depends to some extent on the behavior of the banking system and the public. How great is the loss of control resulting from these sources?

If we consider a short period, such as one to two months, uncertainty about the money multiplier results in a serious loss of money supply control for the Federal Reserve. The variables that affect the money supply and are outside the direct control of the Federal Reserve—the currency/deposit ratio and the excess reserve/deposit ratio—cannot be predicted with precision in the short run. Notice that, although we made simplifying assumptions in our discussion, such as a fixed currency/deposit ratio, in fact the currency/deposit and excess reserve/deposit ratios are *variables* that depend on the decisions of the banking system and the public. These decisions depend, in turn, on the behavior of other economic variables. For example, the excess reserve/deposit ratio depends on the cost of holding such reserves—the interest rate that could be earned on loans and securities. The introduction in the 1980s of accounts that pay a market-determined interest rate created the added complication that the currency/checkable deposit ratio will fluctuate with movement in this rate. Precise control of the money supply would require highly accurate predictions of those variables, among others. Although no one would deny that movements in the monetary base are an important determinant of money growth from month to month, uncertainty concerning short-run variations in the money multiplier makes precise monetary control difficult over such a time horizon.

For a longer period, such as six months to one year, difficulties in monetary control caused by uncertainty about the money multiplier are less serious. Although the Federal Reserve may not be able to predict in a given month the response of the money supply to a given change in the monetary base, policymakers can monitor the month-to-month behavior of the money supply and make the adjustments in the monetary base required

[5]Borrowing in the federal funds market is included in the "Other liabilities and capital" item in Table 16-5.

to achieve the desired *average* rate of growth in the money supply over a period of several months. To see how this averaging might be done, consider the following example.

Suppose that the Federal Reserve wished to achieve a growth rate for the money supply (Ml) of 5 percent for a given calendar year. If no change in the money multiplier was expected, the Federal Reserve could attempt to achieve this target by increasing the monetary base at an annual rate of 5 percent. Assume that in February of that year, the data show that for January, with a 5 percent growth (all growth rates expressed at annual rates) in the monetary base, the money supply grew by only 1 percent. There was a fall in the money multiplier. The Federal Reserve could then, in February and the following months, cause the monetary base to grow by more than 5 percent to offset this fall in the money multiplier. If the action taken in one month was insufficient to get the money supply back on the 5 percent growth path, a further adjustment to the growth rate in the monetary base could be made. Even over periods as long as six months or one year, such control is not perfect. If the Federal Reserve set a target growth rate for the money supply of 5 percent and concentrated all its policy actions on achieving that target, we might end up with growth of 4.8 percent or 5.2 percent. We would not, however, end up with 2 percent or 8 percent.

In actual historical experience, the Federal Reserve has announced growth-rate targets for 6- to 12-month periods and has ended up wide of the mark. If the Federal Reserve *can* control the money supply with a reasonable degree of precision over periods of this length, what explains its failure to hit its own preannounced money growth targets? Why in practice has the Federal Reserve often not closely controlled the money supply?

We previously assumed that the Federal Reserve controlled the monetary base and *concentrated its policy actions* on achieving a money supply target. The reason monetary growth targets are not achieved in practice is that the Federal Reserve is unwilling to concentrate all its efforts on this one policy goal. The Federal Reserve has also been interested in controlling the behavior of other financial market variables, the most important being interest rates. Conflicts arise between hitting target levels of money supply growth and achieving desirable behavior of these other variables. When such conflicts arise, the Federal Reserve has sometimes chosen to miss the money growth target rather than accept what is viewed as the cost of hitting such targets: the resulting undesirable behavior of interest rates.

Figure 16-1*a* reproduces an earlier graph showing the money demand and supply schedules (M^d and M^s) intersecting to determine the equilibrium interest rate r^*. We assume, as we did earlier, that the money supply is exogenous. In terms of this chapter's analysis, we assume that the Federal Reserve uses control of the monetary base to achieve its money supply target (M^*). Also suppose that the equilibrium interest rate r^* shown in Figure 16-1*a* is regarded by the Federal Reserve as the desired level of the interest rate.

Now consider the effects of shifts in the money demand schedule, as shown in Figure 16-1*b*. Such shifts could result from changes in income, which change money demand for a given interest rate. Alternatively, such shifts could represent the effects of actual shifts in the money demand *function*—changes in the amount of money demanded at given levels of both income and the interest rate. Changes in the demand for money might shift the money demand schedule to positions such as M_1^d (an increase in money demand) and M_2^d (a decline in money demand) in Figure 16-1*b*. What will the Federal Reserve do in response to such shifts? If it sticks to its money supply target and maintains the money supply at M^*, the interest rate will move away from r^*, the Federal Reserve's desired level for the interest rate. A decline in money demand

FIGURE 16-1 Interest Rate versus Money Supply Control

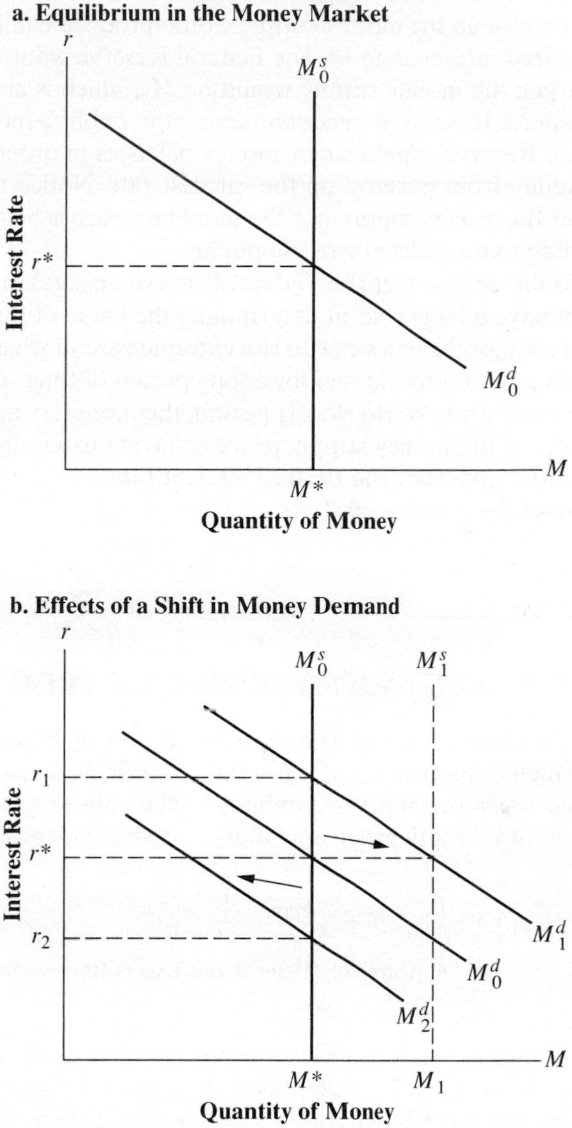

Part *a* shows money market equilibrium with interest rate r^* and money supply M^*. If, however, as shown in part *b*, the money demand function shifts from M_0^d to either M_1^d or M_2^d, then if the Federal Reserve keeps the money supply at M_0^s, the interest rate must diverge from the target level r^*. Alternatively, the Federal Reserve could accommodate the shift in money demand, to M_1^d, for example, by raising the money supply to M_1^s. In this case the money supply target, M^*, will not be achieved.

(a shift in the money demand schedule from M_0^d to M_2^d) would cause the interest rate to fall to r_2; an increase in money demand (a shift in the money demand schedule from M_0^d to M_1^d) would cause an undesirable rise in the interest rate to r_1.

The Federal Reserve can prevent or mitigate these movements in the interest rate only by changing the monetary base and hence the money supply. In the case of an increase in money demand, the Federal Reserve could, by increasing the monetary base, move the money supply to the level given by the M_1^s schedule in Figure 16-1*b*. This increase in the money supply would produce equilibrium in the money market at the desired interest rate r^*. The Federal Reserve would, however, miss the money supply target; the money supply would be M_1, which is above M^*. This is a case in which the Federal Reserve is *accommodating* the public's increased demand for money. The Federal Reserve supplies new money balances in order to keep the increased demand for money from pushing up the interest rate. Notice that with such accommodation, neither the money supply nor the monetary base is being set exogenously. Both are responding to the behavior of the public.

To the degree that the Federal Reserve engages in such accommodation, the public will have a large role in determining the value of the money supply even over periods of six months to a year. In the extreme case in which the Federal Reserve pegs the interest rate at a fixed level for a long period of time, as was done in the United States in the early post–World War II period, the monetary authority plays a completely passive role in the money supply process, having to supply whatever amount of money is required to maintain the desired interest rate.

Read Perspectives 16-1.

PERSPECTIVES 16-1

THE MONEY SUPPLY DURING THE GREAT DEPRESSION

The monetary collapse during the Great Depression, which demonstrates the potential importance of banks and the nonbank public in the money supply process, is illustrated in Figure 16-2. Part *a* of the figure charts the behavior of two factors that affect the value of the money multiplier (m): the currency/deposit ratio (CU/D) and the excess

FIGURE 16-2 Monetary Statistics, 1927–34

a. Currency/Deposit and Excess Reserve/Deposit Ratios

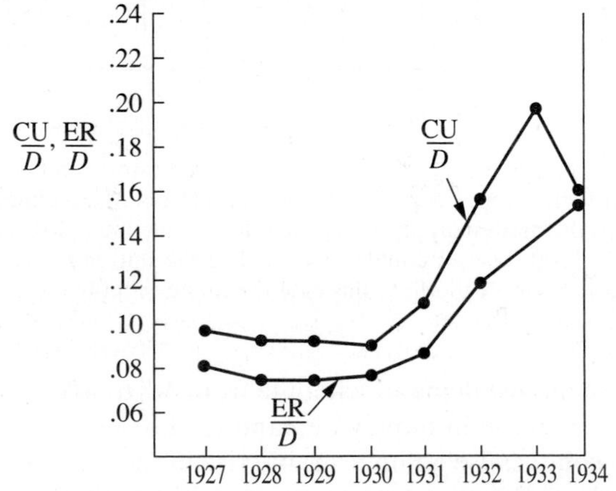

reserve/deposit ratio (ER/D). The first of these is determined by the public and the second by banks. Both of these ratios rose sharply in the early 1930s. The cause of the rise in both ratios was the large number of bank failures; more than 9,000 banks failed between 1929 and 1933. The bank failures caused a loss of confidence in bank deposits. As a consequence, the public held more of their money balances in the form of currency. Banks that did not fail held more excess reserves to ward off "runs" by depositors that could result in the banks' insolvency.

As discussed in this chapter, a rise in either the currency/deposit ratio or the excess reserve/ deposit ratio causes the money multiplier to fall. This effect can be seen from the plot of the money multiplier (m) in part *b* of Figure 16-2. Besides the multiplier, the other factor determining the money supply is the monetary base (MB). Part *b* of the figure shows that the monetary base increased over this period. As can be seen from part *c*, however, the increase in the base was too small to keep the M1 measure of the money supply from declining sharply. Between 1929 and 1933, M1 fell by 26.5 percent. The decline in M2 was even larger (33.3 percent).

The behavior of the Federal Reserve during this period has been criticized, especially by monetarists, who see the decline in the money supply as the cause of the Depression. There is, however, a question of whether the Federal Reserve in the early 1930s had adequate tools to prevent the collapse.[a] In any case, the fall in the money multiplier and the consequent fall in monetary aggregates in the early 1930s do indicate that the public and the banks can be major players in the money supply process.

FIGURE 16-2 *(Continued)*

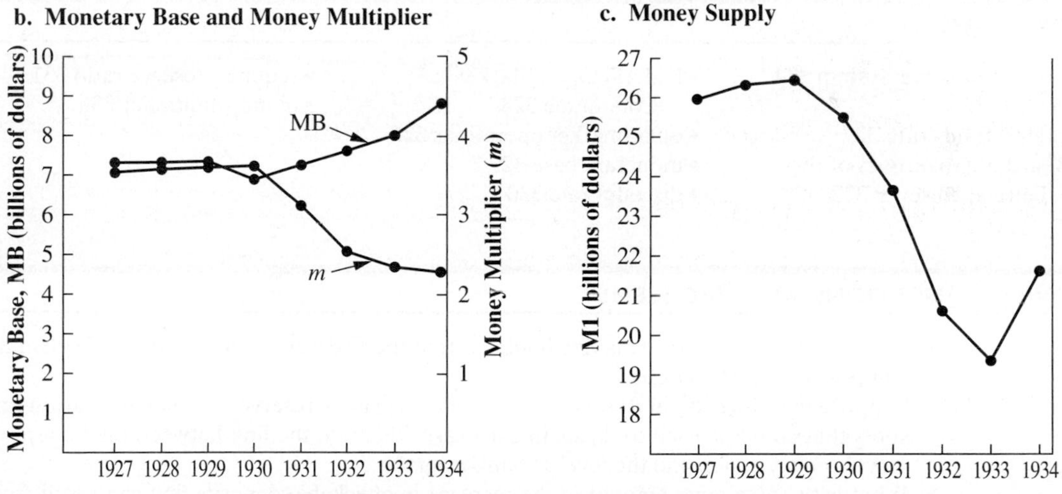

[a]On these issues, see Milton Friedman and Anna Schwartz, *A Monetary History of the United States* (Princeton N.J.: Princeton University Press, 1963); Peter Temin, *Did Monetary Forces Cause the Great Depression?* (New York: Norton, 1976); and Peter Temin, *Lessons from the Great Depression* (Cambridge, Mass.: MIT Press, 1990).

16.6 CONCLUSION

The first four sections of this chapter explained how the Federal Reserve controls the monetary base (currency plus bank reserve deposits) and the link between the monetary base and the money supply. We have seen that, because of uncertainty about the money multiplier, precise Federal Reserve control of the money supply in the very short run (one or two months) is quite difficult. The behavior of the public and the banking system have a substantial influence on such short-term variations in the money supply. Over longer periods (six months to a year, for example), the Federal Reserve can control the money supply with reasonable precision by altering the monetary base to offset any undesirable changes in the money supply as a result of the behavior of the banking system or the nonbank public. When the Federal Reserve does not control the money supply over such long periods, the failure to do so is one of will rather than ability.

The reason the Federal Reserve does not always concentrate solely on controlling the money supply is that to do so would result in what the Federal Reserve regards as undesirable fluctuations in the interest rate. To prevent such undesirable interest-rate movements, the Federal Reserve at times accommodates changes in the public's demand for money, with the effect that the monetary base and the money supply are no longer exogenous. The reasons for the Federal Reserve's concern over fluctuations in interest rates and the relative desirability of controlling interest rates or the money supply are discussed in Chapter 17, where we analyze the Federal Reserve's operating procedures in more detail.

KEY TERMS

- Federal Reserve System 324
- M1, M2 325
- federal funds rate 327
- Board of Governors of the Federal Reserve 327
- Federal Open Market Committee 328
- open-market operations 328
- monetary base 329
- discount rate 330
- required reserve ratio 331
- money multiplier 336

REVIEW QUESTIONS AND PROBLEMS

1. What are the major policymaking bodies within the Federal Reserve System? Explain their composition and functions.
2. Suppose that the Federal Reserve wants to increase bank reserves. Explain the various measures that could be used to do so. In each case, illustrate the link between the Federal Reserve's policy action and the level of bank reserves.
3. What is the maximum amount of the increase in checkable deposits that can result from a $1,000 increase in legal reserves if the required reserve ratio for checkable deposits is 10 percent? Explain how this increase comes about in the banking system. Give two reasons why the actual increase may fall short of the theoretical maximum.
4. Suppose that the level of the required reserve ratio on checkable deposits was 0.10. Also assume that the public's holdings of currency were constant, as were banks' desired excess reserves. Analyze the effects on the money supply of a $1,000 open-market sale of securities by the Federal Reserve. In your answer, explain the role of the banking system in adjusting to this monetary policy action.

5. Explain the concept of the money multiplier. What factors determine the size of the money multiplier?
6. Within the *IS–LM* schedule model used in Chapters 6 and 7, show how income and the interest rate will be affected by each of the following changes:
   a. An increase in the required reserve ratio for checkable deposits.
   b. An open-market sale of securities by the Federal Reserve.
   c. A decrease in the Federal Reserve discount rate.
7. Thc chapter stated that the Federal Reserve would find it very difficult to closely control the rate of growth in the money supply over very short periods but would be able to achieve much greater control over somewhat longer periods. What is the nature of the difficulties in short-run monetary control on a month-to-month basis? Why are these difficulties less serious over longer periods?
8. Within the *IS–LM* schedule model, illustrate the conflict the Federal Reserve faces between trying to control the money supply and trying to achieve "desirable" interest-rate levels.
9. How would the federal funds rate be affected by a Federal Reserve sale of securities in the open market? Would the rate rise or fall? Explain.

CHAPTER 17

Optimal Monetary Policy

Uncertainty is not just an important feature of the monetary policy landscape; it is the defining characteristic of that landscape.

Alan Greenspan

The focus of this chapter is on the optimal conduct of monetary policy. What should central banks *do*? The first section discusses the structure of the U.S. central bank, the Federal Reserve System. We then examine the competing monetary policy strategies from which the Federal Reserve can choose and the choices that have been made. The final section looks at monetary policy in other countries. Dissatisfaction with the conduct of monetary policy under existing legal frameworks has led to institutional changes in the central banks of a number of countries. These reforms address the question of how we can get central banks to "do the right thing."

17.1 THE MONETARY POLICYMAKING PROCESS

As explained in Chapter 16, the key bodies within the Federal Reserve System are the Board of Governors of the Federal Reserve and the Federal Open Market Committee (FOMC). The Board of Governors is composed of seven governors, appointed by the president of the United States, with Senate confirmation, to terms of 14 years, with one of the governors designated by the president as chairman for a four-year term. The FOMC has 12 voting members, the 7 governors and 5 of the presidents of the 12 regional Federal Reserve banks. Presidents of regional Federal Reserve banks serve on a rotating basis, with the exception of the president of the Federal Reserve Bank of New York, who is a permanent voting member.

Also discussed in Chapter 16, open-market operations are the major tool the Federal Reserve uses to conduct monetary policy, and our discussion in this chapter focuses on the behavior of the FOMC.

An important feature of the Federal Reserve's situation is the considerable degree of independence given to the monetary policymaking authority. The 14-year terms for which the governors are appointed and the fact that they cannot be reappointed provide insulation from the political process. The chairman of the Board of Governors is appointed for a four-year term, but this term is not concurrent with that of the president of the United States. Therefore, an incoming president does not immediately get to appoint his choice of chairman. The other members of the FOMC, the regional bank presidents, are appointed by the directors of the regional banks with the approval of the Board of Governors.

In the 1970s, Congress passed legislation requiring periodic reports from the Federal Reserve on the conduct of policy, but monetary policy decisions, such as the target growth rate in the money supply or the target level for interest rates, are not subjects on which Congress legislates. Those decisions are made by the FOMC. Further, the Federal Reserve has a degree of independence from the budget appropriations process because its expenses are paid by its interest earnings on holdings of government securities.

All this is not to say that the Federal Reserve is completely autonomous or that monetary policy is conducted in an apolitical setting. The chairman of the Board of Governors comes up for reappointment (as chairman) during the course of a president's term. For example, President Jimmy Carter declined to reappoint Arthur Burns as chairman in 1978, replacing him with G. William Miller. In 1983, President Ronald Reagan did reappoint Paul Volcker (who was appointed by Carter in 1979 when Miller became Secretary of the Treasury), but only after much speculation that Reagan would prefer his own nominee. In 1987, when Volcker asked not to be considered for a third term as chairman and was replaced by Alan Greenspan, there was speculation that he did so because President Reagan had failed to signal directly that he wanted Volcker to stay. Greenspan, a Republican, came up for and was granted reappointment by President Bill Clinton in 1996 and 2000. Also, because board members often resign before the end of their terms, a president can sometimes make several appointments to the board and, therefore, change the course of monetary policy. By 2007, for example, President George W. Bush had appointed all the members of the board, including Ben Bernanke as chairman.

Perhaps most important, Federal Reserve independence is itself the result of congressional legislation, and the Federal Reserve recognizes that new legislation could weaken this independence. In fact, at times of severe conflict between the Federal Reserve and the administration or Congress over the proper course of monetary policy, bills to limit Federal Reserve independence are often proposed in Congress. The Federal Reserve recognizes this threat and the fact that there are limits on how far it can go in pursuing goals that deviate from those of Congress and the president.

The FOMC meets approximately eight times a year. At these meetings, members review the current domestic and international economic situation. They also consider forecasts of the Federal Reserve staff concerning future economic events. On the basis of this information, they formulate a "directive" to the Open Market Desk at the New York Federal Reserve Bank explaining how open-market operations should be conducted during the period until the next FOMC meeting. The question of an optimal monetary policy strategy can then be viewed as the choice of a directive by the FOMC.

Read Perspectives 17-1.

17.2 COMPETING STRATEGIES FOR MONETARY POLICY: TARGETING MONETARY AGGREGATES OR INTEREST RATES

In one sense, what the Federal Reserve should do is clear. Monetary policy should be conducted in a way that leads to stable growth in aggregate demand. The Federal Reserve should keep demand from growing too rapidly, with resulting inflation, or too slowly, with resulting high unemployment and slow economic growth.

But as the quote from Alan Greenspan that began the chapter indicates, monetary policy must be conducted in an uncertain world. Given that fact, what strategy

PERSPECTIVES 17-1

CENTRAL BANK INDEPENDENCE AND ECONOMIC PERFORMANCE

The degree of central bank independence has at times varied greatly among countries. Some central banks have had virtually complete independence; others have been subservient to their country's finance ministry. The horizontal axis of Figure 17-1 measures central bank independence as of the late 1980s using an index constructed by Alberto Alesina and Lawrence Summers for a sample of industrialized countries.[a] The higher the index value, the greater the independence. The most independent central banks in the sample were those of Switzerland and Germany, followed by the U.S. Federal Reserve. The least independent at that time was the Bank of New Zealand.

The vertical axis of the figure plots the average inflation rate for these countries for the 1955–88 period. Notice the downward slope of the scatter of points; the countries with more independent central banks had lower inflation rates. This better inflation performance has led a number of countries, including New Zealand, the United Kingdom, and Canada, to grant greater independence to their central banks. The European Central Bank set up by the 11 (now 13) countries that have adopted the euro as a common currency was given a high degree of independence. These increases in central bank independence are among the institutional reforms discussed in Section 17.5.

FIGURE 17-1 Central Bank Independence and the Average Inflation Rate; Rankings are from Least (1) to Most (5) Independent

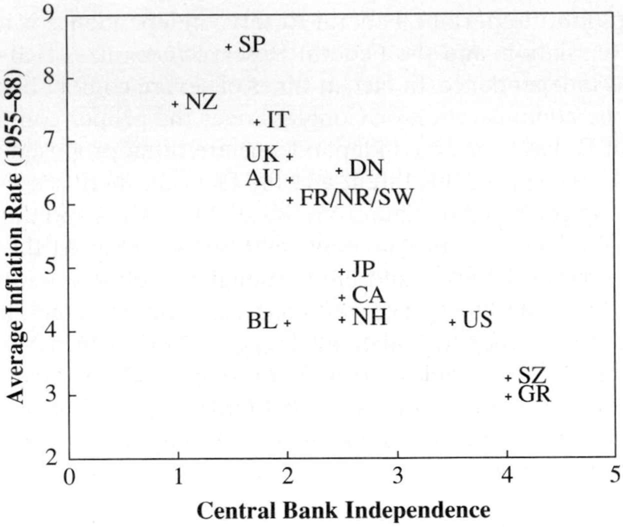

Legend: SP = Spain, NZ = New Zealand, IT = Italy, UK = United Kingdom, AU = Australia, FR = France, NR = Norway, SW = Sweden, DN = Denmark, JP = Japan, CA = Canada, NH = Netherlands, BL = Belgium, US = United States, SZ = Switzerland, GR = Germany

[a] Alberto Alesina and Lawrence Summers, "Central Bank Independence and Macroeconomic Performance," *Journal of Money, Credit and Banking,* 25 (May 1993), pp. 151–62.

will best guide monetary policy? U.S. monetary policy over the past two decades has alternated between strategies that placed primary emphasis on monetary aggregates and, more often, ones that emphasized interest rates. As we saw in the previous chapter, there is a conflict between close control of the money supply and the level of the interest rate; these are competing strategies. In this section we describe how each strategy works in practice. Then we consider the relative merits of the two strategies.

Targeting Monetary Aggregates

The ultimate *targets* that the monetary authority would like to control are macroeconomic goal variables such as the unemployment rate, the inflation rate, and growth in real GDP. Rather than simply adjusting monetary policy instruments, primarily the level of open-market operations, on the basis of past observations on these variables and forecasts of their future behavior, in the short run the Federal Reserve has at times tried to influence these ultimate targets by influencing intermediate target variables.

An intermediate target is a variable that the Federal Reserve controls not because the variable is important in its own right but because, by controlling it, the policymakers believe they are influencing the ultimate policy targets in a predictable way. With a monetary aggregate as an intermediate target, the implicit assumption in Federal Reserve strategy is that, other things being equal, higher rates of growth in the money supply increase inflation while lowering unemployment (raising the level of economic activity) in the short run. Slower monetary growth rates are, again, other things being equal, associated with lower inflation rates and higher short-run rates of unemployment.

What is the rationale for such intermediate targeting? Even if there is a predictable relationship between money growth rates and ultimate economic targets that the Federal Reserve wants to control, why use an intermediate target rather than control the ultimate targets directly? To understand the possible usefulness of the intermediate targeting approach, we must recognize that monetary policy must be made under conditions of imperfect information and, therefore, uncertainty about the behavior of the economy. If the ultimate targets of policy can be observed at less frequent intervals (e.g., quarterly versus weekly) than financial market variables such as interest rates, bank reserves, and monetary aggregates, then as information about such financial market variables becomes available, it can be used to adjust the previous policy setting. The intermediate targeting approach is one way of employing such financial market information.

As implemented by the Federal Reserve, intermediate targeting on a monetary aggregate proceeds as follows. At the beginning of each calendar quarter, the FOMC chooses the money growth rate target that it views as consistent with its ultimate policy goals for the next year. The committee makes this choice based on past data and staff forecasts of the behavior of the economy for given money growth rates. After this choice has been made, monetary policy during the quarter proceeds *as if the chosen money growth target is the ultimate target of monetary policy.* Policy actions within the quarter are aimed at hitting this money target. At the beginning of the next quarter, the money target is reviewed and adjusted on the basis of new forecasts and the experience within the quarter.

Targeting Interest Rate

The alternative to targeting monetary aggregates is to target an interest rate. Interest rate targeting is the current strategy of the Federal Reserve and of the central banks of the other major industrialized economies. We will use current Federal Reserve strategy as an example to explain interest rate targeting.

The Federal Reserve sets a target rate for the federal funds rate. As explained in Chapter 16, the federal funds rate is the rate that banks charge on Interbank loans. In June 2007, for example, the target federal funds rate was 5.25 percent. Like money supply targets, the target for the federal funds rate is chosen at each FOMC meeting to be consistent with hitting the ultimate policy targets.

Once the target federal funds rate is set, the Open Market Desk at the Federal Reserve Bank of New York conducts open-market operations to keep the actual rate at or near the target rate. Thus, for example, if the actual rate began to rise above the target rate, the desk would buy government securities to increase bank reserves. This would increase lending and decrease borrowing in the federal funds market (as explained in Section 16.4) and would bring the rate back down.

Note that in carrying out open-market purchases or sales, the Open Market Desk increases or decreases bank reserves, bank deposits, and therefore the money supply. For example, keeping the federal funds rate at the target level might require large open-market purchases or sales, and therefore large changes in the money supply. The point is that a focus on the interest rate is in fact *an alternative* to targeting a monetary aggregate. The Federal Reserve cannot, in general, do both.

Before going on, it is useful to mention some additional features of the processes of interest rate and money supply control. Short-term interest rates can be observed contemporaneously and closely controlled. The Open Market Desk just looks at a computer screen and sees the current federal funds rate. Therefore, the federal funds rate is a *short-term operating target*. The money supply is only observed with a lag of a week or two and then only with error. If the money supply is a target, some other variable that is more frequently observable, such as the level of the bank reserves, must serve as an operating target. Another point to note is that interest rate targeting focuses on a *short-term* interest rate such as the federal funds rate. Long-term interest rates can also be observed contemporaneously but cannot be closely controlled by central banks. We ignore the distinction between long and short-term rates in the next two sections but return to this point later.

17.3 MONEY VERSUS INTEREST RATE TARGETS IN THE PRESENCE OF SHOCKS

When asked his recipe for monetary policy, Mervyn King, the Governor of the Bank of England, replied that "The secret to good policy is to think through what are the economics of the shocks hitting the economy at present." This is what we will do in this section with reference to the choice of the money supply versus the interest rate as a policy target.

To keep the analysis as simple as possible, we neglect questions such as difficulty of monetary control or the choice of which interest rate to target. These enter our discussion in Section 17.4, where we summarize the relative merits of the two strategies.

FIGURE 17-2 Ideal Case for Targeting a Monetary Aggregate

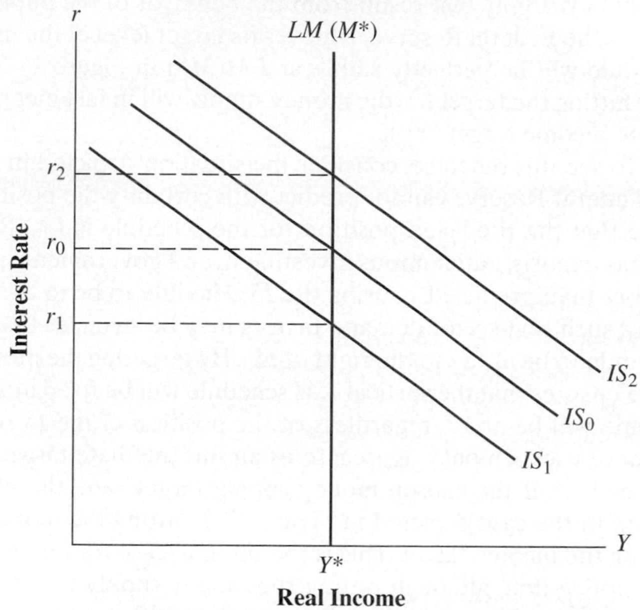

If the demand for money is totally interest-inelastic and perfectly stable, then by hitting the money supply target M^*, the Federal Reserve fixes the vertical LM schedule at $LM(M^*)$. Income will be at the target level Y^* regardless of the IS schedule.

Implications of Targeting a Monetary Aggregate

We begin with the strategy of targeting a monetary aggregate. Here and when we examine the case of interest rate targeting, we employ the *IS–LM* model.

The Ideal Case for Targeting a Monetary Aggregate

We first consider the ideal case for targeting a monetary aggregate, in which this is clearly the optimal strategy. This case is depicted within the *IS–LM* framework in Figure 17-2. Suppose the Federal Reserve has one ultimate target: the level of real income (Y), the desired level of which is Y^*.[1] Also assume that in a given quarter, on the basis of forecasts, the monetary policy authority concludes that the target level of income will be achieved if the money supply is set at M^*.[2]

The LM schedule in Figure 17-2 is vertical, reflecting an assumption that the demand for money is totally interest-inelastic. Money demand depends only on income. Further, we assume that the demand-for-money function is perfectly stable. There are no shifts in the function—no changes in the amount of money demanded for a given

[1] We assume that the Federal Reserve does not want income to fall below Y^* because that would cause excessive unemployment. Levels of income above Y^* are undesirable because of their future inflationary consequences.

[2] An important early analysis of the relative merits of an interest rate versus a monetary aggregate as a target under conditions of uncertainty is William Poole, "Optimal Choice of Monetary Policy Instruments in a Simple Stochastic Macro Model," *Quarterly Journal of Economics,* 84 (May 1970), pp. 197–216.

income level. On the supply side, the Federal Reserve is assumed to offset changes in the money supply that result from the behavior of the public and the banking system. Thus, if the Federal Reserve achieves its target level of the money supply (M^*), the LM schedule will be perfectly stable at $LM(M^*)$ in Figure 17-2. This means that successfully hitting the target for the money supply will in fact mean successfully hitting the ultimate income target (Y^*).

To see this outcome, consider the situation depicted in the figure. We assume that the Federal Reserve cannot predict with certainty the position of the IS schedule. Assume that the predicted position for the schedule is IS_0. Real-sector demand factors such as exports, autonomous investment, and government spending may turn out to be weaker than predicted, causing the IS schedule to be to the left of IS_0, at IS_1. Alternatively, such real-sector demand factors may be stronger than predicted, causing the IS schedule to be at IS_2, to the right of IS_0. By targeting the money supply, the Federal Reserve ensures that the vertical LM schedule will be fixed at $LM(M^*)$, and consequently income will be at Y^*, regardless of the position of the IS schedule. When the Federal Reserve uses a money aggregate as an intermediate target, within the quarter, policy proceeds as if the chosen money supply target *were* the ultimate target of monetary policy. In the case depicted in Figure 17-2, hitting the money supply target guarantees hitting the income target. This is the optimal case for targeting money.

Notice that, although hitting the money supply target guarantees that we will hit the income target, unpredicted shocks that shift the IS schedule will cause volatility in the interest rate. If the position of the IS schedule is IS_1 or IS_2 instead of the Federal Reserve's predicted position, IS_0, the interest rate will be r_1 or r_2 instead of the predicted level, r_0. If the Federal Reserve also had a desired level for the interest rate, for example r_0, the Federal Reserve would miss this interest-rate target.

Less Than Ideal Cases for Targeting a Monetary Aggregate

Figure 17-3 illustrates cases in which achieving the money supply target does not generally mean that the income target will be achieved. In Figure 17-3*a*, we still assume that if the Federal Reserve hits its money supply target, it will fix the position of the LM schedule. For this to be the case, we must assume that the money demand function is perfectly stable. There are no unpredictable shifts in money demand that will shift the LM schedule for a given value of the money supply. In Figure 17-3*a*, we do not assume that money demand is totally interest-inelastic; the LM schedule is therefore not vertical.

In this case, notice that even though the Federal Reserve achieves its target level of the money supply, it will hit the ultimate income target only if the IS schedule is at the predicted position, IS_0—only if the Federal Reserve's real-sector forecast, on which the choice of the money supply target was predicated, was correct. If real-sector demand was weaker than predicted and the IS schedule was at IS_1 in Figure 17-3*a* instead of IS_0, income would be at Y_1, below Y^*. If real-sector demand was stronger than predicted and the IS schedule was at IS_2, income would exceed the target level. In both cases, the income target is missed even though the Federal Reserve hits the money supply target M^*. With a nonvertical LM schedule, fixing the money supply does not fix the level of income.

In Figure 17-3*b*, we consider a case in which the money demand function is not perfectly stable. There are unpredicted shifts in money demand for given levels of

FIGURE 17-3 Less Than Ideal Cases for Targeting a Monetary Aggregate

a. Nonvertical *LM* Schedule

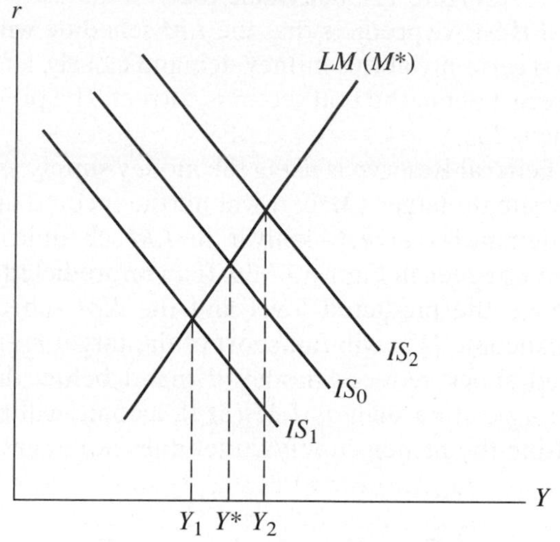

b. Unstable *LM* Schedule

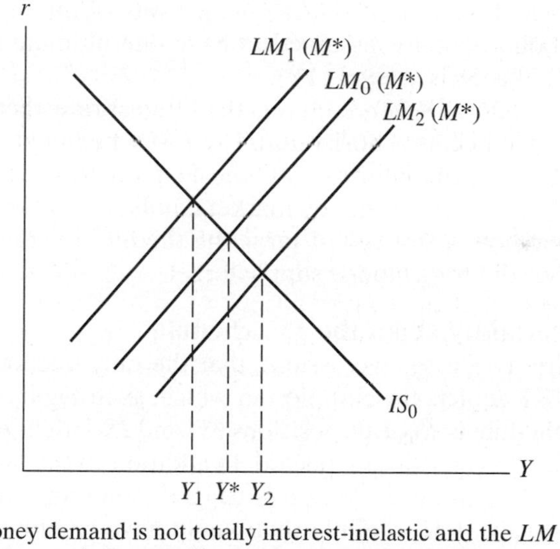

Part *a* shows that, if money demand is not totally interest-inelastic and the *LM* schedule is upward-sloping, hitting the money supply target will cause income to be at the target level Y^* only if the *IS* schedule is at the predicted position IS_0. If, because of unpredicted shocks, the *IS* schedule is instead at IS_1 or IS_2, income will be away from Y^*, at Y_1 or Y_2, even though M is at M^*. In part *b*, we assume that the Federal Reserve hits the money supply target M^*, which, on the basis of its forecast of money demand, should set the *LM* schedule at LM_0 (M^*) and hit the income target Y^*. If, because of an unpredicted shock to the money demand function, the *LM* schedule shifts to either $LM_1(M^*)$ or $LM_2(M^*)$, income will be at Y_1 or Y_2 and the income target will be missed even if the money supply is at the target level M^*.

income and the interest rate. Such shocks to money demand shift the *LM* schedule. In this case, even if the Federal Reserve hits its money supply target, the *LM* schedule will not be fixed. In Figure 17-3*b*, assume that, on the basis of a forecast of money demand, the Federal Reserve predicts that the *LM* schedule will be at $LM_0(M^*)$. To isolate the effects of uncertainty about money demand clearly, let us assume that the Federal Reserve's forecast about the real sector is correct: The predicted and actual position of the *IS* schedule is IS_0.

If the Federal Reserve is using the money supply as an intermediate target and hits the money supply target (M^*), it will hit the income target (Y^*) only if the prediction of money demand is correct—only if the *LM* schedule is at $LM_0(M^*)$ as predicted. This outcome can be seen in Figure 17-3*b*. If an unpredicted shock increases the demand for money above the predicted level and the *LM* schedule is at $LM_1(M^*)$ instead of $LM_0(M^*)$, income (Y_1) will fall short of the target level.[3] In the reverse case, when an unpredicted shock reduces money demand below the predicted level and the *LM* curve is at a position such as $LM_2(M^*)$, income will be at Y_2, above the target level. Again, hitting the money supply target does not guarantee that the income target will be hit.

Implications of Targeting the Interest Rate

Next consider a strategy of targeting the rate of interest. As with a money supply target, the policymaker is assumed to have one ultimate target, that of keeping real income (Y) at a desired level (Y^*).

If the Federal Reserve targets the interest rate, then in the *IS–LM* framework the *LM* schedule becomes horizontal. The *LM* schedule depicts equilibrium in the money market. To peg the interest rate, the Federal Reserve supplies whatever amount of money is necessary for money market equilibrium at the target interest rate.

To see how a strategy of targeting the interest rate works, we consider the same cases as we did for a money supply target.

Uncertainty about the *IS* Schedule

In the first two cases, we assume that the only uncertainty is about the *IS* schedule. Figure 17-4 depicts the situation in which, as in Figure 17-2, the predicted position of the *IS* schedule is IS_0. But positions IS_1 and IS_2 might occur, respectively, if demand is weaker or stronger than expected. In addition to the horizontal *LM* schedule, which is relevant when the interest rate is pegged (solid line), we show (as a dashed line) the position of the *LM* schedule that would have resulted if we had targeted the money supply (at M^*). In Figure 17-4, we assume that money demand is totally interest-inelastic (zero interest elasticity). Therefore, if the money supply were the intermediate target, the *LM* schedule would be vertical.

We see from Figure 17-4 that, with the interest rate targeted at r^*, we will hit the income target, Y^*, only if the *IS* schedule turns out to be in the predicted position IS_0. If, for example, business investment demand were lower than predicted and the *IS* schedule were at IS_1, income would fall below the desired level (to $Y_{r,1}$). In the case depicted

[3]A shock that reduces (or increases) money demand is a shift in the money demand function that reduces (or increases) the quantity of money demanded for a given level of income and the rate of interest. The way this shifts the *LM* schedule is explained in section 6.2.

FIGURE 17-4 Targeting the Interest Rate with *IS* Uncertainty: Zero Interest Elasticity of Money Demand

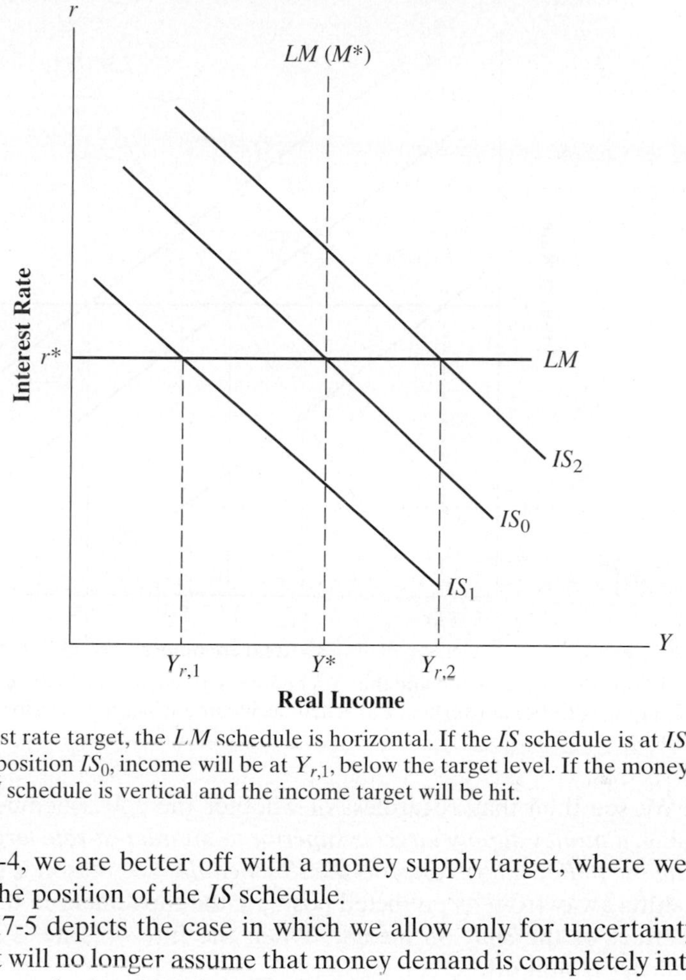

With an interest rate target, the LM schedule is horizontal. If the IS schedule is at IS_1 instead of at the predicted position IS_0, income will be at $Y_{r,1}$, below the target level. If the money supply is the target, the LM schedule is vertical and the income target will be hit.

in Figure 17-4, we are better off with a money supply target, where we stay at Y^* regardless of the position of the IS schedule.

Figure 17-5 depicts the case in which we allow only for uncertainty about the IS schedule but will no longer assume that money demand is completely interest-inelastic. (This is the case depicted in Figure 17-3*a*.) The assumption about the interest elasticity of money demand has no effect on the LM schedule when the interest rate is the target. That LM schedule (the solid LM line in the figure) is horizontal because the Federal Reserve supplies whatever money is required to keep the interest rate at r^*. The LM schedule with a money supply target, shown as a dashed line in Figure 17-5, $LM(M^*)$, will be upward-sloping, not vertical.

Again, the predicted position of the IS schedule is IS_0, but the schedule may turn out actually to be at IS_1 or IS_2, respectively, if private-sector demand is weaker or stronger than predicted. As in Figure 17-4, the money supply target is superior to the interest rate in keeping income close to Y^* when the IS schedule is not at the predicted level. If the IS schedule turns out to be at IS_1 or IS_2, income will be at Y_1 or Y_2, respectively, with a money supply target. With an interest-rate target, income would be at $Y_{r,1}$ or $Y_{r,2}$, respectively, for the same positions of the IS schedule; both levels are farther from Y^*.

FIGURE 17-5 Targeting the Interest Rate with *IS* Uncertainty: Nonzero Interest Elasticity of Money Demand

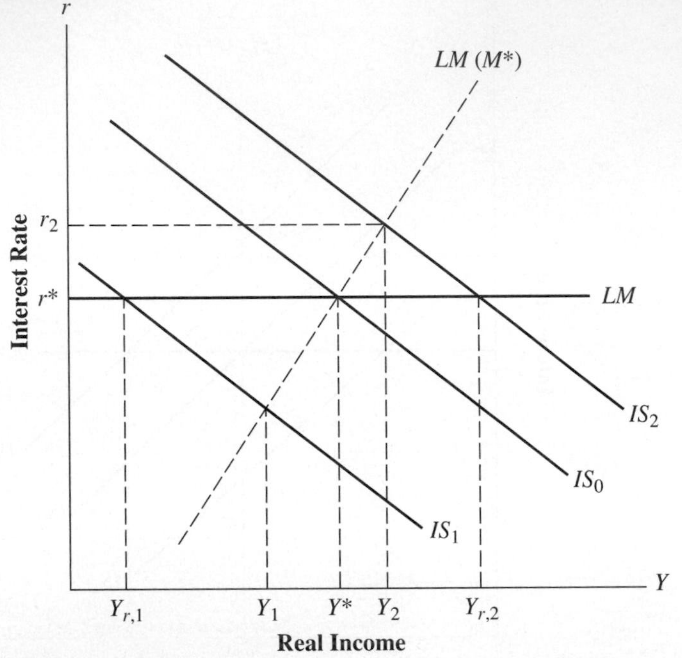

If the interest rate is targeted and the *IS* schedule is at IS_1, income will be at $Y_{r,1}$. If the money supply is the target, with the nonvertical *LM* schedule, income will also fall below the target level, but by less, to Y_1.

We see then that, regardless of whether the *LM* schedule is vertical or upward-sloping, *a money supply target is superior to an interest-rate target when the uncertainty facing the policymaker concerns the IS schedule.* The reason is that, when the *IS* schedule shifts away from its predicted position, the movement in the interest rate *dampens* the effect of the shift on income. When the interest rate is targeted, this *monetary dampener* is shut off.

Consider the effects of an autonomous rise in investment demand (e.g., a shift from IS_0 to IS_2 in Figure 17-5). If the money supply is the target, as the rise in investment causes income to rise, money demand rises and, with a fixed money supply, the interest rate must rise (to r_2 in Figure 17-5). The rise in the interest rate will work against the autonomous rise in demand and cause investment to rise by less than it otherwise would. If the Federal Reserve is targeting the interest rate, this will not happen. As income increases, to keep the interest rate at r^*, the Federal Reserve must carry out open-market purchases to expand the money supply by enough to satisfy the increased demand for money.

Uncertainty About Money Demand

Figure 17-6 depicts the case in which money demand is not perfectly stable (the case shown in Figure 17-3*b*). With the interest rate as a target, the *LM* schedule is horizontal and does *not* shift when there is a shift in the money demand function. For example,

FIGURE 17-6 Targeting the Interest Rate with *LM* Uncertainty

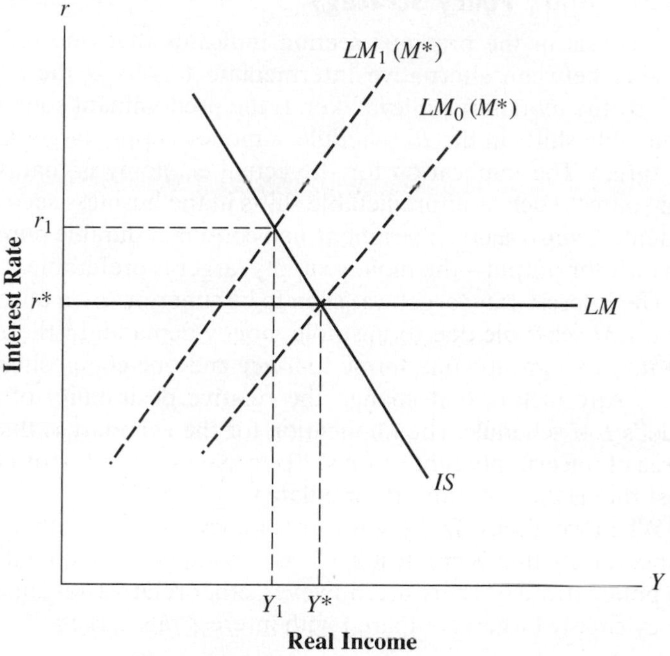

If the interest rate is targeted, the *LM* schedule is horizontal and does not shift when there is a shock to money demand. The money demand shock does not displace income from the target level. If the money supply is the target, a positive shock to money demand will shift the *LM* schedule from $LM_0(M^*)$ to $LM_1(M^*)$; income will fall below the target level to Y_1.

if a positive shock (a desirable new type of bank deposit) increases the demand for money at a given level of income and the interest rate, the Federal Reserve increases the money supply. Shocks to money demand, therefore, do *not* affect income with an interest-rate target. Real income remains at the target level Y^*.

With a money supply target, however, a positive shock to money demand *does* shift the position of the *LM* schedule away from the predicted level even if the target level of the money supply is achieved. If with the money target, M^*, the expected position of the *LM* schedule were the dashed line $LM_0(M^*)$, then a positive shock to money demand would shift the schedule to $LM_1(M^*)$. The interest rate would be pushed up to r_1, and income would fall to Y_1, below Y^*.

We see, then, that *if uncertainty centers on instability in money demand, an interest-rate target is preferable to a money supply target.* If the interest rate is the target, the real sector (output market) is *insulated* from shocks to money demand; the money supply adjusts to maintain the target level of the interest rate. In the case of a money supply target, the shock to money demand *does* affect the interest rate, and therefore income is displaced.

17.4 THE RELATIVE MERITS OF THE TWO STRATEGIES

What can we conclude about the relative advantages and disadvantages of a monetary aggregate versus an interest rate as a target for monetary policy?

The Sources of Uncertainty and the Choice of a Monetary Policy Strategy

The analysis in the previous section indicates that one important consideration in choosing between alternative intermediate targets is the source of the uncertainty faced by the monetary policymaker. If the predominant sources of uncertainty are unpredictable shifts in the *IS* schedule, a money supply target is superior to an interest-rate target. The implication for the actual economy is that, when uncertainty comes from sources such as unpredictable shifts in the business sector's investment spending, residential construction investment, and consumer durable purchases—all private-sector demands for output—the money supply target is preferable.

The interest-rate target was seen to be superior when uncertainty stems from shifts in the *LM* schedule due to unstable money demand. In the *IS–LM* model, assets are split into two groups: one termed *money* and one composite, nonmoney asset termed *bonds*. Any factors that change the relative desirability of the two assets shift the model's *LM* schedule. The implication for the economy is that when the predominant source of uncertainty centers on shifts in asset demands (for bonds and money), the interest rate is the superior intermediate target.

When we discuss Federal Reserve policy, we will see that consideration of the type of uncertainty that is greatest has been an important element in the choice of a monetary policy strategy. There are, however, other relative advantages and disadvantages of money supply targets compared with interest-rate targets.

Other Considerations

One additional advantage of a money supply target is that a strong commitment to keeping the money supply growing in a target range ensures control over inflation for medium-term periods (e.g., three to five years). Virtually all economists believe that sustained high inflation requires accommodating money supply growth. Strict adherence to money supply targets severely limits monetary accommodation.

Advocates of targeting monetary aggregates argue that by setting low, noninflationary money supply targets *and hitting them*, the Federal Reserve can build up anti-inflationary *credibility*; the public starts to believe that the Federal Reserve will carry out announced policies. This strategy has the advantage of keeping inflationary expectations at a low level.

An interest-rate target provides no such anti-inflationary guarantee. If the central bank targets the interest rate, it must increase the money supply to accommodate any increases in money demand. If a potentially inflationary boom begins, money demand will increase (higher transactions demand). The Federal Reserve may then unwittingly be led to fuel inflation by an accommodating increase in the money supply. This outcome is not inevitable; the Federal Reserve may instead observe the potential for inflation and raise the target level of the interest rate. The point here is that simply hitting a particular interest-rate target does not provide the inflation protection that targeting monetary aggregates does.

However, some considerations favor an interest-rate target. For one thing, interest rates are not subject to the measurement problems concerning monetary aggregates (e.g., new deposit types). Interest-rate stability, at least in the short run, is another advantage cited for an interest-rate target. To hit a money supply target, the Federal Reserve must let the interest rate fluctuate freely (see Figure 17-3*a*). Some economists and central bankers worry that a freely fluctuating interest rate will cause instability in financial markets. Recall, for example, that sharp rises in interest rates cause significant capital losses on bonds. These losses may, in turn, lead to instability for financial institutions that hold large quantities of bonds.

A final point concerning the interest-rate strategy is related to the distinction between short and long-term interest rates. The interest rate that the Federal Reserve or other central banks can control is a short-term interest rate such as the federal funds rate in the United States. But private-sector spending may depend more heavily on long-term interest rates such as corporate bond rates. Long-term interest rates are subject to many other influences beyond central bank control. In particular, long-term bonds will be around for many years and will compete in the market with short-term financial assets that will be issued in the future. Thus, in assessing the desirability of long-term bonds, investors will take into account expectations of future short-term interest rates and therefore expectations of future monetary policy actions. The market for long-term bonds, like the stock market, is a *forward*-looking market and beyond the central bank's close control. This was illustrated between 2004 and 2006, when the Federal Reserve raised the federal funds rate from 1 percent to 5.25 percent while the 10-year government bond rate failed to budge.

17.5 THE EVOLUTION OF FEDERAL RESERVE STRATEGY

In the years since 1970, the Federal Reserve's emphasis has varied between controlling the interest rate and targeting monetary aggregates. Twice during this time period, the Federal Reserve dramatically shifted from one strategy to another. Federal Reserve strategy, as well as the reasons for these shifts, can be best explained by looking at several subperiods.

1970–79: Targeting the Federal Funds Rate

The Federal Reserve's strategy in the 1970s was one of interest rate targeting. As is the case today, the rate targeted was the federal funds rate. The strategy was not to peg the rate at any one value for a long period of time. The target rate was reconsidered at each FOMC meeting and adjusted as deemed necessary in light of the state of the economy.

Monetary aggregates were not neglected in the 1970s. Although on a month-to-month basis the interest-rate target was given precedence, the Federal Reserve attempted to hit annual targets for growth in several money supply measures. Still, at several points in the 1970s, the Federal Reserve allowed money supply targets to be missed in order to achieve the interest-rate target.

1979–82: Targeting Monetary Aggregates

The first dramatic switch in Federal Reserve policy came on October 6, 1979, when the Federal Reserve abandoned targeting the federal funds rate. It instead adopted a strategy of directly controlling bank reserves to increase its ability to hit target ranges for growth in the monetary aggregates (M1 and M2). Our analysis in this chapter is helpful for understanding the reasons for this shift.

In 1979, the inflation rate was accelerating rapidly. The recession that many had expected during the year had not materialized. There was a great deal of uncertainty about the strength of private-sector demand. In this situation of uncertainty about the *IS* schedule, a monetary aggregate is superior to an interest rate as an intermediate target.

We have also seen that a commitment to achieving low money growth targets virtually guarantees that high inflation rates will not be sustained, whereas a nominal interest-rate target provides no such guarantee. With the inflation rate over 13 percent in 1979, this was a considerable advantage.

1982–2007: A Gradual Return to Federal Funds Rate Targeting

Although the Federal Reserve was not entirely successful in hitting money supply targets during the 1979–82 period, most observers credit the shift toward a more restrictive monetary policy in 1979 for the decline in inflation to around 4 percent by 1982, albeit at the cost of a serious recession in 1981–82.

The Federal Reserve, however, abandoned the strategy of intermediate targeting on monetary aggregates in the summer of 1982, the second of the policy shifts. Although it later returned to specifying target growth rates for the M2 aggregate, and in some years for the M1 aggregate as well, these targets did not assume as much importance in the post-1982 period as during 1979–82.

The reason for the deemphasis of monetary aggregates was the breakdown of the money–income relationship that occurred in the 1980s. There was substantial instability in money demand during this period. Swings in money demand did not reflect underlying economic conditions but were more heavily influenced by innovations in the deposit market as deregulation took place and banks offered many new types of deposits.

Instability of money demand, and consequent uncertainty about the *LM* schedule, is the condition that favors the interest rate as an intermediate target. The Federal Reserve was reluctant to go all the way back to the strategy of targeting the federal funds rate, partly because of fears that, as in the 1970s, this strategy would provide insufficient protection from accelerated inflation. Therefore, throughout the 1980s, the Federal Reserve continued to monitor closely the behavior of the broader aggregates, especially M2, to be sure that growth in the money supply was not fast enough to generate inflationary pressure. During the recovery from the 1990–91 recession, however, M2 began also to "misbehave." Despite a climate of low interest rates and economic expansion, the demand for the M2 aggregate grew very slowly. Put differently, M2 velocity grew rapidly. The Federal Reserve responded with a further deemphasis of monetary aggregates. By 1995, monetary policy had returned to a strategy of almost complete concentration on the federal funds rate. This reversion to the monetary policy strategy of the 1970s was made explicit in 1997, when the FOMC policy directive was reworded to set a specific target for the federal funds rate.

1994–2007: A Move toward Greater Transparency

The following is a famous quote from Alan Greenspan, "I know you believe you understand what you think I said, but I am not sure you realize that what you heard is not what I meant." Greenspan was known for his opaqueness. Still, under his leadership the Federal Reserve began to move to greater transparency in 1994. We have just noted that in 1997 the FOMC directive began to set an explicit target for the federal funds rate. Earlier, in 1994, they had begun to issue a press release after each FOMC meeting announcing their actions. Other steps followed. In 1999, they began to announce their perceived "balance of risks," indicating their relative concerns about inflation and output growth. In 2003 they began to make a forward-looking statement about the probable direction of the target federal funds rate over the next one or more meetings. Each of these actions was aimed at providing more guidance to financial markets about current and future monetary policy.[4]

Read Perspectives 17-2.

PERSPECTIVES 17-2

THE TAYLOR RULE

With a strategy of federal funds rate targeting, monetary policy can be represented by an interest-rate *reaction function* that shows the response of the interest rate to the state of the economy. John Taylor, at the time a member of the U.S. Council of Economic Advisors (later Under Secretary of the Treasury for International Affairs), proposed a rule for setting the federal funds rate, which has received a great deal of attention.

The rule Taylor proposed was the following:

$$\text{RF} = \text{pdot} + 0.5(\text{pdot} - \text{pdot}^*) + 0.5(Y - Y^*) + \text{RF}^* \qquad \textbf{(17.1)}$$

where: RF = the federal funds rate
pdot = the inflation rate
Y = real output

and the superscript (*) is the target level for each of these variables.

The rule suggested by Taylor would have the Federal Reserve increase the interest rate automatically by 1 percentage point for each percentage point increase in the inflation rate (the first term in the rule). The federal funds rate would also rise by an additional 0.5 percentage point for each 1 percentage point increase in the inflation rate relative to its target level (pdot*) or in output relative to the target output level (Y^* = potential output). Monetary policy would become more restrictive as inflation rose and more expansionary as output fell, both relative to target levels. The last term in equation (17.1) is the equilibrium *real* federal funds rate, the rate, adjusted for inflation, that would be chosen if both output and inflation were at their target levels.

Much of the attention given to the Taylor rule has come from the fact that equation (17.1) did a good job of tracking the actual behavior of monetary policy in the late 1980s and early 1990s. Did the Federal Reserve perhaps follow something like a Taylor rule during those years? In addition, Taylor argued that had policy followed a Taylor rule, mistakes would have been avoided in earlier years. Policy, he stated, would have been more restrictive during the inflationary 1970s. As a consequence, policy could have been less restrictive in the early 1980s, reducing unemployment during that period.

Discussion of the Taylor rule is one example of the growing interest in monetary policy by rules rather than by the discretion of central bankers. The Taylor rule is not an "optimal rule" but more in the spirit of Milton Friedman's belief that in choosing a course for monetary policy, "The best should not be the enemy of the good."

[a] See John Taylor, "Discretion versus Monetary Policy Rules in Practice," *Carnegie-Rochester Conference Series on Public Policy*, 39 (1993), pp. 195–214.

[4] For a description of these moves toward more transparency in Federal Reserve policy, see William Poole, "How Predictable Is U.S. Macroeconomic Policy?" Federal Reserve Bank of St. Louis *Review* 87 (November–December 2006), pp. 659–68.

17.6 CHANGES IN CENTRAL BANK INSTITUTIONS: RECENT INTERNATIONAL EXPERIENCE

In the United States, monetary policy strategy has changed as the economic environment has varied. The institutional structure of the Federal Reserve has, however, not changed in any significant manner. Other industrialized countries, beginning in the late 1980s, have made major changes in central bank structure. In response to what governments have believed to be subpar macroeconomic performance, many countries have changed the mandates and accountability of their central banks.

The most common change has been to instruct central banks to target inflation as the sole goal of monetary policy. Countries that have adopted inflation targeting as a mandate to their central banks include Canada, New Zealand, the United Kingdom, and Sweden. In addition, the new European Central Bank has adopted inflation targeting.

Read Perspectives 17-3.

In the United States, as in all of those countries, low inflation has always been one monetary policy goal. In the 1990s, these countries decided to make low inflation *the* goal of monetary policy. Why?

time inconsistency problems arise when a future policy plan is no longer optimal at a later date even when no new information has arrived in the meantime

Here we examine two strands in the argument for the move to inflation targeting in many industrialized countries. The first, which grows out of the new classical macroeconomic perspective, is the recognition of **time inconsistency** problems that arise when monetary policy is conducted under discretion. The second involves more pragmatic considerations. Both bring us back to the arguments for rules versus discretion in macroeconomic policy formation.

The Time Inconsistency Problem

Our analysis so far suggests that monetary policy strategy should change over time as the sources of uncertainty facing policymakers vary. This view argues for flexibility, or policy by discretion. Recognition of time inconsistency problems in policy formation, however, lends support to the argument for policy by rules.

A time (or dynamic) inconsistency problem for policy arises when, as Stanley Fischer explains, a "future policy that forms part of an optimal plan formulated at an initial date is no longer optimal from the viewpoint of a later date, even though no new information has appeared in the meantime."[5] In other words, a policy announcement will be time-inconsistent if economic agents know that the policymaker will want to renege on the decision when it comes time to act.

As applied to monetary policy under discretion, the time inconsistency problem arises in the following way.[6] Suppose that, because of some distortion in the economy, social welfare would be increased if output were pushed above the *natural rate*, the

[5] Stanley Fischer, "Rules versus Discretion in Monetary Policy," in Benjamin M. Friedman and Frank H. Hahn, eds., *Handbook in Monetary Economics,* vol. 2 (Amsterdam: North Holland, 1990), pp. 1169–70.

[6] Two important papers on the time inconsistency problem are Finn Kydland and Edward Prescott, "Rules versus Discretion: The Time Inconsistency Problem," *Journal of Political Economy*, 85 (June 1977), pp. 473–91; and Robert J. Barro and David B. Gordon, "Rules, Discretion and Reputation in a Model of Monetary Policy," *Journal of Monetary Economics,* 12 (July 1983), pp. 101–21.

PERSPECTIVES 17-3

INFLATION TARGETING IN PRACTICE: THE NEW ZEALAND EXPERIMENT

After two decades with inflation rates that exceeded the OECD (Organization for Economic Cooperation and Development) average and growth rates that fell short of that average, the New Zealand government adopted a very strict form of inflation targeting in 1990. The main provisions for monetary policy are contained in the Reserve Bank Act of 1989.[a] The act specifies that the prime function of the Reserve Bank of New Zealand is to "maintain stability in the general level of prices." The act mandates that the Minister of Finance and the Governor of the Reserve Bank agree on monetary policy targets to achieve price stability. For much of the 1990s, price stability was defined as an inflation rate within a range of 0–2 percent. In 1997, this definition was loosened a bit to a range of 0–3 percent.

The Reserve Bank is then free to choose the strategy that it believes will best achieve the policy target. If inflation is not kept within the target range, the Reserve Bank governor is subject to dismissal. Thus, the arrangement has been termed a *performance contract* for a central bank.

This type of inflation targeting leaves the Reserve Bank with little leeway to directly pursue goals other than price stability; that constraint was the point of the act. The fact that the inflation target is a range does provide some scope to consider economic growth or unemployment in formulating monetary policy. Also, the policy agreement between the Minister of Finance and the Reserve Bank allows for adjustment of the target inflation range if there are special circumstances such as changes in indirect taxes (sales and excise taxes) or the international terms of trade that cause one-time changes in the price level. Still, the New Zealand plan is a very strict form of inflation targeting.

After an initial adjustment period, the performance of the New Zealand economy under inflation targeting has been reasonably good. Real GDP growth and inflation both averaged between 2 and 3 percent on an annual basis over 1992–2006. This compares favorably with the performance of most industrialized nations.

Inflation targeting has not, however, been without difficulties. The focus of monetary policy on inflation has at times forced the Reserve Bank to raise New Zealand's short-term interest rates to very high levels. This, in turn, leads to large capital inflows and a resulting appreciation of the New Zealand dollar. The high value of the currency is hard on exporters. In mid-2007, with the short-term interest rate at 8 percent, for example, the Reserve Bank intervened in the currency market to try to lower the value of the New Zealand dollar in response to complaints from exporters.

[a]The New Zealand experiment with inflation targeting is described in Andreas Fischer, "New Zealand's Experience with Inflation Targets," in Leonardo Leiderman and Lars E. O. Swensson, eds., *Inflation Targets* (Paris: Center for Economic Policy Research, 1995).

level discussed in Chapter 10 that is consistent with price and wage setters accurately predicting the price level. A possible reason might be that noncompetitive features of labor and product markets lead to a natural rate that is too low (e.g., the outcome in the insider–outsider model in Section 12.2). Moreover, suppose that, consistent with the rational expectations hypothesis examined in Chapter 11, the monetary policymaker can push output above the natural rate by generating an unexpectedly high rate of monetary growth. Finally, assume that, as is reasonable, wages and prices are set at less frequent intervals (e.g., annually) than monetary policy actions are implemented (e.g., monthly).

At one point, say the beginning of the year, the policymaker might announce a noninflationary rate of monetary growth of zero. But later in the year, after wages and prices have been set, the policymaker may find it optimal to renege on this commitment and generate "surprise" inflation. Firms and workers, knowing the policymaker's preferences (remember, here we assume rational expectations), will anticipate that the policymaker will *cheat*. There will be no output gain. There will be higher inflation than at zero money growth. The time inconsistency problem causes an inflationary bias in monetary policy.

If, instead, a monetary policy rule bound the policymaker to a zero inflation policy, society would be better off than with policy by discretion. The rule would give credibility to the policymaker's announcement.

It is worth noting that time inconsistency problems exist in contexts other than monetary policy. For example, consider the patent system. Before inventions are made, it is optimal to offer patents as an incentive. After the new devices exist, however, it is optimal to invalidate the patents to avoid monopolistic inefficiency.

Other Arguments for Inflation Targeting

Are time inconsistency problems important for monetary policy? Alan Blinder, a Princeton professor and former vice chairman of the Board of Governors of the Federal Reserve, argues that academic economists who have worried about time inconsistency problems "have been loudly barking up the wrong tree."[7] Or perhaps, as is the problem with dogs, they are barking up what used to be the right tree.

Time inconsistency problems might partly explain inflationary monetary policies during the 1970s. By the late 1980s and into the early 1990s, however, disinflation had been achieved in most industrialized countries. An analogy to the patent system might be useful here. The industrialized countries do not renege on patents even though, in the short run, doing so may seem optimal. They do not because of reputational considerations, the way their present actions affect the behavior of future generations of inventors. Central banks might have learned a lesson from the 1970s and, though tempted to achieve output gains through surprise inflation, now tell themselves, "just don't do it."

If not to solve the time inconsistency problem, what is the motivation behind the move to inflation-targeting rules in many countries? There seem to be more pragmatic considerations. One is to reduce the effect of political pressures on central

[7]Alan S. Blinder, "What Central Bankers Could Learn from Academics and Vice Versa," *Journal of Economic Perspectives,* 11 (Spring 1997), p. 13.

banks. In general, the move to inflation targeting coincides with a grant of greater independence to central banks. Giving the central bank independent control of its policy instruments and a clear mandate to target inflation greatly limits a government's ability to manipulate monetary policy for political purposes. Even before explicit inflation-targeting rules were common, central bank independence was positively associated with lower inflation (see Perspectives 17-1). Inflation targeting is a way of giving central banks independence for their *instruments* while keeping them accountable for *goals*.

Another pragmatic motivation for the move to inflation targeting in several countries was that they experienced problems similar to those the United States experienced with monetary aggregates as intermediate targets. As the money–income relationship became more unstable, they relied more on short-term interest rates to implement monetary policy. As explained previously, this approach leaves monetary policy without any anchor that serves as an anti-inflation guarantee. Direct targeting on inflation provides such an anchor.

Read Perspectives 17-4.

PERSPECTIVES 17-4

INFLATION TARGETING FOR THE UNITED STATES: THREE INFLUENTIAL VIEWS

While, as we have seen, many central banks adopted inflation targeting in the post-1990 period, under the leadership of Alan Greenspan the U.S. Federal Reserve did not. As the quote that begins this chapter indicates, Greenspan sees uncertainty as the key feature of the monetary policy process. What he asks, then, are the "implications of this largely irreducible uncertainty for the conduct of monetary policy?"[a] In answer to this question, he suggests that monetary policy must follow a risk-management approach: "[T]he conduct of monetary policy in the United States at its core involves crucial elements of risk management, a process that requires an understanding of the many sources of risk and uncertainty that policymakers face." Moreover, Greenspan believes that "risk management often involves significant judgment on the part of policymakers, as we evaluate the risks of different events and the probability that our actions will alter those risks."

To critics who argue that such an approach is too undisciplined—too judgmental, seemingly discretionary, and difficult to explain, he responds that tying "policy to the prescriptions of a formal rule is unlikely to lead to an improvement in economic performance." Greenspan's view on this issue reflects an earlier statement of his that after a long search for a rule for monetary policy, he concluded that an ideal rule lies in the realm of Don Quixote.

Ben Bernanke, who succeeded Greenspan as Chairman of the Board of Governors, is an advocate of inflation targeting. He does not favor a rigid rule for monetary policy. Instead, he sees inflation targeting as a framework within which monetary policy can be conducted. Specifically, he has suggested that the Federal Reserve announce an inflation target that he terms an "optimal long-run inflation rate (OLIR)." This would be a target for the long term, not any particular quarter or year. "Variation in actual inflation around the OLIR over the business cycle would be expected and acceptable."[b]

The main benefit Bernanke sees from this type of inflation targeting is "a reduction of uncertainty in financial markets and in the economy more broadly." The transparency and thus the credibility of monetary policy would be enhanced. Moreover, setting an inflation target "would serve as a reminder to policymakers to keep one eye on the long run at the same time they are reacting to current developments in the economy." An inflation targeting regime that concentrated on the long run would, in his view, improve the communication and conduct of policy "without the costs feared by those concerned about a potential loss of flexibility."

Benjamin Friedman of Harvard University has written many in influential articles and conference papers on monetary policy over the past 35 years. He is highly critical of inflation targeting as "best-practice monetary policy." He does not agree that inflation targeting increases the transparency of monetary policy. He believes that inflation targeting "is a framework not for communicating the central bank's goals and policies but for obscuring them. In crucial ways it is not a window but a screen. It promotes not transparency . . . but opaqueness."[c] The problem is that the Federal Reserve has a dual mandate: to pursue high employment as well as price stability. To quantify one goal only begs the question of how the policymaker acts in a framework of multiple goals.

Perhaps worse, in Friedman's view, is that "the inflation-targeting framework affects not just what the central bank says but what it does." He fears that the regime will skew policy too much toward inflation fighting, with too little regard given to employment and output matters—"the point is, language matter."

[a]The quotes in this perspective from Alan Greenspan are taken from his Opening Remarks at the Federal Reserve Bank of Kansas City Conference on Monetary Policy and Uncertainty, August 2003, as published in the conference proceedings.

[b]Quotes here from Ben Bernanke are taken from his comments at a Federal Reserve Bank of St. Louis Conference on Inflation Targeting: Prospects and Problems, as published in the Federal Reserve Bank of St. Louis *Review* (July–August 2004).

[c]Quotes from Benjamin Friedman are from his commentary at the same conference as those from Bernanke, as published in the same volume.

17.7 CONCLUSION

This chapter has considered questions of optimal monetary policy: how should central banks conduct monetary policy? In the case of U.S. Federal Reserve, in practice, strategy has varied with the degree of emphasis placed on the money supply versus the interest rate. Over the past two decades in response to changes in economic conditions, most importantly the growing instability of the money–income relationship, the Federal Reserve has moved to interest-rate targeting. The same has been true in other major industrialized nations. The move to interest-rate targeting has left monetary policy without an anti-inflation *anchor* such as that provided by a money supply target. In response, many central banks, though not the Federal Reserve, have moved to a strategy of inflation targeting.

For both inflation-targeting central banks and noninflation targeters, recent years have been fairly successful ones. Average inflation rates among the industrialized economies have been kept low, and business cycle fluctuations have been moderate by historical standards. Not everyone attributes these developments to improved monetary policy, but central bankers have had more cause for patting each other on the back during the past decade than in the 1970s and 1980s.

KEY TERMS

- time inconsistency 262

REVIEW QUESTIONS AND PROBLEMS

1. What is the Federal Open Market Committee (FOMC)? What role does this committee play in formulating monetary policy?
2. Evaluate the arguments for and against intermediate targeting of a monetary aggregate.
3. Using the *IS–LM* framework, analyze whether an increase in the instability of the money demand function would increase or decrease the desirability of intermediate targeting a monetary aggregate.
4. Describe the shift that took place in Federal Reserve policy in 1979. Explain the reasons for this shift.
5. Suppose that the Federal Reserve is using an interest rate as a target, while real income is the ultimate policy target, and there is an autonomous drop in business investment that the Federal Reserve had not predicted. Use the *IS–LM* model to show the effects of the shock. Would income have been affected less or more if the Federal Reserve had been using a money supply target?
6. Explain the time inconsistency problem as it pertains to monetary policy.
7. What relationship do you see between the problems many countries have experienced with money supply targeting and the move to inflation targeting?
8. Suppose that the *IS* schedule is vertical because the interest elasticity of investment demand is zero; investment is completely insensitive to the interest rate. Is it still true that for the case of *IS* shocks a money-supply target is preferable to an interest-rate target? Show why or why not using the *IS–LM* graphs.
9. Currently, no major central bank closely targets the money supply. Why do you think this is the case? Still, no major central bank completely ignores money growth numbers. Why?

CHAPTER 18

Fiscal Policy

For outside observers, it has been hard to keep track of U.S. fiscal policy debates over recent decades. Debates in the 1980s and 1990s focused on the budget deficit. Large deficits were perceived as a problem, but were they "the devil at the door" or, as others suggested, more like "termites in the basement"? Before the question had been answered, budget agreements between the Clinton administration and Republican-controlled Congresses, abetted by rapid economic growth, had by the late 1990s replaced the budget deficits with surpluses, and even larger surpluses were projected for the medium-term future. By 2001, however, the budget had again fallen into deficit. By 2004, the deficit had risen to levels not seen since the 1980s. Over a 10-year period, projections had shifted from a cumulative surplus of over $3 trillion to a deficit of over $2 trillion, a swing of over $5 trillion. Further complicating the budget picture are long-term projections of huge federal budget deficits due to the demands on Medicare and Social Security that have come as the baby boomer generation has reached retirement age.

In Parts II and III, we looked at fiscal policy along with monetary policy as tools to stabilize the economy. How does this stabilization role fit in with the other considerations that have been driving the federal budget? What role, for example, have stabilization considerations played in causing the dramatic swings in budget deficits we have just described? One long-standing question we address is whether fiscal policy is best conducted by rules, such as ones that would mandate balancing the federal budget (in some sense), or whether policy is best left to the discretion of policymakers.

We begin by examining the goals of fiscal policy and the possibility that the goals of the policymakers, who in the case of fiscal policy are Congress and the administration, may diverge from the goals of the public. Some economists use this divergence to argue in favor of constraining the behavior of fiscal policymakers. Next, we consider the behavior of the federal budget over the post–World War II period and the relationship between the federal budget and the state of the economy. With this background, we examine the long-standing objections of Keynesian economists to balanced-budget rules, as well as the perhaps confusing positions of different schools of economists on proper budget policies for the first part of the twenty-first century.

18.1 THE GOALS OF MACROECONOMIC POLICY

What are the goals of macroeconomic policy? Low unemployment and price stability are agreed-upon policy goals, although, as we saw in Parts II and III, there is considerable disagreement about the ability of policymakers to achieve those goals by managing aggregate demand. There are also differences of opinion about the relative weights that should be assigned to each goal. Economic growth is a third policy goal and one that is closely related to the low unemployment goal, because creating new jobs requires a growing economy.

Suppose we agree that the goals of macroeconomic policy should be to achieve target levels of inflation, unemployment, and economic growth. The question of optimal conduct of macroeconomic policy would then be how to set the policy *instruments*, variables such as the levels of government spending and various tax rates in the case of fiscal policy, in order to come as close as possible to the target levels. One way of formulating this problem is to assume that the policymaker minimizes a social-loss function of the following form:

$$L = a_1(U - U^*)^2 + a_2(\dot{P} - \dot{P}^*)^2 + a_3(\dot{Y} - \dot{Y}^*)^2 \quad a_1, a_2, a_3 > 0 \qquad \textbf{(18.1)}$$

In this equation, L measures the social loss that results when macroeconomic goal variables deviate from target levels—for example, the costs of excessively high unemployment. The goal variables themselves are the level of unemployment (U), the inflation rate ($\dot{P}$), and the rate of growth in real income ($\dot{Y}$). The target levels for these variables are U^*, $\dot{P}^*$, and $\dot{Y}^*$, respectively. In the form given by equation (18.1), the loss in social welfare depends on the squared deviations of the goal variables from the target levels. The social loss from a given increase in the deviation of a goal variable from the target level increases as we get further from the target level; large deviations from desired levels receive especially heavy weights. The coefficients a_1, a_2, and a_3 in equation (18.1) represent the relative weights attached to the different targets.

Equation (18.1) is only one representation of the social-welfare-loss function that is relevant to macroeconomic policies. The key assumption for formulating this type of optimal policy is simply that the policymaker minimizes some social-welfare-loss function. The problem is, then, to find the setting of the instruments that results in the minimum loss. We can further investigate whether various rules, such as a balanced-budget rule, outperform more activist policy prescriptions.

18.2 THE GOALS OF MACROECONOMIC POLICYMAKERS

There is literature questioning the realism of the preceding formulation of the optimal policy question. We examine two strands in this literature: the **public-choice** view and the **partisan theory**. A common element in both is that politics plays a more important role in macroeconomic policymaking than was suggested in the previous section.

public choice is the application to macroeconomic policymaking of the microeconomic theory of how decisions are made

The Public-Choice View

Proponents of the public-choice view argue that macroeconomic policymakers act to maximize their own welfare rather than to maximize the social good.[1] As Gordon Tullock, a proponent of the public-choice view, puts it: "Bureaucrats are like other men. . . . If bureaucrats are ordinary men, they will make most (not all) [of] their decisions in terms of what benefits them, not society as a whole."[2] Rather than a social-welfare-loss function as given by equation (18.1), the

[1]More generally, the term *public choice* is defined as the application of choice-theoretic economic analysis to political decision making. See, for example, Dennis Mueller, *Public Choice II* (Cambridge: Cambridge University Press, 1989).

[2]Gordon Tullock, *The Vote Motive* (London: Institute of Economic Affairs, 1976).

partisan theory views macroeconomic policy outcomes as the result of ideologically motivated decisions by leaders of different political parties. The parties represent constituencies with different preferences concerning macroeconomic variables

relevant loss function is one that measures variables of direct importance to policymakers. In the case of elected officials making fiscal policy decisions, this alternative approach emphasizes votes as the central goal motivating policymakers.

Within the public-choice framework, one representation of the appropriate loss function that the policymaker seeks to minimize is

$$L = b_1 \text{VL} \qquad b_1 > 0 \tag{18.2}$$

where VL is vote loss and b_1 is the weight given to votes lost. Macroeconomic goal variables enter the picture because the behavior of the economy affects votes.

For example, vote loss might be represented as

$$\text{VL} = c_0 + c_1(U - U^*)^2 + c_2(\dot{P} - \dot{P}^*)^2 + c_3(\dot{Y} - \dot{Y}^*)^2 \tag{18.3}$$

The macroeconomic goal variables and their target levels are the same as in equation (18.1). The parameters c_1, c_2, and c_3 represent the loss of votes resulting from deviations of the macroeconomic goal variables from target levels. This particular representation assumes that vote loss depends on the squared deviation from the target level, assuming as before that an especially heavy weight is given to large deviations from desired target levels. The c_0 parameter represents other influences on voter behavior (e.g., foreign policy questions or other domestic issues).

Suppose that vote loss is given by equation (18.3) and the policymaker acts to minimize vote loss; the relevant loss function is equation (18.2). Will policy actions differ from those that would result from the policymaker's acting altruistically and minimizing the social loss function given by equation (18.1)? Advocates of the public-choice view of policymaker behavior argue that they would. To see why, we examine the condition necessary for behavior in the two cases to be the same and then explain why the advocates of the public-choice view do not believe that this condition will be met in practice.

First, assume that voter behavior is governed by what we may call *collective rationality*, meaning that vote loss because of macroeconomic concerns is proportional to social-welfare loss. This assumption means that when macroeconomic variables affect voting behavior, voters reward or punish incumbent politicians, depending on their performance in minimizing social-welfare loss. In this case, the optimal strategy to minimize vote loss [equation (18.2)] is to minimize social-welfare loss [equation (18.1)]. As has been recognized in the public-choice literature, when this type of collective rationality does not exist, the behavior of the vote-maximizing policymaker will deviate from social-welfare–maximizing behavior.

The following hypotheses about voter behavior have been advanced in the public-choice literature.[3]

1. ***Voters are myopic.*** Advocates of the public-choice view argue that voting behavior is heavily influenced by the state of the economy over the few quarters before the election and that the level of economic activity, not the inflation rate,

[3]See, for example, James M. Buchanan and Richard E. Wagner, *Democracy in Deficit* (New York: Academic Press, 1977); and Edward R. Tufte, *Political Control of the Economy* (Princeton, N.J.: Princeton University Press, 1978).

is the variable whose recent performance determines votes. "Incumbent politicians desire re-election and they believe that a booming preelection economy will help to achieve it."[4] As a consequence, we have a *political business cycle*, in which aggregate demand is overly stimulative in the preelection period, with inflation following after the election.

2. ***Unemployment is more likely to result in vote loss than is inflation.*** The inflation process is presumed to be sufficiently complex and ill-understood so that politicians can avoid blame for inflation more easily than they can avoid blame for unemployment: "At any moment of time the inflation is blamed on events which are not under the control of the political party in power, but ideally on the political party previously in power."[5] As a consequence, advocates of the public-choice view argue that elected officials rarely respond to inflation with restrictive policies, but respond to unemployment with expansionary policies. Thus, the fiscal policy process has an inflationary bias.[6]
3. ***A deficit bias exists in the budget process.*** This inflationary bias is reinforced by the inherent bias toward budget deficits that public-choice writers believe to be characteristic of democratic government fiscal policies. For example, as James Buchanan and Richard Wagner argue:

> Elected politicians enjoy spending public monies on projects that yield some demonstrable benefits to their constituents. They do not enjoy imposing taxes on these same constituents. The pre-Keynesian norm of budget balance served to constrain spending proclivities so as to keep governmental outlays roughly within the revenue limits generated by taxes. The Keynesian destruction of this norm, without an adequate replacement, effectively removed the constraint. Predictably politicians responded by increasing spending more than tax revenues, by creating budget deficits as a normal course of events.[7]

If we accept the public-choice characterization, how can this deficit bias in the fiscal policy process be corrected? Buchanan and Wagner believe that we must restore the "pre-Keynesian norm of budget balance"; we must avoid *all* deficit spending. They favor an amendment to the U.S. Constitution that would require Congress and the president to balance the budget.

Also, because new or expanded government spending programs would have to be financed by new taxes in a balanced-budget system, the growth of the government sector would be curtailed by such an amendment. In the public-choice view, optimal fiscal policy does not mean designing policies to stabilize the macroeconomy. Rather, it involves imposing rules on the policymakers that eliminate the destabilizing effects of deficit spending.

[4]Tufte, *Political Control of the Economy*, p. 5.

[5]Morris Perlman, "Party Politics and Bureaucracy in Economic Policy," in Tullock, *The Vote Motive*, p. 69.

[6]In terms of equations (18.1) and (18.3), these public-choice writers argue that, although inflation does cause significant social-welfare loss [a_2 in equation (18.1) may be large], inflation does not result in much of a vote loss [c_2 is small in equation (18.3)]. Therefore, the vote-maximizing policymaker does not respond.

[7]Buchanan and Wagner, *Democracy in Deficit*, pp. 93–94.

The Partisan Theory

In the partisan theory, political factors also affect macroeconomic policy. The partisan theory, however, views politicians as *ideologically* motivated leaders of competing parties.[8] The parties, in turn, represent different constituencies with different preferences concerning macroeconomic outcomes. In the most common partisan party model, there is a liberal (or labor) party and a conservative party. The liberal party primarily emphasizes full employment and income redistribution, whereas the conservative party values price stability most highly.

Rather than a political business cycle, the partisan theory predicts *party cycles* as macroeconomic policy varies, depending on which party is in power. In the case of fiscal policy, for example, the partisan model predicts that if the liberal party gains office, government spending will rise as politicians try to stimulate demand and, hence, employment. Government outlays may also rise as transfer payments are increased to redistribute income. In most circumstances, the more expansionary fiscal policy will also increase the rate of inflation. If the liberal party loses office at a later point, fiscal policy will become more restrictive as the conservatives seek to combat inflation. Unemployment will rise, and a recession may result.

Like political business cycles, partisan party cycles would be prevented or at least mitigated by a fiscal policy rule such as a balanced-budget rule. A rule for fiscal policy would limit the ability of each party to pursue its goals by manipulating aggregate demand. Also, redistribution efforts by the liberal party would be hampered if any increased transfer payments required new taxes.

Read Perspectives 18-1.

Public-Choice and Partisan Theories from the Perspective of 2007

By 1999, as previously noted, the U.S. federal budget had moved into surplus. Many European countries had also successfully reduced or eliminated their budget deficits. One might have thought that the public in these countries had become more sophisticated in understanding the inflationary consequences of deficits and other long-run costs of accumulating a large national debt. Perhaps politicians came to believe that large deficits would cause them to lose votes. This view is consistent with polls in the United States before the 1996 and 2000 elections, which showed that voters ranked deficit reduction ahead of tax cuts as an issue.

In Europe, countries that had adopted the euro as a common currency had bound themselves to the Stability Pact, which limited deficits to 3 percent of GDP except during recessions. In other countries such as New Zealand, rules were legislated for monetary and fiscal policy. Have political factors ceased to influence government budget deficits because of a combination of increased voter sophistication and budget rules?

From the perspective of 2007, things look different. The U.S. budget went from surplus to deficit after 2001 in part due to a recession. The subsequent recovery reduced the size of the deficit somewhat, but there is little prospect of budget balance in the

[8] An early contribution to the partisan theory is Douglas Hibbs, "Political Parties and Macroeconomic Policy," *The American Political Science Review*, 71 (December 1977), pp. 1467–87. See also Thomas Havrilesky, "A Partisan Theory of Fiscal and Monetary Regimes," *Journal of Money, Credit and Banking*, 19 (August 1987), pp. 308–25; and Alberto Alesina, "Macroeconomics and Politics," *NBER Macroeconomics Annual* (1988), pp. 13–61.

PERSPECTIVES 18-1

RATIONAL EXPECTATIONS AND THE PARTISAN THEORY

The original forms of the political business cycle model and the partisan model did not assume that expectations were *rational* and therefore forward-looking. In fact, the myopic behavior of voters in the political business cycle model is clearly inconsistent with rational expectations.

The partisan model of fiscal policy has been modified to assume rational expectations in a paper by Alberto Alesina and Jeffrey Sachs.[a] As before, assume that there are two parties—one liberal, whose constituency is most concerned about unemployment, and one conservative, with a constituency most concerned about inflation.

The economic environment assumed by Alesina and Sachs is consistent with the new classical model in that expectations are rational, but it has the Keynesian element that money wages are set by contracts of several years' duration. In such a framework, elections create uncertainty concerning the future behavior of the inflation rate and therefore the money wage demands workers (or their unions) should make.

Consider the situation in the year before a general election. Workers might presume that if the liberals win, the inflation rate will be high, say 7 percent, whereas if the conservatives win, it will be low, say 3 percent. Even if expectations are rational, the best the workers can do is form an expectation of inflation that is a weighted average of the two possible outcomes. If they view the election of each party as equally likely, then in the previous example the rational expectation of inflation would be 5 percent. Firms and workers would set money wages accordingly.

Now consider what will happen after the election. If the liberals win, the actual inflation rate (7 percent) will exceed the expected inflation rate (5 percent) on the basis of which money wages were set. This higher rate will cause rapid expansion of output as firms hire additional workers because the real wage will be unexpectedly low for firms. On the other hand, if the conservatives win, actual inflation (3 percent) will be below expected inflation (5 percent), and money wages will have been set too high. Unemployment will rise, and a recession may ensue.

Party cycles are then possible in the partisan model even if expectations are rational. The theory predicts that recessions are most likely in the first couple of years following the election of a conservative president—a prediction borne out in 1981–82 and again in 1990–91. The accelerated pace of the recovery from the 1990–91 recession after President George H. W. Bush was defeated by Bill Clinton in 1992 is also consistent with the rational expectations version of the partisan theory.

Later evidence does not entirely support the Alesina and Sachs hypothesis, but there are relatively few observations that provide a test. Administrations have changed party only every 4, 8, or sometimes 12 years during the sample period considered. The replacement of the Democratic Clinton administration by the Republican administration of George W. Bush provided a fresh observation to test the hypothesis. A recession did begin in March 2001. This may be too soon after the election to fit the party cycles hypothesis.

[a] Alberto Alesina and Jeffrey Sachs, "Political Parties and the Business Cycle in the United States, 1948–84," *Journal of Money, Credit and Banking*, 20 (February 1988), pp. 63–82.

near term. In Europe, many countries exceeded the 3 percent deficit limit set by the Stability Pact. The pact was made more flexible in 2005. Part of the problem is cyclical. Slow growth or recession lowers tax revenues and increases the deficit. In the United States, however, by 2007 none of the deficit was due to cyclical factors. The economy was running at potential output according to calculations by the Congressional Budget Office. Over the period from 2001 to 2007, new domestic spending projects such as the prescription drug benefit added to Medicare were popular. Tax cuts were also popular. Vice President Richard Cheney was quoted as saying that "Reagan proved that deficits don't matter" (politically, that is).

The public-choice models we have considered are too simple to explain all the swings in budget policy that have taken place. Still, public-choice theorists continue to stress political motivations as prime movers of fiscal policy decisions.

18.3 THE FEDERAL BUDGET

Two fiscal policy variables, government spending and tax collections, were included in the theoretical models in Parts II and III. The government spending variable (G) was the spending component in national income, which includes federal, state, and local government spending on *currently produced goods and services*. The tax variable (T) included federal, state, and local tax collections. Fiscal stabilization policy is conducted by the federal government. States and localities have limited ability to run budget deficits. The levels for both their expenditures and revenues are determined by local needs and the state of the economy rather than being set to influence macroeconomic goals. Therefore, our discussion here focuses on federal budget policy.

Figure 18-1 shows figures for total federal government receipts and outlays (expenditures) for 1959–2006. The figures reveal rapid growth in both outlays and revenues. But the economy has been growing as well. Figure 18-2 expresses budget items as percentages of GDP. There we can see more clearly how the government has grown relative to the economy as a whole.

In 1929, the federal government was a very small portion of the economy. Total federal outlays were less than 3 percent of GDP. Fiscal policy changes typically represented minor budget adjustments and were of little significance to the overall economy. Both outlays and revenues rose modestly during the 1930s. Outlays rose more than revenues, with a resulting budget deficit. World War II brought a huge expansion in government military spending that was only partly paid for by increasing tax revenues. Budget deficits in the early 1940s rose as high as 25 percent of GDP, the equivalent of a deficit of over $2,500 billion in terms of GDP today. These huge wartime deficits were financed by massive sales of bonds to the public.

After the war, both expenditures and tax revenues declined as proportions of GDP. Yet federal government outlays did not fall back to the level of the 1920s. By the mid-1950s, both outlays and revenues were about 17 to 18 percent of GDP. The federal government had taken on new domestic functions in the 1930s: regulatory agencies, the Social Security system, price supports for agricultural products, and rural electrification, among others. Also, with the onset of the Cold War in the late 1940s, defense spending remained high even in peacetime.

FIGURE 18-1 Federal Receipts and Outlays, Annual, 1959–2006

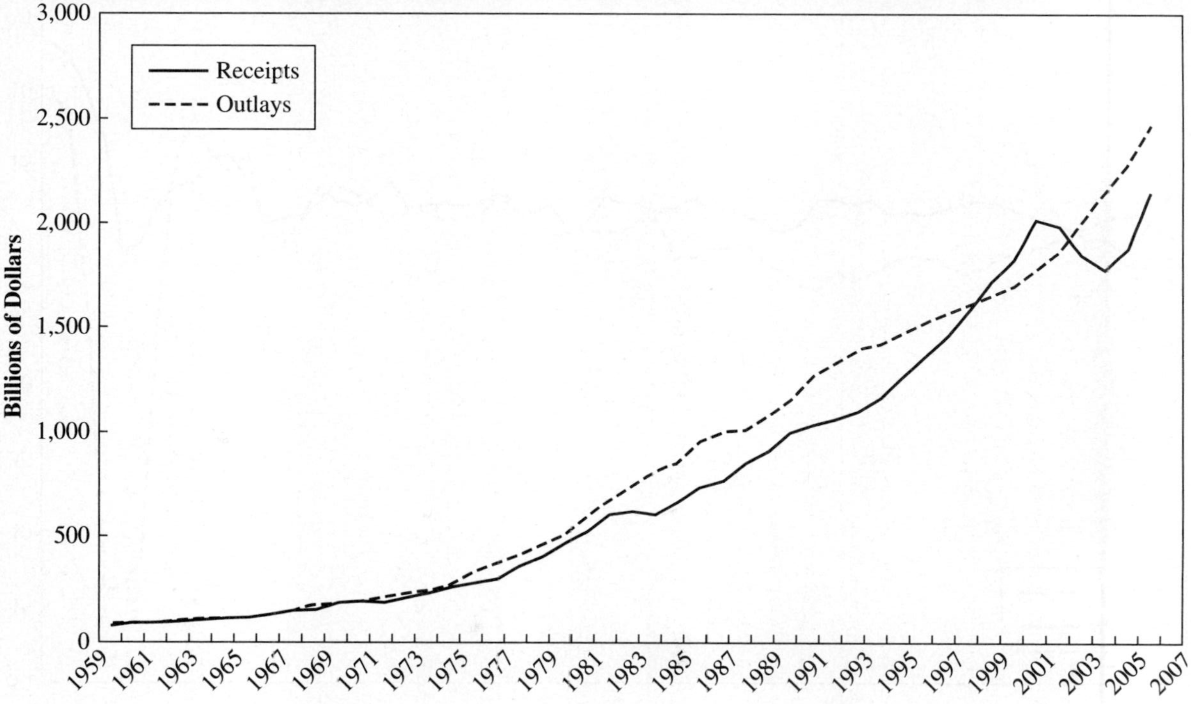

FIGURE 18-2 Outlays and Receipts of the Federal Government as Percentage of GDP, Selected Years

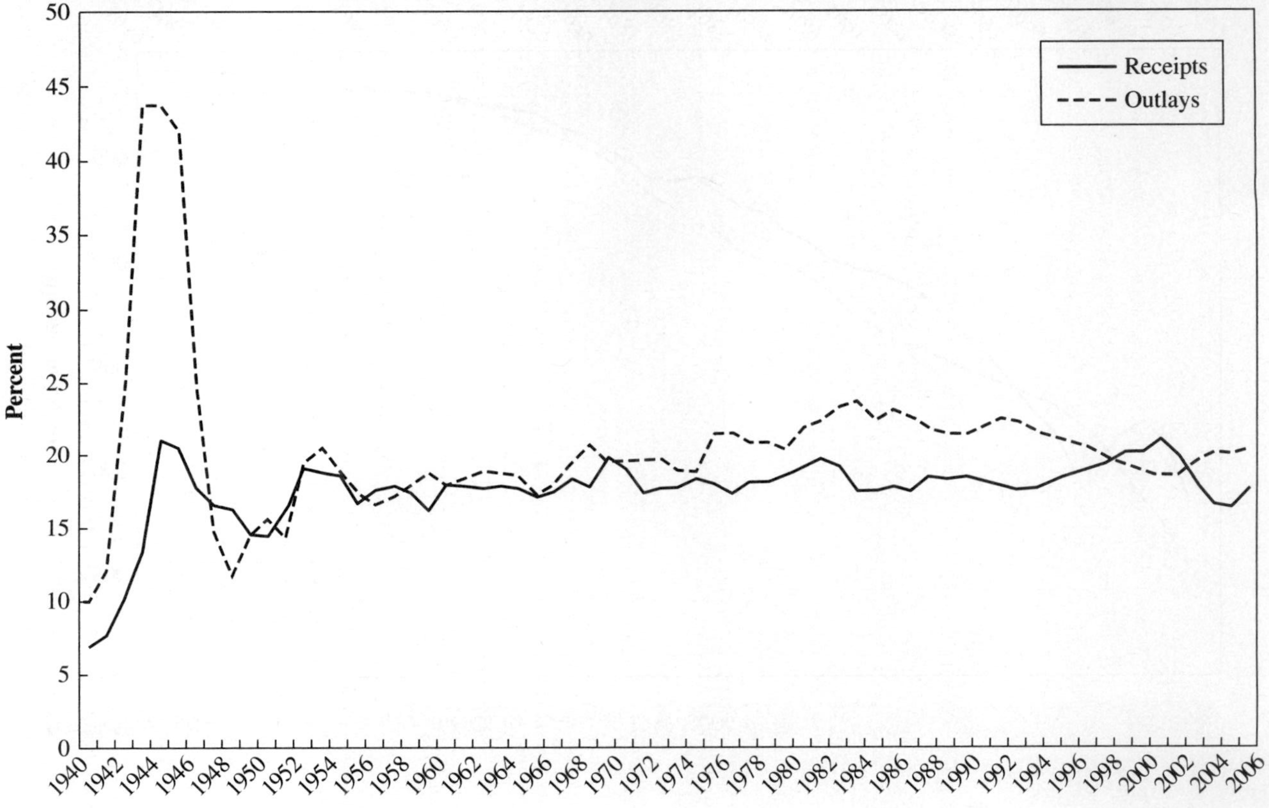

Figure 18-2 shows that in recent decades outlays have grown as a percentage of GDP, from 17 percent in 1955 to 21 percent in 2006. Tax revenues have grown as well, but beginning in the late 1960s, growth in spending outpaced revenue growth, resulting in persistent deficits. The budget deficit grew rapidly during the first half of the 1980s as the upward trend in outlays continued, while revenues declined slightly as a percentage of GDP. By 1986, the budget deficit was roughly 5 percent of GDP. The deficit declined in absolute terms from 1987 to 1989 and then rose sharply with the recession of 1990–91. The deficit began to decline again in 1993 when the Clinton deficit reduction plan was passed. Further spending cuts virtually eliminated the deficit by early 1998, and the budget then moved into surplus. Strong economic growth as well as legislative actions led to the budget turnaround.

After 2001, the budget returned to deficit. As was the case in the late 1990s, both legislative actions, primarily the tax cuts in the Bush administration, and the state of the economy, in this case the recession in 2001, were responsible for the turnaround in the budget. By 2007, however, the deficit was completely the result of tax cuts and policy changes that increased federal outlays, the economy having returned to potential output.

Read Perspectives 18-2.

PERSPECTIVES 18-2

STATE AND LOCAL GOVERNMENT FINANCES

Although our discussion of fiscal stabilization policy centers on the federal government, we should not ignore state and local government finances. State and local government spending currently accounts for 8 percent of GDP, up from 6 percent in 1959. State and local governments spend to provide for education, public welfare, health and hospitals, correction and police protection, and additional services. They raise funds through taxation of income (both corporate and individual), sales, and property. They also levy various fees and specific taxes, such as those on alcohol and tobacco.

Between 2002 and 2004, state and local governments, especially states, faced their most severe budget crisis since World War II. Figure 18-3 shows state and local government revenues and expenditures for the years since 1960. Typically, during recession periods (1974–75, 1981–82, 1990–91) revenues fell short of expenditures. The shortfall was especially sharp following the 2001 recession, and even when an economic recovery began, state finances continued to worsen. By fiscal 2003, states faced prospective deficits of approximately $80 billion, forcing spending cuts and increases in taxes and fees, including tuition at state universities. States have limited ability to run deficits. Most have rules that force them to balance their budget, even though some can carry over deficits for a year or resort to other short-run stopgaps.[a] These spending cuts and tax increases acted as a dampener on the recovery of aggregate demand.

[a]It is the current operating budget that must be balanced. States and localities do issue bonds to fund investment projects such as school or hospital construction. Also, there are exceptions to budget balancing; California approved a bond issue of $15 billion to finance a budget deficit in 2004.

FIGURE 18-3 State and Local Government Receipts and Expenditures, 1960–2006

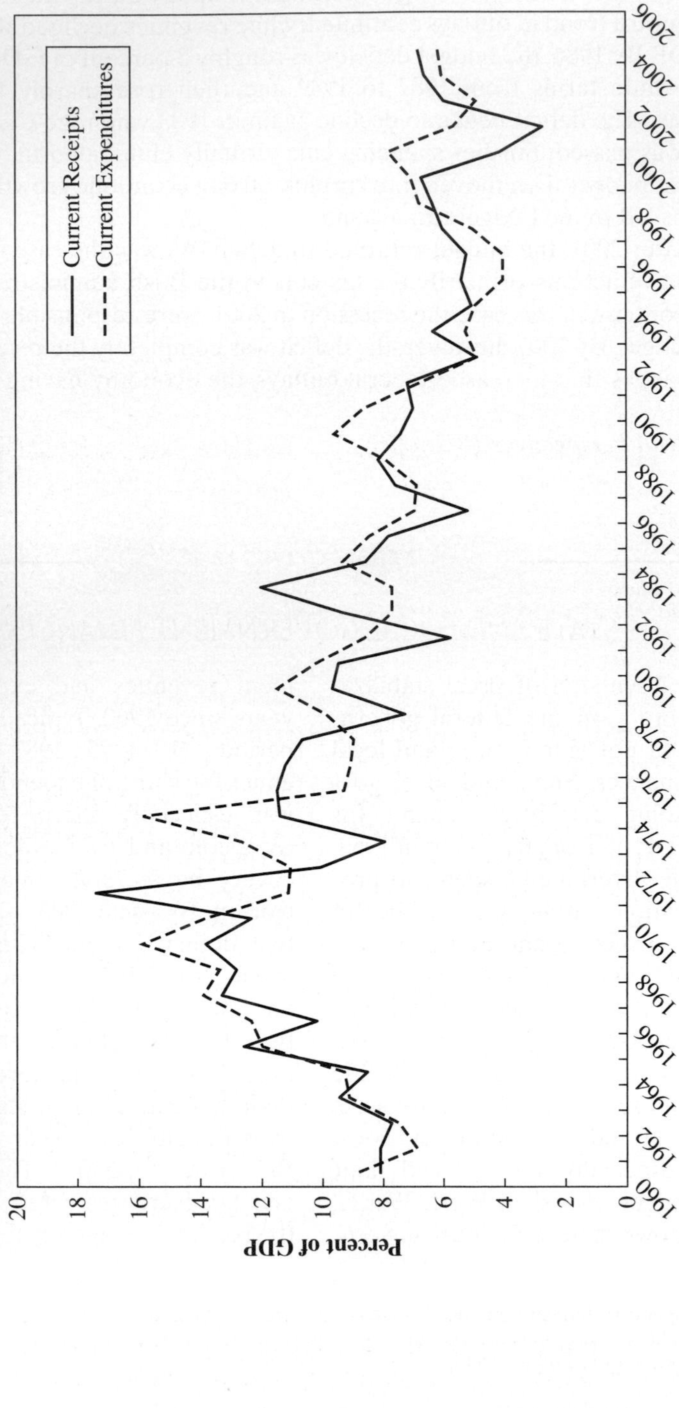

What caused this crisis in state and local government finance, and what are likely trends for the future? Figure 18-3 shows that revenues declined sharply after the recession began in 2001. This was part of the problem but, as noted, this is typical in a recession. What was different this time is that as revenues increased during the prosperous 1990s, states responded by cutting both income and sales taxes. Notice that revenues had begun to fall before the recession began. Spending continued to rise. Some components, in particular Medicaid spending, are entitlements that states are largely unable to reduce. The budget crisis was primarily the result of states financing permanent tax cuts with revenue from the temporarily booming economy and then finding it difficult to reduce spending.

What about the current and future budget situation for states and localities? From Figure 18.3, it can be seen that state and local government revenues rebounded sharply beginning in 2003 due to the strong national economy. By 2007, many state budgets had projected surpluses. Several states, including Texas and Florida, were contemplating large cuts in their property taxes. Still, there are reasons for pessimism about longer-term developments in state and local finances. The growth in Medicaid and state worker health insurance costs will put pressure on the spending side. Many states and localities also have underfunded pension plans. On the revenue side, the move to a service economy has eroded the revenue from state and local sales taxes that fall primarily on goods.

18.4 THE ECONOMY AND THE FEDERAL BUDGET: THE CONCEPT OF AUTOMATIC FISCAL STABILIZERS

The federal budget contains three variables that affect macroeconomic goals: government purchases of goods and services, government transfer payments (including grants to state and local governments), and government tax receipts. In Part II, we analyzed the effects of changes in government spending, specifically spending on goods and services, and changes in tax receipts. In the models in Part II, tax receipts were net of transfers (taxes minus transfer payments); therefore, an increase in transfer payments would have the same effects in those models as a reduction in taxes. In this section, we reverse the question and instead ask how the level of income affects items in the federal budget. In doing so, we see how changes in the government budget work as an **automatic stabilizer** for economic activity.

automatic stabilizers are changes in taxes and government transfer payments that occur when the level of income changes

To consider how the level of economic activity affects the government budget, we modify our assumption that the level of net tax receipts (gross tax receipts minus government transfer payments) is exogenous. An assumption more in line with reality is that the schedule of tax *rates* is exogenously set, but the level of net tax collections depends on the level of income. With this assumption, we can specify *net* tax collections (T) as determined by the following *net tax function*:

$$T = t_0 + t_1 Y, \qquad t_0 < 0, \qquad t_1 > 0 \tag{18.4}$$

where t_0 and t_1 are parameters that represent the tax structure. The parameter t_1 is the marginal net tax rate, giving the increase in taxes (net of transfers) per unit increase in income ($t_1 = \Delta T/\Delta Y$). If the tax system were proportional, the other parameter in the tax function, t_0, would be zero; tax collections would be equal to t_1Y. Notice that, in this case, the marginal tax rate $\Delta T/\Delta Y$ would be equal to the average tax rate T/Y, both being given by t_1. The negative term t_0 allows the average tax rate, which from equation (18.4) would be $(t_0/Y + t_1)$, to be less than the marginal rate (t_1). The negative term t_0 also allows for transfers, negative net taxes, which are independent of income.

From the net tax function given by equation (18.4), it follows that as income rises, net tax collections increase and the government budget surplus increases (or the deficit declines); at higher levels of economic activity, more tax revenue is collected at any given set of tax rates. The positive relationship between *net* tax revenues and economic activity also results from the fact that transfer payments, especially payments for unemployment compensation, decline as economic activity rises. On the expenditures side of the budget, in the absence of discretionary policy shifts, there is no reason to expect government spending (G) to respond to changes in the level of economic activity.[9] Our previous assumption that government spending was exogenous can be maintained.

Consequently, the net effect of a rise in income is to increase the federal budget surplus or decrease the size of an existing deficit. An expansion in economic activity therefore causes fiscal policy, as measured by the budget surplus, to become more restrictive. This more restrictive policy dampens the expansion. Similarly, a shock that causes economic activity to fall automatically results in a decline in the federal budget surplus or a rise in the deficit, which cushions the fall in income. This is the essence of the concept of *automatic fiscal stabilizers*.

To examine automatic fiscal stabilizers in more detail, we return to the multiplier analysis of the Keynesian model in Chapter 5. We considered the way in which aggregate demand responded to exogenous shocks such as changes in autonomous investment demand or government spending. In effect, automatic fiscal stabilizers reduce the response of aggregate demand, and hence income, to such exogenous shocks. To show this outcome, we analyze the effects on the multiplier expressions, the expressions giving the aggregate demand response to these shocks, which result from allowing for endogenous changes in net tax revenues.

The equilibrium condition for income from Chapter 5 is

$$Y = C + I + G \tag{18.5}$$

Consumption (C) is assumed to be given by

$$C = a + bY_D \tag{18.6}$$

where Y_D is disposable income, defined as national income minus net tax collections $(Y - T)$. Investment, government spending, and the level of tax collections are all taken to be exogenous in that simple version of the Keynesian system. Similar to the procedure followed in Chapter 5, we substitute equation (18.6) into the equilibrium condition for income given by equation (18.5), and using the definition of Y_D, we compute an expression for equilibrium income ($\overline{Y}$):

$$\overline{Y} = \frac{1}{1 - b}(a - bT + I + G) \tag{18.7}$$

[9]Here and later, the term *government spending* refers to federal government purchases of goods and services only, with transfer payments included in the net tax variable.

From equation (18.7) we compute the effects on equilibrium income of exogenous changes in investment (I), government spending (G), and *exogenous* tax collections (T) as follows:

$$\frac{\Delta\bar{Y}}{\Delta I}=\frac{1}{1-b}, \frac{\Delta\bar{Y}}{\Delta G}=\frac{1}{1-b}, \frac{\Delta\bar{Y}}{\Delta T}=\frac{-b}{1-b} \tag{18.8}$$

The task here is to see how these expressions are modified when the net tax function given by equation (18.4) is substituted for the assumption that tax collections are exogenous.

To begin, consider the form of the consumption function given by equation (18.6) with our new assumption about taxes. Using the definition of disposable income ($Y_D = Y - T$) and with T defined by equation (18.4), we can write the consumption function as

$$\begin{aligned} C &= a + b(Y - T) \\ &= a + bY - bt_0 - bt_1Y \\ &= a - bt_0 + (b - bt_1)Y \\ &= a - bt_0 + b(1 - t_1)Y \end{aligned} \tag{18.9}$$

Substituting equation (18.9) into the condition for equilibrium income given in equation (18.5), we can derive the revised expression for the equilibrium level of income as follows:

$$\begin{aligned} Y &= \overbrace{a - bt_0 + b(1 - t_1)Y}^{C} + I + G \\ Y[1 - b(1 - t_1)] &= a - bt_0 + I + G \\ \bar{Y} &= \frac{1}{1 - b(1 - t_1)}(a - bt_0 + I + G) \end{aligned} \tag{18.10}$$

Like the previous expression (18.7), equation (18.10) specifies equilibrium income as determined by an autonomous expenditure multiplier, in this case $1/[1 - b(1 - t_1)]$, and the autonomous influences on income given by $a - bt_0 + I + G$. As before, we can compute the effects on equilibrium income of a change in investment or in government spending.

$$\frac{\Delta\bar{Y}}{\Delta I}=\frac{\Delta\bar{Y}}{\Delta G}=\frac{1}{1-b(1-t_1)} \tag{18.11}$$

Note that the autonomous expenditure multiplier and hence the effect on income from a change in autonomous expenditures (changes in I or G, for example) is *smaller* when tax collections depend on income than when the level of tax collections is exogenous; that is,

$$\frac{1}{1-b(1-t_1)} < \frac{1}{1-b}$$

For example, if b, the marginal propensity to consume, were equal to 0.8, and t_1, the marginal tax rate, were 0.25, we would have

$$\frac{1}{1-b}=\frac{1}{1-0.8}=5$$

$$\frac{1}{1-b(1-t_1)}=\frac{1}{1-0.8(1-0.25)}=\frac{1}{1-0.6}=2.5$$

In this example, the marginal tax rate of 0.25 cuts the value of the multiplier in half.

A marginal net income tax rate lowers the effect on equilibrium income of shocks to autonomous expenditure, such as an autonomous change in investment demand. In this sense, the income tax functions as an automatic stabilizer. This stabilizing effect of an income tax can be explained with reference to our earlier discussion of the multiplier process (see Section 5.5). An initial shock to investment demand, for example, changes income and has an induced effect on consumption spending. This induced effect on consumption demand causes equilibrium income to change by a multiple of the original change in investment demand. With a marginal income tax rate of t_1, each 1-dollar reduction in GDP reduces an individual's disposable income, the determinant of consumption, by only $(1 - t_1)$ dollars, because the individual's tax liability falls by t_1 dollars. Disposable income is affected less per unit change in GDP, so the induced effects on consumer demand are smaller at each round of the multiplier process. The total effects on income of a change in autonomous investment, which consists of the original shock to investment plus the induced effects on consumption, are therefore smaller when there is a marginal income tax rate than when tax collections are assumed to be exogenous.

The automatic response of taxes and transfers to the level of economic activity has been a substantial stabilizing force in the U.S. economy since World War II, generally moving the budget sharply into deficit during recessions, with falling deficits or at times (in the 1950s and late 1990s) surpluses during expansionary periods. The increased size of the federal budget in the postwar period relative to the prewar period has increased the effectiveness of automatic fiscal stabilizers; in terms of our tax function, the marginal net tax rate is higher now than it was in a period such as the 1920s, and thus the multiplier is lower.

Substituting the net tax function given by equation (18.4) for the assumption that the level of tax collections is exogenous also requires modifying the analysis of the effects of discretionary tax changes in the model. In the revised expression for equilibrium income given by equation (18.10), tax policy is represented by two variables: t_0, the intercept of the tax function, and t_1, the marginal income tax rate.

The analog to a lump-sum change in tax collections in the revised income equation is a change in t_0. Such a change could represent a lump-sum tax rebate to each taxpayer, for example, or a lump-sum change in transfer payments. From equation (18.10), the effects of a change in t_0 can be computed as

$$\frac{\Delta \overline{Y}}{\Delta t_0} = \frac{1}{1 - b(1 - t_1)}(-b) = \frac{-b}{1 - b(1 - t_1)} \qquad \textbf{(18.12)}$$

Taking account of the change in the autonomous expenditure multiplier, this expression is the same as the tax multiplier where tax collections were exogenous [see equation (18.8)]. Again, the effect of a tax change, here a change in the intercept of the tax function, is opposite in sign from the effect of a change in government spending or autonomous investment given by equation (18.11). An increase in t_0, for example, causes equilibrium income to fall. Also, the effect of a 1-dollar change in t_0 is smaller in absolute value than the effect of a 1-dollar change in I or G. As in the earlier case, at a given level of GDP (Y), a 1-dollar change in taxes changes autonomous expenditures [the term in parentheses in equation (18.10)] by only b (< 1) dollars, with the remaining $(1 - b)$ dollars absorbed by a change in saving. A 1-dollar change in government spending or autonomous investment changes autonomous expenditures by 1 full dollar.

FIGURE 18-4 Effect of an Increase in the Marginal Income Tax Rate (t_1)

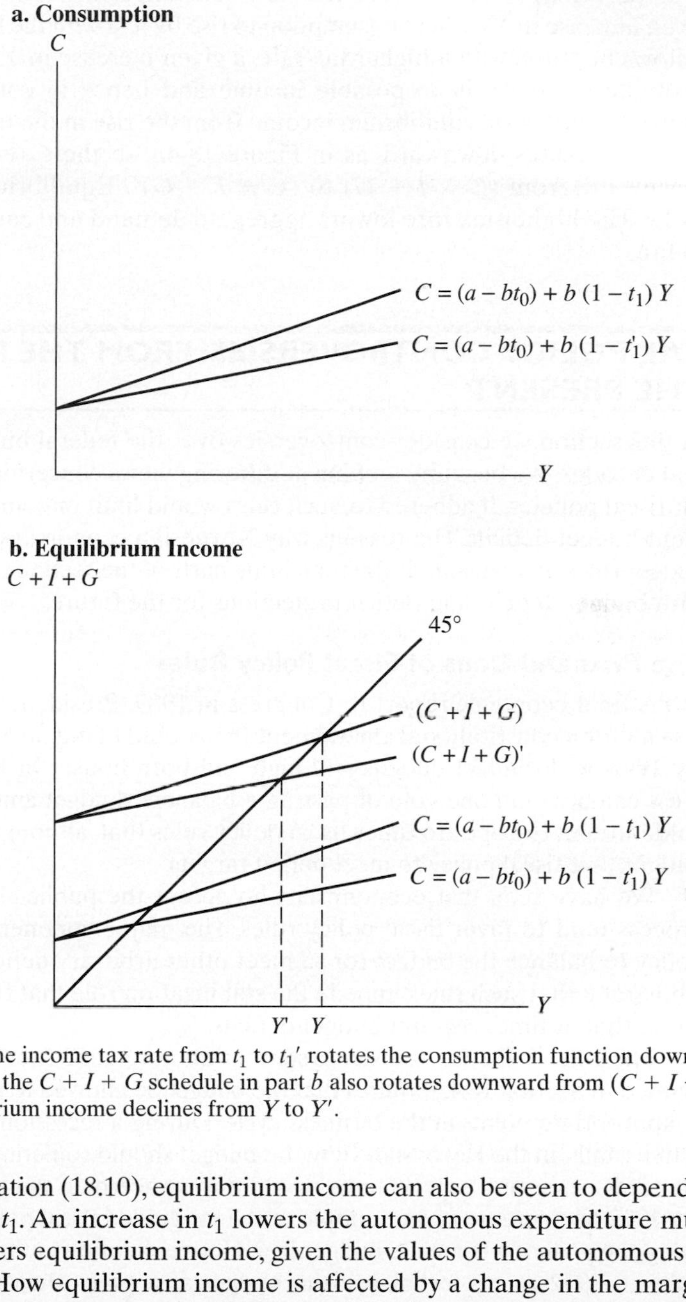

An increase in the income tax rate from t_1 to t_1' rotates the consumption function downward in part *a*. Consequently, the $C + I + G$ schedule in part *b* also rotates downward from $(C + I + G)$ to $(C + I + G)'$. Equilibrium income declines from Y to Y'.

From equation (18.10), equilibrium income can also be seen to depend on the marginal tax rate, t_1. An increase in t_1 lowers the autonomous expenditure multiplier, and therefore lowers equilibrium income, given the values of the autonomous expenditure components. How equilibrium income is affected by a change in the marginal income tax rate can best be seen graphically. Figure 18-4 illustrates the effects of an increase in the marginal tax rate from t_1 to t_1'. Figure 18-4*a* shows the effect of the increase in the tax rate on the consumption function.

With an income tax, consumption is given by equation (18.9). Before the increase in the marginal tax rate, the consumption line is $C = (a - bt_0) + b(1 - t_1)Y$ in the graph.

The increase in the income tax rate rotates the function downward to the schedule $C = (a - bt_0) + b(1 - t_1')Y$. The new consumption line is flatter, indicating that a given increase in Y causes consumption to rise by less with the higher tax rate. This result follows because, with a higher tax rate, a given increase in Y, national income, causes a smaller increase in disposable income and hence in consumption. Figure 18-4*b* shows the effect on equilibrium income from the rise in the tax rate. The consumption function rotates downward, as in Figure 18-4*a*, so the $C + I + G$ line also rotates downward, from $(C + I + G)$ to $(C + I + G)'$. Equilibrium income falls from Y to Y'. The higher tax rate lowers aggregate demand and causes equilibrium income to fall.

18.5 FISCAL POLICY CONTROVERSIES: FROM THE REAGAN YEARS TO THE PRESENT

In this section we consider controversies over the federal budget during the past several decades. We begin by looking at differing views concerning balanced-budget rules for fiscal policies. If adhered to, such rules would limit or completely eliminate government budget deficits. The reasons why Keynesian economists have opposed balanced-budget rules are explained. The remaining parts of the section review the U.S. experience with budget deficits and deficit projections for the future.

The Pros and Cons of Fiscal Policy Rules

In his final economic report to Congress in 1989, President Ronald Reagan renewed his call for a constitutional amendment that would mandate a balanced federal budget. By 1995, with budget deficits still high and both houses in Republican control, Congress came within one vote of passing a balanced-budget amendment. The Maastricht guidelines in Europe are other fiscal policy rules that, although not calling for balanced budgets, set fiscal policy to meet deficit targets.

We have seen that economists who accept the public-choice view of the budget process tend to favor fiscal policy rules. The major opponents of rules that set fiscal policy to balance the budget (or to meet other arbitrary deficit goals) are Keynesians, who argue that such rules impede the stabilization role that fiscal policy should play—a role that at times *requires* budget deficits.

The role of the tax-transfer system as an automatic fiscal stabilizer, which was explained in Section 18.4, requires that the budget be allowed to go into deficit (or surplus) at appropriate points in the business cycle. During a recession, as the level of economic activity falls, in the Keynesian view, the budget should sometimes go into deficit. Raising tax rates or cutting expenditures would only exacerbate the recession. Keynesians cite the 1932 tax increase as an example of the misguided fiscal policies that result from pursuing the goal of a balanced budget. The Hoover administration raised tax *rates* substantially in 1932 to try to balance the budget at a time when tax *revenues* were falling because of the Depression. The tax-rate increase came at a time when the unemployment rate was 24 percent. The policy did not succeed in balancing the budget because of the sharp decline in income, which was partly the result of the tax increase. During the 1974–75 recession, the federal budget deficit soared to nearly $70 billion. Keynesians believe that we would have risked a rerun of the Great Depression had we tried to balance the budget or seriously limit the size of the deficit under such conditions.

In addition to impeding the working of automatic stabilizers, a balanced-budget rule would limit the ability of policymakers to take *discretionary* countercyclical fiscal actions. These are changes in government spending and in tax rates aimed at stabilizing private-sector aggregate demand—the real-economy equivalents of the fiscal policy shifts discussed in previous chapters. Keynesians do not deny that there are past examples of ill-timed, and at times destabilizing, discretionary fiscal policy actions, as well as stabilizing ones. Moreover, Keynesians agree that some of the failures of discretionary fiscal policy stem from interactions between the political process and macroeconomic policymaking. Keynesians opposed to constitutional budget-balancing amendments or other rules for fiscal policy argue, however, that the record for discretionary policy is not uniformly bad and that the cost of interfering with automatic fiscal stabilizers through such amendments is great.

What About the Deficit?

In 1963, Senator Harry Byrd, Sr., asked Budget Director Kermit Gordon, a Keynesian economist, what balancing the budget would do for the country. Gordon replied, "It probably would add about 2.5 million people to the rolls of the unemployed, delay the recovery about four years, and knock 10 percent off U.S. output."[10] Yet, by the mid-1980s, Keynesian economists were among the harshest critics of the large budget deficits that emerged in the Reagan years. What had changed?

Cyclical versus Structural Deficits

One useful distinction in understanding the differing Keynesian positions on the deficits of the early 1960s versus those of the 1980s and 1990s is between **cyclical deficits** and **structural deficits**. We have seen that the federal budget deficit depends in part on the level of economic activity. The *cyclical deficit* is the portion of the deficit that results from a low level of economic activity. In the Keynesian view, cyclical deficits that reflect the working of automatic stabilizers are desirable.

cyclical deficits are the portion of the federal deficit that result from the economy's being at a low level of economic activity

The portion of the deficit that would exist even if the economy were at its potential output is called the *structural deficit*. A structural deficit is not directly attributable to the behavior of the economy and is the part of the deficit for which policymakers are directly responsible. In other words, the structural deficit is the result of decisions policymakers have made about tax rates, the level of government spending, and benefit levels for transfer programs.

structural deficits are the portion of the federal deficit that would exist even if the economy were at its potential level of output

To break the deficit into cyclical and structural components, we need a measure of potential output—the level of output achieved when both capital and labor are utilized at their highest sustainable rates. We can then compute the changes in tax revenues and transfer payments that would have taken place if the economy had moved from actual

[10]Walter Heller, "Kermit Gordon," *Brookings Papers on Economic Activity*, 2 (1976), pp. 283–87.

FIGURE 18-5 Structural and Actual Federal Government Budget Deficit, 1962–2006

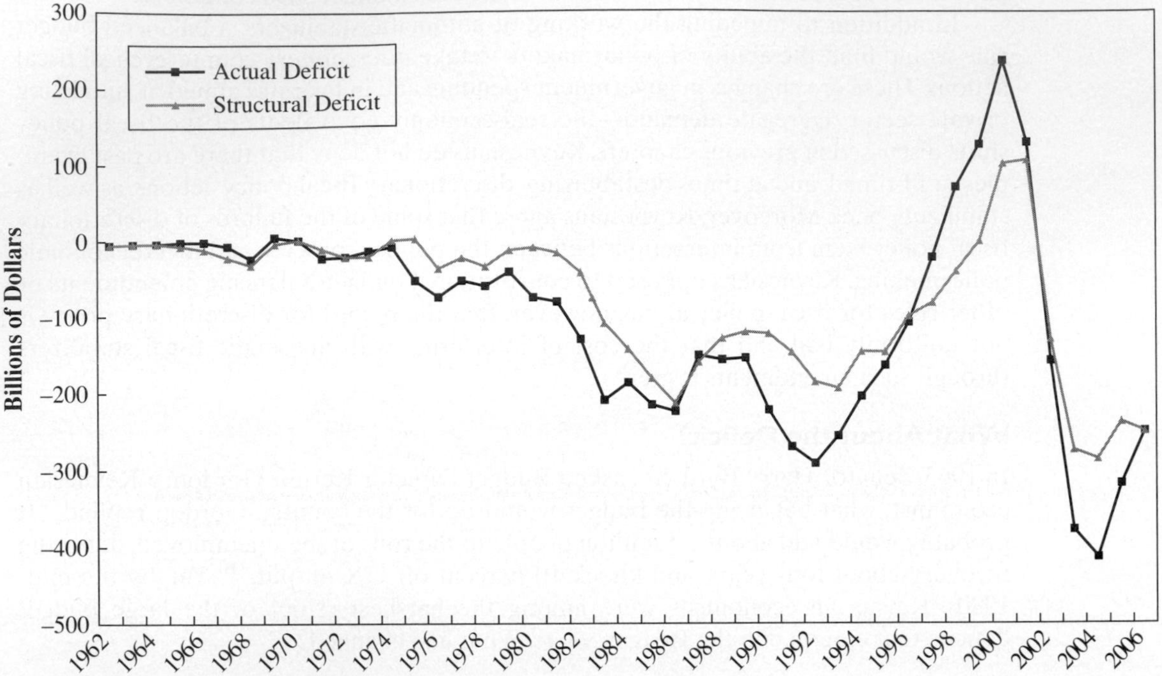

to potential output. Using these figures, we can find the structural deficit. For example, suppose the actual deficit is $300 billion, but the economy is below potential output. If the level of economic activity increased to the potential level, tax revenues would rise, let us assume by $100 billion. Transfer payments would fall, say by $30 billion, because unemployment compensation payments would decline as employment rose. The structural deficit—the deficit at potential output— is then $170 billion (300 − 100 − 30).

There is no one agreed-upon definition of potential output, and consequently, there are different measures of the structural deficit. Figure 18-5 shows the measure based on the Congressional Budget Office's (CBO) estimate of potential output. Notice that in recession periods such as 1981–82 and 1990–91, the actual deficit was much larger than the structural deficit. These were periods of significant cyclical deficits. Notice also, however, that the structural deficit rose rapidly in the post-1982 period and remained high for more than a decade.

Although Figure 18-5 is based on revised data, earlier estimates indicated that the deficits of the early 1960s were cyclical deficits. In 1963, for example, when Kermit Gordon gave his previously quoted response to Senator Byrd, rather than a deficit measured at potential output (as it was estimated at the time), the budget showed a surplus of $13 billion; there was a structural *surplus*.[11] Gordon and other Keynesians opposed balancing the budget in 1963 because the deficit reflected the working of

[11]Keith Carlson, "Estimates of the High-Employment Budget 1947–67," Federal Reserve Bank of St. Louis *Review*, 49 (June 1967), p. 11.

automatic fiscal stabilizers at a time when the economy was apparently operating substantially below potential output.

The Keynesian View of Deficits in the 1980s

In the 1980s, Keynesians were critical of Reagan administration policy because they believed that the large structural deficits reflected a mistaken *mix* of fiscal and monetary policies. Specifically, they believed that the deficits resulted from an overly expansionary fiscal policy. This fiscal policy was composed of the Reagan administration's large tax cuts and increased defense spending that more than counterbalanced cuts in nondefense spending. In the view of Keynesians, the overly expansionary fiscal policies meant that, throughout much of the 1980s, monetary policy had to be especially restrictive to keep the level of aggregate demand from growing too quickly. Keynesians believe that this mix of an easy fiscal policy and a tight monetary policy had unfavorable effects on the *composition* of output in the following ways.

Keynesians believed that the tight monetary and easy fiscal policies resulted in high U.S. interest rates during much of the 1980s. They believed that this policy mix discouraged investment at the expense of consumption. They also believed that the high U.S. interest rates pushed up the value of the U.S. dollar as foreign investment was attracted; this, in turn, encouraged imports and discouraged exports, leading to what were at the time record trade deficits.

Keynesians favored a policy mix of tighter fiscal and easier monetary policies that would have led to higher capital formation (more investment) and higher exports (a lower trade deficit).

The Federal Budget in the Late 1990s and into the Twenty-First Century

Beginning in the mid-1990s, a combination of tax increases and spending cuts, aided by rapid economic growth, moved the budget from large deficits to a surplus. Huge future surpluses were forecast for the medium term. There was concern about the effects of erasing the national debt that was forecast to go to zero by 2011. This concern was premature because, as noted in the introduction, by 2004 10-year budget projections showed a cumulative deficit of over $2 trillion, compared to a surplus of over $3 trillion projected at the beginning of 2001.

Part of this shift was the result of the recession in 2001. This can be seen from Figure 18-5, which shows that in 2002–2004 the actual deficit substantially exceeded the structural deficit. By 2006, almost the whole of the deficit was structural. The current and projected medium-term deficits result from legislated actions, primarily the large tax cuts of the Bush administration. This shift in fiscal policy rekindled the debates of the 1980s and 1990s over the economic effects of large structural deficits. Moreover, as in the 1980s, large government budget deficits were accompanied by record foreign trade deficits, raising additional concerns.

A new element in these debates was concern over long-term budget pressures. These long-term budget pressures result from the gradual retirement of the large baby boom generation and the growing lifespan of the population. Both factors will put a strain on the Social Security and Medicare system. Increases in the cost of health care at a rate higher than the general price level will, if they continue, put

FIGURE 18-6 Projected Growth of the U.S. Economy and Federal Spending for Major Mandatory Programs

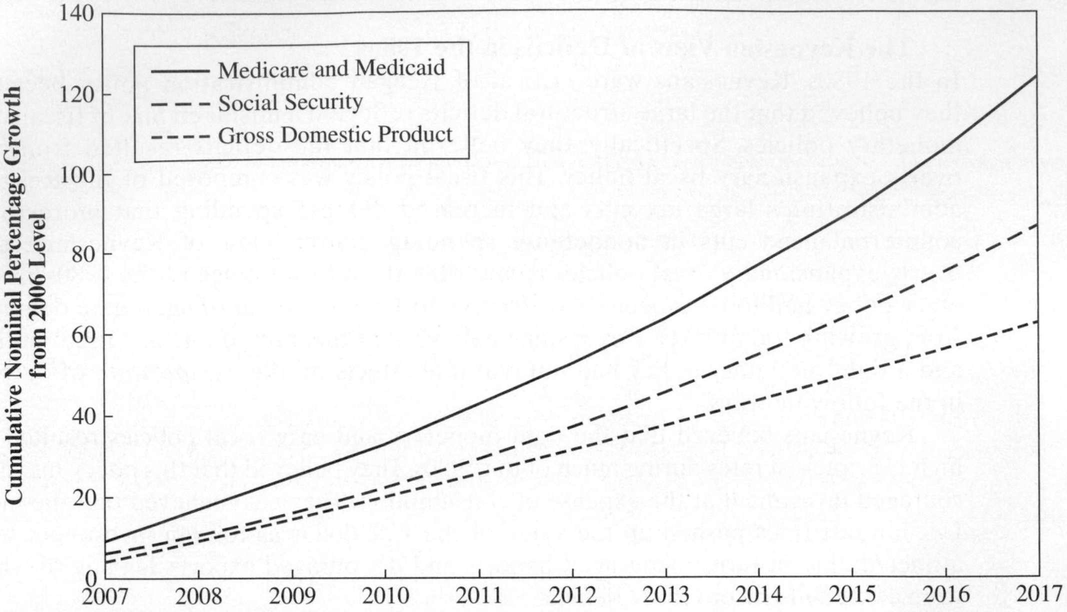

SOURCE: Congressional Budget Office (CBO).

further strain on the Medicare system and increase the cost of the Medicaid program. Figure 18-6 shows CBO projections of the growth in these mandated federal programs relative to growth in U.S. GDP out to 2017. As the programs grow faster than GDP, either higher tax rates or lower spending on other federal programs will be required. Projections out to 2050 are even more dire, especially for Medicare and Medicaid spending.

Critics of Bush administration fiscal policy, especially of the large tax cuts, argue that we should be running budget surpluses now to reduce outstanding debt and prepare for these huge future expenditures. Supporters of the tax cuts counter that lower tax rates will increase economic growth and thus the future tax base to finance higher expenditures. These arguments about the relationships between fiscal policy and economic growth are at the center of the discussion in Chapter 19.

18.6 CONCLUSION

The deficit dominated the debate over fiscal policy in the 1980s and 1990s. Over the next several decades, the longer-run pressures on the budget discussed in this chapter are likely to be the center of attention. Any potential stabilization role for fiscal policy is complicated by the presence of these alternative concerns. In this environment, the major role for stabilization policy has fallen to monetary policy. This has been true not only in the United States but in most industrialized countries.

KEY TERMS

- public choice 369
- partisan theory 370
- automatic stabilizers 379
- cyclical deficits 385
- structural deficits 385

REVIEW QUESTIONS AND PROBLEMS

1. Some economists who accept the public-choice view of the fiscal policymaking process have concluded that a constitutional amendment to mandate a balanced federal budget would be desirable. Summarize their arguments in favor of such an amendment.
2. Explain the central element of the *partisan* theory of fiscal policymaking. Contrast the implications of the partisan theory concerning the relationship of fiscal policy to the business cycle with those of the public-choice view.
3. Explain the concept of an automatic fiscal stabilizer. Give examples.
4. Suppose that, within the simple Keynesian model used in Section 18.4, the level of government spending (G) was 100, the level of investment spending (I) was 75, and consumption (C) was given by

$$C = 25 + 0.8Y_D$$

Net taxes (T) are initially given by the tax function

$$T = -50 + 0.30Y$$

Calculate equilibrium income ($\overline{Y}$). Now suppose that the tax rate is decreased from 0.30 to 0.25. Find the new level of equilibrium income. Compute the values of the autonomous expenditure multiplier before and after the tax cut.
5. Explain the Keynesians' objections to fixed rules for fiscal policy, such as a constitutional amendment that would mandate a balanced federal budget.
6. Refer to the first equilibrium income you calculated in problem 4. Now suppose that the intercept of the net tax function (t_0) changes from -50 to -40. Find the new level of equilibrium income.
7. Explain the concept of the structural budget deficit. How do structural deficits differ from cyclical deficits?
8. Suppose that the marginal propensity to consume out of disposable income is 0.8 and the marginal income tax rate is 0.1. What is the value of the autonomous expenditure multiplier? Now suppose that the marginal income tax rate rises to 0.2. What is the new value of the multiplier? Explain the difference.

PART SIX

Economic Growth

The chapters in this part extend the time frame of our analysis to periods longer than business cycles. In Chapter 19 we consider periods too long for our assumptions about the short run, but we will not assume that the economy is on a long-run equilibrium growth path. In calendar time, these might be periods of a decade or two. Chapter 20 considers models of long-run economic growth. There we will look at the factors that determine what Adam Smith termed "the wealth of nations."

CHAPTER 19

Policies for Intermediate-Run Growth

This chapter considers the factors that determine the growth of output over periods longer than the short run but not necessarily periods of long-run equilibrium: the awkward but important intermediate run. President Bill Clinton liked to talk about "growing the economy." The specific focus of this chapter is on policies to do just that: foster sustained growth over periods of a decade or more.

The short-run period in our earlier analysis was characterized by the assumptions of a constant capital stock, a fixed labor force, and an unchanged technology. Output changes came as the level of employment varied. When considering changes in output in the intermediate run, perhaps over 10 to 15 years rather than 2 to 4 years, we are not entitled to make those assumptions. Variations in the rates of capital formation, growth in the labor force that results from growth in the working-age population as well as changes in labor force participation rates, and variations in the rate of technological change are factors that determine growth rates of output in the intermediate run. What about the importance of demand? Economists who accept the classical, real business cycle, or new classical views see little direct role for aggregate demand as a significant factor in determining the growth path of output over periods of intermediate length. In the classical or real business cycle theories, aggregate demand does not play a role in determining output even in the short run. In the new classical model, only unanticipated demand changes affect output. Therefore, only deviations of demand growth from the average rather than the average rate of growth in demand over a period of 10 to 15 years would affect output.

The situation is different with respect to the monetarist and Keynesian (or new Keynesian) views. As we have explained, the long-run equilibrium growth rate is supply-determined, but both monetarists and Keynesians believe that changes in demand affect output over periods of several years. If we look at any 10- to 15-year period, the average rate of growth may be affected by demand-induced recessions or expansions within that period. Demand factors might, for example, explain why the growth rate of output was approximately zero for the 1929–39 decade of the Great Depression.

Thus, as with analysis of the short run, economists disagree over the relative importance of supply and demand in determining output over intermediate-run periods. We will examine the position of a group called *supply-side* economists. As their name indicates, the supply-side economists emphasize supply factors as the determinants of the behavior of output. The origins of their views are in classical economics; consequently, their theories share elements with real business cycle theories and the new classical economics. There are, however, additional questions that arise in considering output growth in the intermediate run and different types of policy issues.

Rather than considering the full range of views on policies in the intermediate run, we will confine ourselves to contrasting the supply-side view with the Keynesian view. In fact, Keynesian economists have been the sharpest critics of supply-side economics. The Keynesian position maintains, as James Tobin has said, that God gave us two eyes so that we could watch both supply and demand (albeit with the danger of becoming a bit walleyed). In addition to the issue of the relative importance of supply and demand, supply-side economists and Keynesians disagree on which policies have favorable (or unfavorable) effects on aggregate supply.

We proceed by laying out the supply-side position as it has evolved over the past three decades and then considering the Keynesian critique. Next, we describe the redirection of macroeconomic policy that took place during the Reagan and first Bush presidencies—a redirection inspired by supply-side economics. In the 1990s, voters seemed to call for policy to move in another direction by twice electing Bill Clinton to the presidency. But in 1994, the House Republicans' "Contract with America," which drew heavily on the precepts of supply-side economics, proved popular. Moreover, in 2000, George W. Bush was elected and followed an economic program of large tax cuts in line with the prescriptions of supply-side economists. We will conclude the chapter with a consideration of these conflicting aspects of the recent policy-making climate.

Before turning to these topics, however, it is useful to review the growth performance of the U.S. economy over the past several decades.

19.1 U.S. ECONOMIC GROWTH, 1960–2006

The growth experience of the United States for the 1960–2006 period is summarized in Table 19-1. As the table shows, the rates of growth in output and labor productivity slowed down after 1973. The rate of capital formation also declined. Growth in the labor force increased in the late 1960s and into the 1970s, as the post–World War II baby boom generation came to adulthood, and then returned to its earlier level in the 1980s.

Then, at some point in the 1990s, a turnaround appears to have occurred. While growth in the labor force continued to decline because of demographic factors, capital formation and growth in both output and labor productivity increased almost to pre-1973 levels.

The facts that supply-side and Keynesian economists must explain are, therefore, the following:

1. The growth rate in U.S. output slowed markedly in the 1973–92 period.
2. The growth rate in labor productivity declined sharply in the 1970s.
3. The rate of capital formation also slowed in the 1970s and 1980s relative to pre-1973 years.
4. After 1992, capital formation and growth in output and labor productivity rose to near pre-1973 levels.

Read Perspectives 19-1.

TABLE 19-1 U.S. Growth Experience, 1960–2006

	Average Annual Percentage Growth Rate					
Item	***1960–68***	***1968–73***	***1973–79***	***1979–91***	***1992–97***	***1998–2006***
Gross domestic output	4.5	3.2	2.4	2.5	3.4	3.2
Labor productivity	2.6	1.0	0.0	1.0	1.7	2.2
Total labor force	1.6	2.4	2.6	1.7	1.3	1.2
Capital formation	5.0	3.7	1.9	2.3	4.0	4.8

SOURCES: *Historical Statistics, 1960–89* (Paris: OECD, 1991); *Economic Report of the President,* 1992, 1997, 2004; OECD *Economic Outlook* (December 1997, June 2003, June 2007).

PERSPECTIVES 19-1

GROWTH AND PRODUCTIVITY SLOWDOWNS IN OTHER INDUSTRIALIZED ECONOMIES

Table 19-2 shows growth rates in output and labor productivity for six major industrialized countries. The data are average annual percentage growth rates for time periods similar to those considered for the United States in Table 19-1. The striking feature in the table is a marked slowdown in output growth and productivity growth in the post-1970 period in *all* these countries.

The data in the tables are for large industrialized economies, but data for smaller ones tell the same story. The growth and productivity slowdown of the 1970s, with relatively slow growth continuing into the 1980s and early 1990s, affected virtually every industrialized economy. This trend suggests that, as we seek explanations of the slowdown, we should look for causes that have broad international effects.

The turnaround in the growth picture in the United States during the 1990s was shared by some but not all of the countries in the table. Canada and the United Kingdom had increased growth in output and in labor productivity. The continental European countries did not. Japan was still mired in deflationary slow growth.

TABLE 19-2 Growth Rate in Output and Labor Productivity, Selected Countries, Annual Averages

Country	*Item*	*1960–68*	*1968–73*	*1973–79*	*1979–89*	*1990–97*	*1998–06*
Canada	Output	5.5	5.4	4.2	3.1	2.6	3.4
	Labor productivity	4.0	3.2	1.4	1.2	1.7	1.3
France	Output	5.4	5.9	3.0	2.1	1.9	2.3
	Labor productivity	4.9	4.7	2.7	2.0	1.5	1.2
Italy	Output	5.7	4.6	2.6	2.5	1.6	1.3
	Labor productivity	6.3	4.9	1.7	2.1	1.9	0.5
Japan	Output	10.4	8.4	3.6	4.1	1.6	1.2
	Labor productivity	8.8	7.3	2.9	3.0	1.5	1.1
Germany	Output	4.1	4.9	2.3	1.8	2.0	1.4
	Labor productivity	4.2	4.1	2.9	1.7	2.1	0.9
United Kingdom	Output	3.1	3.2	1.5	2.3	2.2	2.7
	Labor productivity	2.7	3.0	1.3	1.7	1.7	1.8

SOURCES: *Historical Statistics*, (Paris: OECD, 1988,1992); OECD, *Economic Outlook* (December 1997, June 2003, June 2007).

19.2 THE SUPPLY-SIDE POSITION

The origins of supply-side economics lie in the classical theories examined in Chapters 3 and 4. In particular, for the intermediate run, supply-side economists accept the classical view that output is determined by real variables—growth of factor supplies and changes in technology. They adhere to a classical view of the saving–investment process, in which the interest rate is the crucial variable. Most fundamentally, supply-side economists share the classical economists' faith in the free-enterprise capitalist system and dislike of government intervention in the economy. To analyze these ideas, we begin by stating some propositions of supply-side economics. We then explain each proposition in terms of its classical roots and show how each applies to current U.S. economic policies.

The following four propositions are central elements of supply-side economics:[1]

1. Output growth in the intermediate run is predominantly supply-determined by rates of growth in factor supplies and the rate of technological change.
2. The rate of growth of capital input is determined primarily by incentives for saving and investment, the incentives being the *after-tax* returns to saving and investment.
3. Growth in labor input, although in the long run determined by demographic factors, can also be affected significantly by incentives, in this case changes in the after-tax real wage.
4. Excessive government regulation of business discouraged capital formation and contributed to the slowdown in the growth of labor productivity in the 1970s and 1980s.

Intermediate-Run Output Growth Is Supply-Determined

In the long run, economic growth depends predominantly on supply factors. Supply-side economists believe that this dependency is also true in the intermediate run. It clearly follows in the classical model, where even in the short run output is supply-determined. Intermediate-run growth in the classical model is illustrated in Figure 19-1. Output increases from Y_0 to Y_1 to Y_2 as the supply schedule shifts to the right, reflecting growth in factor supplies and changes in technology. If the aggregate demand schedule remains at Y_0^d in Figure 19-1, prices will fall successively to P_1 and then to P_2. Instead, if demand is increased as a result of growth in the money supply proportional to the growth in output, the price level will be maintained at P_0. Whichever is the case, the growth in output is determined solely by shifts in the supply schedule.

It is overly restrictive to say that Figure 19-1 represents the supply-side view. Most supply-side economists accept that demand plays a role in the *short-run* determination of income; the very-short-run aggregate supply schedule is upward-sloping to the right rather than vertical, as classical economists would have drawn it. Consequently, to avoid short-run disruptions, many supply-side economists would favor a policy strategy

[1]Early expositions of the supply-side position may be found in George Gilder, *Wealth and Poverty* (New York: Basic Books, 1981), especially chapters 4, 15, and 16; Paul Craig Roberts, *The Supply-Side Revolution* (Cambridge, Mass.: Harvard University Press, 1983); Arthur B. Laffer and Jan P. Seymour, eds., *The Economics of the Tax Revolt: A Reader* (New York: Harcourt Brace Jovanovich, 1979); and Laurence Meyer, ed., *The Supply-Side Effects of Economic Policy* (St. Louis: Center for the Study of American Business, 1981). The last two sources also contain critiques of the supply-side positions. Two useful analyses of supply-side economics are James Barth, "The Reagan Program for Economic Recovery: Economic Rationale (A Primer on Supply-Side Economics)," Federal Reserve Bank of Atlanta *Review* (September 1981), pp. 4–14; and John Tatom, "We Are All Supply-Siders Now!" Federal Reserve Bank of St. Louis *Review,* 63 (May 1981), pp. 18–30. Later evaluations are Martin Feldstein, "Supply-Side Economics: Old Truths and New Claims," *American Economic Review,* 76 (May 1986), pp. 26–30; Lawrence Chimerine and Richard Young, "Economic Surprises and Messages of the 1980s," *American Economic Review,* 76 (May 1986), pp. 31–36; Paul Krugman, *Peddling Prosperity* (New York: Norton, 2000), chapters 1–3; and Bruce Bartlett, *Imposder: How George W. Bush Bankrupted America and Betrayed the Reagan Legacy* (New York: Doubleday 2006).

FIGURE 19-1 Intermediate-Run Growth in the Classical System

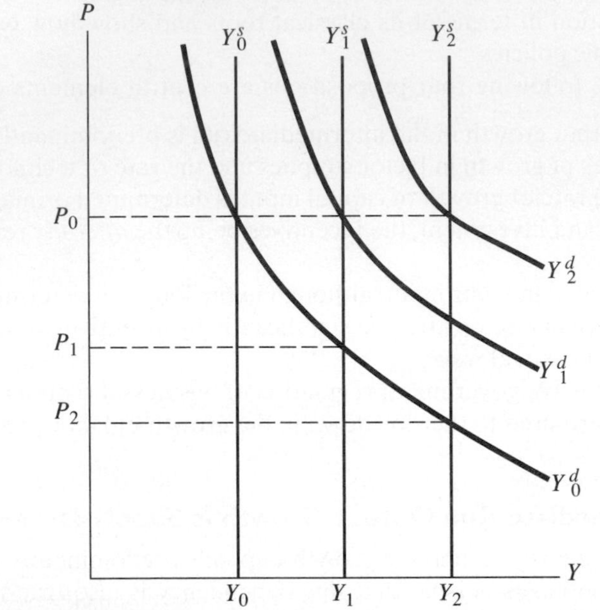

Growth in factor supplies shifts the supply schedule to the right (from Y_0^s to Y_1^s to Y_2^s). If demand is unchanged, the price level falls (from P_0 to P_1 to P_2). Appropriate increases in the quantity of money would increase demand sufficiently (from Y_0^d to Y_1^d to Y_2^d) to maintain the initial equilibrium price level (P_0).

in which demand was raised sufficiently to avoid the need for deflation (the fall in prices from P_0 to P_2 in Figure 19-1). Still, a central element in the supply-side position is that for *intermediate-run* periods, growth in output is supply- and not demand-determined.[2]

Saving and Investment Depend on After-Tax Rates of Return

Supply-side economics stresses the after-tax rate of return to investment as a primary determinant of investment and therefore the rate of capital formation. The after-tax rate of return is the pretax profit rate multiplied by 1 minus the rate at which profits are taxed. Similarly, supply-side economists believe the after-tax return for saving is an important influence on the saving rate. Here the relevant rate of return is the aftertax *real* interest rate, which equals the after-tax nominal interest rate (the nominal rate multiplied by 1 minus the rate at which interest payments are taxed) minus the expected inflation rate.

This view of saving and investment is a classical one. Recall our discussion of the theory of interest in the classical model, as illustrated in Figure 19-2. The equilibrium (real)

[2]On this issue and those discussed later, we can distinguish between a moderate and an extreme supply-side position. On many issues, moderate supply-side economists differ from the Keynesians only in ascribing more importance to supply-side factors. The more extreme supply-side positions virtually ignore the demand side. For example, Martin Feldstein, chairman of the Council of Economic Advisors under President Reagan, whose work on incentives for investment is described later, is an economist who has emphasized the importance of supply-side variables but has been at odds with extreme supply-siders.

FIGURE 19-2 Classical Theory of Interest

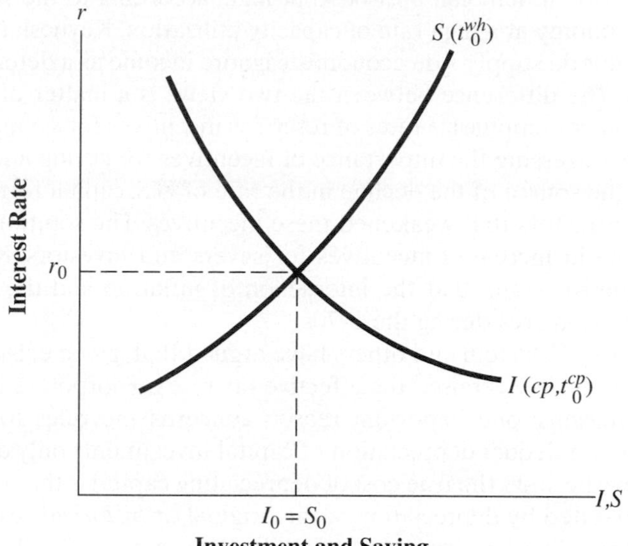

The position of the saving schedule depends on the tax rate for interest and dividend income (t_0^{wh}). The position of the investment schedule depends on the effective tax rate on corporate profits (t_0^{cp}) as well as on the pretax corporate profit rate (cp). These tax rates, t_0^{wh} and t_0^{cp}, therefore, affect the equilibrium real interest rate (r).

interest rate is determined by the intersection of the saving and investment schedules. This outcome reflects the assumption we make for the moment that the government deficit $(G - T)$ is zero. Otherwise, government deficit financing would be an additional demand for loanable funds. The position of the investment schedule is shown to depend on cp, the pretax corporate profit rate, and t^{cp}, the effective tax rate on corporate profits, to be explained later. The position of the saving schedule depends on t^{wh}, the tax rate for income earned on saving (wealth). In the classical model, income earned from savings would be interest income on bonds. In the real economy, t^{wh} would also represent tax rates on dividend income and tax rates on capital gains produced by changes in asset prices. In our earlier analysis, we established that the real interest rate (r) was determined by what the classical economists called the *forces of productivity and thrift*, productivity reflected in the profit rate and therefore the position of the investment schedule, and thrift reflected in the position of the saving schedule (both for a given structure of taxes). Here the important point is that in the classical view, productivity and thrift, *as well as the structure of taxes*, determine saving and investment, and consequently the rate of capital formation.

Supply-side economists need not accept the particular specification of the saving and investment functions in our simple version of the classical system. For example, in predicting the level of investment for the United States in 2008, supply-side economists would use a much more complex investment function than that plotted in Figure 19-2. They would take account of factors such as lags and adjustment costs. The essentially classical feature in supply-side economists' view is their stress on rates of return as influences on the rates of saving, investment, and thus capital formation. Where else might the emphasis be placed? The answer is on income and, hence, on aggregate demand. Keynesians believe that income is the most important determinant of investment. Investment can best be kept high, according to the Keynesian view, by keeping the economy at a high rate of capacity utilization. Keynesians do not ignore rates of return, nor do supply-side economists ignore income as a determinant of saving or investment. The difference between the two views is a matter of emphasis, and supply-side economists emphasize rates of return as incentives for saving and investment.

By stressing the importance of incentives for saving and investment, we are led to seek the source of the decline in the rate of U.S. capital formation in the post-1970 period in factors that weakened these incentives. The solution to slow capital formation may lie in increased incentives for savers and investors. Martin Feldstein and other economists claim that the interaction of inflation and the U.S. tax system weakened these incentives during the 1970s.

First, Feldstein and others have argued that, given existing tax laws, the high inflation of the 1970s raised the effective tax rate on corporate income.[3] They offered several reasons; one important reason concerns the rules for depreciation allowances. Firms can deduct depreciation of capital investments only at the *original* cost. In inflationary periods, the true cost of depreciating capital is the replacement cost. This cost is understated by depreciation at the original or *historical* cost, so profits are overstated, and the effective corporate tax liability was increased in the inflationary 1970s.

Supply-side economists also argue that the combination of inflation and the U.S. tax system reduced the incentives to save during the 1970s. The income tax an individual pays is based on the *nominal* interest, dividends, or capital gains earned on invested savings. Two examples will illustrate how increased inflation and taxation of nominal interest payments or capital gains lower the real return on saving. Suppose that initially the nominal interest rate is 6 percent and the rate of inflation is 2 percent (a pretax real rate of 4 percent). At a 50 percent marginal tax rate, an investor would have an after-tax *nominal* return of 3 percent [6 percent $\times (1 - t^{wh})$ = 6 percent $\times (1 - 0.5)$] and an after-tax real return of 1 percent (3 percent − 2 percent). Now suppose that the nominal interest rate is 16 percent, with an inflation rate of 12 percent (again a pretax real rate of 4 percent). The after-tax nominal return will be 8 percent [16 percent $\times (1 - 0.5)$], which means that the after-tax real return is now −4 percent (8 percent − 12 percent).

Or consider the taxation of nominal capital gains on corporate equities, for example. Suppose that an individual purchased a share of stock at a price of $100 in 1967 and sold it in 1980 for $200. Because the price level rose by over 150 percent in this period while the price of the stock doubled, or rose 100 percent, the individual's real return is negative even before taxes. Still, the individual must pay a capital gains tax on the nominal capital gain (of $100), increasing the size of the real loss. Supply-side economists argue that taxing nominal capital gains and interest earnings during inflationary periods results in an increased effective tax rate on real returns and will retard saving.

The effects of overtaxing both corporate profits and the return to saving during inflationary periods are illustrated in Figure 19-3. Suppose that we move from a period of relatively low inflation rates such as the 1950s and 1960s to a period of higher inflation rates such as the 1970s. Because of historical cost depreciation, this change results in an increase in the effective tax rate on corporate profits from t_0^{cp} to t_1^{cp} in Figure 19-3. For a given

[3]See Martin Feldstein and Lawrence Summers, "Inflation and the Taxation of Capital Income in the Corporate Sector," *National Tax Journal*, 32 (December 1979), pp. 445–70.

FIGURE 19-3 Inflation, the Tax System, and the Saving–Investment Process

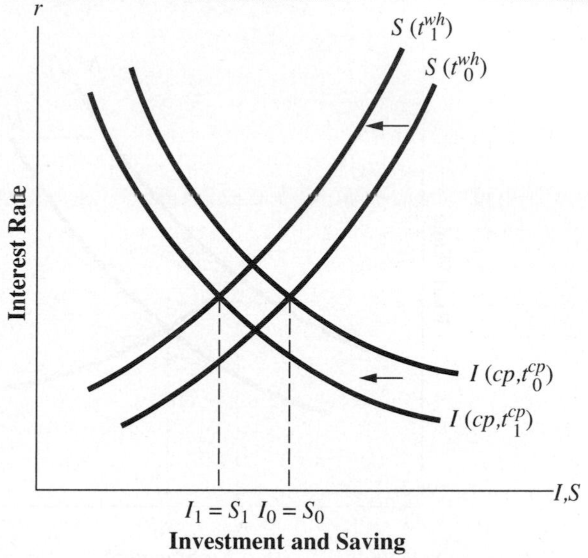

An increase in the effective corporate tax rate due to increased inflation caused the investment schedule to shift leftward from $I(cp, t_0^{cp})$ to $I(cp, t_1^{cp})$. An inflation-induced increase in the effective tax rate on interest income and capital gains shifts the saving schedule leftward from $S(t_0^{wh})$ to $S(t_1^{wh})$. The equilibrium levels of saving and investment fall from $I_0 = S_0$ to $I_1 = S_1$

before-tax profit rate *cp,* this increase in the effective tax rate will shift the investment schedule to the left, as shown in the graph. Further, owing to the taxing of nominal interest payments and capital gains, the effective tax on the return to saving is increased from t_0^{wh} to t_1^{wh}, and the saving schedule shifts to the left in Figure 19-3. After the adjustment to a new equilibrium, saving and investment are reduced from I_0 and S_0 to S_1 and I_1 in Figure 19-3. The rate of capital formation is reduced by the interaction of inflation and the tax system.

Labor Supply Is Responsive to Changes in the After-Tax Real Wage

Supply-side economists argue that labor supply is responsive to changes in *after-tax* real wages. Here again the supply-side view is rooted in classical economics—in this case, building on the classical analysis of the supply-side effects of changes in the marginal income tax rate (see Section 4.3). Figure 19-4 illustrates the determination of equilibrium employment in the classical system and the effect of a change in the after-tax real wage as a result of a change in the marginal income tax rate t^y. Initially, assume that the income tax rate is set at t_0^y. The labor supply schedule is given by $N^s(t_0^y)$ and intersects the labor demand schedule at N_0, the equilibrium level of employment.

Now assume that the income tax rate is raised to a higher level, t_1^y. According to the supply-side view, labor supply depends on the after-tax real wage, which will equal $(1 - t^y)$ W/P. For example, with a marginal tax rate of 0.20, the after-tax real wage will be 0.80 times the pretax real wage. The marginal income tax rate thus forms a "wedge" between the wage paid by the employer, W/P, and the wage received by the worker, $(1 - t^y)$ W/P. Increasing the tax rate from t_0^y to a higher level, t_1^y, causes the labor supply schedule to shift to the left from $N^s(t_0^y)$ to $N^s(t_1^y)$. Less labor is supplied at each level of

FIGURE 19-4 Taxes and Labor Supply in the Classical System

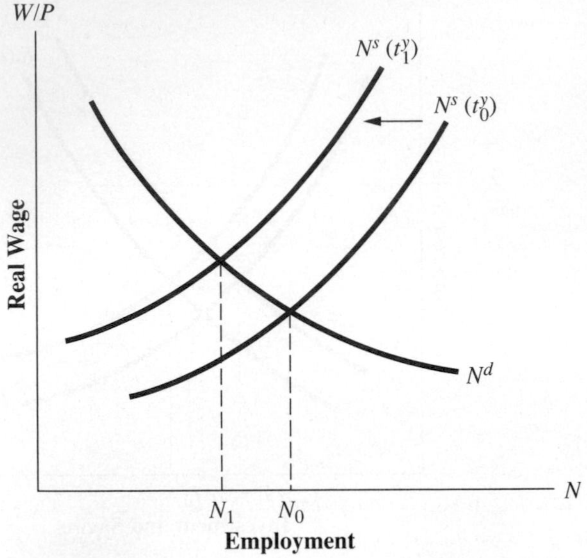

An increase in the income tax rate from t_0^y to t_1^y reduces the after-tax real wage and causes the labor supply schedule to shift to the left. Employment declines from N_1 to N_1.

the pretax real wage because, with a higher tax rate, a given pretax real wage represents a *lower* after-tax real wage. Employment declines from N_0 to N_1.

Supply-side economists believe that rising marginal tax rates in the United States during the 1970s increased the size of the wedge that the income tax creates between the real wage paid by the employer and the after-tax wage received by the employee (see Perspectives 4-2). They claim that work incentives were reduced, with negative effects on employment and output. Here again, inflationary aggregate demand policies and a tax system not well designed to cope with the effects of inflation deserve much of the blame. The U.S. income tax system in the 1970s was progressive, so as *nominal* incomes went up due to inflation, individuals moved into higher marginal tax brackets.

Read Perspectives 19-2.

Government Regulation Contributed to the Slowdown in the U.S. Economic Growth Rate

Supply-side economists argue that the proliferation of government regulation of business contributed significantly to the slowdown in U.S. economic growth during the 1970s. A new wave of government regulatory activity began in the 1960s. New agencies were set up, and laws were passed for pollution control, protection of worker safety, consumer product safety, and pension reform. Supply-side economists argue that this increase in government regulatory activity slowed economic growth in two ways.

First, complying with such regulations increases the cost of producing a given output. Increases in government regulation therefore have the same effects as the supply shocks considered in Chapter 8. The aggregate supply schedule shifts to the left, reducing output. Note that some of the increase in cost comes from employing workers not

PERSPECTIVES 19-2

THE LAFFER CURVE

A "simplified" income tax form circulated as a joke reads

Form "1040"
This year's income ________.
SEND IT IN

A tax system represented by this form, that of a 100 percent tax rate, would not collect any revenue. Who would work and report income? At the other end of the tax rate spectrum, a rate of 0 percent would also yield no revenue. Therefore, we know that if we plot a relationship between tax *revenue*, and the tax *rate*, with revenue on the vertical axis, the curve will first rise as the tax rate moves up from zero, but at some point, before the tax rate hits 1, it will decline. For example, the relationship might be as shown in Figure 19-5.

This curve showing tax revenue collected at each tax rate (or overall level of tax rates) is called the *Laffer curve*. The curve is named after its popularizer, Arthur B. Laffer. The Laffer curve received much attention because it illustrated the possibility that increases in tax rates may *reduce* tax revenue. Conversely, a cut in tax rates may *increase* revenue. The latter effect will occur if tax rates are initially in the range to the right of point A in Figure 19-5.

A number of supply-side economists, including Laffer, argued that this was the case for the United States in the early 1980s. Tax cuts would expand the economy through the supply side. This expansion would increase the tax base. Moreover, supply-siders argued that tax avoidance (e.g., through the use of tax shelters) and tax evasion (e.g., failure to report taxable income) would decline. Together, it was argued, these effects would lead to increased tax revenues even at lower tax rates.

Critics of supply-side economics, and many moderate supply-siders, did not believe the U.S. economy was on the downward-sloping portion of the Laffer curve. They saw the huge deficits that emerged in the 1980s after tax cuts as support for their view.

FIGURE 19-5 The Laffer Curve

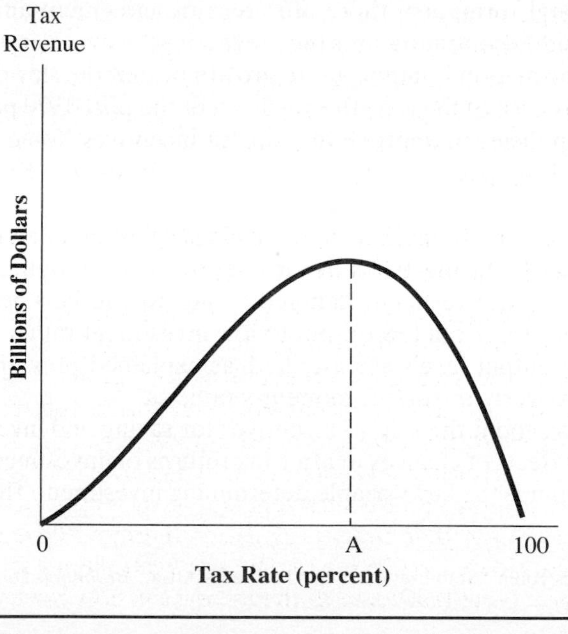

directly for production of output—steel, for example—but for cleaning smokestacks to comply with pollution controls, eliminating on-the-job safety hazards, or other activities to comply with regulations. Thus, increased government regulation is a possible explanation for the decline in the growth of labor productivity.

Second, supply-side economists argue that government regulatory activity retarded capital formation, at least capital formation that contributed to increased productivity in terms of measured output.

19.3 THE KEYNESIAN CRITIQUE OF SUPPLY-SIDE ECONOMICS

Supply-side economics can be regarded as the intermediate-run counterpart to the monetarist and new classical attacks on the Keynesian orthodoxy that dominated by the mid-1960s; those attacks were also based on classical notions. In this section, we analyze the Keynesian critique of the supply-side position in terms of each of the supply-side propositions discussed in the preceding section.

The Supply-Determined Nature of Intermediate-Run Growth

The Keynesian position is that for periods of a decade or so, both supply and demand factors are important in determining output growth. For example, in explaining the lower growth in the United States in the 1970s, James Tobin sees as the primary causes supply shocks, the most important from the energy sector, and monetary policy "overkill," meaning overly restrictive policy actions imposed to slow the economy when a slowdown was already underway. Tobin blames such mistimed monetary actions in part for the severity of the recessions of the 1970s, which resulted in the lower growth rate for the decade.[4]

Saving and Investment and After-Tax Rates of Return

On the question of whether depressed rates of return have lowered saving, investment, and capital formation, there are areas of agreement and disagreement between the supply-side economists and the Keynesians. Keynesian economists do not deny that capital formation is important to growth or that the slowdown in net capital formation was one cause of the growth slowdown of the post-1970 period. Nor do the Keynesians oppose policies to improve investment incentives. Tobin points out, for example, that the first investment tax credit was passed during the Kennedy administration, a high point of Keynesian influence.

Still, in the Keynesian view, the primary explanation for the slowdown in net capital formation in the 1970s lies in the low level of output growth during that period, which caused investment demand to lag. Keynesians believe that, *for the most part*, causation runs from low output to low investment rather than in the reverse direction. The low output levels are ascribed, as explained previously, to supply shocks and, at times, to overly restrictive monetary policies.

What about the role of incentives for saving and investment? Although not ignoring the effects of changes in after-tax returns on investment demand, Keynesians argue that output is the key variable determining investment. Thus, the best way to encourage

[4]See James Tobin, "Stabilization Policy Ten Years After," *Brookings Papers on Economic Activity,* 1 (1980), pp. 19–71.

investment is to keep the economy near potential output. In the case of saving, the Keynesians would not deny that the rate of return (after taxes) is a determinant of saving. Nor would Keynesians deny that a decline in this rate of return may have caused the saving rate to decline in the late 1970s. They believe, however, as Tobin states, that "an explanation of the slowdown in business capital formation in the 1970s may be sought in investment demand rather than saving supply."

The Effect of Income Tax Cuts on Labor Supply

Keynesian economists do not believe that vast increases in labor supply will result from lowering marginal income tax rates. They do not believe that current income tax rates are a serious impediment to labor supply. As evidence, Keynesian economists cite the high labor force participation ratios in Western European countries (Germany, for example), where marginal tax rates are substantially higher than in the United States. Further, they point out that, although inflation due to a progressive income tax will push individuals into higher tax brackets, actual tax rates paid will increase only if the tax schedule is unchanged. If, instead, Congress periodically lowers tax rates to offset the effects of inflation (or for some other reason), actual marginal tax rates may not rise. According to estimates cited by Tobin, the federal marginal rate of personal income tax averaged over all brackets was actually lower in 1975 than in 1960—18.0 percent compared with 18.8 percent. In 1975–80, there does appear to have been some "bracket creep" because of inflation, with the average marginal tax rate increasing to 21.6 percent. But Tobin found no evidence of a weakened "propensity to supply labor."

In rebuttal, supply-side economists point to the large increase in payroll taxes over recent decades. Payroll (Social Security) taxes are an additional element in the wedge between the wage paid by the employer and that received by the worker. In addition, the supply-side economists point to empirical studies indicating that, given secular trends that have increased labor force participation rates, income and payroll tax rates have negative effects on labor supply.[5]

The issues, then, appear to be the empirical ones of whether increases in marginal tax rates have been sufficient to create an important work disincentive and, further, whether reductions in marginal tax rates affect labor supply strongly enough to increase employment and output substantially.

Regulation as a Source of Inflation and Slow Growth

Regarding the effects of government regulation on inflation and growth, the issues are broad, and it is incorrect to argue that there is a single Keynesian position that contrasts with the supply-side position. As stated previously, there is no doubt that government regulations increased from the late 1960s to 1980. There is also no doubt that complying with many of these regulations was costly to firms and that much of the cost was passed on to consumers. Nor is it doubtful that many of the regulations were cost-ineffective, in that more efficient ways exist to achieve the same benefits.

[5]See, for example, Jerry Hausman, "Income and Payroll Tax Policy and Labor Supply," in Meyer, ed., *The Supply-Side Effects of Economic Policy;* Jerry Hausman, "Labor Supply," in Henry Aaron and Joseph Pechman, eds., *How Taxes Affect Economic Behavior* (Washington, D.C.: The Brookings Institution, 1981); and Jerry A. Hausman and James M. Poterba, "Household Behavior and the Tax Reform Act of 1986," *Journal of Economic Perspectives,* 1 (Summer 1987), pp. 101–20.

Economists who would not go as far as the supply-siders in dismantling the regulatory structure that arose since the 1960s believe either that the benefits are greater than the supply-side economists claim or that the costs, in terms of lost growth, are lower. In addition, they may be more optimistic about the possibility of improving regulatory effectiveness. The prospective benefits from these new regulations include cleaner air, cleaner water, safer workplaces, and safer consumer products. These are, of course, desirable to all, but opinions differ as to how much government intervention in the economy is needed to achieve them.

19.4 GROWTH POLICIES FROM RONALD REAGAN TO GEORGE W. BUSH

Economic Redirection in the Reagan Years

After the high inflation and unemployment of the 1970s, voters in the United States were ready in 1980 for an experiment with supply-side economics. To be sure, Ronald Reagan's economic proposals and, to an even greater degree, his policies as enacted, contained elements of theories other than those of the supply-siders. Still, the central elements of what became known as *Reaganomics* were supply-side proposals.

Personal Income Tax Reductions

As enacted by Congress, the Reagan tax cut act reduced marginal income tax rates, in three stages, by a total of 23 percent. The act also lowered the top rate on income earned from capital from 70 to 50 percent. Beginning in 1985, the tax bill indexed tax brackets to inflation to prevent bracket creep. As discussed in Section 19.2, in the view of supply-side economists, such income tax cuts should increase labor supply and therefore output (supply-side proposition 3). Personal income tax cuts should also increase personal saving. The reduction in the maximum tax bracket from 70 to 50 percent was especially aimed at increasing saving. In addition, to encourage saving, the tax act extended the opportunity to use tax-deferred accounts for retirement saving.

In the second Reagan administration, the centerpiece was *tax reform*—touted by President Reagan as a "second American Revolution." The aims of tax reform were, first, to broaden the tax *base* by eliminating many deductible items and, second, to reduce *marginal tax rates.* The combination of these actions was to be offsetting, so that total revenues would neither rise nor fall. However, lower marginal tax rates would improve incentives for labor supply, saving, and investment. Congress passed a tax reform act in August 1986 that reflected not only the president's wishes but also the goals of tax reformers in Congress from both political parties. The act lowered the highest tax rate from 50 percent to 28 percent, the lowest top rate since 1931. The act also raised personal exemptions so that approximately 6 million low-income recipients were removed from the tax rolls. To keep tax reform from reducing tax revenues, the act removed many deductions and eliminated a number of tax shelters.

Reductions in Business Taxes

The first Reagan administration's tax act had several features aimed at encouraging capital formation by increasing the after-tax return to investment. The most important of these was the accelerated cost recovery system (ACRS), which was a set of accelerated depreciation allowances for business plant and equipment. In addition, the investment tax credit for certain types of equipment was increased to encourage capital formation.

These business tax cuts were aimed at offsetting the inflation-induced increase in the effective tax rate on business profits, which was discussed in Section 19.2. Such tax cuts are consistent with the supply-side view (proposition 2) that the way to encourage capital formation is by increasing the after-tax return to investment.

Reductions in Nondefense Government Spending

According to the supply-side view, personal and business tax cuts should increase aggregate supply and, therefore, produce noninflationary real output growth. Also, supply-siders hoped that such growth would increase the tax base and therefore increase tax revenues to offset, largely (or completely), the revenue lost due to the lower tax rates. However, to ensure that demand was not overly stimulated and to keep the budget deficit as small as possible, the Reagan program proposed cuts in nondefense government spending in areas such as housing, education, and income maintenance programs. Such cuts were also needed, in part, to finance a proposed increase in defense spending.

After some early success, cuts in nondefense spending met more resistance. Given the increase in defense spending, the overall lack of much success in cutting nondefense spending meant that government spending as a percentage of GNP *rose* rather than fell during President Reagan's first term. Failure to cut spending, together with tax reduction, led to high government budget deficits in both the first and second terms of the Reagan administration.

Reductions in Government Regulation

Consistent with the supply-side view that government regulation in areas such as air quality, worker safety, and consumer product safety has been overly costly and has retarded economic growth (proposition 4), the Reagan administration began a regulatory review. The aim was to eliminate "wasteful or outdated regulation and to make necessary regulation more efficient and more flexible." Some specific regulatory initiatives in the first Reagan administration shifted some responsibilities for air pollution control to the states, decontrol of petroleum markets, proposals to abolish the Departments of Energy and Education, and an executive order calling for a cost-benefit analysis before issuing any new federal regulation.

Initiatives in the First Bush Administration

President George (H. W.) Bush was at first highly critical of supply-side economics, terming it "voodoo economics." Moreover, when he took office in 1989, both houses of Congress had substantial Democratic majorities that had always been skeptical of supply-side policy prescriptions. Still, some of Bush's proposals were certainly consistent with supply-side positions.

When he ran for president in 1988, a central plank in Bush's economic platform was his pledge of "no new taxes." This pledge conformed to the supply-side view of the disincentive effects of higher taxes. Unfortunately from a supply-sider's view, as the budget deficit ballooned in 1990 and 1991, Bush abandoned this pledge to reach a deficit reduction compromise with Congress. A second Bush proposal was to lower the capital gains tax. The supply-side analysis suggests that such a reduction would have a favorable effect on saving and thus on capital formation. Bush was, however, unable to push a capital gains tax cut through Congress.

Growth Policies During the Clinton Administrations

In 1992, the public appeared to choose a new direction in macroeconomic policy. Clintonomics would replace Reaganomics. President Bill Clinton's program envisioned a more activist role for government, one that "recognizes both the market's efficiencies *and* its imperfections." He proposed a "stimulus package" consisting of public investment in infrastructure, worker retraining, and partnerships between business and government to move resources from "sunset" to "sunrise" industries.

Given concern about the large government budget deficit at the time, Congress was unwilling to pass the stimulus package. Prospects for such an activist approach became even bleaker when voters returned Republican majorities to both houses of Congress in the 1994 election. In that election, the House Republicans' "Contract with America," with its provisions for cuts in taxes and spending, a line–item veto, a moratorium on new federal regulation, and a constitutional amendment to balance the budget, was rooted in supply-side economics. But House Republicans were unable to achieve veto-proof margins for the elements of their program; gridlock developed over budget issues, and at one point there was a temporary shutdown of much of the federal government.

After President Clinton was reelected and Republican majorities were returned to the House and Senate in the 1996 election, both sides were ready for compromise. Republicans got tax cuts, including the long-sought reduction in the capital gains tax. Provisions for retirement savings accounts were liberalized to make them more desirable and so encourage saving. President Clinton limited the extent of tax cuts and targeted some of them for subsidizing education and worker retraining.

Most importantly, during President Clinton's second term, budget agreements were reached that led to perennial deficits being replaced by surpluses and (at that time) even larger projected future budget surpluses. The role this change in the federal budget played in the stronger performance of the U.S. economy in the late 1990s is still controversial.

U.S. economic growth was strong in the late 1990s, and the rate of growth in labor productivity rose (see Table 19-1). But factors other than fiscal policy were also at work. Many attribute the strong performance of the U.S. economy during these years to the revolution in information technology and to the conduct of monetary policy. Stronger growth in labor productivity, and thus output growth, in the United States relative to other industrialized countries is attributed to faster U.S. implementation of advances in information technology.

Tax Cuts During the Administration of George W. Bush

In 2000, George W. Bush won a very close election. From the start of his administration, tax cuts were the centerpiece of economic policy. At first, during the recession of 2001, tax cuts were offered as a short-run stimulus for recovery. The central motivation for the tax cuts was, however, to stimulate growth over the medium term. Even after the recovery was well underway, new tax cuts were passed and more proposed. The economic rationale offered for these tax cuts draws heavily from the proposition of supply-side economics. In fact, it is often said that on economic policy, George W. Bush is the heir of Ronald Reagan, not his father, George W. H. Bush.

The packages of tax cuts passed by 2004 included cuts in the income tax, cuts in the tax on corporate dividends and capital gains, and a phaseout of the inheritance tax. The income tax cuts were expected to have a positive effect on labor supply and therefore aggregate supply (the reverse of the effects of a tax increase in Figure 19-4). The reduction of the capital gains tax and the tax on dividends was aimed at increasing saving and investment by raising the after-tax return to these activities (the reverse of the effect of negative changes in these rates of return, illustrated in Figure 19-3). The inheritance tax affected very few estates, so it is hard to see significant supply-side effects from its abolition.

Keynesians, as well as a number of other economists, opposed tax cuts of the size favored by President Bush, especially after the recovery from the 2001 recession became robust. As we saw in Chapter 18, the tax cuts were by 2006 responsible for current and projected future structural federal budget deficits. Keynesians argued that the deficits would push up interest rates and cancel out any beneficial effects on saving and investment. Keynesians also remained doubtful that income tax cuts have significant effects on labor supply. Another ground on which many criticized the tax cuts was their effect on income distribution. Tax cuts on capital gains, dividends, and inheritances directly benefit the wealthy, who are the main recipients of these forms of income and wealth.

Read Perspectives 19-3.

PERSPECTIVES 19-3

EQUALITY AND EFFICIENCY: THE BIG TRADE-OFF

By the early years of this century, it became apparent that a marked rise in income inequality had occurred over the preceding several decades. There are many measures of the distribution of income and numerous concepts of equality or inequality, so this area defies precision. Still, the evidence for growing inequality of both income and wealth is compelling.

One statistic that makes headlines is that the ratio of the pay of U.S. corporate chief executive officers to average wages rose from 27 in 1973 to 300 in 2005. A more comprehensive comparison shows that the top 1 percent of wage earners accounted for 11.2 percent of wage earnings in 2005, up from 8.7 percent a decade ago and 6 percent three decades ago. The change in personal income, which includes income from interest and dividends, is more striking. The share of the top 1 percent rose from 8.2 percent in 1980 to 17.4 percent in 2005. Another aspect of inequality is income mobility, the ability to move through the income distribution. There is some evidence that this is also falling in the United States and that it is lower here than in other countries. An OECD study in 2007 indicates that a child born into the lowest 20 percent of the income distribution in the United States in recent decades had a 40 percent probability of remaining there. In Britain and Denmark that probability is less than 30 percent.

What is causing the growing U.S. income inequality and what, if anything, should be the public policy response? As to causes, a growing skill premium in part due to globalization is an important factor. It is the share of lower-skilled workers that is declining both in the United States and in other highly industrialized economies. Some economists also see a role for the types of policies to increase incentives that we have been discussing. They see a shifting political environment with weaker unions, lower marginal income tax rates, and more favorable tax treatment for investment income as "allowing winners in the economy to expand their winnings."

As to a public policy response, the evidence of growing inequality is strong enough to have attracted the attention of Ben Bernanke, Chairman of the Federal Reserve. He argues that we don't want to interfere with the dynamism that has resulted in the flexibility and adaptability of our economy.[a] But "That said, we also believe that no one should be allowed to slip too far down the economic ladder, especially for reasons beyond his or her control." He goes on to say, "another difficult question is how to balance the need for maintaining strong market-based incentives, which support economic growth and efficiency but may be associated with greater inequality of results, against the goal [of] insuring individuals against the most adverse outcomes, which may reduce inequality but also tends to diminish the strength of incentives."

Bernanke brings us to the trade-off thoughtfully examined by Arthur Okun over 30 years ago in the book from which the title of this perspective is taken.[b] One distinction Okun makes is between rights and markets. We have some guarantees that come from being citizens, "part of the club." These are not determined in the market. Defining institutional arrangements that determine where a guarantee of rights should lead, for example, to interference with the market results in "uneasy compromises."

A theme of his analysis is that "the market needs a place, and the market needs to be kept in its place." We need the incentives the market provides. In their absence, "society would thrash about for alternative incentives—some unreliable, like altruism; some perilous, like collective loyalty; some intolerable like coercion or oppression." The market, however, has its failings. "Given the chance, it would sweep away all other values, and establish a vending-machine society." We don't really want everything to be for sale. Nor would this be acceptable in a democracy.

Okun provided no simple answers. He believed that the conflicts between equality and efficiency are inescapable. He concluded that "capitalism and democracy are really a most improbable mixture. Maybe that is why they need each other—to put some rationality into equality and some humanity into efficiency."

In the current context of globalization, Martin Wolf, a perceptive observer of the process, argues that the return of the "gilded age" in the United States would be bad domestically and for the rest of the world. In the United States, public support for protectionism would rise. Other high-income countries would reject even the good points of the U.S. economic model. He believes that "The right policy is to combine openness to trade with a politically acceptable sharing of the gains in high income countries. The challenge is huge. But it is one at which we cannot afford to fail."[c]

---

[a]Ben Bernanke, "The Level and Distribution of Economic Well-Being," speech (February 2007).

[b]Arthur Okun, *Equality and Effciency: The Big Tradeoff* (Washington D.C.: The Brookings Institution, 1975).

[c]Martin Wolf, "Employment Policies Can Insure a Fair Share of the Feast," *Financial Times*, April 11, 2007, p. 11.

19.5 Conclusion

Even modest changes in the rate of economic growth have large cumulative effects over several decades. Proper policy to help "grow" the economy is an important and controversial subject for economic analysis. Public opinion, and therefore public policy, as to the best approach to fostering economic growth has shifted several times. The proposals of supply-side economics have been central to this debate.

Review Questions and Problems

1. Outline the main features of a supply-sider's prescription for policies to foster noninflationary economic growth. How do these policy prescriptions differ from those of the Keynesians?
2. Compare the Keynesian and supply-siders' positions on the effects of reduction in the income tax rate.
3. Compare the Keynesian and supply-siders' positions on the determinants of saving, investment, and capital formation.
4. Within the supply-side theory, what is the proper role for aggregate demand management policies?
5. An investment tax credit allows firms to deduct a portion of investment spending from their corporate tax liability. Analyze the effect on output of such a tax credit in the Keynesian model and, alternatively, within the supply-side framework.
6. Outline recent (post-1998) trends in U.S. growth rates in GDP and labor productivity. What are the possible factors responsible for these trends?
7. Use the *IS–LM* and aggregate demand–aggregate supply diagrams to present the case in favor of the George W Bush administration tax cuts as a stimulus to growth. What criticisms would Keynesian economists put forward to refute this case?

CHAPTER 20

Long-Run Economic Growth: Origins of the Wealth of Nations

We have examined classical economics within the context of the cyclical behavior of the economy. The main focus of classical economists such as Adam Smith and David Ricardo was, however, the long-run growth of the world economy. Adam Smith, often referred to as the father of modern economics, was writing during the early stages of the industrial revolution. He witnessed the expansion of industrial capitalism and tried to explain the process that was beginning to sustain economic growth in some but not all parts of the world. In this chapter, as in Smith's famous book, the subject is "the nature and causes of the Wealth of Nations."

Living standards across countries vary greatly. Wealth is spread very unequally among nations. Using official measurements of prices and exchange rates, per capita incomes in the United States and wealthy European countries are about 50 times those of the poorest African and Asian countries. This is surely an overstatement, but even correcting for such factors as more nonmarket economic activity in poor countries, per capita income estimates are still 20 times larger in the richest relative to the poorest countries. Within the developed nations, the standard of living has also improved greatly over time. Between 1870 and 2005 in the United States, national income grew at an annual rate of 3.5 percent. Over the same period, per capita income grew at an annual rate of 1.8 percent. The latter figure implies that per capita income doubled approximately every 40 years.

Even small variations in growth rates have large effects when compounded over time. If, for example, U.S. per capita income had grown at only 0.8 percent over this time period, in 2005 per capita income would have been 2.8 times rather than 10 times the 1870 level. The growth rate matters.

20.1 THE NEOCLASSICAL GROWTH MODEL

In the 1950s, macroeconomists developed formal models of the growth process. An important set of these were called *neoclassical* growth models. The name came from the type of production structure in the models that originated in classical (or neoclassical) microeconomics.

Growth and the Aggregate Production Function

As noted in the introduction, over the period 1870–2005, national income in the United States increased at an annual rate of 3.5 percent. Per capita output increased at an annual rate of 1.8 percent. What factors account for such sustained growth? One way to approach this question employs the *aggregate production function* seen in the previous chapters. The aggregate production function relates the level of output to the level of factor inputs.

For the purposes of this chapter, the aggregate production function can be written as

$$Y = A(t)F(K, N) \tag{20.1}$$

Equation (20.1) differs from expressions for the short-run aggregate production function in Chapter 3 in two respects. First, there is the additional term $A(t)$. This term represents technological change, which for now is taken simply to depend on time; that is, as time passes, the $A(t)$ term increases, meaning that more output will be produced for a given amount of factor inputs. In equation (20.1), the $A(t)$ term enters multiplicatively. With this specification, technological change is assumed not to affect the relative marginal productivities of the two factors, as determined by the $F(K, N)$ part of the production function. In other words, technological change results in equal increases in the productivities of both factors. Such technological change is termed *neutral* (favoring neither capital nor labor) technological change. Robert Solow, studying shifts in the aggregate production function over time, found evidence that, for the United States, technological change had in fact been neutral.[1]

A second difference between equation (20.1) and previous specifications of the production function is the absence of the bar over the K variable, indicating that here we are not assuming that the capital stock is constant. We are now dealing with the long run.

On the basis of equation (20.1), we follow Solow's method in the previously mentioned study and write the following specification for the growth in output over time:

$$\frac{\dot{Y}}{Y} = \frac{\dot{A}}{A} + w_k\frac{\dot{K}}{K} + w_n\frac{\dot{N}}{N} \tag{20.2}$$

where the dot over a variable indicates the time rate of change in that variable (e.g., $\dot{N}$ is the rate at which the labor force is increasing). Equation (20.2) specifies the proportional rate of increase in output ($\dot{Y}/Y$) as depending on the proportional rate of technological change ($\dot{A}/A$) and the proportional rates of change in the capital stock and the number of workers employed ($\dot{K}/K$) and ($\dot{N}/N$). The weights (w_k, w_n) attached to these latter two variables are their shares in national output, reflecting their importance in the production process. Equation (20.2) indicates that the growth in output depends on the rate at which technological progress occurs over time and the rate at which factor supplies grow over time.

constant returns to scale
means that increasing all inputs by a certain proportion (e.g., 100 percent) will cause output to rise by the same proportion (100 percent)

If the production function given by equation (20.1) exhibits **constant returns to scale**, it can be written in an alternative form that will provide some insights into the way each factor enters into the growth process. Constant returns to scale mean that if all inputs rise in some proportion, output will increase in the same proportion. A doubling of the amount of both capital and labor used in production would, for example, double the amount of output produced. With constant returns to scale, it follows that for a given technology, fixing $A(t)$, output per worker (Y/N) will

[1] See Robert Solow, "Technical Change and the Aggregate Production Function," *Review of Economics and Statistics,* 39 (August 1957), pp. 312–20. Also relevant to the discussion here is Solow's book, *Growth Theory,* 2nd ed. (London: Oxford University Press, 2000).

FIGURE 20-1 Aggregate Production Function: Equation (20.3)

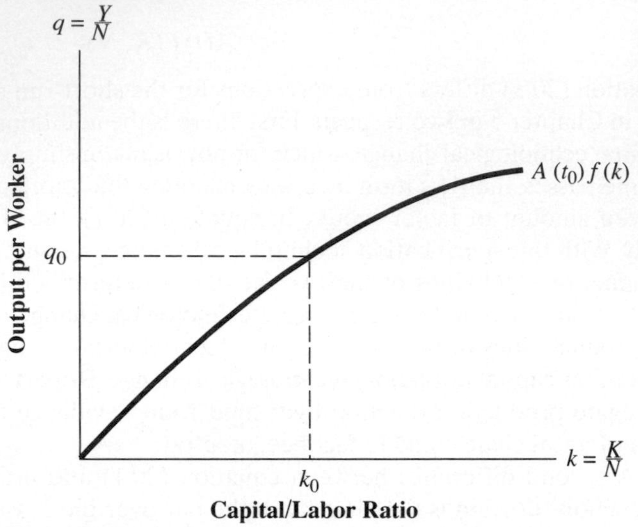

The intensive form of the production function shows output per worker ($q = Y/N$) corresponding to each capital/labor ratio ($k = K/N$) for a given technology [$A(t_0)$]. As the capital/labor ratio rises, output per worker increases but at a declining rate, reflecting diminishing returns to increases in capital per worker.

depend only on the amount of capital employed per worker, the capital/labor ratio.[2] Letting q equal output per worker (Y/N) and k equal capital per worker (K/N), we can rewrite equation (20.1) as

$$\frac{Y}{N} = A(t)f\left(\frac{K}{N}\right)$$

or

$$q = A(t)f(k) \qquad \textbf{(20.3)}$$

where $f(k)$ is the function relating output per worker to the capital/labor ratio for a given technology—what is called the *intensive* form of the aggregate production function.

The relationship given by equation (20.3) is shown in Figure 20-1. The state of technology is assumed to be $A(t_0)$, which fixes the position of the production function relating output per worker to capital per worker. As we move to the right along the production function, output per worker increases with the increase in capital per worker (k). The shape of the production function in Figure 20-1 reflects the assumption that there are diminishing returns to increases in capital per worker. The increment

[2] With constant returns to scale, output per worker (Y/N) does not depend on the level of output. Therefore, with technology fixed, once we fix the capital/labor ratio (K/L), no other variable affects output per worker; Y/N is also fixed.

FIGURE 20-2 Growth in Output per Worker

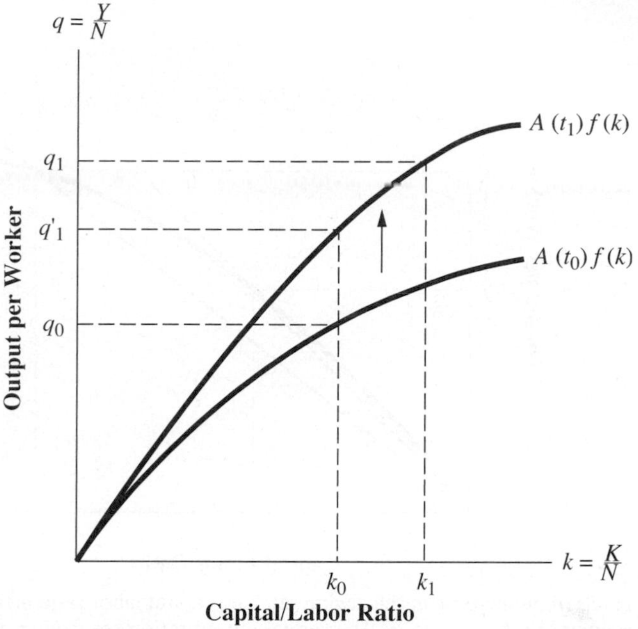

Output per worker increases from q_0 to q'_1 when, as the result of technological progress, the production function shifts upward from $A(t_0)f(k)$ to $A(t_1)f(k)$. There is a further increase in output per worker from q'_1 to q_1 as a result of an increase in the capital/labor ratio from k_0 to k_1.

to output per worker declines with successive increases in capital per worker.[3] At an assumed initial capital/labor ratio of k_0, output per worker would be q_0 in the figure.

Figure 20-2 illustrates the process of growth in output per worker between two points of time, t_0 and t_1. Technological change causes the production function to shift upward from $A(t_0)f(k)$ to $A(t_1)f(k)$. By itself, this technological change would increase output per worker, at the initial capital/labor ratio k_0, from q_0 to q'_0 in Figure 20-2. In addition, however, we assume that the capital/labor ratio increases over time, a process called **capital deepening**. This is illustrated in the graph by a movement to a capital/labor ratio k_1. As a result, output per worker increases further to q_1.

capital deepening is the process by which capital grows at a faster rate than labor and the capital/labor ratio rises

The framework illustrated in Figure 20-2 [the graph of equation (20.3)] suggests that the growth of output per worker is the result of two factors:

1. Technological change, which increases output per worker for a given capital/labor ratio.
2. Capital deepening, as the capital/labor ratio increases.

If we consider the growth rate in total output, as opposed to output per worker, growth in the labor force is an additional source of growth.

[3]Notice that this assumption of diminishing returns to increases in capital intensity is not at odds with the assumption that the production process exhibits constant returns to scale. The latter assumption refers to the effect of proportional increases in *all* factors of production. Diminishing returns to increases in capital intensity refer to the effects of increases in the amount of one factor (capital) per unit of the other factor (labor).

FIGURE 20-3 Effects of an Increase in the Saving Rate

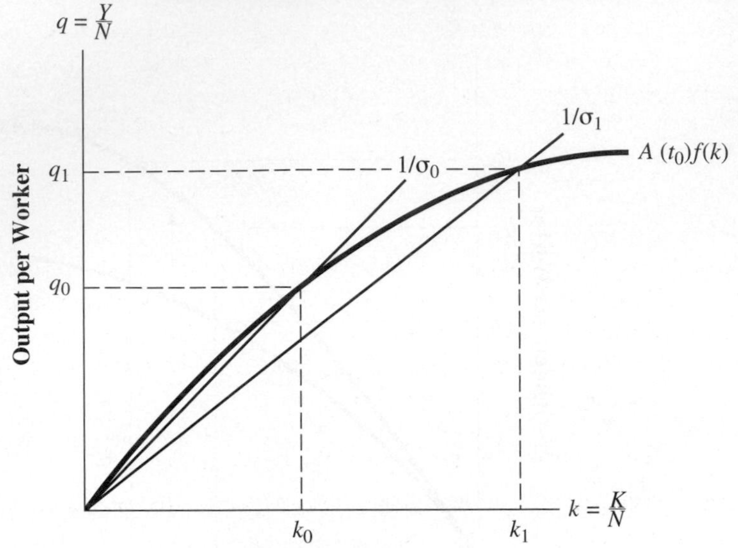

As a result of an increase in the saving rate, the capital/labor ratio increases from k_0 to k_1. Output per worker increases from q_0 to q_1. The capital/output ratio rises from σ_0 to σ_1. Once q_1 is reached, there is no further increase in output per worker. The initial equilibrium growth rate in output is restored.

Sources of Growth in the Neoclassical Model

The analysis in the previous section indicates that within the neoclassical model the factors that determine a country's long-run equilibrium growth rate are those that affect the rate of technological change, labor force growth, and rate of capital formation. Influences on these magnitudes are the ultimate sources of economic growth. We begin with a somewhat paradoxical result: Within the neoclassical growth model, the long-run equilibrium growth rate does not depend on a nation's saving rate ($s = S/Y$).

The independence of a nation's growth rate of the saving rate is at first surprising, because we would expect the saving rate to affect the rate of capital formation and therefore the equilibrium growth rate. To see why the equilibrium growth rate does not depend on the saving rate within the neoclassical model, let us analyze the effect of an increase in the saving rate within the framework of the preceding section.

In Figure 20-3, assume that initially the saving rate is s_0 and that the economy is in equilibrium, with the capital/labor ratio k_0 and output per worker equal to q_0. Consider the ray marked $1/\sigma_0$ coming from the origin and intersecting the production function at a level of output per worker equal to q_0. Each point along the line corresponds to a constant ratio of the variable on the vertical axis Y/N to the variable on the horizontal axis K/N—that is, a constant output/capital ratio—because

$$\frac{Y}{N} \div \frac{K}{N} = \frac{Y}{K} = \frac{1}{\sigma}$$

where σ is the capital/output ratio (K/Y). Initially, the capital/output ratio is σ_0 in Figure 20-3.

Now consider an increase in the saving rate to some higher value, s_1 (say, 15 percent of income as opposed to 10 percent of income). Initially, the economy was assumed to be in equilibrium at the capital/labor ratio k_0; capital and labor were growing at the same rate. With the increase in the saving rate, the rate of capital formation will initially increase. To see this relationship, we need to specify the relationship between capital formation and the saving rate. The rate of capital formation can be written as

$$\frac{\dot{K}}{K} = \frac{I}{K} - \frac{D}{K} \qquad \textbf{(20.4)}$$

where I is gross investment and D is depreciation. In long-run equilibrium, output will grow as supply grows, so we ignore the problem of inadequate demand. We assume that all saving (S) is channeled into investment ($I = S$). We also assume that depreciation is a constant fraction (δ) of the capital stock. Using these facts, we can rewrite equation (20.4) as

$$\frac{\dot{K}}{K} = \frac{S}{K} - \frac{\delta K}{K} = \frac{sY}{K} - \frac{\delta K}{K} \qquad \textbf{(20.5)}$$

where the second equality follows from the fact that saving is equal to the saving rate times the level of income. From equation (20.5) it follows that an increase in the saving rate (s) will *initially* increase the rate of capital formation.

Because the rate of capital formation has increased with no change in the rate of growth in the labor force, the capital/labor ratio will rise. A new equilibrium will be reached, as shown in Figure 20-3, at a capital/labor ratio k_1 and with higher output per worker, q_1. After this adjustment, however, there will be no further increase in output per worker and, because labor force growth is unchanged, the equilibrium growth rate will return to its initial level.

To see why, look at the ray labeled $1/\sigma_1$, which crosses the production function at the new level of output per worker, q_1 in Figure 20-3. As explained previously, each point along such a ray corresponds to a fixed capital/output ratio. The $1/\sigma_1$ ray is flatter than the initial $1/\sigma_0$ ray, indicating that the ratio of Y/N to K/N, the output/capital ratio, is lower after the increase in the saving rate. The capital/output ratio (K/Y) is therefore *higher.* At a higher capital/output ratio, a larger saving rate ($s = S/Y$) is required just to maintain a constant growth rate in the capital stock. Once the capital/output ratio has reached σ_1, capital formation will have returned to the initial equilibrium rate equal to the growth rate in the labor force. There will be no further increases in output per worker or the capital/labor ratio.

The effect on the rate of economic growth is shown in Figure 20-4. Assume that the equilibrium growth rate for income is g. If the rise in the saving rate occurs at time t_0, the growth rate ($\dot{Y}/Y$) will rise temporarily as the economy moves from the initial level of output per worker, q_0, to the higher level of output per worker, q_1. At this new higher level of output per worker, the growth rate will return to g, as shown at time t_1 in Figure 20-4. The increased saving rate causes a temporary period of faster growth but does not affect the equilibrium growth rate.

None of the preceding discussion implies that the saving rate is unimportant in the neoclassical growth model. The temporary period during which a change in the saving rate does affect the growth rate (from t_0 to t_1 in Figure 20-4) may be a long period in calendar time. Also, notice that even after the full adjustment to a change in the saving rate (after we reach t_1 in Figure 20-4 and k_1 and q_1 in Figure 20-3), the higher saving rate has resulted in a *permanent* increase in both capital and output per worker. An

FIGURE 20-4 Effect on the Growth Rate of an Increase in the Saving Rate

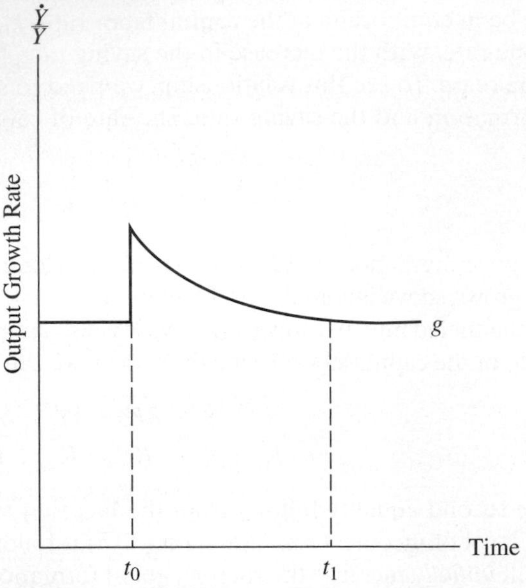

At time t_0, the saving rate increases. Initially, the rate of growth in output rises. This is the period when output per worker is increasing from q_0 to q_1, as shown in Figure 20-3. At time t_1, when output per worker has reached q_1 in Figure 20-3, the initial equilibrium growth rate g has been restored.

economy with a higher saving rate will therefore have a higher standard of living due to a more capital-intensive production process.

Read Perspectives 20-1

20.2 RECENT DEVELOPMENTS IN THE THEORY OF ECONOMIC GROWTH

After an active period in the 1950s and 1960s, interest in the theory of long-run economic growth declined in the 1970s due to doubts about whether it really told us much about growth. The neoclassical growth model explained the dynamics of the growth process, but it ended up telling us that the long-run equilibrium growth rate depended on two exogenous variables: the rate of population growth and the rate of technological change. Because these variables were exogenous, the theory did not isolate the fundamental sources of long-run growth. For this reason, few policy conclusions were derived from the traditional theory of long-term growth.

The latter 1980s witnessed a resurgence of interest in growth theory. Paul Romer, one of the developers of the *new growth theory*, states: "From the point of view of policy advice, growth theory had little to offer. In models with exogenous technological change and exogenous population growth, it never really mattered what the government did."[4]

[4]Paul Romer, "Capital Accumulation and Long-Run Growth," in Robert J. Barro, ed., *Modern Business Cycle Theory* (Cambridge, Mass.: Harvard University Press, 1989), p. 51. Keep in mind that we are discussing the long run. In the previous section, we saw that the saving rate could affect the growth rate, perhaps for a substantial period of time. There are certainly government policies that can influence saving. Only the long-run equilibrium growth rate was exogenous.

Endogenous Growth Models

Recent research extends the traditional analysis by making the rate of technological change or of population growth (or both) endogenous. Having done this, we can ask what factors will speed up or impede the growth process. How will various government policies affect the growth in these variables? The new growth theory is not an attack on the traditional theory. It is, rather, an extension that goes more deeply into the ultimate sources of growth. To see the lines along which this research is proceeding, we examine a model of endogenous technological change.

PERSPECTIVES 20-1

GROWTH ACCOUNTING FOR THE UNITED STATES: AN EXAMPLE

Edward Denison carefully studied economic growth in the United States. Table 20-1 summarizes his findings concerning the sources of growth in U.S. output for 1929–82. As the table indicates, real output grew at an annual rate of 2.9 percent over this period. The other numbers in the table show the percentage (proportion of the total) contribution to the growth rate of several factors. These factors are broken into two groups.

The first group, containing one factor, is growth in labor input. This is growth in output due to the increase in the quantity of labor. Denison estimated that 32 percent, approximately one-third, of the growth in output between 1929 and 1982 came from this source.

The other sources of growth are factors that increase the amount of output per unit of labor input (referred to as output per worker in the previous section)—in other words, factors that increase *labor productivity*. Let us consider each in turn.

EDUCATION PER WORKER

The first of these other sources of growth listed in Table 20-1 is education per worker. As explained by Denison:

> Educational background decisively conditions both the types of work an individual is able to perform and his proficiency in any particular occupation. The distribution of American workers by highest school grade completed has shifted upward continuously and massively, and this shift has been a major growth source.[a]

Denison estimated that 14 percent of U.S. economic growth is due to increased education of the labor force.

CAPITAL FORMATION

Denison estimated that capital formation was responsible for 19 percent, just less than one-fifth, of U.S. economic growth between 1929 and 1982.

TABLE 20-1 Sources of U.S. Economic Growth, 1929–82 (percent)

Annual growth rate of output (percent)	2.9
Percentage of growth due to:	
Growth in labor input	32
Growth in labor productivity	
Education per worker	14
Capital formation	19
Technological change	28
Economies of scale	9
Other factors	−2

SOURCE: Edward F. Denison, *Trends in American Economic Growth, 1929–82* (Washington, D.C.: The Brookings Institution, 1985), p. 30.

TECHNOLOGICAL CHANGE

The next factor in Table 20-1 is technological change. This includes changes in technological knowledge (e.g., ways to employ robots in the production process) as well as new knowledge about how to organize businesses (managerial strategies). In Denison's estimates, technological change accounted for 28 percent of growth and was the most important influence on labor productivity.

ECONOMIES OF SCALE

Denison found that, rather than the constant return to scale we assumed in the previous section, the United States has experienced economies of scale; even given the state of technology, an increase in the quantity of inputs has resulted in a more than proportional increase in output. Denison estimated that 9 percent of U.S. growth from 1929 to 1982 resulted from this source.

OTHER FACTORS

Denison considered other factors that either stimulate or retard the growth process (e.g., changes in allocation of resources among industries, effects of weather on farm output, work stoppages). Taken together, these factors had a net negative effect equal to 2 percent of economic growth.

[a]Edward F. Denison, *Trends in American Growth 1929–82* (Washington, D.C.: The Brookings Institution, 1985), p. 15.

Beginning with the assumption that technological change is a process to model, rather than taking it as exogenous, seems sensible. As two of the new growth theorists cogently argue,

> Innovations do not fall like manna from heaven. Instead they are created by human beings, operating under the normal range of human motivations, in the process of trying to solve production problems, to learn from experience, to find new and better ways of doing things, to profit from opening up new markets, and sometimes just to satisfy their curiosity. Innovation is thus a social process. . . . Thus economic growth involves a two-way interaction between technology and economic life: technology transforms the very economic system that creates it.[5]

To model endogenous technology, we modify the production structure of the neoclassical growth model. First, we specify production of final goods, which we continue to refer to as *output* (Y). The modified form of equation (20.1) is as follows:

$$Y_t = F((1 - \alpha_k)K_t, (1 - \alpha_n)N_t, A_t) \qquad \textbf{(20.6)}$$

As before, output depends on the levels of the capital (K) and labor (N) inputs. The fractions of the economywide levels of capital and labor used in the production of output are $(1 - \alpha_k)$ and $(1 - \alpha_n)$, respectively. Output also depends on the level of technology (A), which we will now term *knowledge*, following the new growth literature. Notice that A_t now appears inside the production function in a more general specification than before. More important, note that all knowledge rather than a fraction appears. Using knowledge in the other sector we will specify—to produce new knowledge—does not keep the final output sector from employing the same knowledge.

[5]Philippe Agion and Peter Howitt, *Endogenous Growth Theory* (Cambridge, Mass.: MIT Press, 1998), p. 1.

Now we turn to the production function for new ideas.

$$\dot{A}_t = G(\alpha_k K_t, \alpha_n N_t, A_t) \tag{20.7}$$

The growth in konwledge ($\dot{A}$) depends on the capital and labor used in producing knowledge, with α_k and α_n being the fractions of the capital stock and labor force used in this sector. The production of new knowledge also depends on the *whole* stock of existing knowledge.

Implications of Endogenous Technological Change

How endogenous technological change affects our conclusions about the process of growth depends on the details of the specification of the two production functions, especially equation (20.7).

In the new growth literature, it is common to assume that the production function for output (equation 20.6) exhibits constant returns to capital and labor. This implies that doubling the amounts of the capital and labor inputs used to produce output with a given stock of knowledge would double the amount of output. This is the assumption in the neoclassical model.

What assumption we should make about the production function for new knowledge (equation 20.7) is less clear. There are several alternatives in the new growth literature. A crucial question here is the effect of the existing stock of knowledge (A) on new discoveries ($\dot{A}$). One might think that a greater existing body of knowledge makes further advances harder; there might be diminishing returns to research and development. Alternatively, new discoveries may foster further advances or at least leave returns to further research constant. It is in these latter cases that endogenous technological change causes the new growth theory to diverge from the neoclassical model in crucial ways.

In the neoclassical model with constant returns to scale and exogenous technology, we saw that an increase in the saving rate initially increased the rate of capital formation. In the neoclassical model, an increase in the rate of capital formation causes a less than proportionate increase in the growth rate of output. The reason is that, with constant returns to scale, the growth rate in the labor input would have to increase by the samc amount as that of capital in order for output growth to rise proportionately. We are assuming that the growth rate in the labor input will be fixed. Although the growth rate in output rises less in proportion to the increase in the growth rate of capital, depreciation rises proportionately because, in both the traditional and newer growth models, depreciation is simply a fraction of the stock of capital, δ in the previous subsection. With the growth rate in output rising less than proportionately while the growth rate in capital and the depreciation rate are rising proportionately, depreciation becomes a larger fraction of output and eventually absorbs the higher saving. The rate of capital formation and the growth rate in output return to their initial levels.

A similar process can occur in an endogenous growth model, but there are other more interesting possibilities. If the response of new knowledge to capital and existing knowledge—the reproducible factors in the model—is sufficiently high, changes that increase growth in the model will lead to a sustained higher growth rate or may lead to explosive growth. The latter would mean that the growth rate moves to an ever-increasing trajectory.

Consider the outcome of explosive growth. Suppose we begin by increasing the proportions of capital (α_k) and labor (α_n) devoted to producing knowledge. If the production function for new knowledge is such that there are increasing returns to knowledge production from existing knowledge, taken together with the resulting increase in capital as output rises, output growth will move to an ever-increasing time path. Of course, the growth rate in output cannot increase forever. Still, a model of this type might be applicable for a period where growth "takes off." Moreover, for other specifications of the production function for knowledge, the result of applying more capital and labor to knowledge production would be a one-time rise in the growth rate that was just sustained rather than explosive growth.

Policy Implications of Endogenous Growth

Endogenous growth models imply that a wide range of government policies may influence a country's long-term growth rate. In our previous example, a policy to increase investment in research and development leads to a permanent change in the long-term growth rate. In some endogenous growth models, knowledge is embodied in new types of capital goods, so investment in capital and new ideas go together. In this case, policies to increase capital formation would be able to permanently increase the growth rate of output for certain specifications of the production function.

In the neoclassical growth model, the long-term growth rate in output is driven by the exogenous growth rate in the labor force and by exogenous technological change. With endogenous technological change there is greater scope for government policy; that is, there are more cases where what the government does will matter.

20.3 INTERCOUNTRY INCOME DIFFERENCES REVISITED

Let us return to where we began this chapter: considering huge intercountry differences in per capita incomes that must be due to differences in past rates of economic growth. How do the theories we have examined explain these differences? What do these theories predict about the future distribution of the wealth of nations?

Much of the discussion of these questions has focused on the hypothesis of *convergence*, the idea that per capita income levels across countries will tend to converge over time, with richer countries growing more slowly than poorer ones.

The neoclassical growth model provides support for the idea of convergence. In that model, an economy that is below the steady-state capital/labor ratio and therefore the steady-state capital/output ratio will have a relatively high growth rate as it moves to the long-run equilibrium growth path. If production functions, saving rates, and investment in human capital were the same across countries and technology could move freely across country boundaries, different countries would be converging to the same steady state. Current intercountry differences in per capita income would in this case be the result of shocks that had taken place in the past. Past wars or colonial domination would have displaced an economy from its steady-state equilibrium. An economy subject to such a negative shock would then grow more rapidly than one that had not been affected as it returned to its steady-state equilibrium.

What does empirical evidence reveal about convergence? First, consider Figure 20-5, which looks at 21 OECD members, a sample of highly industrialized countries. In the

FIGURE 20-5 Convergence in the OECD, 1960–97

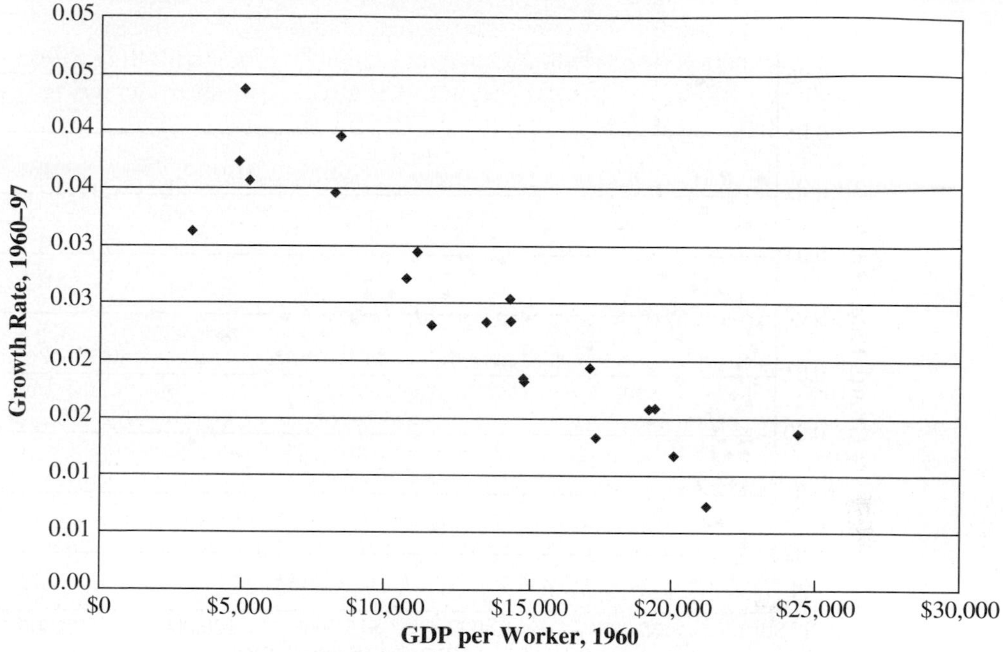

figure, the average annual growth rate in GDP for 1960–97 is measured along the vertical axis and the initial (1960) GDP level is on the horizontal level. The scatter of points has the negative slope consistent with the convergence hypothesis: Countries with the highest initial GDP per capita had lower growth rates than countries that were poorer at the outset.

An examination of data for U.S. states, which compares post-1880 growth in per capita income with the 1880 income level, also provides support for convergence.[6] The states with the highest 1880 income levels grew more slowly in subsequent years.

But now look at Figure 20-6. Here we examine a broader sample of countries. In addition to the OECD countries considered in Figure 20-5, the sample includes middle-income countries and some very poor countries, 71 countries overall. As can be seen from the figure, this data set does not support convergence. Notice in particular that some of the countries with the lowest initial levels of per capita income had low and in some cases negative rates of growth in subsequent years.

How should we interpret the disparate findings about convergence? One interpretation of the data from OECD countries and U.S. states is that the assumption that these groups had similar economic features is reasonable. Thus, they may have the same steady-state equilibrium income levels. Countries or states with lower initial income levels were below their steady-state equilibrium point. The economic infrastructure in some OECD countries, for example, certainly sustained more damage in World

[6]See Robert J. Barro and Xavier Sala-i-Martin, "Convergence," *Journal of Political Economy,* 100 (April 1992), pp. 223–51.

FIGURE 20-6 Convergence in OECD and Non-OECD Countries, 1960–97

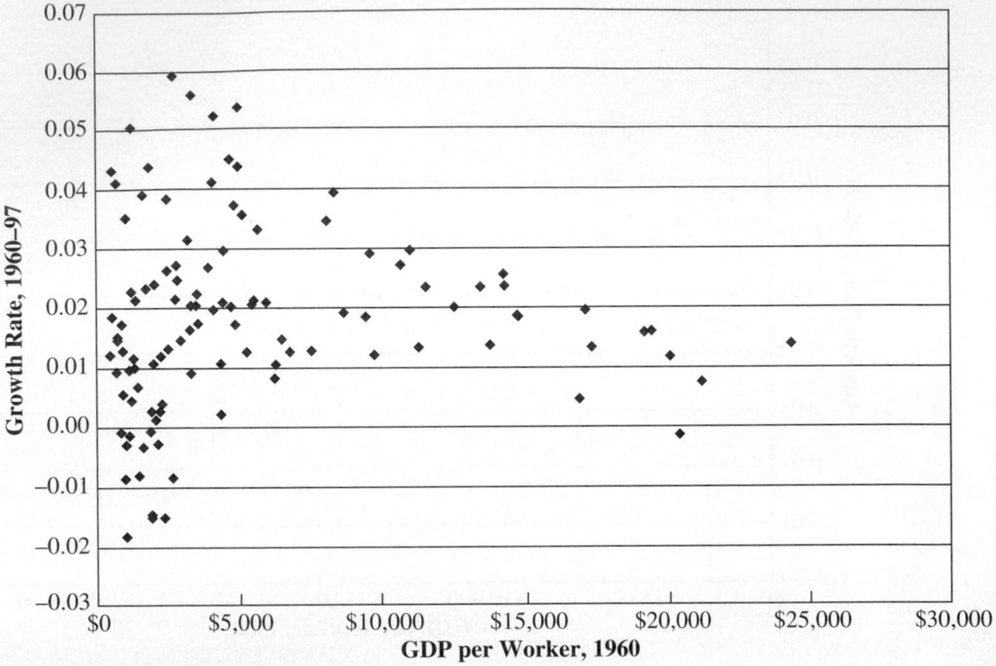

War II than in others. In the case of U.S. states, the economies of southern states were devastated by the Civil War, while those of the northern states were not.

When we go to the broad sample of countries, the assumption of similar economic structures across countries may become untenable. Thus, these countries have very different steady states. Consequently, they are not moving to any one capital/labor or capital/output ratio. Their income levels are not converging.

The concept of convergence we have considered so far is called *absolute* convergence. Countries with lower initial income will have higher subsequent growth rates period. A weaker concept is *conditional* convergence. An economy will grow more rapidly if it is below its own steady-state per capita income level. Steady-state levels will, however, differ across countries due to the different features of their economies. Conditioned upon these different economic features, countries with higher initial income levels will have lower growth rates in later years.

A number of studies have found support for conditional convergence across a broad set of countries such as that in Figure 20.6.[7] Important control variables, those that influence the steady-state income level across countries, include the level of human capital per capita, adherence to the rule of law, the degree of openness to foreign trade, and some macroeconomic variables such as inflation rates and government consumption ratios. Given these variables, the initial income level has the expected negative effect. Still, these studies indicate that convergence is a slow process occurring over many decades.

Read Perspectives 20-2.

[7]See, for example, Robert J. Barro, and Xavier Sala-i-Martin, *Economic Growth,* 2nd ed. (New York: McGraw-Hill, 2004), chapter 12.)

PERSPECTIVES 20-2

MUCK, MONEY, AND THE MORAL CONSEQUENCES OF ECONOMIC GROWTH

A nineteenth-century adage in the Midlands of England was "Where there's muck there's money." Economic growth came with environmental damage even then. In this chapter, we have been concerned with the factors that determine the rate of growth of output, a question of *positive economics.* What about the desirability or undesirability of economic growth, a question of *normative economics*?

The muck is one concern. Today an example would be carbon emissions into the environment and the resulting global warming. Other types of air and water pollution are also examples of negative externalities from economic growth. If growth has negative effects that are not priced in the market, then, rather than policies to promote growth, we should be willing to implement policies that, by properly pricing the consequences of growth, will have the effect of reducing it. Carbon taxes are an example.

In a recent book, however, Benjamin Friedman argues that there are some positive externalities to growth that should not be ignored.[a] He argues that more rapid economic growth fosters movement toward openness, tolerance, fairness, and democracy in societies. Slow growth or stagnation moves societies in the opposite directions.

Friedman believes that we use two benchmarks to measure our economic well-being: where we stand relative to the past and where we are relative to others. In a rapidly growing economy, most people see themselves as improving according to the first of these benchmarks. There is thus less need to be concerned about the second. With slow grow or stagnation, the feeling develops that current living standards are threatened by anyone else's gains or by new groups entering the society to compete. Openness and tolerance decline. Discrimination, inwardness, and defensiveness thrive. Friedman provides support for his thesis with a broad historical survey of the post–Civil War United States and of nineteenth- and twentieth-century Western Europe.

From a policy standpoint, he argues that "To the extent that economic growth brings not only higher private incomes but also greater openness, tolerance and democracy—benefits that the market does not price—and to the extent that these benefits outweigh any unpriced harm that might ensure, market forces alone will systematically provide too little growth."[b] The externalities along this dimension favor policies to foster growth.

So, as is so often the case in questions of economic policy, we are left saying: on the one hand, but then on the other hand. There *is* the muck to consider. The English writer J. B. Priestly, on a trip to the Midlands in the 1930s, noted that "But now there is not much money, there is still a lot of muck. It must last longer." The cost of avoiding more environmental damage may, however, have consequences beyond fewer gas guzzlers and mini-mansions if it lowers the rate of economic growth.

[a]Benjamin Friedman, *The Moral Consequences of Economic Growth* (New York: Alfred A. Knopf, 2005).
[b]Ibid. p. 15.

20.4 Conclusion

The neoclassical growth model implies that the rate of technological change is the primary determinant of the steady-state equilibrium rate of growth in per capita income. The saving rate and therefore the rate of investment in both physical and human capital will affect the growth rate for a considerable period of time and will also influence the steady-state capital/labor and capital/output ratios. In endogenous growth models, the saving rate and thus the rate of capital formation can have permanent effects on a nation's growth rate.

Because of intercountry differences in these variables, there have been large differences across countries in growth experiences. Past shocks such as wars, civil unrest, rapacious dictators, and colonial domination no doubt also influenced cross-country differences in growth rates. Consequently, there are very large disparities in per capita income levels across countries. The gains that could be made in a country by a generation of rapid growth are huge. Per capita income in Taiwan grew by 6.4 percent per year between 1960 and 2000. This growth increased the level of per capita income by a factor of 13. Singapore, Hong Kong, and South Korea all had growth rates of over 5 percent per year. This is what has been called the *Asian miracle*. In contrast, in the Democratic Republic of Congo, per capita income *fell* at an annual rate of 3.2 percent over these years and the level of per capita income by 2000 was one-third of the level of 1960.

Concerning the factors that lead to rapid growth in some countries and stagnation in others, Robert Lucas has written, "The consequences for human welfare involved in questions like these are simply staggering: Once one starts to think about them, it is hard to think about anything else."[8]

Key Terms

- constant returns to scale 411
- capital deepening 413

Review Questions and Problems

1. Explain why, in the neoclassical growth model with exogenous technological change, the long-run equilibrium rate of growth in output is independent of the saving rate (S/Y).
2. According to Denison's estimates, which factors were most important in accounting for the growth in real output over the 1929–82 period?
3. What features of the neoclassical growth model led to the criticism that the model did not really *explain* the processes that generated economic growth? How do endogenous growth models try to remedy this possible weakness of the neoclassical model?
4. Explain the convergence hypothesis. How does the hypothesis of absolute convergence differ from that of conditional convergence?
5. What does it mean to say that growth is exogenous or endogenous? How does the production structure of an endogenous growth model differ from that of the neoclassical growth model?
6. Why do many economists think that large cross-country income differences are hard to reconcile with implications of the neoclassical growth model?

[8]Robert Lucas, Jr., "On the Mechanics of Economic Development," *Journal of Monetary Economics,* 22 (July 1988), pp. 3–42.

Glossary

A

The **accelerator model** is a model of business investment that in its simplest form relates the level of investment to the rate of change in output. More complex forms take account of adjustment costs and borrowing costs.

Aggregate demand is the sum of the demands for current output by each of the buying sectors of the economy: households, businesses, the government, and foreign purchasers of exports.

The **aggregate demand curve** measures the demand for total output at each value of the aggregate price level.

The **aggregate supply function** is the macroeconomic analog to the individual market supply function, which shows the output forthcoming at each level of product price. The aggregate supply function, shows the total output firms will supply at each value of the aggregate price level.

Automatic stabilizers are changes in taxes and government transfer payments that occur when the level of income changes.

The **autonomous expenditure multiplier** gives the change in equilibrium output per unit change in autonomous expenditures (e.g., government spending).

Autonomous expenditures are expenditures that are largely determined by factors other than current income.

The **average propensity to consume (APC)** is the ratio of consumption to income.

The **average propensity to save (APS)** is the ratio of saving to income.

B

The **balanced-budget multiplier** gives the change in equilibrium output that results from a 1-unit increase or decrease in *both* taxes and government spending.

The **balance of payments accounts** record economic transactions between the home country and foreign residents for both goods and assets.

The **Board of Governors of the Federal Reserve** is composed of seven members (governors) appointed by the president of the United States with the advice and consent of the Senate for a term of 14 years. One member of the board is appointed chairman.

The **Bretton Woods system** was a pegged exchange rate system set up at the end of World War II.

C

The **Cambridge approach** is a version of the quantity theory of money that focuses on the demand for money ($M^d = kPY$).

The **capital account** in the balance of payments is a record of purchases of U.S. assets by foreign residents (capital inflows) and purchases of foreign assets by U.S. residents (capital outflows).

Capital deepening is the process where by capital grows at a faster rate than labor and the capital/labor ratio rises.

Capital formation is growth in the stock of plant and equipment.

A **capital gain** is the increase in the market value of any asset above the price originally paid.

Capital goods are capital resources such as factories, machinery, and railroads used to produce other goods.

A **capital loss** is the decrease in the market value of any asset below the price originally paid.

Constant returns to scale means that increasing all inputs by a certain proportion (e.g., 100 percent) will cause output to rise by the same proportion (100 percent).

The **consumer price index (CPI)** measures the retail prices of a fixed "market basket" of several thousand goods and services purchased by households.

Consumption is the household sector's demand for output for current use. *Consumption expenditures* consist of purchases of durable goods (e.g., autos and televisions), nondurable goods (e.g., food and newspapers), and services (e.g., haircuts and taxi rides).

The **consumption function** is the Keynesian relationship between income and consumption.

Corporate bonds are formal IOUs that require the corporation to pay a fixed sum of money (interest payment) annually until maturity and then, at maturity, a fixed sum of money to repay the initial amount borrowed (principal).

The **current account** in the U.S. balance of payments is a record of U.S. merchandise exports and imports as well as trade in services and foreign transfer payments.

The **cyclical deficit** is the portion of the federal deficit that results from the economy's being at a low level of economic activity.

Cyclical unemployment results from fluctuations in the level of economic activity and consequent fluctuations in industry demand for workers.

D

The **deposit multiplier** gives the increase in bank deposits per unit increase in bank reserves.

Depository institutions are financial intermediaries whose main liabilities are deposits. Depository institutions include commercial banks, savings and loan associations, mutual savings banks, and credit unions.

Depreciation is the portion of the capital stock that wears out each year.

The **discount rate** is the rate the Federal Reserve charges on loans to depository institutions.

E

Economies of scale are present when a doubling of all inputs results in *more* than a doubling of output.

The **effective tax rate** is the taxpayer's tax bill divided by her or his total income.

In **efficiency wage models,** the productivity of labor depends on the real wage workers are paid. In such models, the real wage is set to maximize the efficiency units of labor per dollar of expenditure, not to clear the labor market.

Elasticity measures the percentage change in one variable per 1 percent change in another variable: for example, the elasticity of money demand with respect to the interest rate.

The **euro** is the new currency of 12 members of the European Union (Greece joined in 2001).

An **exchange rate** is the value of one country's currency in terms of foreign currencies.

An **exchange rate system** is a set of rules organizing the determination of exchange rates among currencies.

F

Factors of production are labor, land, capital, and entrepreneurship.

The **federal budget deficit** is the excess of federal government outlays over revenues.

The **federal funds rate** is the rate at which banks make loans to one another.

The **Federal Reserve System** (Federal Reserve, or the Fed, for short) is composed of 12 regional Federal Reserve banks and the Board of Governors located in Washington, D.C.

Financial intermediaries are institutions that accept funds from savers and make loans to ultimate borrowers (e.g., firms).

Fiscal stabilization policy is the use of government spending and tax policies to affect the level of economic activity.

Foreign exchange is a term used for foreign currencies in general.

Frictional unemployment is unemployment due to the time workers spend between jobs and to the time entrants or reentrants to the labor force need to find jobs.

G

Government purchases of goods and services are the part of current output that goes to the government sector—the federal government as well as state and local governments.

Government spending refers to government outlays for purchases, transfer payments, and subsidies.

The **Gramm–Rudman–Hollings Act** mandated a move to a balanced budget in steps over five years by *automatic* spending cuts if Congress failed to balance the budget by legislation.

Gross domestic product (GDP) is a measure of all currently produced final goods and services.

Gross national product (GNP) is, like gross domestic product, a measure of aggregate national production. There are two differences between the two measures, both of which concern foreign transactions. GNP includes foreign earnings of U.S. corporations and earnings of U.S. residents working overseas; GDP does not include these items. Conversely, GDP includes earnings from current production in the United States that accrue to foreign residents and foreign-owned firms, whereas GNP excludes those items.

H

Human capital is the accumulation of investments in schooling, training, and health that raises people's productive capacity.

A **hyperinflation** is a period when the price level explodes. In the worst hyperinflation, inflation rates reach several thousand percent *per month.*

Hysteresis describes the tendency for a variable shocked away from an initial value to not return to that value even after the shock is over. Persistently high unemployment rates in many European countries have led economists to argue that unemployment exhibits hysteresis.

I

The **implicit gross national/domestic/deflator** is an index of the prices of goods and services included in gross national/ domestic/product.

Indirect business taxes are general sales and excise taxes.

Induced expenditures are expenditures determined primarily by current income.

Inflation is an increase in the general level of prices as measured, for example, by a price index.

Insider–outsider models provide one explanation of hysteresis in unemployment. Insiders (e.g., union members) are the only group that affect the real wage bargain. Outsiders (e.g., those who want jobs) do not. Recessions cause insiders to become outsiders. After the recession, with fewer insiders, the real wage rises and unemployment persists.

Intermediate targeting on a monetary aggregate is a monetary policy strategy that aims at hitting money growth targets, with the ultimate goal of controlling the level of economic activity.

The **inventory theoretic approach** to the transactions demand for money regards money as an inventory of the medium of exchange held similarly to a firm's holding of an inventory of goods.

Investment is the part of gross national product purchased by the business sector plus residential construction.

L

Labor comprises the physical energy, manual skill, and mental ability that humans apply to the production of goods and services.

Legal reserve requirements specify that banks must hold a certain percentage (fraction) of deposits either in the form of vault cash (currency) or as deposits at regional Federal Reserve banks. They are called *fractional reserve requirements.*

The **life cycle hypothesis** about consumption asserts that saving and consumption decisions of households reflect a plan for an optimal consumption pattern over their lifetime, subject to the constraint of their resources.

The **liquidity trap** is a situation at a very low interest rate where the speculative demand for money schedule becomes nearly horizontal.

M

M1 is the narrower of the two money supply measures in the United States. It consists of currency plus *checkable* deposits. Another measure, M2, is broader. It includes all the components of M1 plus some additional bank deposits that have no or only limited provisions for checks.

The **Maastricht Treaty** of 1991 was a key step in the move to the euro as a common currency for the 12 members of the European Union. The treaty set guidelines for the economies of member countries that had to be satisfied before they could adopt the common currency.

A **managed float** for a country's exchange rate is a system in which, at some times, the exchange rate is allowed to respond to market forces, while at other times the central bank *intervenes* to influence the exchange rate.

Marginal cost is the extra, or additional, cost of producing 1 more unit of output.

The **marginal product** of an input is the addition to total output due to the addition of an extra unit of that input (the quantity of other inputs being held constant).

The **marginal propensity to consume (MPC)** is the increase in consumption per unit increase in disposable income.

The **marginal propensity to save (MPS)** is the increase in saving per unit increase in disposable income.

Marginal revenue is the added revenue associated with the sale of 1 more unit of output.

The **marginal revenue product (MRP)** of any resource input is the extra revenue the firm gains by using 1 more unit of the input, holding other inputs constant.

The **marginal tax rate** is the rate paid on each additional dollar earned from an activity.

The **marginal utility** of a good is the additional satisfaction a consumer derives from consuming 1 additional unit of that good.

Menu costs refer to any type of cost that a firm incurs if it changes its product price.

The **merchandise trade balance** measures exports minus imports in the U.S. balance of payments.

The **monetary base** is equal to currency held by the public plus bank reserves.

Monetary policy is the central bank's use of control of the money supply and interest rates to influence the level of economic activity.

Money is whatever is commonly accepted as payment in exchange for goods and services (and payment of debts and taxes).

The **money multiplier** gives the increase in the money supply per unit increase in the monetary base.

N

National income is the sum of the earnings of all factors of production that come from current production.

Natural rates of output, employment, and therefore unemployment in the monetarist model are determined by *real* supply-side factors: the capital stock, the size of the labor force, and the level of technology. In our simple model, the natural rates of output, employment, and unemployment are the classical equilibrium levels of these variables (unemployment being confined to frictional and structural forms).

Net exports are total (gross) exports minus imports.

Net national product (NNP) is gross national product minus depreciation.

The **new classical policy ineffectiveness proposition** asserts that systematic monetary and fiscal policy actions that change aggregate demand will *not* affect output and employment even in the short run.

Nominal GDP is GDP measured in current dollars.

O

Oligopoly is closer to monopoly than to perfect competition because it is typified by few firms (as few as two or three) and by moderately difficult entry. In product-type oligopoly, markets may have either standardized or differentiated products.

The **open market** is the market of dealers in government securities in New York City.

The **Open Market Committee** is composed of 12 voting members: the 7 members of the Board of Governors and 5 of the presidents of regional Federal Reserve banks. Presidents of the regional banks serve on a rotating basis, with the exception of the president of the Federal Reserve Bank of New York, who is vice chairman and a permanent voting member of the committee.

Open-market operations are purchases and sales of government securities in the open market by the Federal Reserve. Open-market operations are the primary tool for control of the monetary base.

The **opportunity cost** of an action is the value of the best forgone alternative.

P

The **partisan theory** views macroeconomic policy outcomes as the result of ideologically motivated decisions by leaders of different political parties. The parties represent constituencies with different preferences concerning macroeconomic variables.

The **permanent income hypothesis** shares with the life cycle hypothesis the view that consumption depends on a long-term average of income earned from labor and asset holdings.

Personal income is the national income accounts measure of the income received by persons from all sources.

The **Phillips curve** is the schedule showing the relationship between the unemployment and inflation rates.

Potential GDP (output) is the level that would be reached if productive resources (labor and capital) were being used at benchmark high levels.

A **price index** measures the aggregate price level relative to a chosen base year.

The **producer price index (PPI)** measures the wholesale prices of approximately 3,000 items.

A **production function** summarizes the relationship between total inputs and total outputs assuming a given technology.

Public choice is the application to macroeconomic policymaking of the microeconomic theory of how decisions are made.

Q

The **quantity theory of money** is the classical theory stating that the price level is proportional to the quantity of money. In the monetarist version, the quantity theory is a theory of nominal GNP.

R

Rational expectations are expectations formed on the basis of all available relevant information concerning the variable being predicted. Moreover, economic agents are assumed to use available information intelligently; that is, they understand the relationships between the variables they observe and the variables they are trying to predict.

Real gross national product measures aggregate output in constant-valued dollars from a base year.

The **real interest rate** is the nominal interest rate minus the anticipated rate of price inflation.

A **recession** is a period when economic activity declines significantly relative to potential output, but less severely than in a depression such as that of the 1930s.

The **required reserve ratio** is the percentage of deposits banks must hold as reserves.

S

Seigniorage revenues are the amount of real resources bought by the government with newly created money.

Sticky price models (or menu cost models) are those in which costs of changing prices prevent price adjustments when demand changes. Consequently, output falls when, for example, there is a decline in demand.

The **structural deficit** is the part of the federal deficit that would exist even if the economy were at its potential level of output.

Structural unemployment, like frictional unemployment, originates in the dynamic nature of the product and job mix in the economy, but structural unemployment lasts longer.

T

Target zones for exchange rates are ranges within which policymakers try to maintain their currency's value. The target zones are jointly set by major industrialized nations.

Technological change includes changes in technological knowledge (e.g., ways to employ robots in the production process) as well as new knowledge about how to organize businesses (managerial strategies).

A **time inconsistency** problem arises when a future policy formulated at an initial date is no longer optimal at a later date even though no new information has appeared.

The **trade deficit** is the excess of imports over exports.

U

The **unemployment rate** expresses the number of unemployed persons as a percentage of the labor force.

The **user cost of capital** is the overall cost to a firm to employ an additional unit of capital for one period.

V

The **velocity of money** is the rate at which money *turns over* in gross national product transactions during a given period: that is, the average number of times each dollar is used in gross national product transactions.

Index

Note: Locators in italics indicate tables and figures.

A

D

F

H

I

J

K

L

O

T

U